Legal and Ethical Issues in the Human Services

Southeastern University

Freeman | Corey/Corey/Callahan

CENGAGE
Learning·

Australia • Brazil • Japan • Korea • Mexico • Singapore • Spain • United Kingdom • United States

CENGAGE
Learning·

**Legal and Ethical Issues in the Human
Services**

Issues and Ethics in the Helping Professions, 8th Edition
Gerald Corey | Marianne Schneider Corey | Patrick Callanan

© 2011 Cengage Learning. All rights reserved.

Ethics: Introduction to Philosophy & Practice, 1st Edition
Stephen J. Freeman

© 2001 Cengage Learning. All rights reserved.

Senior Project Development Manager:
 Linda deStefano

Market Development Manager:
 Heather Kramer

Senior Production/Manufacturing Manager:
 Donna M. Brown

Production Editorial Manager:
 Kim Fry

Sr. Rights Acquisition Account Manager:
 Todd Osborne

For product information and technology assistance, contact us at
Cengage Learning Customer & Sales Support, 1-800-354-9706
For permission to use material from this text or product,
submit all requests online at **cengage.com/permissions**
Further permissions questions can be emailed to
permissionrequest@cengage.com

This book contains select works from existing Cengage Learning resources and
was produced by Cengage Learning Custom Solutions for collegiate use. As such,
those adopting and/or contributing to this work are responsible for editorial
content accuracy, continuity and completeness.

Compilation © 2012 Cengage Learning

ISBN-13: 978-1-285-55161-6

ISBN-10: 1-285-55161-3

Cengage Learning
5191 Natorp Boulevard
Mason, Ohio 45040
USA
Cengage Learning is a leading provider of customized learning solutions with
office locations around the globe, including Singapore, the United Kingdom,
Australia, Mexico, Brazil, and Japan. Locate your local office at:
international.cengage.com/region.

Cengage Learning products are represented in Canada by Nelson Education, Ltd.
For your lifelong learning solutions, visit **www.cengage.com/custom.**
Visit our corporate website at **www.cengage.com.**

Printed in the United States of America

Brief Contents

Excerpted from:
Ethics: Introduction to Philosophy & Practice, 1st Edition
Stephen J. Freeman

Excerpted from:
Issues and Ethics in the Helping Professions, 8th Edition
Gerald Corey | Marianne Schneider Corey | Patrick Callanan

Brief Contents

1

✳

Problems of Ethics in the Helping Professions

This book was written to provide a framework through which helping professionals can begin to develop a process for understanding the basic values that support and determine their appropriate actions. Helping professionals need to study and internalize a sound theoretical foundation and process for ethical thinking and decision making because they are often confronted with dilemmas that have no apparent correct or good solutions. In the helping professions, almost anything an individual does has potential ethical ramifications. We do not just behave according to instincts or impulse, nor do we live in a vacuum. We acquire values and ideals, form goals, and generally conform to patterns of acceptable social behavior. We usually obey the law. However, on occasion we disagree with some particular aspect of it on the basis of some higher principle. No matter how personal and individual we consider our values to be, we demonstrate agreement with society in our acceptance of certain general assumptions such as the right to live and be happy and the importance of doing the right thing—even though we cannot always agree on what exactly that is. People disagree in particular cases or in general philosophy because each of us believes we are objectively right. But ethics, unlike food, is not just a matter of taste or preference. Assuming that the study of ethics, theories, and concerns is a smorgasbord from which each person can pick and choose is grossly erroneous. Our moral judgments and subsequent actions may be challenged and we are expected to have a sound rationale for them.

The study of ethics should help us think about our actions in real-life situations and help us organize our opinions, beliefs, ideals, and values about what is right and wrong. It should make us aware of the ripple effect our actions create, setting a precedent for future behavior, both our own and that of others. Like the domino effect, where one falling domino sets in motion a series of falling dominos, our actions may provide the impetus or validation for another's action though circumstances may or may not justify the action. This awareness adds a new dimension to our thinking and to our potential for action. Kant (trans. 1963) summarized this well in saying that ethics without reference to particular actions are empty, but actions devoid of ethics are blind.

The study of ethics involves not only our humanness but the appreciation of worthy beliefs, goals, ideals, and values. From the time of the earliest philosophers there has been agreement that there is a correct theory or approach to ethics—one that forms a consistent, coherent, and comprehensive system. Philosophers have, however, disagreed on which approach is the most consistent, coherent, and correct, with each attempting to improve or surpass the others. Many of their theories will be described in this book for the reader's own evaluation.

The following summaries of ethical dilemmas as well as those at the end of various chapters are true stories taken from my experience in clinical practice and university teaching. Significant changes have been made to protect the identity of all characters. Inclusion of real cases, instead of fictitious examples, demonstrates the complexity and untidiness that occurs in real life. These cases demonstrate the need for a well-grounded practical approach to clinical ethical judgments. My comments on the various ethical dilemmas and their resolution are post hoc.

As you read the following summaries of ethical dilemmas, record your actions and the rationale for them in detail for later reference. Refer as necessary to the various codes of ethics in the appendices. (The codes of ethics of related helping professions have been included because we do not work in isolation and increasingly must be able to interface and work as part of a multidisciplinary team. Effective multidisciplinary functioning and related problem solving requires one to have a working understanding of the ethical standards of the other team members.) After responding to these questions, read the rest of the book, including the codes in the appendices. In reviewing the codes of ethics of the various professional organizations be acutely aware of the similarities and differences that exist. When you have finished reading, you may wish to return to the summaries; you may wish to revise and/or add to your original answers. The stimulus questions posed at the end of the dilemmas are to stimulate more in-depth thought for your second round of responses as well as your rationale(s) for them. The goal of this process is to increase self-awareness and insight into the underlying reasons for your actions, leading to the formation of an informed ethical conscience and an increasingly sound ethical basis for decision making.

ETHICAL DILEMMA 1

You are a counselor working independently in a private practice setting. After a lapse of some years, Mrs. M. calls for an appointment. You had originally worked with Mrs. M. when she sought counseling for bereavement after the death of her spouse from cancer some years ago. Your records reflect that she appeared to have made successful resolution of her bereavement. During this second intake appointment, you discover that Mrs. M. has remarried (approximately 2 years ago) and she reports a very happy life until three months ago when she was diagnosed with bone cancer. After numerous consultations, her case was labeled terminal and she was referred to hospice. She has come to see you again because she remembers how much you helped her after the death of her first husband. She states she knows you will be able to help her now. Following her diagnosis and dim prognosis, she had come across the book *Final Exit*. After reading it she decided that rather than suffering the ravages of bone cancer she would take her life ("self deliver" as she expresses it). Knowing you would understand, she requests that you see both her and her new husband to help him understand and cope with her decision, which he neither understands nor approves. You are not altogether sure Mrs. M. is not seeking counseling in order to bolster her resolve in this area of her own commitment.

The Problem

As a supposedly unbiased counselor, should you agree to support Mrs. M. in her decision to commit suicide given her terminal diagnosis? What about her current husband and Mrs. M's request that you help him understand and cope with her decision?

The Dilemma

The dilemma faced here is multifaceted and requires the counselor to address and consider the principles of autonomy, nonmaleficence, beneficence, compassion, fidelity, and justice.

1. Does an individual have the right to control his or her own body and his or her own life, including ending it?
2. Is morality defined by the wishes of the client? Is morality defined by the humane and compassionate values of those involved?

   To assist you in the decision–making process answer the following questions:

1. What are the counselor's responsibilities to Mrs. M.?
2. What are the counselor's responsibilities to Mr. M.?

3. What impact do the wishes of Mrs. M. have on your recommendations?

4. What are the counselor's responsibilities to society (in the welfare of this individual and others and the issue of life and death)?

5. What are your possible alternative courses of action and why would you choose them?

6. What are the possible and probable consequences of the actions you take?

7. How do the ethical codes in the appendices apply to this case? How does this affect your decision?

8. In the final analysis, what are the implications for this particular case? For cases involving ethical questions of life and death?

9. As the counselor, what would you do and why?

ETHICAL DILEMMA 2

You are on the graduate faculty of a small university in the counseling department. You teach various counseling related classes and serve as an advisor to many students. You also maintain an active private counseling practice away from the university. You are licensed and have appropriate academic credentials. One of your current graduate students approaches you with a request for personal counseling. You are not this student's advisor, though you have had her in class before. She is not currently enrolled in any of your classes, though it is possible she would be in the future. However, there are enough other faculty members teaching similar courses that she could switch to one of their courses.

The Problem

Should a professor see a student in personal counseling?

The Dilemma

The dilemma here has to do with dual relationships. Several points concerning dual relationships are seen here.

1. Is it ethical to draw clients from the ranks of your students (or other faculty's students)?
2. Does the role of professor bias the role of counselor, or the role of student dilute or bias the role of client? Does the role of client dilute or bias the role of student?

To assist you in the decision-making process, answer the following questions:

1. What is your responsibility as a professor to this student?
2. What is your responsibility as a professor to your other students?
   a. To the other faculty?
   b. To your profession?
   c. To yourself?
3. What are your possible alternative courses of action and why would you choose them?
4. What are the possible and probable consequences of the actions taken?
5. Review the codes of ethics in the appendices. Are there any statements that would apply here? How do they affect your decision?
6. As the professor, what would you do and why?

ETHICAL DILEMMA 3

As a counselor working independently in a private practice setting, you had previously seen Mr. and Mrs. S. in marital counseling. During the course of counseling, it became clear that Mr. S. desired to leave the relationship. He discontinued conjoint counseling, and divorce followed his move from the home. Mrs. S. continued to see you for individual counseling until after the divorce, and terminated based on mutual agreement between you. Approximately two years following the initial conjoint counseling, you receive a letter in the mail from a court-appointed ombudsman. The letter explains that the couple is engaged in a custody battle and your records will be used to aid the ombudsman in making a recommendation to the court on the issue of custody. You have serious questions regarding the applicability of your records of marital counseling to the question of custody. On further investigation, you determine the ombudsman is a volunteer with "appropriate training." This person appears to have no related academic training in the field, and no certifications or licenses.

The Problem

You have signed releases from both Mr. and Mrs. S., but should you release the information?

The Dilemma

The dilemma involves the clients' rights to information about themselves but also how and by whom this information will be used. There is a serious question as to whether or not your records contain information appropriate for drawing inferences about parental suitability for custody. In addition, there is the ethical question of disclosure of records to an individual unqualified to interpret them.

To help you in the decision-making process answer the following stimulus questions:

1. Exactly who is the client?
2. What are the counselor's responsibilities to Mr. and Mrs. S.?
    a. To Mr. and Mrs. S.'s children?
    b. To the court?
    c. To society?
3. What impact do the wishes of the couple have on the counselor's actions?
4. What are your possible alternative courses of action and why would you choose them?
5. What are the possible and probable consequences of actions taken?
6. What do the ethical codes offer as assistance in resolution of this dilemma?
7. As the counselor, what would you do and why?

ETHICAL DILEMMA 4

You are a school counselor in an expanding middle school. Your responsibilities have increased in proportion to the school's expansion, which is significant. Despite the school's expansion there are no funds currently available to increase the counseling staff. You had previously been able to provide various counseling services to the students, including several groups. Now you face the undesirable possibility of having to discontinue these groups due to increasing administrative duties. Another counselor with whom you are acquainted and who is familiar with your situation approaches you with a possible solution. She says she has been approached by a private psychiatric hospital and asked if she would be willing to provide community counseling services for which they would reimburse her. She further explains she would be willing to do the groups that you have been doing as a community service paid for by the hospital. The school would in effect be gaining a free part-time counselor. You would then be free to attend to your other administrative duties and the students would not lose the experience of group, which you think is very beneficial to them. Your situation is growing more unmanageable and you know that very soon you will have to do something—but what?

The Problem

As a competent school counselor you are concerned about direct services to your students. You are also aware that your job has necessary administrative duties, which take you out of direct contact with students. Are there any problems with the offer made by the other counselor?

The Dilemma

Does the hospital not have the right to engage in community service? Who is the employer of the new counselor in this situation? Does this present any potential problems? Do the benefits outweigh the risks?

To assist you in the decision-making process answer the following questions:

1. What are the school counselor's responsibilities?
   a. To the school?
   b. To her students?
2. What are the other counselor's responsibilities to the students?
   a. To the hospital paying her?
   b. To the school?
3. What are the counselors' responsibilities to their profession?
4. What are the counselors' responsibilities to society (the welfare of the students and others)?
5. What are your possible courses of action and why would you choose them?

6. What are the possible and probable consequences of the action you take?
7. How do the ethical codes in the appendix apply to this situation? How does this affect your decision?

ETHICAL DILEMMA 5

As a counselor working in an agency setting, you have seen Mr. and Mrs. D. in marital counseling for several weeks. Mr. D. requests some individual counseling with you in addition to the conjoint sessions. In the individual session Mr. D. discloses the fact that he had an affair some time ago, and he is experiencing significant guilt feelings. His desire to discuss this with you is several-fold. First, he feels significant guilt over the brief affair, especially because the marital relationship has improved so much since counseling. Second, he is concerned that if Mrs. D. should find out about the affair she would leave him. He points to her statement of such some time ago and to the fact that she is a somewhat fragile individual emotionally, something you as a counselor have also noticed. In stating his dilemma to you, Mr. D. expresses a strong desire to make his relationship work but is caught in a bind of guilt on one side and fear (possibly justified) on the other. He turns to you for assistance.

The Problem

Mr. D. wishes to deal with his guilt feelings by confessing to his wife, but he is afraid she will leave him if he does.

The Dilemma

The counselor is placed in a precarious position by Mr. D.'s disclosure. Should the counselor inform Mrs. D. or have Mr. D. inform her about the affair? What about confidentiality? What about the relationship? What about Mrs. D.'s emotional well being? What about Mr. D.'s increasing feelings of guilt?

Answer the following stimulus questions to help you decide what to do:

1. Who is (are) the client(s)?
2. What are the counselor's responsibilities to Mr. D?
    a. To Mrs. D?
    b. To the agency?
3. Review the ethical codes. Are there any guidelines that may apply?
4. What are your possible courses of action and why would you choose them?
5. What are the possible and probable consequences of each action listed in Question 4?
6. As the counselor, what would you do and why?

ETHICAL DILEMMA 6

You are a female counselor employed in an agency setting. You have been on staff for approximately four years. You have appropriate academic credentials and are also licensed. While working at the agency you were once aware of feeling a significant attraction toward a client you were counseling. Your solid academic background made you conscious of your professional responsibility and you did not allow this to interfere with the therapeutic relationship. Your client successfully completed counseling and you had not seen him since. Now, some years later, you meet this individual several times in a social setting. You again become aware of feeling a significant attraction toward him, and begin to think he may also be attracted to you. When he realizes that you both are single, he asks you out on a date. He does this by saying he was attracted to you during your counseling together and now finds himself feeling the same attraction again.

The Problem

Should you accept the offer of a date from a person who was once a client long ago?

The Dilemma

As a counselor, should you engage in relationships with former clients? When does the professional relationship end? Or does it?

To assist in the decision-making process answer the following questions:

1. What is the effect of the therapeutic relationship on the counselor and the client?
2. When does the counselor's "influence" on the client end, if ever? When does the client cease to be a client?
3. What are the counselor's responsibilities to the client?
   a. To herself?
   b. To the agency?
   c. To the profession?
   d. To society?
4. What are your possible alternative courses of action and why would you choose them?
5. What are the possible and probable consequences of these actions?
6. What would you do and why?

ETHICAL DILEMMA 7

You are a school counselor working in a high school setting. During the first few weeks of school, a student approaches you and requests individual counseling for some adjustment problems. The student is new, having transferred from another city to your school. Several teachers have approached you noting the student's request to be allowed to leave class to see you. They voice concerns that the student's behavior is a little odd in class and ask if you know what is wrong. During one of the early sessions with the student, she revealed that the reason her family moved was that her father had committed suicide approximately six months ago. Her mother had moved the family here to be close to her family of origin. At her old school, the response from the teachers and peers to her father's suicide had been negative. Fearing this reaction again, she asked you not to disclose this to anyone. The student's grief over her father's death is also affecting her schoolwork in that she finds it difficult to concentrate or attend to tasks while in class. The family has not sought counseling and now are attempting, according to the student, to put their lives together as if nothing had ever happened. She feels she can trust you but does not want anyone else to know. At about this same time the principal approaches you stating that several teachers have voiced concerns about this student and they want to know what she (the student) has told you in counseling.

The Problem

One of the most difficult areas for school counselors concerns the disclosure of information obtained in a counseling session. The problem here is whether or not a counselor should disclose to a teacher or administrator what was disclosed in a counseling session if the material may have impact on school performance. The counselor is in a precarious position given the student's and the principal's requests. Should the counselor inform the principal of the student's problem?

The Dilemma

When does the student's need for confidentiality outweigh the right of school officials to know? What if the principal and school policy mandate disclosure?

To assist you in the decision-making process answer the following stimulus questions:

1. What are the counselor's responsibilities to the student?
   a. To the principal?
   b. To the school district?
   c. To the profession?
   d. To society?
2. What guidance is offered by the ethical codes?
3. What are your possible courses of action and why would you choose them?
4. What are the possible and probable consequences of each action?
5. What would you do and why?

ETHICAL DILEMMA 8

You are a school counselor in a junior high school working primarily with eighth-grade students. Last semester you had seen J. M., who is now a freshman, in individual vocational counseling sessions. During the course of one of the sessions, J. M. confessed that for several years he has been cheating on tests in order to receive good grades because he thinks this is his only way to ensure entry into a good college. J. M. further confided that increasing parental pressure to receive good grades and attend a good college is making him a "wreck." He related a recent incident in which he became so nervous before an exam he became physically ill. J. M. said he had tried to talk to his parents but they just wouldn't listen and continue to pressure him. He is afraid that if he does not achieve at the level his parents expect that they will forever be disappointed in him. Following this disclosure, J. M. became very concerned that what he had told you might not be held in confidence. He said that if his parents ever found out about his cheating he would kill himself. This semester, J. M. has been caught cheating on a midterm exam. J. M. pleads with the teacher, stating that he has never cheated before and panicked because he was unprepared for the exam. The teacher seeks consultation from the freshman counselor, who is a personal friend of J. M.'s parents and believes J. M. is sincere but is unsure of what action to take. The counselor, being unfamiliar professionally with J. M., sends you a note requesting a consultation regarding this incident. In the note are the following questions: Are you familiar with J. M.? Have you seen him for counseling? Are you aware of any reasons for this behavior or previous incidents? You are also asked for a recommendation on whether or not J. M. should be allowed to retake the exam.

The Problem

The information you have has potential implications, both academic and personal. The problem is whether or not you should share the information you have about J. M. in a professional consultation.

The Dilemma

When is academic counseling academic and when does it cross the line and become personal counseling and subject to different professional guidelines? When is it necessary and/or appropriate to consult with another professional without a student's/client's consent?

To assist you in the decision-making process answer the following stimulus questions:

1. What are the counselor's responsibilities to the student?
   a. To the school?
   b. To the profession?
   c. To society?
2. What guidance is offered by the ethical codes?

3. What are your possible courses of action and why would you choose them?

4. What are the possible and probable consequences of each action?

5. What would you do and why?

ETHICAL DILEMMA 9

You are a counselor in a middle-class junior high school. You are seeing a 13-year-old female student for both academic and personal counseling. Her parents have recently divorced and she is having difficulty coping, as evidenced by a significant drop in grades and changes in social behaviors. Soon after her parents' divorce she had changed her peer group from other local junior high students to a mixed group of high school students and some recent dropouts. During one session she relates to you that she is sexually active with her new boyfriend, who is much older and a high school student. She tells you that they do not use any form of birth control as they see it as unnatural. She confidently tells you that she knows your concerns, but she won't be one who gets pregnant. Later in the session she acknowledges her desire to become pregnant and have a baby. She sees this as a remedy for her current family dilemma. She states that her new boyfriend is unaware of her desire to have a baby and that she has no intention of telling him until she is sure she is pregnant.

The Problem

This situation presents several ethical as well as potential legal problems. The obvious is that your client is a minor and engaging in sexual activity which, given the age of the boyfriend, may be a crime. Another is her unwillingness to disclose to her partner her desire to have a child out of this relationship.

The Dilemma

If a client, in this case a minor, is involved in potentially dangerous behavior, what should the counselor's response be? Also, if a client's behavior is placing another person at risk, what should the counselor do?

To assist you in the decision-making process answer the following questions:

1. What is the counselor's responsibility to the client?
    a. To the boyfriend?
    b. To the school?
    c. To the student's parents?
    d. To society?

2. What guidance is offered by the ethical codes (the law)?

3. What are your possible actions and why would you choose them?

4. What are the possible and probable consequences of each action taken?

5. What would you do and why?

ETHICAL DILEMMA 10

You are one of six counselors in a fairly large high school with approximately 4,000 students. You are a new counselor who just completed your master's degree and counselor certification. Your school has a mentor program and you are assigned a mentor who has her doctorate and has been a school counselor for over ten years. You find the mentoring relationship rewarding and your mentor a very good role model. During an informal conversation with your mentor, you find out that she is in private practice. She acknowledges to you that her practice is doing well and inquires if you are interested in some part-time private counseling work. She says she has observed you and acknowledges that you have good counseling skills and would be a complement to her in her practice. She further states that both of you working at the school would be beneficial, as the majority of her referrals come directly or indirectly from the school. Because you are new to the field, you ask whether or not this is acceptable practice. Your mentor responds that as long as you do not engage in personal counseling with any students that you are seeing privately during school time there is no problem. You have a great deal of respect for your mentor, and, having just completed graduate school, you have a student loan on which you must begin to make payments. The offer sounds good but there is a nagging question in the back of your mind that prevents you from making a decision.

The Problem

Should you dismiss your concern and take your mentor up on her offer? Should you, as a novice counselor, not accept the guidance of a much more experienced counselor, especially one you admire?

The Dilemma

Do school counselors have a right to pursue private practice? What, if any, restrictions or concerns exist in a situation like this with respect to dual relationships?

To assist you in the decision-making process answer the following questions:

1. What are the counselor's responsibilities to the students?
    a. To the school?
    b. To her mentor?
    c. To herself?
2. What impact do her mentor's concerns or lack of concerns have on the decision?
3. What are your possible alternative courses of action and why would you choose them?
4. What are the possible and probable consequences of the actions taken?
5. How do the ethical codes in the appendices apply to this situation? How does this affect your decision?

ETHICAL DILEMMA 11

You have just graduated with your master's in counseling and are interviewing for a job as a school counselor. The principal with whom you are interviewing appears interested in offering you the position. She hands you the job description and asks if you have any questions. You notice the job description includes responsibilities for testing and assessment. You query the principal, who explains that there is no diagnostician in the district currently and that the counselors have taken over that role. She goes on to say that the counselors are doing such a fine job that the district is in no hurry to find a diagnostician. Your master's program included only one course in testing and assessment and that was a survey course. You acknowledge to the principal that though you feel qualified in all the other duty areas listed, you question your qualifications and competency in the area of testing and assessment. Her response is that the district has the tests and the test manuals so it's not hard to give a test and figure out what it means. The other counselors are doing fine. She goes on to say she knows that with your background and teaching experience you will do fine also. After further discussion the principal says she thinks you are the best applicant and that the job is yours if you want it.

The Problem

Should you accept a position when the duties include responsibilities you feel you are not competent to perform? What about taking a position in a school where you feel you cannot support the policies of the institution?

The Dilemma

Does an individual have the right to employment even though they may not agree with the policies of the institution in which they are seeking employment? What about the fact that other counselors are performing the duties you are concerned about without apparent problems?

To assist you in the decision-making process answer the following questions:

1. What are the counselor's responsibilities to herself?
   a. To the school?
   b. To the students?
   c. To the profession?
2. What impact does the fact that others are apparently doing well with the testing responsibilities have on your decision?
3. What are your possible alternative courses of action and why would you choose them?
4. What are the possible and probable consequences of the actions taken?
5. How do the ethical codes in the appendices apply to this situation? How does this affect your decision?

ETHICAL DILEMMA 12

You are the lead counselor in a middle school. The principal calls you in to inform you of an "experiential" learning exercise she and a teacher have planned for the students. She relates that on Thursday afternoon an announcement will be made that the president has been assassinated. This is planned to coincide with the history classes' study of the presidents and the assassination of President Kennedy. She hopes that the students will experience firsthand the importance of the office of the president in a democratic system and how disruptive the loss of the president can be. She knows that some students may have a strong reaction to the announcement and wants you and the other counselors to be prepared. She asks you to tell the other counselors to treat the announcement as real. The students will be told at the end of the day, before leaving school, that this has been an experiential learning experience and that the president is alive and well. Your first response is disbelief, but after a few moments, you realize that your principal is serious. You voice concerns but they are ignored. The plan is not going to change and your assistance is required.

The Problem

As a counselor, you see the potential for emotional harm to the students. The principal and the history teacher disagree with you and plan to proceed with the exercise. Should you agree to participate because your superior and another teacher think it is all right and you are expected to cooperate?

The Dilemma

Is it ethical to use human subjects in an experiment or to expose them to an experiential form of learning without consent? In a given situation, is it ethical to perform an action you believe is wrong because a superior told you to?

To assist you in the decision-making process answer the following questions:

1. What is the counselor's responsibility to the students?
   a. To the school?
   b. To the profession?
   c. To society?
2. What impact does your principal's "order" have on you and your decision?
3. What are your possible alternative courses of action and why would you choose them?
4. What are the possible and probable consequences of the actions you take?
5. How do the ethical codes in the appendices apply to this situation? How does this affect your decision?

3

✳

Introduction to Ethics

The unexamined life is not worth living (Socrates). What is right? What is wrong? Hamlet wonders, "To be or not to be," but according to Levine (1986), that is not the question. The question is, "How to be?"

In contemporary society there is an increasing opinion that there is no justification for moral judgments. A prevailing nihilism states that everything is relative and so there is no particular meaning (right or wrong) in the decisions you make today about how you act.

> Are all standards of what is right and wrong, what constitutes a good personal life or a good society merely relative to the individual person or to a particular social group expressing nothing more than habit or prejudice and serving individual or group interests and needs? These are the questions of the branch of philosophy called ethics. Ethics asks if there is a highest good for human beings, an absolute good? What is the meaning of right and wrong in human action? What are our obligations? And why should we be moral? (Lavine, 1984, p. 3)

Ethics is a topic that holds some interest for everyone. Abortion, civil rights, civil war, ethnic cleansing, and politics are all issues that overtly or covertly provide us a steady stream of ethical questions. This short list suggests we are well aware of and have an interest in ethics.

WHAT IS ETHICS?

The concept of ethics is not new. For centuries philosophers have wrestled with Lavine's question: What is the meaning of right and wrong in human action? Our founding fathers struggled with the concept of morality when in the Declaration of Independence they wrote, "All men are created equal . . ." So what happened? Blacks and women were excluded from the category of "all men" for generations; discrimination, gender bias, and other contradictions to these concepts linger today. Following W.W. II and Nazi Germany's crimes against humanity, the slogan was "Never again. The world must never forget." Unfortunately, since that time we have seen the killing fields of the Khmer Rouge in Cambodia, the "disappeared" in Argentina, and the ethnic cleansing in Bosnia.

ETHICS AS PHILOSOPHY

To begin to understand or unravel this maze of apparent contradictions, we must first find the meaning of ethics. Webster defines ethics as "the study of standards of conduct and moral judgment; moral philosophy." Simply stated, ethics is the study of morality. What then is "moral"? According to Webster it is "the principles and practices in regard to right, wrong and duty; general conduct or behavior." A moralist, it could then be said, is concerned with behavior—sustaining worthwhile values, warning people of the dangers of their ways, and guiding them toward what is right. An ethicist is concerned with the examination of the underlying assumptions and principles of that which is considered right and wrong.

Ethics and morals are intricately connected but, as numerous writers note, have different denotations. Mowrer (1969) suggests that moral refers to the goodness or badness of a behavior while ethics is an objective inquiry about behavior. Van Hoose and Paradise (1979) suggest ethics is a theoretical examination of morals or morality. Peterfreund and Denise (1992) view moralists as those who tell us what they think is good, while ethicists question the underlying principles of what is good or right. The Roman poet Ovid acknowledged the relationship between ethics and morals when he wrote, "We know and approve the better course but follow the worse."

Returning to the question of what ethics is, we may say ethics is the branch of philosophy concerned with living a good life, being a good person, and doing the right thing. Ethics includes reasoning about general principles and using the process of reasoning to determine an appropriate action to take in a given situation. It attempts to identify explicit standards that are applicable to numerous situations. These standards identify for people the criteria necessary to judge an action or life moral. Ethics goes beyond formulating statements of general principles and attempts to find justification for the standards. It attempts to show that some standards are better or more sound than others. The study of ethics requires that we develop some objective rationale for the standards we use to guide us. Recent episodes of genocide show us that the discipline of ethics is necessary if humankind is to survive in this pluralistic society.

Morality is both the product of our pluralistic society and one of its constitutive features. Our personal values are in large measure learned and shared by many others like ourselves. The choice of values is an important and often confusing topic in the discussion of ethics. Do we choose our values, and does everyone have their own totally subjective values? Most scholars agree that we choose between already established possibilities and already available reasons. The choices are not unlimited, but have been preselected by tradition and culture. One chooses between these preselected choices. Values by their very nature are shared and transcend (go beyond) those who embrace them. The values that we cherish most, our personal values, are typically not idiosyncratic, but are those we share with the greatest numbers of others like ourselves (e.g., respect for life; compassion for others; quest for justice). However, our current society does not have one uniform set of moral standards. There are many different standards or customs and some of these contradict each other. Customs tell people how to live, what to do, and how to evaluate other people and what they do. If a person learns the customs of his or her society, do ethical or moral problems arise? Of course they do. People have many different reasons for not wanting to adopt some of the customs of their society. As standards of behavior, morals always place restrictions on individual behavior and gratification of desires. It is not uncommon, then, for people to question why they should follow the standards and customs of the group or society. Some people believe that they should be responsible for themselves and actively decide on their own standards, morals, and ethics. To them, what they receive from society is not really theirs until it has been explicitly chosen by them. To these individuals, making standards their own requires that they think about them and have a rationale for their actions and the lives they live. This is what Socrates meant when he stated, "the unexamined life is a life not worth living."

Ethics as a discipline refers to both the study of our values and their justification, and to the actual values and standards of conduct by which we live. A word of caution here—it would be a mistake to assume that ethical positions are just different personal opinions and that any opinion or position is as good as any other. Most people think there is an objective good; there are ways of behaving and treating others that are objectively good and others that are objectively bad. Morality is seen not just as a matter of personal opinion or customs. If we, at least in part, believe in objective goodness, then it behooves us to be sure that the standards we choose to live by are the truest according to our knowledge. It is not good enough to just do what we are told or what custom dictates; it is just as important to know the reason behind the action and to be able to say no when the action is wrong. Moral rules and the rationale for them form the preconditions necessary for the very functioning of society. The moral rule that it is wrong to lie seems to be a precondition to believing what others say, and even to communication itself. It is important not only to know the rule but to know why the rule is important. Watzlawick (1967) provides us an interesting example of the confusion that might exist if this were not so in the following case: A Cretin sage was brought before the King and said "All Cretins are liars. . . ." The ensuing problem is immediately apparent. Though this is an example of a principle in communication theory, it also points out that moral rules are the necessary framework that enables society to function. Without such rules we, like the king, would be left wondering, "If the Cretin Sage is lying when he says all Cretins are liars, what is one to believe?" It is necessary to study ethics in order to determine if our standards are true, and if not, to determine what standards are true. Ethics is more than a collection of do's and don'ts; it is a system of values and standards tied together in a coherent and reasonable way serving to show us the path toward the good life.

RELATIVISM

In addressing relativism, the distinction between ethical relativism and cultural relativism is of paramount importance. Ethical relativism is a highly controversial philosophical theory, while cultural relativism is an accepted sociological description of some important differences between cultures (Westermark, 1932; Ladd, 1963). Ethical relativism concerns itself with the question, "What actions are morally right?" Cultural relativism concerns itself with the question, "What actions do different cultures believe to be morally right?" Because differing cultures have diverse moral beliefs, there is no way to decide whether an action is morally right or morally wrong other than by asking the people of that particular culture to judge. Ethical relativism may be seen as the view that if the members of a certain culture believe that a certain action is morally right, then it is morally right to perform that act in that culture. Likewise, if the members of a different culture view the same act as morally wrong, then in that culture to perform that act would be morally wrong (Westermark, 1932; Wellman, 1963; Brandt, 1959). With that basic difference noted, the larger questions involving relativism can be addressed.

Who are you to judge someone else's behavior? What gives you the right to impose your values on others? Some people doubt that the moral judgments of others can be valid. They reject the idea that there are valid universal moral principals applicable to everyone. Ethical relativism questions whether what is right for one person or culture or society is any indication that it is right for another. Relativism states that morality is relative to something else. It denies that there are any absolute moral standards and states that different moral standards exist for different cultures and societies. Relativism is one of the largest areas of controversy in the study of ethics. Holmes (1993, p. 20) distinguishes three theses relevant to relativism.

1. Moral beliefs and practices vary from culture to culture.
2. Morality depends on: (a) human nature (e.g., reason, motivation, emotions, and capacity for pleasure and pain); (b) the human condition (the natural order places constraints on human life such as death); (c) specific

social and cultural circumstances, or some combination of all three of the above.

3. What is right and wrong may vary from person to person and culture to culture.

Holmes (1993) states that thesis 1 simply affirms cultural diversity. Variations in moral beliefs and practices, some of which might be pronounced, are possible but not required in different cultures.

Thesis 2, the dependency thesis, states that morality is dependent on or conditioned by human nature and/or the world people live in. This view states that morality's function is to guide human conduct, and that it has evolved over time in response to human needs.

Thesis 3 is ethical relativism. It contains both theses 1 and 2 and goes beyond them. It is, according to Holmes, a statement about what is right and wrong and not just what is thought to be (pp. 20–21).

Ethical relativists believe in right and wrong; however, they contend that what is right for one person or culture has the possibility of being wrong for another. Relativism allows for the possibility of differing moral judgments about the same behavior being (relatively) correct at the same time.

ABSOLUTISM

Throughout history there have been those who believe, in contrast to relativism, that there are absolute moral standards. Absolute moral standards are both universal and objective. They are universal in that they apply to everyone at all times and also apply to all situations equally. Consistency without contradiction is a key factor in this universal application. Absolute moral standards are objective in that they do not depend on a person's or culture's beliefs, thoughts, feelings, or customs. Objective moral standards have an existence that is independent of one's belief in them. Universal moral standards cannot be discovered by studying empirical data such as human desires or inclinations because by their very nature these vary from person to person. They are referred to as a priori, or existing prior to the creation of any particular situation or moral judgment. As such, they are not derived from experience but they are universally applicable to experience; and, they are the necessary preconditions of empirical knowledge. It is precisely this independence, this objectivity, that creates the categories of right and wrong relative to experience and one's belief about morality. Philosophers have always questioned whether truly absolute immutable moral standards (truths) are knowable by human beings. The agreed-upon answer has been no. Therefore, in an attempt to approximate this absolute moral standard the measure becomes the consistency with which the moral standard can be applied without contradiction.

The issue between absolutism and relativism is not about identifying the correct moral judgments. The issue between them concerns itself with the relationship among the correct moral judgments, whatever those judgments are;

specifically, whether those judgments are consistent with one another. Relativism allows for different judgments concerning similar actions to both be viewed as being true at the same time, thus holding that correct or valid moral judgments are not all consistent with one another. Universalists hold a contrasting view that the true moral standards or principles (knowable to us) are the same for all people and all situations.

MOTIVATION IN MORALS

What motivates human beings to choose one action over another? Do we always act for the sake of our own self-interests, or do we sometimes act for the sake of others, or out of a sense of duty? The dichotomy between acting out of one's self-interest and acting for the benefit of others has been labeled egoism and altruism. Egoism is acting out of a sense of self-interest based in part on the belief that one ought to always act to maximize one's own personal good as an end. The term egoism or egoist should not be confused with the term egotistical or selfish. Egoists are no more conceited than anyone else, nor do they disregard the well-being of others, promoting their own welfare at the expense of others. Altruism is acting for the benefit of others based at least in part on the belief that one ought to act for the benefit of others as an end. This belief does not exclude the fact that the doer may also benefit from the action or act. Altruism may be based on some sense of compassion or possibly solely on principle. Egoism has as its basis for action the benefiting of self. Altruism has as its basis for action the benefiting of others. Motivation for acting is the primary meaning attached to both these terms.

Both egoism and altruism are subdivided into two distinct positions, ethical and psychological. Ethical egoism is the view that one ought to act in such a manner as to maximize one's own interests. Psychological egoism is the view that one is egotistically motivated and that everything that one does is for one's own interests and well being, self-love. Ethical altruism is the view that one ought to act for the benefit of others rather than self. Psychological altruism is the view that one is intrinsically motivated to act for the benefit of others.

Many ethical dilemmas arise as a result of the dichotomous demands between self-interest (egoism) and the interests of others (altruism). The problem is one of motivation—why should we be moral? This question has serious implications. In a society based on individual freedom, which cherishes virtues such as self-reliance and living up to your potential, self-interest (egoism) becomes more than a theory of moral motivation, it becomes a paradox. The paradox of self-interest grows out of egoism's implications for judgments about the conduct of others who are in their quest for their self-interest. In certain circumstances what is good for and in the interest of one person will conflict with what is good for and in the interest of another. A confirmed egoist would realize that both individuals should pursue what would maximize their own good. This means that each individual is obligated to follow his or her own course of action even though they (the actions) are incompatible. The question remaining unanswered is if moral actions are not based (at least partially) on self-interest, what rationale exists for the moral principle that people should act against their own self-interests and in the interests of others? The answer requires reasoning, reflection, and the need to justify one's actions. To act for reasons means that the question of justification or the "why" is relevant and important.

SUMMARY

Moral rules are considered a basic prerequisite for the existence of society. Most people would agree some actions are right and others are wrong. The implication is that some actions are moral, what one ought to do, and others are not. To suggest some action "ought" to be taken implies that the action has meaning or purpose. Aristotle, in his theory of final cause (reason or purpose or intention of an event in existence), stated: To account for something, describe it in terms of that reason it has for being or the end (goal or purpose) toward which it is intending. The implied cause is that which is indicated to be intended, or desired. A teleological approach to the question of "what one ought to do" indicates the quest for one or more other causes in addition to the final cause (moral/ethical reasons for actions).

Moral relativism takes the position that there are no absolute standards, and indeed, in our introduction to ethics, we have found several variations in what different people, different customs, and different cultures believe is right and wrong. Absolutists insist that absolute moral standards exist and are both objective and universal. They are objective in that they transcend the customs and beliefs of a given culture or society. They are universal in that they apply to all people at all times. The actions dictated or allowed by societal norms are judged truly moral only if they agree with the absolute standards. Relativists argue against the existence of absolute moral standards, pointing out that different groups have had and continue to have different moral standards.

Which viewpoint is correct? What is the truth? Does true knowledge have its source in observation or human reason? Is truth fixed, absolute, or relative? What are the motivating factors in human beings' quest to live morally? Do we always act out of our own self-interest? Egoism is the term used to describe action taken out of self-interest. Altruism is the term used to describe action taken to benefit others. The primary meaning of egoism and altruism is in terms of motivation for moral action. One can, despite bad intentions, benefit others, but such action could hardly be called altruistic. One can also fail in an effort to help another and end up personally benefiting, but such action is not solely self-interest. The question has been asked, if one does not at least in part act out of self-interest, then why act morally? The relevant question is one of justification. In subsequent chapters we will survey some of the many ways philosophers have attempted to justify actions.

Values and beliefs are critical in determining behavior, but are they the same? Some might argue that they are, or at least that they are closely related. To look closely is to ascribe a somewhat different meaning to each term. Beliefs are convictions, aspirations, or ideals regarding how things ought to be. Values more closely align themselves with behavior. It is what we truly value that we choose. Values are hierarchically related to a greater or lesser degree of desirability. Values have to do with choice. The reason we select or choose an action, and the value we place on it are most important in determining the priority of the moral obligations. We must look behind the words (beliefs) to discover the reality (values) behind the facade. The congruence or lack of congruence between these two personal concepts has implications for ethics.

In closing our introduction to ethics, a note of caution seems in order. Dietrich Bonhoeffer, a Protestant clergyman imprisoned by the Nazis in World War II, reflected that action comes directly not from thought but from a readiness for responsibility. Carl Menninger, in his 1973 book *What Ever Became of Sin?,* identified this as a growing problem and joined Bonhoeffer in noting that there was a need for a return to common assent to the concept of personal responsibility and answerability both for ourselves and for others.

QUESTIONS FOR ADDITIONAL
REFLECTION AND THOUGHT

1. Pause for a moment to reflect upon conscious choices that you have made that have shaped your life. Every choice reflected the values and commitments that you held at the time you made those choices. Which do you now regret and which remain central to defining your identity?

2. What do you mean when you use the term ethics? How does it differ from morality?

3. What is meant by moral relativism? How does it differ from cultural relativism?

4. You are on a moral quest in search of maturity and integrity. Genuine choice is a matter of ethics. The moral quest is to set goals and to act decisively with conviction. How acutely aware are you of your moral/ethical values and choices and how they have shaped your life thus far? More importantly how can you heighten your moral/ethical awareness and use it to shape your life in the future?

5. How would you define the concept of virtues? Are you better having them or not having them? What role do virtues play in your choice of moral/ethical actions?

6. How influential are a culture's or society's customs, values, and practices in determining an individual's ethics/morals?

7. In your opinion, how do males and females differ in the way each approaches moral/ethical dilemmas?

8. In your opinion, should moral/ethical action be dictated by rules and principles or by the uniqueness of the situation?

9. Think about people who are determined to live their lives with integrity. Do they have the most comfortable, trouble-free lives?

10. What price are you willing to pay for integrity?

9

Moral and Ethical Development

Morality has to do with the conscious adoption of standards related to right and wrong. These standards are established when certain behaviors are labeled as good and others are labeled as bad, beginning in childhood. With age and experience these standards of morality come to include complex ideas, values, and beliefs (Carroll & Rest, 1982).

The process of moral ethical development is analogous to Hegel's theory of Dialectic with each stage, its conflicts, and its resolutions forming the cornerstone for the next developmental progression. Hegel's theory of Dialectic is triadic, consisting of three stages. The first involves the formation of a thesis, or in the case of moral ethical development, a principle based on a paradigm. This is followed by a second (developmental) stage where the first principle is challenged, opposed, or negated by the formation of a new opposing principle, or antithesis. This new principle or paradigm formation causes cognitive dissension leading to the third stage, synthesis. Here a new concept (paradigm) or principle emerges which transcends the two previous theses. Synthesis, or the resolution of this developmental conflict, has three functions: (a) It cancels or resolves the conflict between the original thesis and its antithesis, (b) it preserves and maintains the elements of truth within each of the conflicting views, and (c) it transcends the opposition and raises up or sublimates the conflict into a higher level understanding or truth.

Both Piaget and Kohlberg recognized that human life involves conflict within the individual person and between the individual and the group. Moral judgments pertaining to the resolution of these conflicts are a given part of life.

At what level of understanding is each situation viewed, and how does this impact moral conflict and choice of solution?

MODELS OF MORAL DEVELOPMENT

To understand how morality is shaped by cognitive awareness, Piaget created pairs of stories and asked children to decide which of the two were naughty. Piaget's conversations with the children led him to a three-stage theory of moral development. The three stages were

Stage 1. Premoral: In this stage awareness of rules and reasons for them is limited if it exists at all.

Stage 2. Moral Realism: This stage demonstrates an increased awareness that rules exist as they are learned from parents. Obedience is based on submission to external authority.

Stage 3. Moral Relativism: Here an awareness of the meaning of rules and the reasons for them exists. Rules become regarded as products of mutual consent and respect, and are understood in relation to the principles they uphold.

Moral development emerges from the interaction between cognitive structures (cognitive development and social experiences). Therefore, to understand the concept of morality, it is necessary not only to understand the logic of the individual but also the experience he/she is attempting to make sense of.

Kohlberg offers a detailed explanation of the development of morality. Like Piaget, he maintains that morality is achieved in a series of stages. Also like Piaget, Kohlberg was interested in understanding moral conflicts and in the process involved in resolution of such conflicts and arriving at decisions about right and wrong. Kohlberg (1969) found that although children might come up with the same answer to moral dilemmas as adults (believing that it is not right to lie or steal), the logic of the children's thinking about values was distinctively different from that of adults. Children's thinking, it was found, was less complex but in its own terms no less logical.

According to Gilligan (1980), Kohlberg's six stages of moral development represent increasingly adequate conceptions of justice and reflect an expanding capacity to take the role or perspective of the other person. In the end, she sees these two as the same because the claims of all are accounted for in one just solution. The explanation of moral perspective, according to Gilligan, signifies an extension of the social universe to which the moral considerations pertain. This expansion in perspective defines the three levels of moral judgment into which Kohlberg's six stages fall.

Level 1. Preconventional At this level an individual's moral reasoning results from the consequences of action (punishment, reward, exchange of favor) and from the physical power of those in authority. Moral dilemmas are seen as conflicts between the individual needs of the people involved.

Stage 1. Decisions result from a blind obedience to power, an attempt to avoid punishment, or an attempt to seek rewards.

Stage 2. Decisions result from a desire to satisfy one's own needs and occasionally the needs of others. Individuals view reciprocity as a matter of "you scratch my back and I'll scratch yours." Reasoning involves little consideration of loyalty, gratitude, or justice.

Level 2. Conventional   At this level an individual's moral reasoning involves consideration of the interests of others (family and peers), a desire to maintain respect and support, and to justify the existing social order. Moral judgments always appeal to authority, but the authority derives its moral claim not from greater power but from its consensual validation or legitimate traditional base.

Stage 3. At this stage decisions result from a desire to please and help others and receive their approval in return. Behavior is frequently judged by intention—he or she "means well" becomes important for the first time.

Stage 4. Decisions made here result from a desire to maintain the existing authority, rules, and social order. Right behavior consists of doing one's duty.

Level 3. Post–Conventional   At this level an individual's moral reasoning incorporates moral values and principles with validity and application beyond the authority of groups. Moral reasoning becomes comprehensive and reflects universal principles.

Stage 5. Here decisions result from recognition of an individual's right within a society that has a social contract. As a result, the individual's reasoning emphasizes the legal point of view but with the emphasis on the possibility of changing laws.

Stage 6. In this, the highest stage, decisions result from an obligation to universal ethical principles that apply to all humankind. The universal principles of justice, reciprocity, quality of human rights, and respect for the dignity of human beings as individuals serve as a basis for individual reasoning.

Kohlberg's third post-conventional level of morality has been labeled by Smith (in his commentary on Gilligan, 1980), as a twentieth-century categorical imperative. Kohlberg encapsulated moral development as a process involving the restructuring of the concept of the self in its relationship to the concept of other people. This takes place in a common social world with social standards.

Van Hoose and Paradise (1979) proposed the ethical orientation could be viewed from a model of five qualitatively different stages of ethical reasoning. The stages are as follows:

Stage 1. Punishment Orientation: In this stage, individual ethical orientation is guided by and relies exclusively upon external resources and strict adherence to rules and standards. Motivation is influenced by awareness of consequences of behavior.

Stage 2. Institutional Orientation: As in the first stage, ethical orientation is externally oriented. The institution with which the individual is associated provides the rationale for ethical decisions. There is strict obedience and compliance with higher authorities within the institution.

Stage 3. Societal Orientation: At this stage, there is an ethical orientation toward adherence to the law. The law reflects the societal goal of the greatest good for the greatest many. Where there is a conflict between the individual and the society, the individual is expected to yield to the societal interests.

Stage 4. Individual Orientation: In this stage, the locus of control (ethical orientation) shifts from external to internal. Concern is now for the needs of the individual while not violating the laws of society or the rights of others. The individual is of primary concern with the societal context being second.

Stage 5. Principle or Conscious Orientation. This is the highest stage of ethical/moral orientation. Concern here is for the individual regardless of the legal, professional, or societal consequences, or situational factors. The individual operating in this stage has defined an internal code of ethics that guides behavior regardless of external pressure or situational factors. (p. 38)

Learning patterns of social interaction is the beginning process whereby moral orientation is organized at the individual level (Youniss, 1978; Kohlberg, 1969; Whitehead, 1929). Individuals interact with other individuals and, as a result of many factors, form groups. Moral bias exists and is in part related to an individual's position in a socially structured environment or group (Douglas, 1982). Paradigms are used by individuals to organize related concepts. Paradigms provide approaches for organizing, interpreting, and evaluating information for decision making. Groups interacting with other groups combine to form social institutions. Gilligan (1980) believed that social institutions influence moral development. She further asserted that social institutions impede or foster moral development by the concept of justice they embody. A conceptual framework for understanding social justice begins with the individual, moves to the group, then to the larger society before reverting again to the individual.

This process is circular, not linear. Individuals interacting with and reacting to other individuals combine to form groups with similar goals, beliefs, or values. These groups exert some potential influence on their members as well as on members of other groups. Multiple groups combine to form institutions that exert influence on the groups that make them up as well as on the individuals who make up the groups. An event begins with the individual affecting the group; the group affecting the institution; the institution affecting the individual; and so on. Different levels of moral understanding are related to group or societal position and paradigm structure. These factors impact the understanding of moral conflicts and the process of resolving moral dilemmas, including principles utilized.

INDIVIDUAL MORAL DEVELOPMENT

Individuals innately struggle to make sense of their experiences both within themselves and in the outside world in which they live. One struggles to know what is good. Piaget's (1932) view of the child making sense of his or her world is coupled with the conception of knowledge as residing neither in the child nor the world but rather in the interaction between them. Piaget saw knowledge of morality as emerging from the interaction between cognitive structures and social experience. Therefore, to understand the individual's concept of morality it is necessary to understand not only the logic used but also the social interactions and experiences of which the individual is attempting to make sense. Piaget's work on the moral judgment of the child suggests that a shift in the child's social position from the hierarchical world of the family to the often more democratic world of peers can lead to a concomitant change in the child's view and practice of rules. To understand this transition is to become aware of the region between the event and the reaction to the event—the region where meaning of the experience is determined. The attention is not on what is believed or seen as being true or even on uncovering the why, but rather on the process by which the individual arrives at those views and practices.

Gilligan (1980), in asserting that social institutions impede or foster moral development by the concept of justice they embody, adds three supporting propositions: (a) moral judgment is advanced by an environment that provides moral stimulation and reasoning one stage above the individual's own; (b) moral judgment is advanced by an environment that exposes the individual to conflicts of value and to attempts at integrating these conflicts; and (c) moral judgment is advanced by a social class and peer environment that provide the individual with the opportunity to take the role of others and with the experience of social membership and participation. Even if these propositions have nothing else, they have a high degree of face validity.

The failure of morality signals a breakdown in the process of interaction through which the individual comes, through experience, to replace more primitive concepts of morality with the understanding of cooperation manifested in the notion of justice (Gilligan, 1980). John Dewey (1916/1966) described the democratic community as possessing a variety of commonly shared interests in a group and a certain amount of interaction and cooperative interchange with other groups. Dewey posited that democracy in the school is the bridge between the family and the outside society that is necessary for providing experiences of democratic participation and community and leads to the development of social responsibility. Ironically, for most adult individuals there seems to be a cessation of the further development of moral judgment beginning around the time they leave school. Rest (1980) suggested that development continues as long as individuals are in school, but plateaus when they leave.

While one must be free to choose for morality to make any sense at all, an action does not become right merely because it is chosen. So what factors influence what one chooses and ultimately does?

VALUES, BELIEFS, AND ATTITUDES

Values, beliefs, and attitudes are a triad that influence choice and behavior. Values are prescriptive beliefs that a certain mode of conduct or way of being is preferable to others. They serve as guides in daily activities. Values are positive and idealistic in character and have similar properties to goals (Schwartz, 1994; Feather, 1994). While seen as enduring and stable over time, values may vary in importance at any given time depending on the context (Schwartz, 1992; Feather, 1994; Braithwaite & Scott, 1991; Braithwaite, 1994). This prioritization suggests that values are dynamic rather than static and change in the level of importance according to contextual scrutiny. Beliefs, on the other hand, can be viewed as information individuals have about other individuals, groups, or situations that are either fact or opinion (Braithwaite, 1994). Attitudes involve evaluations of other individuals, groups, or situations in a direct way often requiring interaction (Fishbein & Ajzen, 1975; Petty & Cacioppo, 1981). Attitudes are relatively peripheral in the belief system and they may change, even with similar objects in different situations (Grube, Mayton & Ball-Rokeach, 1994). Attitudes are instrumental for and serve more central values. Therefore, while individuals may possess a plethora of attitudes, there are but a few core values that underpin them.

Attempts to change the attitudes of an individual have limited success if they are not congruent with the more enduring underlying values that support the attitudes and behavior. It is precisely for this reason that a change in one value may precipitate numerous changes in functionally related values, attitudes, and behaviors (Grube et al., 1994). Rokeach (cited in Braithwaite & Scott, 1991) differentiated between values that encompassed ideal end states and values that are concerned with modes of conduct. In doing so, he distinguished between goals of thought and goals of action. It is viewed as being most likely that individuals will act in accordance with their underlying values but not always. Schwartz (1994) provides an example of pursuit of achievement values as a personal value conflicting with values relating to cooperation and benevolence, an institutional requirement. Value conflicts can be seen as potentially existing between the individual and the group or institution within which the individual must function, with the resolution being unpredictable.

Social institutions have a profound impact on individuals' values and view of morality, as do environmental factors. Some of those are briefly examined in the next section.

SOCIAL ENVIRONMENTAL FACTORS

It has been said that where you stand determines what you see, and what you see determines where you stand. Applying a pragmatic interpretation, Douglas (1982) suggests that specific dimensions of social environments are important in determining an individual's moral reasoning. Her concept of grid/group analysis identifies specific social environments in which each of the various types of moral reasoning are most likely to occur. According to Douglas, grid describes the extent of regulation or constraint imposed on an individual, while group refers to the individual's degree of commitment or allegiance to a given group (p. 5). She links alternative visions of a just society and moral bias directly to an individual's position in a socially structured environment.

Douglas analyzed four social relationships as defined by grid/group analysis, which she labeled A, B, C, and D. Type A, the low grid; low group environment, is characterized by individualism. Here individuals often feel little commitment to the group and the pursuit of individual freedoms is seen as unconstrained. Self-motivated entrepreneurial types are examples of Type A. Type B, the high grid; low group, is an environment where individual behavior is highly limited by those in power. In this environment certain individuals are in positions not necessarily of their choice and must do as they are told. Douglas conjectures that in a highly competitive society most women and children (and possibly minorities) are in such positions. Type C, the high grid; high group, is viewed as an ascribed hierarchy. This is similar to the environment of large institutions or the military, where loyalty to the group and its rules are rewarded and the hierarchy respected. The orientation here is toward authority, fixed rules, and the maintenance of social order for its own sake. Type D, the low grid; high group, is composed of small groups formed in disagreement with, and withdrawal from, the larger society. Egalitarianism is expounded while at the same time there is exclusive commitment to the group above all else. Radical groups and cults are examples of Type D.

Feather (1994) appears to agree with Douglas and argues that some research suggests that moral judgments and value preferences are the outcome of socialization experiences rather than the product of developmental sequence. This research suggests that moral decision making involves more complex processes than an attribution to a developmental stage would allow.

As society has grown in size, it has grown in complexity of its organizations. Any organization, regardless of its size or purpose, is similar in that it involves the cooperative endeavor of several people acting to influence and direct other people. All involved have a similar focus and goal, that being the one

provided by the group or organization. That which would be quickly abandoned or identified as wrong if done by a single individual can be carried out
by the group without hesitation or apparent culpability. Isolation is thought to
encourage the development of groupthink as a result of decreased interaction
and cooperative interchange with other groups.

Additionally, these factors, to a greater or lesser degree, make it difficult for
individuals in various groups to see the same issues and dilemmas in complex
real-life situations or events. This is especially true when the issue or dilemma
is one in which they all participate, but do so from different group perspectives.
Cooperative interchanges may be possible for some individuals depending on
their perspective, but not for others because they do not identify the situation
or event as important or even controversial. How and if the group or organization allows participation in decision making or legislates to its members is a
potent factor in determining the process outcome of moral judgments.

Grid/group analysis is consistent with the idea that moral development
plateaus after leaving school (Rest, 1980). According to grid/group analysis,
moral judgment does not result from an advance in reasoning to a qualitatively
higher, more complex structuring of the content of moral knowledge. Instead,
it occurs as a strategic response by the individual who realizes that others in a
given environment find this type of justification appropriate under the circumstances. Changes in moral orientation, according to Douglas, are therefore
not a result of logic, but the result of movement to a new grid/group position.
Acceptance or nonacceptance of a particular moral view is dictated by association rather than logical reasoning. Opportunities for groups or organizations
to "cause the effect" or "effect the cause" regarding moral judgments are
vividly clear.

Let us return to Dewey's idea that democracy in the school is the necessary
bridge to provide the experience that leads to the development of social responsibility, and let us substitute groups or organizations for school. Facilitation
of cooperative interchange with and among different groups on a variety of social and moral issues allows for individual participation in the exchange of ideas.
This participation and the differing roles, much as in school, discourage isolation and tendencies toward groupthink. Groups and organizations become
sources of stimulation and interchange instead of static havens where one finds
others in this environment accepting, without question, a particular justification appropriate under the circumstances. Isolating and compartmentalizing
groups allows for and encourages groupthink and similar phenomena that contribute to the effect.

However, the problem of agreement (not groupthink) remains and can still
be heard in the echo of Aristotle's comment that there is no agreement as to
what young people [or adults] should learn . . . all people do not appreciate the
same kind of goodness, so it is expected that they would differ (Burnet, 1903).

To understand more fully how these social environmental factors, groups,
and organizations go about the process of influencing the perception of social
justice one must explore the paradigm(s) by which they work.

THE PARADIGM OF PRINCIPLES

Gilligan (1980) returns to the individual by stating that moral judgment is related to [individual] moral action. Smith (1980) stated in his commentary on Gilligan that he heard her message as saying adults influence the moral judgments of children, for better or worse. However, those adults who are themselves adrift in a sea of moral relativism are without maps by which their offspring can chart a course toward what is right and good in human life. This statement, especially the importance of a map, can be generalized to our discussion of the process of social justice. Individuals, groups, and organizations all possess knowledge of principles of morality they believe to be correct. The map or principles of morality that are transmitted or taught, regardless of their correctness, are based or constructed on paradigms.

Paradigms provide approaches for organizing, interpreting, and evaluating information for the purpose of making decisions. These are expressed as principles, rules, or laws. Individuals often act as though moral rules or principles are exhaustive and justice requires only an understanding of and adherence to some code of ethics or rules. In given environments or situations a behavior is judged appropriate under the circumstances based on the principles or rules derived from the paradigm. Moral orientation, as viewed by Douglas (1982), is a strategic move to a new grid/group position whose principles support or justify a given action.

The public rhetoric on various aspects of social justice, (e.g., affirmative action, equal rights, abortion, and similar issues) has increasingly become discourse that focuses on matters of principle. Jonsen and Toulmin (1988) have described discourse involving matters of principle as often ending up in a head-butting that pits unqualified and unconditional rights against unqualified and unconditional rights. The very process employed (arguing on high-level theory and general principles) assures that on a practical level no resolution is possible. The more that principles become mottos and slogans, eventually evolving into battle cries, the more the fervent devotees on both sides are driven to frustration and even violence. Pitting contradictory and/or incompatible ethical principles against one another guarantees deadlock. Therefore, solutions must be sought elsewhere. In looking for a pragmatic solution, one must acknowledge that in accepting [universal] rules and principles as the basis for ethics, little if any middle ground can be found between absolutism and relativism (Jonsen & Toulmin). In dealing with real-life ethical dilemmas, one finds that rules and principles apply to some situations without ambiguity but only apply marginally to others. This makes the marginal situation just as problematic as the situations in which different rules or principles conflict with each other.

As we have seen, a given paradigm results in the establishment of rules and principles associated with a certain reference point, often that of the group or organization. The adherence to rules and principles as unchallengable results in what Jonsen and Toulmin have called a principled tyranny. The principle itself, rather than the reason for it, is the treatise on which action is taken. The principle then becomes more important than its underlying rationale. The problems that principled tyranny brings about are not confined to the theoretical level but permeate functioning at all levels. In part, the inability to engage in cooperative interchange is due to a groupthink-type skewed perception of moral problems and/or the inability to identify the situation as important or controversial. The resulting behavior is a "head in the sand" type of denial of the opposing view that further polarizes already differing groups. Another view of this type of situation might be framed as the rigidly dogmatic versus the overly flexible tolerant permissive. The problem again is not as it appears, rigid versus permissive; rather, it lies in the inability to make a paradigm shift to see how, if, and under what conditions justice is served by tolerance of exception. In situations like this, if remediation is possible, one is forced to go beyond the principle or rule and examine the process that underlies it.

DEVELOPMENT OF PRUDENCE

In the application of principles to the process of moral decision making the question remains, "What kind of understanding of human conduct does ethics provide?" Aristotle (trans. 1987) declared ethics is not and could not be a science; therefore, it cannot provide universal principles for particular judgments. Rather, ethics is a field of experience that calls for prudence; prudence being practical experience that cannot be gained in social isolation. Practical wisdom is born of experience and deals with the particulars of a given situation and also with universally applicable concepts. The experience and resulting moral ethical development is analogous to a major part of Smith's moral map. Principles derived from the paradigm are used to judge appropriate behaviors under the circumstances. Granting that some general principles are universal and are to be taken as ethically binding, no matter what their source, one must learn (through the process of moral development) to fit them to particular cases (Arras, 1986, 1994; Kuczewski, 1994).

For pragmatic judgments regarding ethics and social justice, practical wisdom is a prerequisite. Aristotle (trans. 1987), explaining practical wisdom argued, "While the young become geometricians and mathematicians, and wise in matters of that sort, they do not seem to be prudent. The reason is that prudence applies to particular cases, and these cases become known by experience" (p. 198). Jonsen and Toulmin (1988, pp. 34–35) distinguish two approaches in dealing with moral ethical dilemmas. One, the theoretical, is concerned with principles, rules, and other general ideas that posit universal rules [axioms] from which particular moral/ethical judgments are deduced. The second, more practical, focuses on specific features of the particular kinds of moral cases, with moral rules serving as maxims that can be understood only in terms of the paradigmatic cases that define their meaning and force. Theoretical arguments are not dependent on the circumstances of their presentation. The argument is a chain of propositions, linked together in such a way as to guarantee its conclusion. Conclusions are deduced from initial axioms or universal principles.

These truths flow downward to provide resolution for the questions at hand. Practical arguments draw on the outcomes of previous experience, carrying over procedures used to resolve earlier problems and reapplying them in new problematic situations. Their validity depends on how closely the present situation resembles those of the earlier precedent cases for which this particular type of argument was originally devised. The task at hand is not about showing what makes one particular ethical view more correct by referring to rules or laws that are held as true with great certainty by various groups or organizations. Rather, resolution may be sought in the manner ascribed:

> The analysis and resolution of moral issues utilizes procedures of reasoning based on paradigms and analogies, leading to the formulation of opinions about the existence and stringency of particular moral obligations, framed in terms of principles that are general but not universal or invariable, since they hold good with certainty only in the special conditions of the agent and circumstances of action. (Jonsen & Toulmin, p. 257)

The process of moral development requires one to understand not only the general principles of morality, but also in what circumstances and situations they do and do not apply. This requires a paradigm shift from traditional inductive (generalizing or drawing conclusions from particular facts) and deductive (generalizing from a known principle to an unknown) reasoning to a more practical problem-solving approach. This approach views principles as general in form but limited in scope of practical application and understanding arrived at through varied experience. The commitment is not to the principles or views of a particular group, institution, or race, but rather to the understanding of human needs. The practical task is to identify and apply general moral rules and other ethical factors relating to the concept of justice to new and increasingly complex circumstances in ways that respect human needs. Concomitantly, this entails a review and redefining of concepts such as autonomy. Autonomy moves from simply a right to self-determination to a broader independence, meaning that an autonomous agent is the source of moral principles and not merely the recipient. This requires individuals, their groups, and institutions, to facilitate cooperative interchange with and among other groups and institutions allowing for varied human experiences, exchange of ideas, and roles leading to the development of prudence. The key to practical wisdom is embodied in the knowledge of the process; application of this knowledge entails education through cooperative human interchange and transmission of knowledge to others through respectful dialogue. Kung (1991) in his book *Global Responsibility* wrote

> . . . the world in which we live has a chance for survival only if there is no longer any room in it for spheres of differing, contradictory and even antagonistic ethics . . . it needs some norms, values, ideals and goals to bring it together and to be binding on it. The obligation is to the whole not to any part. (p. xvi)

SUMMARY

Moral ethical development is a complex process involving interaction of the individual with one's self and with others. The level of cognitive understanding at which a situation is viewed impacts the conflict as well as the solution. Various models of moral development have been proposed, all of which involve cognitive development and social experiences. Each model views development as a tiered or staged progression, with each stage possessing its own unique logical approach to problem solving. Each stage represents an increasingly adequate conception of fairness or justice. Interaction between the society and the individual leads to the establishment of values, beliefs, and attitudes that influence individual choice and behavior.

Paradigms provide approaches for organizing, interpreting, and evaluating information for the purpose of decision making. Expressed as principles, they are transmitted through the interactional process of moral ethical development. Based on developmental levels, group, or societal position, all individuals, their groups, and organizations possess knowledge of principles of morality that they believe to be true, regardless of their actual correctness.

Moral ethical dilemmas involving matters of principle often reflect a given paradigm, which results in rules or principles associated with a certain inflexible reference point. The inflexibility reflects a lower level of moral ethical development, (e.g., the inability to take another's point of view or to see how principles might apply differently in different situations).

Moral ethical development is a process that involves both the individual and the environment, to include other individuals. The process is seen as interactive and circular, not linear. The sum of the products of this interaction is the development of Aristotelian prudence or what one may call moral ethical maturity.

QUESTIONS FOR ADDITIONAL REFLECTION AND THOUGHT

1. Using the information presented in this chapter, respond to the following statement: What you see depends upon where you stand and where you stand depends upon what you see.

2. Can groups or organizations function autonomously apart from the individuals that comprise them? If so, what are the implications for the moral and ethical functioning of these groups?

3. List some of the groups or institutions in which you have or have had affiliation (e.g., church, school, social organization). How influential have they been in your moral/ethical development? Do the same for significant others in your life. In the process of moral/ethical development which comes first, the individual or the group?

4. List some of the groups or institutions that hold different moral/ethical beliefs from yours. How have these influenced your moral/ethical development?

5. Are your values dynamic or static? Do they change in relative importance depending on situational context?

6. Describe the relationship between values, beliefs, and attitudes.

7. Do females and males differ in their moral development? If so, can you explain the differences and their possible sources?

USING THEORY FOR CONCRETE ETHICAL JUDGMENTS

Ethical Dilemma

You are a nontraditional counseling student who is in the final stages of her program and is taking a practicum in counseling. Before returning to graduate school to become a school counselor you were a social worker (CSW–ACP) and are still licensed to practice in your state. You had worked in a psychiatric hospital for a number of years but after marriage and children you made a career change to teaching. After several years of teaching, you decided to return to your original field and began working on certification as a school counselor. You have completed all your required course work and are seeking a school site to do your practicum. You approach your school district about placement at a local school and they are elated. They inform you that they want to place you in a school where they need experienced counselors, especially licensed counselors. The district has devised a plan by which the licensed counselors (or in this case a social worker) can bill for third–party reimbursement of counseling services rendered to students. Even though you are technically a student, you are a licensed social worker with advanced clinical practitioner certification and experience. The principal and other counselors at the school are excited about having you as a practicum student and desire to know how soon you can begin. The reception you have received is flattering. You are now expected to give them a date when you can begin.

The Problem

As a student, are you agreeable to the practicum placement and the staff's expectations? As a licensed professional, should you agree to the billing of your services for third–party reimbursement? When does a student stop being a student, or when does a professional stop being a professional and become a student? Is it ethical, when working in the role of a student, to bill for services rendered even if you are competent and licensed to do so legally?

The Decision-Making Process

In the current situation a critical question that emerges is how much responsibility for ethical behavior is borne by the institution and how much by you? Who makes the decision? Many actions later shown or acknowledged to be unethical have been defended by the statement: I was only doing what I was told to do by my superior. This statement, considered a rationalization, makes it clear who has the final responsibility. Are your beliefs about what is right and ethical consistent with what you value in this situation? What, if any, effect is your school district's response to you and to this situation having on you and your thoughts about what to do? Is this situation a special one in which the existing principles do not apply?

What are your college's or university's rules regarding practicum students? What are the school district's rules? Imagine yourself belonging to another group and looking in at this situation—what would you see? How would you assess the situation? Is it different from the way you see it currently?

12

✳

Ethics and the Law

INFORMED CONSENT

Before a person becomes a client, he or she must consent to treatment. Obtaining consent precedes any treatment and recordkeeping. In order to consent to treatment, the client must first be made aware of what he or she is agreeing to become a participant in. Minimally, the client should be made aware of the who, what, when, and how. The qualifications of the professional counselor who will be treating the client should be clearly acknowledged. The particular goals of counseling must be identified, as well as the risks and benefits associated with counseling. When results, if any, may be expected and how financial considerations are arranged should be specified.

A client's consent to treatment can occur only after certain requirements are met, defined as the elements of informed consent (Bray, Shepard, & Hays, 1985; Schwitzgebel & Schwitzgebel, 1980). The elements of informed consent are competence, voluntariness, full information, and comprehension. Competence is the client's ability to make a rational decision with regard to participation in treatment. Voluntariness means that the client is free to make the decision to participate or not to participate in treatment. Full information is provided to the client regarding the probable risks and the potential rewards of participation in treatment. Comprehension means that all information provided is expressed in simple language the average person would be expected to easily understand. The actual amount of information to give a client continues to be a subject of controversy. Professional judgment must be used when seeking a balance between the client's desires and right to make an informed decision about treatment and the potential therapeutic compromise resulting from overdisclosure.

CONFIDENTIALITY

The obligation of practitioners to maintain the confidentiality of their relationships with their clients is a cornerstone of the therapeutic process and an essential prerequisite for the therapeutic relationship. Confidentiality, according to Siegel (1979), involves professional ethics rather than legalism and expresses a promise or contract to reveal nothing about an individual except under certain conditions agreed to by the client. Confidentiality may also be based in statute or case law (Swoboda et al., 1978). Confidentiality is thought of as being similar to, but not interchangeable with, privileged communication and privacy because they have different meanings. Distinguishing between confidentiality, privilege, and privacy is critical in understanding a variety of legal/ethical problems. Confidentiality, as defined by Shah (1969), relates to matters of professional ethics. Confidentiality protects the client from unauthorized disclosures of any sort by the practitioner without informed consent of the client. Confidentiality, however, is not absolute. State and federal regulations and court decisions have mandated the disclosure of information in certain situations, even if it means breaking confidentiality. Understanding the concepts of privilege and privacy will better enable practitioners to maintain confidentiality.

PRIVILEGED COMMUNICATION

Privileged communication is "a legal right which exists by statute and which protects [clients] from having [their] confidences revealed publicly from the witness stand during legal proceedings without [their] permission" (Shah, 1969, p. 57). Siegel (1979) defines privileged communication as

> . . . a legal term involving the right not to reveal confidential information
> in a legal procedure. Privilege is granted by statute, protects the client
> from having his/her communications revealed in a judicial setting without
> explicit permission, and is vested in the client by legislative authority.
> (p. 251)

Privileged communication, then, is a legal concept and refers to the right of the client not to have his or her confidential communications revealed without his or her consent. If the client waives this privilege, then the information must be revealed. Privilege belongs to the client and is meant for the protection of the client. Privilege may be claimed by the client or by a representative of the client acting on the client's behalf. A professional may claim privilege only on behalf of the client, not himself. However, it is important to note that the privileged communication for the counselor–client relationship is not legally supported in many states. This means that privileged communication only exists for clients of professionals specifically enumerated in the statute. In other words, only those "professionals" (e.g., physicians or psychiatrists) specifically defined are included. In the absence of specific enumeration in the statute, inclusion may be provided by meeting the qualifications of one who is defined as a professional. Texas, for example, uses the following definition of professional to determine where privilege applies:

> (1) A professional means any person . . . licensed or certified by the State of Texas in the diagnosis, evaluation, or treatment of any mental or emotional disorder, or involved in the treatment or examination of drug abusers; or reasonably believed by the patient to be included in any of the preceding categories. (2) A patient means any person who consults, or is interviewed by a professional for the purpose of diagnosis, evaluation, or treatment of any mental or emotional disorder, including alcoholism, and drug addiction; or is being treated voluntarily or being examined for admission to voluntary treatment for drug abuse (Rule 510, Texas Rules of Civil Evidence).

PRIVACY

Privacy, with regard to counseling and psychotherapy, has been defined as "freedom of individuals to choose for themselves the time and the circumstances under which the extent to which their beliefs, behaviors, and opinions are to be shared or withheld from others" (Siegel, 1979, p. 251). The concept of privacy is addressed by the Fourth Amendment to the United States Constitution, which offers protection against invasion of privacy by the government. Everstine et al. (1980) raise some important questions pertaining to privacy: To what extent should beliefs and opinions be protected from the scrutiny of others? Who may intrude on a person's privacy and how and under what circumstances is this decided? These questions are of particular importance when they include a prospective employer's access to an applicant's psychological tests, parental access to a child's school records, or insurance company or other third-party payer access to information regarding counseling or psychotherapy, or when counseling professionals are bound by law or professional codes of ethics to break confidentiality.

Of central issue here is the question of whose behalf the counselor or therapist is acting on as agent. Shah (1970) notes that in some governmental agencies and institutions the counselor or therapist is not primarily the client's agent. In these situations, counselors or therapists are faced with conflicts between their obligations to their clients and their obligations to their agency or institution. Shah maintains that any potential conflicts should be clarified before entering into a diagnostic or therapeutic relationship with the client. Denkowski and Denkowski (1982), in support of Shah's position, contend that counseling professionals should inform clients of potential breaches of confidentiality. Furthermore, they note that it is ethically incumbent on counseling professionals that all reasonable steps be taken to restrict the legally sanctioned dissemination of confidential client information to its bare minimum (p. 374).

DUTY TO WARN

Because confidentiality is not absolute, it is essential that the counseling professional determine under what circumstances it cannot be maintained. Ethical guidelines (ACA, AMA, APA and others) maintain that disclosure of information is necessary or required in order to protect the welfare of the individual or the community, or where there is a clear and imminent danger to the individual or to the community. What represents a need to protect or clear and imminent danger is usually left to the discretion of the counseling professional. The best-known case regarding clear and imminent danger and duty to warn is the Tarasoff case (*Tarasoff v. Regents of the University of California,* 1976). The facts of the case are as follows:

In the fall of 1969, Prosenjit Poddar, a citizen of India and a naval architecture student at the University of California's Berkeley campus, shot and stabbed to death Tatiana Tarasoff, a young woman who had spurned his affections. Poddar, prior to killing Tarasoff, was seeing a psychologist as an outpatient at the student health service on the Berkeley campus of the university. Poddar had confided to the psychologist that he intended to kill an unnamed woman (who was readily identifiable as Tatiana Tarasoff) when she returned from a trip out of the country. The psychologist consulted with colleagues and then made the assessment that Poddar was dangerous and should be evaluated for civil commitment. The psychologist called the campus police and told them of the death threat and of his conclusion that Poddar was dangerous. The campus police did take Poddar into custody for questioning, but after finding him rational and obtaining a promise that he would stay away from Tarasoff, they concluded he was not dangerous and released him. Poddar never returned to the student health service center, and two months later, killed Tarasoff.

Tarasoff's family filed suit against the University of California Board of Regents, the student health center staff members involved, and the police for failing to notify the intended victim of the threat. A lower court dismissed the suit, and the family appealed to the Supreme Court of California, who in 1976 ruled in favor of the parents, holding that the psychologist did indeed have a duty to warn the victim or her family of the danger. The court's ruling requires that counseling professionals breach confidentiality in cases where the general welfare or safety of others is involved. This was a California case, so counseling professionals in other states are not bound by this court ruling.

Differing opinions, however, do exist. Siegel (1979) contends that "this was a day in court for the law and not for the mental health professions" (p. 253). He contends that, if Poddar's psychologist had accepted the absolute and inviolate confidentiality position, Poddar might well have been kept in psychotherapy and the life of Tatiana Tarasoff might have been saved. Other professionals (Everstine et al., 1980) accept the duty to warn, seeing that there are certain conditions under which counseling professionals must exchange their professional role for the role of a concerned citizen.

Corey, Corey, and Callanan (1984) offer guidelines for counseling professionals to follow if they determine a client poses a serious threat of violence to others.

1. The counseling professional should inform the client of the possible action they must take to protect a third party in situations where there is a threat of violence.

2. When a client makes a threat against others, the counseling professional should document everything observed and stated in the session.

3. If the counseling professional is under supervision, he or she should notify the supervisor verbally and in writing of the threat.

4. The counseling professional should seek professional consultation on how to proceed, and document the consultation.

5. The appropriate authorities should be notified.

6. The intended victim must be notified; in the case of a minor, the minor's parents should be notified also.

SUICIDE AND DUTY TO PROTECT

Clients can pose not only a danger to others, but also to themselves. Most professional counselors inform their clients that they have an ethical and legal responsibility to break confidentiality when they have valid reason to suspect active suicidal intent on the part of the client. In the previous discussion, it was emphasized that professional counselors have a duty to warn and to protect others; these principles also apply to the client. Despite the argument that states, "It's my life and I have a right to do as I desire, including ending it," professional counselors have an ethical duty to protect their clients as well as others.

The debate over individual rights, including the right to take one's own life, has intensified in recent years. Szasz (1986) challenges the position that mental health professionals have an absolute duty to try and prevent suicide. He argues that suicide is the act of a moral agent who is ultimately responsible, and opposes coercive methods of suicide prevention, such as involuntary commitment to a psychiatric hospital. Guided by the principle of autonomy, Szasz takes the stance that it is the client's responsibility to choose to live or die. Szasz contends that if the client seeks professional help for suicidal tendencies, then the professional has an ethical obligation to provide the help being sought. However, according to Szasz, if the client does not seek such help or actively rejects it, then the professional's duty is either to persuade the client to accept help or to leave the client alone. The core of his argument is seen in the following:

Because I value individual liberty highly and am convinced that liberty and responsibility are indivisible, I want to enlarge the scope of liberty and responsibility. In the present instance, this means opposing policies of suicide prevention that minimize the responsibility of the individual for killing themselves and supporting policies that maximize their responsibility for doing so. In other words, we should make it more difficult for suicidal persons to reject responsibility for deliberately taking their own lives and for mental health professionals to assume responsibility for keeping such persons alive. (p. 810)

Szasz is not stating that suicide is always a good or moral option; rather he is insisting that the individual and not the government be responsible for the decision to take one's own life. The right to suicide implies that individual rights supersede the power or right of the government to coercively prevent it.

In an opposing view, this author (Freeman, 1993) also sees responsibility and choice as central concepts; however, responsible rational choice and therefore autonomy is not possible when the individual feels compelled to make one choice over another, often out of desperation, as in the case of suicide. The option of suicide is necessitated by a constricted narrowing of choices that an individual sees as open to them. The goal is not death, but freedom or escape from that which is oppressive or undesirable. A responsible choice is seen here as severely limited at best and, in the worst case, not available as the need to escape is overwhelming. The option of surrender or suicide presents a struggle, a dilemma. The question is to die or not to die (not how to address the overwhelming or insurmountable oppressive problem that has driven the individual to the point of desperation). If suicide is an option in resolving a conflict, then the individual must guard against it, watching with one eye, so that the back is never completely turned. To turn away might result in unwillingly becoming a victim of one's own hand. However, dealing with the problem requires the individual's full attention and energy, which cannot be given up because of the vigil required over one's own death impulse. Intervention, then, is seen as an ethical requirement, not to take away from but to return to the individual the task of responsible choice. Utilizing Schneidman's (1984, p. 310) succinct statement that "suicide is not a 'right' any more than is the right to belch, but if compelled to the individual will do it," the point is made that if forced or compelled to do it, suicide will be the choice regardless of interventions. This author does not say that suicide is never an acceptable option, but an individual should be given the time and resources whereby he or she may be allowed to give up the option of suicide and not be compelled to automatically accept it. I agree with Schneidman that the election of suicide by the individual cannot be taken away, for if driven to take their lives, many will. Many times, with appropriate intervention and help, other options are found.

When faced with the risk of potential suicide by a client, the professional counselor is immediately placed in a precarious situation. The conservative response might be to safeguard the client through hospitalization. The less conservative approach might be to continue to do outpatient work, but on a more frequent basis. Regardless of which approach one chooses, it should be based on a clear and thorough understanding of one's own values underlying the counselor's role and responsibility in preventing suicide. Additionally, counseling professionals should have knowledge and understanding of legal obligations that require action on their part. A determination of lethality should also be made, because what may appear on the surface as a mild suicidal risk, when assessed, could actually be much more serious. Readers are referred to Schneidman's work on assessing suicidal lethality.

Counseling professionals have an obligation to inform clients that the duty to protect exists. Additionally, clients should be told that the counseling professional has a duty to report suspected or substantiated instances of child abuse, incest, and/or other actions that constitute a threat to others or to the clients themselves. These conditions or limitations should be made clear to the client at the beginning of the therapeutic relationship.

ACCESS TO RECORDS

Professional counselors maintain records on clients for various reasons, such as legal obligation, documentation of service, communication to other professionals, and maintenance of a chronological therapeutic history. These records, by their very nature, will contain confidential information; and as long as they exist, someone other than the professional counselor who collected the material may seek access to them.

Requirements for retaining records will vary as a function of the applicable state and or federal regulations, age of the client, and whether the file or record is considered a business record, medical record, school record, or research record. The legal requirements regarding retention of medical, school, and research records are usually more available and specific than those regarding a mental health practitioner's records. Many states do not specifically mention counseling or mental health records, making the requirements unclear. In the absence of clearly defined retention guidelines, the U.S. Internal Revenue Service (IRS) requirements on record retention for professional businesses may provide an alternative and defendable guideline. The IRS requires that professional businesses retain bookkeeping records for seven years. Following this guideline, the counseling professional can show a good faith effort in following established criteria for retention of records.

Time of retention of records begins with the termination of professional services to the client. In the case of a minor client, the retention clock begins when they have attained their legal majority. This means that in the case of a minor the record may need to be kept much longer than seven years.

Disposal of confidential records after the mandatory retention time should be performed in a manner consistent with their confidential nature. Shredding of records is a common method of disposing of confidential material. Other methods such as incineration are equally common and acceptable. The disposal of confidential records in any way that compromises their confidentiality must be avoided at any cost. An example of potential compromise might be placing records in plastic bags and depositing them in a Dumpster. This exposes the records to unauthorized examination and culling by third parties, as well as accidental exposure due to various traumas while in route to a final disposal point.

While records exist, the obvious points to consider are how, under what circumstances, and to whom should access to client records be allowed? To begin, the professional counselor must decide how to obtain the client's informed consent for the release of confidential information. Second, the circumstances under which the information is being sought by a third party or parties and the purpose for which it is sought must also be determined. Finally, who is going to be the recipient of the information, and is the information appropriate for disclosure to them?

INFORMED CONSENT AND THE RELEASES OF RECORDS

The elements of informed consent have been identified as competence, voluntariness, full information, and comprehension. The client's informed consent for the release of confidential information should meet those criteria and also follow the guidelines outlined in the Code of Federal Regulations (42 C.F.R, Part 2). A consent or release of information form should contain the following information: the name of the person, persons, or agency to whom the records will be released; specific description of which records, containing what information about the client (psychological or other testing, diagnosis, prognosis, treatment, or case notes) and the intended use of the information; the date the release was signed; the date the release expires, as well as a statement that the consent may be revoked at any time by the client (except when action has already been taken); any limitations on the information provided; the name and signature of the individual providing authorization to release the information (identify the individual's relationship to the client if not the client him/herself); and the signature of at least one witness. Furthermore, a disclaimer is usually included stating that this information is confidential and further disclosure or release of this information to anyone other than the identified recipient may be a violation of confidentiality.

Access of client records by the court is yet another issue to be considered. It is not unusual for a subpoena duces tecum to be issued requiring the professional counselor to appear in court and bring "any and all files, case notes, tests and reports generated, billing records and correspondence" regarding the case in question. In such cases the practitioner is wise to seek consultation with legal counsel regarding the law and any resulting obligations. Should it be ultimately determined that the demand for records has been appropriately issued, the professional counselor may be in an awkward position, especially if disclosure is viewed by the practitioner as potentially detrimental to the client's well-being or if the client does not wish the information disclosed. There are times when ethical behavior will be at odds with legal requirements. In such cases, the professional counselor may be accused of breaking the law should the disclosure not be made as demanded. A counselor could be fined or jailed for contempt. On the other hand, allowing access to the client's confidential information may be an ethical violation. In the absence of clear guidelines provided by the ethical codes, one must rely on a thorough knowledge of professional ethics and the process as it is applied to a given situation. As Cervantes advised, "Forewarned is forearmed." Consultation with and representation by legal counsel is strongly recommended.

CLIENT ACCESS TO RECORDS

Clients' rights to access their mental health records remain a potential area of conflict that is not directly addressed in the various ethical codes. This is further compounded by the type of records sought, as well as open-records laws governing public and private information. Legislative, ethical, and other practice guidelines regarding clients' rights to access their files have fueled debate and opposing views. Given the recurrence of legal and ethical debate regarding client access, the right of clients to have access to their files merits attention.

Access to institutional or agency records is usually governed by institutional or governmental policy. Federal law such as The Family Educational Rights and Privacy Act of 1974 (The Buckley Amendment) and other federal and state legislation specify a right to access institutional or agency records. The way records are defined will often determine their accessibility. Records can be categorized in three basic types: institutional (e.g., school, agency/clinic, or hospital), testing (scored standardized tests requiring test security), and working or case notes. It is this latter category, working notes or case notes, that causes the greatest concern.

Advocates of more open access to records cite improved client knowledge as helpful and claim improving consumer rights aids in consumer behavior (Roth et al., 1980). Mappes, Robb and Engels (1985) provide the following:

> Feedback provided by such access may be valuable to both the client and the practitioner. It seems logical that counselors who are not willing to explain and to be open and honest with clients, to the extent of allowing clients to see their own files, cannot be expected to create an atmosphere and relationship of trust and safety sufficient to allow the clients to examine their problems openly and experiment with new ways of handling their lives. Preventing client's access to their own counseling files risks limiting potential for growth and strength and may suggest a lack of therapist confidence in the client's self-help abilities. (p. 251)

Previous studies performed at the University of Vermont and Pittsburgh's Western Psychiatric Institute suggest that a more open records policy may reduce clients' anxiety and improve cooperation, while no adverse effects were noted (Roth et al., 1980).

Those who oppose clients' rights to openly access their files note that the information contained may be unintelligible to the client or may be misleading and possibly detrimental if taken out of context (Strassburger, 1975). When a professional denies a client's request for release of mental health records, he or she should provide the client a reason for the refusal in writing and file a copy in the client's file. The statement should specify what part or parts of the file access is being denied, the reason, and duration of rejection.

An additional concern with regard to access of a client's records occurs when the client is a child or has been deemed legally incompetent, and a parent or guardian has been appointed and may be entitled to legal access. The professional counselor must recognize the potential uniqueness of this situation with regard to the individual client's right to privacy and confidentiality. From the onset, all parties should be informed about the confidential nature of the therapeutic relationship. Discussion and subsequent agreement regarding what type of information might be shared and with whom should be made. Information such as imminent danger to self or others or the general progress or course of treatment would be appropriate to disclose.

Third-party insurers represent yet another group that may seek access to confidential client records. Clients sometimes authorize the release of information to third parties without realizing the full implications of their actions. Clients often do not realize that submitting a claim for mental health service benefits to their insurance company may authorize (or require) the professional counselor who provides the services to disclose certain information (e.g., diagnosis, type and duration of treatment, and other data). In some situations, the insurer may require a chart review or audit that requires a peer review group or person to access detailed information from the case file. This information may include detailed case notes, psychological test results, treatment plan, diagnosis, and prognosis. Some insurance companies share certain data obtained on their insured individuals with other insurance companies to aid in determining future insurability (or denial of insurance). Clients are not always aware that they are authorizing the potential release of such information when signing a claim form for submission of benefits. The potential implications of using third-party insurance for payment of mental health services should be made clear to clients, as it involves access to confidential information.

Professional Review Committees (e.g., state boards and professional associations' ethics committees) constitute another type of third party that may request access to a client's confidential information. This type of request usually involves a complaint filed against the practitioner by a client or other party. When asked to respond by such a committee, the professional counselor should first determine if a consent to release information has been obtained. It is unethical for any committee to institute an inquiry about a client without first obtaining written consent by the client to the practitioner for the release of information. When a complaint is made to an ethical committee by a client or a client's representative, the professional counselor against whom the complaint is being made must be allowed sufficient response; therefore, a consent to release confidential information must be made in order for the practitioner to defend himself or herself. The same principle applies in malpractice litigation. Confidentiality must be waived in order for the practitioner to defend himself or herself.

In the final analysis of the ethical and legal provisions regarding confidentiality and access to client mental health records, it is important to remember that ethical requirements and laws applicable to confidentiality of records are constantly changing. Answers that may have been correct in the past may now be incorrect. Continued vigilance on the part of the counseling professional is required to remain informed and updated on this keenly important and constantly changing issue.

CLIENTS' RIGHTS

Ethical practice requires that professional counselors acknowledge the legitimate rights of the individuals they serve and have an awareness and understanding of the subsequent duties involved. In the past, those who sought mental health services have enjoyed few if any rights. Initially thought to be possessed by evil spirits, they were isolated and exposed to cruel and often inhumane conditions. Though individuals such as Phillippe Pinel, Dorothea Dix, and others were able to improve the treatment of the mentally ill, it was not until the 1960s that legal reform began to take place in the mental health arena.

The client's right to confidentiality and informed consent was discussed previously. This section is intended to provide a brief overview of the subject of client rights, such as the right to treatment, the right to refuse treatment, commitment, confinement and release from confinement, and related issues. While legislation enacted at both the federal and state levels has recognized, supported, and regulated mental health services, the courts have also rendered numerous decisions with direct influence on the actions of counseling professionals.

THE RIGHT TO TREATMENT

Treatment may be defined as a course of planned intervention designed to bring about behavioral changes in an individual considered aberrant or dangerous (Brent, 1984; Schwitzgebel & Schwitzgebel, 1980). Treatment, by this definition, may include a variety of possible procedures (e.g., psychological [counseling or psychotherapy], sociological, or medical). Medical procedures (such as electroconvulsive therapy) can also be integrated with psychological and sociological treatments at the direction of the attending physician. Additionally, the development of major tranquilizers and other psychotropic drugs beginning in the 1950s has had and continues to have a profound effect on the treatment of the mentally ill.

The right to treatment was significantly influenced by the 1966 landmark case of *Rouse v. Cameron*. The Federal Court of Appeals in the District of Columbia held that Rouse—charged with a misdemeanor, found not guilty by reason of insanity, and involuntarily committed—had a statutory right to treatment, which he had not received in four years of confinement. Although this decision was based on a state statute, the judge deciding the case discussed a constitutional right to treatment under the Eighth Amendment (forbidding cruel and unusual punishment) and the Fourteenth Amendment (providing for due process and equal protection rights). In the 1971 case, *Wyatt v. Strickney,* a federal district court and a federal court of appeals ruled that the mentally ill have a constitutional right to treatment and that not to provide treatment would be a violation of the mentally ill person's due process under the Fourteenth Amendment. The ruling, which applied to the Alabama State School for the Mentally Retarded, has had far-reaching effects on treatment institutions across the United States. Individualized treatment plans and the least restrictive setting for treatment were two of the most significant and far-reaching results of the court ruling. In addition, addressing the mental patient's right to be free from harm, the Wyatt decision discussed the use of restraints and/or seclusion in the treatment of mental patients. The court mandated certain guidelines, many of which have been incorporated in other state statutes. These specify who can institute restraint or seclusion procedures; how long an individual can be kept in restraint and/or seclusion; what documentation is required before, during, and after; and what the individual's rights are while in restraint and/or seclusion.

In the case of *O'Conner v. Donaldson* (1975), the U.S. Supreme Court recognized for the first time a constitutional right to treatment for the nondangerous, mentally ill person. The court ruled that the state could not confine or otherwise commit a mentally ill person unless treatment was provided. The civilly committed mentally ill person has a constitutional right to be released if he is not dangerous to himself or others, is capable of surviving in the community with help, and is receiving only custodial care. In addition to addressing a mentally ill person's right to treatment, this ruling provided for an alternative or least restrictive placement of mentally ill persons who are judged not to be a danger to themselves or others.

It is clear that the right to treatment and to the least restrictive environment has been assured by the courts. The reality, however, can be different. These rights are not always consistently enforced due to many factors including a lack of financing, inadequate staff, and inadequate monitoring of these rights. Professional counselors should consult state statutes and determine which of these rights discussed have been incorporated into those statutes. They should work with other mental health professionals in assuring and providing these rights. Participation in and documentation of treatment plans, actual practices, and procedures is one way of concretely contributing to and helping to assure the rights of clients.

RIGHT TO REFUSE TREATMENT

There are instances in which institutionalized clients, though guaranteed by law the right to treatment, have refused it. This may include not only medical treatment but also psychological treatment (counseling or psychotherapy). In recent years, this right of the individual to refuse treatment has received increasing attention. The issue of an individual's right to refuse treatment is a multifaceted one. To begin with, the commitment or labeling of an individual as mentally ill does not automatically mean legal incompetence. Therefore, generally speaking, a mentally ill individual can refuse treatment if there is no court document determining that the individual is incompetent. Swenson (1997) and Schwitzgebel and Schwitzgebel (1980) note that some obvious legal problems are the patient's competency to decide to refuse treatment, procedures for obtaining informed consent of a legally competent but severely disturbed individual, handling of objections on religious grounds, and potential liability if a client who refused treatment injures himself or herself or others.

Obtaining consent to treatment from a minor presents another unique set of issues. Usually a parent's consent is required to undertake counseling or psychotherapy with a client who is a minor. According to Melton (1981), when a child wishes to refuse treatment, even if the proposed treatment involves inpatient hospitalization, no legal recourse exists under most circumstances. In the past, the assumption appears to have been that the mental health professional contracted to treat the child at the parent's request was an unbiased third party who could assess what would be in the best interest of the child.

Refusal of treatment may also include refusing medication. The Wyatt ruling stated that no medication may be administered without a written order of a physician. Furthermore, medication cannot be used as a punishment or as a substitute for a treatment program, or merely for the convenience of the staff or facility. In the case of *Winters v. Miller* (1971), medication was administered to a patient in violation of her religious beliefs (Christian Science). The court held that, absent a finding of special incompetence (mere mental illness was not considered a special incompetence), a mental patient retains the right to refuse medication on First Amendment grounds.

The right to refuse treatment, including medication, is a complex issue. In the event of an emergency where the individual is judged to be a danger to self or others, most state mental health codes provide for the assessment and/or treatment of the individual even though he or she may refuse it. At this point, the distinction between voluntary and involuntary confinement may be appropriate.

CIVIL COMMITMENTS: VOLUNTARY, INVOLUNTARY AND COURT ORDERED

An individual may be admitted to a mental health facility in several ways. One way is through the criminal justice system, as when one is charged and found not guilty of a crime by reason of insanity and is required to have treatment for the illness. Another way that an individual can become admitted to a mental health facility is through civil commitment proceedings. Most states have two categories of admissions: voluntary and involuntary (Swenson, 1997; Brent, 1984; Schwitzgebel & Schwitzgebel, 1980).

Voluntary Commitment

Although voluntary admissions are included as a type of civil commitment category, it is the individual and not the civil authority that determines the need for treatment. It is also the individual who signs himself or herself into the facility (at least in theory). As in general hospitals, the individual who voluntarily admits himself or herself to a mental health facility is free to leave at any time. In either case, the individual may be required to sign a statement that he or she is leaving against medical advice if the attending physician disagrees with the discharge of the individual for medical reasons. The time required for a mental hospital to physically release an individual after request for discharge has been made varies, and during that time commitment proceedings to challenge the individual's release may be instigated. In actual practice, voluntary admission and release may not be as benign as they appear.

Involuntary Commitment

The second category of civil commitment procedure in most states is involuntary commitment. There are usually two types of involuntary detention and/or commitment: emergency and court ordered. Procedures and terminology can vary greatly from state to state and even county to county within some states. Emergency detention or temporary commitment of another individual may be sought by a concerned party (police, mental health professional, or other third party) by alleging that the individual is in need of treatment and is a danger to self or others. Usually the requirements for emergency detention or commitment include having the person examined within a specified amount of time by one or two physicians who certify that there is a need for emergency hospitalization. In addition, the individual may only be held for a limited amount of time under an emergency commitment prior to a preliminary hearing. The preliminary hearing is required to determine whether there is probable cause for the continued detention of the individual. Prior to the hearing, the detained individual must be given notice of his or her rights under the law. The individual has the right to legal counsel; however, other procedural details vary from state to state.

Commitment by Court Order

The second type of involuntary commitment is court ordered. The courts have ruled that mental illness alone is not a sufficient condition for involuntary civil commitment. Most state statutes typically require that a person be mentally ill and meet at least one of the following minimum conditions: (a) represent a danger to self or others if allowed to remain at liberty; (b) present a probability or likelihood of serious harm to self or others; (c) be gravely disabled so as to be unable to provide for his or her basic physical needs; (d) lack sufficient insight or capacity to make responsible decisions regarding hospitalization; and/or (e) be in need of care and treatment in a hospital.

Formal commitment procedures (Brent, 1984; Schwitzgebel and Schwitzgebel, 1980; Swenson, 1997) usually begin with a concerned person other than the individual in question petitioning the court for an examination of a supposedly mentally ill person. The supposedly mentally ill individual must physically be in the county where the petition is signed, but neither the petitioner nor the individual in question need be a resident of the county. The petition goes to a judge who determines if the individual in question is possibly mentally ill and in need of intervention of some type. A court-ordered examination need not result in immediate detention of the allegedly mentally ill individual. The court's options are basically two: one is to notify the individual of an order of examination; the other option is to issue an order of protective custody. Individuals not judged to be a danger to self or others and capable of providing for their physical needs may be allowed to stay at home until a determination is made as to their need for hospitalization. However, if the individual is judged a danger to self or others and/or unable to provide for their physical needs then an order for protective custody and emergency admission may be ordered.

A police officer, sheriff's deputy, or mental health worker must personally serve the individual with the petition and court order. Within a specified amount of time, the individual must be examined and determination made as to their need for treatment. The court then holds a hearing to determine whether or not the individual is in need of treatment and/or involuntary hospitalization.

RELEASE FROM CONFINEMENT
OR DISCHARGE

When the mentally ill individual recovers from the illness, he or she has the right to be released. These rights are usually described in the state's mental health statutes that cover patient's rights to release or discharge in voluntary and involuntary situations. Recall that individuals admitted under voluntary conditions must also be released upon request within the time period provided by state statute. Individuals who are involuntarily admitted have more restrictions placed on them in terms of discharge. It is up to the court to determine whether or not the individual is in need of continued confinement. This determination is made based on feedback from the treating physician.

Individuals involuntarily confined may contest their confinement legally through a Writ of Habeas Corpus (Swenson, 1997; Schwitzgebel & Schwitzgebel, 1980). The writ is used to obtain a judicial determination of the legal grounds of continued treatment. It requires immediate review and determination by the court, and if support for continued confinement is not substantiated, the individual must be released.

Counseling professionals have both an ethical and legal obligation to protect the rights of clients they serve. Often the client will not be fully aware of his or her rights and therefore is particularly vulnerable. As a professional, one has the responsibility to make appropriate disclosures to clients with regard to their rights. Failure to act judiciously with regard to clients' rights may result in liability for negligence or malpractice.

MALPRACTICE

Malpractice may be defined as the negligent (or otherwise improper) performance, by a professional person, of the duties that are incumbent upon him or her by reason of a professional relationship with a client (*Cochran's Law Lexicon,* 1973, p. 189). Negligence may be defined as conduct that falls below the standard established by law for the protection of others against unreasonably great risk or harm. Four elements must be present to constitute malpractice litigation: (a) a duty on the part of the practitioner, (b) a breach of that duty, (c) actual loss or injury, and (d) a causal relationship between the breach of duty and the resultant injury (Swenson, 1997; Schwitzgebel & Schwitzgebel, 1980).

Additionally, there must be an expressed or implied professional relationship between the counseling professional and the client resulting in the counselor having a duty to the client. The conduct or behavior of the counseling professional must fall below the acceptable general professional standards resulting in a breach of duty. Some examples of breach of duty are improper diagnosis, violation of confidentiality, liability for suicide or homicide, and failure to supervise properly. Negative effects or injury resulting from the practitioner's neglect may include exacerbation of symptoms (depression), appearance of new symptoms, or other related maladies. The injury or loss incurred by the client must be a direct result of the practitioner's action or inaction.

Ethical responsibilities and legal responsibilities often intertwine and neither can be ignored. One of the best and most effective ways to protect yourself against malpractice is to practice ethically and keep informed about changes in the law that affect your discipline.

SUMMARY

As professions come forth and develop, they take on certain responsibilities designed to safeguard and strengthen their service to the public and at the same time protect and amplify the profession itself. Ethical and legal guidelines are prerequisites to credibility and are central to deserving the public trust. The ethical and legal issues and responsibilities are complex and intertwined. What is ethical may not always be lawful and what is lawful may not always be ethical. However, laws may become necessary in order to give [enforceable] status to professional ethical standards. As is most often the case, ethical responsibilities equate with legal responsibilities; neither can be ignored.

QUESTIONS FOR ADDITIONAL REFLECTION AND THOUGHT

1. Informed consent is extremely important; however, is it possible to give too much information? How much information is sufficient to establish informed consent?

2. Describe a situation in which ethics and law come into conflict. In this situation, which one takes precedence? What is the rationale for your answer?

3. Respond to this statement: It's my life and I can do with it as I choose, including ending it.

4. In keeping with how you answered the above question, answer this one: Am I my brother's keeper?

5. Personal rights are what our country was built on, but how far do our personal rights extend (e.g., how much privacy or confidentiality do you have a right to)?

6. Whose job is it to decide what is in the best interest of a client?

7. Some sectors of the mental health profession are debating if mental illness is a fact or a myth. How would you respond to this question, and what implications does your answer have?

8. It has been said that what is legal is not always ethical and what is ethical is not always legal. Given a situation in which a difference exists, which is more important, ethics or the law?

USING THEORY FOR CONCRETE ETHICAL JUDGMENTS

Ethical Dilemma

You are a counselor working independently in private practice. Mr. S. is a self-referred new client. During your initial intake, Mr. S. relates that he suffers from severe bipolar disorder, which is currently controlled by medication. He reports terrifying and tormenting episodes of depressive psychosis before starting his current medication. His presenting problem has to do with feelings of helplessness and hopelessness related to his mental illness. Mr. S. acknowledges that his illness is not "curable" and that there is a high probability that he will experience psychotic breaks in the future. The thought of future episodes of psychosis is overwhelming, and he is unsure he could or even would want to survive another episode. Through the course of treatment, Mr. S. begins to experience symptoms, which in the past have been precursors to psychotic episodes. Medication adjustments by his psychiatrist have failed to alleviate the advancing symptoms. He announces in session that, after significant reflection, he has decided to commit suicide rather than fight his recurrent mental illness and will refuse further intervention or hospitalization. He goes on to say that his quality of life is so compromised by his illness that he logically and rationally chooses suicide, and asks that you not interfere.

The Problem

Your client confides in you that he is planning to commit suicide rather than face another psychotic episode. Should you notify Mr. S.'s psychiatrist and attempt to have him committed against his will, or is there a case here for individual autonomy and self-determination and/or other factors?

The Decision-Making Process

Utilizing any of the various ethical approaches you have learned and the information contained in this chapter on ethics and the law, determine your course of action and the appropriate rationale that effectively supports it.

B

＊

Ethical Standards for School Counselors

American School Counselor Association

PREAMBLE

The American School Counselor Association is a professional organization whose members have a unique and distinctive preparation grounded in the behavioral sciences with training in clinical skills adapted to the school setting. The counselor assists in the growth and development of each individual and uses his/her specialized skills to ensure that the rights of the counselee are properly protected within the structure of the school program. School counselors subscribe to the following basic tenets of the counseling process from which professional responsibilities are derived:

1. Each person has the right to respect and dignity as a human being and to counseling services without prejudice as to person, character, belief or practice.
2. Each person has the right to self-direction and self-development.
3. Each person has the right of choice and the responsibility for decisions reached.
4. Each person has the right to privacy and thereby the right to expect the counselor–client relationship to comply with all laws, policies and ethical standards pertaining to confidentiality.

In this document, the American School Counselor Association has specified the principles of ethical behavior necessary to maintain and regulate the high standards of integrity and leadership among its members. The Association recognizes

the basic commitment of its members to the *Ethical Standards* of its parent organization, the American Counseling Association (ACA), and nothing in this document shall be construed to supplant that code. *The Ethical Standards for School
Counselors* was developed to complement the ACA standards by clarifying the nature of ethical responsibilities for present and future counselors in the school setting. The purposes of this document are to:

1. Serve as a guide for the ethical practices of all school counselors regardless
    of level, area, population served, or membership in this Association.

2. Provide benchmarks for both self-appraisal and peer evaluations regarding
    counselor responsibilities to students, parents, colleagues and professional
    associates, school and community, self, and the counseling profession.

3. Inform those served by the school counselor of acceptable counselor prac-
    tices and expected professional deportment.

A. RESPONSIBILITIES TO PUPILS

The school counselor:

1. Has a primary obligation and loyalty to the pupil, who is to be
    treated with respect as a unique individual, whether assisted individu-
    ally or in a group setting.

2. Is concerned with the total needs of the student (educational, voca-
    tional, personal, and social) and encourages the maximum growth de-
    velopment of each counselee.

3. Informs the counselee of the purposes, goals, techniques, and rules of
    procedure under which she/he may receive counseling assistance at or
    before the time when the counseling relationship is entered. Prior no-
    tice includes confidentiality issues such as the possible necessity for
    consulting with other professionals, privileged communication, and
    legal or authoritative restraints. The meaning and limits of confiden-
    tiality are clearly defined to counselees.

4. Refrains from consciously encouraging the counselee's acceptance of
    values, lifestyles, plans, decisions, and beliefs that represent only the
    counselor's personal orientation.

5. Is responsible for keeping abreast of laws relating to students and
    strives to ensure that the rights of students are adequately provided for
    and protected.

6. Avoids dual relationships which might impair his/her objectivity
    and/or increase the risk of harm to the client (e.g., counseling one's
    family members, close friends or associates). If a dual relationship is
    unavoidable, the counselor is responsible for taking action to elimi-
    nate or reduce the potential for harm. Such safeguards might include
    informed consent, consultation, supervision, and documentation.

7. Makes appropriate referrals when professional assistance can no longer
    be adequately provided to the counselee. Appropriate referral necessi-
    tates knowledge of available resources.

8. Protects the confidentiality of student records and releases personal
    data only according to prescribed laws and school policies. Student

information maintained through electronic data storage methods is treated with the same care as traditional student records.

9. Protects the confidentiality of information received in the counseling relationship as specified by law and ethical standards. Such information is only to be revealed to others when informed consent of the counselee and consistent with the obligation of the counselor as a professional person. In a group setting, the counselor sets a norm of confidentiality and stresses its importance, yet clearly states that confidentiality in group counseling cannot be guaranteed.

10. Informs the appropriate authorities when the counselee's condition indicates a clear and imminent danger to the counselee or others. This is to be done after careful deliberation and, where possible, after consultation with other professionals. The counselor informs the counselee of actions to be taken so as to minimize confusion and clarify expectations.

11. Screens prospective group members and maintains an awareness of participants' compatibility throughout the life of the group, especially when the group emphasis is on self-disclosure and self-understanding. The counselor takes reasonable precautions to protect members from physical and/or psychological harm resulting from interaction within the group.

12. Provides explanations of the nature, purposes, and results of tests in language that is understandable to the client(s).

13. Adheres to relevant standards regarding selection, administration, and interpretation of assessment techniques. The counselor recognizes that computer-based testing programs require specific training in administration, scoring, and interpretation which may differ from that required in more traditional assessments.

14. Promotes the benefits of appropriate computer applications and clarifies the limitations of computer technology. The counselor ensures that (1) computer applications are appropriate for the individual needs of the counselee, (2) the counselee understands how to use the application, and (3) follow-up counseling assistance is provided. Members of underrepresented groups are assured of equal access to computer technologies and the absence of discriminatory information and values within computer applications.

15. Has unique ethical responsibilities in working with peer programs. In general, the school counselor is responsible for the welfare of students participating in peer programs under her/his direction. School counselors who function in training and supervisory capacities are referred to the preparation and supervision standards of professional counselor associations.

B. RESPONSIBILITIES TO PARENTS

The school counselor:

1. Respects the inherent rights and responsibilities of parents for their children and endeavors to establish a cooperative relationship with parents to facilitate the maximum development of the counselee.

2. Informs parents of the counselor's role, with emphasis on the confidential nature of the counseling relationship between the counselor and counselee.

3. Provides parents with accurate, comprehensive, and relevant information in an objective and caring manner, as appropriate and consistent with ethical responsibilities to the counselee.

4. Treats information received from parents in a confidential and appropriate manner.

5. Shares information about a counselee only with those persons properly authorized to receive such information.

6. Adheres to laws and local guidelines when assisting parents experiencing family difficulties which interfere with the counselee's effectiveness and welfare.

7. Is sensitive to changes in the family and recognizes that all parents, custodial and noncustodial, are vested with certain rights and responsibilities for the welfare of their children by virtue of their position and according to law.

C. RESPONSIBILITIES TO COLLEAGUES AND PROFESSIONAL ASSOCIATES

The school counselor:

1. Establishes and maintains a cooperative relationship with faculty, staff, and administration to facilitate the provision of optimum guidance and counseling services.

2. Promotes awareness and adherence to appropriate guidelines regarding confidentiality, the distinction between public and private information, and staff consultation.

3. Treats colleagues with respect, courtesy, fairness, and good faith. The qualifications, views, and findings of colleagues are represented accurately and fairly to enhance the image of competent professionals.

4. Provides professional personnel with accurate, objective, concise, and meaningful data necessary to adequately evaluate, counsel, and assist the counselee.

5. Is aware of and fully utilizes related professions and organizations to whom the counselee may be referred.

D. RESPONSIBILITIES TO THE SCHOOL AND COMMUNITY

The school counselor:

1. Supports and protects the educational program against any infringement not in the best interest of students.

2. Informs appropriate officials of conditions that may be potentially disruptive or damaging to the school's mission, personnel, and property.

3. Delineates and promotes the counselor's role and function in meeting the needs of those served. The counselor will notify appropriate officials of conditions which may limit or curtail their effectiveness in providing programs and services.

4. Assist in the development of (1) curricular and environmental conditions appropriate for the school and community, (2) educational pro-

cedures and programs to meet student needs, and (3) a systematic evaluation process for guidance and counseling programs, services, and personnel. The counselor is guided by the findings of the evaluation data in planning programs and services.

5. Actively cooperates and collaborates with agencies, organizations, and individuals in the school and community in the best interest of counselees and without regard to personal reward or remuneration.

E. RESPONSIBILITIES TO SELF

The school counselor:

1. Functions within the boundaries of individual professional competence and accepts responsibility for the consequences of his/her actions.
2. Is aware of the potential effects of her/his own personal characteristics on services to clients.
3. Monitors personal functioning and effectiveness and refrains from any activity likely to lead to inadequate professional services or harm to a client.
4. Recognizes that differences in clients relating to age, gender, race, religion, sexual orientation, socioeconomic, and ethnic backgrounds may require specific training to ensure competent services.
5. Strives through personal initiative to maintain professional competence and keep abreast of innovations and trends in the profession. Professional and personal growth is continuous and ongoing throughout the counselor's career.

F. RESPONSIBILITIES TO THE PROFESSION

The school counselor:

1. Conducts herself/himself in such a manner as to bring credit to self and the profession.
2. Conducts appropriate research and reports findings in a manner consistent with acceptable educational and psychological research practices. When using client data for research, statistical or program planning purposes, the counselor ensures protection of the identity of the individual client(s).
3. Actively participates in local, state, and national associations which foster the development and improvement of school counseling.
4. Adheres to ethical standards of the profession, other official policy statements pertaining to counseling, and relevant statutes established by federal, state, and local governments.
5. Clearly distinguishes between statements and actions made as a private individual and as a representative of the school counseling profession.
6. Contributes to the development of the profession through the sharing of skills, ideas, and expertise with colleagues.

G. MAINTENANCE OF STANDARDS

Ethical behavior among professional school counselors, Association members and nonmembers, is expected at all times. When there exists serious doubt as to the ethical behavior of colleagues, or if counselors are forced to work in situations or abide by policies which do not reflect the standards as outlined in these *Ethical Standards for School Counselors* or the ACA *Ethical Standards*, the counselor is obligated to take appropriate action to rectify the condition. The following procedure may serve as a guide:

1. If feasible, the counselor should consult with a professional colleague to confidentially discuss the nature of the complaint to see if she/he views the situation as an ethical violation.
2. Whenever possible, the counselor should directly approach the colleague whose behavior is in question to discuss the complaint and seek resolution.
3. If resolution is not forthcoming at the personal level, the counselor shall utilize the channels established within the school and/or school district. This may include both informal and formal procedures.
4. If the matter still remains unresolved, referral for review and appropriate action should be made to the Ethics Committees in the following sequence:
   —local counselor association
   —state counselor association
   —national counselor association
5. The ASCA Ethics Committee functions in an educative and consultative capacity and does not adjudicate complaints of ethical misconduct. Therefore at the national level, complaints should be submitted in writing to the ACA Ethics Committee for review and appropriate action. The procedure for submitting complaints may be obtained by writing the ACA Ethics Committee, c/o The Executive Director, American Counseling Association, 5999 Stevenson Avenue, Alexandria, VA 22304.

H. RESOURCES

School counselors are responsible for being aware of, and acting in accord with, the standards and positions of the counseling profession as represented in official documents such as those listed below.

Code of Ethics (1989). National Board for Certified Counselors. Alexandria, VA.

Code of Ethics for Peer Helping Professionals (1989). National Peer Helpers Association. Glendale, CA.

Ethical Guidelines for Group Counselors (1989). Association for Specialists in Group Work. Alexandria, VA

Ethical Standards (1988). American Association for Counseling and Development. Alexandria, VA

Position Statement: The School Counselor and Confidentiality (1986). American School Counselor Association. Alexandria, VA

Position Statement: The School Counselor and Peer Facilitation (1984). American School Counselor Association. Alexandria, VA.

Position Statement: The School Counselor and Student Rights (1992). American School Counselor Association. Alexandria, VA.

Ethical Standards for School Counselors was adopted by the ASCA Delegate Assembly, March 19, 1984. This revision was approved by the ASCA Delegate Assembly, March 27, 1992.

As of July 1, 1992 the American Association for Counseling and Development (AACD) becomes the American Counseling Association (ACA).

Reprinted by permission of the American Counseling Association.

E

*

Ethical Standards of Human Service Professionals

National Organization for Human Service Education Council for Standards in Human Service Education

PREAMBLE

Human services is a profession developing in response to and in anticipation of the direction of human needs and human problems in the late twentieth century. Characterized particularly by an appreciation of human beings in all of their diversity, human services offers assistance to its clients within the context of their community and environment. Human service professionals, regardless of whether they are students, faculty or practitioners, promote and encourage the unique values and characteristics of human services. In so doing human service professionals uphold the integrity and ethics of the profession, partake in constructive criticism of the profession, promote client and community well-being, and enhance their own professional growth.

The ethical guidelines presented are a set of standards of conduct which the human service professional considers in ethical and professional decision making. It is hoped that these guidelines will be of assistance when the human service professional is challenged by difficult ethical dilemmas. Although ethical codes are not legal documents, they may be used to assist in the adjudication of issues related to ethical human service behavior.

Human service professionals function in many ways and carry out many roles. They enter into professional–client relationships with individuals, families, groups, and communities who are all referred to as "clients" in these standards. Among their roles are caregiver, case manager, broker, teacher/educator, behavior changer, consultant, outreach professional, mobilizer, advocate, community planner, community change organizer, evaluator, and administrator. The following standards are written with these multifaceted roles in mind.

THE HUMAN SERVICE PROFESSIONAL'S RESPONSIBILITY TO CLIENTS

Statement 1 Human service professionals negotiate with clients the purpose, goals, and nature of the helping relationship prior to its onset as well as inform clients of the limitations of the proposed relationship.

Statement 2 Human service professionals respect the integrity and welfare of the client at all times. Each client is treated with respect, acceptance, and dignity.

Statement 3 Human service professionals protect the client's right to privacy and confidentiality except when such confidentiality would cause harm to the client or others, when agency guidelines state otherwise, or under other stated conditions (e.g., local, state, or federal laws). Professionals inform clients of the limits of confidentiality prior to the onset of the helping relationship.

Statement 4 If it is suspected that danger or harm may occur to the client or to others as a result of a client's behavior, the human service professional acts in an appropriate and professional manner to protect the safety of those individuals. This may involve seeking consultation, supervision, and/or breaking the confidentiality of the relationship.

Statement 5 Human service professionals protect the integrity, safety, and security of client records. All written client information that is shared with other professionals, except in the course of professional supervision, must have the client's prior written consent.

Statement 6 Human service professionals are aware that in their relationships with clients power and status are unequal. Therefore they recognize that dual or multiple relationships may increase the risk of harm to, or exploitation of, clients, and may impair their professional judgment. However, in some communities and situations it may not be feasible to avoid social or other nonprofessional contact with clients. Human service professionals support the trust implicit in the helping relationship by avoiding dual relationships that may impair professional judgment, increase the risk of harm to clients or lead to exploitation.

Statement 7 Sexual relationships with current clients are not considered to be in the best interest of the client and are prohibited. Sexual relationships with previous clients are considered dual relationships and are addressed in Statement 6 (above).

Statement 8 The client's right to self-determination is protected by human service professionals. They recognize the client's right to receive or refuse services.

Statement 9 Human service professionals recognize and build on client strengths.

THE HUMAN SERVICE PROFESSIONAL'S RESPONSIBILITY TO THE COMMUNITY AND SOCIETY

Statement 10 Human service professionals are aware of local, state, and federal laws. They advocate for change in regulations and statutes when such legislation conflicts with ethical guidelines and/or client rights. Where laws are harmful to individuals, groups or communities, human service professionals consider the conflict between the values of obeying the law and the values of serving people and may decide to initiate social action.

Statement 11 Human service professionals keep informed about current social issues as they affect the client and the community. They share that information with clients, groups, and community as part of their work.

Statement 12 Human service professionals understand the complex interaction between individuals, their families, the communities in which they live, and society.

Statement 13 Human service professionals act as advocates in addressing unmet client and community needs. Human service professionals provide a mechanism for identifying unmet client needs, calling attention to these needs, and assisting in planning and mobilizing to advocate for those needs at the local community level.

Statement 14 Human service professionals represent their qualifications to the public accurately.

Statement 15 Human service professionals describe the effectiveness of programs, treatments, and/or techniques accurately.

Statement 16 Human service professionals advocate for the rights of all members of society, particularly those who are members of minorities and groups at which discriminatory practices have historically been directed.

Statement 17 Human service professionals provide services without discrimination or preference based on age, ethnicity, culture, race, disability, gender, religion, sexual orientation or socioeconomic status.

Statement 18 Human service professionals are knowledgeable about the cultures and communities within which they practice. They are aware of multiculturalism in society and its impact on the community as well as individuals within the community. They respect individuals and groups, their cultures and beliefs.

Statement 19 Human service professionals are aware of their own cultural backgrounds, beliefs, and values, recognizing the potential for impact on their relationships with others.

Statement 20 Human service professionals are aware of sociopolitical issues that differentially affect clients from diverse backgrounds.

Statement 21 Human service professionals seek the training, experience, education, and supervision necessary to ensure their effectiveness in working with culturally diverse client populations.

THE HUMAN SERVICE PROFESSIONAL'S RESPONSIBILITY TO COLLEAGUES

Statement 22 Human service professionals avoid duplicating another professional's helping relationship with a client. They consult with other professionals who are assisting the client in a different type of relationship when it is in the best interest of the client to do so.

Statement 23 When a human service professional has a conflict with a colleague, he or she first seeks out the colleague in an attempt to manage the problem. If necessary, the professional then seeks the assistance of supervisors, consultants or other professionals in efforts to manage the problem.

Statement 24 Human service professionals respond appropriately to unethical behavior of colleagues. Usually this means initially talking directly with the colleague and, if no resolution is forthcoming, reporting the colleague's behavior to supervisory or administrative staff and/or to the professional organization(s) to which the colleague belongs.

Statement 25 All consultations between human service professionals are kept confidential unless to do so would result in harm to clients or communities.

THE HUMAN SERVICE PROFESSIONAL'S RESPONSIBILITY TO THE PROFESSION

Statement 26 Human service professionals know the limit and scope of their professional knowledge and offer services only within their knowledge and skill base.

Statement 27 Human service professionals seek appropriate consultation and supervision to assist in decision making when there are legal, ethical or other dilemmas.

Statement 28 Human service professionals act with integrity, honesty, genuineness, and objectivity.

Statement 29 Human service professionals promote cooperation among related disciplines (e.g., psychology, counseling, social work, nursing, family and consumer sciences, medicine, education) to foster professional growth and interests within the various fields.

Statement 30 Human service professionals promote the continuing development of their profession. They encourage membership in professional associations, support research endeavors, foster educational advancement, advocate for appropriate legislative actions, and participate in other related professional activities.

Statement 31 Human service professionals continually seek out new and effective approaches to enhance their professional abilities.

THE HUMAN SERVICE PROFESSIONAL'S RESPONSIBILITY TO EMPLOYERS

Statement 32 Human service professionals adhere to commitments made to their employers.

Statement 33 Human service professionals participate in efforts to establish and maintain employment conditions which are conducive to high-quality client services. They assist in evaluating the effectiveness of the agency through reliable and valid assessment measures.

Statement 34 When a conflict arises between fulfilling the responsibility to the employer and the responsibility to the client, human service professionals advise both of the conflict and work conjointly with all involved to manage the conflict.

THE HUMAN SERVICE PROFESSIONAL'S RESPONSIBILITY TO SELF

Statement 35 Human service professionals strive to personify those characteristics typically associated with the profession (eg., accountability, respect for others, genuineness, empathy, pragmatism).

Statement 36 Human service professionals foster self–awareness and personal growth in themselves. They recognize that when professionals are aware of their own values, attitudes, cultural background, and personal needs, the process of helping others is less likely to be negatively impacted by those factors.

Statement 37 Human service professionals recognize a commitment to life-long learning and continually upgrade knowledge and skills to serve the populations better.

October 1994

[1.] Southern Regional Education Board (1967). Roles and Functions Mental Health Workers: A Report of a Symposium. Atlanta, GA: Community Mental Health Worker Project.

Reprinted by permission of William L. McKinney, University of Rhode Island.

G

✳

National Association of Social Workers Code of Ethics

PREAMBLE

The primary mission of the social work profession is to enhance human well-being and help meet the basic human needs of all people, with particular attention to the needs and empowerment of people who are vulnerable, oppressed, and living in poverty. A historic and defining feature of social work is the profession's focus on individual well-being in a social context and the well-being of society. Fundamental to social work is attention to the environmental forces that create, contribute to, and address problems in living.

Social workers promote social justice and social change with and on behalf of clients. "Clients" is used inclusively to refer to individuals, families, groups, organizations, and communities. Social workers are sensitive to cultural and ethnic diversity and strive to end discrimination, oppression, poverty, and other forms of social injustice. These activities may be in the form of direct practice, community organizing, supervision, consultation, administration, advocacy, social and political action, policy development and implementation, education, and research and evaluation. Social workers seek to enhance the capacity of people to address their own needs. Social workers also seek to promote the responsiveness of organizations, communities, and other social institutions to individuals' needs and social problems.

The mission of the social work profession is rooted in a set of core values. These core values, embraced by social workers throughout the profession's history, are the foundation of social work's unique purpose and perspective:

service

social service

dignity and worth of the person

importance of human relationships

integrity

competence.

This constellation of core values reflects what is unique to the social work profession. Core values, and the principles that flow from them, must be balanced within the context and complexity of the human experience.

PURPOSE OF THE NASW CODE OF ETHICS

Professional ethics are at the core of social work. The profession has an obligation to articulate its basic values, ethical principles, and ethical standards. The *NASW Code of Ethics* sets forth these values, principles, and standards to guide social workers' conduct.

The *Code* is relevant to all social workers and social work students, regardless of their professional functions, the settings in which they work, or the populations they serve.

The *NASW Code of Ethics* serves six purposes:

1. The *Code* identifies core values on which social work's mission is based.
2. The *Code* summarizes broad ethical principles that reflect the profession's core values and establishes a set of specific ethical standards that should be used to guide social work practice
3. The *Code* is designed to help social workers identify relevant considerations when professional obligations conflict or ethical uncertainties arise.
4. The *Code* provides ethical standards to which the general public can hold the social work profession accountable.
5. The *Code* socializes practitioners new to the field to social work's mission, values, ethical principles, and ethical standards.
6. The *Code* articulates standards that the social work profession itself can use to assess whether social workers have engaged in unethical conduct. NASW has formal procedures to adjudicate ethics complaints filed against its members. (For information on NASW adjudication procedures, see *NASW Procedures for the Adjudication of Grievances.*) In subscribing to the *Code*, social workers are required to cooperate in its implementation, participate in NASW adjudication proceedings, and abide by any NASW disciplinary rulings or sanctions based on it.

The *Code* offers a set of values, principles, and standards to guide decision making and conduct when ethical issues arise. It does not provide a set of rules that prescribe how social workers should act in all situations. Specific applications of the *Code* must take into account the context in which it is being considered and the possibility of conflicts among the *Code*'s values, principles, and standards. Ethical responsibilities flow from all human relationships, from the personal and familial to the social and professional.

Further, the *NASW Code of Ethics* does not specify which values, principles, and standards are most important and ought to outweigh others in instances when they conflict. Reasonable differences of opinion can and do exist among social workers with respect to the ways in which values, ethical principles, and ethical standards should be rank ordered when they conflict. Ethical decision making in a given situation must apply the informed judgment of the individual social worker and should also consider how the issues would be judged in a peer review process where the ethical standards of the profession would be applied.

Ethical decision making is a process. There are many instances in social work where simple answers are not available to resolve complex ethical issues. Social workers should take into consideration all the values, principles, and standards in this *Code* that are relevant to any situation in which ethical judgment is warranted. Social workers' decisions and actions should be consistent with the spirit as well as the letter of this *Code*.

In addition to the *Code*, there are many other sources of information about ethical thinking that may be useful. Social workers should consider ethical theory and principles generally, social work theory and research, laws, regulations, agency policies, and other relevant codes of ethics, recognizing that among codes of ethics social workers should consider the *NASW Code of Ethics* as their primary source. Social workers also should be aware of the impact on ethical decision making of their clients' and their own personal values and cultural and religious beliefs and practices. They should be aware of any conflicts between personal and professional values and deal with them responsibly. For additional guidance social workers should consult the relevant literature on professional ethics and ethical decision making and seek appropriate consultation when faced with ethical dilemmas. This may involve consultation with an agency-based or social work organization's ethics committee, a regulatory body, knowledgeable colleagues, supervisors, or legal counsel.

Instances may arise when social workers' ethical obligations conflict with agency policies or relevant laws or regulations. When such conflicts occur, social workers must make a responsible effort to resolve the conflict in a manner that is consistent with the values, principles, and standards expressed in this *Code*. If a reasonable resolution of the conflict does not appear possible social workers should seek proper consultation before making a decision.

The *NASW Code of Ethics* is to be used by NASW and by individuals, agencies, organizations, and bodies (such as licensing and regulatory boards, professional liability insurance providers, courts of law, agency boards of directors, government agencies, and other professional groups) that choose to adopt it or use it as a frame of reference. Violation of standards in this Code does not automatically imply legal liability or violation of the law. Such determination can only be made in the context of legal and judicial proceedings. Alleged violations of the *Code* would be subject to a peer review process. Such processes are generally separate from legal or administrative procedures and insulated from legal review or proceedings to allow the profession to counsel and discipline its own members.

A code of ethics cannot guarantee ethical behavior. Moreover, a code of ethics cannot resolve all ethical issues or disputes or capture the richness and complexity involved in striving to make responsible choices within a moral community. Rather, a code of ethics sets forth values, ethical principles, and ethical standards to which professionals aspire and by which their actions can be judged. Social workers' ethical behavior should result from their personal commitment to engage in ethical practice. The *NASW Code of Ethics* reflects the commitment of all social workers to uphold the profession's values and to act ethically. Principles and standards must be applied by individuals of good character who discern moral questions and, in good faith, seek to make reliable ethical judgments.

ETHICAL STANDARDS

The following ethical standards are relevant to the professional activities of all social workers. These standards concern (1) social workers' ethical responsibilities to clients, (2) social workers' ethical responsibilities to colleagues, (3) social workers' ethical responsibilities in practice settings, (4) social workers' ethical responsibilities as professionals, (5) social workers' ethical responsibilities to the social work profession, and (6) social workers' ethical responsibilities to the broader society.

Some of the standards that follow are enforceable guidelines for professional conduct, and some are aspirational. The extent to which each standard is enforceable is a matter of professional judgment to be exercised by those responsible for reviewing alleged violations of ethical standards.

ETHICAL PRINCIPLES

The following broad ethical principles are based on social work's core values of service, social justice, dignity and worth of the person, importance of human relationships, integrity, and competence. These principles set forth ideals to which all social workers should aspire.

Value *Service*

Ethical Principle *Social workers' primary goal is to help people in need and to address social problems.*

Social workers elevate service to others above self-interest. Social workers draw on their knowledge, values, and skills to help people in need and to address social problems. Social workers are encouraged to volunteer some portion of their professional skills with no expectation of significant financial return (pro bono service).

Value *Social Justice*

Ethical Principle *Social workers challenge social injustice.*
Social workers pursue social change, particularly with and on behalf of vulnerable and oppressed individuals and groups of people. Social workers' social change efforts are focused primarily on issues of poverty, unemployment, discrimination, and other forms of social injustice. These activities seek to promote sensitivity to and knowledge about oppression and cultural and ethnic diversity. Social workers strive to ensure access to needed information, services, and resources; equality of opportunity; and meaningful participation in decision making for all people.

Value *Dignity and Worth of the Person*

Ethical Principle *Social workers respect the inherent dignity and worth of the person.*
Social workers treat each person in a caring and respectful fashion, mindful of individual differences and cultural and ethnic diversity. Social workers promote clients' socially responsible self–determination. Social workers seek to enhance clients' capacity and opportunity to change and to address their own needs. Social workers are cognizant of their dual responsibility to clients and to the broader society. They seek to resolve conflicts between clients' interests and the broader society's interests in a socially responsible manner consistent with the values, ethical principles, and ethical standards of the profession.

Value *Importance of Human Relationships*

Ethical Principle *Social workers recognize the central importance of human relationships.*
Social workers understand that relationships between and among people are an important vehicle for change. Social workers engage people as partners in the helping process. Social workers seek to strengthen relationships among people in a purposeful effort to promote, restore, maintain, and enhance the well–being of individuals, families, social groups, organizations, and communities.

Value *Integrity*

Ethical Principle *Social workers behave in a trustworthy manner.*
Social workers are continually aware of the profession's mission, values, ethical principles, and ethical standards and practice in a manner consistent with them. Social workers act honestly and responsibly and promote ethical practices on the part of the organizations with which they are affiliated.

Value *Competence*

Ethical Principle *Social workers practice within their areas of competence and develop and enhance their professional expertise.*

Social workers continually strive to increase their professional knowledge and skills and to apply them in practice. Social workers should aspire to contribute to the knowledge base of the profession.

ETHICAL STANDARDS

1. **Social Workers' Ethical Responsibilities to Clients**
   1.01 Commitment to Clients

   Social workers' primary responsibility is to promote the well-being of clients. In general, clients' interests are primary. However, social workers' responsibility to the larger society or specific legal obligations may on limited occasions supersede the loyalty owed clients, and clients should be so advised. (Examples include when a social worker is required by law to report that a client has abused a child or has threatened to harm self or others.)

   1.02 Self-Determination

   Social workers respect and promote the right of clients to self-determination and assist clients in their efforts to identify and clarify their goals. Social workers may limit clients' right to self-determination when, in the social workers' professional judgment, clients' actions or potential actions pose a serious, foreseeable, and imminent risk to themselves or others.

   1.03 Informed Consent
   (a) Social workers should provide services to clients only in the context of a professional relationship based, when appropriate, on valid informed consent. Social workers should use clear and understandable language to inform clients of the purpose of the services, risks related to the services, limits to services because of the requirements of a third-party payer, relevant costs, reasonable alternatives, clients' right to refuse or withdraw consent, and the timeframe covered by the consent. Social workers should provide clients with an opportunity to ask questions.
   (b) In instances when clients are not literate or have difficulty understanding the primary language used in the practice setting, social workers should take steps to ensure clients' comprehension. This may include providing clients with a detailed verbal explanation or arranging for a qualified interpreter or translator whenever possible.
   (c) In instances when clients lack the capacity to provide informed consent, social workers should protect clients' interests by seeking

permission from an appropriate third party, informing clients consistent with the clients' level of understanding. In such instances social workers should seek to ensure that the third party acts in a manner consistent with clients' wishes and interests. Social workers should take reasonable steps to enhance such clients' ability to give informed consent.

(d) In instances when clients are receiving services involuntarily, social workers should provide information about the nature and extent of services and about the extent of clients' right to refuse service.

(e) Social workers who provide services via electronic media (such as computer, telephone, radio, and television) should inform recipients of the limitations and risks associated with such services.

(f) Social workers should obtain clients' informed consent before audiotaping or videotaping clients or permitting observation of services to clients by a third party.

1.04 Competence

(a) Social workers should provide services and represent themselves as competent only within the boundaries of their education, training, license, certification, consultation received, supervised experience, or other relevant professional experience.

(b) Social workers should provide services in substantive areas or use intervention techniques or approaches that are new to them only after engaging in appropriate study, training, consultation, and supervision from people who are competent in those interventions or techniques.

(c) When generally recognized standards do not exist with respect to an emerging area of practice, social workers should exercise careful judgment and take responsible steps (including appropriate education, research, training, consultation, and supervision) to ensure the competence of their work and to protect clients from harm.

1.05 Cultural Competence and Social Diversity

(a) Social workers should understand culture and its function in human behavior and society, recognizing the strengths that exist in all cultures.

(b) Social workers should have a knowledge base of their clients' cultures and be able to demonstrate competence in the provision of services that are sensitive to clients' cultures and to differences among people and cultural groups.

(c) Social workers should obtain education about and seek to understand the nature of social diversity and oppression with respect to race, ethnicity, national origin, color, sex, sexual orientation, age, marital status, political belief, religion, and mental or physical disability.

1.06 Conflicts of Interests

(a) Social workers should be alert to and avoid conflicts of interest that interfere with the exercise of professional discretion and impartial judgment. Social workers should inform clients when a real or potential conflict of interest arises and take reasonable steps to resolve the issue in a manner that makes the clients' interests primary and protects clients' interests to the greatest extent possible. In some cases, protecting clients' interests may require termination of the professional relationship with proper referral of the client.

(b) Social workers should not take unfair advantage of any professional relationship or exploit others to further their personal, religious, political, or business interests.

(c) Social workers should not engage in dual or multiple relationships with clients or former clients in which there is a risk of exploitation or potential harm to the client. In instances when dual or multiple relationships are unavoidable, social workers should take steps to protect clients and are responsible for setting clear, appropriate, and culturally sensitive boundaries. (Dual or multiple relationships occur when social workers relate to clients in more than one relationship, whether professional, social, or business. Dual or multiple relationships can occur simultaneously or consecutively.)

(d) When social workers provide services to two or more people who have a relationship with each other (for example, couples, family members), social workers should clarify with all parties which individuals will be considered clients and the nature of social workers' professional obligations to the various individuals who are receiving services. Social workers who anticipate a conflict of interest among the individuals receiving services or who anticipate having to perform in potentially conflicting roles (for example, when a social worker is asked to testify in a child custody dispute or divorce proceedings involving clients) should clarify their role with the parties involved and take appropriate action to minimize any conflict of interest.

1.07 Privacy and Confidentiality

(a) Social workers should respect clients' right to privacy. Social workers should not solicit private information from clients unless it is essential to providing services or conducting social work evaluation or research. Once private information is shared, standards of confidentiality apply.

(b) Social workers may disclose confidential information when appropriate with valid consent from a client or a person legally authorized to consent on behalf of a client.

(c) Social workers should protect the confidentiality of all information obtained in the course of professional service, except for compelling professional reasons. The general expectation that social workers will keep information confidential does not apply when disclosure is necessary to prevent serious, foreseeable, and imminent harm to a client or other identifiable person or when laws or regulations require disclosure without a client's consent. In all instances, social workers should disclose the least amount of confidential information necessary to achieve the desired purpose, only information that is directly relevant to the purpose for which the disclosure is made should be revealed.

(d) Social workers should inform clients, to the extent possible, about the disclosure of confidential information and the potential consequences, when feasible before the disclosure is made. This applies whether social workers disclose confidential information on the basis of a legal requirement or client consent.

(e) Social workers should discuss with clients and other interested parties the nature of confidentiality and limitations of clients' right to confidentiality. Social workers should review with clients circumstances where confidential information may be requested and where disclosure of confidential information may be legally required. This discussion should occur as soon as possible in the social worker–client relationship and as needed throughout the course of the relationship.

(f) When social workers provide counseling services to families, couples, or groups, social workers should seek agreement among the parties involved concerning each individual's right to confidentiality and obligation to preserve the confidentiality of information shared by others. Social workers should inform participants in family, couples, or group counseling that social workers cannot guarantee that all participants will honor such agreements.

(g) Social workers should inform clients involved in family, couples, marital, or group counseling of the social worker's, employer's, and agency's policy concerning the social worker's disclosure of confidential information among the parties involved in the counseling.

(h) Social workers should not disclose confidential information to third-party payers unless clients have authorized such.

(i) Social workers should not discuss confidential information in any setting unless privacy can be ensured. Social workers should not discuss confidential information in public or semipublic areas such as hallways, waiting rooms, elevators, and restaurants.

(j) Social workers should protect the confidentiality of clients during legal proceedings to the extent permitted by law. When a court of law or other legally authorized body orders social workers to disclose confidential or privileged information without a client's consent and such disclosure could cause harm to the client, social workers should request that the court withdraw the order or limit the order as narrowly as possible or maintain the records under seal, unavailable for public inspection.

(k) Social workers should protect the confidentiality of clients when responding to requests from members of the media.

(l) Social workers should protect the confidentiality of clients' written and electronic records and other sensitive information. Social workers should take reasonable steps to ensure that clients' records are stored in a secure location and that clients' records are not available to others who are not authorized to have access.

(m) Social workers should take precautions to ensure and maintain the confidentiality of information transmitted to other parties through the use of computers, electronic mail, facsimile machines, telephones and telephone answering machines, and other electronic or computer technology. Disclosure of identifying information should be avoided whenever possible.

(n) Social workers should transfer or dispose of clients' records in a manner that protects clients' confidentiality and is consistent with state statutes governing records and social worker licensure.

(o) Social workers should take reasonable precautions to protect client confidentiality in the event of the social worker's termination of practice, incapacitation, or death.

(p) Social workers should not disclose identifying information when discussing clients for teaching or training purposes unless the client has consented to disclosure of confidential information.

(q) Social workers should not disclose identifying information when discussing clients with consultants unless the client has consented to disclosure of confidential information or there is a compelling need for such disclosure.

(r) Social workers should protect the confidentiality of deceased clients consistent with the preceding standards.

1.08 Access to Records

(a) Social workers should provide clients with reasonable access to records concerning the clients. Social workers who are concerned that clients' access to their records could cause serious misunderstanding or harm to the client should provide assistance in interpreting the records and consultation with the client regarding the records. Social workers should limit clients' access to their records, or portions of their records, only in exceptional circumstances when there is compelling evidence that such access would cause serious harm to the client. Both clients' requests and the rationale for withholding some or all of the record should be documented in clients' files.

(b) When providing clients with access to their records, social workers should take steps to protect the confidentiality of other individuals identified or discussed in such records.

1.09 Sexual Relationships

(a) Social workers should under no circumstances engage in sexual activities or sexual contact with current clients, whether such contact is consensual or forced.

(b) Social workers should not engage in sexual activities or sexual contact with clients' relatives or other individuals with whom clients maintain a close personal relationship when there is a risk of exploitation or potential harm to the client. Sexual activity or sexual contact with clients' relatives or other individuals with whom clients maintain a personal relationship has the potential to be harmful to the client and may make it difficult for the social worker and client to maintain appropriate professional boundaries. Social workers—not their clients, their clients' relatives, or other individuals with whom the client maintains a personal relationship—assume the full burden for setting clear, appropriate, and culturally sensitive boundaries.

(c) Social workers should not engage in sexual activities or sexual contact with former clients because of the potential for harm to the client. If social workers engage in conduct contrary to this prohibition or claim that an exception to this prohibition is warranted because of extraordinary circumstances, it is social workers—not their clients—who assume the full burden of demonstrating that the former client has not been exploited, coerced, or manipulated, intentionally or unintentionally.

(d) Social workers should not provide clinical services to individuals with whom they have had a prior sexual relationship. Providing clinical services to a former sexual partner has the potential to be harmful to the individual and is likely to make it difficult for the social worker and individual to maintain appropriate professional boundaries.

1.10 Physical Contact

Social workers should not engage in physical contact with clients when there is a possibility of psychological harm to the client as a result of the contact (such as cradling or caressing clients). Social workers who engage in appropriate physical contact with clients are responsible for setting clear, appropriate, and culturally sensitive boundaries that govern such physical contact.

1.11 Sexual Harassment

Social workers should not sexually harass clients. Sexual harassment includes sexual advances, sexual solicitation, requests for sexual favors, and other verbal or physical conduct of a sexual nature.

1.12 Derogatory Language

Social workers should not use derogatory language in their written or verbal communications to or about clients. Social workers should use accurate and respectful language in all communications to and about clients.

1.13 Payment for Services

(a) When setting fees, social workers should ensure that the fees are fair, reasonable, and commensurate with the services performed. Consideration should be given to clients' ability to pay.

(b) Social workers should avoid accepting goods or services from clients as payment for professional services. Bartering arrangements, particularly involving services, create the potential for conflicts of interest, exploitation, and inappropriate boundaries in social workers' relationships with clients. Social workers should explore and may participate in bartering only in very limited circumstances when it can be demonstrated that such arrangements are an accepted practice among professionals in the local community, considered to be essential for the provision of services, negotiated without coercion, and entered into at the client's initiative and with the client's informed consent. Social workers who accept goods or services from clients as payment for professional services assume the full burden of demonstrating that this arrangement will not be detrimental to the client or the professional relationship.

(c) Social workers should not solicit a private fee or other remuneration for providing services to clients who are entitled to such available services through the social workers' employer or agency.

1.14 Clients Who Lack Decision–Making Capacity

When social workers act on behalf of clients who lack the capacity to make informed decisions, social workers should take reasonable steps to safeguard the interests and rights of those clients.

1.15 Interruption of Services

Social workers should make reasonable efforts to ensure continuity of services in the event that services are interrupted by factors such as unavailability, relocation, illness, disability, or death.

1.16 Termination of Services

(a) Social workers should terminate services to clients and professional relationships with them when such services and relationships are no longer required or no longer serve the clients' needs or interests.

(b) Social workers should take reasonable steps to avoid abandoning clients who are still in need of services. Social workers should withdraw services precipitously only under unusual circumstances, giving careful consideration to all factors in the situation and taking care to minimize possible adverse effects. Social workers should assist in making appropriate arrangements for continuation of services when necessary.

(c) Social workers in fee-for-service settings may terminate services to clients who are not paying an overdue balance if the financial contractual arrangements have been made clear to the client, if the client does not pose an imminent danger to self or others, and if the clinical and other consequences of the current nonpayment have been addressed and discussed with the client.

(d) Social workers should not terminate services to pursue a social, financial, or sexual relationship with a client.

(e) Social workers who anticipate the termination or interruption of services to clients should notify clients promptly and seek the transfer, referral, or continuation of services in relation to the clients' needs and preferences.

(f) Social workers who are leaving an employment setting should inform clients of appropriate options for the continuation of services and of the benefits and risks of the options.

Chapter 1

The Focus of This Book

Working both independently and together over the years, the three of us have confronted a variety of professional and ethical issues that have no clear-cut solutions. Conversations with students and colleagues describe similar struggles. Exchanging ideas helps us deal with these issues. We are convinced that students in the helping professions must anticipate and be prepared for these kinds of problems before their first fieldwork experience, and certainly before they begin practicing.

We have discovered that many of the issues relevant to beginning professionals resurface and take on different meanings at various stages in a professional's life. We try to avoid dispensing prescriptions or providing simple solutions to complex situations. Our main purpose is to establish a basis for you to develop a personal perspective on ethical practice within the broad limits of professional codes and divergent theoretical positions. We raise what we consider to be central issues, present a range of views on these issues, discuss our position, and provide you with many opportunities to refine your thinking and actively develop your own position.

As you read this book, it will be apparent that we have certain biases and viewpoints about ethical behavior. We try to identify and clarify these stances as our perspective rather than as universal truths. We state our position not to sway you to adopt our views, but to help you develop your own position on a variety of ethical and professional issues.

Identifying our own personal misconduct is far more challenging than pointing out the misconduct of our colleagues, yet it is incumbent on each of us to continually reflect on what we are doing personally and professionally. In the end, you are responsible for your own ethical practice. Codes of ethics provide general standards, but these are not sufficiently explicit to deal with every situation. It is often difficult to interpret ethics codes, and opinions differ over how to apply them in specific cases. In all cases, the welfare of the

Introduction
to Professional Ethics

client demands that you become familiar with the guiding principles of the ethics codes and accepted standards of practice of your profession. You will encounter many situations that demand the exercise of sound judgment to further the best interests of your clients, and we recommend that you begin to consider these issues now.

The various mental health professions have developed codes of ethics that are binding on their members. As a professional, you are expected to know the ethics code of your specialty and to be aware of the consequences of practicing in ways that are not sanctioned by your professional organization. Responsible practice requires that you use informed, sound, and responsible judgment. It is essential to demonstrate a willingness to consult with colleagues, to keep yourself up to date through reading and continuing education, and to continually monitor your behavior.

Be prepared to reexamine many of the issues that are raised in this book throughout your professional life. Even when you resolve some of these ethical and professional issues at the initial stage of your development as a counselor, these topics are likely to take on new dimensions as you gain experience. Many students think they should resolve all possible issues before they begin to practice; this is an impossible task. The definition and refinement of such concerns is an evolutionary process that requires an open mind and continual reexamination.

Some Suggestions for Using This Book

In this book we cover the central professional and ethical issues you are likely to encounter in your work. Our goal is to provide you with a flexible framework and a direction for working through ethical dilemmas.

We frequently imagine ourselves in conversations with you, our students. We state our own thinking and offer a commentary on how we arrived at the positions we hold. We hope you will try to integrate your own thoughts and experiences with the positions and ethical dilemmas we raise for consideration. In this way you will absorb information, deepen your understanding, and develop an ethical way of thinking.

We offer specific suggestions for getting the most from this book and from your course. Many of these ideas have come from students in our classes. In general, you will get from this book and course whatever you are willing to invest of yourself, so it is important to clarify your goals and to think about ways of becoming actively involved. Here are some suggestions that can help you become an active learner.

• *Be prepared.* You can best prepare yourself to become active in your class by spending time reading and thinking about the questions we pose. Completing the exercises and responding to the questions and open-ended cases will help you focus on where you stand on controversial issues.

• *Identify your expectations.* Students often have unrealistic expectations of themselves. If you have limited experience in counseling clients, you can think about situations in which friends sought your help and how you dealt with them. You can also reflect on the times when you were experiencing conflicts and needed someone to help you gain clarity. This is a way to relate the material to events in your own life.

• *Complete the self-assessment survey.* The multiple-choice survey at the end of this chapter is designed to help you discover your attitudes concerning most of the issues we deal with in the book. Take this inventory before you read the book to determine where you stand on these issues at this time. We suggest that you take the inventory again after you complete the book. You can then compare your responses to see what changes, if any, have occurred in your thinking.

• *Identify your viewpoint by reviewing the self-inventories.* Each chapter begins with an inventory designed to encourage reflection on the issues to be explored in the chapter. Bring your responses to class and discuss your views with those of fellow students. You can retake the inventory after you finish reading the chapter to see if your views have changed.

• *Think about the examples, cases, commentaries, and questions.* Many examples in this book are drawn from actual counseling practice in various settings with different types of clients. (Elements of these cases have been changed to protect confidentiality.) We ask you to consider how you might have worked with a given client or what you might have done in a particular counseling situation. We provide our commentary on each of the cases to guide you in clarifying the specific issues involved and in helping you think about the course of action you might take for each case presented. We also provide illustrations of possible therapist responses to the various ethical dilemmas in the cases, not all of which are ethical or appropriate. Reflect on our commentaries and the questions raised as you respond to the cases in each chapter.

- *Terminology.* In the wide variety of mental health professions covered in this book, professional mental health workers are designated by a variety of terms: *mental health professional, practitioner, therapist, counselor, social worker, school counselor, rehabilitation counselor, addictions counselor, community worker, couples and family therapist, helper,* and *clinician.* Throughout this book, we generally use these terms interchangeably, reflecting the differing nomenclature of the various professions. Substitute your own profession's terminology in specific cases to make the information more meaningful to you.

- *Do the end-of-chapter suggested activities.* Each chapter ends with suggested activities intended to help you integrate and apply what you have learned. These exercises challenge you to be active both in class and on your own, and they give you a chance to apply your ideas about the issues to various situations.

Involve yourself in thinking about the issues we raise. Focus on the questions, cases, commentaries, and activities that have the most meaning for you at this time, and remain open to new issues as they assume importance for you. Strive to develop your thoughts and positions on the ethical dilemmas presented. As you become actively involved in your ethics course, you will discover additional ways to look at the process of ethical decision making.

Professional Codes of Ethics

Various professional organizations (counseling, social work, psychiatry, psychology, marriage and family therapy, human services) have established codes of ethics that provide broad guidelines for mental health practitioners. (A box at the end of the chapter titled "Professional Organizations and Codes of Ethics" lists 17 professional organizations with links to their websites.) The codes of these national professional organizations have similarities, and they also have differences. In addition, national certification boards, other professional associations, specialty areas within the counseling profession, and state regulatory boards all have their own ethics or professional practice documents. Specialty guidelines are available to cover areas not adequately addressed by the general ethics codes. For example, the American Psychological Association (APA) has some of the following specialty guidelines:

- Guidelines for providers of psychological services to ethnic, linguistic, and culturally diverse populations (APA, 1993)
- Guidelines for psychotherapy with lesbian, gay, and bisexual clients (APA, 2000)
- Guidelines on multicultural education, training, research, practice, and organizational change for psychologists (APA, 2003a)

- Guidelines for psychological practice with older adults (APA, 2004)
- Evidence-based practice in psychology (APA Presidential Task Force, 2006)
- Record keeping guidelines (APA, 2007)

The National Association of Social Workers (NASW) also has developed some practice guidelines, two of which are especially helpful in the area of end-of-life care:

- Client self-determination in end-of-life decisions (NASW, 2003)
- NASW standards for social work practice in palliative and end-of-life care (NASW, 2004)

Publications by the various professional organizations contain many resources to help you understand the issues underlying the ethical decisions you will be making in your professional life.

Common Themes of Codes of Ethics

Each major mental health professional organization has its own code of ethics, and we strongly recommend that you obtain a copy of the ethics code of the profession you are planning to enter and familiarize yourself with their basic standards for ethical practice. Pleading ignorance of the specifics of the ethics code of one's profession is not an excuse when engaging in unethical behavior. The ethics codes offered by most professional organizations are broad and general, rather than precise and specific. These codes do not provide specific answers to the ethical dilemmas you will encounter, but they do offer general guidance. Although there are specific differences among the ethics codes of the various professional organization, Koocher and Keith-Spiegel (2008) note a number of similar themes:

- Promoting the welfare of consumers
- Practicing within the scope of one's competence
- Doing no harm
- Protecting client's confidentiality and privacy
- Acting ethically and responsibly
- Avoiding exploitation
- Upholding the integrity of the profession by striving for aspirational practice

Limitations of Codes of Ethics

Your own ethical awareness and problem-solving skills will determine how you translate the various ethics codes into professional behavior. As Welfel (2010) indicates, codes of ethics are not cookbooks for responsible professional behavior; they do not provide recipes for healthy ethical decision making. Indeed, ethics codes offer unmistakably clear guidance for only a few problems. For example, the APA's (2002) ethics code is quite clear that it neither provides all the answers nor specifically addresses every dilemma that may confront a practitioner. In short, ethics codes are necessary, but not sufficient, for exercising ethical responsibility. It is essential that you be aware of the limitations of such codes (see Herlihy & Corey, 2006a; Herlihy & Remley, 1995; Pope & Vasquez, 2007). Here are some limitations and problems you might encounter as you strive to be ethically responsible:

- Some issues cannot be handled solely by relying on ethics codes.
- Some codes lack clarity and precision, which makes assessment of an ethical dilemma unclear.
- Simply learning the ethics codes and practice guidelines will not necessarily make for ethical practice.
- Conflicts sometimes emerge within ethics codes as well as among various organizations' codes.
- Practitioners who belong to multiple professional associations, are licensed by their state, and hold national certifications may be responsible to practice within the framework of numerous codes of ethics, yet these codes may not be uniform.
- Ethics codes tend to be reactive rather than proactive.
- A practitioner's personal values may conflict with a specific standard within an ethics code.
- Codes may conflict with institutional policies and practices.
- Ethics codes need to be understood within a cultural framework; therefore, they must be adapted to specific cultures.
- Codes may not align with state laws or regulations regarding reporting requirements.
- Because of the diverse viewpoints within any professional organization, not all members will agree with all elements of an organization's ethics code.

In the *Code of Ethics* of the National Association of Social Workers (2008), the limits of the code are succinctly described:

> A code of ethics cannot guarantee ethical behavior. Moreover, a code of ethics cannot resolve all ethical issues or disputes or capture the richness and complexity involved in striving to make responsible choices within a moral community. Rather, a code of ethics sets forth values, ethical principles, and ethical standards to which professionals aspire and by which their actions can be judged. (Purpose of NASW Code of Ethics.)

The code of ethics for the Canadian Counselling Association (2007) makes it clear that professionals are challenged to make sound decisions based on their own values:

> Although a Code of Ethics is essential to the maintenance of ethical integrity and accountability, it cannot be a substitute for the active process of ethical

decision-making. Members increasingly confront challenging ethical demands and dilemmas in a complex and dynamic society to which a simple and direct application of this code may not be possible. Also, reasonable differences of opinion can and do exist among members with respect to how ethical principles and values should be rank-ordered when they are in conflict. Therefore, members must develop the ability and the courage to exercise a high level of ethical judgement. (Preamble.)

Using Ethics Codes as Guides

Ethics codes are not intended to be blueprints for resolving every ethical dilemma; nor do they remove all need for judgment and ethical reasoning. Formal ethical principles can never be substituted for an active, deliberative, and creative approach to meeting ethical responsibilities (Pope & Vasquez, 2007). Ethics codes cannot be applied in a rote manner because each client's situation is unique and calls for a different solution. When practitioners weigh multiple and often competing demands and goals, they must use their professional judgment (Barnett, Behnke, Rosenthal, & Koocher, 2007). Handelsman, Gottlieb, and Knapp (2005) remind us that becoming an ethical practitioner is a more complex process than simply following a set of rules. Becoming a professional is somewhat like learning to adjust to a different culture, and both students and professionals experience an ethical acculturation process. Handelsman and colleagues recommend that ethics courses provide opportunities for students to explore their acculturation and begin to develop an ethical identity. Handelsman and colleagues add that "ethics is the study of right and wrong but is often taught as the study of wrong. Many ethics courses are devoted to laws, disciplinary codes, and risk management strategies and do not focus on best practices" (p. 59). From our perspective, practitioners are faced with assuming the responsibility of making ethical decisions and ultimately taking responsibility for the outcomes. This process takes time, and it should include consultation.

Herlihy and Corey (2006a) suggest that codes of ethics fulfill three objectives. The first objective is to *educate professionals* about sound ethical conduct. Reading and reflecting on the standards can help practitioners expand their awareness and clarify their values in dealing with the challenges of their work. Second, ethical standards provide a *mechanism for professional accountability*. Practitioners are obliged not only to monitor their own behavior, but also to encourage ethical conduct in their colleagues. One of the best ways for practitioners to guard the welfare of their clients or students and to protect themselves from malpractice suits is to practice within the spirit of the ethics codes. Third, codes of ethics serve as *catalysts for improving practice*. When practitioners must interpret and apply the codes in their own practices, the questions raised help to clarify their positions on dilemmas that do not have simple or absolute answers. You can imagine the chaos if people were to practice without guidelines so that the resolution of ethical dilemmas rested solely with the individual clinician.

We must never forget that the primary purpose of a code of ethics is to safeguard the welfare of clients by providing what is in their best interest. Ethics codes are also designed to safeguard the public and to guide professionals in their work so that they can provide the best service possible. The *community standard* (what professionals *actually* do) is generally less rigorous than the ethical standard (what professionals *should* do). It is important to be knowledgeable of what others in your local area and subspecialties are doing in their practices.

Bersoff (2003a) makes a distinction between the ideal and realistic purpose of a code of ethics. Ideally, ethics codes provide guidance in resolving moral problems encountered by members of the profession:

> Realistically, however, what a code of ethics does is validate the most recent views of a majority of professionals empowered by their colleagues to make decisions about ethical issues. Thus, a code of ethics is, inevitably, anachronistic, conservative, ethnocentric, and the product of political compromise. But recognition of that reality should not inhibit the creation of a document that fully realizes and expresses fundamental moral principles. (p. 1)

At this point, what do you think it takes to be an ethical professional? Is it primarily knowing and following the ethics code of your profession? What else does it take to be an ethical practitioner? You may find that you answer differently depending on the situation.

Ethics Codes and the Law

Ethical issues in the mental health professions are regulated by both laws and professional codes. The Committee on Professional Practice and Standards (2003) of the American Psychological Association differentiates between ethics and law as follows: **Ethics** pertains to the standards that govern the conduct of its professional members; **law** is the body of rules that govern the affairs of people within a community, state, or country. Laws define the minimum standards society will tolerate, which are enforced by government. An example of a minimum standard is the legal obligation mental health professionals have to report suspected child abuse. All of the codes of ethics state that practitioners are obligated to act in accordance with relevant federal and state statutes and government regulations. It is essential that practitioners be able to identify legal problems as they arise in their work, because many of the situations they encounter that involve ethical and professional judgment will also have legal implications.

Remley and Herlihy (2010) note that counselors sometimes have difficulty determining when there is a legal problem, or what to do with a legal issue once it has been identified. To clarify whether a legal issue is involved, Remley and Herlihy suggest assessing the situation to determine if any of the following apply: (a) legal proceedings have been initiated, (b) lawyers are involved, or (c) the practitioner is in danger of having a complaint filed against him or her for misconduct. When confronted with a legal issue, it is important to consult a lawyer to determine which course of action to take. Remley and Herlihy do not advise consulting with counselor colleagues about how to deal with legal problems, because counselors do not have expertise in legal matters.

One of the reviewers of this book, Mary Hermann, an attorney and counselor educator, teaches a course in legal and ethical issues in counseling. She finds that her students get frustrated because they expect her to provide them with concrete answers to legal problems. Hermann believes that much of the time even legal scholars can only speculate about the answers to these questions. Stating this reality immediately helps to get students thinking about their options and making the best choices they can make under the circumstances rather than searching for some mythical "right answer" to a legal issue (personal communication, January 30, 2009).

To avoid legal ambiguities, some professionals increasingly limit their scope of practice and the range of clients they will work with to reduce their fear of a possible lawsuit. This raises a potential ethical issue of delivering less than effective services, especially if this narrowing of available options to clients is not clearly expressed during the initial interview. In situations such as this, "high-risk clients" may not have access to services they need.

Laws and ethics codes tend to emerge from what has occurred rather than from anticipating what may occur. Limiting your scope of practice to obeying statutes and following ethical standards is inadequate. It is important to acquire an ethical sense of striving for the highest level of functioning at the beginning of your professional program. It is well to remember that the basic purpose of practicing ethically is to further the welfare of your clients (you will hear this many times throughout this book).

At times you may encounter conflicts between the law and ethical principles, or competing ethical standards may appear to require incompatible courses of action (Barnett & Johnson, 2010). In these cases the values of the counselor come into play. Conflict between ethics codes and the law may arise in areas such as advertising, confidentiality, and clients' rights of access to their own files. The APA's Committee on Professional Practice and Standards (2003) suggests that if obeying one's professional code of ethics would result in disobeying the law, it is essential to seek legal advice. A licensed mental health professional might also contact his or her state licensing board for consultation. On this point, the National Association of Social Workers (2008) guideline is clear:

> When such conflicts occur, social workers must make a responsible effort to resolve the conflict in a manner that is consistent with the values, principles, and standards expressed in this Code. If a reasonable resolution of the conflict does not appear possible, social workers should seek proper consultation before making a decision. (Purpose of NASW Code of Ethics.)

When laws and ethics collide, Knapp, Gottlieb, Berman, and Handelsman (2007) state that practitioners need first to verify what the law requires and determine the nature of their ethical obligations. At times, practitioners do not understand their legal requirements and may assume a conflict exists between the law and ethics when there is no such conflict. If there is a real conflict between the law and ethics, and if the conflict cannot be avoided, "psychologists should either obey the law in a manner that minimizes harm to their ethical values or adhere to their ethical values in a manner that minimizes the violation of the law" (p. 55). They add that apparent conflicts between the law and ethics can often be avoided if clinicians anticipate problems in advance and take proactive measures.

One example of a potential conflict between legal and ethical standards involves counseling minors. This is especially true as it pertains to counseling children or adolescents in school settings. Counselors may be committed to following ethical standards in maintaining the confidentiality of the sessions with a minor, yet at times parents/legal guardians may have a legal right to information that is disclosed in these sessions. Practitioners will often struggle between doing what they believe to be ethically appropriate for their client and their legal responsibilities to parents/legal guardians.

In ethical dilemmas involving legal issues, it is imperative to seek advice from legal counsel and discuss the issues with colleagues familiar with the law (Remley, 1996). In those cases where neither the law nor an ethics code resolves an issue, therapists are advised to consider other professional and community standards and their own conscience as well. This subject is addressed more fully in Chapters 5 and 6.

Evolution of Ethics Codes

Codes of ethics are established by professional groups for the purpose of protecting consumers, providing guidelines for practitioners, and clarifying the professional stance of the organizations. As such, these codes do not convey ultimate truth, nor do they provide ready-made answers for the ethical dilemmas practitioners must face. Ethics codes undergo periodic revisions. For instance, the current American Counseling Association (ACA) (2005) and APA (2002) ethics codes replace codes from 10 years earlier.

In addition to codes of ethics, some professional organizations also provide casebooks, which interpret and explain various ethical standards contained with the code. Three examples are *A Guide to the 2002 Revision of the American Psychological Association's Ethics Code* (Knapp & VandeCreek, 2003a), *The Social Work Ethics Casebook: Cases and Commentary* (Reamer, 2008), and *ACA Ethical Standards Casebook* (Herlihy & Corey, 2006a). Two excellent desk reference manuals are also available: *Ethics Desk Reference for Psychologists* (Barnett & Johnson, 2008), which interprets the APA code and provides guidelines for ethical and effective practice; and *Ethics Desk Reference for Counselors* (Barnett & Johnson, 2010), which interprets the ACA code and offers recommendations for preventing ethical problems. However useful these casebooks and desk reference manuals may be, they can never replace the informed judgment and goodwill of the individual counselor. We emphasize again the need for a level of ethical functioning higher than merely following the letter of the law or the code. For instance, you might avoid a lawsuit or professional censure by ignoring cultural diversity, but many of your ethnically diverse clients would likely suffer from your insensitive professional behavior.

Walden, Herlihy, and Ashton (2003) surveyed ACA Ethics Committee chairs in addressing the evolution of ethics codes. One trend emerging as a future issue in the field of counseling ethics relates to cultural considerations and a continued emphasis on the role of diversity in counseling practice. The ethics chairs surveyed predicted the development of a culturally competent code of ethics, increased globalization of counseling, and health care models that take into account the place of diversity in counseling. Other emerging issues that were perceived as necessary to consider in revising ethics codes included the influence of technology on counseling and proactively addressing the impaired professional. Walden and her colleagues concluded that it is important that codes of ethics be evolving documents that are responsive to the needs of counselors, the clients they serve, and society in general.

Professional Monitoring of Practice

The legal and ethical practice of most mental health professionals is regulated in all 50 states. State licensing laws establish the scope of practice of professionals and how these laws will be enforced by licensing boards. State licensing boards have the task of monitoring the conduct of professionals they have licensed (Koocher & Keith-Spiegel, 2008). Some psychotherapy professions are regulated through registration and certification; others, such as social workers, marriage and family therapists, professional counselors, and psychologists, are regulated through licensure. The major duties of regulating boards are (1) to determine standards for admission into the profession, (2) to screen applicants applying for certification or licensure, (3) to regulate the practice of psychotherapy for the public good, and (4) to conduct disciplinary proceedings involving violations of standards of professional conduct as defined by law. Mental health professionals can lose their certification or license if their state regulating board finds that they have engaged in unethical practice or illegal behavior.

In addition to state regulatory boards, most professional organizations have ethics committees—elected or delegated bodies that oversee the conduct of members of the organization. The main purposes of these ethics committees are to educate the association's membership about ethics codes and to protect the public from unethical practices. These committees meet regularly to process formal complaints against individual members of the professional organization. Ethics committees also revise and update their organization's code of ethics.

When necessary, practitioners must explain to clients how to lodge an ethical complaint. When a complaint is lodged against a member, the committee launches an investigation and deliberates on the case. Eventually, a disposition is reached. The complaint may be dismissed, specific charges within the complaint may be dismissed, or the committee may find that ethical standards have been violated and impose sanctions. Possible sanctions include a reprimand; a recommendation that a specific course of remedial action be taken, such as obtaining ongoing supervision or personal therapy; probation or suspension for a specified period of time; a recommendation that the member be allowed to resign from the organization; or a recommendation that the member be expelled.

Expulsion or suspension of a member is a major sanction. Members have the right to appeal the committee's decision. Once the appeals process has been completed or the deadline for appeal has passed, the sanctions of suspension and expulsion are communicated in writing to the members of the professional organization. Practitioners who are expelled from the association may also face the loss of their license or certificate to practice, but only if the state board conducts an independent investigation. Cases that result in expulsion are often serious enough to involve law enforcement and criminal charges. Many cases also result in civil court proceedings, which are usually published in the local press.

How effective are ethics committees of professional organizations in monitoring professional practice and protecting consumers? Koocher and Keith-Spiegel (2008) question their effectiveness and identify some specific criticisms of ethics committees:

- Conflict of interests or bias among committee members
- Lack of training and experience of ethics committee members to adequately carry out their functions
- Excessive time taken to adjudicate cases, resulting in harm to consumers
- Failure to follow due process
- Timid procedures due to fear of lawsuits
- Reactive rather than proactive stances

Mental health professionals facing ethics violations are at times not given fair treatment, and they may take action against the ethics committee. Koocher and Keith-Spiegel state: "Frustrated complainants are increasingly contacting lawyers or the media when sources of redress are inefficient or reach unwelcome conclusions" (p. 50).

Ethical Decision Making

Some Key Terms

Although values and ethics are frequently used interchangeably, the two terms are not identical. **Values** pertains to beliefs and attitudes that provide direction to everyday living, whereas **ethics** pertains to the beliefs we hold about what constitutes right conduct. Ethics are moral principles adopted by an individual or group to provide rules for right conduct. **Morality** is concerned with perspectives of right and proper conduct and involves an evaluation of actions on the basis of some broader cultural context or religious standard.

Ethics represents aspirational goals, or the maximum or ideal standards set by the profession, and they are enforced by professional associations, national certification boards, and government boards that regulate professions (Remley, 1996). Codes of ethics are conceptually broad in nature and generally subject to interpretation by practitioners. Although these minimum and maximum standards may differ, they are not necessarily in conflict.

Community standards (or *mores*) vary on interdisciplinary, theoretical, and geographical bases. The standard for a counselor's social contact with clients may be different in a large urban area than in a rural area, or between practitioners employing a humanistic versus a behavioral approach. Community standards often become the ultimate *legal* criteria for determining whether practitioners are liable for damages. Community standards define what is considered reasonable behavior when a case involving malpractice is litigated. Courts have consistently found that mental health care providers have a duty to exercise a reasonable degree of skill, knowledge, and care. **Reasonableness** is usually defined as the care that is ordinarily exercised by others practicing within that specialty in the professional community.

Professionalism has some relationship to ethical behavior, yet it is possible to act unprofessionally and still not act unethically. For instance, not returning a client's telephone calls promptly might be viewed as unprofessional, but it would probably not be considered unethical unless the client were in crisis.

Some situations cut across these concepts. For example, sexual intimacy between counselors and clients is considered unethical, unprofessional, immoral, and illegal. Keep the differences in the meanings of these various concepts in mind as you read.

Levels of Ethical Practice

One way of conceptualizing professional ethics is to contrast mandatory ethics with aspirational ethics. **Mandatory ethics** describes a level of ethical functioning wherein counselors act in compliance with minimal standards, acknowledging the basic "musts" and "must nots." The focus is on behavioral rules, such as providing for informed consent in professional relationships. **Aspirational ethics** describes the highest standards of thinking and conduct professional counselors seek, and it requires that counselors do more than simply meet the letter of the ethics code. It entails an understanding of the spirit behind the code and the principles on which the code rests. Practitioners who comply at the first level, mandatory ethics, are generally safe from legal action or professional censure. Courts of law and state licensure boards now require minimal standards to which all mental health professionals will be held accountable. At the higher level of ethical functioning, aspirational ethics, practitioners go further and reflect on the effects their interventions may have on the welfare of their clients. An example of aspirational ethics is providing services for no fees (pro bono) for those in the community who cannot afford needed services. In the most recent revision of the ACA's (2005) *Code of Ethics*, each section begins with an introduction, which sets the tone and addresses what counselors should aspire to with regard to ethical practice.

When the word **unethical** is used, people think of extreme violations of established codes. In reality, most violations of ethics probably happen quite inadvertently in clinical practice. The ethics codes of most professional organizations require practitioners to engage in self-monitoring and to take responsibility for misconduct. Welfel (2005) indicates that the professional literature focuses on preventing misconduct and on responding to serious ethical violations. However, the literature has not offered much guidance regarding minor infractions committed by professionals. Welfel states that by taking minor ethical violations seriously and by seeking honest ways to remediate such infractions, counselors can demonstrate their professionalism and personal commitment to benefiting those they serve.

Welfel's (2005) model progresses from awareness, through reflection, to a plan of action whereby counselors can ethically repair damage when they recognize they have violated ethics codes in minor ways. She emphasizes that the first step in recovering from an ethical violation is for the practitioner to recognize that he or she has acted in a way that is likely to be ethically problematic. If a practitioner is not aware of the subtle ways his or her behavior can adversely affect the client, such behavior can go unnoticed, and the client will suffer. For instance, a professional who is struggling financially in her private practice may prolong the therapy of her clients and justify her actions on theoretical grounds. She is likely to ignore the fact that the prolongation of therapy is influenced by her financial situation.

Practitioners can easily find themselves in an ethical quagmire based on competing role expectations. The best way to maintain a clear ethical position is to focus on your clients' best interests. School counselors may be so focused on academic and scheduling issues that they do not reach out to the community and develop the network with other helping professionals needed to make productive referrals for families and students in crises.

In school systems teachers and others sometimes label students and families as dysfunctional or unmotivated. The counselor needs to advocate and help others look for strengths and reframe limitations if progress is to be made. The counselor can be an ethical model in a system where ethics is not given much consideration.

Clients' needs are best met when practitioners monitor their own ethics. Ethical violations may go undetected because only the individual who committed the violation knows about it. Rather than just looking at others and proclaiming "That's unethical!" we encourage you to honestly examine your own thinking and apply guidelines to your behavior by asking yourself, "Is what I am doing in the best interests of my clients? Would the codes of my professional organization agree?"

Principle Ethics and Virtue Ethics

Several writers have developed models for ethical decision making, including Barnett and Johnson (2008, 2010), Cottone (2001), Cottone and Claus (2000), Cottone and Tarvydas (2007), Frame and Williams (2005), Hill, Glaser, and Harden (1995), Jordan and Meara (1990), Kitchener (1984), Koocher and Keith-Spiegel (2008), Meara, Schmidt, and Day (1996), Smith, McGuire, Abbott, and Blau (1991), and Welfel (2010). This section is based on an amalgamation of elements from these various models and our own views.

In a major article titled "Principles and Virtues: A Foundation for Ethical Decisions, Policies, and Character," Meara, Schmidt, and Day (1996) differentiate between principle ethics and virtue ethics. **Principle ethics** is a set of obligations and a method that focuses on moral issues with the goals of (a) solving a particular dilemma or set of dilemmas and (b) establishing a framework to guide future ethical thinking and behavior. Principles typically focus on acts and choices, and they are used to facilitate the selection of socially and historically acceptable answers to the question "What shall I do?"

A thorough grounding in principle ethics opens the way for another important perspective, virtue ethics. **Virtue ethics** focuses on the character traits of the counselor and nonobligatory ideals to which professionals aspire rather than on solving specific ethical dilemmas. Simply stated, principle ethics asks "Is this situation unethical?" whereas virtue ethics asks "Am I doing what is best for my client?" Even in the absence of an ethical dilemma, virtue ethics compels the professional to be conscious of ethical behavior. Meara and her colleagues maintain that it is not a question of subscribing to one or the other form of ethics. Rather, professional counselors should strive to integrate virtue ethics and principle ethics to reach better ethical decisions and policies.

According to the Canadian Counselling Association (CCA, 2007), the virtue ethics approach is based on the belief that counselors are motivated to be virtuous and caring because they believe it is the right thing to do. Virtue ethics emphasizes the counselor's responsibility in making complex ethical decisions. The CCA ethics code suggests asking the following questions when making virtue-based ethical decisions:

- What emotions and intuition am I aware of as I consider this ethical dilemma, and what are they telling me to do?
- How can my values best show caring for the client in this situation?
- How will my decision affect other relevant individuals in this ethical dilemma?
- What decision would I feel best about publicizing?
- What decision would best define who I am as a person?

Some mental health practitioners concern themselves primarily with avoiding malpractice suits. They tend to commit themselves to a rule-bound approach to ethics as a way to stay out of trouble. Other professionals, although concerned with avoiding litigation, are first and foremost interested in doing what is best for their clients. These professionals would consider it unethical to use techniques that might not result in the greatest benefit to their clients or to use techniques in which they were not thoroughly trained, even though these techniques might not lead to a lawsuit.

Meara and colleagues (1996) identify four core virtues—prudence, integrity, respectfulness, and benevolence—that are appropriate for professionals to adhere to in making ethical decisions. They also describe five characteristics of virtuous professionals, which they see as being at the heart of virtue ethics.

- Virtuous agents are motivated to do what is right because they judge it to be right, not just because they feel obligated or fear the consequences.
- Virtuous agents rely on vision and discernment, which involve sensitivity, judgment, and understanding that lead to decisive action.
- Virtuous agents have compassion and are sensitive to the suffering of others. They are able to take actions to reduce their clients' pain.
- Virtuous agents are self-aware. They know how their assumptions, convictions, and biases are likely to affect their interactions with others.
- Virtuous agents are connected with and understand the mores of their community and the importance of community in moral decision making, policy setting, and character development. They understand the ideals and expectations of their community.

Virtue ethics focuses on ideals rather than obligations and on the character of the professional rather than on the action itself. To meet the goals, ideals, and needs of the community being served, consider both principles and virtues because both are important elements in thinking through ethical concerns.

■ A Case Illustrating Virtue Ethics.

Your client, Kevin, is making good progress in his counseling with you. Then he informs you that he has lost his job and will not be able to continue seeing you because of his inability to pay your fees. Here is how four different therapists handled a similar situation:

Therapist A: I'm sorry but I can't continue seeing you without payment. I'm giving you the name of a local community clinic that provides low-cost treatment.

Therapist B: I don't usually see people without payment, but I appreciate the difficulty you find yourself in through no fault of your own. I'll continue to see you, and you pay whatever portion of my fee you can afford. In addition I want you to seek out a community agency and do volunteer work in lieu of the full payment.

Therapist C: I suggest that you put therapy on hold until you can financially afford it.

Therapist D: I can't afford to see you without payment, but I am willing to suggest an alternative plan. Continue writing in your journal, and once a month I will see you for half an hour to discuss your journal. You pay what you can afford for these sessions. When your financial situation has been corrected, we can continue therapy as usual.

How do you react to the various therapists' responses? Which response appeals to you and why? Can you think of another response? Would you be willing to see a client without payment? Why or why not? Do you have concerns about the responses of any of these therapists?

In considering what you might do if you were the therapist in this case, reflect on the standards pertaining to **pro bono services** found in the ethics codes of NASW (2008), ACA (2005), and APA (2002). All three codes encourage practitioners to contribute to society by devoting a portion of their professional time and skills to services for which there is no expectation of significant financial return.

Commentary. In essence, there is no simple solution to this situation. It involves the therapist, the client, the setting, and the situation, all of which need to be considered in context. When a client can no longer pay for services, the therapist must not abandon the client. If treatment is to be terminated, at least a few sessions should be offered to assist Kevin in working through termination issues (Barnett, MacGlashan, & Clarke, 2000). Because you would not want to abandon your client, you could refer Kevin to an agency that would see him without a fee, such as a qualified counselor in a community mental health center, or to a professional who utilizes a sliding fee scale, or to a beginning therapist who is building his or her practice. Alternatively, you could continue to see Kevin as part of your pro bono services, or, as therapists B and D above, you might find a creative strategy to help Kevin remain in counseling while changing your fee or the frequency of counseling. In response to Kevin's job loss, you must still promote his best interests and minimize harm, while simultaneously remaining realistic about your own financial situation and the realities of your work setting.

Moral Principles to Guide Decision Making

Building on the work of others, especially Kitchener (1984), Meara and colleagues (1996) describe six basic moral principles that form the foundation of functioning at the highest ethical level as a professional: *autonomy, nonmaleficence, beneficence, justice, fidelity,* and *veracity.* Applying these ethical principles and the related ethical standards is not as simple as it may seem, especially when dealing with culturally diverse populations. (See Chapters 4 and 13 for more on this issue.) These moral principles involve a process of striving that is never fully complete. We describe each of these six basic moral principles, cite a specific ethical guideline from the ACA, APA, or NASW, and provide a brief discussion of the cultural implications of using each principle.

- **Autonomy** refers to the promotion of self-determination, or the freedom of clients to be self-governing within their social and cultural framework. Respect for autonomy entails acknowledging the right of another to choose and act in accordance with his or her wishes, and the professional behaves in a way that enables this right of another person. Practitioners strive to decrease client dependency and foster client empowerment. The ACA's (2005) introduction to Section A states it this way:

> Counselors encourage client growth and development in ways that foster the interest and welfare of clients and promote formation of healthy relationships. Counselors actively attempt to understand the diverse cultural backgrounds of the clients they serve. Counselors also explore their own cultural identities and how these affect their values and beliefs about the counseling process.

The helping services in the United States are typically based on traditional Western values of individualism, independence, interdependence, self-determination, and making choices for oneself. It often appears as though Western cultures promote individualism above any other cultural value.

However, many cultures follow a different path, stressing decisions with the welfare of the family and the community as a priority. As the ACA standard described here implies, ethical practice involves considering the influence of cultural variables in the counseling relationship.

We cannot apply a rigid yardstick of what is a value priority in any culture without exploring how a particular client views priorities. For instance, what are the implications of the principle of autonomy when it is applied to clients who do not place a high priority on the value of being autonomous? Does it constitute an imposition of values for counselors to steer clients toward autonomous behavior when such behavior could lead to problems with others in their family, community, or culture? What about promoting autonomy for those incapable of it (for example, dependent youths)?

▪ **Nonmaleficence** means avoiding doing harm, which includes refraining from actions that risk hurting clients. Professionals have a responsibility to minimize risks for exploitation and practices that cause harm or have the potential to result in harm. The APA (2002) principle states,

> Psychologists strive to benefit those with whom they work and take care to do no harm.

What are the cultural implications of the principle of nonmaleficence? Traditional diagnostic practices can be inappropriate for certain cultural groups. For instance, a therapist may assign a diagnostic label to a client based on a pattern of behavior the therapist judges to be abnormal, such as inhibition of emotional expression, hesitation to confront, being cautious about self-disclosing, or not making direct eye contact while speaking. Yet these behaviors may be considered normal in certain cultures. Another example may be a school counselor who inappropriately labels a boy ADHD, which may color the perceptions of other staff members in a negative way so they pressure the parents to put the boy on medication. Practitioners need to develop cultural awareness and sensitivity in using assessment, diagnostic, and treatment procedures.

▪ **Beneficence** refers to doing good for others and to promoting the well-being of clients. Beneficence also includes doing good for society. Ideally, counseling contributes to the growth and development of clients within their cultural context. Whatever practitioners do can be judged against this criterion. The following ACA (2005) guideline illustrates beneficence:

> The primary responsibility of counselors is to respect the dignity and to promote the welfare of clients. (A.1.a.)

Consider the possible consequences if a therapist encourages a Vietnamese client to behave more assertively toward his father. The reality of this situation may be that the father would refuse to speak again to a son who confronted him. Even though counselors may be operating with good intentions and may think they are being beneficent, they may not always be doing what is in the best interest of the client. Is it possible for counselors to harm clients unintentionally by encouraging a course of action that has negative consequences? How can counselors know what is in the best interest of their clients? How can counselors determine whether their interventions will lead to growth and development in their clients? As we have previously stated, there are no simple answers to complex questions.

- **Justice** means to be fair by giving equally to others and to treat others justly. Practitioners have a responsibility to provide appropriate services to all clients. Everyone, regardless of age, sex, race, ethnicity, disability, socio-economic status, cultural background, religion, or sexual orientation, is enti-tled to equal access to mental health services. An example might be a social worker making a home visit to a parent who cannot come to the school because of transportation, child care matters, or poverty. NASW's (2008) guideline illustrates this principle:

> Social workers pursue social change, particularly with and on behalf of vulner-able and oppressed individuals and groups of people. Social workers' social change efforts are focused primarily on issues of poverty, unemployment, dis-crimination, and other forms of social injustice. These activities seek to promote sensitivity to and knowledge about oppression and cultural and ethnic diver-sity. Social workers strive to ensure access to needed information, services, and resources; equality of opportunity; and meaningful participation in decision making for all people. (Ethical Principles, Social Justice.)

Traditional mental health services may not be just and fair to everyone in a culturally diverse society. If intervention strategies are not relevant to some segments of the population, justice is being violated. How can practitioners adapt the techniques they use to fit the needs of diverse populations? How can new helping strategies be developed that are consistent with the world-view of culturally different clients?

- **Fidelity** means that professionals make realistic commitments and keep these promises. This entails fulfilling one's responsibilities of trust in a relationship. ACA's (2005) code encourages counselors to inform cli-ents about counseling and to be faithful in keeping commitments made to clients:

> Clients have the freedom to choose whether to enter into or remain in a coun-seling relationship and need adequate information about the counseling pro-cess and the counselor. Counselors have an obligation to review in writing and verbally with clients the rights and responsibilities of both the counselor and the client. Informed consent is an ongoing part of the counseling process and counselors appropriately document discussions of informed consent through-out the counseling relationship. (A.2.a.)

Fidelity involves creating a trusting and therapeutic relationship in which people can search for solutions. However, what about clients whose culture teaches them that counselors are experts whose job is to provide answers for specific problem situations? What if a client expects the counselor to behave in this way? If the counselor does not meet the client's expectations, is trust being established?

- **Veracity** means truthfulness, which involves the practitioner's obligation to deal honestly with clients. Unless practitioners are truthful with their clients, the trust required to form a good working relationship will not develop. An example of the principle of veracity is found in the Code of Ethics of the Association for Addiction Professionals (NAADAC, 2008):

> I understand that effectiveness in my profession is largely based on the ability to be worthy of trust, and I shall work to the best of my ability to act consistently within the bounds of a known moral universe, to faithfully fulfill the terms of both personal and professional commitments, to safeguard fiduciary relationships consistently, and to speak the truth as it is known to me. (Principle 4.)

The six principles discussed here are a good place to start in determining the degree to which your practice is consistent with promoting the welfare of the clients you serve. To the list above, Barnett (2008) adds **self-care,** which involves taking adequate care of ourselves so that we are able to implement the preceding virtues. If mental health professionals fail to practice self-care, their ability to effectively implement the other principles will be impaired (Barnett, Johnston, & Hillard, 2006).

Steps in Making Ethical Decisions

When making ethical decisions, ask yourself these questions: "Which values do I rely on and why? How do my values affect my work with clients?" When making ethical decisions, the National Association of Social Workers (2008) cautions you to be aware of your clients' as well as your own personal values, cultural and religious beliefs, and practices. Acting responsibly implies recognizing any conflicts between personal and professional values and dealing with them effectively. The American Counseling Association's (2005) *Code of Ethics* states that when counselors encounter an ethical dilemma they are expected to carefully consider an ethical decision-making process. To make sound ethical decisions, it is necessary to slow down the decision-making process and engage in an intentional course of ethical deliberation, consultation, and action (Barnett & Johnson, 2010). Although no one ethical decision-making model is most effective, mental health professionals need to be familiar with at least one of the following models or an amalgam that best fits for them.

Ethical decision making is not a purely cognitive and linear process that follows clearly defined and predictable steps. Indeed, it is crucial to acknowledge that emotions play a part in how you make ethical decisions. As a practitioner, your feelings will likely influence how you interpret both your client's behavior and your own behavior. Furthermore, if you are uncomfortable with an ethical decision and do not adequately deal with this discomfort, it will certainly influence your future behavior with your client. An integral part of recognizing and working through an ethical concern is discussing your beliefs and values, motivations, feelings, and actions with a supervisor or a colleague.

In the process of making the best ethical decisions, it is also important to *involve your clients* whenever possible. Because you are making decisions about what is best for the welfare of your clients, it is good to strive to discuss with them the nature of the ethical dilemma that pertains to them. The **feminist model** for ethical decision making calls for maximum involvement of the client at every stage of the process, a strategy based on the feminist principle that power should be equalized in the therapeutic relationship (Hill, Glaser, & Harden, 1995).

Consulting with the client fully and appropriately is an essential step in ethical decision making, for doing so increases the chances of making the best possible decision. Walden (2006) suggests that important therapeutic benefits can result from inclusion of the client in the ethical decision-making process, and she offers some strategies for accomplishing this goal at both the organizational and individual levels. When we make decisions about a client *for* the client rather than *with* the client, Walden maintains that we rob the client of power in the relationship. When we collaborate with clients, they are empowered. By soliciting the client's perspective, we stand a good chance of achieving better counseling results and the best resolution for any ethical questions that arise. Potential therapeutic benefits can be gained by including clients in dealing with ethical concerns, and this practice represents functioning at the aspirational level. In fact, Walden questions whether it is truly possible to attain the aspirational level of ethical functioning *without* including the client's voice in ethical concerns. By adding the voice and the unique perspective of the consumers of professional services, we indicate to the public that we as a profession are genuinely interested in protecting the rights and welfare of those who make use of our services. Walden sees few risks in bringing the client into ethical matters, and there are many benefits to both the client and the professional.

The **social constructionist model** of ethical decision making shares some aspects with the feminist model, but focuses primarily on the social aspects of decision making in counseling (Cottone, 2001). This model redefines the ethical decision-making process as an interactive rather than an individual or intrapsychic process and places the decision in the social context itself, not in the mind of the person making the decision. This approach involves negotiating, consensualizing, and when necessary, arbitrating.

Garcia, Cartwright, Winston, and Borzuchowska (2003) describe a **transcultural integrative model** of ethical decision making that addresses the need for including cultural factors in the process of resolving ethical dilemmas. They present their model in a step-by-step format that counselors can use in dealing with ethical dilemmas in a variety of settings and with different client populations. Frame and Williams (2005) have developed a model of ethical decision making from a multicultural perspective based on universalist philosophy. In this model cultural differences are recognized, but common principles such as altruism, responsibility, justice, and caring that link cultures are emphasized.

Barnett and Johnson (2010) remind us that many of the ethical dilemmas we will encounter do not have a readily apparent answer. Keeping in mind the feminist model of ethical decision making, Walden's (2006) views on including the client's voice in ethical concerns, a social constructionist approach to ethics, and a transcultural integrative model of ethical decision making, we present our approach to thinking through ethical dilemmas. Following these steps may help you think through ethical problems.

1. *Identify the problem or dilemma.* It is important to determine whether a situation truly involves ethics. The distinction between unorthodox and poor professional practice may be unclear (Koocher & Keith-Spiegel, 2008). To determine the nature of the problem or dilemma, gather all the information that sheds light on the situation. Clarify whether the conflict is ethical, legal, clinical, professional, or moral—or a combination of any or all of these. The first step toward resolving an ethical dilemma is recognizing that a problem exists and identifying its specific nature. Because most ethical dilemmas are complex, it is useful to look at the problem from many perspectives. Consultation with your client begins at this initial stage and continues throughout the process of working toward an ethical decision, as does the process of documenting your decisions and actions. Frame and Williams (2005) suggest reflecting on these questions to identify and define an ethical dilemma: "What is the crux of the dilemma? Who is involved? What are the stakes? What values of mine are involved? What cultural and historical factors are in play? What insights does my client have regarding the dilemma? How is the client affected by the various aspects of the problem? What are my insights about the problem?" Taking the time to engage in reflection is an essential first step.

2. *Identify the potential issues involved.* After the information is collected, list and describe the critical issues and discard the irrelevant ones. Evaluate the rights, responsibilities, and welfare of all those who are affected by the situation. Consider the cultural context of the situation, including any relevant cultural dimensions of the client's situation. It is important to consider the context of power and also to assess acculturation and racial identity development of the client (Frame & Williams, 2005). Part of the process of making ethical decisions involves identifying and examining the ethical principles that are relevant in the situation. Consider the six fundamental moral principles—autonomy, nonmaleficence, beneficence, justice, fidelity, and veracity—and apply them to the situation, including those that may be in conflict. It may help to prioritize these ethical principles and think through ways in which they can support a resolution to the dilemma. Reasons can be presented that support various sides of a given issue, and different

ethical principles may sometimes imply contradictory courses of action. When it is appropriate, and to the degree that it is possible, involve your client in identifying potential issues in the situation.

3. *Review the relevant ethics codes.* Consult available guidelines that could apply in your situation. Ask yourself whether the standards or principles of your professional organization offer a possible solution to the problem. Consider whether your own values and ethics are consistent with, or in conflict with, the relevant codes. If you are in disagreement with a particular standard, do you have a rationale to support your position? It is imperative to document this process to demonstrate your conscientious commitment to solving a dilemma. You can also seek guidance from your professional organization on any specific concern relating to an ethical or legal situation. Most of the national professional organizations provide members with access to a telephone discussion of ethical and legal issues. These consultations focus on giving members guidance in understanding and applying the code of ethics to a particular situation and in assisting members in exploring relevant questions. However, these consultations do not tell members what to do, nor does the organization assume responsibility for making the decision.

4. *Know the applicable laws and regulations.* It is essential for you to keep up to date on relevant state and federal laws that might apply to ethical dilemmas. In addition, be sure you understand the current rules and regulations of the agency or organization where you work. This is especially critical in matters of keeping or breaching confidentiality, reporting child or elder abuse, dealing with issues pertaining to danger to self or others, parental rights, record keeping, assessment, diagnosis, licensing statutes, and the grounds for malpractice. However, realize that knowledge of the laws and regulations are not sufficient in addressing a dilemma. As Welfel (2010) aptly puts it: "Rules, laws, and codes must be fully understood to act responsibly, but they are the starting point of truly ethical action, not the end point" (p. 24).

5. *Obtain consultation.* One reason for poor ethical decisions stems from our inability to view a situation objectively because of our prejudices, biases, personal needs, or emotional investment (Koocher & Keith-Spiegel, 2008). At this point, it is generally helpful to consult with one or more trusted colleagues to obtain different perspectives on the area of concern and to arrive at the best possible decision. Do not limit the individuals with whom you consult to those who share your viewpoint. If there is a legal question, seek legal counsel. If the ethical dilemma involves working with a client from a different culture or who has a different worldview than yours, it is prudent to consult with a person who has expertise in this culture. If there is a clinical issue involved, seek consultation from a professional with clinical expertise in the situation. After you present your assessment of the situation and your ideas of

how you might proceed, ask for feedback on your analysis. Are there factors you are not considering? Have you thoroughly examined all of the ethical, clinical, and legal issues involved in the case? It is wise to document the nature of your consultation, including the suggestions provided by those with whom you consulted. In court cases a record of consultation illustrates that you have attempted to adhere to community standards by finding out what your colleagues in the community would do in the same situation. In an investigation the "reasonable person" standard may be applied: "What would a professional in your community with 3 years' experience have done in your situation?"

6. *Consider possible and probable courses of action.* At this point, take time to think about the range of courses of actions. Brainstorm to identify multiple options for dealing with the situation. Generate a variety of possible solutions to the dilemma (Frame & Williams, 2005). Consider the ethical and legal implications of the possible solutions you have identified. By listing a wide variety of courses of action, you may identify a possibility that is unorthodox but useful. Of course, one alternative is that no action is required. As you think about the many possibilities for action, discuss these options with your client as well as with other professionals and document these discussions.

7. *Enumerate the consequences of various decisions.* Consider the implications of each course of action for the client, for others who are related to the client, and for you as the counselor. Examine the probable outcomes of various actions, considering the potential risks and benefits of each course of action. Other potential consequences of a decision include psychological and social costs, short- and long-term effects, the time and effort necessary to implement a decision, and any resource limitations (Koocher & Keith-Spiegel, 2008). Again, collaboration with your client about consequences for him or her is most important, for doing this can lead to your client's empowerment. Use the six fundamental moral principles (autonomy, nonmaleficence, beneficence, justice, fidelity, and veracity) as a framework for evaluating the consequences of a given course of action. Realize that there are likely to be multiple outcomes, rather than a single desired outcome in dealing with an ethical dilemma. A useful strategy is to continue brainstorming and reflecting on other options, as well as consulting with colleagues who may see possibilities that have not occurred to you (Remley & Herlihy, 2010).

8. *Choose what appears to be the best course of action.* To make the best decision, carefully consider the information you have received from various sources. The more obvious the dilemma, the clearer the course of action; the more subtle the dilemma, the more difficult the decision will be. After deciding, try not to second-guess your course of action. You may wonder if you have made the best decision in a given situation, or

you may realize later that another action might have been more beneficial. Hindsight does not invalidate the decision you made based on the information you had at the time. Once you have made what you consider to be the best decision, evaluate your course of action by asking these questions (Frame & Williams, 2005): "How does my action fit with my profession's code of ethics? To what degree does the action taken consider the cultural values and experiences of the client? How have my own values been affirmed or challenged? How might others evaluate my action? What did I learn from dealing with this ethical dilemma?" Reflecting on your assessment of the situation and on the actions you have taken is essential if you are to learn from your experience. Review your notes and follow up to determine the outcomes and whether further action is needed. To obtain the most accurate picture, involve your client in this process. Again we stress the importance of adequately documenting each phase of your ethical decision-making process.

The goal of any ethical decision-making process is to help you take into account all relevant facts, use any resources available to you, and reason through the dilemma in a way that points to the best possible course of action. The procedural steps we have listed here should not be thought of as a simple and linear way to reach a resolution on ethical matters. However, we have found that these steps do stimulate self-reflection and encourage discussion with clients and colleagues. Using this process, we are confident that you will find a solution that is helpful for your client, your profession, and yourself.

Dealing With Suspected Unethical Behavior of Colleagues

In our classes and workshops we are often asked the question, "What should I do when I suspect other mental health professionals or colleagues are engaging in questionable behavior?" You may wonder whether it is your place to judge the practices of other practitioners. Even if you are convinced that the situation involves clear ethical violations, you may be in doubt about the best way to deal with it. Should you first discuss the matter with the person? Assuming that you do and that the person becomes defensive, what other actions should you consider? When would a violation be serious enough that you would feel obligated to bring it to the attention of an appropriate local, state, or national committee on professional ethics? Most professional organizations have specific ethical standards that clearly place the responsibility for confronting recognized violations squarely on members of their profession. Ignoring evidence of peer misconduct is considered to be an ethical violation in itself (see the Ethics Code box titled "Unethical Behavior of Colleagues").

Professionals have an obligation to deal with colleagues when they suspect unethical conduct. Koocher and Keith-Spiegel (2008) discuss the role of

Ethics Codes

Unethical Behavior of Colleagues

Commission on Rehabilitation Counselor Certification (CRCC, 2010)

When rehabilitation counselors have reason to believe that another rehabilitation counselor is violating or has violated an ethical standard, they attempt first to resolve the issue informally with the other rehabilitation counselor if feasible, provided such action does not violate confidentiality rights that may be involved. (L.3.a.)

National Association of Social Workers (2008)

Social workers should take adequate measures to discourage, prevent, expose, and correct the unethical conduct of colleagues. (2.11.a.)

National Organization for Human Services (2000)

Human service professionals respond appropriately to unethical behavior of colleagues. Usually this means initially talking directly with the colleague and, if no resolution is forthcoming, reporting the colleague's behavior to supervisory or administrative staff and/or to the professional organization(s) to which the colleague belongs. (Statement 24.)

informal peer monitoring as a way to assume responsibility for watching out for each other. Informal peer monitoring provides an opportunity for corrective interventions to ethically questionable acts. Actions can be taken directly by confronting a colleague, or indirectly by advising clients how to proceed when they have concerns about another professional's actions. If your efforts at an informal resolution of apparent unethical behavior by a colleague are ineffective, you have an ethical obligation to file a formal complaint (Barnett & Johnson, 2008).

Generally, the best way to proceed when you have concerns about the behavior of colleagues is to tell them directly, unless doing so would compromise a client's confidentiality. In cases of egregious offenses, such as sexual exploitation of clients or general incompetence, the situation calls for going beyond informal measures. Depending on the nature of the complaint and the outcome of the discussion, reporting a colleague to a professional board would be one of several options open to you.

Self-Assessment: An Inventory of Your Attitudes and Beliefs About Ethical and Professional Issues

This inventory surveys your thoughts on various professional and ethical issues in the helping professions. It is designed to introduce you to issues and topics presented in this book and to stimulate your thoughts and interest. You may want to complete the inventory in more than one sitting, giving each question full concentration.

This is not a traditional multiple-choice test in which you must select the "one right answer." Rather, it is a survey of your basic beliefs, attitudes, and values on specific topics related to the practice of therapy. For each question, write in the letter of the response that most clearly reflects your view at this time. In many cases the answers are not mutually exclusive, and you may choose more than one response if you wish. In addition, a blank line is included for each item so you can provide a response more suited to your thinking or to qualify a chosen response.

Notice that there are two spaces before each item. Use the space on the left for your answer at the beginning of the course. At the end of the course, take this inventory again, placing your answer in the space on the right. Cover your initial answers so as not to be influenced by how you originally responded. Then you can see how your attitudes have changed as a result of your experience in the course.

Bring the completed inventory to a class session to compare your views with those of others in the class. Such a comparison can stimulate debate and help the class understand the complexities in this kind of decision making. In choosing the issues you want to discuss in class, circle the items that you felt most strongly about. Ask others how they responded to these items in particular.

_____ _____ 1. **Fees.** If I were working with a client who could no longer continue to pay my fees, I would most likely

   a. see this person at no fee until his or her financial position changed.

   b. give my client the name of a local community clinic that provides low-cost treatment.

   c. suggest bartering of goods or services for therapy.

   d. lower my fee to whatever the client could afford.

   e. _____

_____ _____ 2. **Therapy for therapists.** For those who wish to become therapists, I believe personal psychotherapy

   a. should be required for licensure.

   b. is not an important factor in the ability to work with others.

   c. should be encouraged but not required.

   d. is needed only when the therapist has some form of psychological impairment.

   e. _____

_____ _____ 3. **Therapist effectiveness.** To be an effective helper, I believe a therapist

   a. must like the client.

   b. must be free of any personal conflicts in the area in which the client is working.

c. needs to have experienced the same problem as the client.

d. needs to have experienced feelings similar to those being experienced by the client.

e. _____

_____ _____ 4. **Ethical decision making.** If I were faced with an ethical dilemma, the first step I would take would be to

a. review the relevant ethics codes.

b. consult with an attorney.

c. identify the problem or dilemma.

d. decide on what appears to be the best course of action.

e. _____

_____ _____ 5. **Being ethical.** For me, being an ethical practitioner *mainly* entails

a. acting in compliance with mandatory ethical standards.

b. reflecting on the effects my interventions are likely to have on the welfare of my clients.

c. avoiding obvious violations of my profession's ethics codes.

d. thinking about the legal implications of everything I do.

e. _____

_____ _____ 6. **Unethical supervisor.** If I was an intern and was convinced that my supervisor was encouraging trainees to participate in unethical behavior in an agency setting, I would

a. first discuss the matter with the supervisor.

b. report the supervisor to the director of the agency.

c. ignore the situation for fear of negative consequences.

d. report the situation to the ethics committee of the state professional association.

e. _____

_____ _____ 7. **Multicultural knowledge and skills.** Practitioners who work with culturally diverse groups without having multicultural knowledge and skills

a. may be insensitive to their clients.

b. may be guilty of unethical behavior.

c. should realize the need for specialized training.

d. may be acting illegally.

e. _____

_____ _____ 8. **Feelings toward clients.** If I had strong feelings, positive or negative, toward a client, I would most likely

a. discuss the feelings with my client.

b. keep my feelings to myself.

      c. discuss my feelings with a supervisor or colleague.

      d. accept my feelings unless they began to interfere with the counseling relationship.

      e. _____

_____ _____ 9. **Being ready.** I won't be ready to counsel others until

      a. my own life is free of major problems.

      b. I have experienced counseling as a client.

      c. I feel confident and know that I will be effective.

      d. I have developed the ability to examine my own life and relationships.

      e. _____

_____ _____ 10. **Client's feelings.** If a client expressed strong feelings of attraction or dislike for me, I would

      a. help the client work through these feelings and understand them.

      b. enjoy these feelings if they were positive.

      c. refer my client if these feelings were negative.

      d. direct the sessions into less emotional areas.

      e. _____

_____ _____ 11. **Dealing with diversity.** Practitioners who counsel clients whose sex, race, age, social class, or sexual orientation is different from their own

      a. will most likely not understand these clients fully.

      b. need to be sensitive to the differences between their clients and themselves.

      c. can practice unethically if they ignore diversity factors.

      d. will probably not be effective with such clients because of these differences.

      e. _____

_____ _____ 12. **Ethics versus law.** If I were faced with a counseling situation where it appeared that there was a conflict between an ethical and legal course to follow, I would

      a. immediately consult with an attorney.

      b. always choose the legal path first and foremost.

      c. strive to do what I believed to be ethical, even if it meant challenging a law.

      d. refer my client to another therapist.

      e. _____

———— ———— 13. **Values.** In terms of appreciating and understanding the value systems of clients who are culturally different from me,

    a. I would not impose my cultural values on them.

    b. I would encourage them to accept the values of the dominant culture for survival purposes.

    c. I would attempt to modify my counseling procedures to fit their cultural values.

    d. I would familiarize myself with the specific cultural values of my clients.

    e. _____

———— ———— 14. **Objectivity.** If a client came to me with a problem and I could see that I would not be objective because of my values, I would

    a. accept the client because of the challenge to become more tolerant of diversity.

    b. tell the client at the outset about my fears concerning our conflicting values.

    c. refer the client to someone else.

    d. attempt to understand my need to impose my values.

    e. _____

———— ———— 15. **End-of-life decisions.** With respect to a client's right to make his or her own end-of-life decisions, I would

    a. use the principle of a client's self-determination as the key in any dilemma of this sort.

    b. tell my client what I would do if I were in this situation.

    c. suggest that my client see a clergy person.

    d. encourage my client to find meaning in life, regardless of his or her psychological and physical condition.

    e. _____

———— ———— 16. **When to refer.** I would tend to refer a client to another therapist

    a. if I had a strong dislike for the client.

    b. if I did not have much experience working with the kind of problem the client presented.

    c. if I saw my own needs and problems getting in the way of helping the client.

    d. if I had strong value differences with my client.

    e. _____

———— ———— 17. **Role of values.** My ethical position regarding the role of values in therapy is that, as a therapist, I should

    a. never impose my values on a client.

    b. expose my values, without imposing them on the client.

c. challenge my clients to find other ways of viewing their situation.

d. keep my values out of the counseling relationship.

e. _____

_____ _____ 18. **Sexual orientation.** If I were to counsel lesbian and gay clients, a major concern of mine would be

    a. maintaining objectivity.

    b. not knowing and understanding enough about their sexual orientation.

    c. establishing a positive therapeutic relationship.

    d. being limited by my own values.

    e. _____

_____ _____ 19. **Unethical behavior.** Of the following, I consider the most unethical form of therapist behavior to be

    a. promoting dependence in the client.

    b. becoming sexually involved with a client.

    c. breaking confidentiality without a good reason to do so.

    d. accepting a client who has a problem that goes beyond my competence.

    e. _____

_____ _____ 20. **Counseling friends.** Regarding the issue of counseling friends, I think that

    a. it is seldom wise to accept a friend as a client.

    b. it should be done rarely, and only if it is clear that the friendship will not interfere with the therapeutic relationship.

    c. friendship and therapy should not be mixed.

    d. it should be done only when it is acceptable to both the client and the counselor.

    e. _____

_____ _____ 21. **Confidentiality.** Regarding confidentiality, I believe it is ethical to

    a. break confidence when there is reason to believe a client may do serious harm to him- or herself.

    b. break confidence when there is reason to believe that a client will do harm to someone else.

    c. break confidence when the parents of a client ask for certain information.

    d. inform the authorities when a client is breaking the law.

    e. _____

_____ _____ 22. **Termination.** A therapist should terminate therapy with a client when

    a. the client decides to do so.

    b. the therapist judges that it is time to terminate.

    c. it is clear that the client is not benefiting from the therapy.

    d. the client reaches an impasse.

    e. _____

_____ _____ 23. **Sex in therapy.** A sexual relationship between a *former* client and a therapist is

    a. always ethically problematic because of the power imbalance.

    b. ethical only five years after termination of therapy.

    c. ethical only when client and therapist discuss the issue and agree to the relationship.

    d. never ethical, regardless of the time that has elapsed.

    e. _____

_____ _____ 24. **Touching.** Concerning the issue of physically touching a client, I think that touching

    a. is unwise, because it could be misinterpreted by the client.

    b. should be done only when the therapist genuinely thinks it would be appropriate.

    c. is an important part of the therapeutic process.

    d. is ethical when the client requests it.

    e. _____

_____ _____ 25. **Sex in supervision.** A clinical supervisor has initiated sexual relationships with former trainees (students). He maintains that because he no longer has any professional responsibility to them this practice is acceptable. In my view, this behavior is

    a. clearly unethical, because he is using his position to initiate contacts with former students.

    b. not unethical, because the professional relationship has ended.

    c. not unethical, but is unwise and inappropriate.

    d. somewhat unethical, because the supervisory relationship is similar to the therapeutic relationship.

    e. _____

_____ _____ 26. **Spirituality and religion.** Regarding the role of spiritual and religious values, as a counselor I would be inclined to

    a. ignore such values out of concern that I would impose my own beliefs on my clients.

b. actively strive to get my clients to think about how spiritual-ity or religion could enhance their lives.

c. avoid bringing up the topic unless my client initiated such a discussion.

d. conduct an assessment of my client's spiritual and religious beliefs during the intake session.

e. _____

_____ 27. **Family therapy.** In the practice of family therapy, I think the

a. therapist's primary responsibility is to the welfare of the family as a unit.

b. therapist should focus primarily on the needs of individual members of the family.

c. therapist should attend to the family's needs and, at the same time, be sensitive to the needs of the individual members.

d. therapist has an ethical obligation to state his or her bias and approach at the outset.

e. _____

_____ 28. **Managed care.** The practice of limiting the number of therapy sessions a client is entitled to under a managed care plan is

a. unethical as it can work against a client's best interests.

b. a reality that I expect I will have to accept.

c. an example of exploitation of a client's rights.

d. wrong because it takes away the professional's judgment in many cases.

e. _____

_____ 29. **Gift-giving.** If a client were to offer me a gift, I would

a. accept it cheerfully.

b. never accept it under any circumstances.

c. discuss the matter with my client.

d. attempt to figure out the motivations for the gift.

e. _____

_____ 30. **Bartering.** Regarding bartering with a client in exchange for therapy services, my position is that

a. it all depends on the circumstances of the individual case.

b. I would consider this practice if the client had no way to pay for my services.

c. the practice is unethical.

d. before agreeing to bartering, I would always seek consultation.

e. _____

_____ _____ 31. **Diagnosis.** Concerning the role of diagnosis in counseling, I believe

    a. diagnosis is essential for planning a treatment program.

    b. diagnosis is counterproductive for therapy, because it is based on an external view of the client.

    c. diagnosis can be harmful in that it tends to label people, who then are limited by the label.

    d. the usefulness of diagnosis depends on the theoretical orientation and the kind of counseling a therapist does.

    e. _____

_____ _____ 32. **Testing.** Concerning the place of testing in counseling, I think that tests

    a. generally interfere with the counseling process.

    b. can be valuable tools if they are used as adjuncts to counseling.

    c. are essential for people who are seriously disturbed.

    d. can be either used or abused in counseling.

    e. _____

_____ _____ 33. **Risks of group therapy.** Regarding the issue of psychological risks associated with participation in group therapy, my position is that

    a. clients should be informed at the outset of possible risks.

    b. these risks should be minimized by careful screening.

    c. this issue is exaggerated because there are very few real risks.

    d. careful supervision will offset some of these risks.

    e. _____

_____ _____ 34. **Internet counseling.** Regarding the practice of counseling via the Internet, I believe

    a. the practice is fraught with ethical and legal problems.

    b. this is a form of technology with real promise for many clients who would not, or could not, seek out face-to-face counseling.

    c. it is limited to dealing with simple problems because of the inability to make an adequate assessment.

    d. I would never provide Internet counseling without having some personal contact with the client.

    e. _____

_____ _____ 35. **Inadequate supervision.** As an intern, if I thought my supervision was inadequate, I would

    a. talk to my supervisor about it.

    b. continue to work without complaining.

    c. seek supervision elsewhere.

    d. question the commitment of the agency toward me.

    e. _____

_____ _____ 36. **Supervision.** My view of supervision is that it is

    a. a place to find answers to difficult situations.

    b. an opportunity to increase my clinical skills.

    c. valuable to have when I reach an impasse with a client.

    d. a way for me to learn about myself and to get insights into how I work with clients.

    e. _____

_____ _____ 37. **Addressing diversity.** In working with clients from different ethnic groups, it is most important to

    a. be aware of the sociopolitical forces that have influenced them.

    b. understand how language can be a barrier to effective multicultural counseling.

    c. refer these clients to some other professional who shares their ethnic and cultural background.

    d. help these clients modify their views so that they will feel more accepted.

    e. _____

_____ _____ 38. **Diversity competence.** To be effective in counseling clients from a different culture, a counselor must

    a. possess specific knowledge about the particular group he or she is counseling.

    b. be able to accurately "read" nonverbal messages.

    c. have had direct contact with this group.

    d. treat these clients no differently than clients from his or her own cultural background.

    e. _____

_____ _____ 39. **Community responsibility.** Concerning the mental health professional's responsibility to the community, I believe

    a. practitioners should educate the community concerning the nature of psychological services.

b. professionals should attempt to change patterns that need changing.

c. community involvement falls outside the proper scope of counseling.

d. practitioners should empower clients in the use of the resources available in the community.

e. _____

___ ___ 40. **Role in community.** If I were working as a practitioner in the community, the major role I would expect to play would be that of

a. a change agent.

b. an adviser.

c. an educator or a consultant.

d. an advocate.

e. _____

Chapter Summary

This introductory chapter focused on the foundations of creating an ethical sense and explored various perspectives on teaching the process of making ethical decisions. Professional codes of ethics are indeed essential for ethical practice, but merely knowing these codes is not enough. The challenge comes with learning how to think critically and knowing ways to apply general ethical principles to particular situations. We encourage you to become active in your education and training (see the Internet Resources box for information on joining a professional association). We also suggest that you try to keep an open mind about the issues you encounter during this time and throughout your professional career. An important part of this openness is a willingness to focus on yourself as a person and as a professional, as well as on the questions that are more obviously related to your clients.

Suggested Activities

Note to the student. At the end of each chapter we have deliberately provided a range of activities for instructors and students to choose from. The questions and activities are intended to stimulate you to become an active learner. We invite you to personalize the material and develop your own positions on the issues we raise. We suggest that you choose those activities that you find the most challenging and meaningful.

1. As a practitioner, how will you determine what is ethical and what is unethical? How will you develop your guidelines for ethical practice?

Make a list of behaviors that you judge to be unethical. After you have thought through this issue by yourself, you may want to explore your approach with fellow students.

2. Take the self-assessment survey of your attitudes and beliefs about ethics in this chapter. Now circle the five items that you had the strongest reactions to or that you had the hardest time answering. Bring these items to class for discussion.

3. Look over the professional codes of ethics of one or more of the professional organizations. What are your impressions of each of these codes? To what degree do they provide you with the needed guidelines for ethical practice? What are the values of such codes? What limitations do you see in them? What do the various codes have in common?

4. Check out at least one of the websites of the professional organizations listed in the box titled "Professional Organizations and Codes of Ethics" at the end of the chapter. What is the main mission of the organization? What does the organization offer you as a student? What are the benefits of being a member? What kinds of professional journals and publications are available? What information can you find about conferences?

Ethics in Action *CD-ROM Exercises*

The *Ethics in Action* CD-ROM and this text deal with the topic of ethical decision making—with emphasis on the eight steps in making ethical decisions. Other topics explored in the first part of the CD-ROM include the role of codes of ethics in making decisions and basic moral principles as they apply to resolving ethical dilemmas.

In Part 1 of the CD-ROM program, three role plays provide concrete examples of applying the steps in making ethical decisions described in this chapter. The role plays illustrate ethical dilemmas pertaining to teen pregnancy, interracial dating, and culture clash between client and counselor. After viewing each of these three vignettes, we strongly encourage you to complete the exercises that are a part of each role-play situation.

To make the fullest use of this integrated learning package, conduct small group discussions in class and engage in role-playing activities. Students can assume the role of counselor for the vignette and demonstrate how they would deal with the dilemma presented by the client. For those not using the CD-ROM, descriptive summaries of the vignettes are provided with these exercises to facilitate role plays and class discussions. We hope that the material in the CD-ROM, and in this text as well, will be a catalyst for students to try out alternative approaches to dealing with each ethical challenge presented.

Professional Organizations and Codes of Ethics

The following ethics codes are reproduced in a supplement to this textbook titled *Codes of Ethics for the Helping Professions*, 4th edition (2011), which is sold at a nominal price when ordered as a bundle with this textbook. Alternatively, you may obtain particular codes of ethics by contacting the organizations directly or by downloading these ethics codes from the organizations' websites.

1. **American Counseling Association (ACA):** *Code of Ethics*, ©2005
   Visit www.counseling.org/ for more information on this organization.
2. **National Board for Certified Counselors (NBCC):** *Code of Ethics*, ©2005
   Visit www.nbcc.org/ for more information on this organization.
3. **Commission on Rehabilitation Counselor Certification (CRCC):** *Code of Professional Ethics for Rehabilitation Counselors*, ©2010
   Visit www.crccertification.com/ for more information on this organization.
4. **Association for Addiction Professionals (NAADAC):** *Code of Ethics*, ©2008
   Visit www.naadac.org/ for more information on this organization.
5. **Canadian Counselling Association (CCA):** *Code of Ethics*, ©2007
   Visit www.ccacc.ca/home.html for more information on this organization.
6. **American School Counselor Association (ASCA):** *Ethical Standards for School Counselors*, ©2004
   Visit www.schoolcounselor.org/ for more information on this organization.
7. **American Psychological Association (APA):** *Ethical Principles of Psychologists and Code of Conduct*, ©2002
   Visit www.apa.org/ for more information on this organization.
8. **American Psychiatric Association:** *The Principles of Medical Ethics With Annotations Especially Applicable to Psychiatry*, ©2009
   Visit www.psych.org/ for more information on this organization.
9. **American Group Psychotherapy Association (AGPA):** *Ethical Guidelines for Group Therapists*, ©2002
   Visit www.groupsinc.org/ for more information on this organization.
10. **American Mental Health Counselors Association (AMHCA):** *Code of Ethics*, ©2000
    Visit www.amhca.org/ for more information on this organization.
11. **American Association for Marriage and Family Therapy (AAMFT):** *Code of Ethics*, ©2001
    Visit www.aamft.org/ for more information on this organization.
12. **International Association of Marriage and Family Counselors (IAMFC):** *Ethical Code*, ©2005
    Visit www.iamfc.com/ for more information on this organization.
13. **Association for Specialists in Group Work (ASGW):** *Best Practice Guidelines*, ©2008
    Visit www.asgw.org/ for more information on this organization.
14. **National Association of Social Workers (NASW):** *Code of Ethics*, ©2008
    Visit www.socialworkers.org/ for more information on this organization.

(*continued on next page*)

15. **National Organization for Human Services (NOHS):** *Ethical Standards of Human Service Professionals,* ©2000
    Visit www.nationalhumanservices.org/ for more information on this organization.
16. **Feminist Therapy Institute (FTI):** *Feminist Therapy Code of Ethics,* ©2000
    Visit www.feminist-therapy-institute.org/ for more information on this organization.
17. **American Music Therapy Association (AMTA):** *Code of Ethics,* ©2008
    Visit www.musictherapy.org/ for more information on this organization.

Chapter 2

Pre-Chapter Self-Inventory

The pre-chapter self-inventories will help you to identify and clarify your attitudes and beliefs about the issues to be explored in the chapter. Keep in mind that the "right" answer is the one that best expresses your thoughts at the time. We suggest you complete the inventory before reading the chapter. Then, after reading the chapter and discussing the material in class, complete the inventory again to see if your positions have changed in any way.

Directions: For each statement, indicate the response that most closely identifies your beliefs and attitudes. Use the following code:

5 = I *strongly agree* with this statement.

4 = I *agree* with this statement.

3 = I am *undecided* about this statement.

2 = I *disagree* with this statement.

1 = I *strongly disagree* with this statement.

_____ 1. Unless therapists have a high degree of self-awareness, there is a real possibility that they will use their clients to satisfy their own needs.

_____ 2. Before therapists begin to practice, they should be free of personal problems and conflicts.

_____ 3. Therapists should be required to undergo their own therapy before they are licensed to practice.

_____ 4. Mental health practitioners who satisfy personal needs through their work are behaving unethically.

_____ 5. Many in the helping professions face a high risk of burnout because of the demands of their job.

The Counselor as a Person and as a Professional

_____ 6. Clinicians who are self-aware are more likely to avoid experiencing overidentification with their clients.

_____ 7. If I have strong feelings about a client, I could profit from personal therapy.

_____ 8. Feelings of anxiety in a beginning counselor indicate unsuitability for the counseling profession.

_____ 9. A competent professional can work with any client.

_____ 10. I fear that I will have difficulty challenging my clients.

_____ 11. Ethics codes apply to the professional role behaviors of members, but it is difficult to distinguish between the personal and the professional.

_____ 12. The person and the professional are often inseparable.

_____ 13. Real therapy does not occur unless a transference relationship is developed.

_____ 14. When therapists are not aware of their own needs, they may misuse their power in the therapeutic situation.

_____ 15. An experienced and competent clinician has little need for either periodic or ongoing psychotherapy.

Introduction

A primary issue in the helping professions is the role of the counselor *as a person* in the therapeutic relationship. As counselors we ask clients to look honestly at themselves and to decide what they want to change. It is essential for us to be open to the same scrutiny. We need to ask these questions: "What makes me think I am capable of helping anyone? What do I personally have to offer others who are struggling with problems? Am I doing in my own life what I ask others to do?"

In our training as counselors, we acquire an extensive theoretical and practical knowledge as a basis for our practice. We also bring our human qualities and life experiences to every therapeutic session. Although well versed in psychological theory and having diagnostic and interviewing skills, we still might not be effective counselors. If we ask our clients to grow and change, we must be willing to promote growth in our own lives. This willingness to live in accordance with what we teach is what makes us "therapeutic persons." Compassion for others and dedication to serving others are the hallmarks of being able to make a difference. Norcross and Guy (2007) capture what makes us effective as individuals and as professionals: "We are convinced that the best of who we are, as therapists and indeed as humans, comes from the vitality of the heart. It is the wellspring of the caring and commitment that give meaning to life inside and outside of the consultation room" (p. 194).

In this chapter we deal with some of the ways therapists' personal needs and problems can present ethical issues for the client–therapist relationship. It is difficult to talk about the counselor *as a professional* without considering the counselor's personal qualities. Pipes, Holstein, and Aguirre (2005) point out that there is often a reciprocal and causal relationship between a practitioner's personal life and his or her professional behavior. For example, problems pertaining to interpersonal competence are a debilitating intrusion of a personal difficulty into the professional realm. Likewise, feelings of pride in professional achievement can ameliorate old feelings of personal insecurity. Pipes and colleagues believe that the personal and the professional are often inseparable and point out that it can be difficult to distinguish between what is personal and what is professional. A clinician's beliefs, personal attributes, level of personal functioning, and ways of living inevitably influence the way he or she carries out a professional role, which to us is central to ethical practice. This point is emphasized in the APA's (2002) ethics code: "Psychologists strive to be aware of the possible effects of their own physical and mental health on their ability to help those with whom they work."

Some of the issues we address are specifically related to the therapist's professional identity. Although these professional issues are dealt with throughout this book, in this chapter we take up problems that are closely linked to the counselor's personal life: self-awareness, influence of counselor's personality traits, goals, personal needs, transference, countertransference, personal dynamics, job stress, balancing life roles, and therapist self-care.

Self-Awareness and the Influence of the Therapist's Personality and Needs

Professionals who work intimately with others have a responsibility to be committed to awareness of their own life issues. Without a high level of self-awareness, mental health professionals are likely to obstruct the progress of their clients as the focus of therapy shifts from meeting the client's needs to meeting the needs of the therapist. Consequently, practitioners must be aware of their own needs, areas of "unfinished business," personal conflicts, defenses, and vulnerabilities and how these can influence their therapeutic work. In this section we consider two specific areas we think you need to examine if you are going to be a helping professional: personal needs and unresolved conflicts.

Motivations for Becoming a Counselor

Ask yourself these two questions: "What are my motivations for becoming a counselor?" and "What are my rewards for counseling others?" There are many answers to these questions. You may experience a sense of satisfaction from being with people who are struggling to achieve self-understanding and who are willing to experience pain as they seek a healthier lifestyle. Addiction counselors who are themselves in recovery, for example, may appreciate being part of the process of change for others with substance abuse problems. Indeed, many counselors have been motivated to enter the field because of their own struggles in some aspect of living. It is crucial to be aware of your motivations and to recognize that your way of coping with life's challenges may not be appropriate for your clients. In many ways therapeutic encounters serve as mirrors in which therapists can see their own lives reflected. As a result, therapy can become a catalyst for change in the therapist as well as in the client.

Of course, therapists *do* have their own personal needs, but these needs cannot assume priority or get in the way of a client's growth. Therapists need to be aware of the possibility of working primarily to be appreciated by others instead of working toward the best interests of their clients. Therapeutic progress can be blocked if therapists use their clients, even unconsciously, to fulfill their own needs.

Out of an exaggerated need to nurture others or to feel powerful, professional helpers may come to believe that they know how others ought to live. The tendency of a counselor to give advice and to direct another's life can be especially harmful because it encourages dependence on the part of clients and promotes a tendency for clients to look to others instead of themselves for solutions. Therapists who need to feel powerful or important may begin to think that they are indispensable to their clients or, worse still, try to *make* themselves so.

The goals of therapy also suffer when therapists with a strong need for approval focus on trying to win the acceptance, admiration, and even awe of their clients. Guy (2000) reminds us of the danger of depending on our clients as the main source for meeting our needs of admiration or belonging. When we are unaware of our needs and personal dynamics, we are likely to satisfy our own unmet needs or perhaps steer clients away from exploring conflicts that we ourselves fear. Clients often feel a need to please their therapist, and thus are easily drawn into taking care of their therapist's psychological needs.

Some therapists feel ill at ease if their clients fail to make immediate progress; consequently, they may push their clients to make premature decisions or may make decisions for them. As a way of understanding your needs and their possible influence on your work, ask yourself these questions:

- How will I know when I'm working for the client's benefit or working for my own benefit?
- If I have personal experience with a problem a client is having, can I be objective enough to relate to this person professionally and ethically?
- How much do I depend on being appreciated by others in my own life? Do I depend primarily on sources outside of myself to confirm my worth?
- Am I getting my needs for nurturance, recognition, and support met from those who are significant in my life?
- Do I feel inadequate when clients don't make progress? If so, how could my attitude and feelings of inadequacy adversely affect my work with these clients?

With the exception of a crisis situation, therapists who tell clients what to do diminish the autonomy of their clients and invite increased dependence in the future. The *NAADAC Code of Ethics* (2008) speaks directly to the need for client autonomy: "I shall not do for others what they can readily do for themselves but rather, facilitate and support the doing. Likewise, I shall not insist on doing what I perceive as good without reference to what the client perceives as good and necessary." Examine your behavior to see if you are depending on your clients to fulfill your need for self-worth as opposed to striving to increase client autonomy.

Personal Problems and Conflicts

Mental health professionals can and should be *aware* of their areas of denial and unresolved problems and conflicts. Personal therapy may reduce the intensity connected with these problems, yet it is not realistic to believe that such problems are ever fully resolved. Clearly, then, we are not implying that therapists should have resolved all their personal difficulties before they begin to counsel others. Indeed, such a requirement would eliminate most of us from the field. In fact, a counselor who rarely struggles or experiences anxiety may have real difficulty relating to a client who feels desperate or caught in a hopeless conflict. The critical point is not *whether* you happen to be struggling with personal problems but *how* you are struggling with them. For example, eating disorder specialists who themselves have struggled with dysfunctional eating patterns can draw upon their life experiences in their work as counselors.

Reflect on the following questions: Do you recognize and try to deal with your problems, or do you invest a lot of energy in denying their existence? Do you find yourself blaming others for your problems? Are you willing to consult with a therapist, or do you tell yourself that you can handle it, even when it becomes obvious that you are not doing so? Can you do in your own life what you challenge your clients to do?

When you are in denial of your own problems, you will be in a poor position to pay attention to the concerns of your clients, especially if their problem areas are similar to yours. Suppose a client is trying to deal with feelings of hopelessness and despair. How can you explore these feelings if in your own life you are denying them? Or consider a client who wants to explore her feelings about her sexual orientation. Can you facilitate this exploration if you feel uncomfortable talking about sexual identity issues and do not want to deal with your discomfort? Can you stay with this client emotionally when she introduces her concerns?

You will have difficulty helping a client in an area that you are reluctant or fearful to deal with in your own life. Recognize the topics that make you uncomfortable, not just with clients but in your personal life as well. Knowing that your discomfort will most probably impede your work with a client can supply the motivation for you to change and to realize that you also have an ethical responsibility to be available to your clients so that they can change.

Personal Therapy for Counselors

Throughout this chapter we stress the importance of counselors' self-awareness. A closely related issue is whether those who wish to become counselors should experience their own personal psychotherapy, and also whether continuing or periodic personal therapy is valuable for practicing professionals. We recommend that you expose yourself to therapeutic experiences aimed at increasing your availability to your clients. There are many ways to accomplish this goal: individual therapy, group counseling, consultation with trusted colleagues, continuing education (especially of an experiential nature), keeping a personal journal, and reading. Other less formal avenues to personal and professional development are reflecting on and evaluating the meaning of your work and life, remaining open to the reactions of significant people in your life, traveling to experience different cultures, meditating, engaging in spiritual activities, enjoying physical exercise, spending time with friends and family, and paying attention to the areas and situations that make you feel uncomfortable.

Experiential Learning Toward Self-Understanding

Experiential learning is a basic component of many counseling programs, providing students with the opportunity to share their values, life experiences, and personal concerns in a peer group. Many training programs in counselor education recognize the value of having students participate in personal-awareness groups with their peers. Such a group experience does not necessarily constitute group therapy; however, it can be therapeutic in that it provides students with a framework for understanding how they relate to others and can help them gain a deeper insight into their shared concerns. A group can be set up specifically for the exploration of personal concerns, or such exploration can be made an integral part of training and supervision groups. Whatever the format, students will benefit most if they are willing to focus on themselves personally and not merely on their clients. Beginning counselors tend to focus primarily on client dynamics, as do many supervisors and counselor educators. Being in a group affords students the opportunity to explore questions such as these: "How am I feeling about being a counselor? How do I assess my relationships with my clients? What reactions are being evoked in me as I work with them?" By being personally invested in their own therapeutic process, students can use the training program as an opportunity to expand their abilities to be helpful.

It is important for counselor educators and supervisors to clarify the fine line between training and therapy in the same way that fieldwork agencies must maintain the distinction between training and service. Although these areas overlap, it is clear that the emphasis for students needs to be on training in both academic and clinical settings, and it is the educator's and supervisor's responsibility to maintain that emphasis. It is essential that students be informed at the outset of the program of any requirement for personal exploration and self-disclosure. Students have a right to know about the nature of courses that involve experiential learning. The informed consent process is especially important in cases where the instructor also functions in the role of the facilitator of a group experience. We discuss this topic at greater length in Chapters 7, 8, and 9.

■ The Case of a Required Therapeutic Group.

Miranda is a psychologist in private practice who is hired by the director of a graduate program in counseling psychology to lead an experiential group. She assumes that the students have been informed about this therapeutic group, and she is given the impression that the students are eagerly looking forward to it. When she meets with the students at the first class, however, she encounters a great deal of resistance. They express resentment that they were not told that they would be expected to participate in a therapeutic group. Some students fear negative consequences if they do not participate.

- If you were a student in this program, how would you react?
- Is it ever ethical to mandate self-exploration experiences?
- If you were the director of the program, how would you handle the situation?
- The students knew from their orientation and the university's literature that this graduate program included some form of self-exploration. In your opinion, was this disclosure sufficient for ethical purposes?
- If you were Miranda, what would you do in this situation? How would you deal with the students' objections?

Commentary. Informing students prior to entering the program that self-exploration will be part of their training only minimally satisfies the requirement for informed consent. Students have a right to be informed about every aspect of the experiential group: the rational for the group, issues pertaining to confidentiality, and their rights and responsibilities regarding participation in experiential activities. In addition to this general orientation by the program, each instructor (in this case, Miranda) has an obligation to ensure that students have been properly informed about these expectations and requirements. In our view, Miranda needs to provide an opportunity for students to share their concerns at the initial group meeting. Miranda also has an obligation to ensure that group participation is genuinely voluntary, and if not, that the experience is clearly related to program training objectives.

Personal Therapy During Training

Studies on personal therapy for trainees. In a study conducted by Coster and Schwebel (1997), psychologists favored recommending personal therapy in general to all students but not requiring it unless it appeared to be professionally necessary. Schwebel and Coster (1998) report that requiring personal therapy for graduate students is overwhelmingly supported by administrators of programs in professional psychology. Dearing, Maddux, and Tangney (2005) emphasize the responsibility of faculty, supervisors, and mentors in educating trainees about appropriate pathways to self-care and prevention of impairment. They suggest that students are more likely to seek personal therapy when faculty members convey favorable and supportive attitudes about student participation in therapy. It is apparent that more attention needs to be paid to the risk factors associated with problems such as compassion fatigue, empathy fatigue, distress, impairment, professional burnout, and self-care (Barnett, 2008; Barnett & Cooper, 2009; Gilroy, Carroll, & Murra, 2002; Kramen-Kahn & Hansen, 1998; Schwebel & Coster, 1998; Skovholt, 2001; Stebnicki, 2008). Some professionals believe that self-care, which may include personal therapy, is a moral imperative for mental health practitioners (Barnett, Johnston, & Hillard, 2006; Gilroy et al., 2002; Norcross & Guy, 2007). Foster and Black (2007) suggest that therapists often neglect self-care to their own detriment and to the detriment of their clients. They add that an integral part of "ethical practice involves the conscious attention of counselors to maintain their health and well-being"(p. 223). Barnett, Johnston, and Hillard (2006) contend that ongoing self-care is not an optional activity but an essential part of a therapist's professional competence and personal wellness program.

Personal therapy can be a valuable component for the growth of clinicians. However, few empirical studies in the literature focus on the benefits or liabilities of personal therapy (Gilroy et al., 2002). Dearing and colleagues (2005) indicate that confidentiality issues, general attitudes about therapy, and the importance of personal therapy for professional development were key predictors for trainees seeking their own therapy. They suggest that students consider the potential benefits, both personally and professionally, of psychotherapy during their training, including alleviation of personal distress, a means of gaining insight into being an effective therapist, and development of healthy and enduring self-care habits.

Holzman, Searight, and Hughes (1996) conducted a survey to investigate the experience of personal therapy among clinical psychology graduate students. Nearly 75% of the respondents reported receiving personal therapy at some point in their lives, most often during graduate school. Of those who had been in therapy prior to or during graduate school, 99% reported that they were still in therapy or would consider getting involved in therapy again. Generally, they saw their experience in personal therapy as being positive. They perceived their therapy as providing them with valuable experiential learning that complemented their education and supervision as clinical psychologists.

This study sheds a positive light on the degree to which many graduate students seek therapy for personal enrichment and as a source of training. It challenges counselor education programs to work with therapy providers outside the program to offer psychological services to graduate students in their programs. Because of the ethical problems of counselor educators and supervisors providing therapy for their students and supervisees, faculty members have an obligation to become advocates for their students by identifying therapeutic resources students can afford. There are both practical and ethical reasons to prefer professionals external to a program (who are not part of a program and who do not have any evaluative role in the program) when providing psychological services for trainees. Practitioners from the community could be hired by a counselor-training program to conduct therapeutic groups, or students might take advantage of either individual or group counseling from a community agency, a college counseling center, or a private practitioner.

In a doctoral dissertation on the effects of personal counseling on the professional counselor in the delivery of clinical services, Newhouse-Session (2004) found that all 10 clinicians who participated in her qualitative study believed that personal therapy was beneficial, not only for them personally but in their delivery of services in clinical practice as well. Personal therapy improved the clinician's awareness of areas of conflict and resolution of his or her own problems. Eight of the 10 clinicians in her study thought that personal counseling should be mandated for any person in the counseling profession, a sentiment echoed by Gilroy and colleagues (2002). The participants in the study reported that their ability to be effective and to form a successful working alliance with clients was enhanced by keeping a check on their own past or current issues through personal counseling.

Reasons for participating in personal psychotherapy.   We highly recommend that you experience your own therapy as a way of taking an honest look at your motivations in becoming a helper. In therapy you can explore how your needs influence your actions, how you use power in your life, and what your values are. Your appreciation for the courage your clients will require in their therapeutic journey will be enhanced through your own experience as a client.

When students are engaged in practicum, fieldwork, and internship experiences and the accompanying individual and group supervision sessions, the following issues may surface:

- A tendency to tell people what to do
- A strong inclination to alleviate clients' pain
- A need for quick solutions
- A fear of making mistakes
- An extreme need to be recognized and appreciated
- A tendency to assume too much responsibility for client change
- A fear of doing harm, however inadvertently
- A tendency to deny or not recognize client issues when they relate to their own issues

As trainees begin to practice psychotherapy, they sometimes become aware that they are taking on a professional role that resembles the one they played in their family. They may recognize a need to preserve peace by becoming caretakers. When trainees become aware of concerns such as these, therapy can provide a safe place to explore them.

Most of us have areas in our lives that limit our effectiveness, both as persons and as professionals. Personal therapy can be instrumental in identifying and exploring your blind spots and potential areas of countertransference. Personal therapy can help you understand your dynamics and enhance your effectiveness as a professional helper.

Psychotherapy for remediation purposes. What is the value of psychotherapy when it is applied to the remediation of the problems of psychology trainees? Elman and Forrest (2004) conducted interviews with the training directors of 14 doctoral programs regarding the use of personal therapy for remediation. They point to the literature that shows a high frequency of recommending personal psychotherapy for remediation purposes during professional training. However, they add that there are limited empirical findings about its effectiveness and ethical concerns about the way personal therapy is sometimes used. A theme that emerged from a qualitative analysis of these exploratory interviews with training directors was balancing confidentiality of the trainee's therapy with accountability of training programs to protect future consumers.

Training programs are charged with providing developmentally appropriate educational experiences for trainees in a safe learning environment and at the same time protecting the public by graduating competent professionals. Vacha-Haase, Davenport, and Kerewsky (2004) found that personal psychotherapy was often endorsed as a remediation measure for students with interpersonal skills deficits, but the efficacy of this approach has not been well established empirically. In short, mandated psychotherapy is not always viewed as an effective intervention.

It is important for graduate programs to provide a safe context for training, and the rights and welfare of students must be considered. However, we believe counselor educators can go too far in the direction of protecting the rights of counselor trainees, for example, by not requiring any form of self-exploratory experience as part of their training program. Educators must also be concerned about protecting the public. One way to ensure that the consumer will get the best help available is to prepare students both academically and personally for the tasks they will face as practitioners.

Ethical issues in requiring personal therapy. Professional organizations often provide guidelines regarding personal therapy for trainees or converting supervision sessions into therapy sessions for supervisees. Certain codes emphasize the right of students and trainees to make informed decisions about disclosing personal matters. For example, APA (2002) has the following standard on mandatory individual or group therapy:

> (a) When individual or group therapy is a program or course requirement, psychologists responsible for that program allow students in undergraduate and graduate programs the option of selecting such therapy from practitioners unaffiliated with the program.

> (b) Faculty who are or are likely to be responsible for evaluating students' academic performance do not themselves provide that therapy. (7.05.)

The Canadian Counselling Association's *Code of Ethics* (2007) guidelines specifically address the training program dealing with students' personal issues and integrating self-growth activities into the program:

> *Dealing with Personal Issues:* Counsellors responsible for counsellor education, training, and supervision recognize when such activities evoke significant personal issues for students, trainees, and supervisees and refer to other sources when necessary to avoid counselling those for whom they hold administrative or evaluative responsibility. (F10.)

> *Self-Growth Activities:* Counsellors who work as counsellor educators, trainers, and supervisors, ensure that any professional experiences which require self-disclosure and engagement in self-growth activities are managed in a manner consistent with the principles of informed consent, confidentiality, and safeguarding against any harmful effects. (F11.)

The Council for Accreditation of Counseling and Related Educational Programs (CACREP, 2009) standards also recommends personal counseling for students from outside professionals: "The institution provides information to students in the program about personal counseling services provided by professionals other than program faculty and students" (Section I, G). Although it is *not* appropriate for supervisors to function as therapists for their supervisees, good supervision is therapeutic in the sense that the supervisory process involves assisting supervisees in identifying their personal challenges so that clients are not harmed. Working with difficult clients can affect trainees in personal ways. It is a challenge for both trainees and experienced therapists to recognize and deal effectively with their countertransference, which can usefully be explored in personal therapy.

Consider the situation of a therapist who himself is a disabled veteran working with other disabled veterans. He may be experiencing a great deal of anger and frustration over the lack of attention to the basic needs of his clients, but he may be suffering from the same neglect. As a result, the therapist's personal struggles may get in the way of focusing on his clients' needs. Countertransference reactions also need to be considered for addiction therapists, especially beginning therapists who are in recovery. For example, in inpatient substance abuse treatment programs, the daily intensity of treatment may affect both client and therapist. In this kind of environment, ongoing supervision is critical. Participating in one's own recovery group is often expected, and personal therapy can be most useful. Both of these counselors would do well to consider personal therapy to assist them in sorting out their countertransference reactions.

We believe it is appropriate for supervisors to encourage their supervisees to consider personal therapy with another professional as a way to becoming more effective both personally and professionally. A more detailed exploration of the multiple roles and responsibilities of supervisors, along with ethical issues in combining therapy with supervision, is included in Chapter 9. At this point, ask yourself these questions:

- What kind of self-exploration have I experienced prior to or during my training?
- How open am I to examining my own personal characteristics that could be either strengths or limitations in my role as a counselor?
- At this time, what am I doing about my personal problems?

Ongoing Therapy for Practitioners

Therapists who have experienced their own therapy report that it improves their self-awareness and self-understanding; increases their openness to and acceptance of their feelings; and enhances their personal relationships (Pope & Tabachnick, 1994). Linley and Joseph (2007) found that "therapists who had either received personal therapy previously, or were receiving personal therapy currently, reported more personal growth and positive changes, and less burnout" (p. 392). It seems clear that experienced practitioners can profit from therapeutic experiences that provide them with opportunities to reexamine their beliefs and behaviors, especially as these factors pertain to their effectiveness in working with clients. Baker (2003) advocates personal psychotherapy as being beneficial to both trainees and experienced practitioners, contending that therapy serves different functions at different stages of life:

> As a young trainee, therapy in the service of deepening self-awareness is invaluable. Granting one's self the option to return to therapy as a seasoned therapist for further psychotherapy work is also potentially very beneficial, personally

and professionally. . . . Therapy is also an appropriate means of addressing the major occupational hazard of consciously or unconsciously using the demands and involvements of work as a way to avoid dealing with our own personal issues. (pp. 84–85)

In a study examining the personal therapy experiences of more than 4,000 psychotherapists of diverse theoretical orientations in more than a dozen countries, Orlinsky and Ronnestad (2005) found that more than 88% rated the experience as positive. In a meta-analysis, more than three-quarters of therapists across multiple studies believed that their personal therapy had a strongly positive influence on their development as psychotherapists (Orlinsky, Norcross, Ronnestad, & Wiseman, 2005). Norcross (2005) has gathered self-reported outcomes of personal therapy that reveal positive gains in multiple areas, including self-understanding, self-esteem, work functioning, social life, emotional expression, intrapersonal conflicts, and symptom severity. The most frequent long-lasting benefits to practitioners pertained to interpersonal relationships and the dynamics of psychotherapy. Some of the lessons learned are the centrality of warmth, empathy, and the personal relationship; having a sense of what it is like to be a therapy client; the need for patience and tolerance in psychotherapy; and learning how to deal with transference and countertransference. Norcross and Guy (2007), who have researched self-care and self-change of mental health professionals for more than 25 years, conclude that "personal therapy is an emotionally vital and professionally nourishing experience central to the self-care of clinicians" (p. 168). They add that personal therapy "fuels and informs a lifetime of effective self-care" (p. 181).

When practitioners have been found guilty of a violation, some licensing boards require therapy as a way for practitioners to recognize and monitor their countertransference. We think this provides a rationale for psychotherapy for both trainees and practitioners as a way of reducing the potential negative consequences of practicing psychotherapy. On an ongoing basis, therapists must recognize and deal with their personal issues as they affect their clients. Barnett, Johnston, and Hillard (2006) state that therapists should not wait to take action until impairment harms us and our clients. They believe therapists should seek personal therapy before distressing life situations lead to impairment. In the next section we explore ways in which transference and countertransference can facilitate or interfere with therapy.

Transference and Countertransference

Although the terms *transference* and *countertransference* derive from psychoanalytic theory, they are universally applicable to counseling and psychotherapy and refer to the client's general reactions to the therapist and to the therapist's reactions in response (Gelso & Carter, 1985). Conceptualizing transference and countertransference broadly, Gelso and Carter believe these processes are universal and that they occur, to varying degrees, in all relationships. The therapeutic relationship can intensify the reactions of both client and therapist, and how practitioners handle both their own feelings and their clients' feelings will have a direct bearing on therapeutic outcomes. If these issues are not attended to, clients' progress will most likely be impeded. Therefore, this matter has implications from both an ethical and a clinical perspective.

Transference: The "Unreal" Relationship in Therapy

Transference is the process whereby clients project onto their therapists past feelings or attitudes they had toward significant people in their lives. Transference is understood as having its origins in early childhood and constitutes a repetition of past material in the present. "It reflects the deep patterning of old experiences in relationships as they emerge in current life" (Luborsky, O'Reilly-Landry, & Arlow, 2008, p. 46). This pattern causes a distortion in the way clients perceive and react to the therapist. The client's feelings are rooted in past relationships, but those feelings are now felt and directed toward the counselor. How the clinician handles this is crucial. If therapists are unaware of their own dynamics, they may miss important therapeutic issues when they should be helping their clients to understand and resolve the feelings they are bringing into the present from their past.

Transference is not a catch-all concept intended to explain every feeling clients express toward a therapist. Many reactions clients have toward counselors may be based on the here-and-now style the counselor exhibits. If a client expresses anger toward you, it may or may not be transference. If a client expresses positive reactions toward you, likewise, these feelings may or may not be genuine; dismissing them as infantile fantasies can be a way of putting distance between yourself and your client. It is possible for therapists to err in either direction—being too quick to explain away negative feelings or too willing to accept positive feelings. To understand the real import of clients' expressions of feelings, therapists have to actively work at being open, vulnerable, and honest with themselves. Although ethical practice implies that therapists are aware of the possibility of transference, they also need to be aware of the potential of discounting the genuine reactions their clients have toward them.

Let's examine two brief, open-ended cases in which we ask you to imagine yourself as the therapist. How do you think you would respond to each client? What are your own reactions?

■ The Case of Shirley.
Your client, Shirley, is extremely dependent on you for advice in making even minor decisions. It is clear that she does not trust herself and often tries to figure out what you might do in her place. She asks you personal questions about your marriage and your family life. She has

elevated you to the position of someone who makes wise choices, and she is trying to emulate you. At other times she tells you that her decisions typically turn out to be poor ones. Consequently, when faced with a decision, she vacillates and becomes filled with self-doubt. Although she says she realizes that you cannot give her the answers, she keeps asking you what you think about her decisions.

- How would you deal with Shirley's behavior?
- How would you respond to her questions about your private life?
- If many of your clients expressed the same thoughts as Shirley, is there anything in your counseling style that you may need to examine?

Commentary. When clients ask you questions about your private life, consider what has prompted these inquiries. The client's reasons for asking the questions may be more important than your answers and can offer useful clinical material to be explored. You may not be inappropriately fostering dependence in Shirley, but you will want to explore the dynamics of Shirley's need to get your opinion. Above all, therapists are ethically obligated to promote client autonomy. If you find yourself offering Shirley advice, it is time to look within yourself and examine your counseling style.

■ The Case of Marisa.

Marisa informs you that she terminated therapy with a prior therapist "because he was unable to understand or help" her. She tends to project blame on others and does not take responsibility for her problems. Marisa tells you that she is disappointed in the way her counseling is going with you. She doesn't know if you care very much about her. She would like to be special to you, not "just another client."

- How would you deal with Marisa's expectations?
- To what extent would you explore with Marisa her experience with her prior therapist?
- Can you see a potential ethical issue in the manner in which you would respond to her?
- Would you tell her how she affects you? Why or why not?

Commentary. Marisa's desire to redefine the therapy process and become special in your eyes should be explored. A therapist with a strong need to please or to be a caretaker may inadvertently promote dependence or role-blurring. If you go out of your way to make Marisa feel special, consider your reasons for doing so. You may want to tell her how she affects you as a person, yet this needs to be done in a respectful and therapeutic way. You may also want to explore with her the tendency she has to project blame onto others.

Countertransference: Ethical Implications

So far we have focused on the transference feelings of clients toward their counselors, but counselors also have emotional reactions to their clients, some of which may involve their own projections. It is not possible to deal fully here with all the possible nuances of transference and countertransference. Instead, we will focus on the ethical implications of improperly handling these reactions in the therapeutic relationship.

Countertransference can be considered, in the broad sense, as any projections by therapists that distort the way they perceive and react to a client. This phenomenon occurs when there is inappropriate affect, when clinicians respond in highly defensive ways, or when they lose their objectivity in a relationship because their own conflicts are triggered. In other words, the therapist's reaction to the client is intensified by the therapist's own experience. Ethically, therapists are expected to identify and deal with their reactions through supervision, consultation, or personal therapy so that their clients are not negatively affected by the therapists' problem. Examples of countertransference reactions include the arousal of guilt from unresolved personal problems, inaccurate interpretations of the client's dynamics because of projection on the therapist's part, experiencing an impasse with a client and frustration over not making progress, and impatience with a client (Norcross & Guy, 2007). Personal therapy can be an effective way for therapists to increase their awareness of potential areas of countertransference.

Countertransference can be either a constructive or a destructive element in the therapeutic relationship. A therapist's countertransference can illuminate some significant dynamics of a client. A client may actually be stimulating reactions in a therapist by the ways in which he or she makes the practitioner into a key figure from the past. The fact that the client may have stimulated the countertransference in the therapist does not make this the client's problem. The key here is how the therapist responds. The clinician who recognizes these patterns can eventually help the client change old dysfunctional themes.

Countertransference can show itself in many ways, as has been described by Watkins (1985). Each example in the following list presents an ethical issue because the therapist's clinical work is obstructed by countertransference reactions:

1. *Being overprotective with a client* can reflect a therapist's deep fears. A counselor's unresolved conflicts can lead him or her to steer a client away from those areas that open up the therapist's own pain. Such counselors may treat those clients as fragile and infantile.

- Are you aware of reacting to certain types of people in overprotective ways? If so, what does this behavior reveal about you?
- Do you find that you allow others to experience their pain, or do you have a tendency to want to take their pain away quickly?

2. *Treating clients in benign ways* may stem from a counselor's fear of their anger. To guard against this anger, the counselor creates a bland counseling atmosphere. This tactic results in superficial exchanges.

- Are you aware of how you typically react to anger directed at you?
- What would you do if you became aware that your exchanges are primarily superficial?

3. *Rejecting a client* may be based on the therapist's perception of the client as needy and dependent. Instead of moving toward the client to protect him or her, the counselor may move away from the client. The counselor remains cool and aloof and does not let the client get too close (Watkins, 1985).

- How do you react to unmotivated clients?
- Do you find yourself wanting to create distance from certain types of people?
- What can you learn about yourself by looking at those people whom you are likely to reject?

4. *Needing constant reinforcement and approval* can be a reflection of countertransference. Just as clients may develop an excessive need to please their therapists, therapists may have an inordinate need to be reassured of their effectiveness. When therapists do not see immediate positive results, they may become discouraged and anxious.

- Do you need to have the approval of your clients? How willing are you to confront them even at the risk of being disliked?
- How effectively are you able to confront others in your own life? What does this behavior tell you about yourself as a therapist?

5. *Seeing yourself in your clients* can be another form of countertransference. This is not to say that feeling close to a client and identifying with that person's struggle is necessarily countertransference. However, beginning therapists often identify with clients' problems to the point that they lose their objectivity. Therapists may become so lost in the client's world that they are unable to separate their own feelings. For example, an addictions counselor who is herself in recovery might be more invested in the recovery of her client than the client is.

- Have you ever found yourself so much in sympathy with others that you could no longer be of help to them? What would you do if you felt this way about a client?

- From an awareness of your own dynamics, list some personal traits of clients that could elicit overidentification on your part.

6. *Developing sexual or romantic feelings* toward a client can exploit the vulnerable position of the client. Seductive behavior on the part of a client can easily lead to the adoption of a seductive style by the therapist, particularly if the therapist is unaware of his or her own dynamics and motivations. It is natural for therapists to be more drawn to some clients than to others, and these feelings do not necessarily mean that they cannot counsel these clients effectively. More important than the mere existence of such feelings is the manner in which therapists deal with them. The possibility that therapists' sexual feelings and needs might interfere with their work is one important reason therapists should experience their own therapy when starting to practice and should consult other professionals when they encounter difficulty due to their feelings toward certain clients. Besides being unethical and countertherapeutic, it is also illegal in many states to sexually act out with clients, a topic that we discuss in detail in Chapter 7.

- What would you do if you experienced sexual feelings toward a client?
- How would you know if your sexual attraction to a client was countertransference?
- What would you do if you found yourself more and more frequently being sexually attracted to your clients?

7. *Giving advice* can easily happen with clients who seek answers. The opportunity to give advice places therapists in a superior position, and they may delude themselves into thinking that they do have answers for their clients. Some therapists experience impatience with their clients' struggles toward autonomous decision making. Such counselors may engage in excessive self-disclosure, especially by telling their clients how they have solved a particular problem for themselves. In doing so, the focus of therapy shifts from the client's struggle to the needs of the counselor. Even if a client has asked for advice, there is every reason to question whose needs are being served when a therapist falls into advice giving.

- Do you ever find yourself giving advice? What do you think you gain from it? In what ways might the advice you give to clients represent advice that you could give yourself?
- Are there times when advice is warranted? If so, when?

8. *Developing a social relationship with clients* may stem from countertransference, especially if it is acted on while therapy is taking place. Clients occasionally let their therapist know that they would like to develop a closer relationship than is possible in the limited environment of the office. They may, for instance, express a desire to

get to know their therapist as "a regular person." Mixing personal and professional relationships often destroys the therapeutic relationship and could lead to a lawsuit. This is a topic we examine in Chapter 7. Ask yourself these questions:

- If I establish social relationships with certain clients, will I be as inclined to confront them in therapy as I would do otherwise?
- Will my own needs for preserving these friendships interfere with my therapeutic responsibilities and defeat the purpose of therapy?
- Will my client be able to return to therapy if we form a social relationship after termination?
- Am I sensitive to being called an "aloof professional," even though I may strive to be real and straightforward in the therapeutic situation?
- What do I know about myself that explains my need to form friendships with clients? Whose interests are being served?

Countertransference: Clinical Implications

Gelso and Hayes (2002) contend that it is important to study and understand all of the therapist's emotional reactions to the client. Countertransference can greatly benefit the therapeutic work if clinicians monitor their feelings during therapy sessions and use their responses as a source for understanding clients and helping clients to understand themselves. Clinicians need to develop some level of objectivity and not react defensively and subjectively when their clients express a range of intense feelings toward them.

Countertransference becomes problematic when it is not recognized, monitored, and managed. Destructive or harmful countertransference occurs when a counselor's own needs or unresolved personal conflicts become entangled in the therapeutic relationship, obstructing or destroying a sense of objectivity. In this way, countertransference becomes an ethical issue, as is illustrated in the following case.

■ The Case of Lucia.

Lucia is a Latina counselor who has been seeing Thelma, who is also a Latina. Thelma's presenting problem was her depression related to an unhappy marriage. Her husband, an alcoholic, refuses to come to counseling with Thelma. She works full time in addition to caring for their three children. Lucia is aware that she is becoming increasingly irritated and impatient with her client's "passivity" and lack of willingness to take a strong stand with her husband. During one of the sessions, Lucia says to Thelma: "You are obviously depressed, yet you seem unwilling to take action to change your situation. You have been talking about the pain of your marriage for several months and tend to blame your husband for how you feel. You keep saying the same things, and nothing changes.

Your husband refuses to seek treatment for himself or to cooperate with your therapy, yet you are not doing anything to change your life for the better." Lucia says this with a tinge of annoyance. Thelma seems to listen but does not respond. When Lucia reflects on this session she becomes aware that she has a tendency to be more impatient and harsh with female clients from her own culture, especially over the issue of passivity. She realizes that she has not invited Thelma to explore ways that her cultural background and socialization have influenced her decisions. In talking about this case with a supervisor, Lucia explores why she seems to be triggered by women like Thelma. She recognizes that she has a good deal of unfinished business with her mother, whom she experienced as extremely passive.

- If you were Lucia's supervisor, what would you most want to say to her?
- Both the therapist and the client share a similar cultural background. To what extent does that need to be explored?
- If you were Lucia's supervisor, would you suggest self-disclosure as a way to help her client? What kind of therapist disclosure might be useful? Can you see any drawbacks to therapist self-disclosure in this situation?
- Because of Lucia's recognition of her countertransference with passive women, would you suggest that she refer Thelma to another professional? Why or why not?
- What reactions do you have to the manner in which Lucia dealt with Thelma? Could any of Lucia's confrontation be viewed as therapeutic? What would make her confrontation nontherapeutic?
- Was Lucia remiss in not attending to the alcohol problem of the husband?
- Are there any ways that Lucia's recognition of her own struggles with her mother could actually facilitate her work with women like Thelma?
- What are the ethical dimensions in this case?

If you found yourself in a situation where your unresolved personal problems and countertransference reactions were interfering with your ability to work effectively with a particular client, what actions would you take?

Commentary. Regardless of how self-aware and insightful counselors are, the demands of practicing therapy are great. The emotionally intense relationships counselors develop with clients can be expected to tap into their own unresolved conflicts. Because countertransference may be a form of identification with the client, the counselor can easily get lost in the client's world and be of little therapeutic value. In the case of Lucia, the ethical course of action we would suggest would be for Lucia to involve herself in personal therapy to address some of her own unresolved personal issues. Supervision would enable her to monitor her reactions to certain behaviors of clients that remind her of aspects in herself that she struggles with. Ultimately, if Lucia's personal issues detract from providing competent care, she should refer Thelma, and clients like her, to another therapist.

When counselors' countertransference interferes with good counseling work, counselors can seek supervision or seek their own personal therapy. Ethical practice requires that practitioners remain alert to their emotional reactions to their clients, that they attempt to understand such reactions, and that they do not inflict harm because of their personal problems and conflicts. We agree with Norcross and Guy (2007) that personal therapy can provide mental health practitioners with a fuller understanding of their personal dynamics and conflictual issues. This increases the chances that they will conduct psychotherapy with clearer perceptions, fewer contaminated reactions to clients, and reduced countertransference potential.

■ The Case of Ruby.

Ruby is counseling Henry, who expresses extremely hostile feelings toward homosexuals and toward people who have contracted AIDS. Henry is not coming to counseling to work on his feelings about gay people; his primary goal is to work out his feelings of resentment over his wife, who left him. In one session he makes derogatory comments about gay people. He thinks they are deviant and that it serves them right if they do get AIDS. Ruby's son is gay and Henry's prejudice affects her emotionally. She is taken aback by her client's comments, and she finds that his views are getting in the way as she attempts to work with him. Her self-dialogue has taken the following turns:

- I should tell Henry how he is affecting me and let him know I have a son who is gay. If I don't, I am not sure I can continue to work with him.
- I think I will express my hurt and anger to a colleague, but I surely won't tell Henry how he is affecting me. Nor will I let him know I am having a hard time working with him.
- Henry's disclosures get in the way of my caring for him. Perhaps I should tell him I am bothered deeply by his prejudice, but not let him know that I have a gay son.
- Because of my own countertransference, it may be best that I refer him without telling him the reason I am having trouble with him.

- Maybe I should just put my own feelings aside and try to work with him on reducing his prejudice and negative reactions toward gays.

Which of Ruby's possible approaches to Henry do you find yourself most aligned with? If Ruby came to you as a colleague and wanted to talk about her reactions and the course she should take with Henry, what would you say to her? In reflecting on what you might tell her, consider these issues:

- Is it ethical for Ruby to work on a goal that her client has not brought up?

- To what degree would you encourage Ruby to be self-disclosing with Henry? What should she reveal of herself to him? What should she not disclose? Why?

- Is it ethical for Ruby to continue to see Henry without telling him how she is affected by him?

Commentary. All of Ruby's self-dialogue statements are potential avenues for productive exploration. Because of her own countertransference, Ruby is experiencing difficulty in refocusing Henry on his stated goal for therapy. If she cannot get beyond her reactions, it will be difficult for her to be therapeutic with him. Ruby may or may not choose to tell Henry, without going into too much detail, that he is having an effect on her personally. Such self-disclosures should always be for the client's benefit, not the therapist's. Ruby can acknowledge her reactions without indulging herself in them. If Henry's comments become abusive, or if Ruby feels she can no longer be therapeutic, Ruby should consider an appropriate referral. If Henry were our client, we would approach him with a sense of interest over his focusing his resentment on gay people when he declared that his goal for therapy is to deal with his resentment toward his ex-wife.

Client Dependence

Many clients experience a period of dependence on counseling or on their counselor. This temporary dependence is not necessarily problematic. Others see the need to consult a professional as a sign of weakness. If these clients finally allow themselves to need others, their dependence does not necessarily mean that the therapist is unethical. An ethical issue does arise, however, when counselors *encourage* and promote dependence on the part of their clients. They may do so for any number of reasons. Counselor interns need clients, and sometimes they may keep clients longer than is necessary because they need more clinical hours or will look bad to the agency if they "lose" a client.

Some therapists in private practice fail to challenge clients who show up and pay regularly, even though they appear to be stymied. Clinicians can foster dependence in their clients in subtle ways. When clients insist on answers, these counselors may readily tell them what to do. Dependent clients can begin to view their counselors as having more wisdom; therapists who have a need to be perceived in this way collude with their clients in keeping them dependent.

When therapists offer quick solutions to clients' problems, they could impede clients' empowerment. With the growth of managed care in the United States as an alternative to traditional fee-for-service delivery systems, the client–counselor relationship is changing in many ways. In the relatively brief treatment and the restricted number of sessions allowed in most managed care plans, client dependence is often less of an issue than it might be with longer term therapy. However, even in short-term, problem-oriented therapy aimed at solutions, clients can develop an unhealthy dependence on their therapist.

Like many other ethical issues discussed here, whether therapists are encouraging dependence in clients is often not clear-cut. To help you to think of possible ways that you might foster dependence or independence in your clients, consider the following case.

■ The Case of Eduardo.

Eduardo, a young counselor, encourages his clients to call him at home when they need to. He expects to be on call at all times. He frequently lets sessions run overtime, lends money to clients when they are destitute, and devotes many more hours to his job than are required. He says that he lives for his work and that it gives him a sense of being a valuable person. The more he can do for people, the better he feels.

- How might Eduardo's style of counseling either help or hinder a client?

- Do you see any potential ethical issues in the way Eduardo treats his clients?

- In what ways could Eduardo's style be keeping his clients dependent on him?

- Can you identify with Eduardo in any ways? Do you see yourself as potentially needing your clients more than they need you?

Commentary. From our perspective, the overriding ethical question to ask is, Do Eduardo's behaviors toward clients demonstrate beneficence or maleficence? In other words, is Eduardo really helping his clients? We also wonder about Eduardo's boundaries with his clients. Some of Eduardo's behaviors are inconsistent with promoting client autonomy and seem aimed more at meeting Eduardo's own needs. We want to be careful not to judge Eduardo's enthusiasm and devotion to his work in a negative way, but Eduardo is at high risk for burnout or empathy fatigue based on this high level of involvement with his clients.

Delaying Termination as a Form of Client Dependence

Most professional codes have guidelines that call for termination whenever further therapy will not bring significant gains, but some therapists have difficulty doing this. They run the risk of unethical practice because of either financial or emotional needs. Therapists who become angry with clients when they express a desire to terminate therapy are showing signs of problematic countertransference. Obviously, termination cannot be mandated by ethics codes alone; it rests on the honesty of the therapist and the willingness to include the client in that process.

Termination is a basic part of the therapeutic process and can contribute to the client's overall success in treatment when managed well (Barnett, MacGlashan, & Clarke, 2000). According to Kramer (1990), more than at any other phase of therapy, the ending demands that therapists examine and understand their own needs and feelings about endings. Kramer emphasizes the therapist's role in enabling clients to understand and accept the termination process: "A general philosophy that is respectful of patients and sees them as autonomous, proactive, and self-directive is essential if the therapist is to facilitate healthy, productive endings" (p. 3). In our view, the ultimate sign of an effective therapist is his or her ability to help clients reach a stage of self-determination wherein they no longer need a therapist.

Most of the ethics codes of the various professions state that practitioners should terminate services to clients when such services are no longer required, when it becomes reasonably clear that clients are not benefiting from therapy, or when the agency or institution limits do not allow provision of further counseling services. Apply the general spirit of these codes to these questions:

- How would you know when services are no longer required?
- What criteria would you use to determine whether your client is benefiting from therapy?
- What would you do if your client feels he or she is benefiting from therapy but you don't see any signs of progress?
- What would you do if you are convinced that your client is coming to you seeking friendship and not really for the purpose of changing?
- What are the ethical issues involved if your agency limits the number of sessions yet your client is clearly benefiting from counseling? What if termination is likely to result in harm to the client?

Imagine yourself as the therapist in the following two cases. Ask yourself what you would do, and why, if you were confronted with the problem described.

■ The Case of Jesse.

After five sessions your client, Jesse, asks: "Do you think I'm making any progress toward solving my problems? Do I seem any different to you now than I did 5 weeks ago?" Before you give him your impressions, you ask him to answer his own questions. He replies: "Well, I'm not sure whether coming here is doing that much good or not. I suppose I expected resolutions to my problems before now, but I still feel anxious and depressed much of the time. It feels good to come here, and I usually continue thinking about what we discussed after our sessions, but I'm not coming any closer to decisions. Sometimes I feel certain this is helping me, and at other times I wonder whether I'm just fooling myself."

- What criteria can you employ to help you and your client assess the value of counseling for him?
- Does the fact that Jesse continues to think about his session during the rest of the week indicate that he is probably getting something from counseling? Why or why not?

Commentary. The fact that Jesse asks this question is a positive sign because it shows that he is involved in the outcomes of his own therapy. This is an opportunity for you to explore Jesse's expectations and his goals for treatment. Avoid being defensive with him and explain how the therapeutic process works. Ask about specific aspects of his therapy that he has found helpful and not helpful. Informed consent as an ongoing process rather than a one-time event, and Jesse's question provides another opportunity for you to extend his knowledge about the therapeutic process.

■ The Case of Enjolie.

Enjolie has been coming to counseling for some time. When you ask her what she thinks she is getting from the counseling, she answers: "This is really helping. I like to talk and have somebody listen to me. You are the only friend I have and the only one who really cares about me. I suppose I really don't do that much outside, and I know I'm not changing that much, but I feel good when I'm here."

- Is it ethical for you to continue the counseling if Enjolie's main goal seems to be the "purchase of friendship"? Why or why not?
- Would it be ethical to terminate Enjolie's therapy without exploring her need to see you?
- Would it be ethical for you to continue to see Enjolie if you were convinced that she was not making any progress?

Commentary. We might ask Enjolie to describe what brought her to therapy and help her to define her current goals for treatment.

We would point out that therapy is not the place to make friends with us, but for a chance for her to learn how to make friends in her outside life. We could explore with her what she is doing to find people who will listen to her and what she could do to establish friendships. We would encourage Enjolie to focus on the extent to which she is achieving her goals outside of therapy. If we were convinced that Enjolie was not benefiting from individual therapy, we would consider referring her to a therapy group as the focus of this modality is on interpersonal relationships.

Stress in the Counseling Profession

The Hazards of Helping

Helping professionals engage in work that can be demanding, challenging, and emotionally taxing. Mental health practitioners are typically not given sufficient warning about the hazards of the profession they are about to enter. Many counselors in training look forward to a profession in which they can help others and, in return, feel a deep sense of self-satisfaction. They may not be told that the commitment to self-exploration and to inspiring this search in clients can be fraught with difficulties. Effective practitioners use their own life experiences and personal reactions to help them understand their clients and as a method of working with them. As you will recall, the process of working therapeutically with people can open up personal issues in the therapist's life. The counselor, as a partner in the therapeutic journey, can be deeply affected by a client's pain. Pain connects with pain. If these countertransference issues are not recognized, they can have ethical and painful implications for the therapist. Clinicians overburdened with stress have trouble working effectively, which certainly make stress an ethical issue.

Graduate training programs in the helping professions need to prepare students for the challenging work they will eventually be doing. Self-care education should start at the beginning of a graduate program to prevent decay in students' future careers. If students are not adequately prepared, they may be especially vulnerable to early disenchantment, distress, and burnout due to unrealistic expectations. Training programs have an ethical mandate to design strategies to assist students in effectively dealing with job stress, in preventing burnout, and in emphasizing the role of self-care as a key factor in maintaining vitality. Ideally, the faculty in graduate training programs will also model self-care attitudes and practices for students.

Stress Caused by Being Overly Responsible

When therapists assume full responsibility for their clients' lack of progress, they are not helping clients to be responsible for their own therapy.

Practitioners who have a tendency to accept too much responsibility for their clients sometimes experience their clients' stress as their own. It is important to recognize when this is happening. Signs to look for are irritability and emotional exhaustion, feelings of isolation, abuse of alcohol or drugs, having a relapse from recovery, reduced personal effectiveness, indecisiveness, compulsive work patterns, drastic changes in behavior, and feedback from friends or partners. **Stress** is an event or a series of events that leads to strain, which often results in physical and psychological health problems. To assess the impact of stress on you both personally and professionally, reflect on these questions:

- To what degree are you able to recognize your problems?
- What steps do you take in dealing with your problems?
- Do you practice strategies for managing your stress?
- To what degree are you taking care of your personal needs in daily life?
- Do you listen to your family, friends, and colleagues when they tell you that they are seeing signs of severe stress?
- Are you willing to ask for help?

Sources of Stress

In his book *Empathy Fatigue: Healing the Mind, Body, and Spirit of Professional Counselors,* Stebnicki (2008) writes about the stress generated by listening to the multiple stories of trauma that clients bring to therapy. These stories are saturated with themes of grief, loss, anxiety, depression, and traumatic stress. When these stories mirror therapists' own personal struggles too closely, **empathy fatigue** may result. Empathy fatigue shares some similarities with other fatigue syndromes such as compassion fatigue, secondary traumatic stress, vicarious traumatization, and burnout. The symptoms of empathy fatigue are common to professionals who treat survivors of stressful and traumatic events; who treat people with mood, anxiety, and stress-related disorders; and who work in vocational settings with people with mental and physical disabilities. According to Stebnicki, counselors who practice with empathy are likely to be profoundly affected by the stories of their clients. Stebnicki emphasizes the importance of counselors preparing their mind, body, and spirit to help them become more resilient in working with people at intense levels of interpersonal functioning.

The work of professional counselors can lead to significantly increased levels of stress, which is often manifested in physical, mental, emotional, occupational, and spiritual fatigue (Stebnicki, 2008). Clearly, the stress clients experience and talk about in their therapy can have a major impact on therapists' experience of stress, especially if they are not practicing self-care.

Other sources of stress are associated with working in managed care and educational systems. For mental health professionals who deal with managed care, pressures involve getting a client's treatment approved, justifying needed treatment, quickly alleviating a client's problem, dealing with paperwork, and the anxiety of being put in an ethical dilemma when clients are denied further clinically necessary treatment. For school counselors, in addition to the expectation that they can immediately solve the behavioral problems of children, there is the added stress of dealing with the frustrations of the family, the teachers, and the administrators in the school system. One of our reviewers observed that stress and burnout are occupational hazards in the school counseling context, which is focused on academics and teacher needs. Although school counselors have a multiplicity of demands on them, they often must function alone with little opportunity for their own supervision or for talking about how their work is affecting them personally.

This is equally true for clinicians in private practice who practice in isolation and do not have the benefits of working with colleagues. In addition, therapists who work with violent and suicidal clients are particularly vulnerable to stress, and it is essential that they develop self-care strategies if they are to avoid burnout (Brems & Johnson, 2009).

If you fail to recognize the inevitable sources of stress that are a part of helping, you will not have developed effective strategies to combat the stresses you encounter. It is not realistic to expect to eliminate all of the strains of daily life, but you can develop practical strategies to recognize and cope with them. Doing so is a key part of being an ethical practitioner. Some professional organizations and state licensing boards have impaired professional or peer support programs. These programs can be a significant resource for dealing with the impacts of stress.

Counselor Burnout and Impairment

Stress, burnout, and vicarious traumatization are ongoing challenges associated with the work of helping professionals (Smith & Moss, 2009). Therapists are vulnerable to the effects of stress; if stress is not adequately addressed, it can result in impaired professional competence. Clinicians who do not engage in self-care practices are at great risk of not being able to carry out their professional duties (Barnett, 2008). Unmanaged stress is a major cause of burnout and eventual impairment. **Burnout** is a state of physical, emotional, intellectual, and spiritual depletion characterized by feelings of helplessness and hopelessness. Maslach (2003) identifies burnout as a type of job stress that results in a condition characterized by physical and emotional exhaustion, depersonalization, and a reduction of personal accomplishments. Baker (2003) refers to burnout as "the terminal phase of therapist distress" (p. 21). Jenaro, Flores, and Arias (2007) describe burnout "as an answer to chronic labor stress that is composed of negative attitudes and feelings toward coworkers and one's job role, as well as feelings of emotional exhaustion" (p. 80). Long work hours, heavy involvement in administrative duties, and the perception of having little control over work activities can place practitioners at high risk for emotional exhaustion (Stevanovic & Rupert, 2009).

Burnout comes at the end of a long process of what we refer to as "therapist decay." Based on our observations over the years, we have identified the following signs of therapist decay:

- An absence of boundaries with clients
- Excessive preoccupation with money and being successful
- Taking on clients that exceed one's level of professional competence
- Poor health habits in the areas of nutrition and exercise
- The absence of camaraderie with friends and colleagues
- Living in isolated ways, both personally and professionally
- Failing to recognize the personal impact of clients' struggles
- Resisting personal therapy when experiencing personal distress

If practitioners do not take steps to remedy burnout or make changes in how they deal with stress, the eventual result is likely to be impairment. **Impairment** is the presence of a chronic illness or severe psychological depletion that is likely to prevent a professional from being able to deliver effective services and results in consistently functioning below acceptable practice standards. A number of factors can negatively influence a counselor's effectiveness, both personally and professionally, including substance abuse, chronic physical illness, and burnout. Impaired professionals are unable to effectively cope with stressful events and are unable to adequately carry out their professional duties. Therapists whose inner conflicts are consistently activated by client material may respond by distancing themselves, which clients may interpret as a personal rejection.

Zur (1994) maintains that psychotherapists often fail to attend to their own needs and pay little attention to the effect their profession has on them. They sometimes avoid examining the effects of their work on their families. Zur believes that being a psychotherapist has both advantages and liabilities for one's family life. It takes a conscious effort for a therapist to minimize the liabilities and maximize the advantages. Therapists face the task of dealing with the negative aspects of their profession, such as emotional depletion, isolation, depression, and burnout. It is essential for therapists to let go of their professional role when they are at home, yet this is easier said than done at times.

In a survey of work–family conflict and burnout among practicing psychologists, Rupert, Stevanovic, and Hunsley (2009) found evidence supporting the interdependence of family- and work-life domains. Family support is related to well-being at work and to lower levels of burnout. Conflict between the work and family domains has a significant impact on how psychologists feel about their work. Rupert and colleagues contend that strategies to reduce burnout among psychologists must extend beyond the work setting to consider the quality of family life and the integration of work and family life. To maintain a balance between work and family, Stevanovic and Rupert (2009) suggest that mental health professionals monitor their emotional reactions and develop strategies for coping with work demands.

We ask you to reflect on the sources of stress in your life. What patterns do you see? How do you manage your stress? What steps are you taking to prevent becoming an impaired practitioner?

- Do you ask peers, colleagues, or supervisors for help?
- Are you willing to take time outside of your regular school or work hours to seek supervision?
- Do you seek personal therapy when doing so might be beneficial?
- Do you have a passion in your life other than your work?
- Is there a balance between your work life and your family life?

Take some important steps toward preventing problems for both yourself and your clients by reflecting on these questions and taking action to improve your strategies for self-care now.

Maintaining Vitality Through Self-Care

Sustaining the personal self can be a serious ethical obligation. To work in a competent and ethical manner, clinicians need to acquire and regularly practice self-care and wellness strategies. Self-care is not an indulgence, It is necessary to prevent distress, burnout, impairment, and to maintain a level of psychological and physical wellness. This pursuit of psychological wellness is an ethical imperative (Barnett, Baker, Elman, & Schoener, 2007; Barnett & Cooper, 2009). Skovholt (2001) states that "maintaining oneself personally is necessary to function effectively in a professional role. By itself, this idea can help those in the caring fields feel less selfish when meeting the needs of the self" (p. 146). Skovholt's idea of **self-care** involves searching for positive life experiences that lead to zest, peace, excitement, and happiness. Professional work suffers when self-care is neglected. Some ethics codes specifically address self-care, such as that of the Canadian Psychological Association (2000):

> Engage in self-care activities that help to avoid conditions (e.g., burnout, addictions) that could result in impaired judgment and interfere with their ability to benefit and not harm others. (II.12.)

Another example of the emphasis on self-care is the ethics code of the Canadian Association of Social Workers (1994):

> A social worker shall maintain an acceptable level of health and well-being in order to provide a competent level of service to a client. (3.4.)

Ethics Codes

Professional Impairment

American Association for Marriage and Family Therapy (2001)

Marriage and family therapists seek appropriate professional assistance for their personal problems or conflicts that may impair work performance or clinical judgment. (3.3.)

National Association of Social Workers (2008)

Social workers whose personal problems, psychosocial distress, legal problems, substance abuse, or mental health difficulties interfere with their professional judgment and performance should immediately seek consultation and take appropriate remedial action by seeking professional help, making adjustments in workload, terminating practice, or taking any other steps necessary to protect clients and others. (4.05.b.)

American Psychological Association (2002)

When psychologists become aware of personal problems that may interfere with their performing work-related duties adequately, they take appropriate measures, such as obtaining professional consultation or assistance, and determine whether they should limit, suspend, or terminate their work-related duties. (2.06.b.)

American Counseling Association (2005)

Counselors are alert to the signs of impairment from their own physical, mental, or emotional problems and refrain from offering or providing professional services when such impairment is likely to harm a client or others. They seek assistance for problems which reach the level of professional impairment and, if necessary, they limit, suspend, or terminate their professional responsibilities, until such time it is determined that they may safely resume their work. (C.2.g.)

Self-care is addressed in the *Feminist Therapy Code of Ethics* (Feminist Therapy Institute, 2000):

> A feminist therapist engages in self-care activities in an ongoing manner outside the work setting. She recognizes her own needs and vulnerabilities as well as the unique stresses inherent in this work. She demonstrates an ability to establish boundaries with the client that are healthy for both of them. She also is willing to self-nurture in appropriate and self-empowering ways. (IV.E.)

In *Caring for Ourselves: A Therapist's Guide to Personal and Professional Well-Being*, Baker (2003) emphasizes the importance of tending to mind, body, and spirit. This involves learning to pay attention to and be respectful of our needs, which is a lifelong task for therapists. Baker makes the point that for us to have enough to share with others in our personal and professional lives, we need to nourish ourselves. It will be difficult to maintain our vitality if we do not find ways to consistently tend to our whole being.

The research of Norcross and Guy (2007), along with other studies and interview surveys, clearly indicates the central importance of self-awareness, self-monitoring of distress, and commitment to self-care. "Self-care is not a narcissistic luxury to be fulfilled as time permits; it is a human requisite, a clinical necessity, and an ethical imperative" (p. 14). Self-care is best viewed as an ongoing preventive activity for all mental health practitioners (Barnett, 2008; Barnett, Baker, Elman, & Schoener, 2007; Barnett & Cooper, 2009). Barnett (2008) proposes creating a culture of self-care and wellness: "Help seeking behavior must not be seen as a sign of weakness or indicative of flaws, but rather as normative ongoing behavior for psychologists throughout all phases of their careers and may include consultation, supervision, and personal psychotherapy" (p. 870).

How can you provide nourishment to your clients if you don't nourish yourself? Those in the helping professions are experts at one-way caring, and Skovholt (2001) warns of the dangers involved in this practice. Those who spend most of their professional time in caring for others need to acquire the art of caring for self by nurturing the emotional self, the financial self, the humorous self, the loving self, the nutritious self, the physical self, the playful self, the priority-setting self, the recreational self, the relaxation–stress reduction self, the solitary self, and the spiritual or religious self. Take some time to ask yourself what basic changes, if any, you are willing to make in your behavior to promote your own wellness. Remember, this is routinely the question you ask your clients.

Chapter Summary

The life experiences, attitudes, and caring that we bring to our practice are crucial factors in establishing an effective therapeutic relationship. If we are unwilling to engage in self-exploration, it is likely that our fears, personal conflicts, and personal needs will interfere with our ability to be present for our clients. No amount of knowledge or technical skill can replace that component of helping.

Personal therapy during training and throughout therapists' professional careers can enhance the counselor's ability to focus on the needs and welfare of their clients. Therapists cannot take clients any further than they have taken themselves; therefore ongoing self-exploration is important. By focusing on your own personal development, you will be better equipped to deal with the range of transference reactions your clients are bound to have toward you. You will also be better able to detect potential countertransference on your part and have a basis for managing your reactions in a therapeutic manner. There is a potential for unethical behavior in mismanaging countertransference, and you may find that you need to review your personal concerns periodically throughout your career. This honest self-appraisal is an essential quality of effective helpers.

Stress and the inevitable burnout that typically results from inadequately dealing with chronic sources of stress also raise ethical questions.

Therapists who are psychologically and physically exhausted can rarely provide effective assistance to their clients. Mental health professionals who have numbed themselves to their own pain are ill equipped to deal with the pain of their clients. Impaired practitioners may do more harm than good for those who seek their assistance. There are no simple answers to the question of how to maintain your vitality, but from an ethical perspective, you are challenged to find your own answers to caring for yourself both personally and professionally.

Suggested Activities

These activities and questions are designed to help you apply your learning. Many of them can be done alone or with another person; others are designed for discussion either with the whole class or in small groups. Select those that seem most significant to you and write on these issues in your journal.

1. In small groups, explore your reasons for going into a helping profession. What do you see yourself as being able to do for others?

2. In your journal or in small groups, explore these questions: To what degree might your personal needs get in the way of your work with clients? How can you recognize and meet your needs—which are a real part of you—without having them interfere with your work with others?

3. In small groups share your own concerns over becoming a counselor. What problems do you expect to face as a beginning counselor? What did you learn about yourself from a discussion of your concerns?

4. "Who has a right to counsel anybody?" In groups of three, take turns briefly stating the personal and professional qualities that you can offer people. Afterward, explore any self-doubts you have concerning your ability to counsel others.

5. Think of the type of client you might have the most difficulty working with. Then become this client in a role play with one other student. Have your partner attempt to counsel you. After you have had a chance to be the client, reverse roles and you become the counselor.

6. In small groups discuss any possible experiences you have had with burnout and what contributed to it. Discuss some possible causes of professional burnout and examine specific ways you would deal with this problem.

Ethics in Action *CD-ROM Exercises*

7. In video role play 2, Big Brother, the client (Richard) reports that his sister is dating an Asian man. Richard is angry and says that he

is not going to let that happen. He adds that his sister is not going to mess with his family like that. The counselor (Nadine) asks Richard if he thinks his sister should live to make him happy. He says, "My sister is going to do what I say and that's just it!"

This vignette shows how a counselor's own unfinished personal issues can get in the way of counseling an upset client. Identify and discuss the ethical issues you see played out in this vignette. Reenact the role play by having several students take the role of counselor to show alternative perspectives.

Chapter 3

Pre-Chapter Self-Inventory

Directions: For each statement, indicate the response that most closely identifies your beliefs and attitudes. Use the following code:

5 = I *strongly agree* with this statement.

4 = I *agree* with this statement.

3 = I am *undecided* about this statement.

2 = I *disagree* with this statement.

1 = I *strongly disagree* with this statement.

_____ 1. It is both possible and desirable for counselors to remain neutral so as to keep their values from influencing clients.

_____ 2. In certain situations, counselors should influence clients to adopt values that seem to be in the clients' best interests.

_____ 3. It is acceptable for counselors to express their values as long as they do not try to impose them on clients.

_____ 4. Counselors can challenge clients to make value judgments regarding their own behavior.

_____ 5. Before I can effectively counsel a person, I have to decide whether our life experiences and values are similar enough for me to understand that person.

_____ 6. Clarifying values is a major part of the counseling process.

_____ 7. I would never try to influence my clients to accept my values.

_____ 8. I have a clear idea of what I value and where I acquired my values.

_____ 9. I tend to have difficulty with people who think differently from the way I do.

Values and the Helping Relationship

_____ 10. Ultimately, the choice of living or dying rests with my clients, and therefore I do not have the right to persuade them to make a different choice.

_____ 11. I have an ethical obligation to ask myself when I would have to refer a client because of a value conflict.

_____ 12. To be helpful to a client, a practitioner must accept and approve of the client's values.

_____ 13. Ethical practice demands that counselors address a client's spiritual or religious background.

_____ 14. There are no fundamental conflicts between counseling and religion or spirituality; therefore, it is possible to consider religious or spiritual concerns in a therapeutic relationship.

_____ 15. If a client complained of a lack of meaning in life, I would be inclined to introduce a discussion of spirituality or religion as a way to find purpose.

Introduction

The question of values permeates the therapeutic process. In this chapter we ask you to think about your values and life experiences and the influence they will have on your counseling. We ask you to consider the possible impact of your values on your clients, the effect your clients' values may have on you, and the possible conflicts that can arise if you and your clients have different values.

Can therapists keep their values out of their counseling sessions? Richards, Rector, and Tjeltveit (1999) address this fundamental question of **value neutrality** by summarizing theoretical and research literature that discredits the notion that therapists can and should keep their values out of therapy.

Research has provided evidence that therapists' values influence every phase of psychotherapy, including the theories of personality and therapeutic change, assessment strategies, goals of treatment, the design and selection of interventions, and evaluation of therapy outcomes. (p. 135)

Falender and Shafranske (2004) agree that the idea that psychotherapy is value neutral is no longer tenable. Clinicians need to take into consideration the role of personal influence in their practice. In our view, it is neither possible nor desirable for counselors to be completely neutral in this respect. Although it is not the counselor's function to persuade clients to accept a particular value system, counselors need to understand how their own values can influence their work with clients, perhaps even unconsciously.

If you cannot maintain objectivity regarding a certain value, it is essential that you make it your problem rather than the client's. Inform your client of the areas in which you think you cannot be neutral. We hope this would be necessary in only a few instances. Your task is not to approve or disapprove of your clients' values but to help them explore and clarify their beliefs and apply their values to solving their problems. The only exceptions to this are values and behaviors that violate the law.

Clarifying Your Values and Their Role in Your Work

Clinicians may not agree with the values of their clients, but they must respect the rights of their clients to hold a different set of values. The way therapists deal with clients' values can raise ethical issues. Richards, Rector, and Tjeltveit (1999) do not think therapists should attempt to teach clients specific moral rules and values because doing so violates clients' autonomy and prevents them from making their own choices. Bergin (1991) writes, "It is vital to be open about values but not coercive, to be a competent professional and not a missionary for a particular belief, and at the same time to be honest enough to recognize how one's value commitments may not promote health" (p. 399). Bergin sees the core challenge as being able to use values to enhance the therapeutic process without abusing the therapist's power or exploiting the client's vulnerability.

Not everyone who practices counseling or psychotherapy would agree with these views. At one extreme are counselors who have definite, absolute value systems. They believe their task is to influence their clients to adopt *better* values. Such counselors would direct their clients toward the attitudes and behaviors that *they* judge to be best for their clients. At the other extreme are counselors who are so anxious to avoid influencing their clients that they keep themselves and their values hidden to avoid contaminating their clients' process.

Counseling is not a form of indoctrination, nor is it the therapist's function to teach clients "proper" behavior. Some well-intentioned mental health professionals believe this is what they are supposed to be doing, and the public supports this myth by tuning into radio and television psychologist shows to watch these celebrities prescribe quick solutions to complex problems. We question the underlying assumption that counselors have greater wisdom than their clients and can prescribe ways of being happier. Unquestionably, teaching is a part of counseling, and clients do learn in both direct and indirect ways from the opinions and examples of their therapists. But counseling is not synonymous with preaching, persuasion, or instruction.

Neither do we favor the opposite extreme of trying so hard to be objective that counselors keep their personal reactions and values hidden from clients. In our opinion, clients have a right to a lot more involvement from therapists than mere reflection and clarification. It is helpful for clients to know where their therapist stands so they can test their own thinking. We believe clients are helped by this kind of connection.

Practitioners will inevitably incorporate certain value orientations into their therapeutic approaches and methods. For example, goals are usually based on values and beliefs, and clients may adopt goals that the therapist thinks are beneficial. But if clients are encouraged to change the direction of their values without being aware of what they are doing, they are being deprived of self-determination (Brace, 1997). It may be appropriate at times for the therapist to do more than merely watch clients make poor decisions without interference. Bergin (1991) contends that it is irresponsible for a therapist to fail to inform clients about alternatives: "We need to be honest and open about our views, collaborate with the client in setting goals that fit his or her needs, then step aside and allow the person to exercise autonomy and face consequences" (p. 397).

The following questions may help you to begin thinking about the role of your values in your work with clients:

- Do you think it is ever justified to influence a client's set of values? If so, when and in what circumstances?

- Do you worry that openly discussing your values with certain clients might unduly influence their decision making?

- Is it possible for therapists to interact honestly with clients without making value judgments?

- If you were convinced that your client was making a self-destructive decision, would you express your concerns, and if so, how would you do it?

- Do you think therapists are responsible for informing clients about a variety of value options?

- How are you affected when your clients adopt your beliefs and values?

- Can you remain true to yourself and at the same time allow your clients the freedom to select their own values, even if they differ from yours?

- How do you determine when a conflict between your values and those of your client necessitates a referral to another professional?

- Do you believe certain values are inherent in the therapeutic process? If so, what are these values?
- How does exposing your clients to your viewpoint differ from subtly influencing them to accept your values?
- What are some potential advantages and disadvantages in having similar life experiences with your client?

Because your values will significantly affect your work with clients, it is crucial for you to clarify your assumptions, core beliefs and values, and the ways in which they influence the therapeutic process. Counselors who have liberal values may find themselves working with clients who have conservative values. If these clinicians privately scoff at conventional values, can they truly respect clients who do not think as they do? Or if counselors have a strong commitment to values they rarely question, whether these values are conventional or unconventional, will they be inclined to promote these values at the expense of their clients' exploration of their own attitudes and beliefs? If counselors rarely reflect on their own values, it is unlikely that they will provide a climate in which clients can reexamine their values.

From time to time your values may present some difficulty for you in your work with clients. In the following sections we examine some sample cases and issues to help you clarify what you value and how your values might influence the goals of counseling and the interventions you make with your clients. As you read these examples, keep the following questions in mind:

- What is my position on this issue?
- Where did I develop my views?
- Are my values open to modification?
- Am I open to being challenged by others?
- Do I feel so deeply committed to some of my values that I might want my clients to accept them? Will I be closed to clients with a different set of values?
- Under what circumstances would I disclose my values to my clients? Why?
- How can I communicate my values without imposing those values on clients?
- Do my actions support respect for the principle of clients' self-determination that is consistent with their culture?
- How are my own values and beliefs reflected in the manner in which I help my clients set their goals?

The Ethics of Imposing Your Values on Clients

Value imposition refers to counselors directly attempting to influence a client to adopt their counselors' values, attitudes, beliefs, and behaviors. It is possible for mental health practitioners to do this either actively or passively.

For example, a key element in some addiction treatment programs is that clients accept that there is a power higher than themselves. Although clients are encouraged to define for themselves what this higher power is, some addiction counselors may be tempted to impose their own personal beliefs of what the higher power is, which raises ethical issues. Counselors are cautioned about this kind of value imposition in their professional work in this ACA (2005) standard:

> *Personal Values.* Counselors are aware of their own values, attitudes, beliefs, and behaviors and avoid imposing values that are inconsistent with counseling goals and respect for the diversity of clients, trainees, and research participants. (A.4.b.)

ASCA's (2004) code specifies that the school counselor "respects the student's values and beliefs and does not impose the counselor's personal values" (A.1.c.).

A national survey found a consensus among a representative group of mental health practitioners that basic values such as self-determination are important for clients to become mentally healthy and to guide and evaluate the course of psychotherapy (Jensen & Bergin, 1988). Other basic values include developing effective strategies for coping with stress; developing the ability to give and receive affection; increasing one's ability to be sensitive to the feelings of others; becoming able to practice self-control; having a sense of purpose for living; being open, honest, and genuine; finding satisfaction in one's work; having a sense of identity and self-worth; being skilled in interpersonal relationships; having deepened self-awareness and motivation for growth; and practicing good habits of physical health. These values were considered to be universal, and practitioners surveyed based their therapy on them.

It is now generally recognized that the therapeutic endeavor is a value-laden process and that all clinicians, to some degree, communicate their values to their clients (Richards & Bergin, 2005). Zinnbauer and Pargament (2000) claim there is an abundance of evidence indicating that therapy not only is value laden but that counselors and clients often have different value systems. They report that researchers have found evidence that clients tend to change in ways that are consistent with the values of their therapists, and clients often adopt the values of their counselors. It will be difficult to avoid communicating your values to your clients, even if you do not explicitly share them. What you pay attention to during counseling sessions tends to direct what your clients choose to explore. The methods you use often provide clients with clues about what you value.

Your nonverbal behavior and body language can give clients indications of how you are being affected. If clients have a need for your approval, they may respond to these cues by acting in ways that they imagine will please you. An unhappily married man, for example, may come to believe that you feel he is wasting good years of his life in the marriage. He proceeds with a divorce mostly because of his perceptions that you want him to get a divorce.

Although you may strive not to impose your values on clients, subtle nonverbal messages that you project can have a powerful influence.

Value Conflicts: To Refer or Not to Refer

Some counselors believe they can work with any client or problem. They may be convinced that being professional means being able to assist everyone. Others are so unsure of their abilities that they are quick to refer anyone who makes them feel uncomfortable. Somewhere between these extremes are the cases in which your values and those of your client clash to such an extent that you question your ability to be helpful.

Ethical therapists recognize when their values clash with a client's values to the extent that they are not able to function effectively. Merely having a conflict of values does not necessarily require a referral; it is possible to work through such conflicts successfully. In fact, we think of a referral as the last resort. Before making a referral, explore your part of the difficulty through consultation. What barriers within you would prevent you from working with a client who has a different value system? Merely disagreeing with a client or not particularly liking what a client is proposing to do is not ethical grounds for a referral. When you recognize instances of such value conflicts, ask yourself this question: "Why is it necessary that there be congruence between my value system and that of my client?"

If you have sought consultation and exhausted all other possibilities and still believe that you are at an impasse, you may need to consider a referral. When you make a referral, *how* it is done is critical. Make it clear to the client that the reason for the referral is *your* problem and not the client's. It can be very burdensome to clients to be saddled with your disclosure of not being able to get beyond value differences. Clients may interpret this as a personal rejection and suffer harm as a result. To avoid such situations, consider disclosing in writing from the outset any values you hold that might make it difficult for you to work effectively with certain value systems of clients. In this way, clients can be empowered to decide whether they want to work with you or not. We hope there would be very few instances in which you would refer a client because of a clash of values. Counseling is not about your values but about working with clients within the framework of their value system.

Referral is the appropriate and ethical course of action to take when a client's needs are outside the scope of your competence. No professional has the expertise required to work with all clients. Your knowledge of specialty standards and a comprehensive assessment of the client will assist you in knowing when to make a referral.

Consider the list of potential clients that follows and indicate whether you believe you could work with the client or would find this a challenge because of a conflict of value systems. You may think it unlikely that you will encounter some of these situations in your counseling career, but you need to be mentally prepared to deal with them if and when they do arise. Use the following code:

A = I *could* work with this person.

B = I *would have difficulty* working with this person.

C = I *could not* work with this person.

_____ 1. A person with fundamentalist religious beliefs

_____ 2. A woman who says that if she could turn her life over to Christ she would find peace

_____ 3. A person who shows little conscience development, who is strictly interested in his or her own advancement, and who uses others to achieve personal aims

_____ 4. A gay or lesbian couple wanting to work on conflicts in their relationship

_____ 5. A man who wants to leave his wife and children for the sake of sexual adventures with other women

_____ 6. A woman who has decided to leave her husband and children to gain her independence but who wants to explore her fears of doing so

_____ 7. A woman who is considering an abortion but wants help in making her decision

_____ 8. A teenager who is having unsafe sex and sees no problem with this behavior

_____ 9. A high school student who is sent to you by his parents because they suspect he is abusing drugs

_____ 10. A person who is very cerebral and is convinced that feelings are a private matter

_____ 11. A man who believes the best way to discipline his children is through corporal punishment

_____ 12. An interracial couple coming for premarital counseling

_____ 13. A high school student who seeks counseling to discuss conflicts she is having with her adopted parent who is from a different culture

_____ 14. A high school student who thinks she may be lesbian and wants to explore this gender identification concern

_____ 15. A gay or lesbian couple wanting to adopt a child

_____ 16. A man who has found a way of cheating the system and getting more than his legal share of public assistance

_____ 17. A woman who comes with her husband for couples counseling while maintaining an extramarital affair

_____ 18. An interracial couple wanting to adopt a child and being faced with their respective parents' opposition to the adoption

_____ 19. A client from another culture who has values very different from yours

_____ 20. A mother who is intent on blaming the school for her son's behavior problems and constantly makes excuses for the child

Look back over the list, and pay particular attention to the items you marked "C." What is your difficulty in working with these people? In assessing the ethical ramifications of declining to work with certain clients, what are the potential risks and benefits of making a referral? If you decide not to make a referral, what are the possible risks and benefits to the client if you work with this person?

Values Conflicts Regarding Sexual Attitudes and Behavior

Mental health practitioners may be working with clients whose sexual values and behaviors differ sharply from their own. Ford and Hendrick (2003) designed a study to assess therapists' sexual values for both themselves and their clients in the areas of premarital sex, casual sex, extramarital sex, open marriages, sexual orientation, and sex in adolescence and late adulthood. They found that when therapists' beliefs conflicted with those of clients, therapists were able to avoid imposing their personal values on clients. However, 40% decided to refer a client because of a value conflict.

This research supports previous conclusions that the practice of therapy is not value free, particularly where sexual values are concerned. Respondents in the study indicated that they valued the following: sex as an expression of love and commitment, fidelity and monogamy in marital relationships, and committed life partnerships. Therapists reported handling value conflicts by (a) referring clients (40%), (b) discussing the issues with their clients (25%), and (c) consulting with a colleague, supervisor, or peer (18%). The respondents in this survey report that they are aware of their personal values and make efforts to keep their values from having a negative impact on their clients.

Examine your values with respect to sexual attitudes and behavior. Do you see them as being restrictive or permissive? Think about each of the following statements and mark "A" in the space provided if you mostly agree and "D" if you mostly disagree with the statement.

_____ 1. Internet sex talk can be a creative way to express sexuality.

_____ 2. Sex is most meaningful as an expression of love and commitment.

_____ 3. Recreational sex is healthy if it is consensual.

_____ 4. Sex with multiple partners is not okay unless you know your partners well.

_____ 5. Safe sexual practices are essential throughout your life.

_____ 6. Extramarital sex is acceptable if you stay in a failed marriage for the sake of children.

_____ 7. Premarital sex promotes intimacy later in a relationship.

_____ 8. Same-gender sex is the right choice for some people.

_____ 9. Swinging or group sex is an acceptable means of sexual expression.

_____ 10. Adolescents should avoid becoming sexually intimate because they cannot deal with the consequences.

Can you counsel people who are experiencing conflict over their sexual choices if their values differ dramatically from your own? If you have liberal attitudes about sexual behavior, will you be able to respect the conservative views of some of your clients? If you think their moral views are giving them difficulty, will you try to persuade your clients to adopt a more liberal view? How will you view the guilt clients may experience? Will you treat it as an undesirable emotion that they need to overcome? Conversely, if you have strict sexual guidelines for your own life, will the more permissive attitudes of some of your clients be a problem for you? Can you respect the self-determination of clients who have sharply different sexual values from your own? Who has influenced your choices pertaining to sexual practices?

As you study the following case, reflect on how your sexual attitudes and values are likely to influence your interventions with Virginia and Tom. Then consult the ethics codes of various helping professions to identify standards that validate the responses given by the counselors in this case.

■ The Case of Virginia and Tom.

Virginia and Tom find themselves in a marital crisis when Virginia discovers that Tom has had several affairs during the course of their marriage. Tom agrees to see a marriage counselor. Tom says that he cannot see how his affairs necessarily got in the way of his relationship with his wife, especially since they were never meaningful. He believes that what is done is done and that it is pointless to dwell on past transgressions. He is upset over his wife's reaction to learning about his affairs. He says that he loves his wife and that he does not want to end the marriage. His involvements with other women were sexual in nature rather than committed love relationships. Virginia says that she would like to forgive her husband but that she finds it too painful to continue living with him knowing of his activities, even though they are in the past. She is not reassured by Tom's reactions to his past activities and fears that he might continue to rationalize these activities.

Counselor A. This counselor tells the couple at the initial session that from her experience extramarital affairs add many strains to a marriage, that people get hurt in such situations, and that affairs do pose some problems for couples seeking counseling. However, she adds that affairs sometimes actually have positive benefits for both the wife and the husband. She says that her policy is to let the couple find out for themselves what is acceptable to them. She accepts Virginia and Tom as clients and asks them to consider as many options as they can to resolve their difficulties.

- Is this counselor neutral or biased? Explain.

- Does this approach seem practical and realistic to you? Explain.

Counselor B. From the outset this counselor makes it clear that she sees affairs as disruptive in any marriage. She maintains that affairs are typically started because of a deep dissatisfaction within the marriage and are symptomatic of other real conflicts. The counselor says she can help Tom and Virginia discover these conflicts in couples therapy. She further says that she will not work with them unless Tom's affairs are truly in the past, because she is convinced that counseling will not be effective unless Tom is fully committed to doing what is needed to work on his relationship with Virginia.

- Is this counselor imposing her values? Explain.

- Is it appropriate for the counselor to openly state her conditions and values from the outset? Why or why not?

- To what degree do you agree or disagree with this counselor's thinking and approach?

- After working with them for a time, the counselor discovers that Tom has begun another affair. What do you think she should do and why?

Counselor C. This counselor views the affairs much as Tom does. She points out that the couple seems to have a basically sound marriage and suggests that with some individual counseling Virginia can learn to get past the affairs.

- With her viewpoint, is it ethical for this counselor to accept this couple for counseling? Should she suggest a referral to another professional? Explain.

- Should the counselor have given more attention to the obvious pain expressed by Virginia?

- Should the counselor have kept her values and attitudes to herself so that she would be less likely to influence this couple's decision?

Commentary. Each of the three therapists' responses indicates definite values regarding marital infidelity. By stating their personal values to Virginia and Tom, all three therapists are standing on shaky ethical ground. It is critical that therapists possess awareness of their personal values, but they should not impose their values either directly or indirectly. Not only do therapists need to recognize how their values pertaining to marriage might influence their work, but they also need to be cognizant of any countertransference elicited by affairs. The therapist's job is to help this couple explore their own values to determine what they hope to accomplish from counseling and how committed they are to their relationship. The therapist might explore this question: Is it possible for this couple to reconcile their differing views on affairs?

Value Conflicts Pertaining to Abortion

People's views about abortion are emotionally charged, and counselors may experience a value clash with their clients on this issue. The following discussion is largely taken from an article by Millner and Hanks (2002) titled "Induced Abortion: An Ethical Conundrum for Counselors." Induced abortion is one of the most controversial moral issues in American culture, yet little professional literature addresses abortion-related legal and ethical issues. Millner and Hanks (a) identify issues relevant to counselors regarding abortion, (b) examine how these issues relate to ethical principles, and (c) suggest practical ways in which counselors can resolve dilemmas involving clients' decisions.

Clients who are exploring abortion as an option often present a challenge to clinicians, both legally and ethically. From a legal perspective, mental health professionals are expected to exercise "reasonable care," and if they fail to do so, clients can take legal action against them for negligence. Counselors can be charged with negligence if they (a) do not act with skill by withholding relevant information or providing inaccurate information; (b) do not refer a client; or (c) make an inadequate referral. For example, a counselor who makes a referral that supports his or her values rather than one in keeping with the client's values is vulnerable to a lawsuit.

Millner and Hanks provide the following recommendations when making ethical decisions in cases involving a discussion of abortion.

1. Make a comprehensive examination of your own moral and ethical views on abortion. As a part of this critical examination, ask yourself these questions: "Under what circumstances, if any, would an abortion be justified? Is abortion warranted if the pregnancy is the result of rape or incest? If the mother's life or health is endangered, is abortion justified? To what degree would abortion be acceptable if the fetus was determined to be an unwanted gender? To what degree would abortion be a viable alternative to birth control measures? How are matters such as age of the mother, financial considerations, and marital status relevant considerations?" Self-examination within the context of a clinician's personal ethics and the application of the principles of autonomy,

fidelity, justice, beneficence, and nonmaleficence are useful in helping counselors resolve dilemmas they encounter pertaining to abortion.

2. Determine when your own personal ethics would make it difficult for you to be objective and respectful of the client's autonomy. If possible, clinicians should decide in advance in what circumstances they might be inclined to misuse their influence to steer clients toward a decision that is consistent with their own values rather than in keeping with the client's values.

3. Be prepared to refer clients to other professionals when it is appropriate. Making a referral is often a complex matter. For instance, it may be easier to make a referral for a client who raises abortion as a consideration at the initial counseling session than to refer a long-standing client, which could raise an issue of client abandonment.

4. Become familiar with state and federal laws pertaining to abortions. This is especially true for school counselors who are dealing with minors. Laws, regulations, and policies vary widely; consult with an attorney when necessary.

5. Anticipate circumstances that would make it difficult for you to maintain a sense of objectivity because of a conflict between your values and those of the client. You cannot foresee every possible situation, but you can reflect on an ethical decision-making model you could apply to a range of cases. If you have clarity on your personal values and ethics, you are in a good position to address the challenges of dealing with clients who are considering abortion.

We suggest that you familiarize yourself with the legal requirements in your state that relate to abortion, especially if you are counseling minors who are considering an abortion. The matter of parental consent in working with minors varies from state to state. For example, in 1987 Alabama enacted the Parental Consent for Abortion Law, requiring physicians to have parental consent or a court waiver before performing an abortion on an unemancipated woman. Consider the situation of an unmarried young woman under the age of 18 who tells her school counselor that she is planning to get an abortion and does not want her parents to know about this. In Alabama this counselor is expected to explain this law to the young woman (including the option of a court waiver of parental consent) and advise her that the counselor is obliged to comply with this law, and not encourage any violation of it. In her discussion of abortion counseling, Stone (2002) concludes that school counselors can discuss the topic of abortion with a student if the school board has not adopted a policy forbidding such a discussion. Stone adds that counselors who impose their values on a minor student are not acting in an appropriate, professional, or reasonable manner.

In the following vignette, we present the case of Candy. In light of our previous discussion, what value conflicts, if any, might you face with Candy? What issues do you find most challenging, and how might you deal with them?

■ **The Case of Candy.**

Candy is a 14-year-old student who is sent to you because of her problematic behavior in the classroom. Her parents have recently divorced, and Candy is having difficulty coping with the breakup. Eventually, she tells you that she is having sexual relations with her boyfriend without using any form of birth control.

- What are your reactions to Candy's sexual activity?
- Would you want to know the age of her boyfriend?
- If you sense that her behavior is an attempt to overcome her feelings of isolation, how might you deal with it?
- Would you try to persuade her to use birth control? Why or why not?

You have been working with Candy for several sessions now, and she discovers that she is pregnant. Her boyfriend is 15 and declares that he is in no position to support her and a child. She has decided to have an abortion but feels anxious about following through with it. To clarify how you might respond if Candy were your client, read the following statements and put an "A" in the space provided if you agree more than disagree with the statement; put a "D" in the space if you mainly disagree.

_____ 1. I would explore Candy's ambivalence relative to the abortion.

_____ 2. I would encourage Candy to consider other options, such as adoption, keeping the child as a single parent, or marrying.

_____ 3. I would reassure Candy about having an abortion, telling her that many women make this choice.

_____ 4. I would consult with a supervisor or a colleague about the possible legal implications in this case.

_____ 5. I would consult with an attorney for legal advice.

_____ 6. If I worked in a school setting, I would familiarize myself with the policies of the school, as well as any possible state law pertaining to minors considering an abortion.

_____ 7. I would attempt to arrange for a session with Candy and her parents as a way to open communication on this issue.

_____ 8. I would encourage Candy to explore all the options and consequences of each of her choices.

_____ 9. I would inform Candy's parents, because I believe they have a right to be part of this decision-making process.

_____ 10. I would refer Candy to an outside agency or practitioner because her problems are too complex for counseling in a school setting.

_____ 11. I would pay particular attention to helping Candy clarify her value system; I would be sensitive to her religious and moral values and the possible implications of specific choices she might make.

_____ 12. I would refer Candy to another professional because of my opposition to abortion.

_____ 13. I would tell Candy that I am personally opposed to (or in favor of) abortion, that I want to remain her counselor during this difficult time, and that I will support whatever decision she makes for herself.

Commentary. Candy's case illustrates several complex problems. What do you do if you cannot be objective due to your personal views on abortion? Do you refer Candy? How affected might Candy be by a referral? If you are firmly opposed to abortion, could you support Candy in her decision to have an abortion? Would you try to persuade her to have the baby because of your personal views? Which of your values are triggered by Candy's case, and how might these values either help or hinder you in working with her?

One possible course of action would be to tell Candy about your values and how you think they would influence your work with her. If you determine that you could not work effectively with her, explore your reasons for making this decision. Why is it crucial that her decision be compatible with your values? Do you have to approve of the decisions your clients make to continue working with them? Do you see a distinction between a counselor suggesting a course of action and helping a client arrive at her own decision on the matter? Do you think it is unethical to fail to discuss all of Candy's options if she has made her choice clear to you from the outset? Explain. Can you imagine telling Candy that your personal view on abortion disqualifies you from working with her effectively, and that you will give her a referral so that she can get the best possible help?

Case Studies of Other Possible Value Conflicts

In this section we present two case studies that highlight value conflicts. Try to imagine yourself working with each of these clients. How do you think your values would affect your work with them?

■ The Case of Paul.

Paul comes to an agency with many difficulties and anxieties, one of which is his antipathy toward interracial marriage. He expresses disappointment in his daughter and in himself as a father because of her engagement to a man of another race. Paul has gone as far as threatening to disinherit her if she marries this man. What this client does not know is that the social worker herself is in an interracial marriage. The therapist, Jill, says she is willing to work with him but discloses that she herself is in an interracial marriage. She asks Paul, "How would it be for you to work with me now that you know that?"

- How do you react to her self-disclosure?
- Would a referral be in order? Why or why not?
- What are your values in this situation, and what might you do or say if you were the counselor?

Your views on racial issues can have an impact on your manner of counseling in certain situations. Think about what your responses to the following statements tell you about how your values might operate in cases pertaining to racial concerns. In the space provided, put an "A" if you agree more than you disagree with the statement, and put a "D" if you disagree more than you agree.

_____ 1. I could effectively counsel a person of a different race.

_____ 2. I would be inclined to refer a person of a different race to a counselor of that race because the client is bound to have more trust in a therapist of the same race.

_____ 3. I would modify my practices and techniques when working with clients who are racially and culturally different.

_____ 4. Interracial marriages in this society are almost doomed to failure because of the extra pressures on them.

_____ 5. Interracial marriages pose no greater strain on a relationship than do interfaith marriages.

_____ 6. I have certain racial (cultural) prejudices that would affect my objectivity in working with clients of a different race (culture) from mine.

Commentary. Jill will not be able to work effectively with Paul if she allows her own feelings to be in the foreground or if she confronts Paul immediately regarding his racist attitudes. By disclosing her personal situation at the outset, Jill may have made it more difficult to establish a trusting relationship with Paul that will enable him to reflect on and explore his racist thinking.

■ The Case of Reggie.

Reggie comes to see Linda, who has been a practicing therapist for two years. Reggie is a married man who has had several affairs, which he blames mostly on his marriage. His goal in therapy is to find some way to ameliorate his guilt. After a few sessions, Linda suggests he consider couples therapy because much of the content of his sessions has had to do with his marriage. He refuses this referral. She then tells him that she cannot, in good conscience, continue to see him because his infidelity bothers her and she sees no way to help him obtain his goal of alleviating his guilt and continuing his affairs. Linda suggests that he seek another therapist and offers him three referrals.

- What is your reaction to Linda's refusal to continue counseling Reggie?
- Is this a case of a therapist exposing or imposing her values on a client?
- Should Linda's informed consent have made it clear that she would have difficulty counseling people who are involved in extramarital affairs?
- What are the ethical considerations in this case?
- How would you deal with Reggie if he were your client?

Commentary. Linda is not being therapeutic by imposing her value system pertaining to affairs on Reggie. This issue is not about her, but about her client. Depending on how Linda handles termination and referral, her client may feel that she has abandoned him. If Reggie were our client, we would tell him that we cannot help him ameliorate his guilt directly, but we may be able to do so indirectly by exploring his marriage in more detail. Reggie seems more than willing to talk about his marriage, and this discussion may eventually lead toward a recommendation for marital counseling. If we made this transition to marital therapy with Reggie, considerable attention to informed consent and sensitivity to the risks of multiple roles would be necessary on our part.

Striving for Openness in Discussing Values

When you experience discomfort due to a client's very different system of values, challenge yourself to develop ways of working with this client. Try to work collaboratively to identify and clarify the client's value system and to determine the degree to which the client is living in accordance with *his or her* core beliefs and values. We question the ethics of resorting to a referral in all cases where the therapist experiences discomfort. If you feel secure in your own values, you will not be threatened by really listening to, and deeply understanding, people who think differently or people who do not share your worldview. Listen to your clients with the intent of understanding what their values are, how they arrived at them, and the meaning these values have for them. Being open to your clients can significantly broaden you as a person, and it will enhance your ability to work ethically and effectively with clients.

The Role of Spiritual and Religious Values in Counseling

Addressing spiritual and religious values in the practice of counseling encompasses particularly sensitive, controversial, and complex concerns. As you read the following section, try to clarify your values in this area and think about how your views might either enhance or interfere with your ability to establish meaningful contact with certain clients.

There is a growing awareness and willingness to explore spiritual and religious matters within the context of the practice of counseling and counselor education programs (Burke et al., 1999; Hagedorn, 2005; Polanski, 2003; Yarhouse & Burkett, 2002). Powers (2005) surveyed the literature on spirituality and counseling and found that very little was being written on this topic prior to the 1950s. However, the topic of spirituality in the practice of counseling has received increasing attention in the literature since the 1970s (Hall, Dixon, & Mauzey, 2004; Sperry & Shafranske, 2005). Survey data of both practicing counselors and counselor educators indicate that spiritual and religious matters are therapeutically relevant, ethically appropriate, and potentially significant topics for the practice of counseling in secular settings (Delaney, Miller, & Bisono, 2007; Walker, Gorsuch, & Tan, 2004; Young, Wiggins-Frame, & Cashwell, 2007). Spiritual issues that clients bring to their therapy can be basic therapeutic considerations.

In a study of religious and spiritual psychotherapy behaviors, Frazier and Hansen (2009) found that professional psychologists are reluctant to discuss these issues not only with their clients but also with their colleagues. They discovered that there is a "large gap between recommendations made in the clinical literature and what practitioners actually do when working with clients with religious/spiritual beliefs" (p. 86). In the course of counseling, practitioners ask many questions about a client's life, yet sometimes omit inquiring about the influence of religion and spirituality in an individual's life. Hage (2006) notes that therapists routinely address a range of sensitive topics, such as race and sexuality, yet religious and spiritual issues are not addressed in therapy. When counselors fail to raise the issue, clients may assume that such matters are not relevant for counseling, and counselors may be guilty of excluding an important issue of diversity and experience (Yarhouse, 2003).

Religion and spirituality are oftentimes part of the client's problem and can be part of the client's solution, which makes discussing these topics relevant to the therapeutic process. Spirituality and religion are critical sources of strength for many clients, offering a direction as they make crucial life decisions. Counselors can make use of the spiritual and religious beliefs of their clients as they explore and resolve their problems (Basham & O'Connor, 2005). Because spiritual and religious values can play a major part in human life, these values should be seen as a potential resource in therapy (Harper & Gill, 2005). Spirituality is an essential quality of being human, and Allen Weber believes it must be addressed in whatever form is appropriate in counseling (personal communication, August 9, 2008).

Counseling can help clients gain insight into the ways their core beliefs and values are reflected in their behavior. For clients who are in a crisis situation, the spiritual domain may be a source of comfort and support, and a rich source of discussion. For some people, their spirituality or religious beliefs are a major sustaining power that keeps them going when all else fails. By contrast, the guilt, anger, and sadness that clients experience may result from a misinterpretation of the spiritual and religious realm, which can lead to depression and a sense of worthlessness. Consequently, clinicians must remain open and nonjudgmental when discussions in this realm occur.

Religious Teachings and Counseling

Religious beliefs and practices affect many dimensions of human experience, both positively and negatively. At their best, both counseling and religion are able to foster healing through an exploration of self by learning to accept oneself; by giving to others; by forgiving others and oneself; by admitting one's shortcomings; by accepting personal responsibility; by letting go of hurts and resentments; by dealing with guilt; and by learning to let go of self-destructive patterns of thinking, feeling, and acting.

Although religion and counseling are comparable in a number of respects, some key differences exist. For example, counseling does not involve the imposition of counselors' values on clients, whereas religion often involves teaching doctrines and beliefs that individuals are expected to accept and practice. Some well-known therapists, from Sigmund Freud to Albert Ellis, have been antagonistic toward religion, and some religious leaders have been equally antagonistic toward psychotherapy.

Ethically, it is important to monitor yourself for subtle ways that you might be inclined to push your values in your counseling practice. For instance, you might influence clients to embrace a spiritual perspective, or you might influence them to give up certain beliefs that you think are no longer functional for them. It is critical to keep in mind that it is the client's place to determine what specific values to retain, replace, or modify.

Spiritual and Religious Values in Assessment and Treatment

In a national survey involving more than 1,000 clinical psychologists, Hathaway, Scott, and Garver (2004) found that the majority believe a client's religion and spirituality are an important aspect of functioning. The majority in this survey also believed they could distinguish between healthy and unhealthy religious functioning, and they reported being familiar with the spiritual beliefs of their client populations. The survey revealed, however, that most clinicians *do not* routinely incorporate spirituality into the assessment and treatment process. This omission might well limit the effectiveness of therapy for some clients, which involves a clear ethical concern. Hathaway and colleagues conclude: "Assessment of client religiousness/spirituality should become a more familiar part of the clinical landscape" (p. 103).

Attention to spirituality can be considered in the context of an integrated and holistic effort in helping clients resolve conflicts and improve health, as well as find meaning in dealing with the challenges of living (Shafranske & Sperry, 2005b). If, during the assessment process or later in counseling, clients indicate that they are concerned about any of their religious beliefs or practices, this is a useful focal point for exploration.

Traditionally, when a client comes to a therapist with a problem, the therapist explores all the factors that might have contributed to the development of the problem. Even though a client may no longer consider him- or herself to be religious or spiritual, a background of involvement in religion needs to be explored as part of the client's history. To understand the client's concerns, it is essential that counselors understand how the client's religious values and beliefs affect his or her daily life and decision making and how these values and beliefs are related to the issues that bring the client to counseling (Belaire, Young, & Elder, 2005). This can be done without implying support for specific religious beliefs.

A number of writers and researchers believe it is essential to understand and respect clients' religious beliefs and to include such beliefs in their assessment and treatment practice (Belaire et al., 2005; Faiver & O'Brien, 1993; Faiver & Ingersoll, 2005; Frame, 2003; Harper & Gill, 2005; Hathaway et al., 2004; Kelly, 1995b; Sperry & Shafranske, 2005). Frame (2003) presents many reasons for conducting assessments when working in the area of spirituality in counseling, some of which include understanding clients' worldviews and the contexts in which they live; assisting clients in grappling with questions regarding the purpose of their lives and what they most value; exploring religion and spirituality as client resources; uncovering religious and spiritual problems; and determining appropriate interventions.

The first step is to include spiritual and religious dimensions as a regular part of the intake procedure and the early phase of the counseling process. Faiver and O'Brien (1993) devised a form to assess the religious beliefs of clients, which they use to glean relevant information on the client's belief system for diagnostic, treatment, and referral purposes. Faiver and Ingersoll (2005) encourage counselors to examine the client's spiritual culture, present circumstances, spiritual and religious beliefs (if any), and worldview. They suggest an assessment format that begins with the global and culminates in the specific. Based on a comprehensive assessment, a determination can be made about the appropriateness of devising a treatment plan that incorporates the client's religious and spiritual beliefs.

Assessment is a process of looking at all the potential influences on a client's problem. The exploration of spirituality or religious influences is just as significant as exploring family-of-origin influences. Practitioners should remain finely tuned to their clients' stories and to the reasons clients seek professional assistance.

■ The Case of Anami.

Anami is a counselor in a university counseling center. Tai, a first-generation Asian American client, is caught between the religion of his parents, who are Buddhist, and his different emerging beliefs. Since entering the university environment, Tai has begun to question his Buddhist upbringing, yet he has not found anything to replace his parents' values. He feels lost and does not know what to believe.

Anami considers herself to be a holistic counselor, and her client assessments include asking questions about family history, personal history, religious and spiritual upbringing, life turning points, physical health, nutrition, and social relationships. In the process of the assessment, she discovers that many of the issues Tai is struggling with pertain to Buddhism. Anami tells Tai: "I think I can assist you in the things you struggle with, but I have limited knowledge of the Buddhist religion. With your permission I would like to consult on specific matters with a colleague who is a Buddhist. I may also recommend a Buddhist teacher to you to help you clarify some specific beliefs you mentioned earlier. Is this acceptable to you?" Tai nods in agreement.

- What do you think of the way Anami handled this case?
- Would you have done anything differently, and if so, what?
- What kind of alternative roles can you think of using in working with Tai?
- Do you think Anami should have referred Tai because of her lack of familiarity with Buddhism?

Commentary. We find little to disagree with in the way Anami handled the case. We like the way she recognized and acknowledged her limitations, for being willing to educate herself on these matters, and also for being willing to consult with someone who has greater expertise than she does.

Personal Beliefs and Values of Counselors

If mental health practitioners are to effectively serve diverse needs of clients, it is essential that they be capable and prepared to look at spirituality and religion when these are important to their clients. Counselors must understand their own spiritual and religious beliefs, or the lack thereof, if they hope to gain an in-depth appreciation of the beliefs of their clients (Faiver et al., 2001; Hagedorn, 2005).

Steen, Engels, and Thweatt (2006) encourage a process of continuous self-examination on the part of counselors to discover their own biases, beliefs, and values pertaining to spirituality or religion within the counseling context. They contend that counselors who hold rigid beliefs about spirituality may hinder the progress of counseling. They state: "The ethics of spirituality in counseling primarily lies with the counselor's openness to discussions regarding values and beliefs different from one's own" (p. 115).

Your personal stance.   As you examine your own position on the place of spiritual and religious values in the practice of counseling, reflect on these questions:

- What connection, if any, do you see between spirituality, religion, and the problems of the client?

- Is there such a thing as professional religious counseling? What are the ethics of guiding a client only within the bounds of your religion?

- Do you think it is ever justified for clinicians to introduce or teach their religious or spiritual values to clients and to base their clinical practice on these values?

- How would you describe the influence of religion or spirituality in your life?

- Are therapists forcing their values on their clients when they decide what topics can be discussed?

- If you have no religious or spiritual convictions, how would you work with clients who hold strong views in these areas?

- Is there an ethical issue when a counseling agency that is attached to a church imposes the church's teachings as part of their counseling practices?

- Are you willing to collaborate with clergy or indigenous healers if it appears that clients have questions you are not qualified to answer?

- How does a counselor in a public school deal with spiritual or religious issues that students may bring up? Do parents need to be informed that spiritual issues may be discussed in counseling?

Working With Clergy and Spiritual Teachers

Ethical practice sometimes demands that mental health professionals be willing and able to refer a client to a member of the clergy or to an indigenous healer. Practitioners should become knowledgeable about members of the religious community and indigenous healers that they can collaborate with and refer clients to when it is appropriate. If a client adheres to religious values and practices, should the therapist get input from the clergy? When is there an ethical responsibility to refer clients for clarification of an issue pertaining to their problem and their faith? A referral might be indicated if it becomes clear to the therapist that the client's understanding of his or her religion came from a single clergy person, and that the client's view did not reflect what the religious body actually taught. McMinn, Aikins, and Lish (2003) conclude that basic competence in collaborating with clergy is sufficient for most practitioners, and that this competence is much like collaboration with physicians and other professionals. They add, "it is important for faculty and supervisors to communicate and model respectful attitudes toward clergy in working with students and supervisees" (p. 202).

We agree that it is important to collaborate with clergy and spiritual teachers, much as we do with physicians in serving clients' needs, but we do not believe this is sufficient in all cases. As with other issues of diversity, if mental health professionals are to work effectively with spiritual and religious themes that a client presents, it is important that they have training and experience in this area.

Training in Dealing With Spiritual and Religious Concerns

Spiritual and religious aspects of living may be as much a part of the context of the presenting problem as are issues of gender, race, or culture. Walker and colleagues (2004) indicate that most therapists lack formal training in incorporating religious and spiritual dimensions into the counseling process. Therapists should not use spiritual and religious interventions inappropriately, such as imposing their own values on clients. Elsewhere Walker and his colleagues (2005) suggest that training programs should incorporate workshops and supervision involving religious and spiritual interventions to teach therapists to use these interventions appropriately and effectively in counseling.

The Association for Spiritual, Ethical, and Religious Values in Counseling (ASERVIC) developed a set of competencies in spirituality and proposed including these competencies in the Standards of the Council for Accreditation of Counseling and Related Educational Programs (CACREP). These competencies outline the knowledge and skills counselors need to master to effectively engage clients in the exploration of their spiritual and religious lives (G. Miller, 1999). Young, Wiggins-Frame, and Cashwell (2007) suggest that counselors need training in using a variety of intervention strategies in working with clients on their spiritual concerns. In a national survey of members of the American Counseling Association, there was strong support for the importance of gaining competence in this area (Young et al., 2007). If mental health professionals are claiming to be competent in dealing with spiritual matters, then they need training. Educational programs can encourage students to look at what they believe and how their beliefs and values might influence their work.

Some cautions. Spirituality is an existential issue. Although it is important to be open to dealing with spiritual and religious issues in counseling, counselors should be cautious about introducing these themes, which could unduly influence the client. Hage (2006) maintains that counselors have a responsibility to carefully monitor themselves so that they do not impose their values pertaining to spirituality and religion on clients. Monitoring is equally important for therapists who exclude spiritual and religious issues from therapy, for they also are in danger of imposing their perspective on clients.

Religious dogma is not part of the theoretical foundation of psychotherapy. Therapists should neither impose their religious views on clients, nor should they pretend to be experts in religion any more than they are in medicine, culture, finances, or any other related area (Terence Patterson, personal communication, December 15, 2008).

■ The Case of Sheila.

Sheila is a rational emotive behavior therapist who claims to be an atheist. She has a strong bias against any kind of spiritual or religious influences, considering these beliefs to be irrational. Her client Brendan describes an unhappy marriage as one of the issues he struggles with. When she suggests to him that perhaps he should consider leaving his marriage, he replies that this is out of the question. He informs her that he has a deep spiritual conviction that this is his destiny. If he were to go against his destiny, he would suffer on some other level. Sheila replies: "Have you ever considered that your convictions may be unhealthy, not only for you but also for your children? Are you willing to look at this?" Brendan seems taken aback. He tells the counselor, "I think that what you just said was not respectful of the way I believe. I am not sure that you can help me." Brendan leaves abruptly.

- How would you assess Sheila's approach?
- Do you see any ethical issues raised in the way Sheila dealt with Brendan? If so, what are the issues?
- Could you see yourself responding as Sheila did? Why or why not?
- Did Sheila take care of her needs or of Brendan's needs?
- Would Sheila necessarily have to agree with Brendan's spiritual beliefs to work with him? Explain.
- How would you work with this client?

Commentary. We have concerns about Sheila describing Brendan's spiritual beliefs as "unhealthy." Brendan's reasons for staying in his marriage (his spiritual values) could have been explored rather than being quickly judged. This kind of approach demonstrates the imposition of the therapist's values, not an exploration of the client's concerns. The *Canadian Code of Ethics for Psychologists* (CPA, 2000) describes the therapist's responsibilities in a case such as this:

Psychologists are not expected to be value-free or totally without self-interest in conducting their activities. However, they are expected to understand how their backgrounds, personal needs, and values interact with their activities, to be open and honest about the influence of such factors, and to be as objective and unbiased as possible under the circumstances. (Principle III.)

It is not the proper role of the therapist to suggest a specific course of action to follow, for this kind of advice is likely to backfire or not be successful. This case illustrates how the personal values of therapists can affect the questions they ask, the assumptions they make, the methods they employ, and what they observe and fail to observe.

■ **The Case of Rory.**

Rory, who has been in counseling for some time with Teresa, sees himself as a failure and cannot move past his guilt. He insists that he cannot forgive himself for his past. He is in great turmoil and berates himself for his aberrant ways. Teresa knows that Rory is a profoundly religious man and asks during one of the sessions, "How would you view and react to a person with a struggle similar to yours? What kind of God do you believe in? Is your God a punitive or loving God? What does your religion teach you about the forgiveness of sin?" Teresa is attempting to utilize Rory's convictions to reframe his thinking. Once he begins to look at his behavior through the eyes of his religious beliefs, his attitudes toward his own behavior change dramatically. Because Rory believes in a loving God, he finally learns to be more forgiving of himself.

- How do you react to how Teresa worked with Rory?
- Would you use Rory's religious beliefs as an intervention? Why or why not?
- By doing this, was Teresa imposing her values? Explain.

Commentary. If Teresa had used her own religious beliefs to reframe Rory's thinking, we would have concerns. If she were his minister, rabbi, or priest, it would be acceptable for her to teach these values. But that is not the role of a counselor. However, Teresa noticed a discrepancy between Rory's religious beliefs and his assessment of his behaviors. By using the client's own belief system, she assisted him in reframing his self-assessment and in the process helped him to be true to his own belief system.

Value Conflicts Regarding End-of-Life Decisions

End-of-life decisions have become an increasingly controversial issue since the Death With Dignity Act became law in Oregon in 1997. Do people who are terminally ill, have an incurable disease, or are in extreme pain have a right to choose the time and the means of their own death by seeking aid-in-dying? What is the appropriate role for counselors in dealing with clients who are making end-of-life decisions? Werth and Holdwick (2000) provide the following definitions for some key concepts related to end-of-life matters:

- **Rational suicide** means that a person has decided—after going through a decision-making process and without coercion from others—to end his or her life because of extreme suffering involved with a terminal illness.
- **Aid-in-dying** consists of providing a person with the means to die; the person self-administers the death-causing agent, which is a lethal dose of a legal medication.
- **Hastened death** means ending one's life earlier than would have happened without intervention. It involves speeding up the dying process, which can entail withholding or withdrawing treatment or life support.

The three of us attended an all day workshop on "End-of-Life Decisions" for a variety of helping professionals. The program consisted of a panel of presenters from different disciplines: clinical psychology, philosophy, medicine, psychiatry, social work, and law. What struck us was the complexity of this topic in practice. Although many of us search for the best answers to difficult life-and-death situations, there are few simple answers. We came away from the conference with an increased awareness and appreciation of the challenging nature of working with people who are dying. It reinforced our belief in how critical it is for helping professionals to be clear about their own values on a range of issues pertaining to end-of-life care.

Mental health professionals who are involved in end-of-life care decisions need to be knowledgeable about the implications of advance directives and their involvement with the client. **Advance directives** pertain to decisions people make about end-of-life care that are designed to protect their self-determination when they reach a point in their lives when they are no longer able to make decisions of their own about their care. These advance directives are written documents that specify the conditions under which people wish to receive certain treatment or to refuse or discontinue life-sustaining treatment.

Although there are no easy answers to right-to-die questions, mental health professionals are likely to face these situations with their clients. Practitioners can assist their clients in making decisions within the framework of clients' own beliefs and value systems. Herlihy and Watson (2004) emphasize the willingness of counselors to examine their own values, beliefs, and fears about death and dying to determine whether they are able and willing to consider a request for aid-in-dying.

Mental health professionals must address both ethical and legal issues regarding end-of-life care and be prepared for work with those who are dying and their family members. Counselors will struggle with the ethical quandaries of balancing the need to protect client rights to autonomy and self-determination with meeting their responsibilities to the legal system, all the while remaining true to their own moral and ethical values (Herlihy & Watson, 2004).

At this point in time, consider the following questions:

- What is your position on an individual's right to decide matters pertaining to living and dying?
- What religious, ethical, and moral beliefs do you hold that would allow you to support any decision a client might make regarding his or her end-of-life care?
- How might your beliefs get in the way of assisting your client in making his or her own decision?

Your role as a counselor is to assist clients in making the best decision in the context of their own values. If you will be working with clients concerned about end-of-life care, it is essential to know the laws in your jurisdiction and state and to be familiar with the ethical guidelines of your professional organization concerning an individual's freedom to make end-of-life decisions. Two states have legalized physician-assisted suicide (Oregon and Washington), and similar legislation is pending in New Mexico, New Hampshire, and Massachusetts. Seek legal consultation in cases involving a client's request for more explicit assistance with hastened death.

Codes of Ethics Regarding End-of-Life Decisions

The National Association of Social Workers (2003) has developed a policy statement pertaining to client self-determination in end-of-life decisions. This statement is based on the principle of client self-determination and the premise that choice should be intrinsic to all aspects of life and death. According to the NASW (2003) document, end-of-life decisions are the choices individuals make about terminal conditions regarding their continuing care or treatment options. These options include aggressive treatment of the medical condition, life-sustaining treatment, medical intervention intended to alleviate suffering (but not to cure), withholding or withdrawing life-sustaining treatment, voluntary active euthanasia, and physician-assisted suicide. A terminal condition is one in which there is no reasonable chance of recovery and in which the application of life-sustaining procedures would serve only to postpone the end of life. The *NASW Standards for Social Work Practice in Palliative and End of Life Care* (NASW, 2004) provides specific guidelines that are very useful for any mental health professional who is working with clients on end-of-life care issues.

The American Psychological Association has been very active in end-of-life care issues. APA has convened four groups to examine end-of-life issues, developed facts sheets for the general public, issued a comprehensive report on the topic, and passed two resolutions related to end-of-life issues. The APA also has continuing education programs on end-of-life issues that have been part of the national convention for many years (Werth & Crow, 2009).

In its revised *Code of Ethics,* ACA (2005) addresses end-of-life care for terminally ill clients. Regarding quality of care, ACA offers this guideline:

> Counselors take measures to ensure that clients: (1) receive high quality end-of-life care for their physical, emotional, social and spiritual needs, (2) have the highest degree of self-determination possible, (3) are given every opportunity possible to engage in informed decision making regarding their end-of-life care, and (4) receive complete and adequate assessment regarding their ability to make competent, rational decisions on their own behalf from a mental health professional who is experienced in end-of-life care practice. (A.9.a.)

The ACA guidelines also address competence, choice, and referral:

> Recognizing the personal, moral and competence issues related to end-of-life decisions, counselors may choose to work or not work with terminally ill clients who wish to explore their end-of-life options. Counselors provide appropriate referral information to ensure that clients receive the necessary help. (A.9.b.)

In addition, the ACA (2005) addressed confidentiality issues when working with terminally ill clients:

> Counselors who provide services to terminally ill individuals who are considering hastening their own deaths have the option of breaking or not breaking confidentiality, depending on the specific circumstances of the situation and after seeking consultation or supervision. (A.9.c.)

Bennett and Werth (2006) state that although this standard provides substantive direction for counselors, it is bound to be controversial. They maintain, however, that "the flexibility this standard offers counselors providing care to dying clients will enable counselors to direct their energy toward helping the client rather than being distracted by concerns about breaking confidentiality" (p. 228).

The policy statement of NASW (2003), the standards on end-of-life care of NASW (2004), and the end-of-life care standards of the ACA (2005) provide social workers and counselors with some general guidelines by which they can examine the ethical and legal issues pertaining to end-of-life decisions. Both the ACA and the NASW encourage mental health professionals not to make ethical judgments in isolation, and to consult with other professionals when in doubt about the ethics of an action or when an action is likely to have serious consequences for the client or for the therapist (Sommers-Flanagan, Sommers-Flanagan, & Welfel, 2009).

Differing Perspectives on End-of-Life Issues

Studies of attitudes toward suicide reveal sharp divisions of opinion regarding the meaning of the decision to end one's life. Some regard suicide as a basic personal right; others consider it morally wrong (Neimeyer, 2000). Kiser and Korpi (1996) suggest that mental health professionals may need to reconsider their views of suicide and how to treat suicidal clients. Instead of considering all individuals who are contemplating suicide as persons who are "mentally ill" and should be prevented from ending their lives, certain individuals should be viewed as being capable of making autonomous and rational decisions about ending their life. Therapists can explore alternatives to suicide and, at the same time, be attentive to the client's autonomy and freedom of choice.

There are arguments both in favor of and in opposition to rational suicide. Most arguments favoring rational suicide center on the premise that individuals should have the right to make appropriate decisions about their lives when they are terminally ill. A study examining the attitudes of counselors toward rational suicide found that about 80% of the respondents believed it was possible for a client to make a decision that death was his or her best option (Rogers et al., 2001). The counselors in this study identified the most typical circumstances under which they would consider a decision to die by suicide as being rational as follows: (a) terminal illness, (b) severe physical pain, (c) a nonimpulsive consideration of alternatives, and (d) an unacceptable quality of life.

Arguments against assisted suicide focus on clients' religious and spiritual beliefs. As Herlihy and Watson (2004) indicate, religious institutions are often part of people's lives from the time they are born. Their religious belief systems may exert a major influence on the way individuals live and on their views pertaining to their own death. Spiritual beliefs are an important part of diversity and should be considered in end-of-life situations. In addition, it is important to understand the faith and beliefs of loved ones who will be affected by the choices clients make (Werth & Crow, 2009).

Importance of Assessment

From an ethical and a legal standpoint, conducting a thorough assessment is critical in situations pertaining to end-of-life decisions. This assessment should consider matters such as diagnosable mental disorders, psychological factors that may be causing distress, quality of relationships, and spiritual concerns (Werth & Crow, 2009). The same kind of assessment can be conducted for those who are making end-of-life decisions as for people with suicidal ideation. Depression, hopelessness, and social isolation can contribute to an individual's suicidality, and these same conditions may be present when terminally ill people are making end-of-life decisions (Bennett & Werth, 2006; Werth & Rogers, 2005).

The NASW (2004) *Standards for End of Life Care* specifically address the importance of conducting a comprehensive assessment as a basis for developing interventions and designing treatment plans with dying persons. Some areas for consideration in this assessment are relevant past and current health situation; family structure and roles; stage in the life cycle; spirituality and faith; cultural values and beliefs; client's and family's goals in palliative treatment; social supports; and mental health functioning. For a more complete discussion, we highly recommend that you read the NASW standards yourself.

Role of Professionals in Helping Clients With End-of-Life Decisions

As a counselor, you need to be willing to discuss end-of-life decisions when clients bring such concerns to you. If you are closed to any personal examination of this issue, you may interrupt these dialogues, cut off your clients' exploration of their feelings, or attempt to provide clients with your own solutions based on your values and beliefs.

Psychological services are useful for healthy individuals who want to make plans about their own future care. Such services are also beneficial to individuals with life-limiting illnesses, families experiencing the demands of providing end-of-life care, bereaved individuals, and health care providers who are experiencing stress and burnout (Haley et al., 2003). Mental health practitioners need to acquire knowledge about the psychological, ethical, and legal considerations in end-of-life care. They can have a key role in helping people make choices regarding how they will die and about the ethical issues involved in making those choices (Kleespies, 2004). Bennett and Werth (2006) state that the functions of a counselor in cases pertaining to end-of-life decisions are "to help clients get their needs met, maximize client self-determination, help clients engage in informed decision making, and conduct an evaluation or refer clients to receive a thorough assessment regarding their capacity to make end-of-life decisions" (p. 227). As a counselor, you are obligated to assist clients in an informed decision-making process, regardless of your personal feelings about the outcome (Werth & Crow, 2009).

Some end-of-life decisions are made more broadly, such as refusing all treatment. Does a therapist have an ethical responsibility to explore the client's decision to refuse treatment? Even though it is not against the law to refuse treatment, the client may have made this decision based on misinformation or a misunderstanding. Thus, a counselor could help the client assess the nature of the information upon which this decision was based. It is also essential to assess for depression when clients decide to forgo treatment.

Albright and Hazler (1995) acknowledge that counselors will be faced with difficult decisions on what actions to take with clients struggling with end-of-life decisions. They suggest the following interventions to provide direction for clients struggling with these kinds of decisions:

- Learn as much as possible about the course of clients' illnesses, prognoses, and available treatments.
- Know the clients' family support systems and what their views are regarding end-of-life decisions.
- Realize that clients who are near death often need help coping with their psychological pain as well as their physical suffering. Explore clients' fears about dying, the impact of their religious beliefs on their decision or how religion provides them with meaning, and assist them in achieving closure on any unfinished business with others.
- Assume the role of a resource person for these clients.

- Help clients understand the importance of various personal and formal documents associated with the end of life.
- Regardless of the decisions clients make, offer compassion, acceptance, and understanding related to the difficulties in dealing with life and death issues.
- Realize the role of offering comfort to loved ones and friends after the death.

Werth and Holdwick (2000) suggest some additional steps therapists can take. These include giving prospective clients information about the limitations of confidentiality as it applies to assisted death, if applicable; making full use of consultation throughout the process; keeping risk management–oriented notes; and assessing the impact of external coercion on clients' decision making.

A Practitioner's Responsibilities

What are the responsibilities of mental health professionals in counseling people who are facing the end of life when a conflict of values exist? If a therapist's values do not allow for the possibility of a hastened death as the best option for an individual or if the therapist is unable to provide assistance to a client, what is the ethical course to follow? According to Werth and Crow (2009), if counselors are unable to help clients in making end-of-life decisions, they should provide a referral so that clients are not abandoned. Some of these resources include local hospices, palliative care centers, and health-focused counselors.

Another question being raised by experts in the field is, "Who should be trained to provide assistance for people contemplating rational suicide and hastened death decisions?" Silverman (2000) is not convinced that all students and professionals should be trained for situations and careers that they probably will not encounter in their practices. Silverman's contention raises some questions. Although some practitioners may not regularly encounter clients who are considering rational suicide, how can they ethically function when a long-term client might bring up an end-of-life decision? If the request for assistance in hastening the end of life came from a new client, perhaps a therapist could refer this client. But a referral can be much more difficult with a long-term client who brings up ending his or her life. First, would the client follow through in making an appointment with a new therapist? Second, if the therapist was able to discuss the situation with the client, there is always the possibility that this person might change his or her mind.

The mental health professions face the challenge of formulating ethical and procedural guidelines on right-to-die issues, especially in light of advances in medical technology, the aging of the population, and the AIDS epidemic. In addition, in all states patients are free to refuse treatment to prolong life. We agree with Herlihy and Watson's (2004) position that "there will be a growing need for specially trained, culturally competent, and ethical counselors to assist clients with end-of-life decision making" (p. 181). Now let's examine some specific cases involving end-of-life decisions.

■ The Case of Festus.

A counselor has been seeing a client named Festus who has been diagnosed with an aggressive and painful cancer. After a series of chemotherapy treatments and pain medication, Festus tells the counselor that nothing seems to work and that he has decided to end his life. They discuss his decision for several sessions, examining all aspects, and Festus becomes even clearer about his decision to end his life. Here are four counselors' responses to the decision Festus has made.

Counselor A: Have you thought about a specific way you would end your life? If so, I have a duty to prevent you from carrying out an actual suicide by encouraging you to seek hospitalization or to give me a written no suicide contract.

Counselor B: I have a great deal of difficulty accepting your decision. I am asking you not to take any action for at least 3 weeks to give us time to talk about this further. Are there possibly ways for you to find meaning in your life in spite of your suffering?

Counselor C: Our relationship has come to mean a lot to both of us, especially at a time like this. I will continue to see you as long as you choose to come, and I will help you deal with your pain in any way that I can.

Counselor D: I need to consider what you are telling me. I want to continue working with you at this crucial point; however, I would like to consult with my attorney to make sure that I am fulfilling my legal and ethical obligations.

Counselor E: May I have your permission to contact your physician to discuss your medical status?

Consider each of these approaches, and then clarify what you would do in this situation by answering these questions.

- What are your thoughts about each counselor's response? Which one comes closest to your thinking?
- What would you want to say to Festus?
- Is it ethical to impose your values on Festus in this case? Why or why not?
- Do you think the state has the right to decide how individuals with terminal illnesses will die?

Commentary. We are not aware of any statute that imposes a reporting duty on mental health professionals when clients have a life-threatening disability and express threats of self-harm. However, state laws are not uniform with regard to reporting and protecting in the case of suicidal threats, so it is imperative that you become familiar with the law in your state or jurisdiction. According to James Werth, who co-authored a book on the duty to protect, the laws of the majority of states and all ethics codes *allow*, but do not mandate, intervention with respect to danger to self (personal communication, September 8, 2008). Mental health professionals would not typically be found negligent for failing to take steps to protect a client who is considering hastening his or her own death if that person is in the final stages of a terminal illness. If a client is suffering from severe depression, yet is not facing a life-threatening disease, therapists may have an obligation to take steps to prevent suicide or self-harm.

In the case of Festus, Counselor A suggested a "no-suicide" contract. This can be a useful clinical intervention, but it would not insulate a practitioner from liability in all cases. This contract is only one factor in assessing whether the therapist went far enough in trying to protect Festus. Counselor D tells Festus that he wants to consult with an attorney to make sure he is attending to the legal and ethical aspects involved in this case, which is an intervention that we think is sound. Counselor E asks permission of Festus to contact his physician to discuss his medical status, which also seems like a useful strategy.

When you encounter this kind of case, the proper ethical and legal course is not always clear. If you do not report, you may be thinking of your client's autonomy, self-determination, and welfare. If your client is of sound mind, you may believe that he has a right to decide not to live in extreme pain. By providing him with the maximum degree of support as long as he wants this, you may think you have discharged your duty to this client. However, if you do not attempt to prevent his suicide and he does end his life, the family could sue you for breach of your professional duty. If you take measures to protect him from ending his life, and if he terminates his therapy because of your interventions, you will not be in a position to offer support or to help him in other ways.

Given the ethical, legal, and clinical complexity present with a terminally ill client who is contemplating hastening his or her own death, we encourage you to develop competence in managing end-of-life issues if you plan to work with this population. Otherwise, be quick to pursue legal and collegial consultation when this issue emerges in your practice.

■ The Case of Bettina.

Bettina lives at boarding school and has made several suicidal attempts. Because these attempts were judged to be primarily attention-getting gestures, her counselor feels manipulated and does not report them to

Bettina's parents. During the last of these attempts, however, Bettina seriously hurts herself and ends up in the hospital.

- Do you see any conflict between what is ethically right and what is legally right in this situation?
- At what point in the client–counselor relationship is the counselor obligated to report Bettina's harm to self to the proper authorities?
- Did the counselor take the "cry for help" too lightly? Explain.
- What are the ethical and legal implications for the counselor in deciding that Bettina's attempts were more manipulative than serious and therefore should be ignored?
- If the counselor told Bettina that she was going to inform the girl's parents about these suicidal attempts and Bettina had responded by saying that she would quit counseling if the counselor did so, what do you think the counselor should do?

Commentary. It is dangerous to assume that a suicidal attempt is merely an attention-getting behavior. Active measures were not taken by this counselor to protect the client from self-harm. Even one suicidal attempt demands a comprehensive assessment of the client's risk for suicide. This was not done, which resulted in the client's injury and hospitalization. The counselor was vulnerable to an accusation of serious negligence, which could have ended in Bettina's death.

For a comprehensive discussion of the issues associated with end-of-life decisions, we highly recommend Werth, Welfel, and Benjamin's (2009) book, *The Duty to Protect: Ethical, Legal, and Professional Considerations for Mental Health Professionals*.

Chapter Summary

This chapter has addressed a variety of value-laden counseling situations and issues. We have focused our attention on the ways your values and those of your clients, the codes of ethics, and the legal system are interrelated in your counseling relationships.

There is widespread interest in the spiritual and religious beliefs of both counselors and clients and in how these beliefs and values can be an integral part of the therapeutic relationship. Because spiritual and religious values play a vital role in the lives of many who seek counseling, these values can be viewed as a valuable resource in therapy rather than as something to be ignored. In short, spirituality is a major source of strength for many clients and an important factor in promoting healing and well-being. It is important for clinicians to be open to addressing spiritual and religious issues in the assessment and therapeutic process. Counselors need to receive specialized training to address these concerns therapeutically. A counselor's role is not to prescribe a particular pathway to clients in fulfilling their spiritual needs but to help clients clarify their own pathway.

End-of-life decisions are another area in which counselors need to clarify their values. Mental health professionals have the challenge of clarifying their own beliefs and values pertaining to end-of-life decisions so that they can assist their clients in making decisions within the framework of clients' beliefs and value systems. In this matter, the counselor's role is to assist clients in making the best possible decisions in their situation. However, it is essential for professionals to be aware of state laws and professional codes of ethics concerning an individual's freedom to make end-of-life decisions.

It is unlikely that mental health professionals can be neutral in the area of values. It takes honesty and courage to recognize how your values affect the way you counsel, and it takes wisdom to determine when you are not able to work effectively with a client due to a clash of values. Ongoing introspection and discussions with supervisors or colleagues are necessary to determine how to make optimal use of your values in the therapeutic relationship.

Suggested Activities

1. Have a panel discussion on the topic "Is it possible for counselors to remain neutral with respect to their clients' values?" The panel can also discuss different ways in which counselors' values may affect the counseling process.

2. Invite several practicing counselors to talk to your class about the role of values in counseling. Invite counselors who have different theoretical orientations. For example, you might ask a behavior therapist and a humanistic therapist to talk to your class at the same time on the role of values.

3. For a week keep a record of situations where your values guide your actions. Prioritize your values as they are reflected in your record. How do you think these values might influence the way you work with others?

4. In pairs discuss counseling situations that might involve a conflict of values. Then choose a specific situation to role play, with one student playing the part of the client and the other playing the part of the counselor.

5. The case examples given in this chapter address a wide variety of value issues. In small groups, select two or three of these vignettes and discuss how you, as a group, might address the ethical issues raised in each of these cases.

6. In pairs, talk to your partner about the circumstances in which you would consider referring a client to another professional because of a value conflict between you and your client. Can you think of ways to effectively manage this value conflict other than by making a referral?

7. Some counselors believe terminally ill clients have the ultimate right to determine if, how, and when they will end their life. Other counselors believe their obligation is to assist clients in finding meaning in life regardless of a particular set of circumstances. In two groups argue for and against rational suicide, addressing both ethical and legal issues.

8. In this exercise one student acts as the counselor and the other as the client. The task of the counselor is to try to persuade the client to do what the counselor thinks would be best for the client. Then switch roles; afterward discuss what this process was like for you.

Ethics in Action *CD-ROM Exercises*

9. In video role play 4, The Divorce, it is clear that the counselor has an agenda for the client, who has decided to leave her husband and get a divorce. The counselor's focus is on the welfare of her children. The client feels misunderstood and does not think the counselor is helping her. Have one student role play Gary (the counselor in the video) while another student role plays his supervisor. As the supervisor, explore the issues you see being played out.

10. In video role play 5, Doing It My Way, Sally (the counselor) is attempting to influence her client to think about the effect of her behavior on her parents. Charlae is seeking increased independence and wants to break away from her parents. Sally is concerned about what Charlae's parents' reaction might be if she moves out without involving her parents in this decision. Have one student role play the counselor, while another student becomes Sally's supervisor. Through role playing, demonstrate how you might approach the counselor as her supervisor. What would you most want Sally to consider?

11. In video role play 6, The Promiscuous One, the client (Suzanne) is having indiscriminate sexual encounters, and her counselor (Richard) expresses concern for Suzanne when he learns about her sexual promiscuity. Richard then focuses on how Suzanne's behavior plays out the recurring theme of abandonment by her father, while she thinks there is no connection. If you were Suzanne's counselor, how would you deal with the situation as she presents it? Is it ethically appropriate for you to strongly influence your client to engage in safer sex practices? Demonstrate how you would approach Suzanne through role playing.

12. In video role play 7, The Affair, the client (Natalie) shares with her counselor that she is struggling with her marriage and is having a long-term affair. The counselor (Janice) says, "Having an affair is not a good answer for someone—it just hurts everyone. I do not think it is a good idea." How would your values influence your interventions in this situation? Have one student role play the counselor and show how he or she might work with Natalie. In a second role play, have one student become the counselor's supervisor and demonstrate what issues you might explore with Janice.

Chapter 4

Pre-Chapter Self-Inventory

Directions: For each statement, indicate the response that most closely identifies your beliefs and attitudes. Use the following code:

5 = I *strongly agree* with this statement.

4 = I *agree* with this statement.

3 = I am *undecided* about this statement.

2 = I *disagree* with this statement.

1 = I *strongly disagree* with this statement.

_____ 1. Well-trained, sensitive, and self-aware therapists who do not impose their own values on clients are better qualified to be multicultural counselors.

_____ 2. To counsel effectively, I must be of the same ethnic background as my client.

_____ 3. Basically, all counseling interventions are multicultural.

_____ 4. I must challenge cultural stereotypes when they become obvious in counseling situations.

_____ 5. Contemporary counseling theories can be applied to people from all cultures.

_____ 6. With the current emphasis on multiculturalism, counselors are vulnerable to overcorrecting for a perceived imbalance when addressing cultural differences.

_____ 7. I will be able to examine my behavior and attitudes to determine the degree to which cultural bias influences the interventions I make with clients.

_____ 8. Special guidelines are needed for counseling members of ethnic or racial minority groups.

Multicultural Perspectives and Diversity Issues

_____ 9. The codes of ethics of most professional organizations contain culturally biased assumptions.

_____ 10. The primary function of majority-group counselors is to alert their clients to the choices available to them.

_____ 11. An effective mental health practitioner facilitates assimilation of the minority client into society.

_____ 12. Ethical practice requires that counselors become familiar with the value systems of diverse cultural groups.

_____ 13. I would have no trouble working with someone from a culture very different from mine because we would be more alike than different.

_____ 14. If I just listen to my clients, I will know all I need to know about their cultural background.

_____ 15. Client resistance is typically encountered in multicultural counseling and must be resolved before changes can take place.

_____ 16. The ability to observe and understand nonverbal communication is an important component of multicultural counseling.

_____ 17. Establishing a trusting relationship is more difficult when the counselor and the client come from different cultures.

_____ 18. Unless practitioners have been educated about cultural differences, they cannot determine their competency to work with diverse populations.

_____ 19. As a condition for licensure, all counselors should have specialized training and supervised experience in multicultural counseling.

_____ 20. At this point in my educational career, I feel well prepared to counsel culturally diverse client populations.

_____ 21. To be considered competent, I think all mental health professionals need to appreciate the ways that diversity influences the client–counselor relationship and the counseling process itself.

_____ 22. A Christian counselor should refer gay, lesbian, and bisexual clients to another professional.

_____ 23. Gay and lesbian clients are best served by gay and lesbian counselors.

_____ 24. I would have difficulty counseling either a lesbian or gay couple who wanted support in adopting a child.

_____ 25. As a mental health practitioner, it is my ethical responsibility to learn about referral resources for gay, lesbian, and bisexual clients and to make appropriate referrals if clients request them.

Introduction

In this chapter we examine the cultural values, beliefs, and assumptions of helping professionals and their clients and discuss how these values may influence therapeutic work. We emphasize the ethical dimensions of becoming aware of our own values and potential biases, as well as understanding the client's worldview and tailoring the therapeutic process to the client's cultural context. Our cultural experiences, values, and assumptions are the basis of our worldview and possible biases, so it is important to be aware of how they may influence our practice. We also discuss sexual orientation and the values surrounding this topic.

One of the major challenges facing mental health professionals is understanding the complex role cultural diversity and similarity play in their work. Clients and counselors bring a great variety of attitudes, values, culturally learned assumptions, biases, beliefs, and behaviors to the therapeutic relationship. Some counselors deny the importance of these cultural variables in counseling; others overemphasize the importance of cultural differences, lose their naturalness, and may fail to make contact with their clients. Working effectively with cultural diversity in the therapeutic process is a requirement of good ethical practice. Pack-Brown, Thomas, and Seymour (2008) emphasize the ethical responsibility of counselors to provide professional services that demonstrate respect for the cultural worldviews, values, and traditions of culturally diverse clients. They contend that "cultural issues affect all aspects of the counseling process, including ethical considerations that emerge from the time the counselor first meets a client to termination of the helping endeavor"(p. 297). Because each of us is unique, all counseling interactions can be seen as multicultural events.

Duran, Firehammer, and Gonzalez (2008) assert that culture is part of the soul: "When the soul or culture of some persons are oppressed, we are all oppressed and wounded in ways that require healing if we are to become liberated from such oppression. When discussing these issues, it is important to realize that we have all been on both sides of the oppression/oppressor coin at different points in our lives" (p. 288). Mental health practitioners must avoid using their own group as the standard by which to assess appropriate behavior in others. In addition, greater differences may exist within the same cultural group than between different cultural groups, and we need to be intraculturally sensitive as well as multiculturally sensitive. Cultural sensitivity is not limited to one group but applies to all cultures. There is no sanctuary from cultural bias.

Cultural diversity, as well as cultural prejudice, is a fact of life in our world. Yet it is only within the past couple of decades that helping professionals have realized that they can no longer ignore the pressing issues involved in serving culturally diverse populations. To the extent that counselors are focused on the values of the dominant culture and insensitive to variations among groups and individuals, they are at risk for practicing unethically (Barnett & Johnson, 2010). It is essential to be mindful of diversity if we are to practice ethically and effectively.

Multicultural Terminology

The word **culture** can be interpreted broadly. It can be associated with a racial or ethnic group as well as with gender, religion, economic status, nationality, physical capacity or disability, and affectional or sexual orientation. Pedersen (2000) describes culture as including demographic variables such as age, gender, and place of residence; status variables such as social, educational, and economic background; formal and informal affiliations; and the ethnographic variables of nationality, ethnicity, language, and religion. Considering culture from this broad perspective provides a context for understanding that each of us is simultaneously a member of many different cultures. Culture can be considered as a lens through which life is perceived. Each culture, through its differences and similarities, generates a phenomenologically different experience of reality (Diller, 2007).

Ethnicity is a sense of identity that stems from common ancestry, history, nationality, religion, and race. This unique social and cultural heritage provides cohesion and strength. It is a powerful unifying force that offers a sense of belonging and sharing based on commonality (Lum, 2004; Markus, 2008).

Ethnic minority group refers to a group of people who have been singled out for differential and unequal treatment and who regard themselves as objects of collective discrimination. These groups have been characterized as subordinate, dominated, and powerless. Thus, minority is often defined by the condition of oppression rather than by numerical criteria. Although the term *minority* has traditionally referred to national, racial, linguistic, and religious groups, it now also applies to women, the elderly, gay men, lesbians, bisexuals, and people with disabilities (Atkinson, 2004).

Multiculturalism is a generic term that indicates any relationship between and within two or more diverse groups. A multicultural perspective takes into consideration the specific values, beliefs, and actions influenced by a client's ethnicity, gender, religion, socioeconomic status, political views, sexual orientation, geographic region, and

(*continued on next page*)

historical experiences with the dominant culture. Multiculturalism provides a conceptual framework that recognizes the complex diversity of a pluralistic society, while at the same time suggesting bridges of shared concern that bind culturally different individuals to one another (Pedersen, 1991, 2000).

Multicultural counseling refers to a helping intervention and process that defines contextual goals consistent with the life experiences and cultural values of clients, balancing the importance of individualism versus collectivism in assessment, diagnosis, and treatment (Sue & Sue, 2008).

Cultural diversity refers to the spectrum of differences that exists among groups of people with definable and unique cultural backgrounds (Diller, 2007).

Diversity refers to individual differences on a number of variables that place clients at risk for discrimination based on age, gender, gender identity, race, ethnicity, culture, national origin, religion, sexual orientation, disability, language, or socioeconomic status (Welfel, 2010). Both multiculturalism and diversity have been politicized in the United States in ways that have often been divisive, but these terms can equally represent positive assets in a pluralistic society.

Cultural diversity competence refers to a practitioner's level of awareness, knowledge, and interpersonal skill when working with individuals from diverse backgrounds.

Cultural empathy pertains to therapists' awareness of clients' worldviews, which are acknowledged in relation to therapists' awareness of their own personal biases (Pedersen, Crethar, & Carlson, 2008; Roysircar, 2004). The Scale of Ethnocultural Empathy measures empathy from a cultural perspective in the client–counselor relationship (see Wang et al., 2003).

Culture-centered counseling is a three-stage developmental sequence, from multicultural awareness to knowledge and comprehension to skills and applications. The individual's or group's culture plays a central role in understanding their behavior in context (Pedersen, 2000).

Stereotypes are oversimplified and uncritical generalizations about individuals who are identified as belonging to a specific group. Such learned expectations can influence how you see the client.

Racism is any pattern of behavior that, solely because of race or culture, denies access to opportunities or privileges to members of one racial or cultural group while perpetuating access to opportunities and privileges to members of another racial or cultural group (Ridley, 2005). Racism can operate on both individual and institutional levels, and it can occur intentionally or unintentionally.

Unintentional racism is often subtle, indirect, and outside our conscious awareness; this can be the most damaging and insidious form of racism (Sue, 2005). Practitioners who presume that they are free of any traces of racism seriously underestimate the impact of their own socialization. Whether these biased attitudes are intentional or unintentional, the result is harmful for both individuals and society.

Cultural racism is the belief that one group's history, way of life, religion, values, and traditions are superior to others. This allows for an unequal distribution of power to be justified a priori (Sue, 2005).

Note about names: There is some concern about how to refer appropriately to certain racial and ethnic groups as preferred names tend to change. For instance, some alternate names for one group are Hispanic, Latino (Latina), Mexican American, or Chicana (Chicano). Practitioners can show sensitivity to the fact that a name is important by asking their clients how they would like to be identified.

In this chapter we focus on the ethical implications of a multicultural perspective or lack thereof in the helping professions. To ensure that the terms we use in this chapter have a clear meaning, we have provided specific definitions in the box titled "Multicultural Terminology." This is a complex and rapidly developing field; practitioners are advised to stay current on these developments.

The Problem of Cultural Tunnel Vision

Many students come into training knowing only their own culture and may assume that there is only one "normal" set of behaviors. This can lead to **cultural tunnel vision,** a perception of reality based on a very limited set of cultural experiences. Trainees could unwittingly impose their values on unsuspecting clients by assuming that everyone shares these values. It is essential that they explore their attitudes and fears of people who are different from themselves. At times, student helpers from the majority group have expressed the attitude, explicitly or implicitly, that racial and ethnic minorities are unresponsive to professional psychological intervention because of their lack of motivation to change, which these student helpers label as "resistance." They may never stop to think that what they call resistance may be a healthy response on the part of the client to the helper's cultural and theoretical bias.

Students are not alone in their susceptibility to cultural tunnel vision. Ridley (2005) points out that racism has been present in mental health delivery systems for quite some time. Studies from the 1950s to the present have documented enduring patterns of racism in mental health care delivery systems. The impact of racism on various racial groups and the existence of racism in a variety of treatment settings is well documented.

Gilbert Wrenn (1962), one of the pioneers in the counseling profession, characterizes a **culturally encapsulated counselor** as having some of the following traits:

- Defines reality according to one set of cultural assumptions
- Shows insensitivity to cultural variations among individuals
- Accepts unreasoned assumptions without proof or ignores proof because that might disconfirm one's assumptions
- Fails to evaluate other viewpoints and makes little attempt to accommodate the behavior of others
- Is trapped in one way of thinking that resists adaptation and rejects alternatives

Years later, Wrenn (1985) maintained that cultural encapsulation continues to be a problem for counseling professionals. Pack-Brown, Thomas, and Seymour (2008) contend that "the cultural encapsulation in the counseling field helps to perpetuate various cultural biases that are antithetical to the worldview, values, and psychological well-being of many persons from diverse cultural groups and backgrounds" (p. 297).

A good place to begin to develop a multicultural perspective is by becoming more aware of your own culturally learned assumptions, some of which may be culturally biased (Pedersen, 2003). This will provide a context for understanding how diverse cultures share common ground and also how to recognize areas of similarity and uniqueness. Pedersen (2008) believes that it is no longer possible for effective counselors to ignore their own cultures or the cultures of their clients through encapsulation. Whether we are aware of it or not, Pedersen claims that culture controls our lives and defines reality for each of us. Cultural factors are an integral part of the helping process and influence the interventions we make with our clients. "Until the multicultural perspective is understood as having positive consequences toward making psychology more rather than less relevant and increasing rather than decreasing the quality of psychology, little real change is likely to occur" (p. 15).

Learning to Address Cultural Pluralism

Cultural pluralism is a perspective that recognizes the complexity of cultures and values the diversity of beliefs and values. To operate as if all our clients are the same is not in accord with reality, and it can result in unethical and ineffective practice. Pedersen (2000) reminds us that culture is complex, yet this complexity can be viewed as friend rather than foe because it helps us avoid searching for easy answers to hard questions.

Roysircar and colleagues (2003) emphasize the importance of cultural self-awareness, which is captured in the motto, "Therapist, know thy cultural self." They assert that therapists' cultural self-awareness is essential for effective and culturally relevant therapy. Therapist self-awareness facilitates the client's therapeutic journey.

The Challenges of Reaching Diverse Client Populations

The multicultural counseling competencies developed by the Association for Multicultural Counseling and Development (Roysircar et al., 2003) provide a framework for the effective delivery of services to diverse client populations. Another useful resource is the APA's (1993) "Guidelines for Providers of Psychological Services to Ethnic, Linguistic, and Culturally Diverse Populations." The APA's guidelines challenge practitioners to respect the roles of family members and the community structures, hierarchies, values, and beliefs that are an integral part of the client's culture. Providers should identify resources in the client's family and the larger community and use them in delivering culturally sensitive services. For example, an entire Native American family may come to a clinic to provide support for an individual in distress because many of the healing practices found in Native American communities are centered on the family and the community.

The *Guidelines on Multicultural Education, Training, Research, Practice, and Organizational Change for Psychologists* (APA, 2003a) address the knowledge and skills needed for the profession as a result of the sociopolitical changes within the United States. These guidelines provide psychologists with a framework for delivering services to an increasingly diverse population, and they can be useful for helpers in various mental health professions. Summary statements for the six guidelines follow:

1. Psychologists are encouraged to recognize that, as cultural beings, they may hold attitudes and beliefs that can detrimentally influence their perceptions of and interactions with individuals who are ethnically and racially different from themselves. (p. 382)

2. Psychologists are encouraged to recognize the importance of multicultural sensitivity/responsiveness to, knowledge of, and understanding about ethnically and racially different individuals. (p. 385)

3. As educators, psychologists are encouraged to employ the constructs of multiculturalism and diversity in psychological education. (p. 386)

4. Culturally sensitive psychological researchers are encouraged to recognize the importance of conducting culture-centered and ethical psychological research among persons from ethnic, linguistic, and racial minority backgrounds. (p. 388)

5. Psychologists are encouraged to apply culturally appropriate skills in clinical and other applied psychological practices. (p. 390)

6. Psychologists are encouraged to use organizational change processes to support culturally informed organizational (policy) development and practices. (p. 392)

These guidelines do not form a dogmatic set of prescriptions. It is recognized that the integration of racial and ethnic factors into psychological theory, practice, and research has only recently begun and is an ongoing process.

Psychology has traditionally been based on Western assumptions, which have not always considered the influence and impact of racial and cultural socialization (APA, 2003a). Many clients have come to distrust helpers associated with the establishment or with social service agencies because of a history of unequal treatment. These clients may be slow to form trusting relationships with counselors, and mental health professionals may have difficulty identifying with these clients if they ignore the history behind this distrust. Helpers from all cultural groups need to honestly examine their own assumptions, expectations, and attitudes about the helping process.

The medical model of clinical counseling is seldom a good fit for people in the lower socioeconomic class. The child care and transportation challenges are insurmountable economic barriers for many. In addition, taking time off from work for medical appointments may mean loss of pay. Therapists must be willing to go outside of the office to deliver services in the community. Home-based therapy has been used extensively with ethnic minority clients and families, mainly because many people in the community often do not trust traditional mental health professionals (Zur, 2008). Zur comments that making a home visit with these clients can be a way to get a firsthand view of their home, rituals, neighborhood, community, and support system. Going outside the office can decrease suspicion and enhance trust. Delivering helping services in nontraditional ways is discussed in detail in Chapter 13.

Sometimes cultural traditions contribute to the underutilization of traditional psychotherapeutic services by minority clients. An Asian American person, for example, may not seek professional help immediately when faced with a problem. Consider Binh's experience of being torn between marrying a person selected by his parents and marrying a woman of his choice. He might first look for a solution within himself through contemplation. If he were unable to resolve his dilemma, he might seek assistance from a family member or a clergy person. Then he might look to some of his friends for advice and support in making the best decision. If none of these approaches resulted in a satisfactory resolution of his problem, Binh might then reach outside his cultural community for an "outside expert" as a last resort. The fact that he did not seek counseling services sooner has little to do with resistance or with insensitivity on the part of counselors; Binh was following a route congruent with his cultural background.

Some argue that ethnic minority clients who use counseling resources may lose their cultural values in the process. Some culturally encapsulated helpers mistakenly assume that a lack of assertiveness is a sign of dysfunctional behavior that should be changed. Labeling this behavior dysfunctional reflects the counselor's value orientation. Practitioners need to consider whether passivity is a problem from the client's culturally learned perspective and whether assertiveness is a useful behavior that the client hopes to acquire.

Ethics Codes From a Diversity Perspective

Most ethics codes mention the practitioner's responsibility to recognize the special needs of diverse client populations. Watson, Herlihy, and Pierce (2006) maintain that counselors have been slow to recognize a connection between multicultural competence and ethical behavior. They further state that reliance on ethics codes alone does not guarantee multicultural competence. Take the time to review the ethics codes of one or more professional organizations to determine for yourself the degree to which such codes take

Ethics Codes

Addressing Diversity

The **Feminist Therapy Institute's** (2000) code of ethics has four separate guidelines pertaining to cultural diversity and oppression:

A. A feminist therapist increases her accessibility to and for a wide range of clients from her own and other identified groups through flexible delivery of services. When appropriate, the feminist therapist assists clients in accessing other services and intervenes when a client's rights are violated.

B. A feminist therapist is aware of the meaning and impact of her own ethnic and cultural background, gender, class, age, and sexual orientation, and actively attempts to become knowledgeable about alternatives from sources other than her clients. She is actively engaged in broadening her knowledge of ethnic and cultural experiences, non-dominant and dominant.

C. Recognizing that the dominant culture determines the norm, the therapist's goal is to uncover and respect cultural and experiential differences, including those based on long term or recent immigration and/or refugee status.

D. A feminist therapist evaluates her ongoing interactions with her clientele for any evidence of her biases or discriminatory attitudes and practices. She also monitors her other interactions, including service delivery, teaching, writing, and all professional activities. The feminist therapist accepts responsibility for taking action to confront and change any interfering, oppressing, or devaluing biases she has.

The **Canadian Counselling Association's** (2007) code of ethics calls for members to respect diversity.

Counsellors actively work to understand the diverse cultural background of the clients with whom they work, and do not condone or engage in discrimination based on age, colour, culture, ethnicity, disability, gender, religion, sexual orientation, marital, or socio-economic status. (B.9.)

The **NAADAC Code of Ethics** (2008) addresses nondiscrimination:

I shall affirm diversity among colleagues or clients regardless of age, gender, sexual orientation, ethnic/racial background, religious/spiritual beliefs, marital status, political beliefs, or mental/physical disability.

In the Preamble of the **Code of Professional Ethics for Rehabilitation Counselors** (CRCC, 2010), the following statement recognizes the value of diversity:

Rehabilitation counselors are committed to facilitating the personal, social, and economic independence of individuals with disabilities. In fulfilling this commitment, rehabilitation counselors recognize diversity and embrace a cultural approach in support of the worth, dignity, potential, and uniqueness of individuals with disabilities within their social and cultural context. They look to professional values as an important way of living out an ethical commitment.

The *Ethical Standards for School Counselors* (ASCA, 2004) addresses the role of diversity in school counseling in Section E.2: School counselors are expected to become aware of their own attitudes, cultural values, and biases that can affect their cultural competence. They are also expected to possess knowledge and understanding about how oppression, racism, discrimination, and stereotyping affect them personally and professionally.

In the **NASW** *Code of Ethics* (2008), cultural competence and recognition of social diversity are clearly linked to ethical practice. Here are two relevant guidelines:

Social workers should have a knowledge base of their clients' cultures and be able to demonstrate competence in the provision of services that are sensitive to clients' cultures and to differences among people and cultural groups. (1.05.b.)

(*continued on next page*)

Social workers should obtain education about and seek to understand the nature of social diversity and oppression with respect to race, ethnicity, national origin, color, sex, sexual orientation, gender identity or expression, age, marital status, political belief, religion, immigration status, and mental or physical disability. (1.05.c.)

The *Code of Ethics* of the **Canadian Association of Social Workers** (1994) has this non-discrimination standard:

A social worker in the practice of social work shall not discriminate against any person on the basis of race, ethnic background, language, religion, marital status, sex, sexual orientation, age, abilities, socio-economic status, political affiliation or national ancestry. (1.2.)

The **APA** (2002) ethics code indicates that part of competence implies understanding diversity:

Where scientific or professional knowledge in the discipline of psychology establishes that an understanding of factors associated with age, gender, gender identity, race, ethnicity, culture, national origin, religion, sexual orientation, disability, language, or socioeconomic status is essential for effective implementation of their services or research, psychologists have or obtain the training, experience, consultation, or supervision necessary to ensure the competence of their services, or they make appropriate referrals. (2.01.b.)

The **ACA** (2005) ethics code infuses issues of multiculturalism and diversity throughout the document, including sections dealing with the counseling relationship, informed consent, bartering, accepting gifts, confidentiality and privacy, professional responsibility, assessment and diagnosis, supervision, and education and training programs.

Multicultural/Diversity Considerations: Counselors maintain awareness and sensitivity regarding cultural meanings of confidentiality and privacy. Counselors respect differing views toward disclosure of information. Counselors hold ongoing discussions with clients as to how, when, and with whom information is to be shared. (B.1.a.)

Cultural Sensitivity and Diagnosis of Mental Disorders: Counselors recognize that culture affects the manner in which clients' problems are defined. Clients' socioeconomic and cultural experiences are considered when diagnosing mental disorders. (E.5.b.)

Multicultural Issues/Diversity in Assessment: Counselors use with caution assessment techniques that were normed on populations other than that of the client. Counselors recognize the effects of age, color, culture, disability, ethnic group, gender, race, language preference, religion, spirituality, sexual orientation, and socioeconomic status on test administration and interpretation, and place test results in proper perspective with other relevant factors. (E.8.)

multicultural dimensions into account. Then consider how you could increase your multicultural competencies beyond what it is suggested by these codes. The Ethics Codes box titled "Addressing Diversity" provides an overview of how the various codes address these issues.

Cultural Values and Assumptions in Therapy

Oppression has resulted in *soul wounding* (deep psychological and spiritual pain) for persons in diverse groups (Duran, Firehammer, & Gonzalez, 2008). Duran and colleagues caution that counselors who operate from culturally biased views of mental health and who use intervention strategies that are not congruent with the values of culturally diverse people perpetuate forms of injustice and institutional racism. Sue and Sue (2008) contend that some therapeutic practices reflect racism, sexism, and other forms of prejudice; this ethnocentric bias has been destructive to the natural help-giving networks of minority communities. Helpers need to expand their perception of mental health practices to include support systems such as family, friends, community, self-help programs, and occupational networks.

Clinicians may misunderstand clients of a different sex, race, age, social class, or sexual orientation. If practitioners fail to integrate these diversity factors into their practice, they are infringing on the client's cultural autonomy and basic human rights, which limits their ability to be helpful. Ethical practice requires that practitioners be trained to address these diversity factors when they become relevant in the therapy process.

In the cases that follow, the therapists impose their values in ways that significantly detracted from the value of therapy and may have resulted in significant harm to the clients. Values imposition can be transparent—as in these cases—or more insidious, but it is always unethical.

■ The Case of Lee.

Stacy is a high school counselor. A Vietnamese student, Lee, is assigned to her because of academic difficulties. Stacy observes that Lee is slow and deliberate in his conversational style, and she immediately assigns him to a remedial speech class. In the course of their conversations, Lee discloses to Stacy that his father wants him to apply to college and major in pre-med. Lee is not sure that he even wants to attend college. Stacy gives Lee a homework assignment, asking him to tell his father that he no longer wants to pursue college plans and wants to follow a direction that appeals to him.

- Was the fact that Lee spoke slowly and deliberately an indication that he needed a remedial speech class? Can you offer other explanations for Lee's slow and deliberate speech?
- If you were Lee's therapist, how would you deal with the conflict between Lee's goals and his father's expectations?

- Was Stacy culturally sensitive when asking Lee to directly confront his father? What other alternatives were available?
- Was Stacy too quick in making her assessments, considering that Lee was sent to the school counselor by a teacher? Would it have made a difference if he had come voluntarily for guidance?
- Would you recommend family counseling? If so, how would you present this to Lee and his parents?
- How would the ethics code guidelines on diversity influence your approach to working with Lee?

Commentary. When there is a cultural difference between the counselor and client, counselors must familiarize themselves with how the client approaches counseling and avoid imposing their worldview on the client. Although we hope the counselor would explore with Lee his choice of a major in college and the conflict with his father over his educational and career plans, we do not think it is appropriate for the counselor to tell Lee what to do. Our assessment skills need to encompass the cultural context and the consequences of proposed interventions on the client's life.

■ The Case of Cynthia.

Ling has recently set up a private practice in a culturally mixed neighborhood. Cynthia comes to Ling for counseling. She is depressed, feels that life has little meaning, and feels enslaved by the needs of her husband and small children. When Ling asks about any recent events that could be contributing to her depression, she tells him that she has discussed with her husband her desire to return to school and pursue a career of her choosing. Her husband threatened a divorce if she followed through with her plans. Cynthia then consulted with her pastor, who pointed out her obligations to her family. Ling is aware of his own cultural biases, which include a strong commitment to family and to the role of the man as the head of the household. Although he feels empathy for Cynthia's struggle, he persuades her to postpone her own aspirations until her children have grown up. She agrees to this because she feels guilty about asserting her own needs, and she is also fearful of being left alone. Ling then works with her to find other ways to add meaning to her life that would not have such a dramatic impact on the family.

- List the potential gender and cultural issues in this case. How might you have addressed each of them?
- Ling did not explore the lack of meaning in Cynthia's life until after he persuaded her to give up her aspirations. What ethical issue does this raise?

- If Cynthia had shared Ling's family values, would his approach have been appropriate?

- Because Ling and Cynthia did not share similar values, was a referral indicated? Why or why not?

- How would the ethics code guidelines on diversity influence your approach to working with Cynthia?

Commentary. Cynthia spoke with two significant people regarding her aspirations, and both of them rejected her goals. The therapist also ignored her aspirations. A more ethical approach would be to provide a supportive environment in which Cynthia could explore her struggles without the therapist imposing his agenda on her. Cynthia should not feel pressured to adopt the therapist's value system, nor let her actions be determined by her need to please the therapist. Ling's ethical duty is to listen to Cynthia's aspirations without judgment and to respect her struggle in her journey toward finding her own answers.

Western Versus Eastern Values

Eastern and Western are not just geographic terms but also represent philosophical, social, political, and cultural orientations. Within these broad divisions even greater differences can be found, but it seems clear that many Eastern values differ from those common to Western thinkers. Writers in the field of multicultural counseling allege that most contemporary theories of therapy and therapeutic practices are grounded in Western assumptions, yet most of the world differs from mainstream U.S. culture (Duran et al., 2008; Ivey et al., 2007; Pedersen, 2003). The strong individualistic bias of contemporary theories and the lack of emphasis on broader social contexts, such as families, groups, and communities, provide little of value for diverse clients. Professional psychological help is not a typical option for many minority groups. Duran and colleagues (2008) claim that Western counseling interventions have at times been used to promote social control and conformity rather than the psychological well-being of people in diverse groups: "The counseling profession has not had the humility to critically assess the depths of the culturally biased nature of its helping methods nor the negative outcomes that commonly ensue from imposing Western helping theories and practices among clients from diverse groups and backgrounds" (p. 290). Other writers also describe ways that culturally biased counseling theories and practices can result in ineffective and unethical counseling practices (Ivey et al., 2007; Pack-Brown, Thomas, & Seymour, 2008).

Practitioners who draw from any of the contemporary therapeutic models would do well to reflect on the underlying values of their theoretical orientation. Many of the therapy systems reflect core value orientations of mainstream U.S. culture. Hogan (2007) summarizes the underlying values of American culture, with its roots in the Anglo-Saxon culture of the English, as being characterized by an emphasis on the patriarchal nuclear family; keeping busy; measurable and visible accomplishments; individual choice, responsibility, and achievement; self-reliance and self-motivation; change and novel ideas; and equality, informality, and fair play. The degree to which these value orientations fit clients from Eastern cultures needs to be carefully considered by practitioners.

Challenging Stereotypical Beliefs and Cultural Bias

Helpers may think they are not culturally biased, yet may continue to hold stereotypical beliefs and cultural biases that could affect their practice. Some examples include these statements: "Failure to change stems from a lack of motivation";"People have choices, and it is up to them to change their lives." To assume that all these people lack is motivation is simplistic and judgmental and does not encourage exploration of their struggles. Furthermore, many people do not have a wide range of choices due to environmental factors beyond their control. Another often held assumption is that "talk therapy" works best. This ignores the fact that many cultures have alternative practices that people rely on for regaining psychological health. Therapists can discover their cultural beliefs and stereotypes by reflecting on their cultural and race-based thoughts and feelings, both positive and negative (Roysircar, 2004).

Practitioners who counsel persons in diverse groups without an awareness of their own stereotypical beliefs, cultural biases, and faulty assumptions can cause harm to their clients. Therapists not trained in addiction treatment can bring harm to their clients dealing with substance abuse due to the therapists' faulty assumptions and misconceptions. One of these assumptions is that willpower alone is sufficient to turn a person's life around. Ethical practice requires that mental health practitioners be aware of the unique cultural realities of their clients. Furthermore, ethical practice implies that counselors actively deal with attitudinal barriers. The *Code of Professional Ethics for Rehabilitation Counselors* (CRCC, 2010) identifies advocacy as a part of ethical practice:

> In direct service with the client, rehabilitation counselors address attitudinal barriers, including stereotyping and discrimination, toward individuals with disabilities. They increase their own awareness and sensitivity to individuals with disabilities. (C.1.a.)

Reflect on these issues as you consider the following case example.

■ The Case of Claudine.

Claudine takes over as director of a clinic that has a large percentage of Asian immigrants as clients. At a staff meeting she sums up her philosophy of counseling in this fashion: "People come to counseling to begin change or because they are already in the process of change. Our purpose is to challenge them to continue their change. This holds true whether the client is Euro-American, Asian, or some other minority. If clients are hesitant to speak, our job is to challenge them to speak, because the expectation in American culture is that people deal with problems through talking. Silence may be appropriate in Asian culture, but it does not work in this non-Asian culture. The sooner clients learn this, the better off they are."

- To what extent do you agree or disagree with Claudine's assumptions, and why?
- Do you see any value in the point she is trying to make?

Commentary. Pedersen (2000) would say that Claudine is a culturally encapsulated counselor because she is defining everyone's reality according to her own cultural assumptions and values. She is minimizing cultural differences by imposing her own standards as criteria for judging the behavior of others. In defense of Claudine, there is some truth in her premise regarding a counselor's role in challenging a client to change. However, the key point is that therapists need to first understand the worldview of their clients and then invite them to decide on change that is congruent with their own values and goals.

Examining Some Common Assumptions

Unexamined assumptions can be harmful to clients, especially assumptions based on cultural biases. What is good for one is not good for all. Pack-Brown, Thomas, and Seymour (2008) emphasize that becoming culturally competent clinicians involves acknowledging that they bring personal cultural biases, prejudices, and stereotypes to their work with clients. When students are helped to recognize their cultural biases and assumptions, they are less likely to act against the best interests of clients who come from diverse groups and backgrounds. Let's look at a few of these commonly held beliefs and assumptions about the therapeutic environment.

Assumptions about self-disclosure. Therapists may assume that clients will be ready to talk about their intimate personal issues, or that self-disclosure is essential for the therapeutic process to work. Sue and Sue (2008) point out that most forms of contemporary therapy value one's ability to self-disclose by sharing intimate personal material. The assumption is that self-disclosure is a characteristic of a healthy personality. The converse is that individuals who are reluctant to self-disclose in therapy possess negative traits such as being guarded and mistrustful. However, it is unacceptable in some cultures to reveal personal problems because it not only reflects on the person individually but also on the whole family. Some clients may view self-disclosure and interpersonal warmth as inappropriate in a professional relationship with an authority figure (Barnett & Johnson, 2010). There are strong pressures on many Asian American clients not to reveal personal concerns to strangers or outsiders. Similar pressures have been reported for Hispanic, American Indian, African American, and many European clients. Therapists need to realize that cultural forces may be operating when clients are slow to disclose personal details. Indeed, for many clients it seems strange, and even absurd, for them to talk about themselves personally to a professional therapist whom they do not know. This is illustrated in Alberto's case.

■ The Case of Alberto.

Alberto, a Latino client, comes to a community college counseling center on the recommendation of his physician, who found no organic basis for his symptoms of depression, chronic sleep disturbance, and the imminent threat of failing his classes. As you begin your initial session with Alberto, you recognize that he is extremely guarded, revealing little about himself or how he is feeling. You believe that self-disclosure and openness to the expression of feelings are necessary for change to occur. In trying to help Alberto, you challenge him to be more self-disclosing.

- How sensitive are you to your client's sense of privacy and to his cultural values?
- Would you encourage Alberto to be more self-disclosing without first understanding the possible consequences to him in his outside life? Explain.
- How might your interventions reflect your lack of understanding of the importance of the extended family in Alberto's culture?
- Can you think of some reasons Alberto's cautiousness may be more adaptive than maladaptive?

Commentary. It is important not to pathologize a client who is cautious during the early phase of therapy. Be aware of and respect the differences that exist among different cultures in establishing trust, especially in the beginning of a therapeutic relationship. For some, it is very foreign to speak to a stranger without first developing a rapport with the person. Some clients have a greater need than others to develop a relationship with a therapist before they make themselves vulnerable. The fact that Alberto followed through on his physician's recommendation is a sign that he is open to help, and your task is to provide the structure that allows him to feel safe enough to express his concerns. It would be especially useful for you to explain to Alberto how the therapeutic process works. The case of Alberto reminds us that counselors must ensure their own competence—in this case cultural competence—before launching into therapy work with culturally different clients.

■ The Case of Lily.

Lily, a licensed counselor, has come to work in a family-life center that deals with many immigrant families. She often reacts impatiently with the pace of her clients' disclosures. Lily decides to teach her clients by modeling for them. With one of her reticent couples she says: "My husband and I fight and disagree a lot. We express our feelings openly and clear the air. In fact, several years ago my husband had an affair, which put our relationship into turmoil. I believe it was my ability to vent my anger and express my hurt that allowed me to work through this terrible event."

- How do you evaluate Lily's self-disclosure? Would such a disclosure be useful to you if you were her client?
- Would you be inclined to make a similar type of disclosure to your clients? Why or why not?
- In your opinion, is such a disclosure ever appropriate? Why or why not?

Commentary. Therapist self-disclosure can be a valuable aspect of the therapeutic process and can assist clients in achieving agreed-upon treatment goals (Barnett, 1998). However, it is important to ensure that it is the client's needs and issues that are the focus of treatment. Self-disclosure that is done for the benefit of the therapist, that burdens the client with unnecessary information, or that creates a role reversal where a client takes care of the therapist can be considered a boundary violation (Zur, 2009). This self-disclosure should never be used to meet the clinician's personal needs at the expense of the client's treatment needs. In this case, without taking the time to really know her clients, Lily burdened them with self-disclosures in her impatience and her rush to find a solution. Lily's disclosure seems designed to justify her own behavior rather than to help her culturally different client couple.

Assumptions about directness and respect.   Western therapeutic approaches tend to stress directness and assertiveness, yet in some cultures directness is perceived as rudeness and something to be avoided. Americans generally want to get to the "bottom line" and tend to get impatient when that does not happen. People from many cultures value less direct styles of communication. For example, Latinos engage in "platica" (small talk) before beginning to address their concerns. The counselor could assume that this lack of directness is evidence of pathology, or at least a lack of assertiveness, rather than a sign of respect. If therapists cannot connect to clients using the techniques in which they were trained, it is incumbent on them to find other ways to connect with their clients. Simply put, when therapists have trouble understanding and working with a client, the client is not the problem. The problem rests with the therapist's inability to come up with a way to facilitate the client's exploration of his or her problem. For example, a counselor could say: "I am trying to find a way to help you articulate your difficulty, but so far I have not been successful. Is there something I am doing that is making it difficult for you to go further?" The case of Miguel provides another example of a therapist's assumptions about directness.

■ The Case of Miguel.

Miguel, a Latino born in the United States, has completed his PhD and is working at a community clinic in family therapy. In his training he has learned about the concepts of directness, assertiveness, and triangulation (the tendency of two persons who are in conflict to involve a third person in their emotional system to reduce the stress). Miguel is watching for evidence of these tendencies. While he is counseling a Latino family, the father says to his son, "Your mother expects you to show her more respect than you do and to obey her." Miguel says to the mother, "Can you say this directly to your son rather than allowing your husband to speak for you?" The room falls silent, and there is great discomfort.

- How might Miguel have handled this situation differently?
- What were Miguel's assumptions?

Commentary. As with many vignettes in this book, we cannot emphasize enough the need for cultural sensitivity. The "great discomfort in the room" was evidence that something had gone astray. To intervene in a respectful and helpful way, Miguel could have begun by acknowledging the patriarchal communication mode common to many Latino families. By focusing on the variables of directness and triangulation, Miguel missed other aspects of the moment. His intervention was ill timed because he had not established a strong connection with the family. Miguel's response to what occurred in this session could be the deciding factor in whether the family returns for another session.

Clinicians may assume that being assertive is better than being nonassertive and that clients are better off if they can tell people directly what they think and what they want. However, every culture deals with interpersonal situations in a unique way. It is critical to recognize that there are different perspectives on the value of being direct and assertive; therapists should avoid assuming that assertive behavior is the norm and is desirable for everyone.

Assumptions about self-actualization and trusting relationships.   Many mental health professionals assume that it is important for the individual to become an authentic person. Counselor may focus on self-actualization for the individual without regard for the impact of the individual's change on the significant people in that person's life or the impact of those significant people on the client. A creative synthesis between self-actualization and responsibility to the group may be a more realistic goal for some clients.

Another assumption pertains to the quality of the personal relationship between therapist and client. In many Western cultures people talk more readily about their personal lives than do those in other cultures. This characteristic is reflected in most therapeutic approaches. Although clinicians expect some resistance, they assume that clients will eventually be willing to explore personal issues. In many cultures this kind of a relationship takes a long time to develop. Many Asian Americans, Hispanics, and Native Americans have been brought up not to speak until spoken to, especially when they are with the elderly or with authority figures. A counselor may interpret the client's hesitancy to speak as resistance when it is really a sign of respect.

Assumptions about nonverbal behavior. Many cultural expressions are subject to misinterpretation, including appropriate personal space, eye contact, handshaking, dress, formality of greeting, perspective on time, and so forth. Westerners tend to feel uncomfortable with periods of silence and tend to talk to ease their tension. In some cultures silence may be a sign of respect and politeness rather than a lack of a desire to continue to speak. Silence may be a reflection of fear or confusion, or it may be a cautious expression and reluctance to do what the counselor is expecting of the client.

Students in the helping professions are often systematically trained in a range of microskills that include attending, open communication, observation, hearing clients accurately, noting and reflecting feelings, and selecting and structuring, to mention a few (Ivey, Ivey, & Zalaquett, 2010). Although these behaviors are aimed at creating a positive therapeutic relationship, individuals from certain ethnic groups may have difficulty responding positively or understanding the intent of the counselor's instructions and behavior. The counselor whose confrontational style involves direct eye contact, physical gestures, and probing personal questions could be seen as intrusive by clients from another culture.

In Western middle-class culture, direct eye contact is usually considered a sign of interest and presence, and a lack thereof can be viewed as being evasive. However, even in this culture an individual often maintains more eye contact while listening and less while talking. Research indicates that some African Americans may reverse this pattern by looking more when talking and looking slightly less when listening. Among some Native American and Hispanic groups, eye contact by the young is a sign of disrespect. Some cultural groups generally avoid eye contact when talking about serious subjects (Ivey & Ivey, 1999; Ivey, Ivey, & Zalaquett, 2010). Clinicians need to acquire sensitivity to cultural differences to reduce the probability of miscommunication, misdiagnosis, and misinterpretation of behavior.

A personal case history. Some time ago Marianne Corey and Jerry Corey conducted a training workshop with counselors from Mexico. Marianne was accused by a male participant of being too direct and assertive. He had difficulty with Marianne's active leadership style and indicated that it was her place to defer to Jerry by letting him take the lead. Recognizing and respecting our cultural differences, we were able to arrive at a mutual understanding of different values.

Jerry had difficulty with the participants showing up after the scheduled time and had to accept the fact that we could not follow a strict time schedule. (For a rigid personality, dealing with this is quite a challenge!) Typically we have thought that if people were late or missed a session, group cohesion would be difficult to maintain. Because the issue was openly discussed in this situation, however, the problem did not arise. We quickly learned that we had to adapt ourselves to the participants' view of time and they to us as well. To insist on interpreting such behavior as resistance would have been to ignore the cultural context.

Addressing Sexual Orientation

Most of the previous discussion on multiculturalism has focused on issues of race and ethnicity. However, the concept of human diversity encompasses much more than racial and ethnic factors; it encompasses all forms of oppression, discrimination, and prejudice, including those directed toward age, gender, religious affiliation, and sexual orientation. In 1973 the American Psychiatric Association stopped labeling **homosexuality**, a sexual orientation in which people seek emotional and sexual relationships with same-gendered individuals, as a form of mental illness. In 1975 the American Psychological Association endorsed this move by recommending that psychologists actively work to remove the stigma that had been attached to homosexuality. Along with these changes came the assumption that therapeutic practices would be modified to reflect this viewpoint: The mental health system had finally begun to treat the *problems* of gay and lesbian people rather than treating *them* as the problem.

The ethics codes of the ACA (2005), the APA (2002), the AAMFT (2001), the CCA (2007), the CRCC (2010), and the NASW (2008) clearly state that **discrimination**, or behaving differently and usually unfairly toward a specific group of people, is unethical and unacceptable. As an example of a nondiscrimination policy, consider this standard of the *Code of Professional Ethics for Rehabilitation Counselors* (CRCC, 2010):

> Rehabilitation counselors do not condone or engage in discrimination based on age, color, culture, disability, ethnicity, gender, gender identity, race, national origin, religion/spirituality, sexual orientation, marital status/partnership, language preference, socioeconomic status, or any basis proscribed by law. (A.2.b.).

Lasser and Gottlieb (2004) identify sexual orientation as one of the most chronic and vexing moral debates plaguing our culture. According to Lasser and Gottlieb, many in our society believe that homosexual or bisexual behavior is morally wrong. Many **lesbian, gay,** and **bisexual** (LGB) individuals have internalized such views, and some are significantly troubled regarding their sexual orientation. They add that therapists are faced with various clinical and ethical issues in working with LGB clients. One of these ethical issues involves therapists confronting their own values regarding homosexual or bisexual desire and behavior.

Working with lesbian, gay, and bisexual individuals presents a challenge to counselors who hold strong personal values regarding sexual orientation. Mental health professionals who have negative reactions to homosexuality are likely to impose their own values and attitudes, or at least to convey strong disapproval. Schreier, Davis, and Rodolfa (2005) remind us that no one is exempt from the influence of societal negative stereotyping, prejudice, and even hatefulness toward LGB people. Furthermore, many gay and lesbian people internalize these negative societal messages and experience psychological pain and conflict because of this. We highlight this topic because it illustrates not only the ethical problems involved in imposing values but also the problems involved in effectively addressing the mental health concerns of gay, lesbian, and bisexual clients.

Negative personal reactions, limited empathy, and lack of understanding are common characteristics in therapists who work with LGB clients (Schreier et al., 2005). Before clinical practitioners can change their therapeutic strategies, they must change their assumptions and attitudes toward the sexual orientation of others. Unless helpers become conscious of their own assumptions and possible countertransference, they may project their misconceptions and their fears onto their clients. Therapists are challenged to confront their personal prejudices, myths, fears, and stereotypes regarding sexual orientation. This is particularly important when a client discloses his or her sexual orientation well into an established therapeutic relationship. In such situations prejudicial, judgmental attitudes and behaviors on the part of the therapist can do serious damage to the client.

The American Psychological Association's Division 44 (APA, 2000) has developed a set of specialty guidelines for psychotherapy with lesbian, gay, and bisexual clients that prohibit unfair discrimination based on sexual orientation. These guidelines affirm that a psychologist's role is to acknowledge how societal stigma affects clients and addresses four main areas of understanding: (1) attitudes toward LGB people and sexual orientation issues, (2) relationships and family concerns, (3) the complex diversity within the LGB community, and (4) the training and education needed to work effectively with this client population. Any therapist who may work with lesbian, gay, or bisexual people has a responsibility to understand the special concerns of these individuals and is ethically obligated to develop the knowledge and skills to competently deliver services to them.

In recent years, the therapeutic needs of transgendered individuals have begun to be addressed as well. The Association for Lesbian, Gay, Bisexual, and Transgender Issues in Counseling (ALGBTIC, 2008) recognize that all mental health professionals need to be well versed in understanding the unique needs of this diverse population. ALGBTIC developed a set of competencies for counselors-in-training to help them examine their personal biases and values pertaining to sexual orientation. These competencies can lead to the development of appropriate intervention strategies that ensure effective service delivery. Among the specific competencies in eight different areas of the counseling profession are the following:

- Competent counselors recognize the societal prejudice and discrimination experienced by LGBT individuals and assist them in overcoming internalized negative attitudes toward their sexual and gender identities.
- Counselors strive to understand how their own sexual orientation and gender identity influences the counseling process.
- Counselors seek consultation or supervision to ensure that their own biases or knowledge deficits do not negatively influence their relationships with LGBT clients.
- Counselors understand that attempting to change the sexual orientation or gender identity of LGBT clients may be detrimental, and further, such a practice is not supported by research and therefore should not be undertaken.

The LGB guidelines of APA and the ALGBTIC competencies can assist practitioners in personally and professionally understanding the unique needs of lesbian, gay, bisexual, and transgendered people and can provide a framework enabling therapists to examine their assumptions and attitudes pertaining to sexual orientation and gender identity. These guidelines and competencies have relevance to all mental health professionals. Consider these questions:

- Which guidelines most help you in challenging your beliefs and attitudes regarding sexual orientation?
- Are there any specific attitudes, beliefs, assumptions, and values you hold that could interfere with your ability to effectively counsel lesbian, gay, bisexual, and transgendered clients?
- What competencies do you think you most need to develop in working effectively with sexual orientation issues?
- If you personally believe that homosexual relationships are morally wrong, would you be able to work effectively in this area?
- How would you react, if after three months into the therapeutic relationship, you discovered that your client was in a gay or lesbian relationship?

One way to increase your awareness of ethical and therapeutic considerations in working with LGBT clients is to take advantage of continuing education workshops sponsored by national, regional, state, and local professional organizations. By participating in such workshops, you can learn about referral resources as well as about specific interventions and strategies that are appropriate for LGBT clients. You may not know the sexual orientation of a client until the therapeutic relationship develops, so even if you do not plan to work with an LGBT population, you need to have a clear idea of your own assumptions, attitudes, and values relative to this issue.

Value Issues of Gay, Lesbian, and Bisexual Clients

Like any other minority group, lesbians, gay men, and bisexuals are subjected to discrimination, prejudice, and oppression when they seek employment or a place of residence. But lesbian, gay, and bisexual clients also have special counseling needs. For instance, the U.S. Department of Defense does not permit openly homosexual individuals to serve in the military; however, they may serve so long as they do not disclose their sexual orientation. Counseling an individual in this workplace environment may raise many ethical issues.

It is a mistake to assume that lesbians or gay men who come to counseling want to explore matters pertaining to their sexual orientation. An array of problems not related to sexual orientation may be of primary concern. In short, therapists need to listen carefully to their clients and be willing to explore whatever concerns they bring to the counseling relationship, as the following case shows.

■ The Case of Myrna and Rose.

Myrna and Rose are seeking relationship counseling, saying that they are having communication problems. They have a number of conflicts that they want to work out. They clearly state that their sexual orientation is not a problem for them. They say they need help in learning how to communicate more effectively.

> **Counselor A.** This counselor agrees to see Myrna and Rose, and during the first session he suggests that they ought to examine their sexual orientation. He expresses concern about excluding any issues from exploration in determining what could be their problem.
>
> - How do you react to the stance of this counselor? Explain.
> - Would it have made a difference if in his informed consent, he had stated that no issue would be excluded from possible exploration in therapy?
> - Is it ethical for a counselor to suggest that there could be a problem when a couple insists there is no problem?
>
> **Counselor B.** This counselor agrees to see the couple. During the initial session he realizes that he has strong negative reactions toward them. These reactions are so much in the foreground that they interfere with his ability to effectively work with the couple's presenting problem. He tells the two women about his difficulties and suggests a referral. He lets them know that he had hoped he could be objective enough to work with them, but that this is not the case.
>
> - Was this counselor's behavior ethical? Is he violating any of the ethics codes in refusing to work with this couple because of their sexual orientation?
> - Given his negative reactions, should he have continued seeing the couple, or would this in itself have been unethical?

- Would it be more damaging to the clients to refer them or to continue to see them?

- Is it ethical for the counselor to charge the couple for this session? Explain your point of view.

Counselor C. This counselor agrees to see the two women and work with them much as she would with a heterosexual couple. The counselor adds that if at any time their sexual orientation causes them difficulties, it would be up to them to bring this up as an issue. She lets them know that if they are comfortable with their sexual orientation she has no need to explore it.

- What are your reactions to this counselor's approach?

In reviewing the approaches of these three counselors, which approach would be closest to yours? To clarify your thinking on the issue of counseling gay and lesbian clients, reflect on these questions:

- Therapists often find that the presenting problem clients bring to a session is not their major problem. Is the counselor justified in introducing homosexuality as a therapeutic issue?

- Do you see any ethical issue in a heterosexually oriented therapist working with same-sex couples?

- What attitudes are necessary for therapists to be instrumental in helping clients with their sexual orientation?

- Can a counselor who is not comfortable with his or her own sexual identity possibly be effective in assisting clients who are struggling with their sexual identity?

- If Myrna and Rose stated they would like to get married, what ethical obligations do therapists have in supporting their gay and lesbian clients who seek a deeper commitment?

Commentary. Counselors sometime mistakenly assume, as did Counselor A, that the sexual orientation of same-sex clients is a problem that needs to be addressed. When counselors feel that they *must* address sexual orientation with a gay or lesbian couple, we suspect the counselors lack competence with this client group. They may be operating according to the biased assumption that homosexual orientation is always linked to the presenting problem.

Generally, we would be inclined to explore the problems presented by the couple. During the course of therapy, if it becomes evident that there is a problem that was not identified initially, we would present our hunches to the couple. As with individual clients, we want to be open to address concerns as they become relevant in their therapeutic work. As therapists we need to ask ourselves what motivates us to introduce a problem to a couple that they have not identified as one of their goals. Is this based on our clinical judgment, or does it reflect our personal biases? Recognizing when our countertransference or value bias could be having a negative effect on our professional work demands a great deal of honesty.

■ The Case of Bernard.

Bernard, a 45 year old male, is married to Rebecca, and they have two boys and two girls. He has a very successful career, and Rebecca is a stay-at-home mom. Bernard has been secretly visiting gay bars for the past 10 years. He has also been in a secret gay relationship for 5 years. Rebecca found out about Bernard's double life, and she confronted him. An altercation occurred, tempers flared, and Bernard physically harmed Rebecca. Bernard was very angry and threatened Rebecca if she disclosed his secret to anyone.

During Bernard's second session with a therapist, Sara, he discloses the threat made to Rebecca. He indicates to Sara that he trusts her and would appreciate it if she would never mention the threat because he wouldn't want this to get back to his work. He admits that he was very angry at the time, but he is no longer angry.

Sara has traditional religious values and objects to homosexuality on moral grounds. Sara discloses this to Bernard during their first session as part of the informed consent process. Sara admits that she is not knowledgeable about gay relationships. She commits to researching the subject and consulting with her colleagues, who have more expertise in this area. Sara now believes that she is qualified to work with Bernard.

After the fifth therapeutic session, it is obvious that Bernard's psychological and physical condition is deteriorating, and chaos prevails at home. Sara believes that to stop counseling Bernard or to terminate the therapeutic session before the final stage means that she has failed. Sara further believes that her existential approach and being a role model will teach Bernard acceptable societal values. Sara begins by taking Bernard to a popular restaurant and bar where straight couples socialize. Sara also takes Bernard to her church, which emphasizes that marriage is a union between a man and woman. Bernard eventually appears to be receptive to the warm, empathic, and mentoring relationship Sara has established. Bernard expresses his gratitude, and Sara believes that counseling has been successful.

- What are the implications from a diversity perspective in this case?
- What are your thoughts about Sara's self-disclosure in this case?
- What ethical, legal, professional, and clinical issues does this case suggest?
- How would you counsel Bernard?

Commentary. Therapists ensure their competence to work with specific presenting problems and client types by undergoing appropriate education, training, and supervised practice. Sara was not competent to work with a gay or bisexual client. Because of her imposition of her values pertaining to homosexuality, and her fear of failure, Sara ignored a serious problem of potential spousal abuse (and child abuse if the children observed the mother's beating). She also blurred boundaries in her treatment plan for Bernard.

The ethical course would have been for Sara to refer Bernard to a professional with competence in this area. The American Association for Marriage and Family Therapy's (2001) ethics code clearly states that "marriage and family therapists do not diagnose, treat, or advise on problems outside the recognized boundaries of their competencies" (3.11.).

In our view, general competence as a mental health practitioner requires the capacity to sit cordially and respectfully with a homosexual client or couple without imposing one's personal views or values. Know the limits of your competence in this arena, and make appropriate referrals when the limits of your competence are reached. It is entirely different and both inappropriate and unprofessional to convey intolerance to gay, lesbian, or bisexual clients.

■ A Court Case Involving a Therapist's Refusal to Counsel Homosexual Clients.

In their article, "Legal and Ethical Issues in Counseling Homosexual Clients," Hermann and Herlihy (2006) describe the case of *Bruff v. North Mississippi Health Services, Inc.* (2001). This interesting case illustrates the complexity counselors confront when their value system and religious beliefs conflict with their client's issues. This section is based largely on Hermann and Herlihy's provocative article.

In 1996 Jane Doe initiated a counseling relationship with Bruff, a counselor employed at the North Mississippi Medical Center, an employee assistance program provider. After several sessions, Jane Doe informed Bruff that she was a lesbian and wanted to explore her relationship with her partner. Bruff refused on the basis of her religious beliefs, but offered to counsel her in other areas. The client (Jane Doe) discontinued counseling, and her employer filed a complaint with Bruff's agency. Bruff again repeated her reason for refusing to work with Jane Doe and added that she would be willing to work with clients on any areas that did not conflict with her religious beliefs.

Eventually, Bruff was dismissed by her employer. Bruff appealed to an administrator of the medical center who asked her to clarify the situations in which she could not work with a client. She reiterated that she would "not be willing to counsel anyone on any subject that went against her religion" (cited in Hermann & Herlihy, 2006). She was offered a transfer to a Christian counseling center, which she refused on the basis that the director of the center was too liberal. She was given another opportunity for a position in the agency, but lost to a more qualified candidate. Another position in the agency became available, but she did not apply, and eventually she was terminated. Bruff filed suit, and a jury trial in a federal court ruled in her favor. However, on appeal the court reversed the jury's findings and found that there was no violation of Bruff's rights. The court noted that the employer had made several attempts to accommodate Bruff but that Bruff remained inflexible.

Legal Aspects of the Case

Hermann and Herlihy (2006) summarize some of the legal aspects of the *Bruff* case:

- The court held that the employer did make reasonable attempts to accommodate Bruff's religious beliefs.
- Bruff's inflexibility and unwillingness to work with anyone who has conflicting beliefs is not protected by the law.
- A counselor who refuses to work with homosexual clients can cause harm to them. The refusal to work on a homosexual client's relationship issues constitutes illegal discrimination.
- Counselors cannot use their religious beliefs to justify discrimination based on sexual orientation, and employers can terminate counselors who engage in this discrimination.

Hermann and Herlihy believe the *Bruff* case sets an important legal precedent. They assert that the appeals court decision is consistent with the Supreme Court's precedent interpreting employers' obligations to make reasonable accommodations for employees' religious beliefs. From a legal perspective, the court case clarifies that refusing to counsel homosexual clients on relationship matters can result in the loss of a therapist's job. A homosexual client who sues a counselor for refusing to work with the client on issues related to sexual orientation is also likely to prevail in a malpractice suit as the counselor could be found in violation of the standard of care in the community. Hermann and Herlihy also note that the *Bruff* case raises an ethical issue that counselors often struggle with: When is it appropriate, and on what grounds, to refer a client?

Ethical Implications of the Case

In discussing the implications of the *Bruff* case, Hermann and Herlihy (2006) emphasize the importance for counselors to develop nonjudgmental and accepting attitudes, regardless of their own value system. In short, counselors who discriminate based on sexual orientation are violating ethical standards. For counselors who are not able to reconcile their religious and moral values with certain values held by a client, Hermann and Herlihy make this recommendation:

To avoid finding themselves in situations like Bruff's, these counselors might choose to work in settings that are compatible with their values and advertise these values to potential consumers of counseling services. If it is not possible to work in a compatible setting, these counselors have an ethical duty to avoid harm to clients by ensuring that counselors' informed consent procedures provide potential clients with adequate information about the counselors' values. (p. 418)

Commentary. We raise the following questions in examining the issues involved in this case:

- How do you deal with (or plan to deal with) issues that conflict with your religious beliefs?
- The court held that Bruff could be fired for refusing to counsel a lesbian client on relationship issues. Should she be held liable for any emotional harm she caused the client?
- Is it possible to provide clients with services consistent with an ethical standard of care if counselors conceal their religious beliefs that homosexuality is wrong?
- What distinction, if any, do you see between prejudice based on one's own private belief system as opposed to a conviction based on the teaching of one's religion?
- If you have sharply different moral beliefs from those of your client, is this equivalent to your not being competent to work effectively with this client? Are referrals justified because of major value conflicts?
- How do you determine that your referral will benefit or harm your client?
- Do counselors have an ethical obligation to reveal their religious beliefs prior to the onset of a professional relationship?
- If you are fully disclosing of your limitations and owning them as your problem, are you behaving ethically and legally?
- Should a client ever be surprised with the fact that you cannot continue working on problems that are problematic for you?
- To what degree does your informed consent document protect you from an ethical or legal violation?
- Does your document in which you disclose your limitations protect clients from harm?
- How would you apply the basic moral principles addressed in Chapter 1 to making ethical decisions in this case?

We find this case very challenging as it exposes ethical issues that have no easy answers and that require a great deal of discussion. A rigid stance on either side of this issue can create a major problem, precluding the kind of discussion this topic requires. It brings to mind the words of Rumi, the mystic, "Out beyond ideas of wrong-doing and right-doing, there is a field. I'll meet you there."

The *Bruff* case illustrates both ethical and legal issues related to value imposition and conflict of values between counselor and client (see Chapter 3). In a counseling relationship, it is not the client's place to adjust to the therapist's values, yet this counselor maintained that she could not work with clients whose beliefs went against her religious views. Bruff demonstrates a lack of understanding that counseling is not about her but about the client's needs and values.

Although we do not question Bruff's right to possess her own personal values, we do have concerns about the manner in which she dealt with the client involved in this case. At a minimum, Bruff should have informed her potential clients in writing (as part of the informed consent document) about her religious convictions and moral opposition pertaining to homosexuality, thereby providing potential clients with an opportunity to consider whether they wanted to work with a counselor holding these views.

We do not believe that all counselors can work effectively with all clients, but we would expect them to avoid using their personal value system as the criteria for how all clients should think and act. We also question whether it was appropriate for this counselor to have a position in a public counseling agency given her inexperience and ineffectiveness working with diverse client populations. Bruff showed inflexibility both in dealing with her clients and in her response to the agency's attempts to accommodate her values by transferring her to another position.

Matching Client and Counselor

As we have seen, diversity includes factors such as culture, religion, race, disability, age, gender, sexual orientation, education, and socioeconomic level. Is matching client and counselor on these various aspects of diversity desirable or possible? Does the clinician have to share the experiential world of the client to be effective? It is impossible to match client and therapist in all areas of potential diversity, which means that all encounters with clients are diverse, at least to some degree. Some argue that successful multicultural counseling is highly improbable due to the barriers between groups. Others argue that well-trained practitioners, even though they differ from their clients, are capable of providing effective counseling.

Lee and Ramsey (2006) observe that one pitfall associated with multiculturalism is that some helping professionals may give up in exasperation, asking: "How can I really be effective with a client whose cultural background is different from mine?" When counselors are overly self-conscious about their ability to work with diverse client populations, they may become too analytical about what they say and do. Counselors who are afraid to face the differences between themselves and their clients, who refuse to accept the reality of these differences, who perceive such differences as problematic, or who are uncomfortable working out these differences may end up failing.

Shared Life Experiences With Your Clients

To what degree do you share the view that you must have had life experiences similar to those of your clients? Counselors do not necessarily need to have experienced each of the struggles of their clients to be effective in working with them. When the counselor and the client connect at a certain level, cultural and age differences can be transcended. Consider for a moment the degree that you can communicate effectively with the following clients:

- An older person
- A person of a different racial, ethnic, or cultural group
- A person with a disability
- A delinquent or a criminal
- A person who is abusing alcohol or drugs
- A person who is in recovery from an addiction

It is possible for a relatively young clinician to work effectively with an elderly client. For example, the client may be experiencing feelings of loss, guilt, sadness, and hopelessness. The young counselor can empathize with these feelings even though they come from a different source. However, it is essential that the counselor be sensitive to the differences in their backgrounds and experiences.

To facilitate your reflection on whether you need to have life experiences similar to those of your client, assess the degree to which you think you could establish a good working relationship with Sylvia.

■ The Case of Sylvia.

At a community clinic, Sylvia, who is 38, tells you that she is an alcoholic. During the intake interview she says, "I feel bad because I've tried to stop my drinking and haven't succeeded. I am fine for a while, and then I begin to think that I could do a lot better. I see all the ways in which I do not measure up—how I let my kids down, the many mistakes I've made with them, the embarrassment I've caused my husband—and then I get so down I start drinking again. I know that what I am doing is self-destructive, but I'm not able to stop. I very much want your advice on what I should do."

- What experiences have you had with alcoholism or its treatment, and how important is that?

- If you do not have competence in dealing with substance abuse, how could you acquire the knowledge and skills to effectively work in this area?
- What plan of action would you select for treating Sylvia's problem?
- Do you see Sylvia as having a disease? as suffering from a lack of willpower? as an irresponsible, indulgent person? How would such views influence your interventions?
- Does the fact that Sylvia is a woman affect your view of her problem?
- Would you encourage Sylvia to attend meetings of Alcoholics Anonymous? Why or why not?
- Would you refer Sylvia to a substance abuse treatment program, either inpatient or outpatient? Explain.
- Is it ethical to treat Sylvia's psychological problems without first attending to her addiction problem? Explain.
- Sylvia wants your advice; what advice would you offer? What danger do you see in offering advice in this kind of situation?

Commentary. We support the thinking that the addiction must be treated before attempting to deal with Sylvia's other psychological difficulties, which brings up the issue of advice giving. When is it appropriate for the therapist to provide advice to a client? There are at least two kinds of advice. One form of advice could be a part of the treatment recommendations. For example, the therapist might suggest that Sylvia consult a physician or attend AA meetings. This form of advice is common and can provide useful adjuncts to therapy.

Another form of advice would be to tell a client like Sylvia specific things she should do, such as turn to religion, start an exercise program, or move to a new area. Telling a client specific actions to take in the face of major life events tends to be counterproductive and should generally be avoided. This kind of advice often backfires. If Sylvia does agree with the advice given, or if she has not followed the advice, she may not return for further therapy sessions. Counselors can assist their clients by brainstorming with them about possibilities leading to solutions for their problems, but they should resist the temptation to provide specific actions in the form of giving advice.

How to Address Differences in Therapeutic Relationships

Some therapists wonder whether differences should be addressed, and if they are, should the clinician or the client initiate this? La Roche and Maxie (2003) observe that not all differences between client and therapist have the same impact on the therapeutic relationship. A dissimilarity in race may not hold the same weight as differences in religious beliefs, for example. What is crucial is the client's perception of difference in the therapeutic process. Some writers maintain that most clients will not initiate discussions of cultural differences due to the power differential that exists, which means that the therapist should directly take responsibility to address these differences. Other writers take the position that it is more appropriate to wait for the client to bring up cultural differences.

Cultural clashes and misunderstandings had painful consequences for a Hmong family, which are detailed in Anne Fadiman's (1997) book, *The Spirit Catches You and You Fall Down*. Even though the cultural clashes were between the helping professions and the family, the same dynamics can be applied to clinicians who work with people who are culturally different from themselves. This book illustrates how well-intentioned people can cause much harm when they do not know and respect cultural differences.

LaRoche and Maxie (2003) make a point that cultural differences are subjective, complex, and dynamic. Clinicians can make a mistake by assuming there is a standard way to work with clients of a certain cultural background. Instead, practitioners need to explore the meanings that clients ascribe to these cultural differences. LaRoche and Maxie describe working with a third-generation Korean American gay client. Do you work with the sexual orientation issue or how his extended family deals with his gayness? We agree that the process is dynamic and that clinicians must stay with the client and be led by the client into the areas that are most important to him or her.

Pedersen (1999) emphasizes that becoming a multiculturally competent counselor entails more than following a list of rules. Gaining competence in this area involves more than a shift in thinking; it demands a shift in attitude. The most important aspects of culture-centered counseling can be learned, but not necessarily taught.

It is our position that clinicians can learn to work with clients who differ from them in gender, race, culture, religion, socioeconomic background, physical ability, age, or sexual orientation. But our stance is tempered by certain reservations and conditions. First, clinicians need to have training in multicultural perspectives, both academic and experiential. Second, as in any other counseling situation, it is important that the client and the practitioner agree to develop a working therapeutic relationship. Third, helpers are advised to be flexible in applying theories and techniques to specific situations. The counselor who has an open stance has a greater likelihood of success than someone who rigidly adheres to a single theoretical system. Fourth, the mental health professional should be open to being challenged and tested. In multicultural counseling, many clients are more likely to exhibit caution. They may use many defenses as survival strategies to protect their true feelings. A counselor may be perceived to be a symbol of the establishment. If helpers act defensively, clients may feel that the clinician's values or solutions are being imposed on them and harm may come to these clients.

Some clients believe that a professional who is not part of the solution to their problem is really part of the problem.

Addressing Unintentional Racism

It is especially important in multicultural counseling situations for counselors to be aware of their own value systems, of potential stereotyping, any traces of prejudice, and of their cultural countertransference. Earlier we described those culture-bound counselors who are unintentional racists. In some ways, such counselors can be more dangerous than those who are more open with their prejudices. According to Pedersen (2000), unintentional racists must be challenged either to become intentional racists or to modify their racist attitudes and behaviors. Pedersen (2006) lists five antiracism strategies:

1. Be aware of the history of racism as a social phenomenon.
2. Note the importance of power differences in promoting racism.
3. Recognize that not all racist behaviors are intentional.
4. Challenge the racist assumptions that encapsulate us.
5. Identify racist behaviors in the cultural context where they were learned and are displayed.

The key to changing unintentional racism lies in examining our basic assumptions. Two forms of covert racism that Ridley (2005) identifies are color blindness and color consciousness. The counselor who says, "When I look at you, I see a person, not a Black person" may encounter mistrust from clients who have difficulty believing that. Likewise, a therapist is not likely to earn credibility by saying, "If you were not Black, you wouldn't have the problem you're facing." These examples of color blindness and color consciousness are rather extreme, but there are many more subtle variations on these themes. For a thought-provoking analysis of the role of racism in counseling practice, we refer you to Ridley (2005).

Increasing Your Sensitivity to Cultural Diversity

Try to identify your own assumptions as you think about these questions:

- Does a counselor need to share the cultural background of the client to be effective?
- If you were to encounter considerable "testing" from a client who is culturally different from you, how would you react? What are some ways in which you could work with such a client?
- What experiences have you had with discrimination? How would your own experiences either help or hinder you in working with clients who have been discriminated against?
- What stereotypes are you aware of having?

When counselors identify "unusual behavior" in a client, it is important to determine whether such behavior is unusual within the client's cultural context. Clients may become suspicious if they sense the therapist has already come to a conclusion. Rather than suffering from clinical paranoia, these clients may be reacting to the realities of an environment in which they have suffered oppression and prejudice. In such cases, clients' responses may make complete sense. Practitioners who appreciate the context of such perceptions are less likely to pathologize clients and are able to begin working with clients from their experiential framework.

Multicultural Training for Mental Health Workers

Although referral is sometimes an appropriate course of action, it should not be viewed as a solution to the problem of inadequately trained helpers. Many agencies have practitioners whose cultural backgrounds are less diverse than the populations they serve. With the increasing number of culturally diverse clients seeking counseling, we recommend that all counseling students, regardless of their racial or ethnic background, receive training in multicultural counseling and therapy (MCT).

The standards established by the Council for Accreditation of Counseling and Related Educational Programs (CACREP, 2009) require that programs provide curricular and experiential offerings in multicultural and pluralistic trends, including characteristics within and among diverse groups nationally and internationally. CACREP standards call for supervised practicum experiences that include people from the environments in which the trainee is preparing to work. It is expected that trainees will study ethnic groups, subcultures, the changing roles of women, sexism, urban and rural societies, cultural mores, spiritual issues, and differing life patterns. The Council on Rehabilitation Education (CORE, 2009) also has accreditation standards that address these issues. It is not realistic to develop expertise with every culture or subculture. However, trainees should take active steps to increase their competence with those groups they plan to serve (Barnett & Johnson, 2010).

Characteristics of the Culturally Skilled Counselor

Part of multicultural competence entails recognizing our limitations and is manifested in our willingness to (a) seek consultation, (b) participate in continuing education, and (c) when appropriate, make referrals to a professional who is competent to work with a particular client population. La Roche and Maxie (2003) state that acquiring cultural competence is an active and lifelong learning process rather than a fixed state that is arrived at. They add that this process may include formal training, critical self-evaluation, and questioning of what is occurring in cross-cultural therapeutic partnerships.

A major contribution to the counseling profession has been the development of **multicultural competencies,** a set of knowledge and skills that are essential to the culturally skilled practitioner. Practitioners do not have to master all of these competencies before they begin to see clients, but gaining proficiency should be an ongoing process. Initially formulated by Sue and colleagues (1982), these competencies were later revised and expanded by Sue, Arredondo, and McDavis (1992). Arredondo and her colleagues (1996) updated and operationalized these competencies, and Sue and his colleagues (1998) extended multicultural counseling competencies to individual and organizational development. The multicultural competencies have been endorsed by the Association for Multicultural Counseling and Development (AMCD), by the Association for Counselor Education and Supervision (ACES), and recently by the American Psychological Association (APA, 2003a). For an updated and expanded version of these competencies, see *Multicultural Counseling Competencies 2003: Association for Multicultural Counseling and Development* (Roysircar et al., 2003). Refer also to the APA's (2003a) "Guidelines on Multicultural Education, Training, Research, Practice, and Organizational Change for Psychologists." The essential attributes of culturally competent counselors, compiled from the sources just cited, are listed in the box titled "Multicultural Counseling Competencies."

Multicultural Counseling Competencies

I. Counselor Awareness of Own Cultural Values and Biases
A. With respect to *attitudes and beliefs,* culturally competent counselors:
- believe that cultural self-awareness and sensitivity to one's own cultural heritage is essential.
- are aware of how their own cultural background and experiences have influenced attitudes, values, and biases about psychological processes.
- are able to recognize the limits of their multicultural competencies and expertise.
- recognize their sources of discomfort with differences that exist between themselves and clients in terms of race, ethnicity, and culture.

B. With respect to *knowledge,* culturally competent counselors:
- have specific knowledge about their own racial and cultural heritage and how it personally and professionally affects their definitions of and biases about normality/abnormality and the process of counseling.
- possess knowledge and understanding about how oppression, racism, discrimination, and stereotyping affect them personally and in their work. This allows individuals to acknowledge their own racist attitudes, beliefs, and feelings.

(*continued on next page*)

- possess knowledge about their social impact on others. They are knowledgeable about communication style differences, how their style may clash or foster the counseling process with persons of color or others different from themselves, and how to anticipate the impact it may have on others.

C. With respect to *skills*, culturally competent counselors:
- seek out educational, consultative, and training experiences to improve their understanding and effectiveness in working with culturally different populations.
- are constantly seeking to understand themselves as racial and cultural beings and are actively seeking a nonracist identity.

II. Understanding the Client's Worldview

A. With respect to *attitudes and beliefs*, culturally competent counselors:
- are aware of their negative and positive emotional reactions toward other racial and ethnic groups that may prove detrimental to the counseling relationship. They are willing to contrast their own beliefs and attitudes with those of their culturally different clients in a nonjudgmental fashion.
- are aware of stereotypes and preconceived notions that they may hold toward other racial and ethnic minority groups.

B. With respect to *knowledge*, culturally competent counselors:
- possess specific knowledge and information about the particular client group with whom they are working.
- understand how race, culture, ethnicity, and so forth may affect personality formation, vocational choices, manifestation of psychological disorders, help-seeking behavior, and the appropriateness or inappropriateness of counseling approaches.
- understand and have knowledge about sociopolitical influences that impinge on the lives of racial and ethnic minorities.

C. With respect to *skills*, culturally competent counselors:
- familiarize themselves with relevant research and the latest findings regarding mental health and mental disorders that affect various ethnic and racial groups. They should actively seek out educational experiences that enrich their knowledge, understanding, and cross-cultural skills for more effective counseling behavior.
- become actively involved with minority individuals outside the counseling setting so that their perspective of minorities is more than an academic or helping exercise.

III. Developing Culturally Appropriate Intervention Strategies and Techniques

A. With respect to *attitudes and beliefs*, culturally competent counselors:
- respect clients' religious and spiritual beliefs and values, including attributions and taboos, because these affect worldview, psychosocial functioning, and expressions of distress.
- respect indigenous helping practices and respect help-giving networks among communities of color.
- value bilingualism and do not view another language as an impediment to counseling.

B. With respect to *knowledge*, culturally competent counselors:
- have a clear and explicit knowledge and understanding of the generic characteristics of counseling and therapy and how they may clash with the cultural values of various cultural groups.
- are aware of institutional barriers that prevent minorities from using mental health services.
- have knowledge of the potential bias in assessment instruments and use procedures and interpret findings in a way that recognizes the cultural and linguistic characteristics of clients.
- have knowledge of family structures, hierarchies, values, and beliefs from various cultural perspectives. They are knowledgeable about the community where a particular cultural group may reside and the resources in the community.
- are aware of relevant discriminatory practices at the social and the community level that may affect the psychological welfare of the population being served.

C. With respect to *skills*, culturally competent counselors:
- are able to engage in a variety of verbal and nonverbal helping responses. They are able to send and receive both verbal and nonverbal messages accurately and appropriately. They are not tied to only one method or approach to helping but recognize that helping styles and approaches may be culture bound.
- are able to exercise institutional intervention skills on behalf of their clients. They can help clients determine whether a problem stems from racism or bias in others so that clients do not inappropriately personalize problems.
- are not adverse to seeking consultation with traditional healers or religious and spiritual leaders and practitioners in the treatment of culturally different clients when appropriate.
- take responsibility for interacting in the language requested by the client and, if not feasible, make appropriate referrals.
- have training and expertise in the use of traditional assessment and testing instruments.
- attend to and work to eliminate biases, prejudices, and discriminatory contexts in conducting evaluations and providing interventions and develop sensitivity to issues of oppression, sexism, heterosexism, elitism, and racism.
- take responsibility for educating their clients to the processes of psychological intervention, such as goals, expectations, legal rights, and the counselor's orientation.

For the complete description of these competencies, along with explanatory statements, refer to "Operationalization of the Multicultural Counseling Competencies" (Arredondo et al., 1996). Also see Sue and colleagues (1998, chap. 4) and Sue and Sue (2008, chap. 1) for detailed listings of multicultural counseling competencies.

■ The Case of Talib.

Talib, an immigrant from the Middle East, is a graduate student in a counseling program. During many class discussions, his views on gender roles become clear, yet he expresses his beliefs in a respectful and nondogmatic fashion. Talib's attitudes and beliefs about gender roles are that the man should be the provider and head of the home and that the woman is in charge of nurturance, which is a full-time job. Although not directly critical of his female classmates, Talib voices a concern that these students may be neglecting their family obligations by pursuing a graduate education. Talib bases his views not only on his cultural background but also by citing experts in this country who support his position that the absence of women in the home has been a major contributor to the breakdown of the family. There are many lively discussions between Talib and his classmates, many of whom hold very different attitudes regarding gender roles.

Halfway through the semester, his instructor, Dr. Felice Good, asks Talib to come to her office after class. Dr. Good tells Talib that she has grave concerns about him pursuing a career in counseling in this country with his present beliefs. She encourages him to consider another career if he is unable to change his "biased convictions" about the role of women. She tells him that unless he can open his thinking to more contemporary viewpoints he will surely encounter serious problems with clients and fellow professionals.

- If you were one of Talib's classmates, what would you want to say to him?
- What assumptions underlie Dr. Good's advice to Talib?
- If you were a faculty member, what criteria would you use to determine that students are not suited for a program because of their values?
- How would you approach a person whose views seem very different from your own? How would you respond to Talib?

Commentary. Dr. Good seemed to assume that because Talib expressed strong convictions he was rigid and would impose his values on his clients. She did not communicate a respect for his value system along with her concern that Talib might impose his values on clients. She did not use this situation as a teaching opportunity in the classroom to explore the issue of value imposition.

As a faculty member, Dr. Good is charged with helping to evaluate whether Talib possess the competence and character to become a mental health professional. Although her concern about his attitudes may be warranted, her supervisory intervention appears to be based on assumptions about how Talib manages his own attitudes when working with clients. Ironically, Dr. Good conveys the very disrespect for cultural differences that she accuses Talib of demonstrating. We cannot assume that Talib will necessarily impose his value system on his clients.

Students such as Talib who express strong values are often told that they should not work with certain clients. As a result, these students may hesitate to expose their viewpoints if they differ from the "acceptable norm." In our view, a critical feature of multicultural counseling and therapy is the personal development of trainees, which includes helping them clarify a set of values and beliefs concerning culture that increases their chances of functioning effectively in working with culturally diverse client populations. We want to teach students that having strong convictions is not the same as imposing them on others. Students are challenged to become aware of their value systems and to be open to exploring them. However, their role is not to go into this profession to impose these values on others. If trainees maintain a rigid position regarding the way people should live, regardless of their cultural background, educators must be prepared to address these issues with trainees.

Our Views on Multicultural Training

We recommend these four dimensions of training in multicultural counseling: (1) self-exploration, (2) didactic course work, (3) internship, and (4) experiential approaches. The first step in the process of acquiring multicultural counseling skills is for students to become involved in a **self-exploratory journey** to help identify any potential blind spots. Ideally, this would be required of all trainees in the mental health professions and would be supervised by someone with experience in multicultural issues.

In addition to self-exploration, students can take course work dealing exclusively with multicultural issues and diverse cultural groups. **Course work** is essential for understanding and applying cultural themes in counseling. It is our position that multicultural topics need to be integrated throughout the curriculum, and not simply limited to a single course.

Stadler and colleagues (2006) address the importance of an expansive, systemic approach to training multiculturally competent professionals. They describe how their program moved diversity from the periphery to a core value. We especially appreciate that students, faculty, and administrators are all included in the modifications and developments of the program.

In a training program that holds diversity as a central value, supervised experiences in the field and internships are given special prominence. Trainees should participate in at least one required **internship** in which they have multicultural experiences or reframe their experiences from a multicultural viewpoint. Ideally, the agency or school supervisor will be experienced in the cultural variables of that particular setting and also be skilled in cross-cultural understanding. Students would also have access to both individual and group supervision on campus from a qualified faculty member. Trainees will be encouraged to select supervised field placements and internships that will challenge them to work on gender and cultural concerns, developmental issues, and other areas of diversity. Through well-selected internship experiences, trainees will not only expand their own consciousness but will increase their knowledge of diverse groups and will have a basis for acquiring intervention skills.

In addition to didactic approaches to acquiring knowledge and skills in multicultural competence, we strongly favor **experiential approaches** as a way to increase self-awareness and to identify and examine attitudes associated with diversity competence. Experiential approaches encourage trainees to pay attention to their thoughts, feelings, and actions in exploring their worldviews. In conjunction with other instructional approaches, experiential learning can assist students in developing self-awareness, knowledge, and the skills required for working with culturally diverse client populations (Arthur & Achenbach, 2002). It is also essential for counselors who work extensively with a specific cultural group to immerse themselves in knowledge and approaches specific to that group through reading, cultural events, workshops, and supervised practice.

To get the most from your training, we suggest that you accept your limitations and be patient with yourself as you expand your vision of how your culture continues to influence the person you are today. Overwhelming yourself by all that you do not know will not help you. You will not become more effective in multicultural counseling by expecting that you must be completely knowledgeable about the cultural backgrounds of all your clients, by thinking that you should have a complete repertoire of skills, or by demanding perfection. Rather than feeling that you must understand all the subtle nuances of cultural differences when you are with a client, we suggest that you develop a sense of interest, curiosity, and respect when faced with client differences and behaviors that are new to you. Recognize and appreciate your efforts toward becoming a more effective person and counselor, and remember that becoming a multiculturally competent counselor is an ongoing process. In this process there are no small steps; every step you take is creating a new direction for you in your work with diverse client populations.

Chapter Summary

Over the last decade mental health professionals have been urged to learn about their own culture and to become aware of how their experiences affect the way they work with those who are culturally different. By being ignorant of the values and attitudes of a diverse range of clients, therapists open themselves to criticism and ineffectiveness. We are all culture-bound to some extent, and it takes a concerted effort to monitor our positive and negative biases so that they do not impede the establishment of helping relationships.

In our view, imposing one's own vision of the world on clients not only leads to negative therapeutic outcomes but also constitutes unethical practice.

Culture can be interpreted broadly to include racial or ethnic groups, as well as gender, age, religion, economic status, nationality, physical capacity or handicap, or sexual orientation. We are all limited by our experiences in these various groups, but we can increase our awareness by direct contact with a variety of groups, by reading, by special course work, and by in-service professional workshops. It is essential that our practices be accurate, appropriate, and meaningful for the clients with whom we work. This entails rethinking our theories and modifying our techniques to meet clients' unique needs and not rigidly applying interventions in the same manner to all clients. We encourage ongoing examination of your assumptions, attitudes, and values so that you can determine how they might influence your practice.

Suggested Activities

1. Select two or three cultures or ethnic groups different from your own. What attitudes and beliefs about these cultures did you hold while growing up? In what ways, if any, have your attitudes changed and what contributed to the changes?

2. Which of your values do you ascribe primarily to your culture? Have any of your values changed over time, and if so, how? How might these values influence the way you work with clients who are culturally different from you?

3. What multicultural life experiences have you had? Did you recognize any prejudices? Have you been the object of prejudice? Are you willing to discuss your experiences in class. Interview students or faculty members who identify themselves as ethnically or culturally different from you. What might they teach you about differences that you as a counselor might benefit from to work more effectively with them?

4. To what degree have your courses and field experience contributed to your ability to work effectively with people from other cultures? What training experiences would you like to have to better prepare you for multicultural counseling?

5. Divide into groups of four in your class for this exercise designed by our colleague, Paul Pedersen. One person role plays a minority client. A second person assumes the counselor role. The third person acts as an alter ego for the client, as the anticounselor. The fourth person acts as an alter ego for the therapist, or the procounselor. You might have the minority client be somewhat reluctant to speak. The counselor can deal with this silence by treating it as a form of resistance, using typical therapeutic strategies. During this time the anticounselor expresses the cultural meaning of the silence. The procounselor shares out loud what he or she imagines the counselor might be thinking. Now, devise a way

to deal with silence from this frame of reference without using traditional therapeutic techniques.

6. Minorities are often pressured to give up their beliefs and ways in favor of adopting the ideals and customs of the dominant culture. What do you think your approach would be in working with clients who feel such pressure? How might you work with clients who see their own ethnicity or cultural heritage as a handicap to be overcome?

7. What was your own "internal dialogue" as you read and reflected on this chapter? Share some of this internal dialogue in small group discussions.

8. In small groups, discuss a few of your assumptions that are likely to influence the manner in which you counsel others. Select one of the assumptions discussed in this chapter from the following list that most applies to you. Explore and share your attitudes.

- What assumptions do you make about the value of self-disclosure on the part of clients?
- What are your assumptions pertaining to autonomy, independence, and self-determination?
- To what degree do you assume that it is better to be assertive than to be nonassertive?
- How would you describe an authentic person?
- Do you perceive indirectness as being an impediment?
- What other assumptions can you think of that might either help or hinder you in counseling diverse client populations?

9. In small groups, explore what you consider to be the main ethical issues in counseling lesbian, gay, and bisexual clients. Review the discussion of the case of *Bruff v. North Mississippi Health Services* on pages 138–141. What legal issues are involved in this case? What are the ethical issues in this case? To what degree do you think the counselor imposed her values on her client? Do you think counselors have a right to refuse to provide services to homosexual clients because of the counselors' personal beliefs?

10. Select any one of the many cases described in this chapter, and reflect on how you would deal with this case from an ethical perspective. After you select the case that most interests you, review the steps in the ethical decision-making process described in Chapter 1, and then go through these steps in addressing the issues involved in the case.

11. In small groups review the list of traits of the culturally encapsulated counselor who exhibits cultural tunnel vision. If you recognize any of these traits in yourself, what do you think you might do about them?

12. *The Color of Fear,* produced and directed by Lee Mun Wah, is an emotional and insightful portrayal of racism in America.* Its aim is to illustrate the type of dialogue and relationships needed if we are to have a truly multicultural society based on equality and trust. After viewing the film in class, share what it brought out in you.

Ethics in Action *CD-ROM Exercises*

13. In video role play 3, Culture Clash, the client (Sally) directly questions the counselor's background. Role play a situation where a clash between you and a client might develop (such as difference in age, race, sexual orientation, or culture).

14. Refer to the section titled "Becoming an Effective Multicultural Practitioner" in the *Ethics in Action* CD-ROM. Complete the self-examination of multicultural counseling competencies. Bring your answers to class and explore in small discussion groups what you need to do to become competent as a counselor of clients whose cultural background differs from your own.

The Color of Fear is available from Stir Fry Productions in Oakland, California. The Stir Fry Productions Company provides trained facilitators (in some areas) to assist with discussion after the film is shown.

Chapter 5

Pre-Chapter Self-Inventory

Directions: For each statement, indicate the response that most closely identifies your beliefs and attitudes. Use the following code:

5 = I *strongly agree* with this statement.

4 = I *agree* with this statement.

3 = I am *undecided* about this statement.

2 = I *disagree* with this statement.

1 = I *strongly disagree* with this statement.

_____ 1. If there is a conflict between a legal and an ethical standard, a therapist must always adhere to the ethical standard.

_____ 2. Practitioners who do not use written consent forms are unprofessional and unethical.

_____ 3. To practice ethically, therapists must become familiar with the laws related to their profession.

_____ 4. Clients in therapy should *not* have access to their clinical files.

_____ 5. Clients should be made aware of their rights at the outset of a diagnostic or therapeutic relationship.

_____ 6. It is unethical for a counselor to alter the fee structure once it has been established.

_____ 7. Ethical practice demands that therapists develop procedures to ensure that clients are in a position to make informed choices.

_____ 8. Therapists have an ethical responsibility to become knowledgeable about community resources and alternatives to therapy and to present these alternatives to their clients.

Client Rights and Counselor Responsibilities

_____ 9. Before entering therapy, clients should be made aware of the purposes, goals, techniques, policies, and procedures involved.

_____ 10. In certain circumstances, it is *not* necessary or appropriate to inform clients at the initial counseling session of the limits of confidentiality.

_____ 11. Clinicians have an ethical responsibility to discuss possible termination issues with clients during the initial sessions and to review these matters with them periodically.

_____ 12. It is primarily the therapist's responsibility to determine the appropriate time for termination of therapy for most clients.

_____ 13. A therapeutic relationship should be maintained only as long as it is clear that the client is benefiting.

_____ 14. Clients have a right to know about both the possible benefits and the risks associated with counseling before entering into a professional relationship.

_____ 15. Counselors should keep detailed clinical notes and share these notes with clients if they express interest in knowing what is in their record.

_____ 16. When a child is in psychotherapy, the therapist has an ethical and legal obligation to provide the parents with information they request.

_____ 17. Minors should be allowed to seek psychological assistance regarding pregnancy and abortion counseling *without* parental consent or knowledge.

_____ 18. Mystification of the client–therapist relationship tends to increase client dependence.

_____ 19. Involuntary commitment is a violation of human rights, even for individuals who are unable to be responsible for themselves or their actions.

_____ 20. Counselors would do well to think about specific ways to protect themselves from malpractice suits.

Introduction

To practice in an ethical and legal manner, the rights of clients cannot be taken for granted. In this chapter we deal with ways of educating clients about their rights and responsibilities as partners in the therapeutic process. Special attention is given to the role of informed consent as well as ethical and legal issues that arise when therapists fail to provide sufficient informed consent. We also deal with some of the ethical and legal issues involved in counseling children and adolescents.

Part of ethical practice is talking with clients about their rights. Frequently, clients are not aware of their rights, and they may find the therapeutic process mysterious. Vulnerable and sometimes desperate for help, clients may unquestioningly accept whatever their therapist says or does. Clients may see their therapist much like they see their doctor and expect the therapist to have the "correct" opinion or answer. For most people the therapeutic situation is a new one, and they may not realize that the therapist's duty is to help clients find their own answers. For these reasons, the therapist is held responsible for protecting clients' rights and teaching clients about these rights. The ethics codes of most professional organizations require that clients be given adequate information to make informed choices about entering and continuing the client–therapist relationship (see the Ethics Code box titled "The Rights of Clients and Informed Consent" for examples from several ethics codes). By alerting clients to their rights and responsibilities, the practitioner is steering them toward a healthy sense of autonomy and personal power.

In addition to the ethical aspects of safeguarding clients' rights, legal parameters also govern professional practice. When we attend continuing education workshops on ethics in clinical practice, the focus is often on legal matters and risk management. It is unfortunate that some of these workshops do not address ethical aspects of practice more fully. Practitioners often express their fears of lawsuits and are eager to learn strategies that will protect them from malpractice. Some counselors seem more focused on protecting themselves than on making sure their clients' rights are protected. The emphasis should be on both nonmaleficence (avoiding doing harm) and beneficence (doing what is best for the client).

Counseling can be a risky venture, and you must be familiar with the laws that govern professional practice. However, we hope you avoid becoming so involved in legalities that you lose sight of the ethical and clinical implications of what you do with your clients. Fisher (2008) puts this notion cogently:"If psychologists are having difficulty seeing the ethical forest for the legal trees, what they need is not more legal training, but clearer ethics-based training" (p. 6). You will surely want to protect yourself legally, but not to the point that you immobilize yourself and inhibit your professional effectiveness. Later in this chapter we address risk management strategies that can protect both you and your clients.

Ethics Codes

The Rights of Clients and Informed Consent

American Psychological Association (2002)

(a) When obtaining informed consent to therapy as required in Standard 3.10, *Informed Consent*, psychologists inform clients/patients as early as is feasible in the therapeutic relationship about the nature and anticipated course of therapy, fees, involvement of third parties, and limits of confidentiality and provide sufficient opportunity for the client/patient to ask questions and receive answers.

(b) When obtaining informed consent for treatment for which generally recognized techniques and procedures have not been established, psychologists inform their clients/patients of the developing nature of the treatment, the potential risks involved, alternative treatments that may be available, and the voluntary nature of their participation. (10.01)

National Association of Social Workers (2008)

Social workers should provide services to clients only in the context of a professional relationship based, when appropriate, on valid informed consent. Social workers should use clear and understandable language to inform clients of the purpose of the services, risks related to the services, limits to services because of the requirements of a third party payer, relevant costs, reasonable alternatives, clients' right to refuse or withdraw consent, and the time frame covered by the consent. Social workers should provide clients with an opportunity to ask questions. (1.03.a.)

American Counseling Association (2005)

Counselors explicitly address to clients the nature of all services provided. They inform clients about issues such as, but not limited to, the purposes, goals, techniques, procedures, limitations, potential risks, and benefits of services; the counselor's qualifications, credentials and relevant experience; continuation of services upon the incapacitation or death of a counselor; and other pertinent information.

Counselors take steps to insure that clients understand the implications of diagnosis, the intended use of tests and reports, fees, and billing arrangements. Clients have the right to confidentiality and to be provided with an explanation of its limitations, including how supervisors and/or treatment team professionals are involved; to obtain clear information about their records; to participate in the ongoing counseling plans; and to refuse any services or modality change, and to be advised of the consequences of such refusal. (A.2.b.)

Feminist Therapy Institute (2000)

A feminist therapist educates her clients regarding power relationships. She informs clients of their rights as consumers of therapy, including procedures for resolving differences and filing grievances. She clarifies power in its various forms as it exists within other areas of her life, including professional roles, social/governmental structures, and interpersonal relationships. She assists her clients in finding ways to protect themselves and, if requested, to seek redress. (II.D.)

(*continued on next page*)

Code of Professional Ethics for Rehabilitation Counselors (CRCC, 2010)

Rehabilitation counselors recognize that clients have the freedom to choose whether to enter into or remain in a rehabilitation counseling relationship. Rehabilitation counselors respect the rights of clients to participate in ongoing rehabilitation counseling planning and to make decisions to refuse any services or modality changes, while also ensuring that clients are advised of the consequences of such refusal. Rehabilitation counselors recognize that clients need information to make an informed decision regarding services and that professional disclosure is required in order for informed consent to be an ongoing part of the rehabilitation counseling process. Rehabilitation counselors appropriately document discussions of disclosure and informed consent throughout the rehabilitation counseling relationship. (A.3.b.)

The American Mental Health Counselors Association (2000)

Mental health counselors are responsible for making their services readily accessible to clients in a manner that facilitates the clients' abilities to make an informed choice when selecting a provider. This therapeutic responsibility includes a clear description of what the client can expect in the way of tests, reports, billing, therapeutic regime and schedules, and the use of the mental health counselor's statement of professional disclosure. In the event that the client is a minor or possesses disabilities that would prohibit informed consent, the mental health counselor acts in the client's best interest. (Principle I.J.)

International Association of Marriage and Family Counselors (2005)

Marriage and family counselors promote open, honest and direct relationships with consumers of professional services. Couples and family counselors inform clients about the goals of counseling, qualifications of the counselor(s), limits of confidentiality, potential risks and benefits associated with specific techniques, duration of treatment, costs of services, appropriate alternatives to marriage and family counseling, and reasonable expectations for outcomes. (A.5.)

The Client's Right to Give Informed Consent

The first step in protecting the rights of clients is the informed consent document. **Informed consent** involves the right of clients to be informed about their therapy and to make autonomous decisions pertaining to it. Informed consent is a shared decision-making process in which a practitioner provides adequate information so that a potential client can make an informed decision about participating in the professional relationship (Barnett, Wise, et al., 2007). One benefit of informed consent is that it increases the chances that clients will become involved, educated, and willing participants in their therapy. Mental health professionals are required by their ethics codes to disclose to clients the risks, benefits, and alternatives to proposed treatment. The intent of an **informed consent document** is to define boundaries and clarify the nature of the basic counseling relationship between the counselor and the client. Although informed consent has both legal and ethical dimensions, it is best viewed "as an integral aspect of the psychotherapy process that is essential for its success" (Snyder & Barnett, 2006, p. 40). Informed consent for treatment is a powerful clinical, legal, and ethical tool (Wheeler & Bertram, 2008).

Informed consent entails a balance between telling clients too much and telling them too little. Most professionals agree that it is crucial to provide clients with information about the therapeutic relationship, but the manner in which this is done in practice varies considerably among therapists. It is a mistake to overwhelm clients with too much detailed information at once, but it is also a mistake to withhold important information that clients need if they are to make wise choices about their therapy. Studies of practitioners' informed consent practices have found considerable variability in the breadth and depth of the informed consent given to clients (Barnett, Wise, et al., 2007).

Professionals have a responsibility to their clients to make reasonable disclosure of all significant facts, the nature of the procedure, and some of the more probable consequences and difficulties. Clients have the right to have treatment explained to them. The process of therapy is not so mysterious that it cannot be explained in a way that clients can comprehend how it works. For instance, most residential addictions treatment programs require that patients accept the existence of a power higher than themselves. This "higher power" is defined by the patient, not by the treatment program. Before patients agree to entering treatment, they have a right to know this requirement. It is important that clients give their consent *with* understanding. It is the responsibility of professionals to assess the client's level of understanding and to promote the client's free choice. Professionals need to avoid subtly coercing clients to cooperate with a therapy program to which they are not freely consenting.

Legal Aspects of Informed Consent

Generally, informed consent requires that the client understands the information presented, gives consent voluntarily, and is competent to give consent to treatment (Barnett, Wise, et al., 2007; Wheeler & Bertram, 2008). Therapists must give clients information in a clear way and check to see that they understand it. Disclosures should be given in plain language in a culturally sensitive manner and must be understandable to clients, including minors and people with impaired cognitive functioning (Goodwin, 2009a). To give valid consent, it is necessary for clients to have adequate information about both the therapy procedures and the possible consequences.

Educating Clients About Informed Consent

A good foundation for a therapeutic alliance is for therapists to employ an educative approach, encouraging clients' questions about assessment or treatment and offering useful feedback as the treatment process progresses. Here are some questions therapists and clients could address at the outset of the therapeutic relationship:

- What are the goals of the therapeutic endeavor?
- What services will the counselor provide?

- What is expected of the client?
- What are the risks and benefits of therapy?
- What are the qualifications of the provider of services?
- What are the financial considerations?
- To what extent can the duration of therapy be predicted?
- What are the limitations of confidentiality?
- What information about the counselor's values should be provided in the informed consent document so that clients can choose whether they want to enter a professional relationship with this counselor?
- In what situations does the practitioner have mandatory reporting requirements?
- If the person is referred for an assessment or for therapy from the court or from an employer, who is the client?

A basic part of the informed consent process involves giving clients an opportunity to raise questions and to explore their expectations of counseling. We recommend viewing clients as partners with their therapists in the sense that they are involved as fully as possible in each aspect of their therapy. Practitioners cannot assume that clients clearly understand what they are told initially about the therapeutic process. Furthermore, informed consent is not easily completed within the initial session by asking clients to sign forms. The *Canadian Code of Ethics for Psychologists* (CPA, 2000) states that informed consent involves a process of reaching an agreement to work collaboratively rather than simply having a consent form signed (Section 1.17).

Informed consent is a collaborative process that helps to establish and enhance the therapeutic relationship (Snyder & Barnett, 2006). The more clients know about how therapy works, including the roles of both client and therapist, the more clients will benefit from the therapeutic experience. Educating clients about the therapeutic process is an ongoing endeavor. Informed consent is not a single event; rather, it is best viewed as a process that continues for the duration of the professional relationship as issues and questions arise (Barnett, Wise, et al., 2007; Barnett & Johnson, 2010; Goodwin, 2009a; Snyder & Barnett, 2006; Wheeler & Bertram, 2008).

The informed consent process is a way of engaging the full participation of the client; it is a means of empowering the client, giving it clinical as well as ethical significance. Especially in the case of clients who have been victimized, issues of power and control can be central in the therapy process. The process of informing clients about therapy increases the chances that the client–therapist relationship will become a collaborative partnership.

Practitioners are ethically bound to offer the best quality of service available, and clients have a right to know that managed care programs, with their focus on cost containment, may have adverse effects on the quality of care available. Clinicians are expected to provide prospective clients with clear information about the benefits to which they are entitled and the limits of treatment.

Miller (1996b) asserts that quality of care is likely to decline under restrictive managed care programs. In her discussion of the ethics of therapy in a managed care environment, Wineburgh (1998) states that informed consent issues are particularly complicated. Clearly, clients have the right to specific information regarding their treatment under managed care and the limitations of their treatment packages. However, professionals are often restricted by managed care organizational contracts from educating clients about treatment allocation decisions. Managed care contracts often have "gag clauses" that prohibit practitioners from sharing any negative information about managed care policies, including options not covered by the plan. Koocher and Keith-Spiegel (2008) contend that these policies are inappropriate when applied to health care. Such a rule can be viewed as a restriction of client advocacy and as a measure of intimidation. These restrictions often work against the mental health worker's ethical obligation to provide clients with information regarding benefits, risks, and costs of various interventions. Limits curtail the freedom of both clients and health care providers. In the managed care environment, consumers in need of therapy may be denied service, clients who are treated may be systematically undertreated, and those with moderate to severe problems requiring longer-term treatment may not receive it. Therapists have an obligation to educate consumers, and managed care programs that promote financial interests to the detriment of quality treatment should be held legally responsible for any adverse impact on clients (Newman & Bricklin, 1991). On one hand, you are ethically obligated to give accurate information to the client, and on the other hand, you may be restricted from giving full information to the client by the managed care company. (Chapter 10 includes a detailed discussion of the ethical issues associated with managed care.)

Informed Consent in Practice

How do practitioners assist clients in becoming informed partners? Some recommend that information about the therapeutic process be provided to clients both verbally and in writing (Barnett, Wise, et al., 2007; Pomerantz & Handelsman, 2004; Snyder & Barnett, 2006). In one study, only 25% of the mental health professionals surveyed acknowledged utilizing written informed consent agreements with their clients (Croarkin, Berg, & Spira, 2003). Pomerantz and Handelsman (2004) state that clients have a right to know what the therapy process entails because they are buying a service from a professional. Some of the topics they have developed include a series of questions pertaining to what therapy is and how it works, the clinician's approach, alternatives, appointments, confidentiality, fees, procedures for filing for insurance reimbursement, and policies pertaining to managed care. Pomerantz and Handelsman believe that an open discussion of a wide range of questions about the therapy process enhances the therapeutic alliance and lays the groundwork for a relationship based on empowerment through information. Grosso (2002) recommends that the written consent form be designed in the form of a therapeutic contract. A written consent agreement can augment all verbal consent discussions (Barnett, Wise, et al., 2007; Barnett & Johnson, 2010). In general, client misunderstanding is reduced through the effective use of informed consent procedures, which also tends to reduce the chances a client will file a liability claim. Both the practitioner and the client benefit from this practice.

We have emphasized the importance of the therapist's role in teaching clients about informed consent and encouraging clients' questions about the therapeutic process. With this general concept in mind, put yourself in the counselor's place in the following case. Identify the main ethical issues in this case, and think about what you would do in this situation.

■ The Case of Dottie.

At the initial interview the therapist, Dottie, does not provide an informed consent form and touches only briefly on the process of therapy. In discussing confidentiality, she states that whatever is said in the office will stay in the office, with no mention of the limitations of confidentiality. Three months into the therapy, the client exhibits some suicidal ideation. Dottie has recently attended a conference at which malpractice was one of the topics of discussion, and she worries that she may have been remiss in not providing her client with adequate information about her services, including confidentiality and its limitations. She hastily reproduces an informed consent document that she received at the conference and asks her client to sign the form at the next session. This procedure seems to evoke confusion in the client, and he makes no further mention of suicide. After a few more sessions, he calls in to cancel an appointment and does not schedule another appointment. Dottie does not pursue the case further.

- What are the ethical and legal implications of the therapist's practice? Explain your position.

- If you had been in Dottie's situation, what might you have done?

- Would you have contacted this client after he canceled? Why or why not? What are your thoughts about Dottie not doing that?

Commentary. This case illustrates the absolute importance of making sure the informed consent process is attended to from the outset of therapy. If we only address critical issues when they arise, clients may be justifiably angry and the quality of the therapeutic relationship may be jeopardized. Unfortunately, Dottie focused solely on her own interests in this case. The belated use of an informed consent form and Dottie's willingness to allow the client to terminate abruptly do not enhance the client's best interests or protect him from harm. When this client canceled the appointment, Dottie had an ethical responsibility to pursue the matter to determine whether he had terminated therapy because of her belated attention to the informed consent process.

Consider the following case as you think about your personal stance on what you might include in your informed consent document regarding your personal beliefs and values.

■ The Case of Kieran.

Kieran is a counselor in community agency setting who has strong religious beliefs. He is open about this in his professional disclosure statement, explaining that his religious beliefs play a major part in his personal and professional life. Carmel comes to Kieran for counseling regarding what she considers to be a disintegrating marriage. Kieran has strong convictions that favor preserving the family unit. After going through an explanation of the informed consent document, Kieran asks Carmel if she is willing to join him in a prayer for the successful outcome of the therapy and for the preservation of the family. Kieran then takes a history and assures Carmel that everything can be worked out. He adds that he would like to include Carmel's husband in the sessions. Carmel leaves and does not return.

- Do you see any potential ethical violations on Kieran's part?
- If Kieran came to you for consultation, what might you say to him?
- Is it appropriate to include your personal values and beliefs in the informed consent process? Do clients have a right to know your personal values? How might this help or hinder their work with you?

Commentary. Although we appreciate Kieran's frankness in presenting his values as part of the informed consent process, we question his approach to Carmel. He does not assess the client's state of mind, her religious convictions, if any, the strength of her convictions, or her degree of comfort with his approach. Carmel may have felt pressured to agree with him in this first session, or she may not have had the strength to disagree openly. We question whether Carmel is able to give truly informed consent under these circumstances. It is not appropriate for the therapist to introduce prayer into the session, even though he tells clients that this is part of his philosophy. If this is important to Carmel, it would be her place to introduce prayer in the session. The ethical issue is captured in this question: "Did Kieran take care of the client's needs, or did he take care of his own needs at Carmel's expense?" Keep in mind that providing clear informed consent about one's convictions does not relieve counselors of the duty to respect clients' cultural traditions—including religious beliefs—and the prohibition regarding imposing one's values on clients.

The Content of Informed Consent

One of the main aims of the first meeting is to establish rapport and create a climate of safety in the therapeutic situation. Realizing that informed consent is an ongoing process, the challenge is to provide clients with just the right amount of information at this session for them to make informed choices. The types and amounts of information, the specific content of informed consent, the style of presenting information, and the timing of introducing this information must be considered within the context of state licensure requirements, work setting, agency policies, and the nature of the client's concerns. The content of informed consent is also determined by the specific client population being served. It should be added that there is no assurance that practitioners can avoid legal action, even if they do obtain written informed consent. Rather than focusing on legalistic documents, we suggest that you develop informed consent procedures that stress client understanding and foster client–counselor dialogue within the therapeutic partnership.

Topics selected for discussion during early counseling sessions are best guided by the concerns, interests, and questions of the client. Let's look in more detail at some of the topics about which clients should be informed.

The Therapeutic Process

Although it may be difficult to give clients a detailed description of what occurs in therapy, some general ideas can be explored. We support the practice of letting clients know that counseling might open up levels of awareness that could cause pain and anxiety. Clients who require long-term therapy need to know that they may experience changes that could produce disruptions and turmoil in their lives. Some clients may choose to settle for a limited knowledge of themselves rather than risking this kind of disruption, and this should be explored but also respected. We believe it is appropriate to use the initial sessions for a frank discussion of how change happens. Clients should understand the procedures and goals of therapy and know that they have the right to refuse to participate in certain therapeutic techniques.

Background of the Therapist

Therapists can provide clients with a description of their training and education, their credentials, licenses, any specialized skills, their theoretical orientation, the types of clients and types of problems in which they have competence, and the types of problems that they cannot work with effectively. State licensure boards often make giving this information a legal requirement. If the counseling will be done by an intern or a paraprofessional, clients should be made aware of this. Likewise, if the provider will be working with a supervisor, this fact should be made known to the client. This description of the practitioner's qualifications, coupled with a willingness to answer any questions clients have about the process, reduces the unrealistic expectations clients may have about therapy. It also reduces the chances of malpractice actions.

When you disclose your values, clients are in a better position to decide whether to work with you or not. However, this disclosure should be based on the client's needs and situation. By disclosing values that would make it difficult for you to maintain objectivity, the client is protected from the effects of your bias. If you fail to make such disclosures and later refer your client due to value conflicts, you may face legal jeopardy related to abandoning your client. The timing of disclosure also is important as too much information at the beginning of therapy, or extraneous information, may only serve to confuse or overwhelm the client.

Costs Involved in Therapy

It is essential to provide information about all costs involved in psychological services at the beginning of these services, including methods of payment. Clients need to be informed about how insurance reimbursement will be taken care of and any limitations of their health plan with respect to fees. If fees are subject to change, this should be made clear in the beginning.

Most ethics codes have a standard pertaining to establishing fees. Matters of finance are delicate and, if handled poorly, can lead to problems between client and therapist. Mental health practitioners put themselves and the therapeutic relationship at risk if they allow a client to accrue a large debt without discussing a plan for payment. Although therapists can initiate legal action against a client for nonpayment of fees, this can result in the client filing a claim against the counselor (Wheeler & Bertram, 2008). The manner in which fees are handled has much to do with the tone of the therapeutic partnership.

Some professional codes of ethics recommend a sliding fee scale because the financial resources of clients are variable. In addition, most codes have a *pro bono* guideline that encourages practitioners to share their expertise with those who cannot afford to pay for services. Individual practitioners will aspire to different standards regarding pro bono work, but denying needed services to clients as soon as their insurance has been exhausted raises concerns regarding ethical practice and standards of care. Clinicians should strive to see that clients obtain the services they need.

The Length of Therapy and Termination

Clients should know that they can choose to terminate therapy at any time, yet it is important for the client to discuss the matter of termination with the therapist. Part of the informed consent process involves providing clients with information about the length of treatment and the termination of treatment. Regardless of the length of treatment, it is important for clients to be prepared for a termination phase. Termination should be addressed from the outset of the professional relationship. An effective termination process is critical in securing trust in the overall therapy process while minimizing the return of symptoms or feelings of exploitation. Termination is a key phase of every client's treatment, and therapists should help clients plan for it, prepare for it, and process it (Barnett, MacGlashan, & Clarke, 2000).

Many agencies have a policy limiting the number of sessions provided to clients. These clients should be informed at the outset that they cannot receive long-term therapy. Under a managed care system, clients are often limited to 6 sessions, or a specified amount for a given year, such as 20 sessions. The limited number of sessions needs to be brought to their attention more than once. Furthermore, clients have the right to expect a referral so that they can continue exploring whatever concerns initially brought them to therapy. If referrals are not possible but the client still needs further treatment, the therapist should explain other alternatives available to the client.

Because practitioners differ with respect to an orientation of long-term versus short-term therapy, it is important to inform clients of the basic assumptions underlying your orientation. In a managed care setting, practitioners will need to have expertise in assessing a client's main psychological issues quickly, and matching each client with the most appropriate intervention. They will also need to acquire competency in delivering brief interventions.

Health maintenance organizations (HMOs) exert considerable influence over basic decisions that affect the therapy process, including length of treatment, number of sessions, the amount of money that will be reimbursed, and even the content of therapy (Smith & Fitzpatrick, 1995). If a health maintenance organization and the therapist disagree about the number of sessions required for effective therapy, the therapist might do well to request in writing from the HMO representative the reasons for not allowing further treatment. Part of informing clients about the therapeutic process entails giving them relevant facts about brief interventions that may not always meet their needs. Clients have a right to know how their health care program is likely to influence the course of their therapy as well as the limitations imposed by the program.

Clients have a right to expect that their therapy will end when they have realized the maximum benefits from it or have obtained what they were seeking when they entered it. The issue of termination needs to be openly explored by the therapist and the client, and the decision to terminate ultimately should rest with the client. Termination of therapy, with or without managed care involvement, is of critical concern in the therapeutic relationship. It demands the same kind of care and attention that initiated the professional relationship. With appropriate disclosure of additional options, a client could continue to see a therapist on new payment terms after insurance coverage has been exhausted if both client and therapist believe this is in the client's best interest.

Consultation With Colleagues

Student counselors generally meet regularly with their supervisors and fellow students to discuss their progress and any problems they encounter in their work. It is good policy for counselors to inform their clients that they may consult with other professionals on their cases. Experienced clinicians often schedule consultation meetings with their peers to focus on how they are serving clients. Even though it is ethical for clinicians to discuss their cases with other professionals, it is wise to routinely let clients know about this. Clients will then have less reason to feel that the trust they are putting in their counselor is being violated.

Interruptions in Therapy

Most ethics codes specify that therapists should consider the welfare of their clients when it is necessary to interrupt or terminate the therapy process. It is a good practice to explain early in the course of treatment with clients the possibilities for both expected and unexpected interruptions in therapy and how they might best be handled. A therapist's absence might appear as abandonment to some clients, especially if the absence is poorly handled. As much as possible, therapists should have a plan for any interruptions in therapy, such as vacations or long-term absences. When practitioners plan vacations, ethical practice entails providing clients with another therapist in case of need. Clients need information about the therapist's method of handling emergencies as part of their orientation to treatment. Practitioners will need to obtain a client's written consent to provide information to their substitutes. McGee (2003) recommends that therapists include in their informed consent document the name of at least one professional colleague who is willing to assume their professional responsibilities in the event of an emergency, such as the therapist becoming incapacitated through injury or death. Who will maintain their files should also be addressed at this time.

Benefits and Risks of Treatment

Clients should have some information about both the benefits and the risks associated with a treatment program. Due to the fact that clients are largely responsible for the outcomes of therapy, it is a good policy to emphasize the role of the client's responsibility. Clients need to know that no promises can be made about specific outcomes, which means that ethical practitioners avoid promising a cure. When therapists use techniques that are not traditionally recognized, they are expected to inform their clients of the potential risks and alternatives to such treatments (Snyder & Barnett, 2006).

Alternatives to Traditional Therapy

According to the ethics codes of some professional organizations, clients need to know about alternative helping systems. Therefore, it is a good practice for therapists to learn about community resources so they can present these alternatives to a client. Some alternatives to psychotherapy include self-help programs, stress management, programs for personal-effectiveness training, peer self-help groups, indigenous healing practices, bibliotherapy, 12-step programs, support groups, and crisis-intervention centers.

This information about therapy and its alternatives can be presented in writing, through an audiotape or videotape, or during an intake session.

An open discussion of therapy and its alternatives may, of course, lead some clients to choose sources of help other than therapy. For practitioners who make a living providing therapy services, asking their clients to consider alternative treatments can produce financial anxiety. However, openly discussing therapy and its alternatives is likely to reinforce many clients' decisions to continue therapy. Clients have a right to know about alternative therapeutic modalities (such as different theoretical orientations and medication) that are known to be effective with particular clients and conditions.

Tape-Recording or Video-Recording Sessions

Many agencies require that interviews be recorded for training or supervision purposes. Clients have a right to be informed about this procedure at the initial session, and it is important that they understand why the recordings are made, how they will be used, who will have access to them, and how they will be stored. Therapists sometimes make recordings because they can benefit from listening to them or by having colleagues listen to their interactions with clients and give them feedback. It is essential for trainees or counselors to secure the permission of clients before making any kind of electronic recording.

Clients' Right of Access to Their Files

Clinical records are kept for the benefit of clients. Remley and Herlihy (2010) maintain that clients have a legal right to inspect and obtain copies of records kept on their behalf by professionals. Clients have the ultimate responsibility for decisions about their own health care, and in most circumstances also have the right of access to complete information with respect to their condition and the care provided. A professional writes about a client in descriptive and nonjudgmental ways. A clinician who operates in a professional manner should not have to worry if his or her notes were to become public information or be read by a client.

Some clinicians question the wisdom of sharing counseling records with a client. They may operate on the assumption that their clients are not sophisticated enough to understand their diagnosis and the clinical notes, or they may think that more harm than benefit could result from disclosing such information to clients. Rather than automatically providing clients access to what is written in their files, some therapists give clients an explanation of their diagnosis and the general trend of what kind of information they are recording. Other clinicians are willing to grant their clients access to information in the counseling records they keep, especially if clients request specific information.

Giving clients access to their files seems to be consistent with the consumer-rights movement, which is having an impact on the fields of mental health, counseling, rehabilitation, and education. One way to reduce the growing trend toward malpractice suits and other legal problems is to allow clients to see their medical records, even while hospitalized. In some situations it would not be in the best interests of clients to see the contents of their records. The clinician needs to make a professional determination of those times when seeing records might be counterproductive. Later in this chapter we discuss procedures for keeping records.

Rights Pertaining to Diagnostic Classifying

One of the major obstacles for some therapists to the open sharing of files with clients is the need to give clients a diagnostic classification as a requirement for receiving third-party reimbursement for psychological services. Some clients are not informed that they will be so classified, what those classifications are, or that the classifications and other confidential material will be given to insurance companies. Clients also do not have control over who can receive this information. For example, in a managed care system office workers will have access to specific information about a client, such as a diagnosis. Ethical practice includes informing clients that a diagnosis can become a permanent part of their file. Indeed, a diagnosis can have ramifications in terms of costs of insurance, long-term insurability, and employment. With this information, clients are at least in the position to decline treatment with these restrictions. Some clients have the means to pay for the kind of therapy they want and may choose not to use a third-party payer.

The Nature and Purpose of Confidentiality

Clients should be educated regarding matters pertaining to confidentiality, privileged communication, and privacy (which we discuss in Chapter 6). All of the professional codes have a clause stating that clients have a right to know about any limitations of confidentiality from the outset. For example, the *Code of Ethics of the American Mental Health Counselors Association* (2000) has the following principle pertaining to confidentiality:

> At the outset of any counseling relationship, mental health counselors make their clients aware of their rights in regard to the confidential nature of the counseling relationship. They fully disclose the limits of, or exceptions to, confidentiality, and/or the existence of privileged communication, if any. (3.a.)

Putting this principle into action not only educates clients but also promotes trust. The effectiveness of the client–therapist relationship is built on a foundation of trust. If trust is lacking, it is unlikely that clients will engage in significant self-disclosure and self-exploration.

Part of establishing trust involves making clients aware of how certain information will be used and whether it will be given to third-party payers. Pomerantz and Handelsman (2004) indicate that clients have a right to expect answers from the therapist on questions such as these:"How do governmental regulations, such as federal Health Information Portability and Accountability Act (HIPAA) regulations, influence the confidentiality of records? How much and what kind of information will you be required to give the insurance company about therapy sessions?"

Clients in a managed care program need to be told that the confidentiality of their communications might well be compromised to some extent. It is important for clients to be informed that the managed care organization has the power to limit reimbursement for services. Furthermore, therapists are generally required to release confidential information to determine how much treatment is deemed necessary. Some therapists are concerned that clients will not engage in self-disclosure if they know that confidential information is given to a managed care organization. It is unethical for therapists to withhold the limits of confidentiality from clients in this context (Kremer & Gesten, 1998). Clearly, when a practitioner contracts with a third-party payer, a client's records come under the scrutiny and review of the system doing the reimbursing. Therapists are required to secure written consent from their clients for any disclosure made to an insurance company.

VandeCreek (in Donner et al., 2008) suggests that mental health professionals teach clients about the risks of sharing their health information with an insurance company for reimbursement from the beginning of service. Some clients may want to safeguard their privacy and confidentiality by seeking treatment that does not involve third-party reimbursement. Clients may choose to opt out of using managed care to finance their therapy when they fully understand its potential impact. This presents an ethical dilemma for therapists bound by managed care contracts.

As you will see in Chapter 6, confidentiality is not an absolute. Certain circumstances demand that a therapist disclose what was said by a client in a private therapy session or disclose counseling records. Fisher (2008) believes clients have a right to be informed about conditions and limitations of confidentiality before they consent to a professional relationship, regardless of the clinical consequences of that conversation. If a conversation about the nature and extent of information that may be disclosed does not take place, clients lose their right to make autonomous decisions regarding entering the relationship and accepting the confidentiality risks. Fisher stresses the importance of obtaining *truly informed consent*, which involves far more than simply having the client sign a consent form.

The Professional's Responsibilities in Record Keeping

From an ethical, legal, and clinical perspective, an important responsibility of mental health practitioners is to keep adequate records on their clients. The standard of care for all mental health professionals requires keeping current records for all professional contacts. Record keeping serves multiple purposes. The primary purpose for keeping records is to provide high-quality service for clients and to maintain continuity of service if other professionals are involved. Good record keeping also documents that adequate care was provided, which could be an issue in a disciplinary hearing (Welfel, 2010). From a *clinical* perspective, record keeping provides a history that a therapist can use in reviewing the course of treatment. From an *ethical* perspective, records can assist practitioners in providing quality care to their clients. From a *legal* perspective, state or federal law may require keeping a record, and many practitioners believe that accurate and detailed clinical records can provide an excellent defense against malpractice claims. From a *risk management* perspective, keeping adequate records is the standard of care (Behnke, 2005; Wheeler & Bertram, 2008; Welfel, 2010). According to Barnett (1999b), accurate, timely, and relevant documentation is useful as a risk management strategy, helps prevent successful malpractice litigation, and helps provide appropriate care in a therapist's absence. Remley and Herlihy (2010) point out that record keeping can benefit the client by assisting in continuity of care when a client is transferred from one professional to another.

Record Keeping From a Clinical Perspective

Maintaining clinical notes has a dual purpose: (a) to provide the best service possible for clients, and (b) to provide evidence of a level of care commensurate with the standards of the profession. Although keeping records is a basic part of a counselor's practice, Remley and Herlihy (2010) suggest that it is critical to balance the need to maintain adequate records with the obligation to provide quality counseling services: "Counselors who find themselves devoting inordinate or excessive amounts of time creating and maintaining records probably need to reevaluate how they are spending their professional time and energy" (p. 130). Practitioners need to balance client care with legal and ethical requirements for record keeping (APA, 2007). Griffin (2007) states that writing progress notes can be a simple and straightforward process that takes little time. He recognizes that some events that occur in a given session may be especially noteworthy and require extra time to document, but most sessions can be adequately documented in a brief way.

It is important to distinguish between progress notes and process notes. **Progress notes** are a means of documenting aspects of a client's treatment and are kept in a client's clinical record. These notes may be used to document significant issues or concerns related to a client's treatment (Griffin, 2007). Progress notes are behavioral in nature and address what people say and do. They contain information on diagnosis, functional status, symptoms, treatment plan, consequences, alternative treatments, and client progress. **Process notes,** or *psychotherapy notes,* are not synonymous with progress notes; process notes deal with client reactions such as transference and the therapist's subjective impressions of a client. Other areas that might be included in the process notes are intimate details about the client; details of dreams or fantasies; sensitive information about a client's personal life; and a therapist's own thoughts, feelings, and reactions to clients. Process notes are not meant to be readily or easily shared with others. They are intended for the use of the practitioners who created them. As a general rule, it is best to exclude from process notes matters pertaining to diagnosis, treatment plan, symptoms, prognosis, and progress.

The law requires clinicians to keep a clinical record (progress notes) on all clients, but the law *does not* require keeping process (psychotherapy) notes. The HIPAA privacy rule allows clinicians to keep two sets of records, but it does not mandate it. The idea of two sets of records is that one set (progress notes) is more general, less private, and more readily accessible to insurers and clients. The other set (process notes) is more private and for the use of the therapist. If a therapist does keep process notes, they must be kept separately from the individual's clinical record. Legal requests for documentation in the context of litigation may include requests for process notes as well as progress notes, so it is prudent to consider that process notes may also someday become the subject of courtroom scrutiny.

A client's clinical record is not the place for a therapist's personal opinions or personal reactions to the client, and record keeping should reflect professionalism. If a client misses a session, it is a good practice to document the reasons. In writing progress notes, use clear behavioral language. Focus on describing specific and concrete behavior and avoid jargon. It may help to assume that the contents of this record might someday be read in a courtroom with the client present. Although professional documentation is expected to be thorough, it is best to keep notes as concise as possible. Be mindful of the dictum, "If you did not document it, then it did not happen." Record client and therapist behavior that is clinically relevant. Include in clinical records interventions used, client responses to treatment strategies, the evolving treatment plan, and any follow-up measures taken.

Some therapists choose to devote their time to delivering service to clients rather than recording process and progress notes. However, these notes are an important part of practice. At times, therapists may operate on the assumption that keeping clinical records is not an effective use of the limited time they have, which means they would likely adopt a minimalist approach to record keeping. Clinicians may not keep notes because they believe that they can remember what clients tell them, because they are concerned about violating a client's confidentiality and privacy, because they do not want to assume a legalistic stance in their counseling practice, or because they think they do not have time to keep notes on their clients. Regardless of the reason for not keeping records, in today's climate this is inexcusable and violates the common standards of practice. As discussed in the case of Noah, in some states it may be illegal and unethical to avoid keeping notes (Grosso 2002).

■ The Case of Noah.

Noah is a therapist in private practice who primarily sees relatively well-functioning clients. He considers keeping records to be basically irrelevant to the therapeutic process for his clients. As he puts it: "In all that a client says to me in one hour, what do I write down? and for what purpose? If I were seeing high-risk clients, then I certainly would keep notes. Or if I were a psychoanalyst, where everything a client said matters, then I would keep notes." One of his clients, Sue, assumed that he kept notes and one day after a session asked to see her file. Noah had to explain his lack of record keeping to Sue.

- What do you think of Noah's attitude on record keeping? Do you consider it unethical? Why or why not?
- Taking into consideration the kind of clientele Noah sees, is his behavior justified? If you disagree, what criteria would you use in determining what material should be recorded?
- What if a legal issue arises during or after Sue's treatment? How would documenting each session help or not help both the client and the counselor?
- Assuming that some of Noah's clients will move to other locales and see new therapists, does the absence of notes to be transferred to the new therapist have ethical implications?
- How do you react to Noah's opinion that keeping notes is irrelevant in his practice? Explain.
- If keeping notes were not mandated, would you still keep notes? Why or why not?

Commentary. Keeping adequate clinical records is a legal and ethical requirement regardless of the degree of functioning of a client. Note taking is a critical component of therapy; it can help the therapist remember relevant information and is useful as a review of clinical procedures used with a client. Few therapists, if any, can remember everything that is covered in a given session over the course of time. Noah may have to justify in a courtroom how his decision not to keep clinical records affected the standard of care for his clients. Bennett and colleagues (2006) remind us that the legal requirement for maintaining clinical records involves much more than following a set of arbitrary rules: "Good documentation demonstrates that you used a reasonable standard of care in conceptualizing, planning, and implementing treatment" (p. 34).

Record Keeping From a Legal Perspective

According to Rivas-Vazquez and his colleagues (2001), the adage "if it is not documented, it did not happen" has never been more relevant than in today's climate of heightened awareness of potential liability exposure. These authors outline the specific domains required for comprehensive documentation practices. Professional ethics codes also outline the requirements of good record keeping (see the Ethics Codes box titled "Record Keeping"). It is a wise policy for counselors to document their actions in crisis situations such as cases involving potential danger of harm to oneself, others, or physical property. However, it is not in the best interests of clients for counselors to be more concerned about record keeping as a self-protective strategy than they are to providing quality services to clients.

Ethics Codes

Record Keeping

Code of Professional Ethics for Rehabilitation Counselors (CRCC, 2010)

Rehabilitation counselors include sufficient and timely documentation in the records of their clients to facilitate the delivery and continuity of needed services. Rehabilitation counselors take reasonable steps to ensure that documentation in records accurately reflects progress and services provided to clients. If errors are made in records, rehabilitation counselors take steps to properly note the correction of such errors according to agency or institutional policies. (B.6.a.)

National Association of Social Workers (2008)

(a) Social workers should take reasonable steps to ensure that documentation in records is accurate and reflects the services provided.

(b) Social workers should include sufficient and timely documentation in records to facilitate the delivery of services and to ensure continuity of services provided to clients in the future.

(c) Social workers' documentation should protect clients' privacy to the extent that is possible and appropriate and should include only information that is directly relevant to the delivery of services.

(d) Social workers should store records following the termination of services to ensure reasonable future access. Records should be maintained for the number of years required by state statutes or relevant contracts. (3.04.)

American Psychological Association (2002)

Psychologists create, and to the extent the records are under their control, maintain, disseminate, store, retain, and dispose of records and data relating to their professional and scientific work in order to (1) facilitate provision of services later by them or by other professionals, (2) allow for replication of research design and analyses, (3) meet institutional requirements, (4) ensure accuracy of billing and payments, and (5) ensure compliance with law. (6.01)

Wheeler and Bertram (2008) state that practitioners who fail to maintain adequate clinical records are vulnerable to claims of professional malpractice because inadequate records do not conform to the standard of care expected of mental health practitioners. "Well-organized and well-documented client counseling records are the most effective tool counselors have for establishing client treatment plans, ensuring continuity of care in the event of absence, and proving that quality care was provided" (p. 115). They maintain that competent record keeping is also one of the most effective tools counselors have for successfully responding to licensing board complaints or threats of a malpractice suit. Even if a mental health provider acts reasonably and keeps good records, there is no guarantee that he or she will not be sued. Occasionally a competent practitioner will be found liable for damages. As unfair as it seems, the law sometimes imposes a legal responsibility on professionals that they did not know they had (Mary Hermann, personal communication, November 27, 2008).

Case notes should *never* be altered or tampered with after they have been entered into the client's record. Tampering with a clinical record after the fact can cast a shadow on the therapist's integrity in court. Enter notes into a client's record as soon as possible after a therapy session, and sign and date the entry. If you are keeping client notes in a computer, it is essential that your program has a time and date stamp so that if your records are subpoenaed there will be no question of altering material at a later date.

The content and style of a client's records are often determined by agency or institutional policy, state counselor licensing laws, or directives from other regulatory bodies. The particular setting and the therapist's preference may determine how detailed the records will be. The APA (2007) lists the following content areas for inclusion in record keeping:

- Identifying data
- Fees and billing information
- Documentation of informed consent
- Documentation of waivers of confidentiality
- Presenting complaint and diagnosis
- Plan for services
- Client reactions to professional interventions
- Current risk factors pertaining to danger to self or others
- Plans for future interventions
- Assessment or summary information
- Consultations with or referrals to other professionals
- Relevant cultural and sociopolitical factors

The *Record Keeping Guidelines* (APA, 2007) also document procedures for practitioners working with multiple individuals in couples, family, or group therapy. When therapists work with multiple clients, the issues involved in record keeping can become complex. Disclosure of information on one client may compromise the confidentiality of other clients. It may be useful to create and maintain a separate record for each person participating in group therapy. When counseling a couple or a family, the identified client may be the system, in which case a practitioner might keep a single record for the couple or the family.

Record Keeping for Managed Care Programs

Practitioners working within a managed care setting are required to maintain adequate documentation of treatment services. Typically, such organizations require documentation for payment to be received (Barnett, 1999b). A managed care program may audit a practitioner's reports at any time. By law, managed care practitioners are required to keep accurate charts and notes and must provide this information to authorized chart reviewers.

Case law, licensure board statutes and rules, and Medicare/Medicaid reimbursement regulations all contribute to defining the minimum information that mental health records must contain in the managed care context. This information includes the following: client-identifying information; client's chief complaints, including pertinent history; objective findings from the most recent physical examination; intake sheet; documentation of referrals to other providers, when appropriate; findings from consultations and referrals to other health care workers; pertinent reports of diagnostic procedures and tests; signed informed consent for treatment form; diagnosis, when determined; prognosis, including significant continuing problems or conditions; the existence of treatment plans, containing specific target problems and goals; signed and dated progress notes; types of services provided; precise times and dates of appointments made and kept; termination summary; the use and completion of a discharge summary; and release of information obtained (Canter et al., 1994; Grosso, 2002). A managed care company may demand a refund for services rendered if the records do not contain a complete description of all the services rendered.

Record Keeping for School Counselors

In some counseling settings, it may be difficult to keep up with record keeping. For example, in school counseling a student-to-counselor ratio of 400:1 (or more) is not uncommon. How realistic is it to expect a school counselor to keep detailed notes on every contact with a student? Birdsall and Hubert (2000) indicate that a well-kept record may be useful to demonstrate that the quality of counseling provided was in line with an acceptable standard of care. Keeping records is particularly important in cases involving moderate to severe social or emotional problems or when students may be at risk of suicide (Remley, 2009). Maintaining records on parent contacts is also essential. School counselors are cautioned about the importance of safeguarding the confidentiality of any records they keep.

The *Ethical Standards for School Counselors* (ASCA, 2004) addresses the issue of record keeping on students:

The professional school counselor:

(a) Maintains and secures records necessary for rendering professional services to the student as required by laws, regulations, institutional procedures and confidentiality guidelines.

(b) Keeps sole-possession of records separate from students' educational records in keeping with state laws. (A.8.)

School counselors need to be concerned about both administrative and clinical records. Administrative records are the cumulative files on students that are available to other school personnel. Clinical records are the case notes documenting important events regarding a counseling relationship with a student (Remley & Hermann, 2000). At times, school counselors may need to educate teachers about what to enter into a student's cumulative folder. One of our colleagues reports that he had to ask teachers to rewrite their observational reports to remove judgmental terms such as "lazy" or "bully." School records are open for parents to review, and it is essential to refrain from making negative comments concerning parents in administrative records. These records also follow the students to other schools and can provide biased opinions. All school staff and counselors need to stick to the facts and limit their personal judgments (John Tweton, personal communication, April 2, 2001).

School counselors need to understand the provisions of the Family Educational Rights and Privacy Act of 1974. This federal law requires that schools receiving federal funds provide access to all school records to parents of students under the age of 18 and to students themselves once they reach 18. This law outlines a method for releasing records to clients. Student records are not to be released to third parties without the written consent of parents of minors, or the written consent of adult students (Remley & Hermann, 2000).

Securing Records Now and in the Future

Clients' records must be handled confidentially. ACA's (2005) *Code of Ethics* provides guidelines for storing, transferring, sharing, and disposing of clinical records (see Section B.6.). Counselors have the responsibility for storing client records in a secure place and exercising care when sending records to others by mail or through electronic means.

Be aware that the information in the client's record belongs to the client, and a copy may be requested at any time. It is mandatory to treat a client in an honest and respectful fashion, and it is also expected that accurate records will be kept. Mental health practitioners bear the ultimate responsibility for what they write, how they store and access records, what they do with these records, and when and how they destroy them (Nagy, 2005). Clinicians are ethically and legally required to keep records in a secure manner and to protect client confidentiality. They are also responsible for taking reasonable steps to establish and maintain the confidentiality of information based on their own delivery of services, or the services provided by others working under their supervision.

Practitioners need to consider relevant state and federal laws and the policies of their work setting in determining how long to retain a client's records. HIPAA requires that all health care records be maintained for at least six years (Welfel, 2010). Behnke, Preis, and Bates (1998) recommend keeping records as long it is reasonably possible. They suggest retaining records for a period of 10 years following termination of treatment, and 10 years after a minor client has turned 21. They also recommend keeping a brief summary of a client's treatment once the client's complete records are destroyed. Because regulations vary from state to state, Moline, Williams, and Austin (1998) advise practitioners to find out the specific time period for retention of records that is required by the jurisdiction in which they practice. Whether records are active or inactive, counselors are expected to maintain and store them safely and in a way in which timely retrieval is possible. Extra care should be taken if information is stored on computer disks.

It is wise to think about what will happen to your clinical records after your death or if you are otherwise incapacitated. Most state laws do not specify how records are to be handled upon a therapist's death, but Riemersma (2000) suggests that you give thought to how you expect your records to be handled before it is too late for you to be involved in the decision making. Consider creating a professional will that names another professional who, at least temporarily, will handle your files and clients if you die or become otherwise incapacitated. Here are some questions to consider:

- Who will have access to your records in the event of your death?
- Should your clients be given an opportunity to obtain their records, or should they be given the opportunity to have their records transferred to another therapist?
- Should the records be placed in the custody of another health care professional with the clients so notified?
- Should the records be destroyed immediately, with or without giving clients the opportunity to retrieve their records?
- Is a therapist in the community willing to take over your practice in the case of your death?

It is important to answer these questions to safeguard your estate. A client can bring suit against your estate after your death if you have failed to consider some of these matters. Even death does not shield us from a malpractice suit!

Ethical Issues in Online Counseling

In this section we consider a few of the key ethical issues in the use of online counseling and the many forms of service delivery via the Internet. This rapidly developing field involves both potential benefits and risks, and just as with any new practice area, practitioners have a primary duty to consider the best interests of the client, to strive to do no harm, and to adhere to legal requirements (Koocher & Morray, 2000). Mental health professionals have the responsibility of evaluating the ethical, legal, and clinical issues related to providing counseling and behavioral services to individuals over a distance (Mallen, Vogel, & Rochlen, 2005). VandenBos and Williams (2000) agree that mental health professionals must make decisions about how they wish to incorporate delivery of services via the Internet into their practices, but they also assert that professional associations should develop standards for these services. We believe it is important for professional organizations to exert their influence in designing effective guidelines for online counseling rather than waiting for case law to determine the rules.

Ethics Codes and Technology

The *Code of Ethics of the American Mental Health Counselors Association* (AMHCA, 2000) includes guidelines for Internet online counseling that address issues pertaining to confidentiality, client and counselor identification, client waiver, establishing the online counseling relationship, competence, and legal considerations. The APA (2002) ethics code states that psychologists who offer services via electronic transmission inform clients/patients of the risks to privacy and limits of confidentiality. The ACA (2005) ethics code states that counselors are expected to inform clients of the benefits and limitations of using technology in the counseling process (A.12.). The Ethics Codes box titled "Technology Applications: American Counseling Association (2005)" sets guidelines for using this new technology.

Emerging Issues in Online Counseling

The ethics of online therapy are currently being vigorously debated in the profession, with major cautions centering on its value for clients experiencing significant psychological distress, recurrent psychopathology, and suicidal or homicidal intent (Welfel, 2009). According to Welfel application of the duty to protect standard when a client discloses threats of harm to self or others via e-mail or another electronic medium is an issue receiving thoughtful attention.

Shaw and Shaw (2006) assessed the current ethical practices of 88 online counselors. Their "Ethical Intent Checklist" included the following results:

- Only one third of the online counselors required an intake procedure and an electronically signed waiver explaining the limits of confidentiality on the Internet.
- Less than half of the online counselors required the client to give his or her full name and address.
- Less than half of the websites provided a statement concerning circumstances when confidentiality must be breached.
- Only one third of the websites provided a statement that the Internet is not completely secure and that confidentiality could not be guaranteed.
- Only half of the websites provided a statement that online counseling is not the same as face-to-face counseling.

In general, Shaw and Shaw found that online counselors lack knowledge about ethics codes and ethical practices. They conclude that "if we, as counseling professionals, do not address the ethics in online counseling directly and specifically, we are allowing online service providers to call themselves counselors and what they do as counseling without their being obligated to operate within the professional boundaries of the field" (p. 51).

Ethics Codes

Technology Applications: American Counseling Association (2005)

A.12. Technology Applications

A.12.a. Benefits and Limitations
Counselors inform clients of the benefits and limitations of using information technology applications in the counseling process and in business/billing procedures. Such technologies include but are not limited to computer hardware and software, telephones, the World Wide Web, the Internet, online assessment instruments, and other communication devices.

A.12.b. Technology-Assisted Services
When providing technology-assisted distance counseling services, counselors determine that clients are intellectually, emotionally, and physically capable of using the application and that the application is appropriate for the needs of clients.

A.12.c. Inappropriate Services
When technology-assisted distance counseling services are deemed inappropriate by the counselor or client, counselors consider delivering services face to face.

A.12.d. Access
Counselors provide reasonable access to computer applications when providing technology-assisted distance counseling services.

A.12.e. Laws and Statutes
Counselors ensure that the use of technology does not violate the laws of any local, state, national, or international entity and observe all relevant statutes.

A.12.f. Assistance
Counselors seek business, legal, and technical assistance when using technology applications, particularly when the use of such applications crosses state or national boundaries.

Advantages and Disadvantages of Online Counseling

Most experts agree that what is being currently offered via Internet counseling cannot be considered traditional psychotherapy, yet many think this form of service delivery may benefit consumers who are reluctant to seek more traditional treatment (Rabasca, 2000a). Chang and Yeh (2003) state that Asian American men tend to underutilize mental health services. They point out that this fact reflects the inadequacies of traditional psychotherapy more than the absence of need in this population. They suggest that online groups enable men to be less constrained by masculine stereotypes by offering a more anonymous context for expressing their emotions and personal concerns.

Ritterband and colleagues (2003) state that the provision of health care over the Internet is rapidly evolving and provides a potentially beneficial means of delivering treatment that may be unobtainable otherwise. The benefits of using Internet interventions are vast because of the potential for greater numbers of people to receive services. Web-based treatment interventions offer an opportunity for practitioners to provide specific behavioral treatments tailored to individuals who may need to seek professional assistance from their own homes. Ritterband and colleagues indicate that ethical and legal issues, including privacy, confidentiality, data validity, credentials of professionals, potential misuse of Internet interventions, and equality of Internet access, must be addressed when using Internet interventions. In addition, Internet interventions must first demonstrate feasibility and efficacy through rigorous scientific testing.

There are advantages and disadvantages in using Internet technology to deliver counseling services. Riemersma and Leslie (1999) suggest these advantages for consumers of Internet counseling:

- Some consumers want brief, convenient, and anonymous therapy service.
- Some clients who are unwilling to participate in traditional therapy may be willing to accept help online.
- For persons with physical disabilities, online services are more accessible.
- This form of counseling is suited to a problem-solving approach, which appeals to many consumers.
- Clients who experience anxiety when talking face-to-face with a therapist, or clients who are extremely shy, may feel more comfortable dealing with their problems by means of a computer.

In addition, Sampson, Kolodinsky, and Greeno (1997) identify some benefits to therapists who deliver counseling services online:

- Access to clients in rural areas
- Facilitates assigning, completing, and assessing client homework
- Enhances record keeping
- Expands the pool of referral services
- Increases flexibility in scheduling
- Increases options for supervision and case conferencing
- Enhances collection of research data

Ravis (2007) maintains that the benefits of distance counseling outweigh the risks. With adequate preparation, support, and resourcefulness, counselors may find that the challenges involved in distance counseling are less daunting than might be imagined. Ravis offers some suggestions for counselors considering online counseling:

- Before offering distance counseling, acquire the appropriate competencies related to this evolving specialty.
- Learn how to adapt traditional methods for effective application to distance counseling.

- Screen clients for suitability with respect to the specific distance services you are considering using.
- As a part of informed consent, educate your clients about the difficult situations that may occur during distance counseling.
- Familiarize yourself with the ethical guidelines that have been developed to inform your specific scope of practice.
- Be aware of the legal issues and state licensure board regulatory policies that govern your specific practices when delivering online counseling.

Freeny (2001) has learned from his practice that online therapy presents a number of therapeutic and ethical concerns, especially with clients in crisis. He underscores the dilemmas clinicians face between honoring the client's desire for anonymity and a therapist's clinical need to be able to respond in an appropriate and timely manner to crisis situations. There are ethical problems involved in using online counseling to deal with a serious crisis, a psychotic individual, or even someone who needs more than a behavioral intervention. According to Freeny, another disadvantage is that insurance companies have not recognized online counseling for reimbursement. Freeny admits that there will be errors as electronic therapy develops, yet he maintains that the risks are worth taking.

Simply having a technology available does not mean that it is appropriate for every client, or perhaps for any client. The potential benefits need to be greater than the potential risks for clients to ethically justify any form of technology that is used for counseling purposes. Here are some of the *disadvantages* we see to the use of online counseling:

- Inaccurate diagnosis or ineffective treatment may be provided due to lack of behavioral clues and the lack of nonverbal information.
- Confidentiality and privacy cannot be guaranteed.
- Therapists' duty to warn or protect others is restricted.
- Clients who are suicidal, suffering extreme anxiety or depression, or who are in crisis may not receive adequate immediate attention.
- Anonymity enables minors to masquerade as adults seeking treatment.
- Transference and countertransference issues are difficult to address.
- Difficult to develop an effective therapeutic alliance with an individual who has never been seen in the traditional face-to-face counseling context.
- Complex long-term psychological problems are not likely to be successfully treated.

Shaw and Shaw (2006) point out that the debate on the usefulness of online counseling will continue until there are adequate data on outcome effectiveness of this medium. They suggest that informed consent documents state that online counseling is not a replacement for traditional face-to-face counseling.

Legal Issues and Regulation of Online Counseling

Because providing counseling services over the Internet is relatively new and controversial, a host of legal questions will not be addressed until lawsuits are filed pertaining to its use, or misuse, in counseling practice. Foxhall (2000) states that the most pressing issue regarding behavioral telehealth or Internet counseling is whether it is legal for a mental health practitioner who is licensed in one state to treat a client in another state by telephone or over the Internet. In some states, licensed mental health professionals cannot practice online counseling in states in which they are not licensed.

Few, if any state legislatures have addressed Internet counseling, although some states have begun restricting physician practice across state lines (Foxhall, 2000). Riemersma and Leslie (1999) write that therapists who choose to offer professional services over the Internet will have to give careful thought to ways of limiting their legal liability and to reducing potential harm to their clients.

Competent Counseling Online

Practitioners need to consider their level of competence in delivering services over the Internet, determine what kinds of services they can and cannot appropriately offer, and assess the benefits and risks of this form of service delivery. Therapists who choose to counsel clients online should acquire special training regarding counseling via the Internet.

Riemersma and Leslie (1999) recommend that therapists address these issues specific to the online counseling environment:

- Evaluate and diagnose a client at the beginning of treatment, ideally through an initial face-to-face session, to determine whether the client is a good candidate for online counseling.
- Require the client to be evaluated by a physician to rule out a physical cause for the client's psychological problem prior to initiating Internet counseling.
- Fully inform the client of the limits and expectations of the online relationship.
- Develop a plan for how emergencies will be dealt with.
- Address with the client, in advance, the limitations involved in confidentiality over the Internet and discuss what actions might be taken in the event that confidentiality is compromised.
- Discuss with the client, in advance, how situations involving technological failure will be handled.

According to Ritterband and colleagues (2003), the use of the Internet is likely to grow in importance as a powerful dimension of successful psychobehavioral treatment. In forecasting future directions, they write:

> It is unlikely that Internet interventions will replace face-to-face psychotherapy; however, this technology may be helpful in the treatment of some psychological problems that might otherwise go untreated. It is also possible that such interventions may enhance traditional therapy as an adjunctive component. (p. 533)

Our Perspective on Online Counseling

Therapists do not have to choose between Internet counseling and traditional face-to-face counseling. Technology can be used in the service of clients and can address some unique needs, especially if therapists combine online and personal sessions. For example, therapists might require one to three face-to-face sessions, if at all possible, to determine the client's suitability for online counseling and to establish a working therapeutic relationship. This will increase the likelihood that online services will be effective. During these face-to-face sessions, time could be allocated for orienting the client to the counseling process and securing informed consent, taking the client's history, conducting an assessment and formulating a diagnostic impression, collaboratively identifying counseling goals, developing a general treatment plan, and formulating a specific plan of action. As the action plan is carried out following these initial sessions, Internet sessions could be used to monitor specific homework assignments. Depending on the client's needs and situation, there might be face-to-face sessions scheduled at regular intervals along with online counseling. Integrating traditional counseling with online counseling in this way can accommodate consumers who would not take advantage of counseling delivered exclusively by face-to-face sessions due to financial considerations or restrictions imposed by traveling long distances.

Some fields of counseling seem better suited for online work than others. For example, career counseling and educational counseling involve gathering information and processing this information. In this endeavor, technology may have some useful applications. Graduate training and continuing education in appropriate technological applications for professional practice are needed (McMinn et al., 1999).

We have reservations about the effectiveness of online counseling for clients with deeply personal concerns or interpersonal issues. Most clinical problems involve complex variables that require human-to-human interaction. At the present time, we do not think online counseling should be used as an exclusive or primary means of delivering services, but in some cases it could be an important adjunct to face-to-face counseling. If you were to make online counseling part of your practice, what ethical considerations would you consider? What are the difficulties that you think most need to be addressed in this area?

Working With Children and Adolescents

The definition of a minor varies from state to state (Barnett & Johnson, 2010). The upper range is 18 to 21 years of age, although some states authorize 16-year-olds to consent to their own health care in some circumstances. Consistent with the increasing concern over the rights of children in general, more attention is being paid to issues such as the minor's right of informed consent. Barnett and Johnson maintain that therapists should clearly discuss the limits of confidentiality with minors as part of the informed consent process, even in those cases when a parent or guardian consents to treatment.

Below are some of the legal and ethical questions faced by human service providers who work with children and adolescents:

- Can minors consent to treatment without parental knowledge and parental consent?
- At what age can a minor consent to treatment?
- To what degree should minors be allowed to participate in setting the goals of therapy and in providing consent to undergo it?
- What are the limits of confidentiality in counseling minors? Would you discuss these limits with minor clients even though a parent or guardian consents to treatment of the minor?
- What does informed consent consist of in working with minors?

We consider some of these questions next and focus on the rights of children when they are clients.

Parental Right to Information About a Minor's Treatment

Each state has specific statutes and regulations that offer guidance to clinicians working with children and adolescents, and it is essential that practitioners become familiar with the laws in their state pertaining to minors (Barnett, Hillard, & Lowery, 2001). In most states, for a minor to enter into a counseling relationship, it is necessary to have informed parental or guardian consent or for counseling to be court ordered (Lawrence & Kurpius, 2000), although there are exceptions to this general rule. A parent is entitled to general information from the counselor about the child's progress in counseling, but parents do not have a right to access a child's records.

Informed consent of parents or guardians may not be legally required when a minor is seeking counseling for dangerous drugs or narcotics, for sexually transmitted diseases, for pregnancy and birth control, or for an examination following alleged sexual assault of a minor over 12 years of age (Lawrence & Kurpius, 2000). The justification for allowing children and adolescents to have access to treatment without parental consent is that some minors might not otherwise seek needed treatment. Some children and adolescents who seek help when given independent access might not do so without the guarantee of privacy.

School Counseling and Parental Consent

It is essential that counselors working with minors know the laws in their state or jurisdiction and understand the policies of the settings in which they work. School counselors do not need to obtain parental consent unless a state statute requires this. Many schools have a student handbook, a part of which typically describes information about counseling services available to students. This handbook is often sent to parents at the beginning of a school year to provide them with school rules and policies, as well as general information about various services offered by the school. At the end of the handbook, there is typically a page that asks for parents' signatures indicating their consent for their children to use the services provided by the school. Such a procedure is a means of securing blanket consent. If parents do not want their children to receive any kind of counseling, this could be indicated at the end of the handbook on the signature page.

In the section on counseling, some handbooks give examples of individual and group counseling activities. For example, counseling sessions may focus on themes such as improving study habits, time management, making good choices, substance abuse prevention, anger management, career development, and other personal or social concerns. At times, specific approval may be required if children want to participate in special counseling (such as a children of divorce group). If parents have questions about any counseling activities, they are given the name of a person to contact at the school. Remley and Herlihy (2010) suggest that parents who object to their child's participation in counseling probably have a legal right to do so.

Seeing Minors Without Parental Consent

Counselors faced with the issue of when to accept minors as clients without parental consent must consider various factors. What is the competence level of the minor? What are the potential risks and consequences if treatment is denied? What are the chances that the minor will not seek help or will not be able to secure parental permission for needed help? How serious is the problem? What are the laws pertaining to providing therapy for minors without parental consent? If practitioners need to make decisions about accepting minors without parental consent, they should know the relevant statutes in their state. They would also be wise to consult with other professionals in assessing the ethical issues involved in each case.

Informed Consent Process With Minors

Minors are not always able to give informed consent. The APA (2002) provides guidance on this matter:

> For persons who are legally incapable of giving informed consent, psychologists nevertheless (1) provide an appropriate explanation, (2) seek the individual's assent, (3) consider such persons' preferences and best interests, and (4) obtain appropriate permission from a legally authorized person, if such substitute consent is permitted or required by law. When consent by a legally authorized person is not permitted or required by law, psychologists take reasonable steps to protect the individual's rights and welfare. (3.10.b.)

The ACA (2005) also addresses this topic:

> When counseling minors or persons unable to give voluntary consent, counselors seek the assent of clients to services, and include them in decision-making as appropriate. Counselors recognize the need to balance the ethical rights of clients to make choices, their capacity to give consent or assent to receive services, and parental or familial legal rights and responsibilities to protect these clients and make decisions on their behalf. (A.2.d.)

Therapists who work with children and adolescents have the ethical responsibility of providing information that will help minor clients become active participants in their treatment. If children lack the background to weigh risks and benefits and if they cannot give complete informed consent, therapists should still attempt to explain the therapy process and general procedures of therapy to them. Even though minors usually cannot give informed consent for treatment, they can give their *assent* to counseling. Assent to treatment implies that counselors involve minors in decisions about their own care, and that to the greatest extent possible they agree to participate in the counseling process (Welfel, 2010).

There are both ethical and therapeutic reasons for involving minors in their treatment. By giving them the maximum degree of autonomy within the therapeutic relationship, the therapist demonstrates respect for them. Also, it is likely that therapeutic change is promoted by informing children about the process and enlisting their involvement in it. In general, the older and more mature a child is, the more he or she can be included in the process of ongoing informed consent. Factors to consider are what the child can and cannot understand, as well as the degree to which the child is able to understand, participate in, and benefit from informed consent.

Involving Parents in the Counseling Process With Minors

To work effectively with a minor it is often necessary to involve the parents or guardians in the treatment process. To the extent that it is possible, it is a good practice for counselors to involve the parents or guardians in the initial meeting with their child to arrive at a clear, mutual agreement regarding the nature and extent of information that will be provided to them. This also gives the therapist an opportunity to see how the child behaves around the parents. This policy makes it possible to create clear boundaries for sharing information and establishes a three-way bond of trust (Lawrence & Kurpius, 2000). The *Ethical Standards for School Counselors* (ASCA, 2004) addresses the matter of the school counselor's responsibilities to parents:

> The professional school counselor respects the rights and responsibilities of parents/guardians for their children and endeavors to establish, as appropriate, a collaborative relationship with parents/guardians to facilitate the student's maximum development. (B.1.a.)

Ethical and Legal Challenges Pertaining to Confidentiality With Minors

Mental health professionals must take special care to protect the rights of minors, but clinicians often experience difficulty when applying ethics codes in their work with children and adolescents (Barnett, Hillard, & Lowery, 2001). According to Benitez (2004), counselors who work with minors are frequently challenged to balance the minor's need for confidentiality and the parents' requests for information about the minor's counseling. Benitez claims that it is a wise policy for practitioners to make it clear to parents of minors that effective counseling requires a sense of trust in the therapist. Information that will or will not be disclosed to parents or guardians must be discussed at the outset of therapy with both the child or adolescent and the parent or guardian. If the matter of confidentiality is not clearly explored with all parties involved, problems can be expected to emerge in the course of therapy.

Therapists cannot guarantee blanket confidentiality to minors. If the parents or guardians of minors request information about the progress of the counseling, the therapist may be expected to provide some feedback. Remley and Herlihy (2010) state that in some circumstances counselors will determine that parents or guardians must be given information that a minor client has disclosed in a counseling session. For example, if a counselor makes the judgment that a minor client is at risk of harm (to self or others), the counselor is required to inform the minor's parents. If a counselor had relevant information and did not take appropriate action to prevent a minor client from injuring him- or herself, or if the minor client harms another person, the counselor may be held legally accountable.

Minors who engage in self-injurious behaviors raise complex issues regarding the limits of confidentiality. Wester (2009) points out that there is little in the ethics codes of the ACA or the APA to assist counselors in determining when to breach confidentiality for minors who engage in self-injurious behavior. It is crucial to set limitations to confidentiality specifically related to self-injurious behavior at the outset of a professional relationship. Also, counselors need to understand the distinction between self-injury and suicidal behavior, as well as have the expertise to identify self-injury when it is presented in counseling by a client. Wester adds that counselors should seek supervision and consultation when necessary so that they are working within the boundaries of their competence.

Although minor clients have an *ethical* right to privacy and confidentiality in the counseling relationship, the law still favors the rights of parents over their children. However, some sensitive information, if revealed or disclosed, may be detrimental to the therapy process. Disclosure of a minor's personal information can result in the child no longer trusting the therapist, fearing that this personal information will be disclosed to parents (Barnett, Hillard, & Lowery, 2001). This should be explained to parents during the informed consent process.

Parents and guardians usually have a *legal* right to information pertaining to counseling sessions with their children, although a court may hold otherwise due to specific state statutes (Remley & Herlihy, 2010). When parents or legal guardians become involved in the counseling process, counselors must acknowledge that these adults have authority over minors (Remley & Hermann, 2000). Marion's case is an example of the challenges a counselor must address in determining how to handle personal information to parents.

■ The Case of Marion.

Marion is a 15-year-old honors student. She discovered that she is pregnant and feels she would be better off dead than being a teenage mom.

Marion was born to teenage parents, so she knows they will never allow her to have an abortion. Marion went to see the school counselor to talk about her situation. The counselor educated Marion on the different options she had in regard to her pregnancy. Marion stated that she wanted to abort her pregnancy. If her parents would not allow her to have an abortion, Marion said she would kill herself. The school counselor persuaded Marion to agree to see a family therapist with her parents, and during the family session Marion's father stated he would not hear of Marion's having an abortion. Marion then stated with conviction that she would kill herself. The family therapist has reason to believe that Marion will act on her threat of suicide.

- If your state had a law requiring parental consent for abortion, how would this influence the interventions you would make in this case?
- Might you encounter a conflict between ethics and the law if you were counseling Marion? How would you deal with her suicidal threat?
- Knowing what Marion told you about her parents' values, would you have involved them in this case? Why or why not?
- Would you use Marion's threat of suicide to influence her parents, or would you ignore this threat? Explain.
- Would you try to involve Marion's spiritual or religious support system in this situation? Why or why not?
- What other options would you consider?

Commentary. The family therapist can act on the suicidal threat, which could result in a 72-hour hospitalization. This takes care of the therapist's legal responsibility, yet this does not solve the problem of Marion's suicidal threats. This case reminds us of the importance of knowing about available resources when there is a suicidal threat, and the need for consultation and documentation. After Marion is released, the therapist will need to continue working with the family. Regardless of what the therapist does and how hard she works to prevent Marion from taking her life, the therapist may not be successful.

Marion's case illustrates the importance of ensuring one's own competence to counsel various types of clients. In this case, the counselor must be competent to work with minors and their families in crisis.

At this point we suggest that you think about some of the legal and ethical considerations in providing counseling for minors.

- Many parents argue that they have a right to know about matters that pertain to their adolescent daughters and sons. They assert, for example, that parents have a right to be involved in decisions about abortion. What is your position?

- If the state in which you practice has a law requiring parental consent for abortion, how would this influence your interventions with minors who were considering an abortion?

- Some people argue for the right of minors to seek therapy without parental knowledge or consent because needed treatment might not be given to them otherwise. When, if at all, would you counsel a minor without parental knowledge and consent?

- What kinds of information should be provided to children and adolescents before they enter a therapeutic relationship?

- If therapists do not provide minors with the information necessary to make informed choices, are they acting unethically? Why or why not?

Counseling Reluctant Children and Adolescents

Some young people resent not having a choice about entering a therapeutic relationship. Adolescents often resist therapy because they become the "identified patient" and the focus is on changing them. These adolescents are frequently aware that they are only *part* of the problem in the family unit. Although many minors indicate a desire to participate in treatment decisions, few are given the opportunity to become involved in a systematic way. Unwillingness to participate in therapy can be minimized if therapists take time to explore the reasons for adolescents' resistance.

■ The Case of Frank.

Frank was expelled from high school for getting explosively angry at a teacher who, according to Frank, had humiliated him in front of his class. Frank was told that he would not be readmitted to school unless he sought professional help. His mother called a therapist and explained the situation to her, and the therapist agreed to see him. Although Frank was uncomfortable and embarrassed over having to see a therapist, he was nevertheless willing to talk. He told the therapist that he knew he had done wrong by lashing out angrily at the teacher, but that the teacher had provoked him. He said that although he was usually good about keeping his feelings inside, this time he had "just lost it."

After a few sessions, the therapist determined that there were many problems in Frank's family. He lived with an extreme amount of stress, and to work effectively with Frank it would be essential to see the entire family. Indeed, he did have a problem, but he was not the entire problem. He was covering up many family secrets, including a verbally abusive stepfather and an alcoholic mother. Hesitantly, he agreed that it would be a good idea to have the entire family come in for therapy. When the therapist contacted the parents, they totally rejected the idea of family therapy. The mother asserted that the problem was with Frank and that the therapist should concentrate her efforts on him. A few days before his next scheduled appointment his mother called to cancel, saying that they had placed Frank in homebound study and that he therefore no longer required counseling.

- What are the ethical responsibilities of the therapist in this situation?
- Should Frank be seen as a condition of returning to school?
- What other strategies could the therapist have used?
- What would you have done differently, and why?
- Should the therapist have seen Frank and the teacher?
- Should the therapist have encouraged Frank to continue his therapy even if his family refused to undergo treatment?

Commentary.   One ethical problem in this case was the treatment of the individual as opposed to the treatment of the family. This case highlights the importance of providing thorough informed consent. If a therapist routinely transitions from individual to marital or family therapy, clients need to understand the circumstances that might prompt the therapist to recommend this role shift.

In this case, there was an alcoholic parent in the family. Frank's expulsion from school could have been more a symptom of the family dysfunction than of his own personal dysfunction. Indeed, he did need to learn anger management, as both the school and the mother contended, yet more was going on within this family that needed attention. In this case it might have been best for the therapist to stick to her initial convictions of family therapy as the treatment of choice. If the parents would not agree to this, she could have made a referral to another therapist who would be willing to see Frank in individual counseling. In many states the therapist would be required to make a child abuse report to Child Protective Services because of the alleged verbal and emotional abuse.

Specialized Training for Counseling Children and Adolescents

Because minors are a special client population, distinct education, training, and supervised practice are required for counselors who expect to work with minor clients (Lawrence & Kurpius, 2000). The ethics codes of the major professional organizations specify that it is unethical to practice in areas for which one has not been trained. It is important not to begin counseling with minors without requisite course work and supervision by a specialist in this area. Many human-service professionals have been trained and supervised in "verbal therapies," but there are distinct limitations in applying these therapeutic interventions to children. Practitioners who want to counsel children may have to acquire supervised clinical experience in play therapy, art and music therapy, and recreational therapy. These practitioners also must understand the developmental issues pertaining to the population with which they intend to work. They need to become familiar with laws relating to minors, to be aware of the limits of their competence, and to know when and how to make appropriate referrals. It is essential to know about community referral resources, such as Child Protective Services.

Involuntary Commitment and Human Rights

The practice of involuntary commitment of people to mental institutions raises difficult professional, ethical, and legal issues. Practitioners must know their own state laws and must be familiar with community resources before taking measures leading to involuntary hospitalization. Good practice involves consulting with professional colleagues to determine the appropriate length and type of treatment (Austin, Moline, & Williams, 1990). The focus of our discussion here is not on specific legal provisions but on the ethical aspects of involuntary commitment.

Under the social policy of "deinstitutionalization," involuntary commitment is sought only after less restrictive alternatives have failed. The main purpose of involuntary hospitalization is to secure treatment for clients rather than to punish them. As it applies to mental health practices, the legal doctrine of using the "least restrictive alternative" requires that treatment be no more harsh, hazardous, or intrusive than necessary to achieve therapeutic aims and to protect clients and others from physical harm (Bednar et al., 1991). Professionals are sometimes confronted with the responsibility of assessing the need to commit clients who pose a serious danger either to themselves or to others. The growing trend is for courts to recognize the therapist's duty to commit such clients. Under most state laws, involuntary civil commitment is based on the following criteria: mental illness, dangerousness to self or others, disability, refusal to consent, treatability, incapacity to decide on treatment, and compliance with the "least restrictive" criterion (Bednar et al., 1991).

Bennett and his colleagues (1990) offer these specific recommendations pertaining to the commitment process:

- Be familiar with your state laws and regulations pertaining to both voluntary and involuntary commitment.
- If you notice that a client's condition is deteriorating, consult with colleagues.
- Carefully consider what you hope to obtain in recommending commitment. Assess the degree to which your client is a danger to self or others.
- Before deciding on a course leading to commitment, consider other options. Also, consider the advisability of referring your client to another professional for evaluation or treatment.

- Ask yourself how commitment might affect the client's attitude toward you as a therapist and toward therapy in general.
- If hospitalization is involuntary, know the procedural steps that must be followed under your state laws.
- Make certain that you can offer reasons for commitment.

Making a decision to commit a client is a serious matter that has implications for you, your client, and members of the client's family. It is essential that you obtain consultation if there is any doubt about the proper course to follow. You need to raise many questions about the appropriateness of choosing commitment over other alternatives. Some writers emphasize practices such as conducting ongoing psychiatric and psychosocial assessments and documenting all examinations and consultations in the client's record. Practitioners are advised to protect themselves from liability associated with involuntary hospitalization by documenting all the steps they take in making this decision (Austin et al., 1990; Bednar et al., 1991).

Malpractice Liability in the Helping Professions

How vulnerable are mental health professionals to malpractice actions? What are some practical safeguards against being involved in a lawsuit? In this section we examine these questions and encourage you to develop a prudent approach to risk management in your practice. It is easy to be anxious over the possibility of being sued, but this is not likely to bring out the best in us as practitioners. We want our discussion of malpractice to lead you to an increased awareness of the range of professional responsibilities and suggest ways to meet these responsibilities in an ethical fashion.

What Is Malpractice?

The word **malpractice** means "bad practice." Malpractice is the failure to render professional services or to exercise the degree of skill that is ordinarily expected of other professionals in a similar situation. Malpractice is a legal concept involving negligence that results in injury or loss to the client. **Professional negligence** can result from unjustified departure from usual practice or from failing to exercise proper care in fulfilling one's responsibilities.

Practitioners are expected to abide by legal standards and adhere to the ethics codes of their profession in providing care to their clients. Unless practitioners take due care and act in good faith, they may be liable in a civil lawsuit for failing to do their duty as provided by law. The primary focus of a negligence suit is determining what **standard of care** to apply in deciding whether a breach of duty to a client has taken place. Clinicians are judged according to the standards that are commonly accepted by the profession; that is, whether a reasonably prudent counselor in a similar circumstance would have acted in the same manner as the counselor acted (Wheeler & Bertram, 2008).

Practitioners need not be infallible, but they are expected to possess and exercise the knowledge, skill, and judgment common to other members of their profession. It is a good policy for practitioners to maintain a reasonable view of the realities involved in dealing with high-risk clients. No matter how ethical and careful you try to be, you can still be accused of malpractice. However, the more careful and ethical you try to be, the less likely you are to be successfully sued. The best defense against becoming embroiled in a malpractice suit is to practice quality client care.

To succeed in a malpractice claim, these four elements of malpractice must be present: (1) a professional relationship between the therapist and the client must have existed; (2) the therapist must have acted in a negligent or improper manner, or have deviated from the "standard of care" by not providing services that are considered "standard practice in the community"; (3) the client must have suffered harm or injury, which must be verified; and (4) there must be a legally demonstrated causal relationship between the practitioner's negligence or breach of duty and the damage or injury claimed by the client. It should be noted that anyone, at any time, can file a suit against you. Even if the suit does not succeed, it can take a toll on you in terms of time and money. You may have to spend many hours preparing and supplying documents and responding to requests for information. However, the burden of proof that harm actually took place is the client's, and the plaintiff must demonstrate that all four elements applied in his or her situation. Let us take a closer look at each of these four elements. This discussion is based on an adaptation of the work of several writers (Austin et al., 1990; Bednar et al., 1991; Bennett et al., 2006; Calfee, 1997; Crawford, 1994; Remley, 2009; Wheeler & Bertram, 2008).

1. **Duty.** There are two aspects of establishing a legal duty: one is the existence of a special relationship, and the other is the nature of that special relationship. A duty exists when a therapist implicitly or explicitly agrees to provide mental health services.

2. **Breach of duty.** After the plaintiff proves that a professional relationship did exist, he or she must show that the duty was breached to the client. Practitioners have specific responsibilities that involve using ordinary and reasonable care and diligence, applying knowledge and skill to a case, and exercising good judgment. If the practitioner failed to provide the appropriate standard of care, the duty was breached. This breach of duty may involve either actions taken by the therapist or a failure to take certain precautions.

3. **Injury.** Plaintiffs must prove that they were injured or damaged in some way—physically, relationally, psychologically—and that actual injuries were sustained. Examples of such injuries include wrongful death (e.g., suicide), loss (e.g., divorce), and pain and suffering.

4. **Causation.** Plaintiffs must demonstrate that the professional's breach of duty was the proximate cause of the injury they suffered. The test in this case lies in proving that the harm would not have occurred if it were not for the practitioner's actions or omissions.

In the case of suicide, for example, two factors determine a practitioner's liability: foreseeability and reasonable care. Most important is *foreseeability*, which involves assessing the level of risk. Failing to conduct a comprehensive risk assessment and to document this assessment would be a major error on the therapist's part. If you are not competent to make such an assessment, then a referral is mandatory so that an assessment can be made. Practitioners need to demonstrate that their judgments were based on data observed and that these judgments were reasonable. The second factor in liability is whether *reasonable care* was provided. Once an assessment of risk is made, it is important to document that appropriate precautions were taken to prevent a client's suicide.

Reasons for Malpractice Suits

The most frequent reasons for disciplinary actions for psychologists from 1994 to 2003 were related to sexual boundary violations, nonsexual multiple relationships, insurance and fee problems, child custody, breach of confidentiality, practicing outside areas of competence, treatment and abandonment, and inadequate diagnosis (Bennett et al., 2006). Other specific areas that constituted grounds for disciplinary actions included conviction of crimes, fraudulent acts, inadequate record keeping, improper or inadequate supervision, impairment, failure to comply with continuing education requirements, and fraud in applying for licensure (Kirkland, Kirkland, & Reaves, 2004).

Malpractice is typically found in the following kinds of situations: (1) the procedure used by the practitioner was not within the realm of accepted professional practice; (2) the practitioner employed a technique that he or she was not trained to use; (3) the professional did not use a procedure that could have been more helpful; (4) the therapist failed to warn others about and protect them from a violent client; (5) informed consent to treatment was not obtained or not documented; or (6) the professional did not explain the possible consequences of the treatment (Wheeler & Bertram, 2008).

Many areas of a therapist's practice could lead to a legal claim, but we will focus on the types of professional negligence that most often put therapists at legal risk. The following discussion of these risk categories is an adaptation of malpractice liability and lawsuit prevention strategies suggested by various writers (Bennett et al., 2006; Calfee, 1997; Kennedy et al., 2003; Kirkland et al., 2004; Knapp & VandeCreek, 2003a; Mitchell, 2007; Stromberg & Dellinger, 1993; Swenson, 1997; VandeCreek & Knapp, 2001; Wheeler & Bertram, 2008).

Failure to obtain or document informed consent.   Therapists need to recognize that they can be liable for failure to obtain appropriate informed consent even if their subsequent treatment of the client is excellent from a clinical perspective. Although written informed consent may not be needed legally, it is wise to have clients sign a form to acknowledge their agreement with the terms of the proposed therapy. Without a written document, it may be very difficult to ascertain whether counselors communicated clearly and effectively to clients about the therapeutic process and whether clients understood the information.

Client abandonment and premature termination.   Younggren and Gottlieb (2008) define **termination** as "the ethically and clinically appropriate process by which a professional relationship is ended" (p. 500). They define **abandonment** as "the failure of the psychologist to take the clinically indicated and ethically appropriate steps to terminate a professional relationship" (p. 500). A central concern associated with termination is avoiding abandonment of a client. Clinical records should give evidence that they were not terminated inappropriately. It is useful to document the nature of a client's termination, including who initiated the termination, how this was handled, the degree to which initial goals were met, and referrals provided when appropriate.

Clients need to be informed about termination and, as much as possible, should be involved in making decisions about when to end their treatment. When both client and therapist agree that the goals of therapy have been achieved and that therapy is no longer required, there is a very low risk that the client will file a malpractice complaint. However, premature termination carries clear risks of a lawsuit when made in the following situations (Younggren & Gottlieb, 2008):

- The practitioner is no longer being compensated by the client or the managed care organization.
- The therapist recognizes he or she is not in the best position to treat the client.
- The client is not making progress toward therapy goals.
- The client lacks motivation or commitment to work toward agreed-upon treatment goals.
- The therapist is abruptly absent.

Courts have determined that the following acts may constitute abandonment: failure to follow up on the outcomes with a client who has been hospitalized; consistently not being able to be reached between appointments; failure to respond to a request for emergency treatment; or failure to provide for a substitute therapist during vacation times. Clients have a case for abandonment when the facts indicate that a therapist unilaterally terminated a professional relationship and that this termination resulted in some form of harm. Under managed care plans, therapists may be accused of abandonment when they terminate a client based on the allocated number of sessions rather than on the therapeutic needs of the client. The codes of ethics apply to practitioners, not to managed care systems.

Sexual misconduct with a client.   Related to the topic of unhealthy transference relationships is the area of sexual boundary violations, one of the most common grounds for malpractice suits. It is *never* appropriate for therapists to engage in sexual contact with clients. This topic is explored in detail in Chapter 7. Court cases suggest that no act is more likely to create legal problems for therapists than engaging in a sexual relationship with a client. Furthermore, initial consent of the client will not be a defense against malpractice actions. Even in the case of sex between a therapist and a former client, courts do not easily accept the view that therapy has ended.

Marked departures from established therapeutic practices. If counselors employ unusual therapy procedures, they put themselves at risk. They bear the burden of demonstrating a rationale for their techniques. If it can be shown that their procedures are beyond the usual methods employed by most professionals, they are vulnerable to a malpractice action. If it is unlikely that an expert can be found to testify to the acceptability of a certain treatment approach, it would be prudent not to employ this approach (Calfee, 1997).

Practicing beyond the scope of competency. Mental health practitioners have been held liable for damages for providing treatment below a standard of care. If the client follows the treatment suggested by a professional and suffers damages as a result, the client can initiate a civil action. Professional health care providers should work only with those clients and deliver only those services that are within the realm of their competence. Accepting a case beyond the scope of a counselor's education and training is not only a breach of ethics but also can result in a malpractice suit.

Mental health professionals have an obligation to work closely with physicians to ensure that a medical condition or side effects from a medication are not causing the psychological symptoms. A client may need to be referred to a physician for a medication evaluation in some instances, and collaboration as well as a referral may become necessary.

If counselors have any doubts about their level of competency to work with certain cases, they should receive peer input or consultation. If a counselor is accused of unethical practice, the counselor must prove that he or she was properly prepared in that area of practice (Chauvin & Remley, 1996). Clinicians can refine their skills by participating in continuing education, taking graduate course work, or seeking direct supervision from a colleague who has relevant clinical experience.

Misdiagnosis. Lacking the ability to demonstrate diagnostic competence can result in making a misdiagnosis or no diagnosis, which could leave the practitioner vulnerable to an allegation of malpractice (Wheeler & Bertram, 2008). It is generally not the court's role to question the therapist's diagnosis. However, in cases where it can be shown through the therapist's records that a diagnosis was clearly unfounded and below the standard of care, a case of malpractice might be successful. In court, an expert witness is often questioned to determine whether the therapist used appropriate assessment procedures and arrived at an appropriate diagnosis. It is wise for mental health practitioners to require a prospective client to undergo a complete physical examination, as the results of this examination might have a bearing on the client's diagnosis and affect his or her treatment (Calfee, 1997).

Repressed or false memory. A memory is considered false if it is arrived at through an untested intervention by the therapist rather than being the client's actual memory. Therapists have been sued and found guilty of such induced memories. A jury in Minnesota awarded more than $2.6 million to a woman who claimed she was injured by false memories of abuse induced after her psychiatrist suggested that she suffered from a multiple personality disorder, which most likely was the result of repeated sexual abuse by relatives (Wheeler & Bertram, 2008). Certainly, the style in which a therapist questions a client can influence memories, particularly for young children. Repeated questioning can lead a person to believe in a "memory" of an event that did not occur. A trusted therapist who suggests past abuse as a possible cause of problems or symptoms can greatly influence the client.

What is the best course for you to follow when you suspect that past sexual abuse is related to a client's present problem? How can you best protect the client, the alleged abuser, and other family members, without becoming needlessly vulnerable to a malpractice suit? Wheeler and Bertram (2008) recommend following these basic clinical and ethical principles:

- Be attentive to the kinds of questions you ask clients.
- Remain nonjudgmental and demonstrate empathy as you talk to a client about possible memories of abuse.
- Avoid prejudging the truth of the client's reports.
- If a client reports a memory, explore it with the person.
- Make use of standard assessment and treatment techniques.
- Avoid pressuring the client to believe events that may not have actually occurred.
- Do not suggest to clients that they terminate the relationship precipitously. (p. 47)

If you are not specifically trained in child abuse assessment and treatment, consult with a supervisor or a professional with expertise in this area, or refer the client for a clinical assessment.

Unhealthy transference relationships.   The importance of understanding how transference and countertransference play out in the therapy relationship was considered in Chapter 2. The mere existence of countertransference feelings is not an ethical or legal issue. However, if a therapist's personal reactions to a client cannot be managed effectively, an abuse of power is likely, and this can have both ethical and legal consequences. In cases involving mishandling of a client's transference or a counselor's countertransference, allegations have included sexual involvement with clients, inappropriate socialization with clients, getting involved with clients in a business situation, and burdening clients with a counselor's personal problems. When a therapist gets involved in multiple relationships with a client, it is always the client who is more vulnerable to abuse because of the power differential. When a client cannot be served in a professional manner due to a practitioner's personal feelings about him or her, it is the therapist's responsibility to seek consultation, to undergo personal therapy, and if necessary, to refer the client to another counselor (Calfee, 1997).

Failure to control a dangerous client. Therapists may have a duty to intervene in cases where clients pose a grave danger to themselves or to others. However, it is difficult to determine when a given client actually poses a danger to self or others. We discuss this topic in greater detail in Chapter 6.

Most states require mental health professionals to warn intended victims of potential harm. States have promulgated statutes to protect mental health professionals who breach confidentiality to report danger to others as well as to protect the public. Even in states where such a warning is not legally mandated, ethical practice demands a proper course of action on the therapist's part.

Risk Management Strategies

Risk management is the practice of focusing on the identification, evaluation, and treatment of problems that may injure clients and lead to filing an ethics complaint or a malpractice action. One of the best precautions against malpractice is personal and professional honesty and openness with clients. Providing quality professional services to clients is the best preventive step you can take. Although you may not make the "right choice" in every situation, it is crucial that you know your limitations and remain open to seeking consultation in difficult cases. Misunderstandings between therapist and client can result in a stronger therapist–client working relationship if the client and the therapist talk through the misunderstanding. Minor errors can become significant, however, and can lead to malpractice actions when they are repeated and are not recognized by the therapist. It is critical that clinicians remain alert for possible misunderstandings that, if not recognized or poorly handled, could lead to a therapeutic break or premature termination of therapy.

Bennett and colleagues (2006) contend that good risk management should involve more than simply following the minimal legal requirements. They claim that "your risk management principles should not be driven by remote or irrational fears but motivated by your deepest values, such as desiring to serve others and to have a rewarding career" (p. 31). Some additional recommendations for improving risk management follow:

- Become aware of local and state laws that pertain to your practice, as well as the policies of any agency for whom you work. Keep up to date with legal and ethical changes by becoming actively involved in professional organizations and attending risk management workshops (Kennedy et al., 2003).

- Make use of treatment contracts that present clients with written information on confidentiality issues, reasons for contacting clients at home, fee structures and payment plans, a policy on termination, and suicide provisions (Kennedy et al., 2003). Review this information with the client and document informed consent with a signature. Recognize that the disclosure statement establishes a contract between you and your client (Chauvin & Remley, 1996).

- Present information to your clients in clear language and be sure they understand the information.
- Contemporaneously engage in assessment and document your decisions (Werth et al., 2009).
- Explain your diagnosis, the treatment plan, and its risks and benefits in sufficient detail to be sure the client understands it, and document this as well.
- Inform clients that they have the right to terminate treatment any time they choose.
- Restrict your practice to clients for whom you are qualified by virtue of your education, training, and experience. Refer clients whose conditions are obviously not within the scope of your competence.
- Documentation is one of the cornerstones of good risk management, and also of quality care (Werth et al., 2009). Carefully document your clients' treatment process.
- Document reasons for a client's termination and any referrals or recommendations given (Kennedy et al., 2003).
- Document not only what you do and why, but what you decided not to do in certain cases (Werth et al., 2009).
- Maintain adequate business and clinical records.
- Recognize your ethical, professional, and legal responsibility to preserve the confidentiality of client records.
- Develop clear and consistent policies and procedures for creating, maintaining, transferring, and destroying client records (Remley & Herlihy, 2010).
- Report any case of suspected child abuse, elder, or dependent abuse as required by law.
- Evaluate how well you keep boundaries in your personal life. If you have clarity and responsibility in your personal life, then you are likely to have the same in your professional life.
- Before engaging in any multiple relationship, seek consultation and talk with your client about the possible repercussions of such a relationship. Realize that such relationships can lead to problems for both you and your client.
- Be especially prudent about informed consent, documentation, and consultation when crossing boundaries or engaging in multiple relationships with high-risk clients (Bennett et al., 2006).
- In deciding whether or not to accept a gift or to engage in bartering, consider the relevant cultural and clinical issues.
- Do not engage in sexual relationships with current or former clients or with current supervisees or students.

- Not keeping your appointments may feel like abandonment to a client. If you have to miss a session, be sure to call the client. Provide coverage for emergencies when you are going away.

- When in doubt, consult with colleagues and document the discussions. Before consulting with others about a specific client, obtain consent from the client for the release of information. Consultation shows that you have a commitment to sound practice and that you are willing to learn from other professionals to further the best interests of your clients.

- Develop a network of consultants who can assist you with considering options without necessarily telling you what to do (Werth et al., 2009).

- Get training in the assessment of clients who pose a danger to themselves or others, or have an experienced and competent therapist to whom you can refer.

- Consult when you are working with a suicidal client. Clearly document the nature of the consultation, including the topics discussed (Kennedy et al., 2003).

- If you make a professional determination that a client is dangerous, take the necessary steps to protect the client or others from harm.

- Obtain written parental or guardian consent when working with minors. This is good practice even if this consent is not required by state law.

- Recognize that a mental health professional is a potential target for a client's anger or transference feelings. Keep the lines of communication open with clients, allowing them to express whatever they feel to you (Chauvin & Remley, 1996). Be attentive to how you react to your clients and monitor your countertransference.

- Treat your clients with respect by attending carefully to your language and your behavior.

- The best protection against malpractice liability is to be concerned first and foremost with providing quality care and secondly to strive for ways to reduce risk (Werth et al., 2009).

- Have a theoretical orientation that justifies the techniques you employ.

- Be clear about what psychotherapy can and cannot do. When initiating a new form of therapy or different method of treatment, be sure you can support the choice of treatment (Calfee, 1997).

- Realize that prevention is a less expensive option than a successful defense against a malpractice suit (Swenson, 1997).

This list of risk management strategies may appear overwhelming. Our intention is to remind you of appropriate actions and also to provide a checklist to expand your awareness of ethical and professional behavior. Most ethical practitioners will already be taking these steps. The best way to reduce the chance of being sued is to know the ethical and legal standards and to follow them. If you develop too many forms of self-protection, however, the therapeutic relationship could be negatively affected. Because of your exaggerated cautiousness, your client may be reluctant to engage in the self-disclosure that is a critical aspect of the therapy process. Increased use of the legal system may lead to excessive caution on the part of therapists because of their concern about being sued. With the encroachment of malpractice issues into ethical thinking, there is increasing emphasis on doing what is safest for the therapist rather than what is best for the client.

It is worth noting that malpractice claims are not reserved exclusively for the irresponsible practitioner. Clients may make allegations of unethical conduct or file a legal claim due to negligence, even though the counselor may have acted ethically and appropriately. As Williams (2000) has noted, there are false complaints against psychotherapists who become victimized by the "victims." Williams reminds us that risk management is based on the assumption that practitioners can control their exposure to lawsuits and licensing complaints by monitoring their behaviors. However, reasonable risk management strategies may not prevent false accusations.

Course of Action in a Malpractice Suit

Even though you practice prudently and follow the guidelines previously outlined, you may still be sued. In the event that you are sued, consider these recommendations by Bennett and his associates (1990):

- Treat the lawsuit seriously, even if it represents a client's attempt to punish or control you.
- Do not attempt to resolve the matter with the client directly, because anything you do might be used against you in the litigation.
- Consult with your professional organization's legal counsel. If you consult with an attorney, prepare summaries of any pertinent events about the case that you can use.
- Become familiar with your liability policy, including the limits of coverage, and contact your insurance company immediately.
- Never destroy or alter files or reports pertinent to the client's case.
- Do not discuss the case with anyone other than your attorney. Avoid making self-incriminating statements to the client, or to his or her attorney, or the press.
- Determine the nature of support available to you from professional associations to which you belong.
- Do not continue a professional relationship with a client who is bringing a suit against you.

Legal assistance is a must if the licensing board has opened an investigation. This usually occurs before the filing of a malpractice claim and can be just as devastating as a lawsuit. You should be aware that the licensing board is an advocate for the consumer, not for the provider (Rahn Minagawa, personal communication, August 14, 2003). If you face going to court, you would do well to have some basic knowledge and take steps to prepare yourself for your appearance.

Legal Liability in an Ethical Perspective

Legal liability and ethical practice are not identical, but they do overlap in many cases. Legal issues give substance and direction to the evolution of ethical issues. Because ethics complaints may lead to civil or criminal lawsuits, Chauvin and Remley (1996) believe the legal aspects of an ethical complaint dictate how counselors must conduct themselves. Thus, clinicians need to know the relationship between ethics complaints and lawsuits, how boards process complaints, and the importance of seeking legal consultation.

If you are involved in a malpractice action, an expert case reviewer will probably evaluate your clinical records to determine if your practice reflected the appropriate standard of care. Records are vital to review the course of treatment. The manner in which you document treatment is likely to determine the outcome of the case (Mitchell, 2007). The case reviewer will probably look for deviations from your process of reasoning and application of knowledge in trying to determine whether there has been a gross deviation from the standards. As a practitioner, you cannot guarantee the outcome, but you are expected to demonstrate that you applied a reasonable and scientifically based approach to the present problem of your client (Rahn Minagawa, personal communication, August 14, 2003). Although you are not expected to be perfect, it is beneficial to evaluate what you are doing and why you are practicing as you are.

Chapter Summary

The ethics codes of all mental health organizations specify the centrality of informed consent. Clients' rights can best be protected if therapists develop procedures that aid their clients in making informed choices. Legally, informed consent entails the client's ability to act freely in making rational decisions. The process of informed consent includes providing information about the nature of therapy as well as the rights and responsibilities of both therapist and client. A basic challenge therapists face is to provide accurate and sufficient information to clients yet at the same time not to overwhelm them with too much information too soon. Informed consent can best be viewed as an ongoing process aimed at increasing the range of choices and the responsibility of the client as an active therapeutic partner.

In addition to a discussion of the rights of clients, this chapter has considered the scope of professional responsibility. Therapists have responsibilities to their clients, their agency, their profession, the community, the members of their clients' families, and themselves. Ethical dilemmas arise when there are conflicts among these responsibilities, for instance, when the agency's expectations conflict with the concerns or wishes of clients. Members of the helping professions need to know and to observe the ethics codes of their professional organizations, and they must make sound judgments within the parameters of acceptable practice. We have encouraged you to think about specific ethical issues and to develop a sense of professional ethics and knowledge of state laws so that your judgment will be based on more than what "feels right."

Associated with professional responsibilities are professional liabilities. If practitioners ignore legal and ethical standards or if their conduct is below the expected standard of care, they may be sued. Practitioners who fail to keep adequate records of their procedures are opening themselves to liability. Good record-keeping practices will help practitioners avoid legal trouble and will enhance the quality of their service to clients. Certainly, it is realistic to be concerned about malpractice actions, and professional practices that can reduce such risks have been described. However, it is our hope that practitioners do not become so preoccupied with making mistakes and self-protective strategies that they render themselves ineffective as clinicians. Being committed to doing what is best for the client is a very powerful risk management strategy.

Suggested Activities

1. In small groups, create an informed consent document. What does your group think clients must be told either before therapy begins or during the first few sessions?

2. In small groups, explore the rights clients have in counseling. One person in each group can serve as a recorder. When the groups reconvene for a general class meeting, the recorders for the various groups share their lists of clients' rights on a 3-point scale: 3 = Extremely important; 2 = Important; 1 = Somewhat important. What rights can your class agree on as the most important?

3. Select some of the open-ended cases presented in this chapter to role play with a fellow student. One of you chooses a client you feel you can identify with, and the other becomes the counselor. Conduct a counseling interview. Afterward, talk about how each of you felt during the interview and discuss alternative courses of action that could have been taken.

4. Providing clients with access to their files and records seems to be in line with the consumer-rights movement, which is having an impact on the human-service professions. What are your own thoughts on providing your clients with this information? What information would you want to share with your clients? In what ways might you go about providing them with this information? What might you do if there were a conflict between your views and the policies of the agency that employed you?

5. Consider inviting an attorney who is familiar with the legal aspects of counseling practice to address your class. Here are some possible questions for consideration: What are the legal rights of clients in therapy? What are the main legal responsibilities of therapists? What are some of the best ways to become familiar with laws pertaining to counselors? What are the grounds for lawsuits, and how can counselors best protect themselves from being sued?

6. Interview practicing counselors about some of their most pressing ethical concerns in carrying out their responsibilities. How have they dealt with these ethical issues? What are some of their legal considerations? What are their concerns, if any, about malpractice suits?

7. Discuss your concerns about professional liability. What can you do to lessen the chances of being accused of not having practiced according to acceptable standards?

Ethics in Action *CD-ROM Exercises*

8. In video role play 7, The Affair, a counselor states, "Having an affair is not a good answer for someone—it just hurts everyone. I just don't think it is a good idea." If you held such a view, should this be a part of your informed consent document? In what value areas might you have difficulty maintaining objectivity? Are there situations in which you would want to get your client to adopt your position?

9. In video role play 4, The Divorce, some interesting points are raised about the rights of clients to know about your values as a counselor if these values influence your approach to counseling them. The client has decided to leave her husband and get a divorce. She tells her counselor that she doesn't want to work on her marriage anymore. The counselor responds: "I hate to hear that. What about your kids? Who will be the advocate for them?" She says, "If I am happy, they will be happy. I will take care of my kids." The counselor concludes by asking, "Is divorce the best way to take care of your children?" If you were counseling couples or families, what would you want to tell clients about your values pertaining to matters such as faithfulness in relationships and divorce? In class, role play a situation in which you are meeting a client (or a couple) for the first session. What would you want to tell them about your role as a counselor? Would you reveal the core values you hold that could either enhance or interfere with their therapeutic progress?

10. In video role play 1, Teen Pregnancy, the client is a 13-year-old who just found out she is pregnant. She begs the counselor not to tell her parents. In this situation, what are the rights of the minor client? What rights do the parents have for access to certain information? What ethical and legal issues are involved in this case? What role would parental consent laws play in this case? What kind of informed consent process would you implement if you were counseling minors?

Pre-Chapter Self-Inventory

Directions: For each statement, indicate the response that most closely identifies your beliefs and attitudes. Use the following code:

> 5 = I *strongly agree* with this statement.
> 4 = I *agree* with this statement.
> 3 = I am *undecided* in my opinion about this statement.
> 2 = I *disagree* with this statement.
> 1 = I *strongly disagree* with this statement.

_____ 1. I am not clear about how much to tell my clients about confidentiality.

_____ 2. There are no situations in which I would disclose what a client had told me without the client's permission.

_____ 3. Absolute confidentiality is necessary if effective psychotherapy is to occur.

_____ 4. If I were working with a client whom I had assessed as potentially dangerous to another person, it would be my duty to protect the possible victim.

_____ 5. Once I make an assessment that a client is suicidal or at a high risk of carrying out self-destructive acts, it is my ethical and legal obligation to take appropriate action.

_____ 6. Counselors should consider evoking guilt to discourage clients from suicidal action.

_____ 7. If a client who is suicidal does not want my help or actively rejects it, I would be inclined to leave the person alone.

_____ 8. I would find the evaluation and management of suicidal risk stressful.

Confidentiality: Ethical and Legal Issues

_____ 9. As a helping professional, it is my responsibility to report suspected child abuse, regardless of when it occurred.

_____ 10. The reporting laws pertaining to child abuse sometimes prevent therapy from taking place with the abuser.

_____ 11. I think reporting child abuse should be left to the judgment of the therapist.

_____ 12. To protect children from abuse, strict laws are necessary, and professionals should be penalized for failing to report abuses.

_____ 13. If my client is HIV-positive, I have a legal duty to warn and protect all of the person's identifiable sexual partners if my client refuses to disclose his or her HIV status to them.

_____ 14. In counseling HIV-positive clients, I would be inclined to maintain confidentiality because failing to do so could erode the trust of my clients.

_____ 15. If an HIV-positive client refused to disclose his or her HIV status to a partner, I would explore with my client the reasons for not doing so.

_____ 16. I am concerned that I won't know what actions to take in situations involving the duty to protect.

_____ 17. Using cell phones jeopardizes confidentiality.

_____ 18. Communication via electronic mail is fraught with privacy problems.

_____ 19. If it became necessary to break a client's confidentiality, I would inform my client of my intended action.

_____ 20. I believe that it is easy to invade a client's privacy unintentionally.

Introduction

Perhaps the central right of a client is the guarantee that disclosures in therapy sessions will be protected. As you will see, however, you cannot promise your clients that *everything* they talk about will *always* remain confidential. In this chapter we consider the ethical and legal ramifications of confidentiality and explore the process, importance, and impact of informing your clients from the outset of therapy of those circumstances that limit confidentiality.

The more you consider the legal ramifications of confidentiality, the clearer it becomes that most matters are not neatly defined. Even if therapists have become familiar with local and state laws that govern their profession, this legal knowledge alone is not enough to enable them to make sound decisions. Each case is unique. There are many subtle points in the law and at various times conflicting ways to interpret the law. Professional judgment plays a significant role in resolving cases, from both an ethical and a legal perspective. Keep in mind that the law is not "fact specific" and that rules of law are considered in light of a particular situation.

Fisher (2008) notes that laws often take center stage, when what is most needed is a language for placing laws into an ethical context. Fisher contends that taking a risk management perspective not only raises practitioners' anxiety but encourages them to focus on avoiding risks to *themselves* rather than focusing on their ethical obligations and the potential risks to *clients*.

Confidentiality, Privileged Communication, and Privacy

Confidentiality is a complex obligation, with several exceptions and nuances, and both legal and ethical implications have to be considered (Benitez, 2004). See the Ethics Codes box titled "Confidentiality in Clinical Practice" for some specific guidelines on the obligations mental health practitioners have to maintain the confidentiality of their relationships with clients. It is essential that therapists become familiar with concepts of confidentiality, privileged communication, and privacy, as well as the legal protection afforded to the privileged communications of clients and the limits of this protection.

Confidentiality

Confidentiality, privileged communication, and privacy are related concepts, but there are important distinctions among them. **Confidentiality**, which is rooted in a client's right to privacy, is at the core of effective therapy; it "is the counselor's ethical duty to protect private client communication" (Wheeler & Bertram, 2008, p. 65). As a general rule, psychotherapists are prohibited from disclosing confidential communications to any third party unless mandated or permitted by law to do so. Therapists are advised to err on the side of being overly cautious in protecting the confidentiality of their clients, unless faced

Ethics Codes

Confidentiality in Clinical Practice

American Counseling Association (2005)

At initiation and throughout the counseling process, counselors inform clients of the limitations of confidentiality and identify foreseeable situations in which confidentiality must be breached. (B.1.d.)

American Psychological Association (2002)

Psychologists have a primary obligation and take reasonable precautions to protect confidential information obtained through or stored in any medium, recognizing that the extent and limits of confidentiality may be regulated by law or established by institutional rules or professional or scientific relationship. (4.01.)

American School Counselor Association (2004)

The professional school counselor informs students of the purposes, goals, techniques and rules of procedure under which they may receive counseling at or before the time when the counseling relationship is entered. Disclosure notice includes the limits of confidentiality such as the possible necessity for consulting with other professionals, privileged communication, and legal or authoritative restraints. The meaning and limits of confidentiality are clearly defined in developmentally appropriate terms to students. (A.2.a.)

Canadian Counselling Association (2007)

Counselling relationships and information resulting therefrom are kept confidential. However, there are the following exceptions to confidentiality:

- when disclosure is required to prevent clear and imminent danger to the client or others;
- when legal requirements demand that confidential material be revealed;
- when a child is in need of protection. (B.2.)

National Association of Social Workers (2008)

Social workers should protect the confidentiality of all information obtained in the course of professional service, except for compelling professional reasons. The general expectation that social workers will keep information confidential does not apply when disclosure is necessary to prevent serious, foreseeable, and imminent harm to a client or other identifiable person. In all instances, social workers should disclose the least amount of confidential information necessary to achieve the desired purpose; only information that is directly relevant to the purpose for which the disclosure is made should be revealed. (1.07.c.)

American Mental Health Counselors Association (2000)

Mental health counselors have a primary obligation to safeguard information about individuals obtained in the course of practice, teaching, or research. Personal information is communicated to others only with the person's written consent or in those circumstances where there is a clear and imminent danger to the client, to others or to society. Disclosure of counseling information is restricted to what is necessary, relevant and verifiable. (Principle 3.)

with a mandatory exception to confidentiality such as reporting child abuse or elder abuse (Benitez, 2004).

Donner, VandeCreek, Gonsiorek, and Fisher (2008) argue that confidentiality is a primary obligation for mental health professionals and must be given priority. These authors point out that the ever-growing list of exceptions to confidentiality, which focus on *protecting the public*, has been given priority over protecting the *privacy of clients*. The fear of liability attached to a complaint for the failure to protect, risk management, continuing education courses focused protecting therapists from litigation, and mandatory reporting laws have diluted the value and meaning of confidentiality. Donner and colleagues believe that any disclosure of confidential information should be a last resort and that mental health professionals must push back to limit the growing list of mandatory and permissible disclosures.

Mental health professionals have an ethical responsibility, as well as a legal and professional duty, to safeguard clients from unauthorized disclosures of information given in the therapeutic relationship. Professionals must not disclose this information except when authorized by law or by the client to do so. Hence, there are limitations to the promise of confidentiality. Court decisions have underscored that there are circumstances in which a therapist has a duty to warn and to protect the client or others, even if it means breaking confidentiality. Also, because confidentiality is a client's right, psychotherapists may legally and ethically reveal a client's confidences if a client waives this right. Confidentiality belongs to the client, and counselors generally do not find it problematic to release information when the client requests that they do so. Challenges arise, however, when third parties demand that counselors release confidential information that clients do not want released (Glosoff, Herlihy, & Spence, 2000).

The APA (2002) ethics code provides the following guidelines for disclosure of confidential information: "Psychologists may disclose confidential information with the appropriate consent of the organizational client, the individual client/patient, or another legally authorized person on behalf of the client/patient unless prohibited by law" (4.05.a.).

The ACA (2005) ethical standard for counselor advocacy has implications for confidentiality. Although counselors are expected to advocate for their clients by working to remove potential barriers and obstacles that might inhibit client access to services or inhibit client growth (A.6.a.), counselors must obtain client consent before engaging in advocacy on behalf of an identifiable client (Herlihy & Corey, 2006c).

Fisher (2008) has designed a six-step ethical practice model for protecting confidentiality rights that places legal mandates in an ethical context. The six steps include the following:

> *Preparation.* To inform your clients about the limits of confidentiality, you must understand the limits yourself. This involves doing your legal homework and engaging in personal soul searching regarding your own moral principles. Devise an informed consent document that reflects your real intentions and that describes confidentiality and

its limits in clear language. Discuss the importance of confidentiality with your clients.

Tell clients the truth "up front." Inform your clients about the limits you intend to impose on confidentiality, and obtain your client's consent to accept these limits as a condition of entering into a professional relationship with you.

Obtain truly informed consent before making a disclosure. Make disclosures only if legally unavoidable; obtain and document your client's consent before disclosing.

Respond ethically to legal requests for disclosure. Notify your client of a pending legal demand for disclosure without his or her consent. Limit disclosure of confidential information to the extent that is legally possible.

Avoid the "avoidable" breaches of confidentiality. Avoid making unethical exceptions to the confidentiality rule; establish and maintain policies aimed at protecting confidentiality; monitor your note taking and record keeping practices; anticipate legal demands and your response to such requirements; and empower clients to act protectively on their own behalf.

Talk about confidentiality. Model ethical behavior and practice; invite a dialogue with clients about confidentiality as needed; teach ethical practices to students and supervisees; and educate attorneys, judges, and consumers.

Fisher's (2008) model can assist mental health professionals to frame ethical questions more clearly help identify questions to explore in the process of consultation. "In short, psychologists can use this practice model to reclaim their status as experts about the confidentiality ethics of their profession" (p. 12).

Privileged Communication

Privileged communication is a legal concept that generally bars the disclosure of confidential communications in a legal proceeding (Committee on Professional Practice and Standards, 2003). All states have enacted into law some form of psychotherapist–client privilege, but the specifics of this privilege vary from state to state. When a client–therapist relationship is covered as privileged communication by statute, clinicians may not disclose confidential information (Remley, 2009). Therapists can refuse to answer questions in court or refuse to produce a client's records in court. These laws ensure that personal and sensitive client information will be protected from exposure by therapists in legal proceedings.

Again, this privilege belongs to the client and is designed for the client's protection rather than for the protection of the counseling professional. If a client knowingly and rationally waives this privilege, the professional has no legal grounds for withholding the information. Professionals are obligated to disclose information that is *necessary and sufficient* when the client requests it, but only the information that is specifically requested and only to the individuals or agencies that are specified by the client.

Generally speaking, the legal concept of privileged communication does *not* apply to group counseling, couples counseling, family therapy, or child and adolescent therapy. However, the therapist is still bound by confidentiality with respect to circumstances not involving a court proceeding. Statements made in the presence of a third party may not be protected in a court proceeding. Members of a counseling group can assume that they could be asked to testify in court concerning certain information revealed in the course of a group session, unless there is a statutory exception. In states where no law exists to cover confidentiality in group therapy, courts may use the ethics codes of the professions regarding confidentiality. If a situation arises, therapists may need to demonstrate the means they used to create safety for the group members. One way of doing this is by using a written group contract, which clearly states that members have the responsibility for maintaining confidentiality of others in the group (Grosso, 2002).

Similarly, couples therapy and family therapy are not subject to privileged communication statutes in many states. In the case of child and adolescent clients, there are restrictions on the confidential character of disclosures in the counseling relationship. No clear judicial trend has emerged for communications that are made in the presence of third persons. Therapists should inform clients about confidentiality and its exceptions from the beginning of the professional contact and should remain open to discussing this matter as the situation may warrant later in the professional relationship. Clients have a right to be informed about any limitations on confidentiality in group work, child and adolescent therapy, couples and family therapy, and organizational consulting (Nagy, 2005).

The *Jaffee* case and privileged communication.   The basic principles of privileged communication have been reaffirmed by case law. On June 13, 1996, the United States Supreme Court ruled that communications between licensed psychotherapists and their clients in the course of diagnosis or treatment are privileged and therefore protected from forced disclosure in cases arising under federal law. The Supreme Court ruling in *Jaffee v. Redmond* (1996), written by Justice John Paul Stevens, states that "effective psychotherapy depends upon an atmosphere of confidence and trust in which the patient is willing to make frank and complete disclosure of facts, emotions, memories, and fears." The 7–2 decision in this case represented a victory for mental health organizations because it extended the confidentiality privilege.

In the *Jaffee* case, an on-duty police officer, Mary Lu Redmond, shot and killed a suspect while attempting an arrest. The victim's family sued in federal court, alleging that the victim's constitutional rights had been violated. The court ordered Karen Beyer, a licensed clinical social worker, to turn over notes she made during counseling sessions with Redmond after the shooting. The social worker refused, asserting that the contents of her conversations with the police officer were protected against involuntary disclosure by psychotherapist–client privilege. The court rejected her claim of psychotherapist–client privilege, and the jury awarded the family $545,000.

The Court of Appeals for the Seventh Circuit reversed this decision and concluded that the trial court had erred by refusing to afford protection to the confidential communications between Redmond and Beyer. Jaffee, an administrator of the victim's estate, appealed this decision to the Supreme Court.

The Supreme Court upheld the appellate court's decision, clarifying for all federal court cases, both civil and criminal, the existence of the privilege. The Court recognized a broadly defined psychotherapist–client privilege and further clarified that this privilege is not subject to the decision of a judge on a case-by-case basis. The Court's decision to extend federal privilege (which already applied to psychologists and psychiatrists) to licensed social workers leaves the door open for inclusion of other licensed psychotherapists, such as licensed marriage and family therapists, licensed professional counselors, and mental health counselors. The issues in this case are critical for psychotherapists, and it is expected that this decision will have far-reaching consequences for licensed psychotherapists and their clients (Hinnefeld & Towers, 1996; Morrissey, 1996; Newman, 1996; Seppa, 1996). According to Newman (1996), the high court's ruling recognizes the societal value of psychotherapy and the importance of confidentiality to successful treatment. This decision may signal the broadening of a trend toward stronger privileged communication statutes.

In discussing the impact on the law of the *Jaffee v. Redmond* case, Shuman and Foote (1999) indicate that the case is not constitutionally based. Instead, *Jaffee* is an interpretation of the Federal Rules of Evidence that apply in actions tried in federal courts. Thus, *Jaffee* applies only in federal cases, both civil and criminal, governed by the Federal Rules of Evidence. Knapp and VandeCreek (1997) conclude that more work needs to be done in extending equal protection to clients across all states. In that way therapists will better be able to inform their clients about the limits to confidentiality. Glosoff and colleagues (1997) support this point of view, saying there needs to be a consistent definition of privilege because therapists may be liable in a legal claim for breach of duty if they neglect to *accurately* describe the limits of confidentiality to their clients.

Privacy

Privacy, as a matter of law, refers to the constitutional right of individuals to be left alone and to control their personal information (Wheeler & Bertram, 2008). Practitioners should exercise caution with regard to the privacy of their clients. It is easy to invade a client's privacy unintentionally. Examples of some of the most pressing situations in which privacy is an issue include an employer's access to an applicant's or an employee's psychological tests, parents' access to their child's school and health records, and a third-party payer's access to information about a client's diagnosis and prognosis.

It is of paramount importance to respect the privacy of your clients and to exercise caution when discussing your work publicly. You must not reveal identifying information about clients, orally or in writing, or even the fact that they consult you, without their formal consent (Nagy, 2005). Nagy adds that you need to understand state and federal laws pertaining to privacy and the rules of your employment setting as well, and how they might affect your work in therapy, research, consulting, and supervision.

If counselors have occasion to meet clients outside of the professional setting, it is essential that they do not violate their privacy. This is especially true in small towns, where such meetings can be expected. In such cases, it is a good practice to talk with your client and discuss how you might interact in these possible meetings. Consider what you might do in the following case.

■ The Case of Erica.

Helena is a counselor in the student services department at a community college. She has been counseling Erica for several months for a variety of problems having to do with her body image and eating behaviors. One evening Helena and a friend go out to a local cafe for a light meal and a coffee. Helena is surprised when the waitress comes up to her cheerily and says hello. She looks up and realizes it is Erica. She chats briefly with Erica who then takes her order and goes off to serve other customers. Erica has not mentioned counseling or any aspect of their relationship in another context. Helena's friend then asks who Erica is and how she knows her?

- If you were the counselor, would you introduce Erica to your friend? If so how?
- If you were the counselor, how would you answer your friend's question?
- If Erica began to discuss her sessions with you, what would you do?

Commentary.   These chance meetings are often unavoidable. If Helena had ignored Erica, not only could this be seen as being rude, but Erica might feel offended. It is inappropriate for Helena to acknowledge to her friend that Erica is her client. If Erica began discussing matters pertaining to her counseling sessions, Helena should find a way to steer the interaction to a general conversation. Helena's dilemma reminds us that during the informed consent process, it is a good idea to discuss how clients would like you to handle chance encounters outside of therapy; this is especially important if you live and practice in a small community.

Most professional codes of ethics contain guidelines to safeguard a client's right to privacy, such as this ACA (2005) standard: "Counselors respect client rights to privacy. Counselors solicit private information from clients only when it is beneficial to the counseling process" (B.1.b.).

Another example of the privacy standard, designed to minimize intrusions on privacy, is found in the APA (2002) ethics code:

Psychologists disclose confidential information without the consent of the individual only as mandated by law, or where permitted by law for a valid purpose such as to (1) provide needed professional services; (2) obtain appropriate professional consultations; (3) protect the client/patient, psychologist, or others from harm; or (4) obtain payment for services from a client/patient, in which instance disclosure is limited to the minimum that is necessary to achieve the purpose. (4.05.b.)

One other area where privacy is an issue involves practitioners who also teach courses, offer workshops, write books and journal articles, and give lectures. If these practitioners use examples from their clinical practice, it is of the utmost importance that they take measures to adequately disguise their clients' identities. Additionally, those who teach counseling courses need to explain to their students that they should adequately disguise identities of their clients in any reports they give in class. Of course, students' personal comments in class are also to be kept confidential.

Confidentiality and Privacy in a School Setting

Managing confidentiality is a challenge most school counselors face. School counselors need to balance their ethical and legal responsibilities with three groups: the students they serve, the parents or guardians of those students, and the school system. When minors are unable to give informed consent, parents or guardians provide this informed consent, and they may need to be included in the counseling process.

School counselors are ethically obliged to respect the privacy of minor clients and maintain confidentiality, yet this obligation may be in conflict with laws regarding parental rights to be informed about the progress of treatment and to decide what is in the best interests of their children (Glosoff & Pate, 2002). An ASCA (2004) guideline indicates that the school counselor "recognizes his/her primary obligation for confidentiality is to the student but balances that obligation with an understanding of the legal and inherent rights of parents/guardians to be the guiding voice in their children's lives" (A.2.g.). School counselors need to approach parents as allies or partners in the counseling process (Glosoff & Pate, 2002).

School counselors have an ethical responsibility to ask for client permission to release information, and they should clearly inform students of the limitations of confidentiality and how and when confidential information may be shared. The ASCA (2004) guideline regarding parents is that the school counselor "informs parents/guardians of the counselor's role with emphasis on the confidential nature of the counseling relationship between the counselor and student" (Section B.2.a.). Although school counselors may be required to provide certain information to parents and school personnel, they need to do so in a manner that will minimize intrusion of the child's or adolescent's privacy and in a way that demonstrates respect for the counselee. To the degree possible, school counselors aim to establish collaborative relationships with parents and school personnel.

Laws regarding confidentiality in school counseling differ. In some states, therapists in private practice are required to demonstrate that attempts have been made to contact the parents of children who are younger than 16, whereas school counselors are not required to do so. Schools that receive federal funding are generally bound by the provisions of the Family Educational Rights and Privacy Act of 1994 (FERPA). It is essential that school counselors exercise discretion in the kind and extent of information they reveal to parents or guardians about their children.

School personnel and administrators may operate under different guidelines regarding confidentiality, and they may not understand the mental health professions' requirements. A trainee or intern in a school who is being supervised for licensure is bound by both the profession's ethics codes and state regulations; therefore, supervisors at this level have a particular obligation to assist trainees and interns in negotiating difficulties regarding confidentiality, informed consent, and treatment expectations in schools (Terence Patterson, personal communication, December 12, 2008). To be sure, this is a complex area that requires careful thought and consideration, as the following case examples illustrate.

■ The Case of Donna.

Donna, a school counselor, shifted her career from private practice to counseling in an elementary school. She was particularly surprised by the differences between private practice and school counseling with respect to confidentiality issues. She remarked that she was constantly fielding questions from teachers such as "Whom do you have in that counseling group?" "How is Johnny doing?" "It's no wonder this girl has problems. Have you met her parents?"

Although Donna talked to the teachers about the importance of maintaining a safe, confidential environment for students in counseling situations, she would still receive questions from them about students, some of whom were not in their classes. In addition to the questions from teachers, Donna found that she had to deal with inquiries from school secretaries and other staff members, some of whom seemed to know everything that was going on in the school. They would ask her probing questions about students, which she, of course, was not willing to answer. For example, although she would not tell a secretary whom she was counseling, a teacher might have told the secretary that she was seeing one of his students. One secretary asked her: "Why are you working with Jimmy Smith? He doesn't have as many problems as some of the other students!"

Donna observed that principals and parents also asked for specific information about the students she was seeing. She learned the importance of talking to everyone about the need to respect privacy. If she had not exercised care, it would have been easy for her to say more than would have been ethical to teachers, staff members, and parents. She also learned how critical it was to talk about matters of confidentiality and privacy in simple language with the schoolchildren she counseled.

- If you were asked some of the questions posed to Donna, how would you respond?
- How would you protect the privacy of the students and at the same time avoid alienating the teachers and staff members?
- How would you explain the meaning of confidentiality and privacy to teachers? staff members? parents? administrators? the children?

Commentary. This case illustrates the importance of a school counselor taking the initiative to educate parents, administrators, and staff members about the need to respect privacy and protect confidentiality of minor clients. Donna took steps to protect the privacy of the children by educating all concerned about the importance of confidentiality in counseling. Because school counselors are part of an educational community, they often consult with parents, teachers, and administrators. In these consultations, school counselors need to make it clear that their primary client is the student (Glosoff & Pate, 2002). Birdsall and Hubert (2000) warn school counselors of their responsibility to safeguard a student's right to privacy when teachers or principals ask counselors to divulge student confidences.

■ The Case of Jeremy.

Jeremy, a third grade boy in an elementary school, reports to his school counselor that he was with his mother when she stole a dress from a store. Jeremy also reports that after he and his mother left the store, she told him that she at times stole food because she couldn't afford it. Jeremy requests that the counselor not say anything to his mother because she has been very depressed about not having a job and he worries about what she might do if she learns that he is talking to a counselor about her. After the session, the counselor initiates a conversation with Jeremy's fourth grade sister, who is a student in the same school, to further explore the allegation of the mother's stealing.

- Was this school counselor behaving inappropriately by initiating a conversation with a client's sibling to further explore an alleged crime?
- As a counselor, do you have a legal obligation in this case?
- What would you have done if you were counseling Jeremy?

Commentary. The therapist cannot automatically assume that Jeremy is telling the truth, but talking to Jeremy's sister is a violation of Jeremy's confidentiality. If the mother is indeed stealing from stores, she may be arrested, which could be traumatic for the children.

The school counselor's primary duty is to address Jeremy's fear and his well-being. The therapist may suggest that Jeremy ask his mother to attend a session with him so Jeremy has an opportunity to express his fears in a conjoint session. A school counselor may have an ethical and legal responsibility to report a parent for an alleged crime, especially when there is risk of harm to the minor such as dealing drugs from the home, driving drunk with children in the car, or leaving the children alone for long periods of time. Even when such a report is necessary, it is important to simultaneously work to keep the minor client engaged.

■ A Case of Academic Dishonesty.

Simon, a high school counselor, is told by Ginger, a student, that she and some friends have stolen a chemistry final exam. Ginger requests that Simon not say a word about it to anyone because she is presently failing chemistry and needs to do well on the final exam to pass the course and graduate from high school. Simon decides not to divulge any information, respecting the student's request to maintain confidentiality.

- What are your thoughts about Simon's decision not to divulge any information?
- How might this dilemma for Simon raise questions concerning the limits to confidentiality?
- What would you have done if you were the counselor in this situation?
- Can school policies be included as you explain the limits to confidentiality to students in your role as a school counselor? Why or why not?

Commentary. The counselor has no obligation to breach confidentiality because there is no danger to life. If it is school policy that such matters must be reported, this information should be clearly stated in an informed consent document. One clinical issue that could be explored is why this student told Simon about the theft.

Ethical and Legal Ramifications of Confidentiality and Privileged Communication

Clients in counseling are involved in a deeply personal relationship and have a right to expect that what they discuss will be kept private. The compelling justification for confidentiality is that it is necessary in order to encourage clients to develop the trust needed for full disclosure and for the other work involved in therapy. Clients must feel free to explore all aspects of their lives without fear that these disclosures will be released outside the therapy room.

Counselors are ethically obligated to help clients appreciate the meaning of confidentiality by presenting it in language the client can understand and that respects the cultural experiences of the client (Barnett & Johnson, 2010).

When it does become necessary to break confidentiality, it is good practice to inform the client of the intention to take this action and also to invite the client to participate in the process. For example, all states now have statutes that require professionals who suspect any form of child abuse to report it to the appropriate agencies, even when the knowledge was gained through confidential communication with clients. A professional who reports suspected child abuse, in good faith, is immune from civil liability and criminal prosecution as a mandated reporter (Jensen, 2006).

Exceptions to confidentiality and privileged communication. Counselors need to help clients understand that confidentiality is not an absolute, and it is essential for counselors to describe the limits and exceptions to confidentiality (Barnett & Johnson, 2010). The circumstances under which confidentiality cannot be maintained are not always clearly defined by accepted ethical standards, and therapists must exercise their own professional judgment. When assuring their clients that what they reveal will ordinarily be kept confidential, therapists should point out that they have obligations to others besides their clients. All of the major professional organizations have taken the position that practitioners must reveal certain information when there is *serious and foreseeable danger* to an individual or to society; therapists are bound to act in such a way as to protect others from harm. The ASCA's (2004) ethical standard states this clearly:

> The professional school counselor keeps information confidential unless disclosure is required to prevent clear and imminent danger to the student or others or when legal requirements demand that confidential information be revealed. Counselors will consult with appropriate professionals when in doubt as to the validity of an exception. (A.2.b.)

It is the responsibility of therapists to clarify the ethical and legal restrictions on confidentiality. Consider these exceptional circumstances in which it is permissible to share information with others in the interest of providing competent services to clients:

- When the client requests a release of information
- When reimbursement or other legal rules require disclosure
- When clerical assistants handle confidential information, as in managed care
- When the counselor consults with experts or peers
- When the counselor is working under supervision
- When other mental health professionals request information and the client has given consent to share
- When other professionals are involved in a treatment team and coordinate care of a client

Remley and Herlihy (2010) and Welfel (2010) provide a detailed discussion of exceptions to confidentiality and privileged communication. Among some of the conditions that warrant disclosure of information shared in the counseling relationship are these legally mandated exceptions to confidentiality and privileged communication:

- Disclosure of confidential information is ordered by a court
- Clients file complaints against their counselors
- Clients claim psychological damage in a lawsuit
- Civil commitment proceedings are initiated
- Statutes involving child abuse or elder abuse mandate disclosure
- Clients pose a danger to others or to themselves

Remley and Herlihy (2010) underscore the importance of consultation (and documentation) whenever practitioners are in doubt about their obligations regarding confidentiality or privileged communication.

The limitations of confidentiality may be greater in some settings and agencies than in others. In addition, exceptions to confidentiality vary by jurisdiction, and counselors are required to know the laws that govern their area of practice. If clients are informed about the conditions under which confidentiality may be compromised, they are in a better position to decide whether to enter counseling. If clients are involved in involuntary counseling, they can decide what they will disclose in their sessions. It is generally accepted that clients have a right to understand in advance the circumstances under which therapists are required or allowed to communicate information about them to third parties. Unless clients understand the exceptions to confidentiality, their consent to treatment is not genuinely informed.

In an addiction treatment center, the policy may be "what is said to one staff member is said to all." This frees the entire treatment staff to share information about patients as a part of the treatment process, and it eliminates concerns about breaching confidentiality. One reason for this practice may be to avoid triangulation of the staff, which would be to the detriment of the patients. Of course, the patients should be made aware of this policy. When patients suffer a relapse during addictions treatment and public safety is jeopardized, counselors have a duty to report. If being intoxicated while on the job can seriously threaten the lives of others, such as when an airline pilot, bus driver, or surgeon is frequently relapsing, counselors have a duty to disclose this (Glaser & Warren, 1999). These situations cannot be ignored.

If you breach confidentiality in an unprofessional manner (in the absence of a recognized exception), you open yourself to both ethical and legal sanctions, including expulsion from a professional association, loss of certification, license revocation, and a malpractice suit. To protect yourself against such liability, it is essential to become familiar with all applicable ethical and legal guidelines pertaining to confidentiality, including state privilege laws and their exceptions, child and elder abuse reporting requirements, and the parameters of the duty-to-protect exceptions in your state.

■ The Case of Larry.

Larry, 16 years old, is sent to a family guidance clinic by his parents. During the first session the counselor sees Larry and his parents together. She tells the parents in his presence that what she and Larry discuss will be confidential and that she will not disclose information acquired through the sessions without his permission. The parents seem to understand that confidentiality is necessary for trust to develop between their son and his counselor.

At first Larry is reluctant to come in for counseling. Eventually, as the sessions go on, he discloses that he has a serious drug problem. Larry's parents know that he was using drugs at one time, but he has told them that he is no longer using them. The counselor listens to anecdote after anecdote about Larry's use of illegal drugs, about how "I am loaded at school every day," and about a few brushes with death when he was under the influence of illegal substances. Finally, she tells Larry that she does not want the responsibility of knowing he is experimenting with illegal drugs and that she will not agree to continue the counseling relationship unless he stops using them. At this stage she agrees not to inform his parents, on the condition that he quits using drugs, but she does tell him that she will be talking with one of her colleagues about the situation.

Larry apparently stops using drugs for several weeks. However, one night while he is under the influence of methamphetamine he has a serious automobile accident. As a result of the accident, Larry is paralyzed for life. Larry's parents angrily assert that they had a legal right to be informed that he was seriously involved in drug use, and they file suit against both the counselor and the agency.

- What is your general impression of the way Larry's counselor handled the case?
- Do you think the counselor acted in a responsible way toward the client? the parents? the agency?
- If you were convinced that Larry was likely to hurt himself or others because of his drug use and his emotional instability, would you have informed his parents, even at the risk of losing Larry as a client? Why or why not?
- Which of the following courses of action could you have taken if you had been Larry's counselor? Check as many as you think are appropriate:

_____ State the legal limits on you as a therapist during the initial session.

_____ Consult with the supervisor of the agency.

_____ Refer Larry for psychological testing to determine the degree of his emotional disturbance.

_____ Refer Larry to a psychiatrist for treatment.

_____ Continue to see Larry without any stipulations.

_____ Insist on a session with Larry's parents as a condition of continuing counseling.

_____ Inform the police or other authorities.

_____ Document your decision-making process with a survey of pertinent research.

- What potential ethical violations do you see in this case?

Commentary. This case emphasizes the seriousness of doing a thorough assessment of a client. When Larry spoke of "a few brushes with death," it was clear that he was a danger to himself, which was cause for the counselor to take immediate action. This therapist wanted to believe Larry's story and failed to take the necessary steps to prevent harmful consequences to her client. This case demonstrates how important it is to set limits to confidentiality based on the counselor's assessment (danger to self or others) and highlights the issue of informed consent. Although the counselor promised confidentiality at the outset, many circumstances and jurisdictional requirements may necessitate disclosure of confidential information to both an official agency and to the parents or legal guardians. When explaining informed consent, counselors who routinely work with minors need to clarify the various exceptions to confidentiality in language minor clients can understand.

Three short cases. We have provided commentaries on many cases involving ethical dilemmas. Based on what you have learned and from your own deliberations, select the most ethical course of action in each of the following cases.

1. You are a student counselor. For your internship you are working with college students on campus. Your intern group meets with a supervisor each week to discuss your cases. One day, while you are having lunch in the campus cafeteria with three other interns, they begin to discuss their cases in detail, even mentioning names of clients. They joke about some of the clients they are seeing, while nearby there are other students who may be able to overhear this conversation. What would you do in this situation?

_____ I would tell the other interns to stop talking about their clients where other students could overhear them and to continue their conversation in a private place.

_____ I would bring the matter up in our next practicum meeting with the supervisor.

_____ I would not do anything because the students who could over-hear the conversation would most likely not be that interested in what was being said.

2. You are leading a counseling group on a high school campus. The members have voluntarily joined the group. In one of the sessions several of the students discuss the drug use on their campus, and two of them reveal that they sell illegal substances to their friends. You discuss this matter with them, and they claim that there is nothing wrong with using these drugs. They argue that most of the students on campus use drugs, that no one has been harmed, and that there isn't any difference between using drugs (which they know is illegal) and using alcohol. What would you do in this situation?

_____ Because their actions are illegal, I would report them to the police.

_____ I would do nothing because their drug use doesn't seem to be a problem for them, and I would not want to jeopardize their trust in me.

_____ I would report the situation to the school authorities but keep the identities of the students confidential.

_____ I would let the students know that I planned to inform the school authorities of their actions and their names.

_____ I would not take the matter seriously because the laws relating to drugs are unfair.

_____ I would explore with the students their reasons for making this disclosure.

_____ I would start an education program pertaining to drug abuse.

3. You are counseling children in an elementary school. Barbara is referred to you by her teacher because she is becoming increasingly withdrawn. After several sessions Barbara tells you that she is afraid that her father might kill her and that he frequently beats her. Until now she has lied about obvious bruises on her body, claiming that she fell off her bicycle and hurt herself. She shows you welts on her arms and back, but tells you not to say anything to anyone because her father has threatened a worse beating if she tells anyone. What would you do in this situation?

_____ I would respect Barbara's wishes and not tell anyone what I knew.

_____ I would report the situation to the principal and the school nurse.

_____ I would immediately go home with Barbara and talk to her parents.

_____ I would report the matter to the police and to the Child Protective Services.

_____ I would ask Barbara why she was telling me about the beatings if she did not want me to reveal them to anyone else.

_____ I would tell Barbara that I had a legal obligation to make this situation known to the authorities but that I would work with her and not leave her alone in her fears.

Privacy Issues With Telecommunication Devices

The use of the telephone, answering machines, voice mail, pagers, faxes, cellular phones, and e-mail can pose a number of potential ethical problems regarding the protection of privacy of clients. Mental health practitioners need to exercise caution in discussing confidential or privileged information with anyone over the telephone. Remley and Herlihy (2010, pp. 152–153) offer these guidelines for counselors using the telephone:

- Do not acknowledge that clients are receiving services or give out information regarding clients to unknown callers.
- Strive to verify that you are actually talking to the intended person when you make or receive calls in which confidential information will be discussed.
- Be aware that there is no way to prevent your conversation from being recorded or monitored by an unintended person.
- Be professional and cautious in talking about confidential information over the telephone; avoid saying anything off the record.
- Avoid making any comments that you would not want your client to hear or that you would not want to repeat in a legal proceeding.

There are also privacy issues involved in using answering machines, voice mail, pagers, and cellular telephones. Remley and Herlihy offer a number of suggestions to protect the privacy of clients:

- Do not allow unauthorized persons to hear answering machine messages in your office as they are being left or retrieved.
- If you use voice mail or an answering service, ensure that your access codes are not disclosed to unauthorized persons.
- When you leave a message on an answering machine, be aware that the intended person may not be the one who retrieves your message. A family member may retrieve a personal message you left for a client. It is a good idea to discuss with clients ahead of time whether you may leave messages on an answering machine, and the best number to reach them.
- If you are talking to a client by cellular phone, assume that he or she is not in a private place. Also, realize that your conversation may be intercepted by an unauthorized person.

- If you use a pager or a cell phone to send text messages, exercise caution. In sending a text message to a client, be mindful of ensuring your client's privacy by exercising the same caution you would if you were sending a voice mail message.

Using fax machines and e-mail to send confidential material is another source of potential invasion of a client's privacy. It is the counselor's responsibility to make sure fax and e-mail transmissions arrive in a secured environment in such a way as to protect confidential information. Before sending a confidential fax or e-mail, it is a good idea to make a telephone call to ensure that the appropriate person will be able to retrieve this information in a safe and sensitive manner (Cottone & Tarvydas, 2007).

Frankel (2000) states that he will not use e-mail to provide services unless all of the following conditions are met: having an existing professional relationship with a client; providing the client with informed consent about the use of e-mail and its attendant confidentiality; and limiting the e-mail exchange to giving a client basic information such as an appointment time. Because e-mail is notoriously unsafe in the way that most people use it, Freeny (2001) contends that security and privacy issues in the use of e-mail must be disclosed in detail to clients.

Good practice dictates that you do not send clients e-mail messages at their workplace or home, because they have no right to privacy in these situations. Furthermore, the courts have ruled that e-mail sent or received on computers used by employees is considered to be the property of the company, and therefore, privacy and confidentiality do not exist. Since there is no reasonable expectation of confidentiality for e-mail, clients need to have input regarding how they want communication to be handled so that their privacy is protected.

This discussion of privacy may appear to be mere common sense, but we have become so accustomed to relying on technology that careful thought is not always given to subtle ways that privacy can be violated. Exercise caution and pay attention to ways that you could unintentionally breach the privacy of your clients when using various forms of communication. Apprise your clients of potential problems of privacy regarding a wide range of technology and discuss how they might best contact you between office visits and how you might leave messages for them. Take preventive measures so that both you and your clients have an understanding and agreement about these important concerns.

Implications of HIPAA for Mental Health Providers

The **Health Insurance Portability and Accountability Act of 1996 (HIPAA)** was passed by Congress to promote standardization and efficiency in the health care industry and to give patients more rights and control over their health information. Patients must be informed of their rights and are required to sign the appropriate forms authorizing a health care provider to obtain and provide information to other health care providers (Robles, 2009). HIPAA includes provisions designed to encourage electronic transactions and requires certain new safeguards to protect the security and confidentiality of health information. The **HIPAA Privacy Rule** was designed to provide a uniform level of privacy and security on the federal level. This Privacy Rule, which applies to both paper and electronic transmissions of protected health information by covered entities, developed out of the concern that transmission of health care information through electronic means could lead to widespread gaps in the protection of client confidentiality (Wheeler & Bertram, 2008). The Privacy Rule requires health plans and other covered entities to establish policies and procedures to protect the confidentiality of health information about their patients. It provides patients with rights concerning how their health information is used and disclosed by health care providers who fall within the domain of HIPAA.

Health care providers need to determine whether they are covered entities under HIPAA. If providers transmit any protected health information in electronic form (such as health care claims, health plan enrollment, or coordination of benefits), or if they hire someone to electronically transmit protected health care information, they must comply with all applicable HIPAA regulations (Bennett et al., 2006; Wheeler & Bertram, 2008). If you submit a claim electronically, even once, you are likely to be considered a covered entity for HIPAA purposes.

What is a **covered entity**? Jensen (2003b) explains that there are three types of covered entities: health plans, health care clearinghouses, and health care providers who transmit health information by electronic means. To determine that you are a "covered entity," you need to answer affirmatively to all three of these questions:

1. Are you a health care provider?
2. Do you transmit information electronically?
3. Do you conduct covered transactions?

According to Jensen, if you do not answer "yes" to all of these questions, or if you do not employ someone to conduct the covered transactions for you, then you are not a covered entity and HIPAA does not apply to you.

If you want to avoid becoming a covered entity, Jensen (2003e) offers these suggestions:

- Do not use your computer to conduct one of the standard/covered transactions.
- Use only your telephone, the mail, or your fax machine.
- Avoid hiring a person to do your billing services to clients if he or she conducts one of the standard/covered transactions electronically.
- Do not allow health plans to communicate with you electronically.

- Make certain that health plans communicate with you about clients only by phone, mail, or fax machine.

In his article, "HIPAA Overview," Jensen (2003b) describes the four standards of HIPAA: (1) privacy requirements, (2) electronic transactions, (3) security requirements, and (4) national identifier requirements. Let's examine each in more detail.

> *Privacy requirements.* The Privacy Rule requires practitioners to take reasonable precautions in safeguarding patient information. Licensed health care providers are expected to have a working knowledge of and guard patients' rights to privacy in disclosure of information, health care operations, limiting the disclosure of protected information, payment matters, protected health information, psychotherapy notes and a patient's medical record, and treatment activities.
>
> *Electronic transactions.* HIPAA aims at creating one national form of communication, or "language," so that health care providers can communicate with one another electronically in this common language.
>
> *Security requirements.* Minimum requirements are outlined in HIPAA that are designed to safeguard confidential information and prevent unauthorized access to health information of patients.
>
> *National identifier requirements.* It is essential that covered entities be able to communicate with one another efficiently. Health care providers and health plans are required to have national identification numbers that identify them when they are conducting standard transactions.

Only mental health providers who fall within the definition of *covered entity* are subject to HIPAA requirements. Those providers who do not fall within this scope of practice are not required to comply with HIPAA requirements, unless they choose to do so (Jensen, 2003e). Wheeler and Bertram (2008) suggest that some HIPAA requirements could be good practices from a risk management perspective even if a practitioner is not technically a covered entity.

Handerscheid, Henderson, and Chalk (2002) state that HIPAA privacy requirements are meant to protect confidential patient information irrespective of the form in which the information is stored. To comply, covered entities first need to review their routine business practices to assess how well patient information is protected against inappropriate disclosures. The second step involves modifying business policies or practices once any problems are detected. The third step involves working with consumers to inform them of their rights, advise them about providing written authorization for release of information, and describe grievance procedures clients can use if they believe their privacy has been violated. (For more background on HIPAA, see U.S. Department of Health and Human Services, 2003.)

The Duty to Warn and to Protect

Mental health professionals, spurred by the courts, have come to realize that they have a dual professional responsibility: to protect other people from potentially dangerous clients and to protect clients from themselves. Wheeler and Bertram (2008) remind us that the competing interests of client privacy and public safety must be assessed by mental health professionals. Balancing client confidentiality and protecting the public is a major ethical challenge (Donner et al., 2008). In this section we look first at therapists' responsibilities to protect potential victims from violence and then at the problems posed by clients who are suicidal.

The Duty to Protect Potential Victims

Practitioners need to integrate legal and professional issues into their clinical practice in such a manner that care of clients is not compromised. Bednar and his colleagues (1991) maintain that counselors must exercise the ordinary skill and care of a reasonable professional to (1) identify those clients who are likely to do physical harm to third parties, (2) protect third parties from those clients judged potentially dangerous, and (3) treat those clients who are dangerous.

One of the most difficult tasks therapists must grapple with is deciding whether a particular client is dangerous. Indeed, it is extremely difficult to decide when it is justified to breach confidentiality and notify and protect potential victims. Although practitioners are not generally legally liable for their failure to render perfect predictions of violent behavior of a client, a professionally inadequate assessment of client dangerousness can result in liability for the therapist, harm to third parties, and inappropriate breaches of client confidentiality. Therapists faced with potentially dangerous clients should take specific steps to protect the public and to minimize their own liability. They should take careful histories, advise clients of the limits of confidentiality, keep accurate notes of threats and other client statements, seek consultation, and record steps they have taken to protect others. Practitioners should consult with a supervisor or an attorney because they may be subject to liability for failing to notify those who are in danger. In cases where a client expresses an intention to harm another person, Bennett et al. (2006) recommend making an assessment for suicidal intentions because there is a correlation between suicidal and homicidal behaviors. If a determination is made that an individual poses a high risk for harming an identifiable third party, it is essential to develop and implement an intervention plan. Bennett and colleagues note that it is necessary to continually reevaluate the potential for dangerous behavior with high-risk clients for the duration of therapy and to modify the treatment plan if conditions change.

Welfel and colleagues (2009) point out that nearly every jurisdiction has a different interpretation of the duty to warn and the duty to protect, with some having no statute or case law related to the issues and others with very specific legal guidelines. Bennett et al. (2006) stress the importance of knowing the law in your state regarding the duty to warn or protect. Most states permit (if not require) therapists to breach confidentiality to warn or protect victims. Some states specify how that duty is to be discharged. Some states grant therapists immunity or protection from being sued for breaching confidentiality if the therapist can demonstrate that he or she acted in good faith to notify or protect third parties. A few states have no mandatory duty to warn and to protect third parties, and therapists have no specific grant of immunity from civil suits for breaching confidentiality in those states.

Welfel, Werth, and Benjamin (2009) differentiate between the duty to warn and the duty to protect. The **duty to warn** applies to those circumstances where case law or statute requires the mental health professional to make a reasonable effort to contact the identified victim of a client's serious threats of harm, or to notify law enforcement of the threat. The **duty to protect** applies to situations where the mental health professional has a legal obligation to protect an identified third party who is being threatened; in these cases the professional generally has other options in addition to warning the person of harm. The duty to protect provides ways of maintaining the client's confidentiality; the duty to warn requires a disclosure of confidential information to the person who is being threatened with harm.

Welfel, Werth, and Benjamin state that exercising a duty to warn can result in inappropriate breaches of confidentiality that damage the therapeutic relationship, which can end treatment. Furthermore, this course of action cannot guarantee another person's safety. Although warning is sometimes the prudent action to take, for most professionals in many situations, warning is not the only option or the best course to follow. Absent specific state laws mandating the duty to warn and to protect, Wheeler and Bertram (2008) believe mental health professionals may have an ethical duty to disclose information when it is necessary "to prevent clear and imminent danger to the client or others" (p. 85). They suggest the real question for counselors to ponder is: "How can I fulfill my legal and ethical duties to protect human life, act in the best interest of the client, and remain protected from potential liability (p. 85)?"

The responsibility to protect the public from dangerous acts of violent clients entails liability for civil damages when practitioners neglect this duty by (1) failing to diagnose or predict dangerousness, (2) failing to warn potential victims of violent behavior, (3) failing to commit dangerous individuals, or (4) prematurely discharging dangerous clients from a hospital (APA, 1985). The first two of these legally prescribed duties are illustrated in the case of *Tarasoff v. Board of Regents of the University of California* (1976), which has been the subject of extensive analysis in the psychological literature. The other two duties are set forth in additional landmark court cases.

The *Tarasoff* case.   In August 1969 Prosenjit Poddar was a voluntary outpatient at the student health service at the University of California, Berkeley and was in counseling with a psychologist named Moore. Poddar had confided to Moore his intention to kill an unnamed woman (who was readily identifiable as Tatiana Tarasoff) when she returned from an extended trip in Brazil. In consultation with other university counselors, Moore made the assessment that Poddar was dangerous and should be committed to a mental hospital for observation. Moore later called the campus police and told them of the death threat and of his conclusion that Poddar was dangerous. The campus officers did take Poddar into custody for questioning, but they later released him when he gave evidence of being "rational" and promised to stay away from Tarasoff. He was never confined to a treatment facility. Moore followed up his call with a formal letter requesting the assistance of the chief of the campus police. Later, Moore's supervisor asked that the letter be returned, ordered that the letter and Moore's case notes be destroyed, and asked that no further action be taken in the case. Tarasoff and her family were never made aware of this potential threat.

Shortly after Tarasoff's return from Brazil, Poddar killed her. Her parents filed suit against the Board of Regents and the employees of the university for having failed to notify the intended victim of the threat. When a lower court dismissed the suit in 1974, the parents appealed, and the California Supreme Court ruled in favor of the parents in 1976, holding that a failure to warn an intended victim was professionally irresponsible. The court's ruling requires that therapists breach confidentiality in cases where the general welfare and safety of others is involved. This was a California case, and courts in other states are not bound to decide a similar case in the same way.

Under the *Tarasoff* decision, the therapist must first accurately diagnose the client's tendency to behave in dangerous ways toward others. This first duty is judged by the standards of professional negligence. In this case the therapist did not fail in this duty. He even took the additional step of requesting that the dangerous person be detained by the campus police. But the court held that simply notifying the police was insufficient to protect the identifiable victim (Laughran & Bakken, 1984).

In the first ruling, in 1974, the lower court cited a **duty to warn**, but this duty was expanded by the 1976 California Supreme Court ruling, which said: "When a therapist determines . . . that his patient presents a serious danger of violence to another, he incurs an obligation to use reasonable care to protect the intended victim against such danger." Richard Leslie (2008) states that the "duty" created by the California Supreme Court in the *Tarasoff* decision was *not* a "duty to warn." According to Leslie, this so-called duty to warn has long been a mischaracterization of the actual duty. Rather, the court described the duty simply as a "duty to exercise reasonable care to protect the foreseeable victim" of the serious danger of violence against him or her.

Therapists can protect others through traditional clinical interventions such as reassessment, medication changes, referral, or hospitalization. Other steps therapists may take include warning potential victims, calling the police, or informing the state child protection agency. Negligence lies in the practitioner's failure to warn a third party of imminent danger, not in failing to predict any violence that may be committed.

The *Tarasoff* decision made it clear that client confidentiality can be readily compromised; indeed, "the protective privilege ends where the public peril begins" (cited in Perlin, 1997). As Bednar and his colleagues (1991) indicate, the mental health professional is a double agent. Therapists have ethical and legal responsibilities to their clients, and they also have legal obligations to society. These dual responsibilities sometimes conflict, and they can create ambiguity in the therapeutic relationship. Welfel (2010) points out that courts interpret the duty to warn and protect to include situations in which therapists *should have known* about the danger. If ignorance about a dangerous situation is the result of incompetent or negligent practice, then professionals have neglected this duty. "The courts simply do not view incompetence or negligence as an adequate defense against a claim of failure to protect" (p. 131). State courts and legislatures vary in their interpretations of *Tarasoff*, and practitioners remain uncertain about the nature of their duty to protect or to warn. However, the codes of ethics of most mental health professions incorporate this concept, and it is generally assumed that the duty to warn and to protect is a national legal requirement.

Mandatory reporting laws only apply to threats regarding future violence (Barnett & Johnson, 2010). Reports by clients of past violence may not be reported and are protected as confidential information. Mental health professionals should be familiar with the warning signs and risk factors for violence and the potential for acting out. Barnett and Johnson recommend that therapists conduct a formal risk assessment with all clients who show any warning signs for violence. Therapists should be familiar with the treatment options and resources for managing high-risk clients in their local area.

Therapists are often concerned about legal responsibility when the identity of the intended victim is unknown. VandeCreek and Knapp (2001) recommend seeking consultation with other professionals who have expertise in dealing with potentially violent people and documenting the steps taken. They add that therapists do well to adhere to risk management strategies in dealing with dangerous clients. In particular, therapists need to be especially careful about grounds for liability including abandonment; failure to consult, refer, or coordinate treatment with a physician; maintaining adequate records; and responding appropriately if a suit is filed.

At the time the *Tarasoff* decision was issued it was binding only in California, and therapists in other states did not know whether courts in their states would comply with this decision (VandeCreek & Knapp, 2001). Not all states have embraced the *Tarasoff* doctrine. In 1999 the members of the Texas Supreme Court unanimously rejected the *Tarasoff* duty (*Thapar v. Zezulka*, 1999). Basing its decision on the Texas statute governing the legal duty of mental health professionals to protect clients' confidentiality, the court found that it was unwise to impose a duty to warn on mental health practitioners.

In July 2004 a California appeals court decision extended the interpretation of the *Tarasoff* warning law (Zur, 2005). In *Ewing v. Goldstein* (2004) the court expanded the practitioner's duty to warn those in danger to include the circumstance in which a family member communicates to a mental health practitioner a belief that the client poses a risk of grave bodily injury to another person. This court decision means that licensed therapists in California could be held liable for failure to issue a *Tarasoff* warning when the information regarding the dangerousness of a client comes from a client's family member rather than from the client. In his discussion of the *Ewing* and *Tarasoff* cases, Jensen (2005) synopsizes the court ruling as follows:

> Communication from a patient's "family member" to the patient's therapist, made for the purpose of advancing the patient's therapy, may create a duty upon the therapist to warn an intended victim of the patient's threatened violent behavior. (p. 33)

Zur (2005) recommends that California therapists add this recent court decision to their informed consent document.

The *Bradley* case. A second case illustrates the duty not to negligently release a dangerous client. In *Bradley Center v. Wessner* (1982) the patient, Wessner, had been voluntarily admitted to a facility for psychiatric care. Wessner was upset over his wife's extramarital affair. He had repeatedly threatened to kill her and her lover and had even admitted to a therapist that he was carrying a weapon in his car for that purpose. He was given an unrestricted weekend pass to visit his children, who were living with his wife. He met his wife and her lover in the home, and shot and killed them. The children filed a wrongful death suit, alleging that the psychiatric center had breached a duty to exercise control over Wessner. The Georgia Supreme Court ruled that a physician has a duty to take reasonable care to prevent a potentially dangerous patient from inflicting harm (Laughran & Bakken, 1984).

The *Jablonski* case. A third legal ruling underscores the duty to commit a dangerous individual. The intended victim's knowledge of a threat does not relieve therapists of the duty to protect, as can be seen by the decision in *Jablonski v. United States* (1983). Meghan Jablonski filed suit for the wrongful death of her mother, Melinda Kimball, who was murdered by Philip Jablonski, the man with whom she had been living. Earlier, Philip Jablonski had agreed to a psychiatric examination at a hospital. The physicians determined that there was no emergency and thus no basis for involuntary commitment. Kimball later again accompanied Jablonski to the hospital and expressed fears for her own safety. She was told by a doctor that "you should consider staying away from him." Again, the doctors concluded that there was no basis for involuntary hospitalization and released him. Shortly thereafter Jablonski killed Kimball. The Ninth U.S. Circuit Court of Appeals found that failure to obtain Jablonski's prior medical history constituted malpractice. The essence of *Jablonski* is a negligent failure to commit (Laughran & Bakken, 1984).

The *Hedlund* case. A fourth legal ruling, *Hedlund v. Superior Court* (1983), extends the duty to warn in California to a foreseeable, identifiable person who might be near the intended victim when the threat is carried out and thus might also be in danger. LaNita Wilson and Stephen Wilson had received psychotherapy from a psychological assistant, Bonnie Hedlund.

During treatment Stephen Wilson told the therapist that he intended to harm LaNita Wilson. Later he did assault her, in the presence of her child. The allegation was that the child had sustained "serious emotional injury and psychological trauma."

In keeping with the *Tarasoff* decision, the California Supreme Court held (1) that a therapist has a duty first to exercise a "reasonable degree of skill, knowledge, and care ordinarily possessed and exercised by members [of that professional specialty] under similar circumstances" in making a prediction about the chances of a client's acting dangerously to others and (2) that therapists must "exercise reasonable care to protect the foreseeable victim of that danger." One way to protect the victim is by giving a warning of peril. The court held that breach of such a duty with respect to third persons constitutes "professional negligence" (Laughran & Bakken, 1984).

In the *Hedlund* case the duty to warn of potentially dangerous conduct applied to the mother, not to her child, against whom no threats had been made. However, the court found that a therapist could be held liable for injuries sustained by the intended victim's child if the violent act was carried out. The court held that a therapist must consider the welfare of the intended victim as well as the welfare of persons in close relationship to the victim when determining how to best protect the potential victim.

Guidelines for Dealing With Dangerous Clients

Most counseling centers and community mental health agencies now have guidelines regarding the duty to warn and protect when the welfare of others is at stake. These guidelines generally specify how to deal with emotionally disturbed individuals, violent behavior, threats, suicidal possibilities, and other circumstances in which counselors may be legally and ethically required to breach confidentiality.

Understandably, many counselors find it difficult to predict when clients pose a serious threat to others. Clients are encouraged to engage in open dialogue in therapeutic relationships, and many clients express feelings or thoughts about doing physical harm to others. But few of these threats are actually carried out, and counselors should not be expected to routinely reveal all verbal threats (Bennett et al., 2006). Notifying a third party of a threat is a relatively rare event. Breaking confidentiality can seriously harm the client–therapist relationship as well as the relationship between the client and the person "threatened." Such disclosures should be carefully evaluated. In making decisions about when to warn, counselors should seek consultation, exercise reasonable professional judgment, and apply practices that are commonly accepted by professionals in the specialty.

Practitioners often lack knowledge of their ethical and legal duties in dealing with potentially dangerous clients. Pabian, Welfel, and Beebe (2009) examined psychologists' knowledge of their legal and ethical responsibilities with dangerous clients and found that most (76% of respondents) were misinformed about their state's laws pertaining to *Tarasoff*-type situations.

Many believed they had a legal duty to warn when they did not; others assumed that warning was their only legal option, when other less intrusive interventions were possible. Pabian and colleagues found no significant relationship between legal knowledge and continuing education in legal and ethical issues, graduate training in ethics, or clinical experience in working with clients who posed a danger to others. They concluded that educational experiences during and after graduate school do not seem to be meeting the needs of professionals in understanding state laws and ethical duties regarding dangerous clients.

In most cases therapists will not have advanced warning that a client is dangerous. Therefore, it is essential for therapists to be prepared for such an eventuality. We offer the following suggestions:

- Examine your informed consent document. Is it clear in terms of the forfeiture of confidentiality because of a threat of violence to self or others?
- Know how to contact the legal counsel of your professional organization.
- Review the code of ethics of your professional organization on matters applicable to your practice.
- Familiarize yourself with professionals who are experienced in dealing with violence and know how to reach them.
- In the initial interview, if there is any hint of violence in the client's history, request clinical records from previous therapists, if they exist.
- Take at least one workshop in the assessment and management of dangerous clients.
- Determine that the limits of your professional liability insurance are adequate.

Wheeler and Bertram (2008) suggest some practical risk management guidelines in dealing with duty to warn and protect situations:

- Consult with an attorney if you are not clear about your legal duty.
- Inquire about a client's access to weapons, homicidal ideation, and intentions, which would include whether a specific victim is involved.
- Consider all appropriate steps to take and the consequences of each.
- Know and follow the policy of your institution.
- Document all the actions you take and the rationale behind each of your decisions.

If you have prepared yourself for the eventuality of a dangerous client, you will have a better sense of what to do in these circumstances. In addition, your liability will be eliminated if you have followed a prudent course of action and can demonstrate that you acted within the standard of care expected of a competent mental health professional.

As you think about the following case, ask yourself how you would assess the degree to which Marvin is potentially dangerous. What would you do if you were the therapist in this case?

■ The Case of Marvin.

Marvin has been seeing Robin, his counselor, for several months. One day he comes to the therapy session inebriated and very angry. He has just found out that a close friend is having an affair with his wife. He is deeply wounded over this incident. He is also highly agitated and even talks about killing the friend who betrayed him. As he puts it, "I am so damn mad I feel like getting my gun and shooting him." Marvin experiences intense emotions in this session. Robin does everything she can to defuse his rage and to stabilize him before the session ends. The session continues for about 2 hours (instead of the usual hour), and she asks him to call her a couple of times each day to check in. Before he leaves, she contracts with him that he will not go over to this man's house and that he will not act out his urges. Because of the strength of the therapeutic relationship, she assessed Marvin as not being a violent person and decided not to follow through with the duty to warn. He follows through and calls her every day. When he comes to the session the following week, he admits to still being in a great deal of pain over his discovery, but he no longer feels so angry. As he puts it, "I am not going to land in jail because of this jerk!" He tells Robin how helpful the last session was in allowing him to get a lot off his chest.

- Do you think Robin followed the proper ethical and legal course of action in this case?
- Did she fulfill her responsibilities by making sure that Marvin called her twice a day?
- Some would say that she should have broken confidentiality and warned the intended victim. What do you think? Explain your reasoning.
- What criteria could you use to determine whether the situation is dangerous enough to warn a potential victim? What is the fine line between overreacting and failing to respond appropriately in this kind of case?
- If Robin had sought you out for consultation in this case immediately after the session at which Marvin talked about wanting to kill his friend, how would you have advised her?

Commentary. Robin did an assessment of dangerousness and received several commitments from Marvin to restrain his behavior. Although a verbal threat of the intent to harm another person is a key factor, other factors to consider include the context in which the threat is made, the intent, Marvin's history of violence, use of drugs and alcohol, and the availability of opportunity. Robin's assessment that Marvin was not dangerous was based on her five-month relationship with him and her trust in him to honor their agreements. From both an ethical and legal perspective, it is critical that Robin seek consultation in the process of making her decision on how to deal with Marvin's threat.

Implications of Duty to Warn and to Protect for School Counselors

In her doctoral dissertation on legal issues in counseling, Hermann (2001) describes the multiple interpretations of the *Tarasoff* duty and the lack of case law as it pertains to the duty to warn and protect in situations of potential violence in school settings. The basic standard of care for school counselors is clear; courts have uniformly held that school personnel have a duty to protect students from foreseeable harm (Hermann & Remley, 2000). School personnel may need to act on student reports of their peers' plans related to intended violence. Furthermore, school officials may be held accountable if a student's writing assignments contain evidence of premeditated violence.

Hermann and Finn (2002) contend that school counselors are legally and ethically obligated to work toward preventing school violence. They state that school counselors may find themselves legally vulnerable because of their role in determining whether students pose a risk of harm to others and deciding on appropriate interventions with these students. Current case law reveals that all indicators of potential violence should be taken seriously.

Hermann (2002) found that 63% of the school counselors in her study believed they were well prepared to determine whether a student posed a danger to others. Preventing students from harming other students seems to be implicit in the duty of school personnel. Courts have consistently found that school counselors have a duty to exercise reasonable care to protect students from foreseeable harm, but they are only exposed to legal liability if they fail to exercise reasonable care (Hermann & Remley, 2000).

In the short space of one month in 2001, two major shooting incidents took place within the same school district in San Diego, California. Both of these events resulted in intense national media coverage and raised the question of how these tragedies might have been prevented. In the first event the boy doing the shooting had told some friends of his intentions, and they searched his knapsack for a gun, which they could not find. The shooter insisted he was joking, and his friends failed to report the matter because they did not want to get him in trouble. He later killed 2 and injured 13 others on the campus. In the second incident, no one was killed, but several were injured. In this case, the student had made prior threats of violence.

School counselors are increasingly being forced to deal with incidents and threats of violence by students (Isaacs, 1997). Costa and Altekruse (1994) recommend that school counselors make an assessment of dangerousness by evaluating the student's plans for implementing the violent act and the student's ability to carry out the act. Waldo and Malley (1992) advise gathering the necessary information to make a determination about the student's potential dangerousness, and when faced with potential dangerousness, counselors should consult with other mental health professionals and with legal counsel about the state's most recent position on *Tarasoff*-type cases. Given the context of emerging case law and the violent climate of today's schools, Hermann and Remley (2000) assert that school counselors would do well to take every threat of violence seriously.

Many schools now search students for weapons, which has resulted in protests over infringement of students' constitutional rights. Hermann and Remley (2000) report that constitutional rights are being restricted in the wake of public outrage over school violence:

> As school violence and school security increase, students are likely to continue to engage in court battles against educators seeking lost constitutional protections. And educators face even more litigation as those injured seek to find someone to blame for the unfortunate societal phenomenon of guns and violence in schools. (p. 439)

The central ethical concern surrounding this issue involves the commitment of mental health professionals to develop organized prevention efforts in response to school violence. Although many psychologists are involved in assessing and treating at-risk youth for violent behavior, Evans and Rey (2001) report that efforts are not often directed toward organized prevention of violence and delinquency. Not only are psychologists being asked to shed light on the community's understanding of the causes of high-profile incidences of violence, but they are increasingly being asked what they might do to help prevent youth violence, both in and out of the school. Evans and Rey believe practicing psychologists represent a critical resource to school districts in designing and implementing a comprehensive violence prevention program.

The following case illustrates a challenge school counselors might face in dealing with students who pose a danger to others.

■ The Case of Matt.

Matt is a high school student who seems to have the potential for violence. During his sessions with you, he talks about his impulses to hurt others and himself, and he describes times when he has seriously beaten his girlfriend, Lucy. He tells you that she is afraid to leave him because she thinks he will beat her even more savagely. He later tells you that sometimes he gets so angry that he feels like killing her. You believe Matt could seriously harm and possibly even kill Lucy. Which of the following would you do? Check all that apply.

_____ 1. I would notify Matt's girlfriend that she might be in grave danger, if I knew of her identity.

      ——————— 2. I would notify the police or other authorities.

      ——————— 3. I would keep Matt's threats to myself because I could not be sure that he would act on them.

      ——————— 4. I would seek a second opinion from a colleague.

      ——————— 5. I would inform my director or supervisor.

      ——————— 6. I would refer Matt to another therapist.

      ——————— 7. I would arrange to have Matt hospitalized.

Would you answer differently if Matt showed real promise in therapy and seemed to really want to change his behavior?

> *Commentary.* Because Matt is voluntarily seeing a therapist and is disclosing his impulses and behavior, he may want to change. However, you must consider specific actions, comments, and threats that Matt has made in determining the appropriate course of action to take. He has seriously beaten Lucy and she is afraid to leave him. He also tells you that sometimes he gets so angry that he feels like killing her, and you believe he is capable of this violence. The seriousness of Matt's actions poses a clear danger to others, which you cannot ethically or legally ignore. Notifying the police may be in order because Matt's girlfriend cannot be relied upon to inform the police. You may be able to continue therapy after notifying the police if Matt agrees to this, or you can help him find other appropriate resources, such as an anger management program.

The Duty to Protect Suicidal Clients

In the preceding discussion we emphasized the therapist's obligation to protect others from dangerous individuals. The guidelines and principles outlined in that discussion often apply to the client who poses a danger to self, but some courts have found there is not the same duty in cases of suicide as in cases of violence (Mary Hermann, personal communication, March 19, 2009). As part of the informed consent process, therapists must inform clients that they have an ethical and legal obligation to break confidentiality when they have good reason to suspect suicidal behavior. Even if clients argue that they can do what they want with their own lives, including taking them, therapists have a legal **duty to protect** suicidal clients. The crux of the issue is knowing when to take a client's hints seriously enough to report the condition. Certainly not every mention of suicidal thoughts or feelings justifies extraordinary measures.

The evaluation and management of suicidal risk can be a source of great stress for therapists. Clinical practitioners must face many troublesome issues, including their degree of influence, competence, level of involvement with a client, responsibility, legal obligations, and ability to make life-or-death decisions. Courts have consistently ruled that when mental health providers fail to provide adequate assessment, treatment, or follow-up, they are liable for a client's death if a reasonable standard of care would have likely prevented the suicide from occurring (Barnett & Porter, 1998). If a client dies by suicide, the risk of a malpractice action is greatly reduced if the therapist can demonstrate that a reasonable assessment and intervention process took place; professional consultation was sought; clinical referrals were made when appropriate; and thorough and current documentation was done (Jobes & O'Connor, 2009). Counselors can be accused of malpractice for neglecting to take action to prevent harm when a client is likely to take the step of suicide, yet they are also liable if they overreact by taking actions that violate a client's privacy when there is not a justifiable basis for doing so (Remley & Herlihy, 2010).

The law does not require practitioners to always make correct assessments of suicide risk, but therapists do have a legal duty to make assessments from an informed position and to carry out their professional obligations in a manner comparable to what other reasonable professionals would do in similar situations. If a counselor makes a determination that a client is at risk for suicide, the counselor should take the least intrusive steps necessary to prevent the harm.

School Counselor Liability for Student Suicide

Suicide by a student is perhaps the greatest tragedy on a campus, and one that shocks the entire school community. Recognizing signs of potential suicide and preventing suicide certainly have to be among the major challenges school counselors face. School counselors are expected to be aware of the warning signs of suicidal behavior and need to have the skills necessary to assess a student's risk for suicide (Capuzzi & Gross, 2008). To manage the legal risks associated with their jobs, school counselors must be prepared to determine whether a student may be at risk for suicide (Capuzzi, 2009).

In her study of legal issues encountered by school counselors, Hermann (2002) reports the most prevalent legal issue involves school counselors determining whether students are suicidal. Hermann found that almost three fourths (72%) of the school counselors surveyed believed they were well prepared to determine whether a client was suicidal. King and colleagues (2000) studied (1) whether high school counselors knew the risk factors associated with suicidal behavior, and (2) whether these counselors knew the appropriate steps to take in intervening with a student who expressed suicidal ideation, had a specific plan, and had the lethal means to carry out the plan. King and colleagues found that the majority of the high school counselors surveyed were knowledgeable about risk factors of adolescent suicide and knew the appropriate steps to take when a student gave indications of suicidal ideation. However, in another study King and colleagues (1999) found that only 38% of the high school counselors surveyed believed they could determine whether a student was at risk for committing suicide. This discrepancy may result from the reality of the very large numbers of students that school counselors are assigned, which makes it difficult for counselors to have personal knowledge about the majority of the students for whom they are responsible. King and colleagues (2000) made a number of suggestions based on their findings:

- Counselors need to educate school employees, especially teachers, about the risk factors associated with adolescent suicide.
- Counselors might institute peer assistance programs to help identify students at risk for suicide.
- It would be useful for school counselors to have increased access to training programs geared to acquiring information about student suicide.
- Given the legal duty to protect students who may pose a danger to themselves, school counselors would do well to take the initiative in obtaining continuing education on recent developments in the field of student suicide to help limit their legal liability.
- Professional journals and professional conferences need to continue highlighting the issue of student suicide.
- Counselor education programs need to better prepare future school counselors to recognize students at risk for suicide.

School counselors who do not possess competency in identifying and managing students who may be suicidal need supervision, consultation, and direction from counselors who possess such expertise (Remley, 2009). Although school counselors are not expected to predict all suicide gestures or attempts, they are expected to use sound judgment in making clinical decisions, and their reasoning should be documented in their notes. In cases where school counselors make an assessment that a student is at risk for suicide, it is imperative that the student's parents or guardians be notified that such an assessment took place. Parents or guardians have a legal right to know when their child may be in danger.

Court cases.   In school settings, courts have found a special relationship between school personnel and students. Hermann (2001) has documented this, and our discussion is based on her work. One of the first cases that addressed school counselor liability for student suicide was *Eisel v. Board of Education* (1991). In this case, 13-year-old Nicole was involved in Satanism. Nicole made a suicide pact with another student, who subsequently shot Nicole and then shot herself. Fellow students had told their school counselor that Nicole wanted to take her own life. When the school counselor confronted Nicole about her suicidal intentions, she denied making any such statements. The counselor did not attempt to contact Nicole's parents. In *Eisel* the court found that school counselors have a duty to use reasonable means to attempt to prevent a suicide when they know about a student's suicidal intentions. The reasoning of the court was that an adolescent is more likely to share thoughts of suicide with friends than with a school counselor, teacher, or parent. The court found that reasonable care would have included notifying Nicole's parents that their daughter was at risk for suicide. Although the suicide occurred off the school premises, the court held that legally the school could be held liable for failure to exercise reasonable care to prevent a foreseeable injury.

Even if the risk of the student actually committing suicide is remote, the possibility may be enough to establish a duty to contact the parents or the guardians and to inform them of the potential for suicidal behavior. Courts have found that the burden involved in making a telephone call is minor considering the risk of harm to a student who is suicidal. In short, school personnel are advised to take every suicide threat seriously and to take every precaution to protect the student.

The courts have addressed the need for training school employees in suicide prevention. The *Wyke v. Polk County School Board* (1997) case involved a 13-year-old named Shawn, who attempted suicide two times at school before finally killing himself at home. School officials were aware of the suicide attempts, yet they failed to notify Shawn's mother. During the trial, several experts in the field of suicide prevention testified about the need for suicide prevention training in schools, including mandatory written policies requiring parental notification, holding students in protective custody, and arranging for counseling services. The experts who testified at the trial believed the school board failed to provide adequate training for school personnel. Without training, school personnel will most likely underestimate the lethality of suicidal thoughts, statements, and attempts. The conclusion of this expert testimony was that Shawn would not have committed suicide if the employees had been adequately trained. Persuaded by this input, the court held that the school could be found negligent for failing to notify the decedent's mother.

If you are aiming for a career as a school counselor, you will need more than this basic knowledge regarding your ethical and legal obligations to respond in a professional manner in situations where students may pose a danger to themselves or others. Continuing education is of the utmost importance, as is your willingness to seek appropriate consultation when you become aware of students who are at risk.

■ The Case of Rupe.

Rupe, a 16-year-old high school student, is being seen by the school psychologist, Vernon, at the request of his parents. Rupe's school work has dropped off, he has become withdrawn socially, and he has expressed to his parents that he has thought of suicide, even though he has not made a specific plan. After the psychologist has seen Rupe for several weeks of individual counseling, his concerned parents call and ask how he is doing. They wonder whether they should be alert to possible suicide attempts. Rupe's parents tell Vernon that they want to respect confidentiality and are not interested in detailed disclosures but that they want to find out if they have cause for worry. Without going into detail, Vernon reassures them that they really do not need to worry.

- Is Vernon's behavior ethical? Would it make a difference if Rupe were 25 years old?
- Does Vernon have an ethical obligation to inform Rupe of the conversation with his parents?
- If the parents were to insist on having more information, does Vernon have an obligation to say more?
- Did Vernon have sufficient information to justify telling the parents that they have no need to worry?
- If Vernon provides details to the parents, does he have an obligation to inform Rupe before talking with his parents?
- Would Vernon be remiss if he had not informed Rupe about the limits of confidentiality?
- Other than doing what this school psychologist did, do you see other courses of action?
- If Rupe were indeed suicidal, what ethical and legal obligations would Vernon have toward the parents? Would he have to inform the school principal?

Commentary. This case shows the importance of knowing the law in your state or jurisdiction pertaining to confidentiality in counseling minors. What are the rights of the parents/guardians? What are the minor client's rights? To prevent later misunderstandings, it is good practice initially to have a dialogue with both the minor client and the parents/guardians regarding what details may be shared regarding the progress of therapy. A discussion of the limits of confidentiality is also in order. Good practice also involves informing the minor client of any times when there is a discussion between the parents and the therapist. When Rupe's parents asked the therapist for information, they could have been invited to a session with their son (with his permission) to express their concerns with him being present. This would enable Rupe to be part of the discussion and, with the counselor's help, to choose what to disclose directly to his parents.

Guidelines for Assessing Suicidal Behavior

Mental health professionals cannot predict or prevent all client suicides (Bennett et al., 2006; Remley, 2009), but they can learn to recognize common crises that may precipitate a suicide attempt and reach out to people who are experiencing these crises. Counselors must take the "cry for help" seriously. Mental health professionals are expected to complete a comprehensive assessment of clients, especially with clients who pose a threat to themselves. Bennett et al. (2006) recommend that therapists ask every client about present and past suicide ideation or attempts during the initial session. In addition to making an initial assessment, it is important to conduct ongoing assessments throughout the course of treatment (Barnett & Porter, 1998). According to Wheeler and Bertram (2008), therapists who fail to conduct an adequate assessment of a client are vulnerable to a malpractice claim. If a client denies suicidal intent, yet shows evidence of serious depression, the therapist should inquire further and possibly make a referral to a psychiatrist for further evaluation. In an assessment interview, it is important to focus on evaluating depression, suicide ideation, suicide intention, suicide plans, and the presence of any risk factors associated with suicide. In the assessment, it is useful to obtain information about a client's past treatment. In crisis counseling, assess your clients for suicidal risk during the early phase of therapy, and keep alert to this issue during the course of therapy. Danger signs, such as the following, should be evaluated:

- Take direct verbal warnings seriously, as they are one of the most useful single predictors of a suicide. Be sure to document your actions.
- Find out if there were previous suicide attempts, as these are the best single predictor of lethality.
- Identify clients suffering from depression, a characteristic common to all suicide victims. Sleep disruption, which can intensify depression, is a key sign. For people with clinical depression the suicide rate is about 20 times greater than that of the general population.
- Be alert for feelings of hopelessness and helplessness, which seem to be closely associated with suicidal intentions. Explore the client's ideational and mood states. Individuals may feel desperate, guilt-ridden, and worthless.
- Explore carefully the interpersonal stressor of loss and separation, such as a relationship breakup or the death of a loved one.
- Monitor severe anxiety and panic attacks.
- Ascertain whether there has been a recent diagnosis of a serious or terminal health condition.
- Determine whether the individual has a plan. The more definite the plan, the more serious is the situation. Suicidal individuals should be asked to talk about their plans and be encouraged to explore their suicidal fantasies.
- Identify clients who have a history of severe alcohol or drug abuse, as they are at greater risk than the general population. Alcohol is a contributing factor in one fourth to one third of all suicides.
- Be alert to client behaviors such as giving away prized possessions, finalizing business affairs, or revising wills.

- Determine whether clients have a history of previous psychiatric treatment or hospitalization. Clients who have been hospitalized for emotional disorders are more likely to be inclined to suicide.
- Assess the client's support system. If there is no support system, the client is at greater risk.

Therapists have the responsibility to prevent suicide if they can reasonably anticipate it. Special attention should be placed on the limits of confidentiality and on the actions the practitioner will take if the client is found to be at risk (Barnett & Porter, 1998). Once it is determined that a client is at risk for serious harm to self, the professional is legally and ethically required to take appropriate action aimed at protecting the person. Liability generally arises when a counselor fails to act in such a way as to prevent the suicide or when a counselor does something that might contribute to it.

The final decision about the degree of suicidal risk is a subjective one that demands professional judgment. According to VandeCreek and Knapp (2001), in evaluating liability courts assess the reasonableness of professional judgment in treating a suicidal person. If a client demonstrates suicidal intent, and the therapist does not exercise reasonable precautions, there are grounds for liability. VandeCreek and Knapp provide this advice regarding therapist liability:

> The courts will not hold the psychotherapist liable only because a patient committed suicide. Instead, the plaintiffs must prove that the psychotherapists were negligent in their assessment or treatment. Psychotherapists can demonstrate the adequacy of their treatment through consulting with other psychotherapists and documenting treatment decisions carefully. (p. 34)

In his discussion of legal issues associated with suicide, Remley (2004) states that although therapists are not required to predict all suicide gestures or attempts, they are expected to exercise sound judgment in making clinical decisions, and their reasoning needs to be recorded in their notes.

The case for suicide prevention.   Suicidal individuals often hope that somebody will listen to their cry. Many are struggling with short-term crises, and if they can be given help in learning to cope with the immediate problem, their potential for suicide can be greatly reduced.

Expectations for action by mental health professionals dealing with suicidal clients differ depending on the setting. In school settings, the law imposes a duty to take precautions to protect students who may be suicidal. A similar standard exists in hospital settings. However, legal opinions are not consistent when addressing suicidal clients in outpatient settings. It should be noted that successful lawsuits have been brought against therapists who did not follow standard procedures to protect a client's life (Austin et al., 1990). The following are recommendations for managing suicidal behavior (see Austin et al., 1990; Barnett & Johnson, 2008, 2010; Bednar et al., 1991; Bennett et al., 1990, 2006; Bonger, 2002; Peruzzi & Bongar, 1999; Pope & Vasquez, 2007;

Remley, 2004, 2009; Rosenberg, 1999; Sommers-Flanagan & Sommers-Flanagan, 1995):

- Know how to determine whether a client may be at risk for attempting suicide.
- Assess each new client for suicidal thoughts, regardless of the reason the client is seeking counseling.
- Be knowledgeable about the legal requirements bearing on mandatory reporting of suicidal clients and limits of confidentiality in your jurisdiction.
- Clearly outline the limits of confidentiality and the steps you will need to take if your client poses a risk of self harm.
- Obtain education, training, and supervision in suicide risk assessment, suicide prevention, and crisis intervention methods.
- Keep up to date with current research, theory, and practice regarding suicide prevention.
- Work with the suicidal client to create a supportive environment.
- Attempt to secure a contract from the client that he or she will not try to commit suicide, but recognize that the existence of a contract will not be a sufficient "defense" if a court determines that more significant intervention was required of the therapist to prevent suicide.
- Periodically collaborate with colleagues and ask for their views regarding the client's condition. Consult with as many colleagues as possible when making difficult decisions and document these discussions.
- Specify your availability to your clients; let them know how they can contact you during your absences.
- Realize that you may have the responsibility to prevent suicide if the act can be reasonably foreseen.
- Recognize the limits of your competence and know when and how to refer.
- Use sensitivity and caution in terminating or referring a client who has been or is currently suicidal. Be careful to ensure that this transition goes smoothly and that the client does not feel abandoned in the process.
- Consider hospitalization, weighing the benefits and the drawbacks.
- For services that take place within a clinic or agency setting, ensure that clear and appropriate lines of responsibility are explicit and are fully understood by everyone.
- Work with clients so that dangerous instruments are not within easy access. If the client possesses any weapons, put them in the hands of a third party.
- Consider increasing the frequency of the counseling sessions.

- Work with clients' strengths and desires to remain alive.
- Attempt to communicate a realistic sense of hope.
- Be willing to communicate your caring.
- As much as possible, involve the client in the decisions and actions being taken. It is important for clients to share in the responsibility for their ultimate decisions.
- Document the client's mental status, your ongoing risk assessments, and your treatment plan decisions in the client's record.
- Know your personal limits and your own reactions to working with suicidal clients. Recognize the stresses involved and the toll this work takes on you personally and professionally. Seek appropriate consultation, practice self-care, and try to limit the number of suicidal clients with whom you work.
- Attempt to develop a supportive network of family and friends to help clients face their struggles. Discuss this with clients and enlist their help in building this resource of caring people.

Remember that clients are ultimately responsible for their own actions and that there is only so much that you can reasonably do to prevent self-destructive actions. Even though you take specific steps to lessen the chances of a client's suicide, the client may still take this ultimate step.

The case against suicide prevention.   Now that we have looked at the case for suicide prevention, we explore another point of view. Szasz (1986) challenges the statement that mental health professionals have an absolute professional duty to try to prevent suicide. He presents the thesis that suicide is an act of a moral agent who is ultimately responsible, and he opposes coercive methods of preventing suicide, such as forced hospitalization. Szasz argues that by attempting to prevent suicide mental health practitioners often ally themselves with the police power of the state and resort to coercion, therein identifying themselves as foes of individual liberty and responsibility. When professionals assume the burden of responsibility of keeping clients alive, they deprive their clients of their rightful share of accountability for their own actions. Szasz believes that it is the client's responsibility to choose to live or to die. He opposes policies of suicide prevention that minimize the responsibility of individuals for taking their own lives and supports policies that maximize their responsibility for doing so.

Szasz is not claiming that suicide is always good or that it is a morally legitimate option; rather, his key point is that the power of the state should not be used to prohibit an individual from taking his or her own life. The right to suicide implies that we must abstain from empowering agents of the state to coercively prevent it.

A new dimension has been added to the suicide prevention debate with the passage of Oregon's Right to Die legislation, which enables a person following standard guidelines with physician assistance to hasten the advent of death. Basic to this proposition is the assumption that not every person contemplating suicide is mentally incompetent. In other words, an argument has been made for rational suicide. (See Chapter 3 for more on this topic.)

Your stance on suicide prevention.   Considering the arguments for and against suicide prevention, what is your stance on this issue? You may want to review the discussion on personal values in Chapter 3 when considering this topic. What is your position with respect to your ethical obligations to recognize, evaluate, and intervene with potentially suicidal clients? To what degree do you agree with the guidelines discussed in this chapter? Which guidelines make the most sense to you? Do you take a contrary position on at least some cases of suicide? How do you justify your viewpoint? To what extent do you agree or disagree with the contention of Szasz that current policies of suicide prevention displace responsibility from the client to the therapist and that this needlessly undermines the ethic of self-responsibility? After clarifying your own values underlying the professional's role in assessing and preventing suicide, reflect on the following case of a client who is contemplating suicide. If Emmanuel were your client, what actions would you take?

■ The Case of Emmanuel.

Emmanuel is a middle-aged widower who complains of emptiness in life, loneliness, depression, and a loss of the will to live. He has been in individual therapy for 7 months with a psychologist. Using psychodiagnostic procedures, she has determined that Emmanuel has serious depressive tendencies and is potentially self-destructive. In their sessions he talks about the history of his failures, the isolation he feels, the meaninglessness of his life, and his feelings of worthlessness and depression. With her encouragement he experiments with new ways of behaving in the hope that he will find reasons to go on living. Finally, after 7 months of searching, he decides that he wants to take his own life. He tells his therapist that he is convinced he has been deluding himself in thinking that anything in his life will change for the better and that he feels good about deciding to end his life. He informs her that he will not be seeing her again.

The therapist expresses her concern that Emmanuel is very capable of taking his life. She acknowledges that the decision to end his life by suicide is not a sudden one, but she lets him know that she wants him to give therapy more of a chance. He says that he is truly grateful to her for helping him. He says firmly that he does not want her to attempt to obstruct his plans in any way. She asks that he postpone his decision for a week and return to discuss the matter more fully. He tells her he isn't certain whether he will keep this appointment, but he agrees to consider it.

The therapist does nothing further. During the following week she hears from a friend that Emmanuel has ended his own life.

- What do you think of the way the therapist dealt with her client?
- What would you have done differently if you had been Emmanuel's therapist?
- How would your viewpoint regarding suicide influence your approach with Emmanuel?
- Which of the following actions might you have pursued?

_____ Committed him to a state hospital for observation, even against his will, for 72 hours

_____ Consulted with another professional as soon as he began to discuss suicide as an option

_____ Respected his choice of suicide, even if you did not agree with it

_____ Informed the police and reported the seriousness of his threat

_____ Informed members of his family of his intentions, even though he did not want you to

_____ Bargained with him in every way possible in an effort to persuade him to keep on trying to find some meaning in life

Discuss in class any other steps you could have taken in this case.

Commentary. Although prediction of both danger to others and to self is difficult, courts may impose liability on therapists who predict incorrectly. Suicidal clients, like dangerous clients, pose a high risk for therapists. In Emmanuel's case, we would be inclined to report the client's suicidal intent to the most appropriate authority in his jurisdiction (a mental health evaluation team or the police department). In light of the fact that Emmanuel is not terminally ill and is suffering from depression, this course of action is required both ethically and legally.

Protecting Children, the Elderly, and Dependent Adults From Harm

Whether you work with children or adults in your practice, you are expected to know how to assess potential abuse and to report it in a timely fashion. Privileged communication does not apply in cases of child abuse and neglect, nor does it apply in cases of elder and dependent adult abuse. Such matters constitute a situation of **reportable abuse**. If children, the elderly, or other dependent adults disclose that they are being abused or neglected, the professional is required to report the situation under penalty of fines and imprisonment. If adults reveal in a therapy session that they are abusing or have abused their children, the matter must be reported. The practice of **mandatory reporting** is designed to encourage reporting of any suspected cases of child, elder, or dependent adult abuse; thus, therapists are advised to err on the side of reporting in uncertain circumstances (Benitez, 2004). The goal of reporting is to protect the child or older person who is being abused. The professional has an obligation to protect those who cannot advocate for themselves.

In 1974 Congress enacted the National Child Abuse Prevention and Treatment Act (PL 93-247), which defines child abuse and neglect as follows:

> Physical or mental injury, sexual abuse or exploitation, negligent treatment, or maltreatment of a child under the age of eighteen or the age specified by the child protection law of the state in question, by a person who is responsible for the child's welfare, under circumstances which indicate that the child's health or welfare is harmed or threatened thereby.

All states now require mental health professionals and school personnel to report incidents of child abuse, or suspected child abuse. Because criteria for reporting vary among the states, there is no substitute for knowing the specific law in your state (Bennett et al., 2006; Welfel, 2010). Increasingly, states are enacting laws that impose liability on professionals who fail to report abuse or neglect of children, the elderly, and other dependent adults. States also provide immunity by law from civil suits that may arise from reporting suspected child abuse and neglect, or of abuse of the elderly or other dependent adults, if the reports are made in good faith. Some states require that professionals complete continuing education workshops on assessment of abuse and proper reporting as a condition of license renewal.

All states have statutes related to elder abuse, and in 45 states mental health professionals are mandated to report neglect or abuse of dependent elders (Welfel, 2010). The duty to protect elders from harm is stronger than a practitioner's obligation to maintain client confidentiality. In 2003 more than 550,000 elderly people were reported abused or neglected in the United States, but the actual number may be four or five times higher than this (Egan, James, & Wagner, 2004). The major types of elder abuse are physical abuse, sexual abuse, psychological abuse, neglect, abandonment, and financial or material exploitation (see the box titled "Types of Elder Abuse"). The National Center on Elder Abuse (NCEA, 2003) states that about 90% of older adults live either alone or with loved ones or caretakers. Abusers of older people can be anyone they depend on or come into contact with.

The National Center on Elder Abuse (NCEA) is dedicated to educating the public about elder abuse, neglect, and exploitation and its tragic consequences. NCEA is an internationally recognized resource for policy leaders, practitioners, prevention specialists, researchers, advocates, families, and concerned citizens. One of the reviewers of this book made the observation that not enough people talk about elder abuse and the legal obligation to report abuse and neglect. We support the position that abuse of older people and other vulnerable adults deserves the same kind of attention that is paid

Types of Elder Abuse

Physical abuse involves the use of physical force that often results in bodily injury, physical pain, or impairment.

Sexual abuse consists of nonconsensual sexual contact of any kind with an older adult.

Psychological or emotional abuse involves inflicting anguish, pain, or distress through verbal or nonverbal acts. This kind of abuse might include verbal assaults, insults, threats, intimidation, humiliation, and harassment.

Neglect is the failure of caregivers to fulfill their responsibilities to provide an elderly person with basic necessities such as food, water, clothing, shelter, medicine, personal safety, and comfort. Neglect can be either intentional or unintentional, and can be either self-inflicted or inflicted by others. Older people, especially those who live alone, may suffer from self-neglect. This can be the result of chronic illness, depression, financial problems, or an older individual's unwillingness to ask for help (Egan et al., 2004).

Abandonment involves the desertion of an elderly person by a person who has assumed responsibility for being a caregiver.

Financial or material exploitation is the illegal or improper use of an elder's funds, property, or assets.

to abuse of children. Mental health providers have an ethical and legal obligation to protect children, older adults, and dependent adults from abuse and neglect.

As mentioned previously, mandatory reporting laws regarding suspected child abuse differ from state to state. In Pennsylvania, for example, therapists are required to file a report if the client appears to be the victim of abuse. In New York, therapists must report abuse whether they learn about the situation from the child in therapy, the abuser who is in therapy, or a relative. The laws of some states now require therapists to report disclosures by adult clients about child sexual abuse that occurred years before treatment.

From both an ethical and legal perspective, mental health practitioners are expected to inform clients about the limits of confidentiality pertaining to the duty to report cases of abuse. A study on confidentiality and its relation to child abuse reporting indicated that respondents were inconsistent in their procedures for informing clients of the limits of confidentiality (Nicolai & Scott, 1994). The findings of this study suggest the need to reassert the importance of providing clients with detailed information about the limits of confidentiality from the onset of therapy.

Although therapists are likely to accept their professional responsibility to protect innocent children, older adults, and dependent persons from physical and emotional mistreatment, they may have difficulty determining how far to go in making a report. It is often difficult to reconcile ethical responsibilities with legal obligations. Therapists may think they have been placed in the predicament of behaving either unethically (by reporting and thus damaging the therapy relationship) or illegally (by ignoring the mandate to report all cases of suspected child or elder abuse). Clinicians must develop a clear position regarding the assessment and reporting of child, elder, and dependent adult abuse. Bennett and colleagues (2006) emphasize that therapists must know the exact law in their state regarding reporting in these cases. Sometimes reporting is mandatory, sometimes it is discretionary. Some states require permission from the elderly client; other states do not.

Many therapists wonder whether they have sufficient information or suspicion to report abuse. In California, for example, therapists are mandated to report child abuse when they have a "reasonable suspicion" that abuse has occurred or is occurring. Mental health professionals who fail to file a mandated report because of the concern that nothing will be done about it, or who fear that a report could make matters worse, or because they are not certain that their suspicions are valid are likely to be in violation of the law and the ethics codes of most professional organizations (Barnett & Johnson, 2010). Fortunately, professional associations in many states have "help lines" that therapists can call to assist them in making a determination about when and whether to report abuse. Child Protective Services is also useful in helping to determine when to report a situation. Consult with a colleague when in doubt about reporting, but if you have a reasonable suspicion that abuse occurred, the best course to follow is to report the matter, for doing so best protects you as a mandated reporter.

Are you prepared to carry out your duty to protect children, the elderly, and other dependent adults from abuse or neglect? Evaluate your preparedness by answering the following questions:

- How well prepared do you think you are in determining when to report suspected abuse of a child, an older person, or a dependent adult?

- Would you consider cultural factors in determining whether a situation indicates actual abuse? How would you account for cultural differences in assessing abuse?

- Can you think of ways in which you could file a report on an adult abuser and continue working with the client therapeutically?

- What struggles, if any, have you encountered with respect to following the laws regarding reporting child, dependent adult, or abuse of older adults?

- If you follow the law in all cases, are you also following an ethical course? What potential conflicts are there between doing what is legal and what is ethical?

- If an adult admits having abused a child, what are your thoughts about a therapist who argues that keeping the client in therapy is the best way to help him or her work through this problem, even if it means failing to report the abuse to authorities?

- Do you think therapists should have some flexibility in deciding when it would be best to make a report? Why or why not?

To help you clarify your position with respect to situations involving child abuse, consider the following two case examples. In the first case, ask yourself how far you should go in reporting suspected abuse. Does the fact that you have reported a matter to the officials end your ethical and legal responsibilities? In the second case, look for ways to differentiate between what is ethical and what is legal practice. Ask yourself what you would be inclined to do if you saw a conflict between ethics and the law.

■ The Case of Martina.

Martina, a high school counselor, has reason to believe that one of her students is being physically abused. As part of the abuse, critical medication is being withheld from the student. Martina reports the incident to Child Protective Services and gives all the information she has to the caseworker. She follows up the phone conversation with the caseworker with a written report. A week later, the student tells her that nothing has been done.

- Has Martina adequately fulfilled her responsibility by making the report? Does she have a responsibility to report the agency for not having taken action?
- If the agency does not take appropriate action, does Martina have a responsibility to take other measures?
- Would it be ethical for Martina to take matters into her own hands and to call for a family session or make a house call, especially if the student requests it?
- Does Martina have an obligation to inform the administration? Does the school have a responsibility to see that action is taken?

Commentary. Suspected physical abuse and denying the child critical medication are immediate reportable matters. Although the therapist complied with her legal duty to protect the child by reporting the matter to Child Protective Services, she has an ethical obligation to follow up on the report until the matter has been officially investigated and actions have been taken. Martina might want to begin with another phone call to the original caseworker. Should this course of action prove unsatisfactory, she might contact the caseworker's supervisor to emphasize the urgent medical issues at hand. Martina should document these efforts.

■ The Case of Sally.

One night, in a moment of rare intoxication, a father stumbles into his 12-year-old daughter's bedroom and briefly fondles her. Sally's cries bring her mother into the room, and the incident does not go further. Later, the father does not recall the incident. There has been no previous history of molestation. During therapy the family is able to talk openly about the incident and is working through the resulting pain. Because of this incident, the father has enrolled in a substance abuse program. The family is adamant that this situation should not be reported to social services. The therapist knows that the statute in her state clearly specifies that she is required to report this incident, even if it had happened in the past and no further incidents had occurred. Listen to the inner dialogue of the therapist as she debates the pros and cons of reporting the incident, and think about your reactions to each course of action she considers:

> There are many hazards involved if I don't report this incident. If this family ever broke up, the mother or daughter could sue me for having failed to report what happened. I would be obeying the law and protecting myself by reporting it, and I could justify my actions by citing the requirement of the law.
>
> But this occurred on one occasion, and the father was intoxicated. The daughter was frightened by the incident, but she seems to be able to talk about it in the family now. If I obey the law, my actions may be more detrimental to the family than beneficial.
>
> But the law is there for a reason. It appears that a child has been abused—that is no minor incident—and there was trauma for some time afterward.
>
> What is the most ethical thing to do? I would be following the law by reporting it, but is that the most ethical course in this case? Is it the best thing for this family now, especially as none of the members want it reported? My ethical sense tells me that my interventions should always be in the best interests of all three members of this family.
>
> I am required to report only if I suspect or believe that abuse has occurred. Some could argue that no abuse has taken place, which is what the parents seem to indicate by their behavior.
>
> The family is now in therapy with me. If I do make a report, the family might terminate therapy. Is reporting this situation worth risking that outcome?
>
> Child protective agencies are often overburdened, and only the most serious cases may be given attention. Because no abuse is presently going on, I wonder if this case will be followed up. Will it be worth risking the progress that has been made with this family?
>
> As an alternative to reporting this matter to the authorities, I could document a clinical plan of action that addresses therapeutic interventions with the father and also the well-being of the others. This course of

action might be the best way to meet my legal and ethical obligations in this particular case.

Before I act, perhaps I should consult an attorney for advice on how to proceed. Or I could call Child Protective Services to find out what I must do. Maybe I should call the Board of Ethics of my professional organization and get some advice on how to proceed.

I don't know what action to take. Maybe I should consult with a colleague before I take any definite action.

Commentary.   This case illustrates some of the difficulties counselors face when it comes to reporting an incident of abuse. Each of the ethics codes in the mental health professions encourages therapists to adhere to the law when there is a conflict between legal and ethical requirements. In this situation the counselor has no choice but to report because the law takes precedence over any concerns she may have about how reporting may affect the therapeutic relationship with this family. At times, therapists err on the side of not making a report because of their fear that doing so will mean an end to the therapeutic relationship. Depending on how the therapist handles the matter with the family, it may be possible to continue a therapeutic relationship in this case.

◼ A Case of Protecting an Older Client.

Emily, an older adult, takes great pride in her independence, her ability to take care of herself, and in not being a burden to her family. Her therapist, Tom, is impressed with her independent spirit. Emily eventually divulges to Tom several episodes of forgetting to turn off the gas flame in the kitchen. She laughs it off by saying, "I guess I'm not perfect." Every so often, Emily discloses similar episodes of forgetfulness that have potential lethal consequences. Tom becomes increasingly concerned and suggests that she notify her family of her problem. Emily lets Tom know that this is not an option because her family has wanted her to move to a nursing home. Emily is adamant in her refusal to go along with their plan. She tells Tom, "If you make me leave my home, there is no point in living."

- If you were Emily's counselor, what course of action would you take?
- What ethical, legal, and medical issues can you identify in this case?
- Is there a duty to protect in this situation?

Commentary.   The therapist cannot afford to become sidetracked by Emily's insistence that there is no reason to worry or by ignoring Emily's hint of suicide. It is more important for the therapist to take action to help the client than it is to have her like the therapist. As Tom suggests, a meeting with the family can be of great benefit to all concerned. In our view, Tom does have a duty to protect Emily from accidentally harming herself, and possibly others, as a result of her cognitive impairment. By working closely with Emily, her family, and appropriate authorities, he may be able to help Emily transition to an arrangement that is both safe and acceptable to her. The counselor might also help Emily see some of the potential positive elements in leaving her home, such as fewer things to worry about and being given useful assistance.

■ A Case of Protecting a Dependent Adult.

You are working with individuals with mental disabilities, many of whom are institutionalized. One of your clients, Mike, who has a severe mental disability and lives in a residential home, leads you to believe that he is being sexually abused by at least one member of the staff. You are not really sure about this because it is difficult to separate fact from fantasy when talking with him about other things.

- What steps would you take to separate fact from fantasy?
- Are you required to make a report to protective services so that they can determine the validity of the allegation?
- Could you be legally liable for not making a report to protective services?

Commentary.   In a case such as this it is better to error on the side of caution rather than assuming there is no reality base to the allegations. When there is a reasonable suspicion of any abuse or neglect, a report must be made to the appropriate agency within the time frame specified in local laws (Barnett & Johnson, 2010). Valuable information can be gleaned from a meeting with the multidisciplinary treatment team to make a more accurate assessment and to determine the course of action to take with Mike.

Confidentiality and HIV/AIDS-Related Issues

AIDS affects a large population with diverse demographics and will continue to gain prominence as a public health and social issue. Most mental health practitioners will inevitably come in contact with people who have AIDS, with people who have tested positive as carriers of the virus, or with people who are close to these people.

People who receive an HIV-positive test are usually in need of immediate short-term help. They need to establish a support system to help them through the troubled times they will endure. Those who are HIV-positive often live with the anxiety of not knowing when or whether they may be diagnosed with AIDS. Many also struggle with the stigma attached to AIDS.

They live in fear not only of developing a life-threatening disease, but also of being discovered and rejected by society and by friends and loved ones. In addition to feeling different and stigmatized, anger, which is likely to be directed toward others, especially those who have infected them, can be extreme. These clients have often been discriminated against, so it is important that professionals respect their situation, obtain informed consent, and educate them about their rights and responsibilities.

Therapists need to inform themselves about the limits of confidentiality, matters of reporting, and their duty to protect third parties, and they need to communicate their professional responsibilities to their clients from the outset. If therapists decide that they cannot provide competent services to HIV-infected people, it is ethically appropriate that they refer these clients to professionals who can provide assistance. We recommend that you review the earlier discussion in this chapter regarding the therapist's duty to protect. Think about how that duty applies to people who have AIDS or are HIV-positive.

As a counselor you may indeed work with clients who are HIV-positive. You might accept a client and establish a therapeutic relationship only to find out months later that this person had recently tested positive. If this were the case, how would you answer the following questions:

- Would it be ethical to terminate the professional relationship and make a referral?
- Would the ethical course be to become informed so that you could provide competent help?
- What would be in the best interests of your client?
- If you are counseling HIV-positive individuals, do you have a duty both to your clients and to their sexual partners?
- Do you have an ethical responsibility to warn or otherwise protect third parties in cases of those who are HIV-positive and who are putting others at risk by engaging in unprotected sex or needle sharing?
- If you do your best to convince your client to disclose his or her HIV status to a partner, and if your client refuses to share this information, what course of action might you take?

Consider your ethical responsibilities to respond to this population *before* you encounter possible difficult situations. The following two cases are designed to help you clarify your position on the ethical dimensions of counseling clients who have AIDS or are HIV-positive. For a wealth of clinical information on many of the topics explored in this section, we recommend *Ethics in HIV-Related Psychotherapy: Clinical Decision Making in Complex Cases* (Anderson & Barret, 2001).

■ The Case of Al and Wilma.

Al and Wilma are seeing Sarina for couples counseling. After a number of sessions Wilma requests an individual session, in which she discloses that she has tested HIV-positive as a result of an affair. Sarina finds herself in a real dilemma: She has concerns for the welfare of the couple and about her duty to protect Al, but she is also concerned about Wilma's painful predicament, especially because Wilma has a sincere desire to make her relationship work.

- Does Sarina have a duty to warn and protect Al? Why or why not?
- What alternatives does she have to warning that would serve to protect Al?
- Would such a duty supersede any implied confidentiality of the private session?
- Would it be more therapeutic for Sarina to persuade Wilma to disclose her condition to Al rather than taking the responsibility for this disclosure herself?
- If Wilma refused to inform her husband, should Sarina discontinue therapy with the couple? If she were to discontinue working with them, how might she ethically explain her decision to the couple?
- If Sarina felt obligated to continue therapy with the couple, how would she handle the secret, and what ethical issues arise from keeping such a secret?
- Are there factors in this situation that would compel Sarina to treat Wilma's secret differently from other major secrets in couples therapy?

Commentary.   The law is not clear pertaining to the duty to warn in cases pertaining to HIV status. It is extremely important to know the specific law in your jurisdiction and to seek consultation from a colleague experienced with reporting requirements. In some states therapists could lose their license to practice if they breached confidentiality by warning in cases involving HIV status. A number of our colleagues who have faced this kind of dilemma report that they are generally successful in convincing the person who is HIV-positive to disclose his or her health status. This is especially true if the therapist is willing to continue to provide support to both of the partners once the disclosure has been made. It is hard to imagine that couple counseling could be successful if this secret is not addressed.

■ The Case of Hershel.

Hershel is a vice-president in a large company. He is married and has young children. Hershel's job necessitates transcontinental travel several times a year. During these trips he spends time with a lover. On his last trip he confided that one of the men that he had recently been sexually involved with had received an HIV-positive diagnosis. Hershel is panic stricken and seeks the help of a counselor, Blanche, who immediately recommends that he be tested. He follows her recommendation, and his test results are negative. He is elated and now sees no reason to continue therapy. Blanche makes no attempt to persuade him to explore other issues. She has no expertise in the treatment of persons with AIDS and lacks essential knowledge pertaining to the latest AIDS research.

- Blanche took the ethical course in suggesting that Hershel be tested for HIV, but was one test sufficient? What else needed to be done?
- Given this therapist's level of knowledge about HIV, should she have referred Hershel? Explain.
- Did the therapist have a duty to protect Hershel's wife from the potential life-threatening situation to which she was now exposed?
- If Hershel had disclosed to Blanche that he and his wife were planning on having more children, how might that have affected the complexity of this case?
- Did Blanche have an ethical obligation to convince Hershel to discuss the matter with his wife because of the risk to her health? Explain.
- What course of action would you have taken in this case?

Commentary. Therapists need to be knowledgeable about the latest research on HIV/AIDS. None of us can assume that we will never encounter this kind of case. Blanche was unaware that more than one test is necessary to establish a negative HIV result, and she has a responsibility to become more informed. Blanche also needs to ascertain whether Hershel intends to continue this risky sexual behavior. Both this case and the previous one involve a secret that will affect the therapy process and all of the individuals involved. Therapists can use their clinical expertise to assist clients in disclosing behavior that could have negative outcomes. In this case, the counselor should also review with Hershel why he came in for treatment and what his specific goals are for his therapy.

Ethical and Legal Considerations in AIDS-Related Cases

Much has been written about the conditions under which confidentiality might be breached in AIDS-related therapy situations. Courts have not applied the duty to protect to mental health professionals in cases involving

HIV infection. Thus, therapists' legal responsibilities for protecting sexual partners of HIV-positive clients remain unclear.

The following guideline from the ACA (2005) ethics code outlines the ethical responsibility of practitioners who might deal with HIV-positive clients who are unwilling to inform their sexual or needle-sharing partners of their HIV status:

> When clients disclose that they have a disease commonly known to be both communicable and life-threatening, counselors may be justified in disclosing information to identifiable third parties, who must be known to be at a demonstrable and high risk of contracting the disease. Prior to making a disclosure the counselors confirm the diagnosis and assess the intent of clients to inform the third parties about their disease or to engage in any behaviors that may be harmful to an identifiable third party. (B.2.b.)

This guideline places the responsibility on the counselor for examining a number of issues and eventually arriving at the best decision in a given case. The guideline holds that counselors *may be justified* in disclosing information to a third party who is at risk, yet counselors are not necessarily *obligated* to take this course of action. In fact, this is an example of where what is ethically appropriate may be in conflict with what is legally acceptable. Practitioners may act in ways they deem to be ethical only to find that they have broken a legal standard. For example, in California the ACA standard regarding reporting a health risk could conflict with state law, placing the individual who divulges this confidential information at risk for fines, civil penalties, incarceration, and loss of license (Rahn Minagawa, forensic psychologist, personal communication, August 14, 2003). From a legal perspective, breaching confidentiality because of a client's HIV status is not one of the exceptions to confidentiality. Until a landmark court case determines a precedent, mental health professionals will have to continue to struggle with doing what they think is morally and ethically right without any guarantee of legal protection.

Duty to protect versus confidentiality.   Earlier in this chapter we discussed the principles involved in situations where therapists may have a duty to protect innocent victims. The duty to protect *may* arise when a therapist is convinced that a client who is HIV-positive intends to continue to have unprotected sex, or to share needles, with unsuspecting but reasonably identifiable third parties.

The HIV-positive duty to protect decision is one of the more controversial and emotion-laden issues practitioners might encounter. For practitioners who work with persons who are HIV-positive, the choice is often between protecting the client–therapist relationship and breaching confidentiality to protect persons at risk of infection. This situation can put practitioners in a moral, ethical, legal, and professional bind.

State laws differ regarding HIV and the limits of confidentiality, and the law is often different for medical professionals than for licensed psychotherapists. All states now have statutes governing reporting of HIV and AIDS cases to public health authorities and corresponding confidentiality duties, but many of the laws that either permit or require reporting are limited to reporting by physicians (Wheeler & Bertram, 2008). Some state laws forbid any disclosure of HIV status to third parties, and others allow some disclosure to at-risk third parties by physicians and psychiatrists, but not by other mental health professionals. Some states prohibit psychotherapists from warning identifiable victims of persons who are HIV-positive (VandeCreek & Knapp, 2001). Under some state laws, therapists who disclose a person's HIV-status to an unauthorized third party are subject to criminal charges and to malpractice action as well. Other states have yet to address this issue by statute. Thus, therapists are advised to know what statutes, if any, define the actions they should take regarding reporting of HIV or AIDS cases; they should then follow the statutory mandate (Wheeler & Bertram, 2008).

Several writers have addressed breaching confidentiality related to the danger to others posed by HIV-positive clients (Ahia & Martin, 1993; Cohen, 1997; Erickson, 1993; Kooyman & Barret, 2009; Lamb et al., 1989; McGuire et al., 1995; Totten, Lamb, & Reeder, 1990; VandeCreek & Knapp, 2001; Wheeler & Bertram, 2008). These writers provide the following recommendations for therapists:

- All limits to confidentiality should be discussed with the client at the onset of treatment. When this is done early in the therapeutic relationship, it is less likely that therapists will lose clients because of breaching confidentiality. The implications of disclosing confidentiality, as well as other alternatives, can be explored with HIV-positive clients within the counseling context at this time.

- Therapists need to keep current with regard to relevant medical information related to the transmission of HIV, know which sexual practices are safer and which are not, and encourage their clients to practice safer sex. Because sharing a contaminated needle is another major means of HIV transmission, therapists should be up to date on approaches to drug education.

- Most mental health professionals and not trained in communicable diseases and should not offer medical advice to clients who have communicable diseases (Kooyman & Barret, 2009).

- Practitioners should seek training for intervening in the crises facing clients who are HIV-positive and for persons with AIDS.

- Therapists need to be aware of their own attitudes, biases, and prejudices as they relate to individuals who are at a higher risk of becoming infected.

- Therapists should speak directly and openly with their clients about their concerns regarding the danger of certain behaviors and the risk to third parties. They can use the therapeutic process to educate their clients about the effects their behavior can have on others, teach safer sex practices, obtain commitments from the client to notify partners, and offer help in communicating information to partners.

- If the client continues to resist using safer sex practices or refuses to inform partners, then the therapist needs to determine what course of action to follow. Practitioners should consult with knowledgeable peers or attorneys, or both, to determine that their intended course of action is ethically and legally sound.

- In disclosing HIV information, therapists need to follow the statutory guidelines and safeguard the client's privacy as much as possible.

- If all other options have been exhausted and the therapist has decided to breach confidentiality by warning or otherwise protecting an identified partner, generally the client should be informed of this intention, and the therapist should attempt to obtain the client's permission.

Bennett and colleagues (2006) recommend thinking about these situations from a clinical perspective. Attempt to understand the reasons a client is not willing to disclose his or her HIV status. Is it because of fear of domestic abuse? fear of being abandoned? social rejection? Or is the nondisclosure due to some other relationship issue? If you explore the clinical aspects of your client's situation, it may not be necessary to take steps to warn or protect others.

VandeCreek and Knapp (2001) believe the duty to warn obligation has received disproportionate attention and that good clinical skills will obviate the need to determine a course of action regarding warning third parties. They assert that warning an identifiable victim should be considered as a last resort. Dr. James L. Werth Jr. (personal communication, October 25, 2008) concurs with VandeCreek and Knapp's analysis. Werth, who has been specializing in seeing persons with HIV for over 15 years, has never broken confidentiality in such cases. He maintains that many courses of action are open to practitioners besides warning a third party and breaking confidentiality. If psychotherapy is given a chance to work, there is a good chance that the client will voluntarily disclose this information to his or her partner.

For a comprehensive and in-depth treatment of duty to protect issues, we highly recommend *The Duty to Protect: Ethical, Legal, and Professional Considerations for Mental Health Professionals* (Werth, Welfel, & Benjamin, 2009).

Special Training on HIV-Related Issues

Mental health professionals have an ethical obligation to be knowledgeable about HIV so they can ask the right questions. You can start by reading about HIV/AIDS-related issues and by attending a workshop on the subject. You can also contact one of the many clinics throughout the country, which are useful resources for treatment and referrals. In many communities, groups of volunteers have been organized to work with AIDS clients.

In summary, dealing responsibly with the dilemmas posed in this section demands an awareness of the ethical, legal, and clinical issues involved in working with clients with HIV/AIDS. There are no simple solutions to the complex issues practitioners face, and this topic is surely one of the more challenging ones. Consulting with both colleagues and attorneys is an excellent practice that can help you make appropriate decisions.

Chapter Summary

Along with their duties to clients, therapists have responsibilities to their agency, to their profession, to the community, to the members of their clients' families, and to themselves. Ethical dilemmas involving confidentiality arise when there are conflicts between responsibilities. Members of the helping professions should know and observe the ethics codes of their professional organizations and make sound judgments that are within the parameters of acceptable practice. We have encouraged you to think about specific ethical issues and to develop a sense of professional ethics and knowledge of state laws so that your judgment will be well-founded.

Court decisions have provided an expanded perspective on the therapist's duty to protect the public. As a result of the *Tarasoff* case, therapists are now becoming aware of their responsibility to the potential victims of a client's violent behavior. This duty spans interventions from warnings to threatened individuals to involuntary commitment of clients. Therapists also have a duty to protect clients who are likely to injure or kill themselves.

States have enacted laws that require professionals to report child, elder, and dependent adult abuse whenever they suspect or discover it in the course of their professional activities. Clients have a right to know that therapists are legally and ethically bound to breach confidentiality in situations involving child, elder, or dependent adult abuse. Therefore, this must be included in your informed consent document.

The duty to protect has also been applied to HIV/AIDS cases. Because state laws vary on breaching confidentiality of a client's HIV status to warn or protect potential victims, practitioners are advised to know their state laws and to consult professional colleagues, and perhaps an attorney, before they take any action. Breaching confidentiality should be the last resort, implemented only after less obtrusive measures have failed, and only if the disclosure does not conflict with state law.

Suggested Activities

1. In small groups discuss the cases and guidelines presented in this chapter on the duty to protect victims from violent clients. If you found yourself faced with a potentially dangerous client, what specific steps might you take to carry out this duty?

2. Structure a class debate around the arguments for and against suicide prevention. Consider debating a specific case of a client who is terminally ill with AIDS and decides that he wants to end his life because of his suffering and because there is no hope of getting better.

3. Ask several students to investigate the laws of your state pertaining to confidentiality and privileged communication and present their

findings to the class. What kinds of mental health providers in your state can offer their clients privileged communication? What are the exceptions to this privilege? Under what circumstances are you legally required to breach confidentiality? Regarding confidentiality in counseling minors, what state laws should you know?

4. In small groups discuss specific circumstances in which you would break confidentiality, and see whether you can agree on some general guidelines.

5. Discuss some ways in which you can prepare clients for issues pertaining to confidentiality. How can you teach clients about the purposes of confidentiality and the legal restrictions on it? Examine how you would do this in various situations, such as school, group work, couples and family counseling, and counseling with minors.

6. In a class debate, have one side take the position that absolute confidentiality is necessary to promote full client disclosure. The other side can argue for a limited confidentiality that still promotes effective therapy.

Ethics in Action *CD-ROM* Exercises

7. Refer to role play 6, The Promiscuous One, and think of ways to reenact a role play with different students demonstrating a variety of ways to deal with this woman who is having unprotected casual sexual encounters. If she told you that she just found out that she is HIV-positive—and that she absolutely does not intend to reveal this news to her husband—what would your stance be? Would you protect the client's confidentiality? Or would you see this as a duty to warn and protect case? Devise alternative role plays showing a variety of approaches for dealing with the ethical and legal dimensions in this case.

Pre-Chapter Self-Inventory

Directions: For each statement, indicate the response that most closely identifies your beliefs and attitudes. Use the following code:

5 = I *strongly agree* with this statement.
4 = I *agree* with this statement.
3 = I am *undecided* about this statement.
2 = I *disagree* with this statement.
1 = I *strongly disagree* with this statement.

_____ 1. A good therapist gets involved in the client's case without getting involved with the client emotionally.

_____ 2. Nonerotic touching is best avoided in counseling because it can easily be misunderstood by the client.

_____ 3. Therapists who hug clients of only one sex are guilty of sexist practice.

_____ 4. Although it may be unwise to form social relationships with clients while they are in counseling, there should be no ethical or professional prohibition against social relationships after counseling ends.

_____ 5. If I were a truly ethical professional, I would never be sexually attracted to a client.

_____ 6. If I were counseling a client who was sexually attracted to me, I would refer this client to another counselor.

_____ 7. I might be inclined to barter my therapeutic services for goods if a client could not afford my fees.

_____ 8. If a client initiated the possibility of exchanging services in lieu of payment, I would consider bartering as an option.

Managing Boundaries and Multiple Relationships

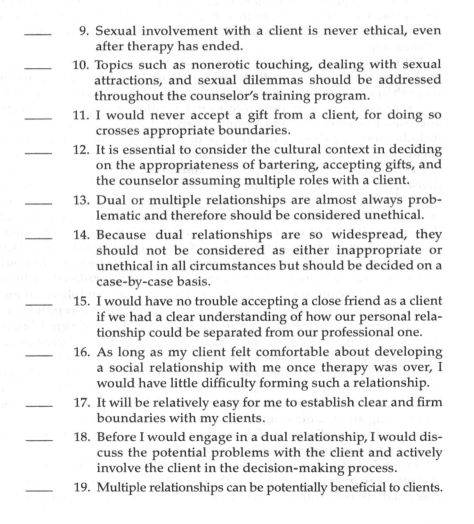

_____ 9. Sexual involvement with a client is never ethical, even after therapy has ended.

_____ 10. Topics such as nonerotic touching, dealing with sexual attractions, and sexual dilemmas should be addressed throughout the counselor's training program.

_____ 11. I would never accept a gift from a client, for doing so crosses appropriate boundaries.

_____ 12. It is essential to consider the cultural context in deciding on the appropriateness of bartering, accepting gifts, and the counselor assuming multiple roles with a client.

_____ 13. Dual or multiple relationships are almost always problematic and therefore should be considered unethical.

_____ 14. Because dual relationships are so widespread, they should not be considered as either inappropriate or unethical in all circumstances but should be decided on a case-by-case basis.

_____ 15. I would have no trouble accepting a close friend as a client if we had a clear understanding of how our personal relationship could be separated from our professional one.

_____ 16. As long as my client felt comfortable about developing a social relationship with me once therapy was over, I would have little difficulty forming such a relationship.

_____ 17. It will be relatively easy for me to establish clear and firm boundaries with my clients.

_____ 18. Before I would engage in a dual relationship, I would discuss the potential problems with the client and actively involve the client in the decision-making process.

_____ 19. Multiple relationships can be potentially beneficial to clients.

_____ 20. I might consider becoming involved in a business venture with a client if I were convinced that doing so would not harm my client.

Introduction

The APA (2002) ethics code defines a **multiple relationship** as one in which a practitioner is in a professional role with a person in addition to another role with that same individual, or with another person who is close to that individual. When clinicians blend their professional relationship with another kind of relationship with a client, ethical concerns must be considered. In these situations, it is often difficult to determine what is in the best interests of the client.

The terms _dual relationships_ and _multiple relationships_ are used interchangeably in various professional codes of ethics, and the ACA (2005) uses the term _nonprofessional relationships._ In this chapter we use the broader term of _multiple relationships_ to encompass both dual relationships and nonprofessional relationships.

Multiple relationships occur when professionals assume two or more roles at the same time or sequentially with a client. This may involve assuming more than one professional role (such as instructor and therapist) or blending a professional and nonprofessional relationship (such as counselor and friend or counselor and business partner). Multiple relationships also include providing therapy to a relative or a friend's relative, socializing with clients, becoming emotionally or sexually involved with a client or former client, combining the roles of supervisor and therapist, having a business relationship with a client, borrowing money from a client, or loaning money to a client. Mental health professionals must learn how to effectively and ethically manage multiple relationships, including dealing with the power differential that is a basic part of most professional relationships, managing boundary issues, and striving to avoid the misuse of power (Herlihy & Corey, 2006b).

Sometimes it is difficult to understand the rationale behind prohibitions, and some boundary limitations may seem arbitrary. The rationale behind the argument to abstain from any boundary crossings or multiple relationships involves the _potential_ for therapists to misuse their power to influence and exploit clients for their own benefit and to the clients' detriment (Zur, 2008). Although codes can provide some general guidelines, good judgment, the willingness to reflect on one's practices, and being aware of one's motivations are critical dimensions of an ethical practitioner. Mental health professionals can fail to heed warning signs in their relationships with clients. They may not always pay sufficient attention to the potential problems involved in establishing and maintaining professional boundaries. Practitioners may be unaware of the implications of their actions and may be blind to the fact they are engaged in unprofessional or problematic conduct.

The underlying theme of this chapter is the need for you to be honest and self-searching in determining the impact of your behavior on clients. In cases that are not clear-cut, it becomes especially crucial to make an honest appraisal of your behavior and its effect on clients. To us, behavior is unethical when it reflects a lack of awareness or concern about the impact of the behavior on clients. Some counselors may place their personal needs above the needs of their clients, engaging in more than one role with clients to meet their own financial, social, or emotional needs.

This chapter focuses on boundary issues in professional practice, the difference between boundary crossings and boundary violations, multiple relationships, role blending, a variety of nonsexual dual relationships, and sexual issues in therapy. We also examine the more subtle aspects of sexuality in therapy, including sexual attractions and the misuse of power. Multiple relationship issues cannot be resolved with ethics codes alone; therapists must think through all of the ethical and clinical dimensions involved in a wide range of boundary concerns.

The Ethics of Multiple Relationships

The codes of ethics of most professional organizations warn of the potential problems of multiple relationships (see the Ethics Codes box titled "Standards on Multiple Relationships"). These codes caution professionals against any involvement with clients that might impair their judgment and objectivity, affect their ability to render effective services, or result in harm or exploitation to clients. It should be noted that none of these codes of ethics state that nonsexual multiple relationships are unethical, and most of them acknowledge that some are unavoidable (Lazarus & Zur, 2002). However, when multiple relationships exploit clients, or have significant potential to harm clients, they are unethical.

A legal perspective on multiple relationships.   Writing from a legal perspective, Hermann (2006a) indicates that dual or multiple relationships exist on a continuum ranging from boundary crossings for a client's benefit to sexual dual relationships that cause major harm to a client. The legal implications pertaining to dual relationships depend on the nature of the relationship and whether the client suffers harm. The mere existence of a multiple relationship does not, in itself, constitute malpractice; rather, it is misusing power, harming, or exploiting a client that is unethical. In cases where a client suffers harm or is exploited due to a multiple relationship, the client could file a malpractice lawsuit against the mental health provider. Hermann suggests that it is wise for counselors to avoid multiple relationships to the extent possible and to document precautions taken to protect clients when such relationships are unavoidable.

Differing Perspectives on Multiple Relationships

There is a wide range of viewpoints on multiple relationships. If you are intent on clarifying your position on this issue, you will encounter conflicting advice. Some writers focus on the problems inherent in multiple relationships.

Ethics Codes

Standards on Multiple Relationships

American Association for Marriage and Family Therapy (2001)

Marriage and family therapists are aware of their influential position with respect to clients, and they avoid exploiting the trust and dependency of such persons. Therapists, therefore, make every effort to avoid conditions and multiple relationships with clients that could impair professional judgment or increase the risk of exploitation. When the risk of impairment or exploitation exists due to conditions or multiple roles, therapists take appropriate precautions. (4.1.)

National Association of Social Workers (2008)

Social workers should not engage in dual or multiple relationships with clients or former clients in which there is a risk of exploitation or potential harm to the client. In instances when dual or multiple relationships are unavoidable, social workers should take steps to protect clients and are responsible for setting clear, appropriate, and culturally sensitive boundaries. (Dual or multiple relationships occur when social workers relate to clients in more than one relationship, whether professional, social, or business. Dual or multiple relationships can occur simultaneously or consecutively.) (1.06.c.)

Feminist Therapy Institute (2000)

A feminist therapist recognizes the complexity and conflicting priorities inherent in multiple or overlapping relationships. The therapist accepts responsibility for monitoring such relationships to prevent potential abuse of or harm to the client. (III.A.)

National Organization for Human Services (2000)

Human service professionals are aware that in their relationships with clients, power and status are unequal. Therefore, they recognize that dual or multiple relationships may increase the risk of harm to, or exploitation of, clients, and may impair their professional judgment. However, in some communities and situations it may not be feasible to avoid social or other nonprofessional contact with clients. Human service professionals support the trust implicit in the helping relationship by avoiding dual relationships that may impair professional judgment, increase the risk of harm to clients, or lead to exploitation.

Association for Addiction Professionals (NAADAC, 2008)

Dual Relationships. I understand that I must seek to nurture and support the development of a relationship of equals rather than to take unfair advantage of individuals who are vulnerable and exploitable. (Principle 7.)

Canadian Psychological Association (2000)

Avoid dual or multiple relationships and other situations that might present a conflict of interest or that might reduce their ability to be objective and unbiased in their determinations of what might be in the best interests of others. (III.33.)

Manage dual or multiple relationships that are unavoidable due to cultural norms or other circumstances in such a manner that bias, lack of objectivity, and risk of exploitation are minimized. This might include obtaining ongoing supervision or consultation for the duration of the dual or multiple relationship, or involving a third party in obtaining consent. (III.34.)

Canadian Counselling Association (2007)

Counsellors make every effort to avoid dual relationships with clients that could impair professional judgment or increase the risk of harm to clients. Examples of dual relationships include, but are not limited to, familial, social, financial, business, or close personal relationships. When a dual relationship cannot be avoided, counsellors take appropriate professional precautions such as role clarification, informed consent, consultation, and documentation to ensure that judgment is not impaired and no exploitation occurs. (B.8.)

American School Counselor Association (2004)

[The school counselor] avoids dual relationships that might impair his/her objectivity and increase the risk of harm to the student (e.g., counseling one's family members, close friends or associates). If a dual relationship is unavoidable, the counselor is responsible for taking action to eliminate or reduce the potential for harm. Such safeguards might include informed consent, consultation, supervision and documentation. (A.4.a.)

American Counseling Association (2005)

Counselor-client non-professional relationships with clients, former clients, their romantic partners, or their family members should be avoided, except when the interaction is potentially beneficial. (A.5.c.)

When a counselor-client non-professional interaction with a client or former client may be potentially beneficial to the client or former client, the counselor must document in case records, prior to the interaction (when feasible), the rationale for such an interaction, the potential benefit, and anticipated consequences for the client or former client and other individuals significantly involved with the client or former client. Such interactions should be initiated with appropriate client consent. When unintentional harm occurs to the client or former client, or to an individual significantly involved with the client or former client, due to the non-professional interaction, the counselor must show evidence of an attempt to remedy such harm. Examples of potentially beneficial interactions include, but are not limited to, attending a formal ceremony (e.g., a wedding or graduation); purchasing a service or product provided by a client or former client (excepting unrestricted bartering); hospital visits to an ill family member, mutual membership in a professional association, organization, or community. (A.5.d.)

American Psychological Association (2002)

(a) A multiple relationship occurs when a psychologist is in a professional role with a person and (1) at the same time is in another role with the same person, (2) at the same time is in a relationship with a person closely associated with or related to the person with whom the psychologist has the professional relationship, or (3) promises to enter into another relationship in the future with the person or a person closely associated with or related to the person.

A psychologist refrains from entering into a multiple relationship if the multiple relationship could reasonably be expected to impair the psychologist's objectivity, competence, or effectiveness in performing his or her functions as a psychologist, or otherwise risks exploitation or harm to the person with whom the professional relationship exists.

(continued on next page)

Multiple relationships that would not reasonably be expected to cause impairment or risk exploitation or harm are not unethical.

(b) If a psychologist finds that, due to unforeseen factors, a potentially harmful multiple relationship has arisen, the psychologist takes reasonable steps to resolve it with due regard for the best interests of the affected person and maximal compliance with the Ethics Code.

(c) When psychologists are required by law, institutional policy, or extraordinary circumstances to serve in more than one role in judicial or administrative proceedings, at the outset they clarify role expectations and the extent of confidentiality and thereafter as changes occur. (3.05.)

Others see the entire discussion of multiple relationships as subtle and complex, defying simplistic solutions or absolute answers. Zur (2008) states that multiple relationships are common, inevitable, unavoidable, normal, and a healthy part of communal life in many settings. Many counselors are rethinking their traditional approach to the therapeutic process and more often are entering into secondary relationships that may have an impact on the counseling relationship (Moleski & Kiselica, 2005). Despite certain clinical, ethical, and legal risks, some blending of roles is unavoidable, and it is not necessarily unethical or unprofessional. Zur (2007) points out that APA's (2002) codes of ethics now provides more flexible guidelines regarding multiple relationships and emphasizes the importance of context in making ethical decisions.

Although the codes of ethics of most professions caution against engaging in nonsexual multiple relationships, such relationships exist in most settings and are not necessarily problematic; indeed, some are beneficial (Herlihy & Corey, 2006b; Herlihy & Corey, 2008). For example, "mentoring" involves blending roles, yet both mentors and learners can certainly benefit from this relationship. Casto, Caldwell, and Salazar (2005) point out that mentors often balance a multiplicity of roles, some of which include teacher, counselor, role model, guide, and friend. They add that the mentoring relationship is a personal one, in which both mentor and mentee may benefit from knowing the other personally and professionally. There are many clear benefits in mentoring relationships, but ethical concerns are associated with these relationships. Ethical problems are likely to arise if the mentor's role becomes blurred, so that he or she is more of a friend than a mentor (Warren, 2005). Casto and colleagues emphasize the importance of maintaining boundaries between mentorship and friendship, which requires vigilance of the power differential and how it affects the mentee. They contend that the focus of mentoring is always on the mentee's personal and professional development.

After reviewing the literature on the topic of multiple relationships, Herlihy and Corey (2006b) conclude that there is no clear consensus regarding nonsexual multiple relationships in counseling. It is the responsibility of practitioners to monitor themselves and to examine their motivations for engaging in such relationships, or face the consequences if they are negligent in these matters. Practitioners should be cautious about entering into more than one role with a client. It is generally a good idea to avoid multiple roles unless there is sound clinical justification for doing so.

Factors to Consider Before Entering Into a Multiple Relationship

Moleski and Kiselica (2005) believe multiple relationships range from the destructive to the therapeutic. Although some multiple relationships are harmful, other secondary relationships complement, enable, and enhance the counseling relationship. Moleski and Kiselica encourage counselors to examine the potential positive and negative consequences that a secondary relationship might have on the primarily counseling relationship. They suggest that counselors consider forming multiple relationships only when it is clear that such relationships are in the best interests of the client.

Younggren and Gottlieb (2004) suggest applying an ethically based, risk-managed, decision-making model when practitioners are analyzing a situation involving the pros and cons of a multiple relationship. They acknowledge that "these types of relationships are not necessarily violations of the standards of professional conduct, and/or the law, but we know enough to recommend that they have to be actively and thoroughly analyzed and addressed, although not necessarily avoided" (p. 260). Younggren and Gottlieb recommend that practitioners address these questions to make sound decisions about multiple relationships (pp. 256–257):

- Is entering into a relationship in addition to the professional one necessary, or should I avoid it?
- Can the multiple relationship potentially cause harm to the client?
- If harm seems unlikely, would the additional relationship prove beneficial?
- Is there a risk that the multiple relationship could disrupt the therapeutic relationship?
- Can I evaluate this matter objectively?

In answering these questions, practitioners need to carefully assess the risk for conflict of interests, loss of objectivity, and implications for the therapeutic relationship. Counselors must discuss with the client the potential problems involved in a multiple relationship, and it is good practice to actively involve the client in the decision-making process. If the multiple relationship is judged to be appropriate and acceptable, the therapist should document the entire process, including having the client sign an informed consent form. In addition, therapists would do well to adopt a risk-management approach to the problem. This involves a careful review of various issues such as diagnosis, level of functioning, therapeutic orientation, community standards and practices, and consultations with professionals who could support the decision.

Younggren and Gottlieb conclude with this advice: "Only after having taken all these steps can the professional consider entering into the relationship, and he or she should then do so with the greatest of caution" (p. 260).

In a study of multiple relationships encountered by lesbian and bisexual psychotherapists, Graham and Liddle (2009) explored the decision-making process these clinicians used in determining whether to become involved in nonsexual multiple relationships and the strategies they used to either prevent or cope with them. In deciding whether to take on multiple roles, the clinicians gave careful thought to the depth of existing relationships, the therapist's objectivity, the likelihood and frequency of outside contact, and the client's ability to appropriately manage multiple roles and relationships. Younggren and Gottlieb (2004) proposed a similar set of standards: evaluate the necessity of multiple roles and relationships, evaluate the potential benefit and potential risk to the client of entering into a multiple relationship, reflect on the clinician's ability to be objective in the situation, and seek consultation with colleagues.

Barnett (in Barnett, Lazarus, et al., 2007) suggests some guidelines to increase the likelihood that a client's best interests are being served:

- The therapist is motivated by what the client needs rather than by his or her own needs.
- The boundary crossing is consistent with a client's treatment plan.
- The client's history, culture, values, and diagnosis have been considered.
- The rationale for the boundary crossing is documented in the client's record.
- The boundary crossing is discussed with the client in advance to prevent misunderstandings.
- Full recognition is given to the power differential, and the client's trust is safeguarded.
- Consultation with colleagues guides the therapist's decisions.

Lamb, Catanzaro, and Moorman (2004) also suggest that nonsexual overlapping relationships be evaluated by considering factors such as context, history, current status of the professional relationship, the reaction of the client to the multiple relationship, and how the therapist explains the purpose of the boundary crossing within the context of the goals of the professional relationship. Lamb and colleagues raise a significant question: How do therapists determine whether a particular action is likely to cause impairment, exploitation, or harm?

Boundary Crossings Versus Boundary Violations

Certain behaviors of professionals have the potential for creating a multiple relationship, but they are not inherently considered to be multiple relationships. Examples of these behaviors include accepting a client's invitation to a special event such as a graduation; bartering goods or services for professional services; accepting a small gift from a client; attending the same social, cultural, or religious activities as a client; or giving a supportive hug after a difficult session. Some writers (Gabbard, 1994, 1995, 1996; Gutheil & Gabbard, 1993; Smith & Fitzpatrick, 1995) caution that engaging in boundary crossings paves the way to boundary violations and to becoming entangled in complex multiple relationships. Gutheil and Gabbard (1993) distinguish between boundary crossings (changes in role) and boundary violations (exploitation of the client at some level). A **boundary crossing** is a departure from commonly accepted practices that could potentially benefit clients; a **boundary violation** is a serious breach that results in harm to clients and is therefore unethical. They note that not all boundary crossings should be considered boundary violations. Interpersonal boundaries are fluid; they may change over time and may be redefined as therapists and clients continue to work together. Yet behaviors that stretch boundaries can become problematic, and boundary crossings can lead to a pattern of blurring of professional roles. The key is to take measures to prevent boundary crossings from becoming boundary violations.

Barnett (in Barnett, Lazarus, et al., 2007) states that even for well-intentioned clinicians, thoughtful reflection is required to determine when crossing a boundary results in a boundary violation. If a therapist's actions result in harm to a client, it is a boundary violation. Failing to practice in accordance with prevailing community standards, as well as other variables such as the role of the client's diagnosis, history, values, and culture, can result in a well-intentioned action being perceived as a boundary violation. Barnett (2007) summarizes this matter thusly: "One person's intended crossing may be another's perceived violation. A thoughtful, premeditated approach with open discussion with the client before engaging in actions that may be misinterpreted or misconstrued is strongly recommended" (p. 403). Barnett also points out that crossing boundaries may be clinically relevant and appropriate in some cases, and that avoiding crossing some boundaries could work against the goals of the therapeutic relationship.

Establishing and maintaining appropriate boundaries. Consistent yet flexible boundaries are often therapeutic and can help clients develop trust in the therapy relationship. Borys (1994) suggests that many clients require the structure provided by clear and consistent boundaries. Such a structure is like "a buoy in stormy, chaotic seas" (p. 270). Koocher and Keith-Spiegel (2008) suggest that "the therapy relationship should remain a sanctuary in which clients can focus on themselves and their needs while receiving clear, clean feedback and guidance" (p. 264).

Conventional wisdom emphasizes the need for stability in the client–therapist relationship. Ira Orchin (2004), a psychologist in private practice, stretches boundaries by taking therapy outdoors. Orchin maintains that going outside the office challenges therapists to manage more fluid boundaries and novel situations, but that doing so can have definite therapeutic benefits. He believes that an outdoor session can be an appropriate way to create ceremonies and rituals to mark transitions, celebrate achievements, and encourage transformation.

Orchin claims that this effective intervention has assisted many of his clients in getting through an impasse in their therapy and moving therapy forward. This approach is an example of a boundary crossing that could have therapeutic benefits if it is carefully applied to certain clients and specific situations.

Zur (2008) also makes a case for taking professional relationships beyond the office walls. He writes about the advantages of out-of-office experiences, such as home visits, attending celebrations of a client, adventure or outdoor therapy, and other encounters with clients. For example, he describes how he accompanied a client to the gravesite of a child for whom she had not grieved. This intervention proved to be therapeutic for the woman who had been depressed for years prior to beginning her therapy with Zur.

We recommend that therapists who make it a practice to venture outside of the office or engage in nontraditional activities with clients make this clear at the outset of therapy during the informed consent process. Furthermore, therapists should consult with their insurance carrier about such practices as these activities may have implications for one's liability exposure.

Role blending.   Some roles that professionals play involve an inherent multiplicity of roles. **Role blending**, or combining roles and responsibilities, is quite common in some professions. For example, counselor educators serve as instructors, but they sometimes act as therapeutic agents for their students' personal development. At different times, counselor educators may function in the role of teacher, therapeutic agent, mentor, evaluator, or supervisor. School counselors must often function in multiple roles such as counselor, teacher, chaperon, and other noncounseling roles. Supervisors typically engage in a multiplicity of roles as well, such as coach, consultant, evaluator, counselor, and mentor. Although supervision and psychotherapy are two different processes, they share some common aspects. The supervisor may need to assist supervisees in identifying ways that their personal dynamics are blocking their ability to work effectively with clients, a topic addressed in more detail in Chapter 9.

Role blending is not necessarily unethical, but it does call for vigilance on the part of the professional to ensure that exploitation does not occur. Herlihy and Corey (2006b) assert that role blending is inevitable in the process of educating and supervising counselor trainees and that this role blending can present ethical dilemmas when there is a loss of objectivity or conflict of interests. Functioning in more than one role involves thinking through potential problems *before* they occur and building safeguards into practice. Whenever a potential for negative outcomes exists, professionals have a responsibility to design safeguards to reduce the potential for harm. Herlihy and Corey (2006b) identify the following measures to minimize the risks inherent in multiple relationships:

- Maintain healthy boundaries from the outset.
- Secure the informed consent of clients and discuss with them both the potential risks and benefits of multiple relationships or any kind of blending of roles.
- Remain willing to talk with clients about any potential problems and conflicts that may arise.

- Seek supervision or consult with other professionals when multiple relationships become particularly problematic or when the risk for harm is high.
- Document any multiple relationships in clinical case notes.
- When necessary, refer clients to another professional.

Issues to consider in addressing multiple relationships.   In *Boundary Issues in Counseling: Multiple Roles and Responsibilities,* Herlihy and Corey (2006b) identify 10 key themes surrounding multiple roles in counseling. These themes summarize the critical issues practitioners face in thinking about multiple relationships.

1. Multiple relationship issues affect virtually all mental health practitioners, regardless of their work setting or clientele.
2. All professional codes of ethics caution practitioners about the potential exploitation in multiple relationships, and more recent codes acknowledge the complex nature of these relationships.
3. Not all multiple relationships can be avoided, nor are they necessarily always harmful.
4. Multiple role relationships challenge us to monitor ourselves and to examine our motivations for our practices.
5. Whenever you consider becoming involved in a multiple relationship, seek consultation from trusted colleagues or a supervisor.
6. Few absolute answers exist to neatly resolve multiple relationship dilemmas.
7. The cautions for entering into multiple relationships should be for the benefit of our clients or others served rather than to protect ourselves from censure.
8. In determining whether to proceed with a multiple relationship, consider whether the potential benefit outweighs the potential for harm. To the extent possible, include the client in making this consideration.
9. It is the responsibility of counselor preparation programs to introduce boundary issues and explore multiple relationship questions. It is important to teach students ways of thinking about alternative courses of action.
10. Counselor education programs have a responsibility to develop guidelines, policies, and procedures for dealing with multiple roles and role conflicts within the program.

Avoiding the slippery slope.   Professionals get into trouble when their boundaries are poorly defined and when they attempt to blend roles that do not mix. A gradual erosion of boundaries can lead to very problematic multiple relationships that bring harm to clients. Gabbard (1994) cites the **slippery slope phenomenon** as one of the strongest arguments for carefully monitoring boundaries in psychotherapy. This argument is based on the premise that certain actions can lead to a progressive deterioration of ethical behavior. Furthermore, if professionals do not adhere to uncompromising standards, their behavior may foster relationships that are harmful to clients. To avoid the slippery slope, therapists are advised to have a therapeutic rationale for every boundary crossing and to question behaviors that are inconsistent with their theoretical approach (Pope, Sonne, & Holroyd, 1993; Smith & Fitzpatrick, 1995).

Managing multiple roles and relationships can be extremely complex, and seasoned professionals are often challenged to follow the most ethical course when it comes to crossing boundaries. Managing multiple relationships can be even more challenging to students, trainees, and beginning professionals. Those with relatively little clinical experience are well advised to avoid engaging in multiple relationships whenever possible.

The Changing Perspectives on Nonsexual Multiple Relationships

In *Boundaries in Psychotherapy*, a thoughtful and comprehensive treatment of the ethical and clinical issues we consider here, Zur (2007) addresses the changing perspectives on professional boundaries. Concerns about therapeutic boundaries came to the forefront during the 1960s and 1970s, largely due to a widespread lack of any sense of boundaries on the part of many mental health professionals and the resulting exploitation of clients. Therapists were instructed to avoid blending sexual relationships with professional relationships and cautioned to avoid any kind of dual relationship. The 1980s saw increased injunctions against boundary crossing and an increased emphasis on risk management practices.

In the 1990s, a shift in thinking about psychotherapeutic boundaries began to emerge. There was increased recognition that some boundary crossings, such as therapist self-disclosure and nonsexual touch, can be clinically valuable. Topics such as appropriate therapeutic boundaries, potential conflicts of interest, and ethical and effective ways of managing multiple relationships were addressed in some ethics codes. Professional organizations began to revise their ethics codes to acknowledge that nonsexual dual relationships were unavoidable in some situations, especially in small communities.

The indiscriminate ban on multiple relationships has been replaced with cautions against taking advantage of the power differential in the therapeutic relationship and exploiting the client, while acknowledging that some boundary crossings can be beneficial (Herlihy & Corey, 2008). Zur (2007) presents a compelling position on ethical thinking and behaving when it comes to professional boundaries. He asserts that risk management and quality care are not mutually exclusive: "The challenge is to find ways to practice ethically with a responsible, clinical foundation while protecting clients and therapists from risk" (p. 11). Many professionals now agree that flexible boundaries can be clinically helpful when applied ethically and that boundary crossings need to be evaluated on a case-by-case basis (Herlihy & Corey, 2006b, 2008; Knapp &

VandeCreek, 2006; Lazarus & Zur, 2002; Moleski & Kiselica, 2005; Schank & Skovholt, 2006; Younggren & Gottlieb, 2004; Zur, 2007, 2008).

Think about the circumstances in which you may decide upon flexible boundaries. What multiple relationships do you consider unavoidable, and what can you do in these situations? What kinds of relationships could place you in professional jeopardy? Consider, for example, how refusing to attend a social event of a client could complicate the therapeutic relationship. In struggling to determine what constitutes appropriate boundaries, you are likely to find that occasional role blending is inevitable. Therefore, it is crucial to learn how to manage boundaries, how to prevent boundary crossings from turning into boundary violations, and how to develop safeguards that will prevent the exploitation of clients.

Controversies on Boundary Issues

Lazarus (1998, 2001) states that a general proscription against dual and multiple relationships has led to unfair and inconsistent decisions by state licensing boards, brought sanctions against practitioners who have done no harm, and sometimes impeded a therapist's ability to perform optimum work with a client. He argues for a nondogmatic evaluation of boundary questions when deciding whether to enter into a secondary relationship.

Lazarus (1994a, 2001, 2006) contends that some well-intentioned ethical standards can be transformed into artificial boundaries that result in destructive prohibitions and undermine clinical effectiveness. Moreover, he believes some dual or multiple relationships can enhance treatment outcomes. Lazarus admits that he has socialized with some clients, played tennis with others, taken walks with some, respectfully accepted small gifts, and given gifts (usually books) to clients. He makes it clear that he is opposed to any form of disparagement, exploitation, abuse, harassment, or sexual contact with clients. Boundaries such as these are essential. Rather than being driven by rules, however, Lazarus calls for a process of negotiation in many areas of nonsexual multiple relationships that some would contend are in the forbidden zone. Lazarus's (1994a) keynote article caused a good deal of controversy, and a number of authors were invited to respond. In this section we present some of the responses to Lazarus's ideas and his rejoinder.

Bennett, Bricklin, and VandeCreek (1994) remind us of the unfortunate reality that too many practitioners have difficulty distinguishing where appropriate boundary lines should be drawn. Bennett and his colleagues agree with Lazarus that competent therapists will use clinical judgment rather than a cookbook approach when working with clients, but they fear that less experienced therapists will misinterpret his position as granting them license to minimize the importance of respecting boundary issues in therapy.

In her response to Lazarus's article, Brown (1994) maintains that the goal of ethical decision making is to take a position where the potential for exploitation is minimized. She recognizes how easy it is for therapists to misuse the power they have and suggests that therapists consider the impact of their behavior on clients. Brown questions the clinical purpose of Lazarus's extra-office encounters with his clients—playing tennis, eating meals, and going for walks—and wonders if he has taken into account the entire therapeutic relationship before deciding to engage in any of these extra-office contacts. She states that violations of boundaries tend to profoundly imbalance the power of an already power-imbalanced relationship by placing the needs of the more powerful person, the therapist, in a paramount position.

Gabbard (1994) fears that Lazarus is "teetering on the precipice." Failing to establish clear boundaries can be very dangerous to both the client and the therapist. Gabbard sees boundaries as providing safety for clients: "Professional boundaries provide an envelope within which a warm, empathic holding environment can be created" (p. 285).

Gutheil (1994) criticizes Lazarus for not considering the potential impact of his interventions on the client. He also stresses his belief that sound risk management is not antithetical to spontaneity, warmth, humanitarian concerns, or flexibility of approach, as Lazarus contends. One of Gutheil's main points is that sound and valid risk management principles need to rest on a solid clinical foundation.

In Lazarus's rejoinder (1994b) he comments that the major difference between his views and those of the respondents is that they dwell mainly on the potential *costs and risks,* whereas he focuses mainly on the potential *advantages* that may occur when certain boundaries are transcended. Elsewhere Lazarus (2001) asserts that there is a widespread sense of mass hysteria where clinicians and licensing boards incorrectly assume that consumers are protected by declaring all forms of dual relationships as harmful, exploitive, and inevitably resulting in sexual misconduct. Lazarus believes that professionals who hide behind rigid boundaries often fail to be of genuine help to their clients.

Advantages of Boundary Crossings

Rigid adherence to boundaries may be just as harmful to a client and the therapeutic relationship as a boundary violation (Barnett & Johnson, 2010). Examples of such rigidity include never touching a client under any circumstances, refusing every small gift, or refusing to extend a session for any reason. In many situations, it may be difficult for clinicians to readily discern the difference between a positive boundary crossing and a boundary violation.

Arnold Lazarus (personal communication, April 25, 2005) provided us with the following two cases (Pete and Rita) in which he contends that boundary crossings had positive outcomes rather than harming or exploiting the client. As you read Lazarus's thoughts on the advantages of selected boundary crossings, ask yourself where you stand on this issue.

■ The Case of Pete.

A few minutes before noon, my client Pete, whom I was scheduled to see from 11 a.m. to 12 p.m. was focusing on some highly significant issues.

I said to him: "What's your program like for the rest of the afternoon?" He said that he had to attend a 4 p.m. meeting, whereupon I said: "I have nothing scheduled until 1:30. Should we pick up some sandwiches from the local deli, come back here, and continue for another hour at no extra cost to you?" He enthusiastically agreed.

As I had anticipated, Pete seemed to be more relaxed and open while munching sandwiches and sipping iced tea, so that pertinent information emerged much sooner than might have been the case had we adhered to the traditionally accepted therapist–client relationship. Subsequently, Pete emphasized how much my largesse had meant to him. That "sandwich session" seemed to be a turning point in the course of his therapy and appeared to have consolidated our working alliance.

I should underscore that the invitation to extend the session and "break bread" was not issued capriciously. Boundary crossings should occur only when they are likely to be helpful to the client. The therapist needs to consider potential benefits, drawbacks, and probable risks beforehand (see Lazarus & Zur, 2002).

■ The Case of Rita.

Rita, a young woman who had graduated from a prestigious law school, felt inferior, considered herself "a loser," and generally belittled herself. She had received years of traditional insight therapy, and whatever gains may have accrued, self-confidence was not one of them. I was using a cognitive-behavior therapy approach, and we were making headway. Possibly because she was now exuding a sense of confidence and competence, a few fortunate events came together. She obtained a position with a law firm in which the senior partner was very supportive. She developed an intimate relationship with a man, which further helped to bolster her ego. She prepared a legal brief that enabled her firm to win an important case. Nevertheless, to use a football analogy, she was still not in the end zone. She felt that I and I alone really understood her "decrepitude." If her boss, her boyfriend, or anyone else were privy to the information she had shared with me, they would demean and reject her. So when she volunteered to critique a rather lengthy book chapter I was working on at the time, I decided to cross a boundary and accepted her offer. (I had mentioned this project *en passant* when she was discussing the rigors of preparing legal briefs.) My sense was that had I played by the rules and declined her offer—no matter how politely and graciously—this would only have reinforced her self-denigration. When the page proofs subsequently arrived, I made a point of showing her how many of her excellent literary suggestions had been incorporated. A few months later, I crossed another boundary. When one of my associates needed an attorney with expertise in Rita's domain, I referred him to her. This proved to her that despite knowing about her previous shortcomings, I nevertheless had respect for her and held her in high regard.

This was a turning point. "If you believe in me, there's every reason for me to believe in myself," she declared.

Boundary crossings that promote healing. In much of the literature on boundaries, the focus is on negative outcomes. Phrases such as "protecting the client," "minimizing the potential for abuse and exploitation," "teetering on the precipice," and the "slippery slope phenomenon" abound. The assumption seems to be that without ethical rules and regulations all practitioners would be violating the rights of clients. We are in agreement with Lazarus that this focus on the negative, emphasizing what the practitioner cannot do, can be detrimental to the client. Greenspan (2002) too is doubtful that the admonition to eschew all dual relationships achieves the objective of protecting clients and promoting healing. Elsewhere Greenspan (1994) states:

> The standard of care itself conspires against the genuine meeting of persons that is the real *sine qua non* of healing. It keeps patient and professional separate even when they do not wish to be. It makes authenticity feel like a bad and dangerous thing. (pp. 199–200)

There are advantages to crossing boundaries in certain circumstances. For instance, consider some of the advantages of out-of-office encounters between school counselors and students. By attending a student's school play, musical recital, or sports event, the counselor can do a lot to build a relationship with a student. However, we recommend that school counselors ask these questions: "How will I respond if this client continues to ask me to participate in other activities?" "How will I respond to other students who make similar requests?" "How will I deal with these extra demands on my time?"

Imagine that you were required to videotape all your sessions with clients and maintain them as your records. Would your behavior with your clients be different in any way? What do you do now that you might hesitate to do if your colleagues were to view your videotaped sessions? Would you be pleased to have your work with the client published? Would you welcome oversight from your peers? If you would not be comfortable with such oversight, take time to examine what makes you uncomfortable.

Consider the client population with whom you are dealing as this will certainly influence the kinds of boundaries of which you need to be sensitive. Not all clients are alike. Age, diagnosis, life experiences such as abuse, and culture are key elements that need to be considered in establishing boundaries. A second element is the character of the therapist. In our opinion, the therapist's character and values have more influence than training and orientation. Consider how boundaries were respected in your family of origin and how you manage boundaries in your own personal life. How sensitive are you to the boundaries of others in your personal life? If we establish and maintain appropriate boundaries in our personal lives, it is unlikely that we will be indifferent to boundaries in our professional lives, or unwittingly ignore them.

Before you read about the various forms of multiple relationships therapists may encounter, clarify your thinking on these issues:

- How do you respond to Lazarus's contention that certain boundaries can diminish therapeutic effectiveness?
- What are your reactions to Lazarus's claim that some multiple relationships and boundary crossings tend to enhance treatment outcomes?
- Do you think nonsexual multiple relationships necessarily lead to exploitation, sex, or harm? What are your thoughts about the "slippery slope" argument?
- Do you think the ethics codes of the various professional organizations are reasonable as they pertain to boundary issues, nonprofessional relationships, and multiple relationships?
- What kinds of boundaries do you maintain in your personal life?
- Might certain multiple relationships alter the power differential between you and your client in such a manner as to facilitate better health and healing?
- How can you assess the impact your interventions and behavior have on your clients?
- Would your fears of a malpractice suit alter the way you deal with boundaries with clients? If so, what are you doing now that could be viewed as being unethical?
- What topics pertaining to managing boundaries, multiple roles, and multiple relationships would you want to address with your clients from the initial session?

As you read the rest of this chapter, think of some challenges you might encounter in managing multiple relationships.

Managing Multiple Relationships in a Small Community

In small communities, including rural communities, mental health practitioners and school counselors have far greater challenges dealing with multiple relationships than those who work in urban areas. Practitioners who work in small communities often have to blend several professional roles and functions. They may attend the same church or community activities as the clients they serve. A therapist who is a recovering alcoholic and attends Alcoholics Anonymous meetings may meet a client at one of these meetings. In an isolated area a clergy person may seek counseling for a personal crisis from the only counselor in the town—someone who also happens to be a parishioner. Consider the roles of these two psychologists who practice in rural settings.

- Dr. Gib Condie lives in Powell, Wyoming, a community of about 5,000 where he holds the multiple roles of psychologist, neighbor, friend, and spiritual leader. As a school psychologist, he is faced with the challenge of balancing multiple roles and relationships in his community. He is also a Mormon bishop to 400 people in Powell. Condie believes that the many benefits associated with a rural practice far outweigh the challenges (cited in Kennedy, 2003, p. 67).

- Dr. Dan Goodkind offers psychological services to an underserved rural community 170 miles outside of Salt Lake City. This Utah psychologist finds that practicing in a rural area poses unique ethical dilemmas. Because the area has limited psychological services, neighbors or friends can become his next clients. Even though he tries to avoid seeing personal acquaintances professionally, this is not always possible (cited in Dittmann, 2003).

Sleek (1994) describes ethical dilemmas that are unique to rural practice. For example, if a therapist shops for a new tractor, he risks violating the letter of the ethics code if the only person in town who sells tractors happens to be a client. However, if the therapist were to buy a tractor elsewhere, this could strain relationships with the community because of the value rural communities place on loyalty to local merchants. Or consider clients who wish to barter goods or services for counseling services. Some communities operate substantially on swaps rather than on a cash economy. This does not necessarily have to become problematic, yet the potential for conflict exists in the therapeutic relationship if the bartering agreements do not work well.

Campbell and Gordon (2003) address some of the unique aspects of rural practice and offer strategies for evaluating, preventing, and managing multiple relationships in rural practice. They point out that the APA ethics code offers three helpful criteria in making decisions about multiple relationships: (1) risk of exploitation, (2) loss of therapist objectivity, and (3) harm to the professional relationship. They also mention that in the everyday professional practice in rural areas, prospective multiple relationships do not often fit precisely into a single ethical category. Campbell and Gordon conclude:

> Multiple relationships in rural practice are inevitable because of the limited number of rural practitioners, access difficulties, characteristics of rural communities, and characteristics of psychologists who practice in these communities. Although the best practice is to abstain from multiple roles and boundary compromises, there are situations in which avoidance of involvement may result in no psychological care for a large portion of the rural community. (p. 434)

The Ethical Standards of the California Association for Alcohol and Drug Educators (CAADE, 2006) clearly state that dual relationships should be avoided:

> The Certified Addictions Treatment Counselor will avoid dual relationships with current or past clients in self-help based recovery groups (such as A. A., N. A., Al-Anon, Smart Recovery) by not sponsoring a current or former client; by not having as a client a former sponsor or sponsee; by avoiding meeting, whenever possible, where clients are present; and by maintaining clear and distinct

boundaries between the professional counselor and self-help sponsor roles. (Principle 8, F.)

Although this is a good standard in theory, it may not be practical in many remote rural communities. Should a counselor who herself is in recovery avoid attending a recovery group in her small town? If a client and a counselor happen to encounter each other at an A. A. meeting, how can this matter best be dealt with? What are some potential difficulties in "maintaining clear and distinct boundaries" in a recovery context?

Barnett (1999a) points out that mental health professionals who are engaged in a rural practice or who work in a closed system (such as the deaf community, religious communities, or the military) often have to become an integral part of the community to be accepted as a credible mental health resource. If these practitioners isolate themselves from the surrounding community, they are likely to alienate potential clients and thus reduce their effectiveness in the settings where they work.

Schank and Skovholt (1997) conducted interviews with psychologists who live and practice in rural areas and small communities and found that they all acknowledged concerns involving professional boundaries. Some of the major themes were the reality of overlapping social or business relationships, the effects of overlapping social relationships on members of the psychologist's own family, and the dilemma of working with more than one family member as clients or with clients who have friendships with other clients. For them to be accepted, many of these psychologists found they had to work within the existing community system. Although the psychologists knew the content of the ethics codes, they admitted that they often struggle in choosing how to apply those codes to the ethical dilemmas they face in rural practice.

For a readable discussion of current concerns in small communities, strategies to minimize risk, and the challenge and hope of working in small communities, we recommend *Ethical Practice in Small Communities: Challenges and Rewards for Psychologists* (Schank & Skovholt, 2006).

■ A Case of a Multiple Relationship in a Small Community.

Millie, a therapist in a small community, experienced heart pain one day. The fire department was called, and the medic on the team turned out to be her client, Fred. To administer proper medical care, Fred had to remove Millie's upper clothing. During subsequent sessions, neither Fred nor Millie discussed the incident, but both exhibited a degree of discomfort with each other. After a few more sessions, Fred discontinued his therapy with Millie.

- Can this case be considered an unavoidable dual relationship? Why or why not?
- What might Millie have done to prevent this outcome?

- Should Millie have discussed her discomfort in the therapy session following the incident? Why or why not?
- If you were in Millie's situation, what would you have done?

Commentary. This case illustrates how some roles can shift and how some multiple relationships are unavoidable, especially in small communities. In small communities, therapists must anticipate frequent, and sometimes uncomfortable, boundary crossings with clients. In our view, Millie should have discussed with Fred how he would like to handle chance encounters in the community during the informed consent process. Even so, we doubt that Millie could have predicted this awkward boundary crossing with Fred. Clinically, Millie might have salvaged the therapy relationship by processing her own discomfort with a colleague, and then processing the event with Fred. By allowing the discomfort to remain hidden, Millie failed to practice with the best interests of her client in mind. In this instance, neither Millie's nor Fred's needs were being met in the therapeutic relationship.

The Challenge of Practicing in a Small Community*

I (Marianne Schneider Corey) would like to share my experience in conducting a private practice in a small community. I practiced for many years as a marriage and family therapist in a small town. This situation presented a number of ethical considerations involving safeguarding the privacy of clients. Even in urban areas, therapists will occasionally encounter their clients in other situations. However, in a rural area such meetings are more likely to occur.

I discussed with my clients the unique variables pertaining to confidentiality in a small community. I informed them that I would not discuss professional concerns with them should we meet at the grocery store or the post office, and I respected their preferences regarding interactions away from the office. Knowing that they were aware that I saw many people from the town, I reassured them that I would not talk with anyone about who my clients were, even when I might be directly asked. Another example of protecting my clients' privacy pertained to the manner of depositing checks at the local bank. Because the bank employees knew my profession, it would have been easy for them to identify my clients. Again, I talked with my clients about their preferences. If they had any discomfort about my depositing their checks in the local bank, I arranged to have them deposited elsewhere.

Practicing in a small town inevitably meant that I would meet clients in many places. For example, the checker at the grocery store might be my client; the person standing in line before me at the store could be a client who wants to talk about his or her week; at church there may be clients or former

*This section is presented from the private practice of Marianne Schneider Corey.

clients in the same Bible study group; in restaurants a client's family may be seated next to the table where my family is dining, or the food server could be a client; and on a hiking event I may discover that in the group is a client and his or her partner. As I was leaving the hairstyling salon in town one day, I encountered a former client of many years ago who enthusiastically greeted me. I stopped and acknowledged her, and she then went on in great detail telling the hairstylist, "This woman saved my life when I was going through a very painful divorce." I did not ask her any pointed questions nor did I engage her in any counseling issues. Instead, I kept the conversation general. Had I not acknowledged her, this most likely would have offended her. All of these examples present possible problems for the therapist. Neither my clients nor I experienced problems in such situations because we had talked about the possibility of such meetings in advance. Being a practitioner in a small community demands flexibility, honesty, and sensitivity. In managing multiple roles and relationships, it is not very useful to rely on rigid rules and policies; you must be ready to creatively adapt to situations as they unfold.

The examples I have given demonstrate that what might clearly not be advisable in an urban area might just as clearly be unavoidable in a rural area. This does not mean that rural mental health professionals are free do whatever they please. The task of managing boundaries is more challenging in rural areas, and practitioners often are called upon to examine what is in the best interests of their client.

Now consider the following questions:

- What ethical dilemmas do you think you would encounter if you were to practice in a rural area?
- Are you comfortable discussing possible outside contacts with clients up front, and are you able to set guidelines with your clients?
- What are some of the advantages and disadvantages of practicing in a small community?
- Is there more room for flexibility in setting guidelines regarding social relationships and outside business contacts with clients in a small community?

Bartering for Professional Services

When a client is unable to afford therapy, it is possible that he or she may offer a **bartering** arrangement, exchanging goods or services in lieu of a fee. For example, a mechanic might exchange work on a therapist's car for counseling sessions. However, if the client was expected to provide several hours of work on the therapist' car in exchange for one therapy session, this client might become resentful over the perceived imbalance of the exchange. If the therapist's car was not repaired properly, the therapist might resent that client. This would damage the therapeutic relationship. In addition, problems of another sort can occur with dual relationships should clients clean houses, perform secretarial services, or do other personal work for the therapist. Clients can easily be put

Ethics Codes

Bartering

American Psychological Association (2002)

Barter is the acceptance of goods, services, or other nonmonetary remuneration from clients/patients in return for psychological services. Psychologists may barter only if (1) it is not clinically contraindicated, and (2) the resulting arrangement is not exploitative. (6.05.)

American Counseling Association (2005)

Counselors may barter only if the relationship is not exploitive or harmful and does not place the counselor in an unfair advantage, if the client requests it, and if such arrangements are an accepted practice among professionals in the community. Counselors consider the cultural implications of bartering and discuss relevant concerns with clients and document such agreements in a clear written contract. (A.10.d.)

American Association for Marriage and Family Therapy (2001)

Marriage and family therapists ordinarily refrain from accepting goods and services from clients in return for services rendered. Bartering for professional services may be conducted only if: (a) the supervisee or client requests it, (b) the relationship is not exploitative, (c) the professional relationship is not distorted, and (d) a clear written contract is established. (7.5.)

National Association of Social Workers (2008)

Social workers should avoid accepting goods or services from clients as payment for professional services. Bartering arrangements, particularly involving services, create the potential for conflicts of interest, exploitation, and inappropriate boundaries in social workers' relationships with clients. Social workers should explore and may participate in bartering only in very limited circumstances when it can be demonstrated that such arrangements are an accepted practice among professionals in the local community, considered to be essential for the provision of services, negotiated without coercion, and entered into at the client's initiative and with the client's informed consent. Social workers who accept goods or services from clients as payment for professional services assume the full burden of demonstrating that this arrangement will not be detrimental to the client or the professional relationship. (1.13.b.)

in a bind when they are in a position to learn personal material about their therapists. The client might feel taken advantage of by the therapist, which could damage his or her therapy. Certainly, many problems can arise from these kinds of exchanges for both therapists and clients.

Ethical Standards on Bartering

Most ethics codes address the complexities of bartering (see the Ethics Codes box titled "Bartering"). We agree with the general tone of these standards, although we would add that bartering should be evaluated within a cultural context. In some cultures, and especially in small communities, bartering is an accepted practice. ACA's (2005) code specifically mentions the cultural dimensions of bartering. Over the years, the APA has softened its prohibitions on bartering and now spells out conditions in which bartering may be acceptable.

Before bartering is entered into, both parties need to talk about the arrangement, gain a clear understanding of the exchange, and come to an agreement. It is also important that problems that might develop be discussed and that alternatives be examined. Using a sliding scale to determine fees or making a referral are two possible alternatives that might have merit. Bartering is an example of a practice that we think allows some room for therapists, in collaboration with their clients, to use good judgment and consider the cultural context in the situation. Barnett and Johnson (2008) and Koocher and Keith-Spiegel (2008) acknowledge that bartering arrangements with clients can be both a reasonable and a humanitarian practice when people require psychological services but do not have insurance coverage and are in financial difficulty. They suggest that bartering arrangements can be a culturally sensitive and clinically indicated decision that may prove satisfactory to both parties. However, bartering entails risks, and they emphasize the importance of carefully assessing such arrangements prior to taking them on. Clinicians should seek consultation from a trusted colleague who can provide an objective evaluation of the proposed arrangement in terms of equity, clinical appropriateness, and the danger of potentially harmful multiple relationships.

Both Holly Forester-Miller and Lawrence Thomas write about their views on the benefits of bartering when clients cannot afford to pay for psychological services. Forester-Miller (2006) writes about the difficulties involved in avoiding overlapping relationships in rural communities. She reminds counselors that values and beliefs may vary significantly between urban dwellers and their rural counterparts and suggests that counselors need to work to ensure that they are not imposing values that come from a cultural perspective different from that of their clients. She uses bartering as an example of one way of providing counseling services in some regions to individuals who could not otherwise afford counseling. Forester-Miller gives an example of adapting her practices in the Appalachian culture, where individuals pride themselves on being able to provide for themselves and their loved ones. Forester-Miller once counseled an adolescent girl whose single-parent mother could not afford her usual fee, nor could she afford to pay a reduced fee, as even a small amount would be a drain on this family's resources. When Forester-Miller informed the mother that she would be willing to see her daughter for free, the mother stated that this would not be acceptable to her. However, she asked the counselor if she would accept a quilt she had made as payment for counseling the daughter. The mother and the counselor discussed the monetary value of the quilt and decided to use this as payment for a specified number of counseling sessions. Forester-Miller reports that this was a good solution because it enabled the adolescent girl to receive needed counseling services and gave the mother an opportunity to maintain her dignity in that she could pay her own way.

Thomas (2002) believes bartering is a legitimate means of making psychological services available to people of limited economic means. He maintains that bartering should not be ruled out simply because of the slight chance that a client might initiate a lawsuit against the therapist. His view is that if we are not willing to take some risks as psychotherapy professionals, then we are not worthy of our position. Thomas believes that venturing into a multiple relationship requires careful thought and judgment. In making decisions about bartering, the most salient issue is the "higher standard" of considering the welfare of the client. Thomas recommends a written contract that spells out the nature of the agreement between the therapist and client, which should be reviewed regularly. Documenting the arrangement can clarify agreements and can help professionals defend themselves if this becomes necessary. Thomas admits that bartering is a troublesome topic, yet he emphasizes that the role of our professional character is to focus on the higher standard—the best interests of the client.

Making a Decision About Bartering

Barnett and Johnson (2008) maintain that, as a general rule, it is unwise to engage in bartering practices with therapy clients. They add that accepting goods or services for professional services can open the door to misunderstandings, perceived or actual exploitation, boundary violations, and reduced effectiveness as a clinician. Although bartering is not prohibited by ethics or law, most legal experts frown on the practice. Woody (1998), both a psychologist and an attorney, argues against the use of bartering for psychological services. He suggests that it could be argued that bartering is below the minimum standard of practice. If you enter into a bartering agreement with your client, Woody states that you will have the burden of proof to demonstrate that (a) the bartering arrangement is in the best interests of your client; (b) is reasonable, equitable, and undertaken without undue influence; and (c) does not get in the way of providing quality psychological services to your client. Because bartering is so fraught with risks for both client and therapist, Woody believes prudence dictates that it should be the option of last resort: "No matter how carefully a bartering agreement is structured, the psychologist remains vulnerable" (p. 177). Even if the client needs special financial arrangements or suggests bartering as a solution to his or her financial problem, the therapist is always left with the liability.

The current economic crisis may present therapists with more frequent requests for bartering. Therapists who are considering entering into a bartering arrangement would do well to consider Hall's (1996) recommendations prior to establishing such an arrangement:

- Evaluate whether the bartering arrangement will put you at risk of professional censure or have a negative impact on your performance as a therapist.
- Determine the value of the goods or services in a collaborative fashion with the client at the outset of the bartering arrangement.
- Determine the appropriate length of time for the barter arrangement.

- Document the bartering arrangement, including the value of the goods or services and a date on which the arrangement will end or be renegotiated.

Woody (1998) presents some additional guidelines to clarify the bartering arrangements:

- Minimize any unique financial arrangements.

- If bartering is used for psychological services, it is better to exchange goods rather than services.

- Both you and your client should reach a written agreement for the compensation by bartering.

- If a misunderstanding begins to develop, the matter should be dealt with by a mediator, not by you and your client.

To these recommendations we add the importance of consulting with experienced colleagues, a supervisor, or your professional organization if you are considering some form of bartering in lieu of payment for therapy services. We highly recommend a straightforward discussion with your client about the pros and cons of bartering in your particular situation, especially as it may apply to the standards of your community. We concur with Thomas (2002), who recommends creating a written contract that specifies hours spent by each party and all particulars of the agreement. If you still have doubts about the agreement, consult with a contract lawyer. Once potential problems have been identified, consult with colleagues about alternatives you and your client may not have considered. Ongoing consultation and discussion of cases, especially in matters pertaining to boundaries and dual roles, provide a context for understanding the implications of certain practices. Needless to say, these consultations should be documented.

Your stance on bartering.   Consider a situation in which you have a client who cannot afford to pay even a reduced fee. Would you be inclined to engage in bartering goods for your services? What kind of understanding would you need to work out with your client before you agreed to a bartering arrangement? Would your decision be dependent on whether you were practicing in a large urban area or a rural area? How would you take the cultural context into consideration when making your decision?

Consider the following cases and apply the ethical standards we have summarized to your analysis. What ethical issues are involved in each case? What potential problems do you see emerging from these cases? What alternatives to bartering can you think of?

■ The Case of Barbara.

Barbara is 20 years old and has been in therapy with Sidney for over a year. She has developed respect and fondness for her therapist, whom she sees as a father figure. She tells him that she is thinking of discontinuing therapy because she has lost her job and simply has no way of paying for the sessions. She is obviously upset over the prospect of ending the relationship, but she sees no alternative. Sidney informs her that he is willing to continue her therapy even if she is unable to pay. He suggests that as an exchange of services she can become the babysitter for his three children. She gratefully accepts this offer. After a few months, however, Barbara finds that the situation is becoming difficult for her. Eventually, she writes a note to Sidney telling him that she cannot handle her reactions to his wife and their children. It makes her think of all the things she missed in her own family. She writes that she has found this subject difficult to bring up in her sessions, so she is planning to quit both her services and her therapy.

- What questions does this case raise for you?
- How would you have dealt with this situation?
- What are your thoughts concerning the therapist's suggestion that Barbara babysit for him?
- To what degree do you think that Sidney adequately considered the nature of the transference relationship with this client?

Commentary. This case illustrates how a well-meaning therapist created a multiple relationship with his client that became problematic for her. In addition, Sidney suggested a bartering arrangement that involved Barbara performing personal services in exchange for therapy; it generally is not a good idea for a therapist to involve his significant others in barter exchanges with the client. Sidney did not explore with Barbara her transference feelings for him, nor did he predict potential difficulties with her taking care of his children. Indeed, countertransference on Sidney's part may have led to the blurring of boundaries. The ethics codes of the ACA (2005), APA (2002), NASW (2008), and AAMFT (2001) all specify that bartering may be ethical only under these conditions: if the client requests it; if it is not clinically contraindicated; if it is not exploitative; and if the arrangement is entered into with full informed consent. None of these standards was met in this case. Sidney should have explored other options such as working pro bono, reducing his fees, or a referral to another agency.

■ The Case of Olive.

Olive is a massage therapist in her community. Her services are sought by many professionals, including Giovani, a local psychologist. In the course of a massage session, she confides in him that she is experiencing difficulties in her marriage. She would like to discuss with him the possibility of exchanging professional services. She proposes that in return for marital therapy she will give both him and his wife massage treatments. An equitable arrangement based on their fee structures can be worked out. Giovani might make any one of the following responses:

Response A: That's fine with me, Olive. It sounds like a good proposal. Neither one of us will suffer financially because of it, and we can each benefit from our expertise.

Response B: Well, Olive, I feel okay about the exchange, except I have concerns about the dual relationship.

Response C: Even though our relationship is nonsexual, Olive, I do feel uncomfortable about seeing you as a client in marital therapy. I certainly could refer you to a competent marital therapist.

What are your thoughts on these response options? Which do you consider to be ethical? unethical? Do you think Olive's proposal is practical? What are the ethical implications in this case? If you were in this situation, how would you respond to Olive?

> *Commentary.* Because of the physically intimate nature of massage work, we would discourage any therapist from entering into this kind of exchange. We do not see any signs that Olive and Giovani adequately assessed the potential risks involved in exchanging these personal services. As with the previous case, other options besides bartering could have been considered.

■ The Case of Exchanging Services for Therapy.

Bryce is a counselor in private practice who has been seeing a client for a few months. Jana is hard working, dedicated to personal growth, and is making progress in treatment. At her last session she expressed concern about her ability to continue funding her sessions. Jana suggested that Bryce consider allowing her husband's pool company to provide summer pool cleaning service for the months of May through August for Bryce's home pool in return for her continued sessions. The fees would be basically equitable, and Bryce is seriously considering this agreement to assist Jana in her ability to continue counseling.

- Does this arrangement seem like a reasonable request to you?
- What ethical issues related to this situation might cause you concern, if any?
- Which ethical standards apply to this situation?

> *Commentary.* The case of Bryce and Jana is less clear-cut. It is important that the arrangement was suggested by Jana and not by Bryce. It would be beneficial for Bryce to consider some consultation in reviewing the pros and cons of this proposal prior to making a decision. Bryce should also consider whether bartering is a commonly accepted practice in his geographical area. If he decides to participate in this bartering arrangement, he will need to have an explicit written contract of the agreed-upon terms of exchange. Exchanging services for therapy, because

of its complexity, is fraught with more inherent problems than is accepting goods from clients. Bryce might suggest an alternative form of bartering, asking Jana to perform some kind of community service for a mutually agreed-upon cause or a nonprofit organization rather than a more direct exchange (Zur, 2007).

Giving or Receiving Gifts

Few professional codes of ethics specifically address the topic of giving or receiving gifts in the therapeutic relationship. The AAMFT (2001) does have such a guideline:

> Marriage and family therapists do not give to or receive from clients (a) gifts of substantial value or (b) gifts that impair the integrity or efficacy of the therapeutic relationship. (3.10.)

The latest version of the ACA ethics code (2005) added a new standard on receiving gifts.

> *Receiving Gifts.* Counselors understand the challenges of accepting gifts from clients and recognize that in some cultures, small gifts are a token of respect and showing gratitude. When determining whether or not to accept a gift from clients, counselors take into account: the therapeutic relationship, the monetary value of the gift, a client's motivation for giving the gift, and the counselor's motivation for wanting or declining the gift. (A.10.e.)

Lavish gifts certainly present an ethical problem, yet we can go too far in the direction of trying to be ethical and, in so doing, actually damage the therapeutic relationship. Some therapists include a policy statement on matters such as not accepting gifts from clients in their informed consent document, so that there will not be a question on this matter. Rather than establishing a hard and fast rule, our preference is to evaluate each situation on a case-by-case basis. Let's examine a few of these areas in more detail.

- *What is the monetary value of the gift?* Most mental health professionals would agree that accepting a very expensive gift is inappropriate and unethical. It would also be problematic if a client offered tickets to the theater or a sporting event and wanted you to accompany him or her to this event. In the novel *Lying on the Couch* (Yalom, 1997), a therapist is offered a $1,600 bonus by a wealthy client to show his appreciation for how a few therapy sessions changed his life. The therapist struggles as he declines this gift, stating that it is considered unethical to accept a monetary gift from a client. The client angrily protests, claiming that rejecting his gift could cancel some of the gains made during their work, and he *insists* that the score be evened. The therapist steadfastly responds that he cannot accept the gift and acknowledges that one topic they did not discuss in therapy was the client's discomfort in accepting help.

- *What are the clinical implications of accepting or rejecting the gift?* It is important to recognize when accepting a gift from a client is clinically contraindicated and that you be willing to explore this with your client. Certainly, knowing the motivation for a client's overture is critical to making a decision. For example, a client may be seeking your approval, in which case the main motivation for giving you a gift is to please you. Accepting the gift without adequate discussion would not be helping your client in the long run. Accepting a small gift typically does not raise ethical problems, but Koocher and Keith-Spiegel (2008) state that accepting certain kinds of gifts (highly personal items) would be inappropriate and require exploring the client's motivation. Practitioners may want to inquire what meaning even small gifts have to the client. Koocher and Keith-Spiegel provide this guideline: "When a gift is no longer a gesture of gratitude, or when even a small gift raises a therapeutic issue or potential manipulation, problems of ethics and competent professional judgment arise" (p. 293). Zur (2007) suggests that any gift must be understood and evaluated within the context in which it is given. He mentions that inappropriately expensive gifts or any gifts that create indebtedness, whether of the client or the therapist, are boundary violations.

- *When in the therapy process is the offering of a gift occurring?* Is it at the beginning of the therapy process? Is it at the termination of the professional relationship? It is more problematic to accept a gift at an early stage of a counseling relationship because doing so may be a forerunner to creating lax boundaries.

- *What are your own motivations for accepting or rejecting a client's gift?* It is essential that you be aware of whose needs are being served by receiving a gift. Some counselors will accept a gift simply because they do not want to hurt a client's feelings, even though they are not personally comfortable doing so. Counselors may accept a gift because they are unable to establish firm and clear boundaries. Other counselors may accept a gift because they actually want what a client is offering.

- *What are the cultural implications of offering a gift?* In working with culturally diverse client populations, clinicians often discover that they need to engage in boundary crossing to enhance the counseling relationship (Moleski & Kiselica, 2005). The cultural context does play a role in evaluating the appropriateness of accepting a gift from a client. Sue (2006) points out that in the Asian cultures gift giving is a common practice to show respect, gratitude, and to seal a relationship. Although such actions are culturally appropriate, Western-trained professionals may believe that accepting a gift would distort boundaries, change the relationship, and create a conflict of interest. However, if a practitioner were to refuse a client's gift, it is likely that this person would feel insulted or humiliated and the refusal could damage both the therapeutic relationship and the client. If you are opposed to receiving gifts and view this as a boundary crossing, address this issue in your informed consent document.

Brown and Trangsrud (2008) conducted a survey to assess the ethical decision making of 40 licensed psychologists regarding accepting or declining gifts from clients. These psychologists were more likely to accept gifts from clients when the gift was inexpensive, was culturally appropriate, and was given as a sign of appreciation at the end of treatment. The participants indicated they were more likely to decline gifts that were expensive, were offered during treatment, and had sentimental or coercive value. Cultural considerations are important in weighing the benefits of accepting a gift against the risk of jeopardizing the therapeutic relationship by refusing the gift.

One of the reviewers of this book stated that students sometimes give school counselors gifts. Such gifts are usually inexpensive, if purchased, or are items made in an art or shop class. He indicates that he could accept the gift and display the gift in his office. If you were a school counselor, would you be inclined to accept inexpensive gifts? Would you display a gift in your office? How would you respond if other students (your clients) or teachers asked you who made the gift that is on display? Under what circumstances, if any, might you be inclined to give a student a gift? To what degree would you be comfortable documenting and having your colleagues learn about a gift you have accepted?

■ The Case of Tomoko.

Toward the end of her therapy, Tomoko, a Japanese client, presents an expensive piece of jewelry to her counselor, Joaquin. Tomoko says she is grateful for all that her counselor has done for her and that she really wants him to accept her gift, which has been in her family for many years. In a discussion with the counselor, Tomoko claims that giving gifts is a part of the Japanese culture. Joaquin discusses his dilemma, telling Tomoko that he would like to accept the gift but that he has a policy of not accepting gifts from clients. He reminds her of this policy, which was part of the informed consent document she signed at the beginning of the therapeutic relationship. Tomoko is persistent and lets Joaquin know that if he does not accept her gift she will feel rejected. She is extremely grateful for all Joaquin has done for her, and this is her way of expressing her appreciation. Joaquin recalls that Tomoko had told him that in her culture gifts are given with the expectation of reciprocity. A few days after this session, Joaquin received an invitation from Tomoko to attend her daughter's birthday party where her family would be present.

Put yourself in this situation with Tomoko. What aspects would you want to explore with your client before accepting or not accepting her gift?

- Do you see a difference between accepting a gift during therapy or toward the end of therapy?
- Would it be important to consider your client's cultural background in accepting or not accepting the gift?
- How would you deal with Tomoko if she insisted that you recognize her token of appreciation and accept her invitation to her daughter's birthday party?
- If you find that clients frequently want to give you gifts, would you need to reflect on what you might be doing to promote this pattern? Explain.

Commentary. Joaquin was clear about his policy on accepting gifts, which was included in his informed consent document, and he understood that Tomoko accepted this guideline. Rather than surrendering to Tomoko's pressure to accept her gift, Joaquin could discuss with her what importance and meaning the gift has for her. He could also explore with her the cultural implications of her offering him this gift. Counselors must weigh cultural influences and implications in professional relationships, but it is important not to yield to a culture-based request that might ultimately harm the client or the counseling relationship. Joaquin must deal with the pressure to accept the gift if it does not seem right for him to do so. With respect to the invitation to the daughter's birthday party, Joaquin would do well to reflect on how he will deal with possible future requests from this client as well as requests from other clients. He needs to decide if he is comfortable meeting his client's family in a nonprofessional setting.

Cases of disciplinary action against therapists.   In 2005 a licensed marriage and family therapist, Judy, was charged with gross negligence in her treatment of a client in that she blurred therapeutic boundaries by creating a dual relationship (CAMFT, 2005, p. 50). In fact, there were multiples charges against Judy. The therapist repeatedly gave gifts to her client and received gifts from the client. Shortly after therapy began with a married woman, Judy began disclosing increasing amount of personal information about herself to her client, including details of her sex life. Judy encouraged the client to increase her sessions to twice a week. These sessions often lasted 2 to 3 hours, and sometimes beyond midnight. Judy invited her client to spend a weekend with her at her home. During this weekend, the therapist smoked marijuana in the client's presence and invited her to smoke it also. During this same weekend, the therapist had a massage in her living room at home and started to undress in front of her client.

Another case involves a disciplinary action against, Matthew, a marriage and family therapist, who did not maintain professional boundaries between his personal life and that of his client. Matthew gave his client gifts of clothes, books, CDs, and household items. He also paid some of the client's bills and gave her a loan for car repairs. The therapist was charged with failing to establish reasonable boundaries with his client and improperly engaging in a dual relationship.

These cases illustrate how lax boundaries can contribute to a number of ethical violations.

- Would you ever consider giving a gift to a client? Why or why not?
- Would you ever consider giving a loan to a client who was in financial difficulty? Why or why not?
- How much personal information do you think you would share with a client? In what circumstances might you do so?

Social Relationships With Clients

Do social relationships with clients necessarily interfere with therapeutic relationships? Some would say no, contending that counselors and clients are able to handle such relationships as long as the priorities are clear. They see social contacts as particularly appropriate with clients who are not deeply disturbed and who are seeking personal growth. Some peer counselors, for example, maintain that friendships before or during counseling are actually positive factors in establishing trust.

Other practitioners take the position that counseling and friendship should not be mixed. They claim that attempting to manage a social and professional relationship simultaneously can have a negative effect on the therapeutic process, the friendship, or both. Here are some reasons for discouraging the practice of accepting friends as clients or of becoming socially involved with clients: (1) therapists may not be as challenging as they need to be with clients they know socially because of a need to be liked and accepted by the client; (2) counselors' own needs may be enmeshed with those of their clients to the point that objectivity is lost; and (3) counselors are at greater risk of exploiting clients because of the power differential in the therapeutic relationship.

Few professional ethics codes specifically mention social relationships with clients. One exception is that of the Canadian Counselling Association (2007), which has the following standard pertaining to relationships with former clients:

> Counsellors remain accountable for any relationships established with former clients. Those relationships could include, but are not limited to those of a friendship, social, financial, and business nature. Counsellors exercise caution about entering any such relationships and take into account whether or not the issues and relational dynamics present during the counselling have been fully resolved and properly terminated. In any case, counselors seek consultation on such decisions. (B.11.)

Cultural Considerations

The cultural context can play a role in evaluating the appropriateness of dual relationships that involve friendships in the therapy context. In Parham and Caldwell (2006) question Western ethical standards that discourage dual and multiple relationships and claim that such standards can prove to be an obstacle or hindrance in counseling African American clients. In an African context, therapy is not confined to a practitioner's office for 50-minute sessions. Instead, therapy involves multiple activities that might include conversation, playful activities, laughter, shared meals and cooking experiences, travel, rituals and ceremony, singing or drumming, storytelling, writing, and touching. Parham and Caldwell view each of these activities as having the potential to bring a "healing focus" to the therapeutic experience.

In a similar spirit, Sue (2006) points out that some cultural groups may value multiple relationships with helping professionals. Some of his points are worth considering in determining when multiple relationships might be acceptable:

- In some Asian cultures it is believed that personal matters are best discussed with a relative or a friend. Self-disclosing to a stranger (the counselor) is considered taboo and a violation of familial and cultural values. Some Asian clients may prefer to have the traditional counseling role evolve into a more personal one.

- Clients from many cultural groups prefer to receive advice and suggestions from an expert. They perceive the counselor to be an expert, having higher status and possessing superior knowledge. To work effectively with these clients, the counselor may have to play a number of different roles, such as advocate, adviser, change agent, and facilitator of indigenous support systems. Yet counselors may view playing more than one of these roles as engaging in dual or multiple relationships. (See Chapter 13 for a more extensive discussion of alternatives to traditional roles for professionals who work in the community.)

Forming Relationships With Former Clients

Grosso (2002) states that mental health professionals are not legally or ethically prohibited from entering into a nonsexual relationship with a client after the termination of therapy. However, Grosso adds that the ethics codes address friendships with former clients, stating that difficulties might arise for both the client and the therapist. For example, a former client might feel taken advantage of, which could result in a complaint against the therapist. Grosso points out that therapists need to know that it is their responsibility to evaluate the impact of entering into such relationships.

Although forming friendships with former clients may not be unethical or illegal, the practice could lead to problems. The safest policy is probably to avoid developing social relationships with former clients. O'Laughlin (2001) reports that some state licensing boards view social relationships with former clients much the same as sexual relationships with former clients. Some state regulations have posttherapy bans on both of these relationships for at least 2 years or more after termination of therapy. This social relationship restriction bars a therapist and a client from dating, becoming friends, or getting married.

In the long run, former clients may need you more as a therapist at some future time than as a friend. If you develop a friendship with a former client, then he or she is not eligible to use your professional services in the future. Additionally, in many situations the imbalance of power never changes. Even in the social relationship, you are either seen as a therapist, or you behave as a therapist. Mental health practitioners should be aware of their own motivations, as well as the motivations of their clients, when allowing a professional relationship to evolve into a personal one, even after the termination of therapy. We question the motivation of helpers who rely on their professional position as a way to meet their social needs. Furthermore, therapists who are in the habit of developing relationships with former clients may find themselves overextended and come to resent the relationships they sought out or consented to. Perhaps the crux of the situation involves the therapist being able to establish clear boundaries regarding what he or she is willing to do.

Your position on socializing with current or former clients.   There are many types of socializing, ranging from going to a social event with a client to having a cup of tea or coffee with a client. There are differences between a social involvement initiated by a client and one instigated by a therapist. Another factor to consider is whether the social contact is ongoing or occasional. The degree of intimacy is also a factor. For instance, there is a difference between meeting a client for coffee as opposed to a candlelight dinner. In thinking through your own position on establishing a dual relationship with a current client, consider the nature of the social function, the nature of your client's problem, the client population, the setting where you work, the kind of therapy being employed, and your theoretical approach. If you are psychoanalytically oriented, you might adopt stricter boundaries and would be concerned about infecting the transference relationship should you blend any form of socializing with therapy. If you are a behavior therapist helping a client to stop smoking, it may be possible to have social contact at some point. Weigh the various factors and consider this matter from both the client's and the therapist's perspective.

Certainly, there are problems when professional and social relationships are blended. Such arrangements demand a great deal of honesty and self-awareness on the part of the therapist. No matter how clear the therapist is on boundaries, if the client cannot understand or cannot handle the social relationship, such a relationship should not be formed—with either current or former clients. When clear boundaries are not maintained, both the professional and the social relationship can sour. Clients may well become inhibited during therapy out of fear of alienating their therapist. They may fear losing the respect of a therapist with whom they have a friendship. They may censor their disclosures so that they do not threaten this social relationship.

Ethics codes generally do not address the issue of friendships with *former* clients; an exception is the Canadian Counselling Association (2007), which provides the following guidelines:

> Counsellors remain accountable for any relationships established with former clients. Those relationships could include, but are not limited to those of a friendship, social, financial, and business nature. Counsellors exercise caution about entering any such relationships and take into account whether or not the issues and relational dynamics present during the counselling have been fully resolved and properly terminated. In any case, counsellors seek consultation on such decisions. (B.11.)

What are your thoughts on this topic? What are the therapist's obligations to former clients? Should the focus be on all relationships with former clients or only those that are exploitative? Should ethics codes address nonromantic and nonsexual posttherapy relationships specifically? Under what circumstances might such relationships be inappropriate or even unethical? When do you think these relationships might be considered ethical?

Sexual Attractions in the Client–Therapist Relationship

Are sexual attractions to be expected in therapy? In a pioneering study, "Sexual Attraction to Clients: The Human Therapist and the (Sometimes) Inhuman Training System," Pope, Keith-Spiegel, and Tabachnick (1986) developed the theme that there has been a lack of systematic research into the sexual attraction of therapists to their clients. They provide clear evidence that attraction to clients is a prevalent experience among both male and female therapists and investigated the following questions:

- What is the frequency of sexual attraction to clients by therapists?
- Do therapists feel guilty or uncomfortable when they have such attractions?
- Do they tend to tell their clients about their attractions?
- Do they consult with colleagues?
- Do therapists believe their graduate training provided adequate education on attraction to clients?

Pope and his colleagues (1986) studied 585 respondents, and only 77 reported never having been attracted to any client. The vast majority (82%) reported that they had never seriously considered actual sexual involvement with a client. An even larger majority (93.5%) reported never having had sexual relations with their clients. Therapists gave a number of reasons for having refrained from acting out their attractions to clients, including a need to uphold professional values, a concern about the welfare of the client, and a desire to follow personal values. Fears of negative consequences were mentioned, but they were less frequently cited than values pertaining to client welfare. Those who had some graduate training in this area were more likely to have sought consultation (66%) than were those with no such training.

Since this pioneering study there has been more research on this topic (see Downs, 2003; Fisher, 2004; Lamb, Catanzaro, & Moorman, 2003; Pope 1994; Pope et al., 1993). According to Pope, Sonne, and Holroyd (1993), the tendency to treat sexual feelings as if they are taboo has made it difficult for therapists to acknowledge and accept attractions to clients. The most common reactions of therapists to sexual feelings in therapy included surprise, guilt, anxiety about unresolved personal problems, fear of losing control, fear of being criticized, confusion about boundaries and roles, and confusion about actions. Given these reactions, it is not surprising that many therapists want to hide rather than to acknowledge and deal with sexual feelings by consulting a colleague or by bringing this to their own therapy.

There is a distinction between finding a client sexually attractive and being preoccupied with this attraction. If you find yourself sexually attracted to your clients, it is important that you monitor these feelings. If you are frequently attracted, you need to examine this issue in your own therapy and supervision. If this happens, consider these questions: "What is going on in my own life that may be creating this intense sexual attraction? What am I not taking care of in my personal life?" We recommend Irvin Yalom's (1997) book, *Lying on the Couch: A Novel*, for an interesting case and discourse on the slippery slope of sexual attraction between therapist and client.

Educating Counselor Trainees

Many training programs spend too little time addressing how to deal with sexual attraction to clients (Fisher, 2004; Hamilton & Spruill, 1999; Housman & Stake, 1999; Pope, 1987; Pope et al., 1986; Pope et al., 1993; Samuel & Gorton, 1998; Wiederman & Sansone, 1999). Training programs have an ethical responsibility to help students identify and openly discuss their concerns pertaining to sexual dilemmas in counseling practice. Prevention of sexual misconduct is a better path than remediation. Ignoring this subject in training sends a message to students that the subject should not be talked about, which will inhibit their willingness to seek consultation when they encounter sexual dilemmas in their practice.

Although transient sexual feelings are normal, intense preoccupation with clients is problematic. Pope and colleagues (1986) found that 57% of the psychologists in their study sought consultation or supervision when attracted to a client. Housman and Stake (1999) found that 50% of the doctoral students in their study reported having experienced a sexual attraction to a client; only half of these students had chosen to discuss the attraction with a supervisor. Seeking help from a colleague or supervision or personal therapy can give therapists access to guidance, education, and support in handling their feelings. Pope, Sonne, and Holroyd (1993) believe that exploration of sexual feelings about clients is best done with the help, support, and encouragement of others. They maintain that practice, internships, and peer supervision groups are ideal places to talk about this issue but that this topic is rarely raised.

Counselors need to ask themselves how they set boundaries when sexual attraction occurs. Practitioners who have difficulty setting and keeping appropriate boundaries in their personal life are more likely to encounter problems in establishing appropriate boundaries with their clients. Heiden (1993) writes that counselors must ask themselves about how they treat clients in different ways, especially with reference to time spent, intimacy, and touch. It is well for counselors to think about how their own needs for intimacy are being met by clients.

Housman and Stake (1999) surveyed sexual ethics training and student understanding of sexual ethics in clinical psychology doctoral programs and found that 94% of the students had received sexual ethics training. Programs provided an average of 6 hours of training. Their findings also call attention to the importance of addressing sexual issues in therapy early in students' training. They note that sexual attraction toward clients is common among students as well as professional practitioners. It was concluded that most students in training do not understand that sexual attractions for clients are normal. Housman and Stake's findings suggest that only half the students who are attracted will seek supervision. They note that even if students refrain from acting on their sexual feelings for clients, they may withdraw emotionally from their clients to avoid feelings they believe are unacceptable. It is crucial that students acknowledge these feelings to themselves and their supervisors and take steps to deal effectively with them.

Wiederman and Sansone (1999) assert that deliberate attention to sexuality issues during training is required for the development of competent mental health professionals. Ideally, this training would involve accurate information and firsthand experience. Hamilton and Spruill (1999) believe it is crucial to increase students' awareness of sexual attraction before they begin seeing clients. They recommend including this topic as a basic component in a preparatory clinical skills course. This training needs to create the expectation that sexual attractions will arise in therapy and to create an atmosphere of trust in which students feel as free as possible to disclose these feelings and experiences in their supervision. If students are not presented with normalizing information, they are likely to continue to regard sexual feelings as proof of a troubled therapy relationship.

Suggestions for Dealing With Sexual Attractions

To prevent sexual feelings of therapists from interfering with therapy, Bennett and colleagues (2006) believe it is important for therapists to recognize their countertransference reactions and deal with them so that their feelings do not go underground. The vulnerability the client shows when revealing painful material is very powerful and appealing. The attention a caring therapist shows in response is also powerful and appealing. This environment creates the possibility of mutual attraction. When these feelings are acknowledged in a safe setting, therapists are more likely to manage their feelings productively.

Jackson and Nuttall (2001) provide the following recommendations regarding sexual attractions to minimize the likelihood of sexual transgressions by clinicians:

- Learn to recognize sexual attractions and how to deal with these feelings constructively and therapeutically.
- Seek professional support during times of personal loss or crisis.
- Make it a practice to examine and monitor feelings and behaviors toward clients.
- Know the difference between having sexual attraction to clients and acting on this attraction.
- Learn about the possible adverse consequences for clients and therapists who engage in sexual activity.
- Establish and maintain clear boundaries when a client makes sexual advances toward you.
- Terminate the therapeutic relationship when sexual feelings obscure objectivity.

Fisher (2004) discourages therapist self-disclosure of sexual feelings to clients and suggests using less explicit interventions: "It appears that direct explicit disclosures of sexual feelings can run the risk of harming clients and may therefore be unethical" (p. 105). Some of the recommendations Fisher makes regarding managing sexual feelings are listed below:

- Rather than making any explicit communication of sexual feelings for clients, therapists might consider acknowledging caring and warmth within the therapeutic relationship.
- Therapists do well to practice a risk management approach if they develop sexual feelings for a client. This would involve awareness of timing and the location of scheduled appointments, nonerotic touch, and general self-disclosure.
- Therapists need to be open to using supervision, consultation, and personal therapy throughout their careers, especially at those times when they are challenged.

■ Put Yourself in This Situation.

Imagine that you are sexually attracted to one of your clients. You believe your client may have similar feelings toward you and might be willing to become involved with you. You often have difficulty paying attention during sessions because of your attraction. Which of the following options do you think are most ethical? Which of the following courses of action would you consider to be unethical?

- I can ignore my feelings for the client and my client's feelings toward me and focus on other aspects of the relationship.
- I will tell my client of my feelings of attraction, discontinue the professional relationship, and then begin a personal relationship.
- I will openly express my feelings toward my client by saying: "I'm glad you find me an attractive person, and I'm attracted to you as well. But this relationship is not about our attraction for each other, and I'm sure that's not why you came here."
- If there was no change in the intensity of my feelings toward my client, I would arrange for a referral to another therapist.
- I would consult with a colleague or seek professional supervision.

Can you think of another direction in which you might proceed? What might you do and why?

Commentary. Some may argue that if you are sexually attracted to a client, he or she will be aware of this and it could easily impede the therapy process. As therapists, we need to control our emotional energy without getting frozen. It is a good practice to monitor ourselves by reflecting on the messages we are sending to a client. It is our responsibility to recognize and deal with our feelings toward a client in a way that does not burden the client. As Fisher (2004) states, therapists have the responsibility to make sure that they take appropriate steps to manage their feelings professionally and ethically.

Koocher and Keith-Spiegel (2008) advise therapists to discuss feelings of sexual attraction toward a client with another therapist, an experienced and trusted colleague, or an approachable supervisor. Doing so can help therapists clarify the risk, become aware of their vulnerabilities when it comes to sexual attraction, provide suggestions on how to proceed, and offer a fresh perspective on these situations. We caution against sharing your feelings of attraction with your client directly; such disclosures often detract from the work of therapy and may be a confusing burden for the client. Koocher and Keith-Spiegel emphasize that therapists are always responsible for managing their feelings toward clients and that shifting blame or responsibility to the client is never an excuse for unprofessional or unethical conduct.

■ The Case of Adriana.

Adriana's husband, a police officer, was killed in the line of duty, leaving her with three school-age boys. She seeks professional help from Clint, the school social worker, and explores her grief and other issues pertaining to one son who is acting out at school. She seems to rely on the social worker as her partner in supporting her son. After 2 years the son is ready to move on to high school. She confesses to Clint that she is finding it increasingly difficult to think of not seeing him anymore. She has grown to love him. She wonders if they could continue to see each other socially and romantically.

At first Clint is taken aback. But he also realizes that throughout the relationship he has come to admire and respect Adriana, and he discloses his fondness for her. He explains to her that because of their professional relationship he is bound by ethical guidelines not to become involved with parents socially or romantically. He proposes to her that they not see each other for a year. If their feelings persist, he will then consider initiating a personal relationship.

- What do you think of Clint's way of handling the situation?
- If Clint was attracted to Adriana but had withheld this information for therapeutic reasons, how would you assess that?
- If you were in a similar situation and did not want to pursue the relationship, how might you deal with your client's disclosure?

Commentary. We applaud Clint for refusing to initiate a romantic relationship with Adriana at this time. However, Clint should carefully consider his ethical obligations bearing on romantic and sexual relationships with former clients or their family members. Further therapy with her son would be closed if they developed a personal relationship at some point in the future. The ACA (2005) code explicitly prohibits such relationships for a period of 5 years following the termination of services, and the APA (2002) code specifies a moratorium of 2 years. If Clint does commence a romantic relationship with Adriana in the future, he will bear the burden of showing that this change in roles was not harmful to her.

If the boundaries involved in the therapeutic relationship are identified in our informed consent document, situations such as this are likely to be less complicated. If we are clear in our personal life about setting boundaries, we will more likely be able to establish and maintain appropriate boundaries in our professional setting. Growing fond of each other is not an ethical violation, but how we act on our feelings toward our clients determines our degree of ethical and professional behavior.

Sexual Relationships in Therapy: Ethical and Legal Issues

The issue of erotic contact in therapy is not simply a matter of whether or not to have sex with a client. Even if you decide intellectually that you would not engage in such intimacies, it is important to realize that the relationship between therapist and client can involve varying degrees of sexuality. Therapists may have sexual fantasies, they may behave seductively with their clients, they may influence clients to focus on sexual feelings toward them, or they may engage in physical contact that is primarily intended to satisfy their own needs. Sexual overtones can distort the therapeutic relationship and become the real focus of the sessions. It is crucial that practitioners learn to differentiate between having sexual feelings and acting on them. We need to be aware of the effects of our sex-related socialization patterns and how they may influence possible countertransference reactions.

During the past decade a number of studies have documented the harm that sexual relationships with clients can cause. As you will see in Chapter 9, there has also been considerable writing on the damage done to students and supervisees when educators and supervisors enter into sexual relationships with them. Later in this section we discuss the negative effects that typically occur when the client–therapist relationship becomes sexualized.

Ethical Standards on Sexual Contact With Clients

Sexual relationships between therapists and clients continue to receive considerable attention in the professional literature. Sexual relationships with clients are clearly unethical, and all of the major professional ethics codes have specific prohibitions against them (see the Ethics Codes box titled "Sexual Contact and the Therapeutic Relationship"). Additionally, most states have declared such relationships to be a violation of the law. If therapists have

Ethics Codes

Sexual Contact and the Therapeutic Relationship

- "Sexual intimacy with clients is prohibited" (AAMFT, 2001, 1.4.).
- "Sexual or romantic counselor-client interactions or relationships with current clients or their family members are prohibited" (ACA, 2005, A.5.a.).
- "The social worker shall not have a sexual relationship with a client" (CASW, 1994, 4.3.).
- "Psychologists do not engage in sexual intimacies with current clients/patients" (APA, 2002, 10.05.).
- "Psychologists do not engage in sexual intimacies with individuals they know to be close relatives, guardians, or significant others of current clients/patients. Psychologists do not terminate therapy to circumvent this standard" (APA, 2002, 10.06.).
- "Psychologists do not accept as therapy clients/patients persons with whom they have engaged in sexual intimacies" (APA, 2002, 10.07.).
- "Social workers should under no circumstances engage in sexual activities or sexual contact with current clients, whether such contact is consensual or forced" (NASW, 2008, 1.09.a.).
- "Social workers should not provide clinical services to individuals with whom they have had a prior sexual relationship. Providing clinical services to a former sexual partner has the potential to be harmful to the individual and is likely to make it difficult for the social worker and individual to maintain appropriate professional boundaries" (NASW, 2008, 1.09.d.).

had a prior sexual relationship with a person, many of the ethics codes also specify that they should not accept this person as a client. It is clear from the statements of the major mental health organizations that these principles go beyond merely condemning sexual relationships with clients. The existing codes are explicit with respect to sexual harassment and sexual relationships with clients, students, and supervisees. However, they do not, and maybe they cannot, define some of the more subtle ways that sexuality can enter the professional relationship.

Sexual misconduct is considered to be one of the more serious of all ethical violations for a therapist, and it is also one of the most common allegations in malpractice suits (see APA, 2003b). Therapist–client sexual contact is arguably the most disruptive and potentially damaging boundary violation (Smith & Fitzpatrick, 1995).

The Scope of the Problem

The report of the APA (2003b) Ethics Committee reveals that the major area of sexual dual relationship allegations continues to be male psychologists with adult female clients. Sexual misconduct played a role in 53% of the complaints opened by the APA in 2002, and all of these sexual multiple relationships involved male psychologist–female client complaints. In a study that focused on psychologists who had sexual relationships with clients, supervisees, and students, Lamb, Catanzaro, and Moorman (2003) found that 3.5% reported at least one sexual boundary violation. Of the total sample in the study, 2% reported a sexual boundary violation with a client, 1% with a supervisee, and 3% with a student. The majority of these violations occurred after the professional relationship had ended (50% after therapy, 100% after supervision, and 54% after teaching). In the sample, 84% were older male psychologists who engaged in sexual relationships with female clients, supervisees, and students.

In her review of research on the sexually abusive therapist, Olarte (1997) likewise notes that a majority of sexual boundary violations (approximately 88%) occur between male therapists and female clients. According to Olarte, the typical composite of a therapist who becomes involved in sexual boundary violations is a middle-aged man who is experiencing personal distress, is isolated professionally, and overvalues his healing abilities. His methods are unorthodox, and he inappropriately discloses personal information that is irrelevant to therapy.

Many professional journals review disciplinary actions taken against therapists who violate ethical and legal standards, and most of these cases involve sexual misconduct. Brief summaries of a few of these cases provide a picture of how therapists can manipulate clients to meet their own sexual or emotional needs.

- A clinical social worker engaged in unprofessional conduct when he exchanged a romantic kiss with a client. The clinician used his relationship with another client to further his own personal, religious, political, or business interests. He engaged in a sexual relationship with a former client, less than 3 years after termination of the professional relationship (CAMFT, 2004b, p. 49).

- A licensed marriage and family therapist engaged in inappropriate sexually based discussions and sexual relationships with a client. The therapist discussed intimate aspects of his personal life with his client, engaged in multiple relationships with the client, watched a sexually explicit movie with her, and accepted a nude photograph of the client. He failed to schedule appointments with the client at appropriate times, scheduling them instead for the evening hours. He failed to refer her to another therapist (CAMFT, 2004c, p. 50).

- A licensed psychologist was charged with gross negligence in using vulgar language with clients and suggesting that they hug and/or kiss him on the cheek, even though doing so made his clients uncomfortable (California Department of Consumer Affairs, Board of Psychology, 1999, pp. 12–13).

- A licensed psychologist, who was a professor, was charged with gross negligence and unprofessional conduct in using his position as a professor to take advantage of a student that involved both giving the student a back massage and inappropriate sexual touching (California Department of Consumer Affairs, Board of Psychology, 1999, pp. 12–13).

- A licensed counselor treated a female client for about 10 years. The counselor asked his client how she felt about taking her clothes off during therapy sessions. She indicated that she would feel very embarrassed. About 3 months later, he urged her to remove her clothing, proposing to use "Reichian" therapy.

The client removed her clothes, except her underwear, but told her counselor about her discomfort in doing this. He assured her that this technique would help her in dealing with her sexual problems. Later, she agreed to take off all her clothes and was nude during her sessions. This occurred between 6 and 12 times and constituted gross negligence on the counselor's part (CAMFT, 1996b, p. 25).

- A licensed counselor told a female client that she needed to have and to express her Oedipal sexual feelings toward her father as a child in a safe place, that he would be that safe place, that she should have sexual feelings for someone other than her father, and that she needed to be sexually attracted to him. During a session in the early phase of her therapy, the counselor instructed the client to sit on his lap and tell him what she wanted to do with him sexually. Later the counselor kissed the client on the mouth. Although she did not experience this kiss as sexual, she did not feel it was right. The therapist later tried to convince her that the kiss was on the cheek and not on the lips. She eventually terminated therapy because she felt that the situation surrounding the kiss operated against any therapeutic gain in continuing therapy with this counselor (CAMFT, 1996c, p. 34).

Sexual violations are currently given priority consideration, and rightly so, yet many other violations can be very damaging, including client abandonment, mismanaging clients who are suicidal, misuse of the power differential with the student in academic settings, and financial ruin resulting from a business relationship with a treating therapist (Orr, 1997).

At-Risk Therapists

In the Lamb, Catanzaro, and Moorman (2003) study of professionals who engaged in sexual boundary violations, respondents cited concurrent dissatisfaction in their own lives as a risk factor leading to sexual misconduct. In their study on sexual boundary violations, Jackson and Nuttall (2001) note that it is critical for clinicians to become aware of their own history and the impact it may have on their relationships with clients. They contend that, although sexual exploitation of clients by therapists is the result of a complex set of factors, one of these factors is a childhood history of severe sexual abuse in the background of offending male therapists.

Jackson and Nuttall conclude that therapists can minimize their potential for sexual boundary violations through a process of self-examination and being willing to seek ongoing support. They urge high-risk clinicians to avoid the isolation of private practice, closely monitor their boundaries with clients, obtain ongoing professional supervision, and seek their own therapy to address any remaining abuse-related issues. In our opinion, these suggestions will only work with those therapists who recognize they have a problem and want to change.

Harmful Effects of Sexual Contact With Clients

Studies continue to demonstrate that clients who are the victims of sexual misconduct suffer dire consequences. Erotic contact is totally inappropriate and is an exploitation of the relationship by the therapist.

Bouhoutsos and colleagues (1983), in a pioneering study of sexual contact in psychotherapy, assert that when sexual intercourse begins, therapy as a helping process ends. When sex is involved in a therapeutic relationship, the therapist loses control of the course of therapy. Sexual contact is especially disruptive if it begins early in the relationship and if it is initiated by the therapist. Of the 559 clients in their study who became sexually involved with their therapists, 90% were adversely affected. This harm ranged from mistrust of opposite-gender relationships to hospitalization and, in some cases, suicide. Other effects of sexual intimacies on clients' emotional, social, and sexual adjustment included negative feelings about the experience, a negative impact on their personality, and a deterioration of their sexual relationship with their primary partner. Bouhoutsos and her colleagues conclude that the harmfulness of sexual contact in therapy validates the ethics codes barring such conduct and provides a rationale for enacting legislation prohibiting it.

Olarte (1997) identifies the harmful effects of sexual boundary violations: distrust of the opposite sex, distrust of therapists and the therapeutic process, guilt, depression, anger, feeling of rejection, suicidal ideation, and low self-esteem. It is generally agreed that sexual boundary violations remain harmful to clients no matter how much time elapses after termination of therapy.

Legal Sanctions Against Sexual Violators

A number of states have enacted legal sanctions in cases of sexual misconduct in the therapeutic relationship, making it a criminal offense. Among the negative consequences for therapists include being the target of a lawsuit, being convicted of a felony, having their license revoked or suspended by the state, being expelled from professional organizations, losing their insurance coverage, and losing their jobs. Therapists may also be placed on probation, be required to undergo their own psychotherapy, be closely monitored if they are allowed to resume their practice, and be required to obtain supervised practice.

Professionals cannot argue that their clients seduced them. Even if clients behave in seductive ways, it is clearly the professional's responsibility to keep appropriate boundaries. Regardless of the client's pathology, the responsibility to hold to ethical standards in a therapy relationship rests solely with the therapist (Olarte, 1997).

Criminal liability is rarely associated with the practices of mental health professionals. However, some activities can result in arrest and incarceration, and the number of criminal prosecutions of mental health professionals is increasing. The two major causes of criminal liability are sex with clients (and former clients) and fraudulent billing practices (Reaves, 2003). In California, the law prohibiting sexual activity in therapy applies to two situations: (1) the therapist has sexual contact with a client during therapy, or (2) the therapist ends the professional relationship primarily to begin a sexual relationship with a client. Therapists who have sex with clients are subject to both a prison sentence and fines (California Department of Consumer Affairs, 2004). For a first offense with one victim, an offending therapist would probably be charged with a misdemeanor, with a penalty of a sentence up to one year in county jail and a fine up to $1,000. For second and following offenses, therapists may be charged with misdemeanors or felonies. For a felony charge, offenders face up to 3 years in prison, or up to $10,000 in fines, or both. In addition to criminal action, civil action can be taken against therapists who are guilty of sexual misconduct. Clients may file a civil lawsuit to seek money for damages or injuries suffered and for the cost of future therapy sessions (California Department of Consumer Affairs, 2004).

Assisting Victims in the Complaint Process

Each of the mental health professional associations has specific policies and procedures for reporting and processing ethical and professional misconduct. (Chapter 1 lists these organizations and provides contact information.) Mental health professionals have an obligation to help increase public awareness about the nature and extent of sexual misconduct and to educate the public about possible courses of action. The California Department of Consumer Affairs (2004) booklet, *Professional Therapy Never Includes Sex*, describes ethical, legal, and administrative options for individuals who have been victims of professional misconduct.

Although the number of complaints of sexual misconduct against therapists has increased, individuals are still reluctant to file complaints for disciplinary action against their therapists, educators, or supervisors. Many clients do not know that sexual contact between counselor and client is unethical and illegal. They are often unaware that they can file a complaint, and they frequently do not know the avenues available to them to address sexual misconduct. Each of the following options has both advantages and disadvantages, and it is ultimately up to the client to decide the best course of action.

Clients can file an ethical complaint with the therapist's licensing board. The board would review the case, and if the allegation is supported, the board has the power to discipline a therapist using the administrative law process. Depending on the violation, the board may revoke or suspend a license. When a license is revoked, the therapist cannot legally practice. In those cases where sexual misconduct is admitted or proven, most licensing boards will revoke the therapist's license. The board's action will often be published in the journal of the therapist's professional organization.

Legal alternatives include civil suits or criminal actions. A malpractice suit on civil grounds seeks compensatory damages for the client for the cost of treatment and for the suffering involved. Criminal complaints are processed based on state and federal statutes.

Sexual Relationships With Former Clients

Most professional organizations prohibit their members from engaging in sexual relationships with former clients because of the potential for harm. Some organizations specify a time period, and others do not. Most of the organizations state that in the exceptional circumstance of sexual relationships with former clients—even after a 2- to 5-year interval—the burden of demonstrating that there has been no exploitation clearly rests with the therapist. (For guidelines for particular professional associations, refer to the Ethics Codes box titled "Sexual Relationships With Former Clients.")

When considering initiating such a relationship, many factors must be evaluated. These include the amount of time that has passed since termination of therapy, the nature and duration of therapy, the circumstances surrounding termination of the professional–client relationship, the client's personal history, the client's competence and mental status, the foreseeable likelihood of harm to the client or others, and any statements or actions by the therapist suggesting a plan to initiate a sexual relationship with the client after termination. Koocher and Keith-Spiegel (2008) state that sexual relationships with former clients involve such a high potential for a number of risks that they strongly discourage them, regardless of the lapse of time stipulated in ethics codes.

Some counselors maintain, "Once a client, always a client." Although a blanket prohibition on sexual intimacies, regardless of the time that has elapsed since termination, might clarify the issue, some would contend that this measure is too extreme. Others point out that there is a major difference between an intense, long-term therapy relationship and a less intimate, brief-term one. A blanket prohibition ignores these distinctions.

It is essential that the therapist be willing to seek consultation or personal therapy to explore his or her motivations and the possible ramifications of transforming a professional relationship into a personal one. Bennett and his colleagues (1990) offer several suggestions to those considering initiating a relationship with a former client:

- Be aware that developing a personal relationship with a former client is illegal in some jurisdictions and that therapists have been sued for malpractice for engaging in this practice.
- Reflect on the reasons for termination. If you, the client, or both of you experienced an attraction before ending therapy, was the professional relationship terminated for an appropriate reason or so that a sexual relationship could develop?
- Ask yourself about the potential benefits and risks of developing a personal relationship with a former client.
- Before initiating such a relationship, consider discussing the matter with a colleague. If you are unwilling to do so, then you are a danger to yourself and your clients.

■ What is Your Position?

At this point, reflect on your own stance on the controversial issue of forming sexual relationships once therapy has ended. Consider these questions in clarifying your position:

- Should counselors be free to formulate their own practices about developing sexual relationships with former clients? Give your reasons.

Ethics Codes

Sexual Relationships With Former Clients

Canadian Counselling Association (2007)

Counsellors avoid any type of sexual intimacies with clients and they do not counsel persons with whom they have had a sexual relationship. Counsellors do not engage in sexual intimacies with former clients within a minimum of three years after terminating the counselling relationship. This prohibition is not limited to the three year period but extends indefinitely if the client is clearly vulnerable, by reason of emotional or cognitive disorder, to exploitative influence by the counselor. Counsellors, in all such circumstances, clearly bear the burden to ensure that no such exploitative influence has occurred, and to seek consultative assistance. (B.12.)

American Psychological Association (2002)

(a) Psychologists do not engage in sexual intimacies with former clients/patients for at least two years after cessation or termination of therapy.

(b) Psychologists do not engage in sexual intimacies with former clients/patients even after a two-year interval except in the most unusual circumstances. Psychologists who engage in such activity after the two years following cessation or termination of therapy and of having no sexual contact with the former client/patient bear the burden of demonstrating that there has been no exploitation, in light of all relevant factors, including (1) the amount of time that has passed since therapy terminated; (2) the nature, duration, and intensity of the therapy; (3) the circumstances of termination; (4) the client's/patient's personal history; (5) the client's/patient's current mental status; (6) the likelihood of adverse impact on the client/patient; and (7) any statements or actions made by the therapist during the course of therapy suggesting or inviting the possibility of a posttermination sexual or romantic relationship with the client/patient. (10.08.)

American Counseling Association (2005)

Sexual or romantic counselor-client interactions or relationships with former clients or their family members are prohibited for a period of five years following the last professional contact. Counselors, before engaging in sexual or romantic interactions or relationships with clients or client family members after five years following the last professional contact, demonstrate forethought and document (in written form) whether the interactions or relationship can be viewed as exploitive in some way, and/or whether there is still potential to harm the former client; in cases of potential exploitation and/or harm, the counselor avoids entering such an interaction or relationship. (A.5.b.)

Commission on Rehabilitation Counselor Certification (2010)

Sexual or romantic rehabilitation counselor–client interactions or relationships with former clients, their romantic partners, or their immediate family members are prohibited for a period of five years following the last professional contact. Even after five years, rehabilitation counselors give careful consideration to the potential for sexual or romantic relationships to cause harm to former clients. In cases of potential

(continued on next page)

exploitation and/or harm, rehabilitation counselors avoid entering such interactions or relationships. (A.5.b.)

National Association of Social Workers (2008)

Social workers should not engage in sexual activities or sexual contact with former clients because of the potential for harm to the client. If social workers engage in conduct contrary to this prohibition or claim that an exception to this prohibition is warranted because of extraordinary circumstances, it is social workers—not their clients—who assume the full burden of demonstrating that the former client has not been exploited, coerced, or manipulated, intentionally or unintentionally. (1.09.c.)

American Association for Marriage and Family Therapy (2001)

Sexual intimacy with former clients is likely to be harmful and is therefore prohibited for two years following the termination of therapy or last professional contact. In an effort to avoid exploiting the trust and dependency of clients, marriage and family therapists should not engage in sexual intimacy with former clients after the two years following termination or last professional contact. Should therapists engage in sexual intimacy with former clients following two years after termination or last professional contact, the burden shifts to the therapist to demonstrate that there has been no exploitation or injury to the former client or to the client's immediate family. (1.5.)

- Does the length and quality of the therapy relationship have a bearing on the ethics involved in such a personal relationship? Would you apply the same standard to a long-term client and a brief therapy client who worked on personal growth issues for six weeks?
- Would you favor changing the ethics codes to include an absolute ban on posttermination sexual relationships regardless of the length of time elapsed? Why or why not?
- What ethical guidelines would you suggest regarding intimate relationships with former clients?
- Although it might not be illegal in your state, what are the potential consequences of engaging in sex with former clients? Explain.
- React to the statement, "Once a client, always a client."

Commentary. We believe the statement "Once a client, always a client" is a dogmatic pronouncement that should be open to discussion. An absolute ban on all sexual relationships with former clients implies that diagnosis and treatment are irrelevant. Is a client who is seen for two sessions to be considered on equal footing with a client who may have been in therapy for 5 years? Clearly there is concern when a therapist marries a former client and, indeed, doing so might be unwise. Yet making all actions that may be unwise into "clearly unethical actions" seems excessive.

A Special Case: Nonerotic Touching With Clients

Although acting on sexual feelings and engaging in erotic contact with clients is unethical, nonerotic contact is often appropriate and can have significant therapeutic value. It is important to stress this point because some counselors perceive a taboo against touching clients. Therapists may hold back when they feel like touching their clients compassionately. They may feel that touching can be misinterpreted as sexual or exploitative; they may be afraid of their impulses or feelings toward clients; they may be afraid of intimacy; they may be overly concerned with risk management; or they may believe that to express closeness physically is unprofessional. With the current attention being given to sexual harassment and lawsuits over sexual misconduct in professional relationships, some counselors are likely to decide that it is not worth the risk of touching clients at all, lest their intentions be misinterpreted.

We include this discussion in this chapter because it is perhaps one of the more controversial boundary crossings. Although some are concerned that nonsexual touching can eventually lead to sexual exploitation, nonerotic touching can be a positive influence in the therapeutic relationship. A therapist's touch can be a genuine expression of caring and compassion, or it can be done primarily to gratify the therapist's own needs. Koocher and Keith-Speigel (2008) contend that therapists must carefully assess the appropriateness of touching clients. They add that it is inappropriate to touch *some* clients under any circumstances. Zur (2007) and Zur and Nordmarken (2009) write that touch needs to be evaluated in the context of client factors, the professional setting, the therapist's theoretical orientation, and the quality of the therapeutic relationship. Client factors include gender, age, culture, class, personal history with touch, presenting problem, diagnosis, and personality. For some clients touching may be appropriate and therapeutic, whereas the same kind of touch may be inappropriate and harmful for other clients. According to Zur and Nordmarken, a growing body of research indicates the potential clinical value of touch as an adjunct to verbal therapy. Clinically appropriate touch can increase a client's trust and ease with the therapist and can be effective in enhancing the therapeutic alliance.

There are two sides to the issue of touching. Some clinicians oppose any form of physical contact between counselors and clients on the grounds that it can promote dependency, can interfere with the transference relationship, can be misread by clients, and can become sexualized. On the other side, Rabinowitz (1991), in writing about a men's therapy group, cites research findings indicating that appropriate touching can foster self-exploration, increase verbal interaction, increase the client's perception of the expertness of the counselor, and produce more positive attitudes toward the counseling process. Rabinowitz states that it may be safer for a hug to occur in group therapy rather than in individual counseling because there are witnesses to the context of the touching, leaving less room for misinterpretation. However, counselors are still responsible for being sensitive to each member of the group and for avoiding meeting their own needs at the expense of the members.

Holub and Lee (1990) assert that the decision to touch or not to touch clients involves more than considering its effectiveness in helping clients or engaging them in therapy. They maintain that this decision should also include deliberating over the correctness, motivations, and interpretations of the touching. The power differential between therapist and client should be considered, and touching often elicits different feelings in men than it does in women. The practice of male therapists' touching only female clients might be interpreted as sexist or at least as poor judgment, and perhaps an indicator of future boundary violations. If touching is consistently and actively used as a therapeutic intervention, Bennett and his colleagues (1990) suggest that it is wise to explain this practice to clients and their families, if appropriate, before therapy begins. Practitioners should consider how their clients are likely to react to touching.

In our view, it is critical to determine whose needs are being met when it comes to touching. If it comes from the therapist alone, and not from the context of the therapeutic relationship, it needs to be carefully examined. If touching occurs, it should be a spontaneous and honest expression of the therapist's feelings and always done for the client's benefit. It should not be done as a technique. It is unwise for therapists to touch clients if this behavior is not congruent with what they feel. A nongenuine touch will most likely be detected by clients and could erode trust in the relationship.

Therapists need to be sensitive to those circumstances when touching could be counterproductive. There are times when touching clients can distract them from what they are feeling, or when clients do not want to be touched. This is often the case with clients who come from a background of physical or sexual abuse. There are also times when a touch given at the right moment can convey far more empathy than words can. Therapists need to be aware of their own motives and to be honest with themselves about the meaning of physical contact. They also need to be sensitive to factors such as the client's readiness for physical closeness, the client's cultural understanding of touching, the client's reaction, the impact such contact is likely to have on the client, and the level of trust that they have built with the client.

Ethical and Clinical Considerations of Nonsexual Touch in Therapy

Practitioners need to formulate clear guidelines and consider appropriate boundaries when it comes to touching. It is sad that the legal climate discourages the appropriate clinical use of this medium of reaching clients. Think about your position on the ethical implications of the practice of touching as part of the client–therapist relationship by answering these questions:

- What criteria could you use to determine whether touching your clients is therapeutic or countertherapeutic?

- Do you think some clients may never be open to touching in therapy?

- How could you honestly answer the question, "Are my own needs being met at the expense of my client's needs?" What might you do if you hugged a client whom you felt needed this kind of physical support and the client suggested that you were meeting your own needs?

- Do you give hugs routinely in your personal life? If not, what motivates you to give hugs as a professional?

- To what degree do you think your professional training has prepared you to determine when touching is appropriate and therapeutic?

- What factors should you consider in determining the appropriateness of touching clients? (Examples are age, gender, the type of client, the nature of the client's problem, and the setting in which the therapy occurs.)

- Imagine your first session with a same-gender client who is crying and in a state of crisis. Might you be inclined to touch this person? Would it make a difference if the client asked you to hold him or her? Would it make a difference if this client were of the opposite gender? of the same gender?

- If you are favorably inclined toward the practice of touching clients, are you likely to restrict this practice to opposite-gender clients? to same-gender clients? Explain.

- What would you do if your client wanted a hug but you were hesitant to do it? How would you explain yourself to the client?

Zur and Nordmarken (2009) note that touch in therapy is not inherently unethical and that none of the codes of ethics of professional organizations view touch as unethical. They also suggest that practicing risk management by rigidly avoiding touch may be unethical. They do suggest that therapists seek consultation in using touch in complex and sensitive cases. Documentation of the type and frequency of touch, along with the clinical rationale for using touch, is an important aspect of ethical practice. Zur and Nordmarken identify the following ethical and clinical guidelines for nonsexual touch in therapy:

- Touch should be employed only when it is likely to have a positive therapeutic effect.

- Touch should be used in accordance with the therapist's training and competence.

- It is essential that therapists create a foundation of client safety and empowerment before using touch.

- In deciding to touch, it is important to thoughtfully consider the client's potential perception and interpretation of touch.

- Special care is important in using touch with people who have experienced assault, neglect, attachment difficulties, rape, molestation, sexual addictions, or intimacy issues.

- It is the responsibility of therapists to explore their personal issues regarding touch and to seek education and consultation regarding the appropriate use of touch in therapy.

- Therapists should not avoid touch out of fear of licensing boards or the dread of litigation.

- Clinically appropriate touch must be used with sensitivity to clients' variables such as gender, culture, problems, situation, history, and diagnosis.

Zur and Nordmarken emphasize that it is critical that therapists be mindful of not abusing the trust and power they have in the therapeutic relationship. They remind us that power by itself does not corrupt; rather, it is the lack of personal integrity on the therapist's part that corrupts.

■ The Case of Ida.

Chee is a warm and kindly counselor who routinely embraces his clients, both male and female. One of his clients, Ida, has had a hard life, has had no success in maintaining relationships with men, is now approaching her 40th birthday, and has come to him because she is afraid that she will be alone forever. She misreads his friendly manner of greeting and assumes that he is giving her a personal message. At the end of one session when he gives his usual embrace, she clings to him and does not let go right away. Looking at him, she says: "This is special, and I look forward to this time all week long. I so much need to be touched." He is surprised and embarrassed. He explains to her that she has misunderstood his gesture, that this is the way he is with all of his clients, and that he is truly sorry if he has misled her. She is crestfallen and abruptly leaves the office. She cancels her next appointment.

- What are your thoughts on this counselor's manner of touching his clients?
- If Chee had asked for Ida's permission to hug her at the end of a session, would that have been more acceptable?
- Was the manner in which he dealt with Ida's embrace ethically sound?
- Would you follow up with Ida about canceling her appointment?

Commentary. In our opinion, this case is a good example of a situation in which the counselor was more concerned with the bind he was in than the bind his client was in. The nature of a therapist's work is to take care of the client's difficulty first. Chee assumed that he correctly understood Ida's message, and his response served his emotional needs rather than Ida's. Had Chee put his client's needs first, he would have encouraged Ida to discuss the meaning for her of the embrace. Chee also must be mindful of his own possible countertransference and how this could be affecting the manner in which he interpreted Ida's comments.

Chapter Summary

In this chapter we have tried to put ethical issues pertaining to multiple relationships into perspective. We have emphasized that dual and multiple relationships are neither inherently unethical nor always problematic. Such relationships are always unethical, however, when they result in exploitation or harm to clients. We have attempted to avoid being prescriptive and have summarized a range of recommendations offered by others to reduce the risk of boundary crossings and boundary violations—recommendations we expect will increase the chances of protecting both the client and the therapist.

Although ethics codes provide general guidance, you will need to weigh many specific variables in making decisions about what boundaries you need to establish in your professional relationships. The emphasis in this chapter has been on guidelines for making ethical decisions about nonsexual multiple relationships, which often tend to be complex and defy simplistic solutions. To promote the well-being of their clients, clinicians are challenged with balancing their own values and life experiences with ethics codes as they make choices regarding how to best help their clients (Moleski & Kiselica, 2005).

Sexual relationships with clients are obviously unethical and detrimental to clients' welfare. It is unwise, unprofessional, unethical, and in many states illegal to become sexually involved with clients. However, it is important that you not overlook some of the more subtle and perhaps insidious behaviors of the therapist that may in the long run cause serious damage to clients. This is not to say that as a counselor you are not also human or that you will never be attracted to certain clients. You are imposing an unnecessary burden on yourself if you believe that you should not have such feelings for clients or if you try to convince yourself that you should not have more feeling toward one client than toward another. What is important is how you decide to deal with these feelings as they affect the therapeutic relationship. Referral to another therapist is not necessarily the best solution, unless it becomes clear that you can no longer be effective with a certain client. Instead, you may recognize a need for consultation or, at the very least, for an honest dialogue with your colleagues. If for some reason your feelings of attraction become known to the client, it is essential that the client be assured that they will not be acted upon. If this creates a problem for the client, a referral should be discussed.

Becoming a therapist does not make you perfect or superhuman. We want to stress the importance of reflecting on what you are doing and on whose needs are primary. A willingness to be honest in your self-examination is your greatest asset in becoming an ethical practitioner. As was mentioned earlier, it is always good to keep in mind whether you would act differently if your colleagues were observing you.

Suggested Activities

1. Investigate the ethical and legal aspects of dual relationships as they apply to the area of your special professional interests. Look for any trends, special problems, or alternatives. Once you have gathered some materials and ideas, present your findings in class.

2. Some say that dual relationships are inevitable, pervasive, and unavoidable and have the potential to be either beneficial or harmful. Form two teams and debate the core issues. Have one team focus on

the potential benefits of dual relationships and argue that they cannot be dealt with by simple legislative or ethical mandates. Have the other team argue the case that dual relationships are unethical because they have the potential for bringing harm to clients and that there are other and better alternatives.

3. Write a brief journal article on your position on dual relationships in counseling. Take some small aspect of the problem, develop a definite position on the issue, and present your own views.

4. What are your views about forming social relationships with clients during the time they are in counseling with you? after they complete counseling?

5. What guidelines would you employ to determine whether nonerotic touching was therapeutic or countertherapeutic? Would the population you work with make a difference? Would the work setting make a difference? How comfortable are you in both receiving and giving touching? What are your ethical concerns about touching?

6. Take some time to review the ethics codes of the various professional associations as they apply to two areas: (a) dual relationships in general and (b) sexual intimacies with present or former clients. Have several students team up to analyze different ethics codes, make a brief presentation to the class, and then lead a discussion on the code's value.

7. Review the discussion on sexual relationships with former clients. Form two teams and debate the issue of whether sexual and romantic relationships with former clients should be allowed after some period of time has elapsed.

8. Form small groups to explore the core issues involved in some of the cases in this chapter. Role play the cases, and then discuss the implications. Acting out the part of the therapist and the client is bound to enliven the discussion and give you a different perspective on the case. Feel free to embellish on the details given in the cases.

9. Divide the class into a number of small groups, and develop your own case illustrating some ethical dilemma in the general area of dual relationships. Come up with a title for your case, creative names for the therapist and the client, and interesting points that will make the case a good discussion tool. Each group can act out its case in class and lead a general discussion.

Ethics in Action *CD-ROM Exercises*

10. Using segment 3 of the CD-ROM (boundary issues), bring your completed responses to the self-inventory to class for discussion.

11. In video role play 8, The Picnic, the client (Lucia) would like to meet with the counselor (John) at the park down the street for their counseling sessions so she can get to know him better and feel closer to

him. She could bring a lunch for a picnic. John is concerned about creating an environment that would help Lucia the most, and she says, "That (meeting in the park) would really help me."Through role playing, demonstrate how you would establish and maintain boundaries with Lucia if she were your client.

12. In video role play 9, The Friendship, at the last therapy session the client (Charlae) says she would like to continue their relationship because they have so much in common and she has shared things with the counselor (Natalie) that she has not discussed with anyone else. Natalie informs Charlae that this puts her in a difficult situation and she feels awkward. Charlae says, "What if we just go jogging together a couple of mornings a week?" Assume your client would like to meet with you socially and this is the final therapy session. Via role playing, demonstrate how you would handle such a request from a former client who is interested in developing a social relationship with you.

13. In video role play 10, The Disclosure, the counselor (Conrad) shares with the client (Suzanne) that he has been thinking about her a lot and that he is attracted to her. Suzanne responds with, "You are kidding, right?" She says she came to him because she was having problems with men taking advantage of her and not respecting her. She has bared her soul to him, and now she feels devalued. Suzanne suggests possibly seeing another counselor, but Conrad thinks they can work it out. What are your thoughts about the way the counselor (Conrad) shared his feelings with the client? If you were sexually attracted to a client, what course of action would you follow? Role play the way you would deal with a client who disclosed to you that he or she found you "quite attractive." Assume that you also found this client "quite attractive."

14. In video role play 11, The Architect, the client (Janice) lost her job and can no longer pay for counseling sessions. She suggests providing architecture services for work on his house. The counselor (Jerry) suggests they discuss the pros and cons and that he wants to be sure that this is in her best interests. He mentions the code of ethics that discourages bartering. Jerry talks about issues of value and timeliness of services. Put yourself into this scene. Assume your client lost her job and could no longer pay for therapy. She suggests a bartering arrangement for some goods or services you value. Role play how you would deal with her. What issues would you want to explore with your client?

15. In video role play 12, Tickets for Therapy, the client (John) shows his appreciation for his counselor (Marianne) by giving her tickets to the theater. John says, "I got tickets for you so you can go and enjoy it and have a good time."Marianne talks about why she cannot accept the tickets, in spite of the fact that she is very appreciative of his gesture. Put yourself in the counselor's place. What issues would you explore with John? Might you accept the tickets, under any circumstances? Why or why not? Demonstrate, through role playing, what you would say to the client.

Chapter 8

Pre-Chapter Self-Inventory

Directions: For each statement, indicate the response that most closely identifies your beliefs and attitudes. Use the following code:

5 = I *strongly agree* with this statement.

4 = I *agree* with this statement.

3 = I am *undecided* about this statement.

2 = I *disagree* with this statement.

1 = I *strongly disagree* with this statement.

_____ 1. Counselors are ethically bound to refer clients to other therapists when working with them is beyond their professional training.

_____ 2. Ultimately, practitioners create their own ethical standards.

_____ 3. Possession of a license or certificate from a state board of examiners shows that a person has therapeutic skills and is competent to practice psychotherapy.

_____ 4. Professional licensing protects the public by setting minimum standards of preparation for those who are licensed.

_____ 5. The present processes of licensing and certification encourage the self-serving interests of the groups in control instead of protecting the public from incompetent practice.

_____ 6. Continuing education course work should be a requirement for renewal of a license to practice psychotherapy.

_____ 7. It is unethical for counselors to practice without continuing their education.

_____ 8. Institutions that train counselors should select trainees on the basis of both their academic record and the degree to

Professional Competence and Training

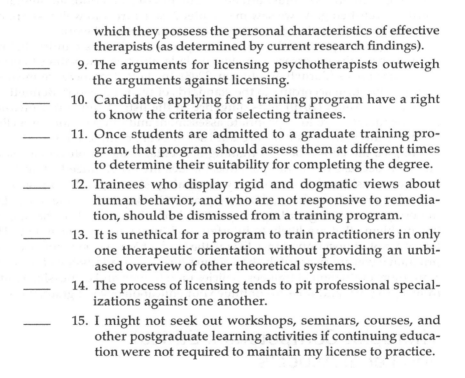

which they possess the personal characteristics of effective therapists (as determined by current research findings).

_____ 9. The arguments for licensing psychotherapists outweigh the arguments against licensing.

_____ 10. Candidates applying for a training program have a right to know the criteria for selecting trainees.

_____ 11. Once students are admitted to a graduate training program, that program should assess them at different times to determine their suitability for completing the degree.

_____ 12. Trainees who display rigid and dogmatic views about human behavior, and who are not responsive to remediation, should be dismissed from a training program.

_____ 13. It is unethical for a program to train practitioners in only one therapeutic orientation without providing an unbiased overview of other theoretical systems.

_____ 14. The process of licensing tends to pit professional specializations against one another.

_____ 15. I might not seek out workshops, seminars, courses, and other postgraduate learning activities if continuing education were not required to maintain my license to practice.

Introduction

In this chapter we focus on the ethical and legal aspects of professional competence and the education and training available for mental health professionals. We discuss issues related to professional licensing and certification as well as approaches to continuing education.

Ability is not an easy matter to assess, but competence is a major concern for mental health professionals. Striving for competence is a lifelong endeavor.

We are called upon to devote the entire span of our careers to developing, achieving, maintaining, and enhancing our competence. Competence at one point in our career does not assure competence at a later time. We must take active steps to maintain our skills. Continuing education is particularly important in emerging areas of practice (Barnett, Doll, et al., 2007; Barnett & Johnson, 2010).

Barnett and Johnson (2010) remind us to consider the scope of our competence. Being competent in one area of counseling does not mean that we are competent in other areas. Practitioners can develop competence both as generalists and as specialists. A generalist is a practitioner who is able to work with a broad range of problems and client populations. A specialist is a worker who has developed competence in a particular area of practice such as career development, addiction counseling, eating disorders, or family therapy. Barnett and Johnson emphasize that to apply our knowledge and skills competently, we must attend to our physical, emotional, mental, and spiritual well-being. As we saw in Chapter 2, self-care and wellness are basic to being able to function competently in our professional work.

Although competence does not imply perfection, it does require that practitioners have the necessary knowledge, skills, abilities, and values to provide effective services (Barnett & Johnson, 2008). In short, "competence means the ability to perform according to the standards of the profession" (Bennett et al., 2006, p. 61). Welfel (2010) adds diligence to the list: "A diligent professional gives deliberate care to appropriate assessment and intervention for a client's problem and maintains that care until services are completed" (p. 84).

We give the education and training of mental health professionals special attention because of the unique ethical issues involved. Indeed, ethical issues must be considered from the very beginning, starting with admission and screening procedures for graduate programs. One key issue is the role of training programs in safeguarding the public when it becomes clear that a trainee has problems that are likely to interfere with professional functioning. These topics are of utmost importance to you, the student. You will get more from your program if you are aware of the basic issues involved in admission of students to a program, evaluation of trainees, policies on retaining and dismissing students from a program, and ways to continue your education beyond graduation.

Therapist Competence: Ethical and Legal Aspects

In this section we examine **therapist competence**, or the skills and training required to effectively and appropriately treat clients in a specific area of practice. We discuss what competence is, how we can assess it, and what some of its ethical and legal dimensions are. We explore these questions: What ethical standards offer guidance in determining competence? What ethical issues are involved in training therapists? To what degree is professional licensing an accurate and valid measure of competence? What are the ethical responsibilities of mental health professionals to continue to upgrade their knowledge and skills?

Ethics Codes

Professional Competence

International Association of Marriage and Family Counselors (2005)

Marriage and family therapists do not attempt to diagnose or treat problems beyond the scope of their training and abilities. They do not engage in specialized counseling interventions or techniques unless they have received appropriate training and preparation in the methods. (C.5.)

American Psychological Association (2002)

Psychologists provide services, teach, and conduct research with populations and in areas only within the boundaries of their competence, based on their education, training, supervised experience, consultation, study, or professional experience. (2.01.a.)

American Psychiatric Association (2009)

A psychiatrist who regularly practices outside his or her area of professional competence should be considered unethical. Determination of professional competence should be made by peer review boards or other appropriate bodies. (2.3.)

American School Counselor Association (2004)

The professional school counselor monitors personal well-being and effectiveness and does not participate in any activity that may lead to inadequate professional services or harm to a student. (E.1.b.)

Feminist Therapy Institute (2000)

A feminist therapist will contract to work with clients and issues within the realm of her competencies. If problems beyond her competencies surface, the feminist therapist utilizes consultation and available resources. She respects the integrity of the relationship by stating the limits of her training and providing the client with the possibilities of continuing with her or changing therapists. (IV.B.)

A feminist therapist recognizes her personal and professional needs and utilizes ongoing self-evaluation, peer support, consultation, supervision, continuing education, and/or personal therapy. She evaluates, maintains, and seeks to improve her competencies, as well as her emotional, physical, mental, and spiritual well-being. When the feminist therapist has experienced a similar stressful or damaging event as her client, she seeks consultation. (IV.C.)

National Association of Social Workers (2008)

Social workers should accept responsibility or employment only on the basis of existing competence or the intention to acquire the necessary competence. (4.01.a.)

Social workers should strive to become and remain proficient in professional practice and the performance of professional functions. Social workers should critically examine and keep current with emerging knowledge relevant to social work. Social workers should routinely review the professional literature and participate in continuing education relevant to social work practice and social work ethics. (4.01.b.)

Canadian Association of Social Workers (1994)

A social worker shall have and maintain competence in the provision of a social work service to a client. (3.)

(*continued on next page*)

The social worker shall not undertake a social work service unless the social worker has the competence to provide the service or the social worker can reasonably acquire the necessary competence without undue delay, risk, or expense to the client. (3.1.)

Canadian Counselling Association (2007)

Counsellors limit their counselling services and practices to those which are within their professional competence by virtue of their education and professional experience, and consistent with any requirements for provincial and national credentials. They refer to other professionals, when the counselling needs of clients exceed their level of competence. (A.3.)

American Counseling Association (2005)

Counselors practice only within the boundaries of their competence, based on their education, training, supervised experience, state and national professional credentials, and appropriate professional experience. Counselors gain knowledge, personal awareness, sensitivity, and skills pertinent to working with a diverse client population. (C.2.a.)

Ethical Standards of the California Association for Alcohol and Drug Educators (CAADE, 2006)

The Certified Addictions Treatment Counselor (C.A.T.C.) shall recognize that the profession is founded on national standards of competency which promote the best interests of society, of the client, of the C.A.T.C., and of the profession as a whole. The C.A.T.C. shall recognize the need for ongoing education and clinical supervision as a component of professional competency. (Principle 3.)

Competence is both an ethical and a legal concept. From an *ethical* perspective, competence is required of practitioners if they are to protect and serve their clients. Even though mental health professionals may not intend to harm clients, lack of competence often is a major contributing factor in causing harm. From a *legal* standpoint, incompetent practitioners are vulnerable to malpractice suits and can be held legally responsible in a court of law (Corey & Herlihy, 2006b).

Perspectives on Competence

We begin this discussion of competence with an overview of specific guidelines from various professional associations. They are summarized in the Ethics Codes box titled "Professional Competence."

These guidelines leave several questions unanswered. What are the boundaries of competence, and how do professionals know when they have exceeded them? How can practitioners determine whether they should accept a client when their experience and training might be questionable? What should be the minimal degree required for entry-level professional counseling? Counselors may need to be both generalists and specialists to be competent to practice with some client populations. Many substance abuse counselors argue that if you are licensed as a generalist, you are not qualified to work in the area of treatment of addictions. To qualify as a substance abuse counselor, the CACREP (2009) standards identify specific knowledge, skills, and practices in the following areas: foundations; counseling, prevention, and intervention; diversity and advocacy; assessment; research and evaluation; and diagnosis.

Questions pertaining to competence become more complex when we consider the criteria used in evaluating competence. In our opinion, assessing competence is an extremely difficult task. What are the criteria for the assessment? How do you measure the competence and objectivity of the assessors? Lichtenberg and colleagues (2007) contend that procedures to assess abilities across specific areas of knowledge, skills and attitudes are not equal. "Psychology does not currently have methods to readily or reliably assess the integration of knowledge, skills, and attitudes in the performance of professional functions that comprise competence" (p. 476). Many people who complete a doctoral program lack the skills or knowledge needed to carry out certain therapeutic tasks. Obviously, a degree or a license alone does not guarantee competence for any and all psychological services. Even with a license, you are not competent to work with all populations. For example, if you work with families, you need specialized knowledge and skills to practice ethically.

When is a therapist ready to practice independently? Is the number of supervised hours a sufficient criterion to evaluate a practitioner's readiness to practice independently? The results of one study indicate that psychology training directors are divided in their opinions of when trainees are competent to practice independently and what constitutes minimal competence (Rodolfa, Ko, & Petersen, 2004).

As mental health professionals, we bear the responsibility of taking adequate steps to ensure that we meet minimal standards of competence. To do so requires that we engage in an ongoing process of self-assessment and self-reflection (Barnett, Doll, et al., 2007) If we are unsure of our ability to provide services in a particular area of counseling practice, it is essential that we consult with colleagues. Barnett and Johnson (2010) point out that none of us can be competent with all client populations and settings, or with all skills and techniques. When it becomes clear that a client's counseling needs exceed our competence, we must either develop the competence necessary to effectively treat the client or refer this client to another professional who possesses the competence to meet this client's counseling needs.

Assessment of Competence

Assessment of competence has received increased attention in the psychological literature. Kaslow and colleagues (2007) suggest that assessment approaches are most effective when they integrate both formative and summative evaluations. **Formative assessment** is a developmentally informed process that provides useful feedback during one's training and throughout one's professional career. **Summative assessment** is an end point evaluation typically completed at the end of a professional program or when applying for licensure status. Together these assessments address an individual practitioner's strengths and provide useful information for developing remedial education plans, if needed, for the person whose competence is being evaluated.

Johnson and colleagues (2008) contend that those who are responsible for educating and training mental health professionals are ethically and professionally obligated to balance their roles as advocate and mentor of trainees with their gatekeeping role. One way to manage these sometimes conflicting roles is to thoroughly and accurately provide routine formative and summative assessment for trainees, carefully document these evaluations, and ensure that multiple professionals give independent evaluations of each trainee. Training faculty are ethically obligated to provide accurate, relevant, and timely feedback for all trainees throughout the program.

As a beginning counselor, if you were to refer all the clients whose problems seemed too difficult for you, it is likely that you would have few clients. You must be able to make an objective and honest assessment of how far you can safely go with clients and recognize when to refer clients to other specialists or when to seek consultations with other professionals. It is not at all unusual for even highly experienced therapists to wonder seriously at times whether they have the personal and professional abilities needed to work with some of their clients. It is more troubling to think of therapists who rarely question their competence. Thus, difficulty working with some clients does not by itself imply incompetence, nor does lack of difficulty imply competence.

One way to develop or upgrade your skills is to work with colleagues or professionals who have more experience, especially when you branch out into new areas of practice. As a general rule, seek consultation before moving outside the areas in which you have received education and training (Bennett et al., 2006). Doll (cited in Barnett, Doll, et al., 2007) believes that practitioners must constantly build competence in new knowledge, skills, and practices, long after they leave their training programs. Doll notes that practitioners typically are the ones who judge their own boundaries of competence as they define the areas of practice they will provide. However, when therapists extend the boundaries of their practice, or when they branch out into an area requiring specialty competence, they should seek consultation with a competent practitioner. "In essence, the judgment of professional competence is a decision that should not be made in isolation, but always incorporate collegial consultation or professional supervision with acknowledged experts" (p. 515).

New skills can be learned by attending conferences and conventions, by reading books and professional journal articles, by taking additional courses in areas you do not know well and in theories that you are not necessarily drawn to, and by participating in workshops that combine didactic work with supervised practice. The feedback you receive can give you an additional resource for evaluating your readiness to undertake certain therapeutic tasks.

Making Referrals

Even if you are competent in a certain area, you still may need to make referrals if the resources are limited in the setting in which you work. For example, a school counselor may make a referral to a mental health professional outside of the school for a student needing individual psychotherapy. If your work setting limits the number of counseling sessions for clients, develop a list of appropriate, qualified referral resources in your area.

The counseling process can be unpredictable at times, and you may encounter situations in which the ethical path is to refer your client. For example, a school counselor was working with Quan, whose presenting problem was anxiety pertaining to academic success in college. This was within the scope of the school counselor's training. However, during the course of therapy, Quan became very depressed and engaged in self-mutilation and other forms of self-destructive behavior. Quan's counselor recognized that these symptoms and behaviors reflected a problem area that was outside the scope of his expertise. Ethical practice required that he make a referral to another professional who was competent to treat Quan's problems.

Possessing the expertise to effectively work with a client's problem is one benchmark, but other circumstances might also make you wonder if a referral is in order. You and a client may decide that a referral is in order because of value conflicts or because the counseling relationship is not productive. The client may want to continue working with another person rather than discontinue counseling. For these and other reasons, you will need to develop a framework for evaluating when to refer a client, and you will need to learn how to make this referral in such a manner that your client will be open to accepting your suggestion rather than being harmed by it. It is of the utmost importance to make skillful referrals when the limits of your competence are reached, ensuring that clients understand the reason for the referral and do not feel rejected or abandoned (Barnett & Johnson, 2008).

Hermann and Herlihy (2006) caution that it is inappropriate and unethical to refer a client on the basis of a client's sexual orientation. Not only is discrimination because of sexual orientation unethical, but doing so could result in the termination of a therapist's job, a complaint to the professional ethics board, and a malpractice suit. We hope you would not see referring a client with whom you have difficulty as a cure-all. Clients can be negatively affected when you refer them too quickly. If you make frequent referrals, you may need to examine your assessment of your competence. In this case, you may need to refer yourself for further help. Consider a referral as a final intervention after you have exhausted other interventions including consulting. Most codes of ethics have a guideline pertaining to conditions for making a referral, for example:

> Social workers should refer clients to other professionals when the other professionals' specialized knowledge or expertise is needed to serve clients fully or when social workers believe that they are not being effective or making reasonable progress with clients and that additional service is required. (NASW, 2008, 2.06.a.)

■ The Case of Helen.

Consider the following exchange between Helen and her counselor. Helen is 45 years old and has seen a counselor at a community mental health center for six sessions. She suffers from periods of depression and frequently talks about how hard it is to wake up to a new day. It is very difficult for Helen to express what she feels, and most of the time she sits silently during the session. The counselor decides that Helen's problems warrant long-term therapy, which he doesn't feel competent to provide. In addition, the center has a policy of referring clients who need long-term treatment to therapists in private practice. The counselor therefore approaches Helen with the suggestion of a referral:

Counselor: Helen, during your intake session I let you know that we are generally expected to limit the number of our sessions to six visits. Since today is our sixth session, I'd like to discuss the matter of referring you to another therapist.

Helen: Well, you did say that the agency generally limits the number of visits to six, but what about exceptions? I mean, I feel as if I've just started with you, and I really don't want to begin all over again with someone I don't know or trust.

Counselor: I can understand that, but you may not have to begin all over again. I could meet with the new therapist to talk about what we've done these past weeks.

Helen: I still don't like the idea at all. I don't know whether I'll see another person if you won't continue with me. Why can't I stay with you?

Counselor: I think you need more intensive therapy than I'm trained to offer you. As I've explained, I'm expected to do only short-term counseling.

Helen: Intensive therapy! Do you think that my problems are that serious?

Counselor: It's not just a question of you having serious problems. I am concerned about your prolonged depressions, and we've talked about my concerns over your suicidal fantasies. I believe it would be in your best interest if you were to see someone who is trained to work with depression.

Helen: I think you've worked well with me. If you won't let me come back, then I'll forget about counseling.

Consider the ethical issues involved in Helen's case by addressing these questions:

- What do you think of the way Helen's counselor approached her? Would you have done anything differently?

- Was the counselor working beyond the scope of his practice, or was Helen not very sophisticated about the process of therapy?
- Is it possible that the counselor was not clear enough regarding the limitation of six visits?
- Would you have waited until the sixth session to remind the client of termination?
- If you were Helen's counselor and you did not think you were competent to treat her, would you agree to continue seeing her if she refused to be referred to someone else? Why or why not?

Commentary.   This exchange reflects a common problem; counselors and clients often have different perspectives on termination and referral issues. It is unethical for this therapist to continue counseling Helen, even though she opposes ending therapy with him. Continued treatment of a client's problem that is beyond the scope of the therapist's competence is a serious violation of the standard of care (Younggren & Gottlieb, 2008).

This counselor would have been wise to suggest a referral before the last session and to reinforce the short-term nature of the help he was qualified to provide. With rare exceptions, a therapist should be able to determine whether he is competent to treat a given client by the end of the initial interview. How the counselor suggests the referral is critical. He should have informed Helen about the limitations of their relationship from the outset. Ultimately, it is the client's choice whether to accept or decline a referral. If this counselor can demonstrate that a referral is in Helen's best interest, there is a greater chance that she will accept the referral.

Ethical Issues in Training Therapists

Training is a basic component of practitioner competence. You will be able to assume an active role in your training program if you have some basic knowledge about policy matters that affect the quality of your education and training. Although providing adequate training is primarily the responsibility of the faculty in your program, you too have a role and a responsibility to ascertain that your training will provide you with the experiences necessary to become a competent practitioner. In this section, our discussion of the central ethical and professional issues in training is organized around questions pertaining to selection of trainees, content of training programs, and best approaches to training.

Selection of Trainees

A core ethical and professional issue involves formulating policies and procedures for selecting appropriate candidates for a training program. Here are some issues to consider:

- What criteria should be used for admission to training programs?
- Should the selection of trainees be based solely on traditional academic standards, or should it take into account factors such as personal characteristics, character, and psychological fitness?
- Is there a good fit between the candidate and the training program?
- To what degree is a candidate for training open to learning and to considering new perspectives?
- Does the candidate have problems that are likely to interfere with training and with the practice of psychotherapy?
- What are some ways to increase applications to programs by diverse groups of candidates?
- How open are training programs to diversity? How open are they to including people who will challenge them as trainers?
- How thorough should an orientation to a program be? What should it include?
- How does a program determine the psychological fitness and character of a candidate?

Training programs have an ethical responsibility to establish clear selection criteria, and candidates have a right to know the nature of these criteria when they apply. Although grade point averages, scores on the Graduate Record Examination (GRE), and letters of recommendation are often considered in the selection process, relying on these measures alone does not provide a comprehensive picture of a candidate.

Personality characteristics, character, and psychological fitness are important variables to consider in selecting applicants. However, "there is currently no consistent approach to screening for character and fitness during graduate school admission; similarly, there is no consistent approach to effectively addressing problems with character and fitness once they are revealed" (Johnson & Campbell, 2002, p. 50). In addition, "no research in psychology demonstrates the efficacy of a screening approach to character and fitness" (Johnson & Campbell, 2004, p. 406). Despite these shortcomings, Johnson and Campbell maintain that being competent requires both moral character and personal psychological fitness. Although character and fitness alone do not ensure competence, Johnson and Campbell point out that their absence greatly increases the risk of both impairment and incompetence. They argue that a lack of psychological fitness threatens to undermine a practitioner's ability to reliably and effectively serve clients.

We think it is important to meet with applicants in some kind of personal or group interview process. We have participated in group screening interviews with candidates applying for a counseling program and found that the group format has some advantages over individual interviews. One of these advantages is being able to observe applicants interacting with others in the group and see how they present their ideas on a range of specific topics.

Although some faculty will protest the time it takes to conduct individual and group interviews as part of the admissions process, it is considerably less time and effort than is expended in dealing with even one problematic student who is admitted and who later faces dismissal from a program for a nonacademic reason.

Many programs ask candidates to write a detailed essay that includes their reasons for wanting to be in the program, their professional goals, an assessment of their personal assets and liabilities, and life experiences that might be useful in their work as counselors. A number of programs have both faculty members and graduate students on the reviewing committee. If many sources are considered and if more than one person makes the decision about whom to select for training, there is less likelihood that people will be screened out on the basis of the personal bias of one individual.

As part of the screening process, ethical practice requires that candidates be given information about what will be expected of them if they enroll in the program. Just as potential therapy clients have a right to informed consent, students applying for a program have a right to know the material they will be expected to learn and the manner in which education and training will take place. In most training programs, students are expected to engage in appropriate self-disclosure and to participate in various self-growth activities. Programs should make sure that applicants understand these requirements. The language in the informed consent document must be unambiguous, and the criteria for successful completion of the program easily understood by all concerned. The Canadian Counselling Association (2007) calls for those in charge of training programs to "take responsibility to orient prospective students and trainees to all core elements of such programs and activities, including to a clear policy with respect to all supervised practice components, both those simulated and real" (F.6.). With this kind of orientation to a program, students are better equipped to decide whether they want to be a part of it.

Screening can be viewed as a two-way process. As faculty screen candidates and make decisions on whom to admit, candidates may also be screening the program to decide if this is right for them.

■ The Case of Leo.

Julius is on a review committee in a graduate counseling program. Leo has taken several introductory courses in the program, and he has just completed an ethics course with Julius. It is clear to this professor that Leo has a rigid approach to human problems, particularly in areas such as interracial marriage, same-sex relationships, and abortion. Over the course of the semester, Leo appeared to be either unwilling or unable to modify his thinking. When challenged by other students in the class about his views, Leo responded by saying that he felt he was in a double bind. His faith gave him very clear guidelines on what is acceptable behavior. At the same time, in this supervision class he is being asked to violate those norms, so he feels that "he is damned if he does, and damned if he doesn't." Nobody offers him a solution. If he refers a future client with whom he has value conflicts he is behaving unethically; if he were to accept such a client, he would be going against his church's teachings. In meeting with the committee charged with determining whether candidates should be advanced in the program, Julius expresses his strong concern about retaining Leo in the program. His colleagues share this concern.

- What reactions do you have to this case? How would you respond to Leo's dilemma?
- Was it made clear to Leo that when he expressed his ideas in his classes they could be held against him? If not, is there an ethical issue in that situation?
- Are any other avenues open in dealing with Leo short of disqualifying him from the program?
- If Leo's values reflected his minority cultural background, would that make a difference? Would the committee be culturally insensitive for rejecting him from the program?
- What if Leo said that when he eventually obtained his license he intended to work exclusively with people from his cultural and religious background? Should he be denied the opportunity to pursue a degree in counseling if his career goal is to work with a specific population that shares his views and values?
- If you were on the committee, how would you handle candidates who seemed to exhibit racism, homophobia, and rigid thinking?

Commentary. Leo's case illustrates the dilemma counselor educators sometimes face when they have serious concerns about trainees who are likely to impose their values on their future clients. Ethically, the client's problems need to be explored and resolved in a way that matches the client's values, not the therapist's values. Although Leo is not seeing clients now, he has the potential to do harm to clients if the rigidity of his value system is not challenged.

Educators and supervisors have several ethical obligations to students and trainees who may be impaired or incompetent. At least one faculty representative should meet with Leo to explore with him how his religious values might affect his work with clients. The faculty should document consistent and clear formative feedback to Leo as well as efforts to encourage remediation or personal development before deciding to dismiss him from the program.

Educators who fail to adequately orient prospective and current students regarding expectations and evaluation procedures heighten the risk of conflicts with ill-informed students (Barnett & Johnson, 2010). Leo should have been clearly oriented to the graduate program's expectations for students, including minimum competencies such as working with culturally different clients and avoiding the imposition of one's own values.

Content of a Program

We hope you ask questions about the content of your own training program and seek ways to become as actively involved as possible in your own learning. What is the content of your training program, and how is it decided? Is the curriculum determined by the preferences of your faculty, or is it based on the needs of your future clients, or both? Some programs are structured around a specific theoretical orientation in two ways: first, by the school itself having a specific orientation, and second, by insisting that students subscribe to one theory at some point in their training. Other programs have a broader content base and are aimed at training generalists who will be able to step into future positions that present evolving challenges. From an ethical perspective, counselor educators and trainers are expected to present varied theoretical positions. Training programs would do well to offer students a variety of therapeutic techniques and strategies that can be applied to a wide range of problems with a diverse clientele.

We recommend that students be exposed to the major contemporary counseling theories and that they be taught to formulate a rationale for the therapeutic techniques they employ. It is a good idea to teach students the strengths and limitations of contemporary counseling theories. Some writers point out the limitations of basing training mainly on these standard counseling models and call for training in alternative theoretical positions that apply to diverse client populations (Sue, Ivey, & Pedersen, 1996). For an overview of the contemporary counseling theories see Corey (2009c), Corsini and Wedding (2008), Ivey et al. (2007), Prochaska and Norcross (2010), and Sharf (2008).

Look at your program and ask how it measures up against these questions:

- Is the curriculum inclusive of many cultures, or is it culturally biased?
- Does the curriculum give central attention to the ethics of professional practice?
- Does your program have a specific course in ethics? Is it enough to hope that ethical issues will be addressed through the supervision process alone?
- What is the proper balance between academic course work and supervised clinical experience?
- What core knowledge is being taught in your training program?

In training programs for various mental health professions, general content areas are part of the core curriculum, which are generally outlined by

CACREP (2009) standards. The following areas are typically required for all students in counseling programs: professional orientation and ethical practice, social and cultural diversity, human growth and development, career development, helping relationships, group work, assessment, and research and program evaluation.

Training programs need to be designed so that students can acquire a thorough understanding of themselves, as well as acquire theoretical knowledge. Ideally, students will be introduced to various content areas, will acquire a range of skills they can utilize in working with diverse clients, will learn how to apply theory to practice through supervised fieldwork experiences, will learn a great deal about themselves personally, and will develop a commitment to acquiring or enhancing personal wellness. A good program does more than impart knowledge and skills essential to the helping process. In a supportive and challenging environment, the program challenges students to examine their attitudes and beliefs, encourages students to build on their life experiences and personal strengths, and provides opportunities for expanding their awareness of self and others. A good training program will infuse in students the importance of self-care and emphasize wellness throughout the program. Although there is some evidence that counselor educators strive to promote a wellness philosophy in students, a study by Roach and Young (2007) indicates that their efforts may not be successful: "Although counselor education students are exposed to many of the concepts of wellness, the means for effectively implementing strategies to educate and evaluate student progress in this area remains vague and largely neglected" (p. 40). Roach and Young recommend that students be taught ways of implementing wellness strategies into their daily lives in a manner similar to the way they are taught to implement techniques into their counseling practice.

Ethics education deserves prominent attention in any program geared to educating and training mental health practitioners. Down's (2003) study suggests that counselor trainees receive inconsistent ethics education. Approximately 30% of the respondents in Down's study report having a separate ethics course. Most of the study's participants received their ethics education through supervision. In their survey investigating ethics education practices in CACREP-approved counselor education programs, Urofsky and Sowa (2004) found that ethics education is combined with legal issues in 39% of the programs; 31% of the programs have a stand alone ethics course; and 11% of the programs report that ethics is infused in various courses in the curriculum. Urofsky and Sowa state that "ethics education is a fairly well-established aspect of the general counselor education curriculum" (p. 44). It is interesting to note that 92% of the responding counselor educators believe that they are adequately prepared to teach an ethics course in the counseling program. Seventy-nine percent of the counselor educators either agree or strongly agree with the statement: "Students feel better able to conduct ethical clinical practice after completing a counseling ethics course" (p. 42).

Although ethics is supposedly incorporated in a number of required courses, seminars, supervision, and practicum and internship experiences, we believe the lack of systematic coverage of ethical issues will hinder students, both as trainees and later as professionals. The topics addressed in this book deserve a separate course as well as infusion throughout all courses and supervised fieldwork experiences.

How Can We Best Train?

Programs geared to educating and training counselors should be built on the foundation of the natural talents and abilities of the students. Ideally, as we have said, counselor educators and supervisors teach students the knowledge and skills they need to work effectively with diverse populations. In our view, one of the best ways to teach students how to effectively relate to a wide range of clients, many of whom will differ from themselves, is for faculty to model healthy interpersonal behavior. It is imperative that counselor educators and supervisors display cohesive relationships among themselves and treat students in a respectful, collegial manner. This is not always the case, however. In some programs the faculty performs somewhat like a dysfunctional family with unaddressed interpersonal conflict, and even hostile behavior. Students are sometimes drawn into these dynamics, being expected to take sides. In an effective program, differences are discussed openly, and there is an atmosphere of genuine respect and acceptance of diversity of perspectives. If a faculty practices the principles they teach, they are demonstrating powerful lessons about interpersonal relating that students can apply to their personal and professional lives.

- What would you do if you found yourself in a program characterized by dysfunctional behavior?
- How would you react to a student who said, "I don't care what they do; I just want to get my degree and get out of here"?
- If you were concerned about the ethics of this program as a student, what actions would be open to you besides quitting?

Effective programs combine academic and personal learning, weave together didactic and experiential approaches, and integrate study and practice. A program structured exclusively around teaching academics does not provide important feedback to students on how they function with clients. In experiential learning and in fieldwork, problem behaviors of trainees will eventually surface and can be ameliorated. Evaluation is an important component of this process, and we turn to this topic next.

Evaluating Knowledge, Skills, and Personal Functioning

As a student in a counselor education program, you have a right to know how you will be evaluated, both academically and personally. If you are aware of the evaluation criteria and procedures, you are in a better position to ask key questions that can influence your degree of satisfaction and your involvement in your educational program.

Evaluation Criteria and Procedures

Every training institution has an ethical responsibility to screen candidates so the public will be protected from incompetent practitioners. Programs clearly have a dual responsibility: to honor their commitment to the students they admit and to protect future consumers who will be served by those who graduate. Just as the criteria for selecting applicants to a program should be clear, the criteria for successful completion and the specifics of the evaluation process need to be spelled out just as clearly and objectively. The criteria for dismissing a student should be equally clear and objective. Academic programs should have written policies that are available to students as part of the orientation to the program.

Students need to know that their knowledge and skills, clinical performance, and interpersonal behaviors will be evaluated at different times during the program. Ongoing evaluation of counselor trainees is crucial to determine whether students are making satisfactory progress in all areas of the training program (Wilkerson, 2006). In addition to assessing knowledge and skills competencies, it is of vital importance to assess *personal* and *interpersonal competencies,* such as the capacity for self-awareness and self-reflection (Orlinsky, Geller, & Norcross, 2005). Consistent with the existing research on psychotherapy outcomes, Orlinsky et al. state that *interpersonal relatedness* is a core aspect of the therapeutic process. They emphasize the *personal* qualities of the therapist, including the therapist's emotional resonance and responsiveness, social perceptiveness, compassion, desire to help, self-understanding, and self-discipline. In our view, possessing personal characteristics such as these lay the foundation for *professional competence.*

We strongly support the standards for performance evaluation of the ACA, NASW, and APA (see the Ethics Codes box titled "Evaluating Student Performance"). In addition to evaluating candidates when they apply to a program, we favor periodic reviews to determine whether trainees should be retained. The CACREP (2009) standard for student evaluations states the following:

> The program faculty conduct a developmental, systematic assessment of each student's progress throughout the program, including consideration of the student's academic performance, professional development, and personal development. . . . If evaluations indicate that a student is not appropriate for the program, faculty members help facilitate the student's transition out of the program and, if possible, into a more appropriate area of study.

Students need feedback on their progress so they can build on their strengths or remediate problem areas. Ideally, trainees will also engage in self-evaluation to determine whether they are "right" for the program and whether the program is suitable for them. The first goal of an evaluation of candidates is to assess progress and correct problems. If shortcomings are sensitively

Ethics Codes

Evaluating Student Performance

American Counseling Association (2005)

Counselors clearly state to students, prior to and throughout the training program, the levels of competency expected, appraisal methods, and timing of evaluations for both didactic and clinical competencies. Counselor educators provide students with on-going performance appraisal and evaluation feedback throughout the training program. (F.9.a.)

National Association of Social Workers (2008)

Social workers who have responsibility for evaluating the performance of others should fulfill such responsibility in a fair and considerate manner and on the basis of clearly stated criteria. (3.03.)

American Psychological Association (2002)

In academic and supervisory relationships, psychologists establish a timely and specific process for providing feedback to students and supervisees. Information regarding the process is provided to the student at the beginning of supervision. (7.06.a.)

Psychologists evaluate students and supervisees on the basis of their actual performance on relevant and established program requirements. (7.06.b.)

pointed out to trainees in a timely way, they can often correct them and continue in the program.

Responsibility of Professional Organizations

The standards for evaluating student performance provided by the various professional organizations are quite general and do not specify what constitutes "incompetent professional performance." For example, it would be helpful if an organization such as CACREP identified the specifics of what constitutes "satisfactory personal and professional development." We believe professional organizations have a key role to play in specifying minimum standards of competence by providing a clear definition of what it means for a candidate to be found unsuitable. This protects both future clients and students who may be facing dismissal from a program. Furthermore, it protects the counseling faculty and administration by having the backing of a professional organization. The absence of such specific guidelines from the professions puts the responsibility solely on faculty to develop these standards. Oftentimes training programs have little power or support when designing criteria and procedures for dismissing students who fail to meet minimum performance standards.

Ideally, we would like to see each professional organization develop specific guidelines pertaining to students' successful completion of a program: NASW for social worker students, AAMFT or IAMFC for students in marital and family therapy programs, APA for students in clinical and counseling psychology, and ACA for students in counselor education programs. Faculty in these respective professional training programs would then have the backing of their professional associations in determining their own specific set of evaluation procedures to be used in making decisions regarding retaining or dismissing students.

Evaluation of Interpersonal Behaviors, Personal Characteristics, and Psychological Fitness

It is essential to evaluate trainees' professional behavior, clinical performance, and psychological fitness to identify those interpersonal behaviors and personality characteristics that are likely to influence trainees' ability to effectively deliver mental health services. It is relatively easy to assess the academic progress of students, but evaluating trainees on the basis of their personal characteristics and psychological fitness is often a challenging task. Interpersonal behaviors of trainees have a direct bearing on their clinical effectiveness, so these factors must be taken into consideration in the evaluation process. Johnson and Campbell (2002) believe that psychology training programs devote only cursory attention to character and fitness criteria for professional psychologists. Johnson and Campbell (2004) define **character** as the honesty and integrity with which a person deals with others. Character includes virtues such as *integrity* (honesty and consistency in behavior), *prudence* (evidence of good judgment), and *caring* (respect and sensitivity to the welfare of others). **Psychological fitness** pertains to the emotional or mental stability necessary to practice safely and effectively. Fitness can be evidenced by the presence of personality adjustment, absence of psychological disorder, and appropriate use of substances. Johnson and colleagues (2008) believe that training faculty "bear a weighty and professional burden to guard entry into the profession and ensure that those who graduate have sufficient character, psychological fitness, and competence to function autonomously" (p. 591).

Johnson and Campbell (2004) found that training directors are very concerned about both character and fitness but that there is a lack of consensus as to what constitutes character and fitness. As they point out, it is easier to identify the absence of character and fitness than it is to confirm their existence. They note that there is no existing research bearing on the practices that programs employ in evaluating character and fitness, either during the application process or during the training itself. The faculty of each training program has a responsibility to develop clear definitions and evaluation criteria for assessing the character and psychological fitness of trainees. Later in this chapter, we address some ways of evaluating students on their psychological fitness.

Scholars across disciplines are engaged in discussions about trainee impairment (Wilkerson, 2006), referring to it variously as problem students; inadequate, unsatisfactory, deficient, substandard behavior; and problematic student behaviors. Elman and Forrest (2007) recommend better terminology and clearer definitions and caution that the term *impairment* overlaps with a specific legal meaning in the Americans With Disabilities Act (ADA), which could create legal risks for programs. They recommend that faculty avoid using the term *impairment* to refer to trainees who are not meeting minimum standards of professional competence and instead refer to such trainees as having *problematic professional competence, professional competence problems,* or *problems with professional competence.* Kress and Protivnak (2009) prefer the term *problematic counseling student behaviors.* They state that "problematic" focuses on student behaviors without labeling the student as incompetent or impaired. Possible problematic behaviors include poor clinical skills; poor interaction with faculty, supervisors, and colleagues; inappropriate self-disclosure with clients; and failure to communicate with clinical supervisors or faculty about needs and concerns.

Sometimes students have personal characteristics or problems that interfere with their ability to function effectively, yet when this is pointed out to them, they may deny the feedback they receive. The helping professions often use *DSM-IV* criteria to classify mental dysfunctions of clients yet show no such clarity in defining the mental, emotional, and personal characteristics required of students entering a training program. A program has an ethical responsibility to take action rather than simply pass on a student with serious academic or personal problems. Students who are manifesting emotional, behavioral, or interpersonal problems could be encouraged to avail themselves of services at the campus counseling center. Elman and Forrest (2004) take the position that training programs need to establish written policies regarding the way that personal psychotherapy might be recommended and required with respect to the remediation of a student's problems.

> Training programs need to reduce their ambivalence about involvement in personal psychotherapy when it is used for remediation. The challenge is to provide developmentally appropriate educational experiences for trainees in a safe learning environment while protecting the public by graduating competent professionals. (p. 129)

Gatekeeper Role of Faculty in Promoting Competence

A key role of clinical training faculty is to promote and facilitate competence and professional behavior of their students. A major problem faced by educators in these training programs is identifying, dealing with, and possibly dismissing students who are not making satisfactory progress toward professional competence (Oliver et al., 2004). The academic faculty in a professional program generally has a **gatekeeper's role,** protecting consumers by identifying and intervening with graduate students who exhibit problematic behaviors (Johnson et al., 2008; Vacha-Haase et al., 2004). Until recently there has been very little examination of problematic student behavior or the evaluation and dismissal of students in professional programs.

With the increased awareness of the damage mental health professionals who do not possess the personal qualities necessary for effective practice can cause, there is an ethical imperative for training faculty to serve as gatekeepers for the profession (Johnson et al., 2008; Lumadue & Duffey, 1999). This gatekeeper role is addressed in the ethics codes of most professional organizations.

Forrest and her colleagues (1999) summarize the ethical obligation of faculty members and clinical supervisors in overseeing trainees' work as follows:

> Ethical standards mandate that educators and trainers: (a) attend to the possibility that their trainees' personal problems might lead to harm of others; (b) make sure that trainees are not harming clients or others under their care; (c) attend to the possibility that trainees may misuse their influence; (d) evaluate whether trainees are performing services responsibly, competently, and ethically; (e) articulate a clear set of professional standards; and (f) evaluate trainees based on these relevant and established requirements. (p. 636)

In their review of the literature, Forrest and colleagues (1999) found these common categories for dismissal: poor academic performance, poor clinical performance, poor interpersonal skills, and unethical behavior. Psychological reasons for dismissal included factors such as emotional instability, personality disorder, psychopathology, and unprofessional demeanor.

Faculty cannot rely on screening procedures during the admissions process alone to identify students who do not have the necessary personality characteristics to become competent clinicians (Kerl et al., 2002). It is essential to operationally define the personality characteristics that are likely to impede a student's ability to practice effectively. In fairness to students, counseling faculty need to develop objective evaluation procedures and processes to communicate to students both their strengths and areas needing improvement with respect to interpersonal behavior and clinical performance. This should begin as early as possible in the program so that a timely intervention might solve the problem and help the student. If a student initiates a legal challenge regarding his or her professional performance, faculty and program administrators must show documentation of the student's lack of competency (Kerl et al., 2002).

Gaubatz and Vera (2002) investigated whether formalized gatekeeping procedures and program-level training standards influence the rates at which problematic trainees are graduated from counseling programs. Their findings indicated that programs with formalized standards and procedures reduce the number of deficient students it graduates. In a later study, Gaubatz and Vera (2006) discovered that "well-designed gatekeeping procedures appear to improve the effectiveness with which [deficient students] are identified and prevented from progressing unremediated into the counseling field" (p. 41). Although Gaubatz and Vera endorse the efforts of individual training programs to address the issue of deficient trainees, they also add that these efforts "should be integrated into the professional standards that guide the field of counselor training as a whole" (p. 41).

■ The Case of a Discouraged Professor.

Prudence was a student at a university with a 48-unit master's degree program in counseling. This core degree and a few additional classes qualified a graduate to apply for the licensed professional counselor examination once the required supervised internship hours were completed. Prudence was identified by the faculty as having a level of affect that indicate a complete lack of empathy. In counseling dyads, group process experiences, and classroom exercises it became clear that Prudence was unable to make empathic connection. Academically, Prudence received good grades; she completed the reading, wrote satisfactory papers, and did well on the examinations. It was in the behavioral dimension—such as reflective listening, being able to establish client rapport, and demonstrating empathic understanding—that her lack of skill was noted.

Prudence progressed through most of the graduate program and entered an intensive group process course, which was a requirement of the program. The professor in this didactic training environment noted Prudence's barriers to building effective counseling relationships and made two or three interventions. These interventions included direct discussion with Prudence as well as referral and recommendation for personal counseling. At the end of the semester, Prudence's behaviors and skills had not improved, and by some measures they had actually deteriorated. The grade for the group process class was the only grade Prudence needed to complete her degree program. After many hours of soul searching, the professor decided that this student should not be allowed to advance because her lack of empathic understanding and her typically bizarre responses in counseling dyads made her, as a potential counseling professional, a risk to others. He gave Prudence a failing grade, which meant that Prudence would not receive her degree without successfully repeating the group process class.

Prudence responded by suing both the professor and the university. An investigation was completed at the university by the academic senate. In addition to the professor and the student, several members of the faculty and many individuals from the group process class were called as witnesses. The senate overruled the professor's grade and awarded a master's degree in counseling to Prudence. Today she is a licensed professional counselor.

Discouraged by the lack of support from the university, the professor reduced his teaching to part time and retired at the first available opportunity. In reflecting on this case, what implications can you draw?

- Was the professor justified in blocking her from a master's degree based on her performance in this one group process course?
- Might Prudence's lack of empathy and connection to others cause potential harm to clients?

- Does Prudence's lack of empathy and connection necessarily imply that she is incompetent?
- What criteria were used to determine her fitness?
- What are your thoughts about the actions taken by the administration?
- Is it the responsibility of professional accrediting agencies to intervene in a situation such as this?
- Did other professors who had noticed Prudence's lack of empathy have an ethical responsibility to address this issue with her earlier in her graduate course work?

Commentary. The gatekeeping function continues to present many challenges to faculty in counseling programs. In addition to possible legal issues, administrative support may be lacking for a program's decision to dismiss a student for nonacademic reasons. The welfare of future clients must be considered when evaluating students who lack competence due to personality issues. Furthermore, students need to know that they will not be endorsed by faculty before a licensing board or for employment if students demonstrate problematic behaviors.

Students should not be allowed to complete a graduate program if they do not successfully remediate personal or interpersonal problems that negatively affect their clinical performance. Prudence was unable to offer the emotional connection that many clients require to profit from therapy. In our view, the professor did the right thing in adhering to both a clear process of feedback and remediation and his obligation to serve as gatekeeper for the profession in protecting the public. When there are conflicts between ethical obligations and institutional policies (e.g., graduating incompetent students), we should make the conflict known to the institution and then stick to our ethical duties. The discouraged professor did this well.

Dismissing Students for Nonacademic Reasons

From our perspective, faculty who are in the business of training counselors should be credited with the ability to have accurate perceptions and observations pertaining to personality characteristics that are counterproductive to becoming effective counselors. When a student has good grades but demonstrates substandard interpersonal behavior, indicating serious unresolved conflicts, action needs to be taken. Dismissal from a program is a measure of last resort. We would hope this option would not be employed unless all other attempts at remediation had failed.

Legal Deterrents to Dismissing Students

Some of the barriers to taking the action of dismissing students from a program include difficulties in giving clear evidence to support the decision to dismiss a student; the lack of adequate procedures in place to support a dismissal decision; concern about the psychological distress for faculty and students; concern about the heightened resistance and defensiveness in the trainee; the potential for receiving criticism from other faculty or supervisors who were not involved in the trainee's remediation; and lack of administrative support (Forrest et al., 1999).

Perhaps the major deterrent to dismissing a student is the fear of legal reprisal by that student. Bernard and Goodyear (2009) have noted that faculty in training programs have traditionally been concerned about their legal standing if they decide to dismiss a student from a program for "nonacademic" reasons. After their review of the literature on evaluating the competence of trainees, Forrest and her colleagues (1999) came to the conclusion that "we are struggling to understand and implement our responsibilities as gatekeepers for professional quality control" (p. 679).

At times, both counselor educators and administrators are reluctant to dismiss students who have interpersonal or clinical skills deficits. This may be especially true if the concerns are about personal characteristics or problematic behavior, even when the faculty is in agreement regarding the lack of suitability of a given student. Some reasons faculty members may be reluctant to assume a gatekeeper function were offered by Brad Johnson (personal communication, April 10, 2009): (1) faculty members are naturally supportive of students and may tend to overlook personality problems or assume that growth will occur; (2) as professors become mentors to students, they frequently have more ambivalence about giving critical feedback; (3) educators and supervisors may not recognize or accept that their roles include a screening or gatekeeping component; and (4) faculty may be very reluctant to render an evaluation that will end a student's career aspirations.

If it can be demonstrated that a program failed to adequately train an individual, the university may be held responsible for the harm the graduate inflicts on clients (Custer, 1994; Kerl et al., 2002). Custer (1994) describes a lawsuit involving a master's level counselor who graduated from Louisiana Tech's College of Education. A female therapy client filed suit against Louisiana Tech, claiming that the program allowed an incompetent practitioner to graduate from the program. The client claimed that her life had been destroyed by incompetent therapy. The claim was that the program itself was inadequate in that it simply did not adequately prepare her counselor. The counselor was named in the malpractice action along with her supervisor and the university. The initial lawsuit was settled in 1994 for $1.7 million. A case such as this makes it clear that specific competency standards for retaining and graduating counseling students are not only useful, but necessary.

Court Cases on Dismissing Students From a Program

Mary Hermann summarized a court case pertaining to dismissing a student for nonacademic reasons (cited in Remley et al., 2002). In *Board of Curators of the University of Missouri v. Horowitz* (1978), the United States Supreme Court considered a case brought by a student who had been dismissed from medical school, in spite of the fact that she had excellent grades. The decision to dismiss the student was based on the faculty's determination that she was deficient in clinical performance and interpersonal relationship skills. Prior to the dismissal, on several occasions, the faculty expressed dissatisfaction with the student's clinical work and informed her that she faced dismissal if she did not exhibit clear improvement. The student continued to receive unsatisfactory evaluations on her clinical work. Prior to the student's dismissal from medical school, she was evaluated by seven independent physicians in the community, all of whom agreed with the medical school professors that her clinical skills were unsatisfactory.

After being dropped from the program, the student filed a lawsuit claiming that her dismissal from medical school violated her constitutional rights. In reviewing the case, the Supreme Court considered that the student had been informed of the faculty's dissatisfaction with her clinical performance, and the student knew that unless she made significant improvement in this area, she would be dismissed from the program. The Court held that the decision to dismiss the student from medical school was based on a careful and deliberate evaluation by the faculty, and thus the student's dismissal was not a violation of her constitutional rights.

The model described for medical students would be an excellent model for counselor education programs to adopt in dealing with a student identified as lacking the necessary qualifications to be an effective helper. Using this model, the problematic student would be evaluated both at the university and in the community, where a number of experienced practitioners would review the findings of the faculty and administration.

In *Shuffer v. Trustees of California State University and Colleges* (1977), a California court addressed a complaint similar to that of the medical student described previously. The student plaintiff was enrolled in a master's degree program in counseling. The faculty determined that Shuffer's work in a practicum was unsatisfactory, and she was required to take a second practicum. The court held that a faculty may require students to complete special requirements as long as the requirements are not arbitrary.

Another case, presented at an ACES conference by Remley and colleagues (2002), illustrates the difficulty of implementing procedures for dismissing students for nonacademic reasons. The university went to great lengths to identify the problem areas and to develop a remediation plan for the student. The faculty offered the student an opportunity to challenge the grade in one class. The decision was made not to advance the student's candidacy. The letter was returned as undeliverable, and a lawsuit was filed against the faculty and the university. The lawsuit was dismissed with prejudice (cannot be refiled) based on an executed confidential settlement agreement.

Systematic Procedures in Evaluation of Student Performance

As mentioned earlier, as a student, you have a right to be clearly informed of the procedures that will be used to evaluate your performance. A key part of the informed consent process involves learning about the policies pertaining to the roles that personal and professional development play in the program. Informed consent requires clear statements about what constitutes ground for concerns, including when and why students may be terminated from a program (Wilkerson, 2006).

Kerl and colleagues (2002) describe the importance of designing systematic procedures for training programs to evaluate students' professional performance. When dismissal from a program is based on interpersonal or clinical incompetence, Kerl and colleagues underscore the importance of sound systematic academic evaluation and adherence to procedural and substantive due process. These authors argue that in counselor education programs the evaluation of students' interpersonal and clinical skills is part of the overall assessment of their academic performance. They conclude that courts have consistently viewed personal characteristics or behaviors as basic to academic performance, which makes this an academic issue. Kerl and colleagues describe an evaluation instrument, *Professional Counseling Performance Evaluation* (PCPE), designed by the counseling faculty at Southwest Texas State University to provide feedback to students on their progress in meeting professional standards and to document deficiencies that are serious enough to result in dismissal from the program.

The PCPE is provided to all students at admission and is discussed during program orientation. The PCPE is completed for each student in every experiential course. Students receive a copy of the evaluation and have an opportunity to discuss their ratings with the faculty member at the end of each course. Kerl and colleagues state that using the PCPE throughout the program has resulted in significantly fewer students finding out about their problematic behavior as they reach the end of their program and significantly fewer dismissals from the program.

Kerl and colleagues describe a legal challenge by a student who was dismissed from the counseling program at Southwest Texas State University. The student exhibited poor impulse and anger control, unethical behavior, and inadequate counseling skills. This student had received three completed PCPE's that identified significant reservations by faculty members regarding the student's professional performance competency. Suggestions for improvement were given to the student at the time each PCPE was shared and discussed with the student. The student failed to follow through with remediation plans and filed suit against the university and the counseling program. Kerl and colleagues describe the outcome of this case:

> The court ruled that the student was provided adequate due process, that the university had the obligation to uphold professional standards, that the university's policies and procedures were enunciated in the graduate catalog and other departmental documents, and that the faculty had followed these procedures. (pp. 330–331)

This court decision identified professional performance competence as an academic concern. The use of the PCPE (along with the clear standards, policies, and procedures developed by the faculty) played a key role in the court's judgment that ruled in favor of the university on all counts (Kerl et al., 2002).

McAdams, Foster, and Ward (2007) and McAdams and Foster (2007) describe their experience and lessons learned from a challenge in federal court when their program dismissed a counseling student on the grounds of deficient professional performance. The student had engaged in unethical behavior during a clinical practicum and then failed to cooperate with a remedial program implemented by the program faculty. Many systematic procedures were implemented prior to making the decision to dismiss the student, who later filed a lawsuit against the counseling program faculty and the university. One of the charges was that the program and the university violated the student's constitutional right to due process. To the credit of this program, the faculty had designed a document detailing specific criteria for systematically evaluating students in their program in their *Professional Performance Review Policy Standards* (PPRP).

A key strength of the program's legal position rested in the steps the faculty took in formally documenting all the remedial actions taken in dealing with the student. In a federal jury trial, the court ruled in favor of the counseling program and the university by upholding the dismissal decision. This court case demonstrates that when counselor trainees are found to be deficient in their professional performance, training programs have a legal obligation to develop a just and fair remedial plan of action (McAdams & Foster, 2007). Although the faculty won the case, there was no sense of victory in the aftermath of a painful and long litigation process that had a huge impact on both the students and the faculty in the program. McAdams, Foster, and Ward (2007) capture the heart of the dilemma that faculty in a training program face in making a dismissal decision:

> When a student's performance necessitates dismissal action, counselor educators are faced with a difficult and seemingly no-win dilemma in responding. They can dismiss the student, thus opening the door for litigation and, given the uncertainty of any court outcome, placing the well-being of their program and institution at considerable risk. Or they can retain the unfit student, thus avoiding litigation, but violating their professional ethics and responsibility to protect the public. (p. 213)

Kress and Protivnak (2009) describe a systematic plan for assisting students in remediating problematic areas. Their professional development plans (PDPs) are detailed contracts that can be used to address problematic student behaviors. PDPs systematically document and address faculty expectations of students; specific behaviors required of students; tasks students need to attend to; and consequences to students if they do not successfully address the specific tasks and engage in the required behaviors. Such concrete, simple, and explicit plans can be integrated into a program's remediation, review, dismissal, and retention policies.

Seattle University's Department of Counseling and School Psychology has developed an excellent form designed to assess students' personal and professional competencies at several junctures in their program. With the permission of the faculty and dean of this program, we are reproducing their assessment form, which is a good model for informing students about expectations of the program and for providing students with regular feedback on both their personal and professional development (see the box titled "Personal and Professional Competencies").

Personal and Professional Competencies

The counseling faculty, Department of Counseling and School Psychology, College of Education, Seattle University, believes that counseling students must be able to demonstrate basic counseling skills and be knowledgeable of a variety of counseling theories. Additionally, they must be able to integrate the learned skills with their own developed philosophical and theoretical constructs. The faculty knows the role of the school counselor, mental health counselor, and post-secondary counselor to be, and, therefore, expects students to meet 18 *Personal and Professional Competencies*. Each student is assessed at candidacy, prior to internship, and at the end of each quarter of the three-quarter internship. Students are aware of the *Personal and Professional Competencies* when they enter the program and know that they will be evaluated as to whether or not they meet these competencies. At the end of internship, the student must have met each competency.

Student _____ Date _____

_____ School _____ Mental Health _____ Post-Secondary _____ Certification-only

_____ On-going/optional _____ Candidacy/required _____ Pre-Internship/required

MC=Meets competency **NM**=Does not meet competency **NO**=Not observed or documented Shaded column=on-going or at candidacy; non-shaded=pre-internship

(*continued on next page*)

A. Counseling Skills and Abilities	MC		NM		NO	
1. The student counselor creates a safe clinical setting with appropriate boundaries regarding such issues as the professional relationship, meeting times and location.						
2. The student counselor listens to the client and conveys the primary elements of the client's story.						
3. The student counselor responds to client feelings, thoughts, and behaviors in a therapeutic manner using appropriate counseling responses.						
4. The student counselor communicates empathy by expressing the perspective of the client, when appropriate.						
5. The student counselor stays in the here and now, when appropriate.						
6. The student counselor is intentional by responding with a clear understanding of the therapeutic purpose.						
B. Professional Responsibility	MC		NM		NO	
7. The student counselor follows professional codes of ethics, the Seattle University Student Honesty Code, civil laws; demonstrates analysis and resolution of ethical issues; and relates to peers, professors, and clients in a manner consistent with professional standards.						
8. The student counselor demonstrates sensitivity to real and ascribed differences of client and counselor roles and manages role differences therapeutically.						
9. The student counselor demonstrates the ability to match appropriate interventions to the presenting clinical profile in a theoretically consistent manner and provides only those services and applies						

	MC	NM	NO
only those techniques for which the student is qualified, or is in the process of being qualified, through education, training, and experience.			
10. The student counselor has a commitment to social justice and demonstrates a respect for individual differences, including those related to age, gender, race, ethnicity, culture, national origin, religion, sexual orientation, disability, language, and socioeconomic status.			
11. The student counselor articulates an understanding of how and when a counselor may take a leadership role.			
12. The student counselor articulates how regional, national, and international issues affect the role of the counselor.			
C. Personal Responsibility	**MC**	**NM**	**NO**
13. The student counselor demonstrates an awareness of the student's own belief systems, values, needs and limitations and the effect of these on personal and professional behavior.			
14. The student counselor demonstrates the ability to receive, integrate, and utilize feedback from peers, faculty, teaching assistants, and supervisors.			
15. The student counselor demonstrates appropriate behavior in and out of the classroom and is dependable regarding assignments, attendance, and deadlines.			
16. The student counselor takes responsibility for personal and professional behavior.			
17. The student has an accurate assessment of personal and professional competencies.			

(*continued on next page*)

18. The student exhibits appropriate levels of self-assurance and confidence.

19. The student counselor expresses thoughts and feelings effectively both orally and in writing.

20. The student counselor demonstrates the ability to manage the stresses of a demanding profession by developing effective coping skills, that include professional and personal support systems.

Comments (refer to specific competency):

Orientation (*to be signed at the new student orientation*)
By signing below, the student is certifying that the student understands: 1) the personal and professional competencies listed above; 2) that the student is expected to meet these competencies; and 3) that the student *may* be evaluated at any time; and *will* be evaluated at candidacy and prior to internship using this document.

Student   Date

Faculty   Date

(copy to student file)
Candidacy (*to be signed at the meeting with the student advisor at candidacy*)
By signing below, the student is certifying that the student has met with the student's advisor and 1) has discussed the student's candidacy status; 2) understands competencies that have not been meet; 2) has a strategy for meeting unmet criteria; 3) and understands that unmet competencies are expected to be met before the student finished the program.

Student   Date

Faculty   Date

Disposition or recommendation:
Pre-Internship (*to be signed at a meeting with the student advisor at the discretion of the student or the advisor prior to internship*)
By signing below, the student is certifying that the student has met with the student's advisor and 1) has discussed the student's pre-internship status; 2) understands competencies that have not been meet; 3) has a strategy for meeting unmet criteria; 4) and understands that unmet competencies are expected to be met before the student finished the program.

Student	Date
Faculty	Date

Disposition or recommendations:
We thank the counseling faculty, Department of Counseling and School Psychology, College of Education, Seattle University, for granting us permission to reproduce the form they use in their program.

Professional Licensing and Credentialing

Most states have established specific requirements of supervised practice beyond the receipt of a master's or doctoral degree for licensing and certification in areas such as clinical social work, clinical or counseling psychology, rehabilitation counseling, mental health counseling, and couples and family therapy. Most licenses are generic in nature, meaning the holder of the license is assumed to have minimal competence in the general practice of counseling or clinical work. In this section we focus on issues pertaining to competence both as a generalist and in an advanced specialization, including basic assumptions of the practice of licensing, arguments for and against licensing and certification for mental health professionals, and the debate over specialty certification.

Purposes of Legislative Regulation of Practice

Sweeney (1995) describes credentialing as an approach to identifying individuals by occupational group, involving at least three methods: registry, certification, and licensure. In its simplest form, **registry** is generally a voluntary listing of individuals who use a title or provide a service. Registration represents the least degree of regulation of practice. Both certification and licensure involve increased measures designed to regulate professional practices.

Although licensing and certification differ in their purposes, they have some features in common. Both require applicants to meet specific requirements in terms of education and training and acceptance from practicing professionals. Both also generally rely on tests to determine which applicants have met the standards and deserve to be granted a credential.

Certification is a voluntary attempt by a group to promote a professional identity. Certification confirms that the practitioner has met a set of minimum standards established by the certification agency. Some types of certification are required for practicing in a certain setting. For example, in most states school counselors must obtain a certificate in order to practice. Although certification gives practitioners the right to use a specific title, it does not ensure quality practice, nor does it govern practice (Hosie, 1995).

Unlike certification, **licensure statutes** determine and govern professional practice. Licensure acts, sometimes called practice acts, specify what the holder of the license can do and what others cannot do (Remley, 1995). Licensure is generally viewed as the most desirable form of legislative regulation of professional practice because it tends to highlight the uniqueness of an occupation and restricts both the use of the title and the practice of an occupation (Sweeney, 1995).

Licensure and certification assure the public that practitioners have completed minimum educational programs, have had a certain number of hours of supervised training, and have gone through some type of evaluation and screening. Licenses and certifications do not, and probably cannot, ensure that practitioners will competently do what their credentials permit them to do. The main advantages of licensure and certification are the protection of the public from grossly unqualified and untrained practitioners and the formal representation to the public that practitioners are part of an established profession.

All states (except California) provide for licensure of professional counselors. The licensure laws specify minimum standards regarding education, experience, and examination. Titles vary by state, but the most common title is Licensed Professional Counselor (LPC). Applicants for licensure must have a master's degree in counseling, and most states require individuals to complete 60 semester hours of graduate study from an accredited program. Applicants for licensure must obtain supervised experience (with a range of 2,000 to 3,000 hours) prior to being licensed. All states require licensed professional counselor applicants to pass a comprehensive examination on counseling practice. For a state-by-state report of licensure requirements for professional counselors, see American Counseling Association (2008).

Most licenses and credentials are generic; that is, they usually do not specify the clients or problems practitioners are competent to work with, nor do they specify the techniques that they are competent to use. A licensed psychologist may possess the expertise needed to work with adults yet lack the training necessary to work with children. The same person may be qualified to do individual psychotherapy yet have neither the experience nor the skills required for family counseling or group therapy. Most licensing regulations do specify that licensees are to engage only in those therapeutic tasks for which they have adequate training, but it is up to the licensee to put this rule into practice. Such a broad definition of practice also applies to many other professions.

Arguments For and Against Professional Licensing and Credentialing

Four main arguments have been put forth in favor of legislation to regulate the delivery of mental health services. The first is that the public is protected by setting minimum standards of service and holding professionals accountable if they do not measure up. This argument contends that the consumer would be harmed by the absence of such standards because incompetent practitioners can cause long-term negative consequences. Second, the regulation of practitioners is designed to protect the public from its ignorance about mental health services. This argument rests on the assumption that the consumer who needs psychological services typically does not know how to choose an appropriate practitioner or how to judge the quality of services received. Most people do not know the basic differences between a licensed professional counselor, a licensed psychologist, a psychiatrist, a licensed clinical social worker, and a licensed marital and family therapist. Third, because insurance companies frequently reimburse clients for the services of licensed practitioners, licensing means that more people can afford mental health care. Fourth, there is the view that licensing allows the profession to define for itself what it will and will not do. In fact, licensure itself is perceived to enhance the profession and is a sign of maturity.

The arguments for licensure revolve around the contention that the consumer's welfare is better safeguarded with legal regulation than without it. Those who challenge this assumption often maintain that licensing is designed more for self-serving purposes than as a protection for consumers. Others are skeptical when it comes to setting up criteria for regulating mental health practitioners. Carl Rogers (1980) maintained that as soon as criteria are set up for certification the profession inevitably becomes frozen in a past image. He noted that there are as many certified charlatans as there are uncertified competent practitioners. Another drawback to licensing, from his viewpoint, is that professionalism builds up a rigid bureaucracy. Merrill (2003) uses the term *licensure anachronisms* to identify these rigid rules and asserts that there is a need for a change in licensure practices. Each state regulates its own standards and practices regarding granting of licenses to psychologists. Interstate reciprocity that would allow a licensed psychologist to practice in a state other than the one that granted the license is rare. Licensing boards claim that their function is to protect the consumer, but Merrill contends that licensing bodies sometimes carry out self-serving and arbitrary actions rather than performing this function.

We have observed that the process of licensing often contributes to professional specializations' pitting themselves against one another. Instead of fostering a collaborative spirit between licensed clinical social workers and licensed marriage and family therapists or between licensed psychologists and licensed professional counselors, the licensing process of each group too often promotes working in the opposite direction. We wonder if the protection of consumers is the main motivation of some licensing boards or whether their motivation may be to limit the number of practitioners. Furthermore, the examinations used to determine competence may have questionable validity. Although we are not opposed to the concept of professional licensing, we do have serious concerns about the criteria and the processes that often are used to determine who is competent to practice and the manner in which candidates are assessed. Regardless of one's personal views about credentialing and licensure, mental health practitioners do have an ethical obligation to ensure their own competence.

Continuing Professional Education and Demonstration of Competence

Professionals are required to engage in ongoing study, education, training, and consultation in their areas of practice. A practitioner's level of competence can diminish over time, which is a rationale for continuing education. Bennett et al. (2006) refer to the failure to maintain one's competence as "practitioner decay." Although some therapists may have been competent when they began to practice, Bennett and colleagues report "some evidence consistent with the theory that the skills of some practitioners fall behind acceptable standards over time" (p. 66). Professionals need to be committed to doing what is necessary to maintain their competence; continuing professional education is one route toward attaining this goal.

Ethics Codes

Continuing Professional Education Requirements

American Counseling Association (2005)

Counselors recognize the need for continuing education to acquire and maintain a reasonable level of awareness of current scientific and professional information in their fields of activity. They take steps to maintain competence in the skills they use, are open to new procedures, and keep current with the diverse populations and specific populations with whom they work. (C.2.f.)

American Psychological Association (2002)

Psychologists planning to provide services, teach, or conduct research involving populations, areas, techniques, or technologies new to them undertake relevant education, training, supervised experience, consultation, or study. (2.01.c.)

National Association of Social Workers (2008)

Social work administrators and supervisors should take reasonable steps to provide or arrange for continuing education and staff development for all staff for whom they are responsible. Continuing education and staff development should address current knowledge and emerging developments related to social work practice and ethics. (3.08.)

American Association for Marriage and Family Therapy (2001)

Marriage and family therapists pursue knowledge of new developments and maintain competence in marriage and family therapy through education, training, or supervised experience. (3.1.)

American Psychiatric Association (2009)

Psychiatrists are responsible for their own continuing education and should be mindful of the fact that theirs must be a lifetime of learning. (5.1.)

Most professional organizations support efforts to make continuing professional education a mandatory condition of relicensing (see the Ethics Codes box titled "Continuing Professional Education Requirements").

Most mental health professionals are required to demonstrate, as a basis for relicensure or recertification, that they have completed a minimal number of continuing education activities. As a condition for relicensure as a social worker, psychologist, or a marriage and family therapist, most states now require specific courses and a minimum number of hours of continuing professional education. Many states now require practitioners to complete a 6-hour course in ethics and the law as part of the continuing education for every license renewal period.

Individual practitioners have an ethical responsibility to seek out ways to keep current with new developments in their field, and administrators of mental health agencies also have responsibilities to provide continuing professional education activities for the staff. Some of these activities can take the form of in-service workshops and training at the agency site; other activities will require therapists to go outside the agency.

Johnson, Brems, Warner, and Roberts (2006) conducted a survey of mental health counselors and psychologists regarding their needs for continuing professional education in ethics. The participants gave high rankings to topic areas of ethical management of clients with special needs, especially in these areas: clients with substance abuse or other addiction problems; clients from diverse cultural backgrounds; clients dealing with terminal illness; and clients with stigmatizing problems or illnesses. Respondents found other topics useful in assisting them in their practice, such as the identification and discussion of clinical mistakes, dealing with professional misconduct of colleagues, and dealing with impaired colleagues. Johnson and colleagues conclude that continuing education efforts are effective, in general, and in promoting ethical awareness, in particular, for licensed mental health professionals. They conclude that continuing professional education can serve mental health professionals by helping ensure that they maintain the knowledge and awareness to avoid potential ethical pitfalls. Continuing education also serves consumers well by helping ensure that they receive up-to-date and ethical care.

A Lifelong Commitment to Maintaining Competence

To assume that our skills never deteriorate or that we know everything we need to know upon graduation is naive. If we rarely or never seek continuing professional education, how do we justify this lack of initiative? One of the best ways to maintain competence is to engage in regular consultation with other professionals throughout your career (Bennett et al., 2006). Learning never ceases; new clients present new challenges. New areas of knowledge and practice demand ongoing education. Even recent graduates may have significant gaps in their education that will require them to take workshops or courses in the future. You may also need to seek supervision and consultation in working with various client populations or to acquire skills in certain therapeutic modalities. For example, your job may require you to conduct groups, yet your program may not have included even one group course in the curriculum. When continuing education is tailored to your personal and professional needs, it can keep you on the cutting edge of your profession.

Consider the following case of a therapist who believes that competence can be attained once and for all.

■ The Case of Conrad Hadanuf.

Dr. Conrad Hadanuf has been a licensed psychologist for 20 years and has always maintained a busy practice. He sees a wide variety of clients. As a condition of license renewal, he is required to attend a 15-hour retraining program on substance abuse. He is indignant. "I have a PhD, I have 3,000 hours of supervised experience, and I have years of experience with all sorts of problems," he says. "This is just a money-making gimmick for those who want to generate workshops!" Knowing that he has no choice if he wants to retain his license, Conrad grudgingly attends the workshop, sits in the back of the room, takes no notes, takes longer breaks than scheduled, and leaves as soon as the certificates of attendance are available.

- What are your reactions to Conrad's statements? Is his rationale for not wanting to participate in the workshops reasonable and justified?
- Although Conrad might claim that he has no desire to deal with substance abuse, can he realistically say that he will never be confronted with clients with substance abuse problems?
- How do you view mandated continuing education as a condition for license renewal?
- Are practitioners being ethically responsible to their clients if they never actively participate in the required continuing education courses?

Commentary. Although Dr. Hadanuf may satisfy the legal licensure requirement in this case, he is certainly violating the spirit of the APA ethics code, which requires psychologists to undertake ongoing efforts to develop and maintain their competence. This counselor's attitude is an example of why continuing education should be required—it is precisely for those who think they do not need it. He may actually learn something by attending workshops as well as meeting people in his field.

This case reminds us of Sidney Jourard's comments about lifelong learning for mental health professionals. Jourard (1968) warns about the delusion that one has nothing new to learn. He maintains that relevant workshops or contact with challenging colleagues can keep therapists growing. He urges professionals to find colleagues whom they can trust so that they can avoid becoming "smug, pompous, fatbottomed and convinced that they have the word. [Such colleagues can] prod one out of such smug pomposity, and invite one back to the task" (p. 69).

Clarifying your stance.   It is important to find ways to maintain and enhance your competence over the course of your career. Use the following questions to clarify your thinking on the issues we have raised. What is your own strategy for remaining professionally competent?

- What effects on individual practitioners do you think the trend toward increased accountability is likely to have? How might this trend affect you?

- Do you think it is ethical to continue practicing if you do not continue your education? Why or why not?

- What is the rationale for stating that maintaining competence as a lifelong endeavor?

- What are some advantages and disadvantages to using continuing education programs solely as the basis for renewing a license? Is continuing education enough? Explain.

- What are your reactions to competence examinations (oral and written) for entry-level applicants and as a basis for license renewal? What kinds of examinations might be useful?

- Should evidence of continuing education be required (or simply strongly recommended) as a basis for recertification or relicensure?

- If you support mandatory continuing education, who should determine the nature of this education? What standards could be used in making this determination?

- What kinds of continuing education would you want for yourself? Through what means do you think you can best acquire new skills and keep abreast of advances in your field?

Review, Consultation, and Supervision by Peers

Peer review is an organized system by which practitioners within a profession assess one another's services. Peer review provides some assurance to consumers that they will receive competent services. In addition to providing peer review, colleagues can challenge each other to adopt a fresh perspective on problems they encounter in their practice. Regarded as a means rather than an end in itself, peer review has as its ultimate goal not only to determine whether a practitioner's professional activity is adequate, but also to ensure that future services will be up to standard. Peer review continues a tradition of self-regulation.

Borders (1991) describes the value of structured peer groups that foster the development of skills, conceptual growth, participation, instructive feedback, and self-monitoring. Peer-supervision groups are useful for counselors at all levels of experience. For trainees, peer groups offer a supportive atmosphere and help them learn that they are not alone with their concerns. For counselors in practice, they provide an opportunity for continued professional growth. Counselman and Weber (2004) contend that peer-supervision groups are valuable for therapists for many reasons, some of which include ongoing consultation and support for difficult cases, networking, and combating professional isolation and potential burnout. Clinicians often recognize a renewed need for supervision at a later point in their careers because they want additional training, because of the emotional intensity of practicing therapy, or because of the stress associated with their professional work. Counselman and Weber cite a number of advantages of group supervision over individual supervision, making this a useful approach to consultation.

Consider your own stance as you answer these questions about peer review and peer consultation:

- Can you think of both advantages and disadvantages to basing license renewal strictly on peer-review procedures?
- Who determines the qualifications of the peer reviewer? What criteria should be used to determine the effectiveness of counseling practice?
- What are your thoughts about a peer-consultation group for yourself? If you would like to be involved in such a group, how might you take the initiative to form one?

Some final thoughts.   Before closing this discussion of competence, we want to mention the problem of rarely allowing yourself to experience any self-doubt and being convinced that you can handle any therapeutic situation. We support the view that supervision is a useful tool throughout one's career. We also see the development of competence as an ongoing process, not a goal that counselors ever finally attain. This process involves a willingness to continually question whether you are doing your work as well as you might and to search for ways of becoming a more effective person and therapist.

Chapter Summary

The welfare of clients is directly affected by ethical issues in the training of therapists and in the debate over whether professional licensure and credentialing are adequate measures of competence. Counselors must acquire new knowledge and skills throughout their professional career. This is particularly true for practitioners wishing to develop a specialty area dealing with certain client populations or problems.

A core ethical and professional issue in training involves the question of how to develop policies and procedures for selecting the candidates who are best suited for the various mental health professions. The challenge is to adopt criteria for choosing people who have the life experiences that will enable them to understand the diverse range of clients with whom they will work. The personal characteristics of trainees, such as attitudes, beliefs, character, and psychological fitness, are critical to success. The ability of trainees to effectively relate to others, including clients, must be assessed throughout the program, and remedial work for students with interpersonal competence problems should be addressed by faculty. The evaluation process encompasses knowledge, skills, and interpersonal relationship dimensions. Training programs have an ethical responsibility to intervene when students have major personal and interpersonal problems that interfere with their professional competence.

Suggested Activities

1. Invite several practicing counselors to talk to your class about the ethical and legal issues they encounter in their work. You might have a panel of practitioners who work in several different settings and with different kinds of clients.

2. In small groups explore the topic of when and how you might make a referral. Role play a referral, with one student playing the client and another the counselor. After a few minutes the "client" and the other students can give the "counselor" feedback on how he or she handled the situation.

3. In small groups explore what you think the criteria should be for determining whether a therapist is competent. Make up a list of specific criteria, and share it with the rest of the class. Are you able as a class to come up with some common criteria for determining competence?

4. Several students can look up the requirements for licensure or certification of the major mental health specializations in your state. What are some of the common elements? Present your findings to the class.

5. Work out a proposal for a continuing education program as a small group activity. Develop a realistic model to ensure competency for professionals once they have been granted a license. What kind of design most appeals to you? a peer-review model? competency examinations? taking courses? other ideas?

6. Assume that you are applying for a job or writing a résumé to use in private practice. Write your own professional disclosure statement in a page or two. Bring your disclosure statements to class and have fellow students review what you have written. They can then interview you,

and you can get some practice in talking with "prospective clients." This exercise can help you clarify your own position and give you valuable practice for job interviews.

7. As a class project several students can form a committee to investigate some of the major local and state laws that apply to the practice of psychotherapy. You might want to ask mental health professionals what major conflicts they have experienced between the law and their professional practice.

8. Form a panel to discuss procedures for selecting appropriate applicants for your training program. Your task as a group is to identify specific criteria for candidates. Consider these questions: In addition to grade point averages, scores on the Graduate Record Examination, and letters of recommendation, what other procedures and criteria might you establish? Would you recommend individual interviews? interviews conducted in small groups? What life experiences would your group look for? What personal qualities are essential? What attitudes, values, and beliefs would be congruent with becoming a counseling professional? What personal characteristics, if any, would you use as a basis for rejecting an applicant? What process should the program use in making selections?

9. Assume that you are a graduate student who is part of the interviewing team for applicants for your training program. Identify six questions to pose to all applicants. What are you hoping to learn about the applicants from your questions?

10. Interview professors or practitioners in schools, agencies, or work settings that interest you. Ask them what they most remember about their training programs. What features were most useful for them? What training do they wish they had more of and wish they had less of? How adequately did their graduate program prepare them for the work they are now doing? What continuing education experiences did they most value?

11. Have several students role play a licensing board to interview candidates for a professional license. Make up a list of questions to pose to the examinees. Several students in the class can volunteer to sit for the interview. This role play can be repeated.

12. Consider the advantages of forming a peer-support group within one of your own classes. Several of you could make a commitment to meet to explore ways to get the most from your training and education. The group could also study together and exchange ideas for future opportunities.

Ethics in Action *CD-ROM Exercises*

13. Reflect on all of the role-playing situations enacted in the *Ethics in Action* CD-ROM. Putting yourself in the place of the counselor, can you

think of any situations in which you would determine that a referral is in the best interests of your client? Consider situations such as sharp value differences between you and your client, a lack of multicultural competence in a particular case, a client to whom you were sexually attracted, or a client who cannot pay you because of losing employment. Select an area where you could envision yourself making a referral and role play this with another student as the client. Assume that your client does not want to accept the referral and insists on remaining with you.

Pre-Chapter Self-Inventory

Directions: For each statement, indicate the response that most closely identifies your beliefs and attitudes. Use the following code:

5 = I *strongly agree* with this statement.

4 = I *agree* with this statement.

3 = I am *undecided* about this statement.

2 = I *disagree* with this statement.

1 = I *strongly disagree* with this statement.

_____ 1. If I am qualified to practice individual therapy, I can effectively conduct group therapy.

_____ 2. Ethical practice requires that prospective group members be carefully screened and selected.

_____ 3. It is important to prepare members so that they can derive the maximum benefit from the group.

_____ 4. Requiring people to participate in a therapy group raises special ethical issues.

_____ 5. It is unethical to allow a group to exert pressure on one of its members.

_____ 6. Confidentiality is less important in groups than it is in individual therapy.

_____ 7. Socializing among group members is almost always undesirable.

_____ 8. One way of minimizing psychological risks to group participants is to negotiate contracts with the members.

Ethical Issues
in Group Work

_____ 9. A group leader has a responsibility to teach members how to translate what they have learned in the group to their outside lives.

_____ 10. It is unethical for counselor educators to lead groups of their students in training.

_____ 11. Group psychotherapy cannot be conducted in an ethical manner over the Internet except in very limited circumstances.

_____ 12. It is the group leader's responsibility to make prospective members aware of their rights and responsibilities and to demystify the process of a group.

_____ 13. Group members should know that they have the right to leave the group at any time.

_____ 14. Before people enter a group, it is the leader's responsibility to discuss the personal risks involved, especially potential life changes, and help them explore their readiness to face these risks.

_____ 15. It is a sound practice to provide written ethical guidelines to group members in advance and discuss them in the first meeting.

Introduction

We are giving group work special attention, as we did with couples and family therapy, because it raises unique ethical concerns. Groups have been increasing in popularity, and in many agencies and institutions they are the primary form of treatment. Along with this increased use of groups has come a rising ethical awareness. Practitioners who work with groups face a variety of ethical quandaries that differ from those encountered in individual therapy.

In tracing the research trends in group counseling and psychotherapy, Barlow, Fuhriman, and Burlingame (2004) state that a set of recognizable factors—such as skilled leaders, appropriately referred group members, and defined goals—have been shown to create positive outcomes in groups. They conclude that group approaches can ameliorate a number of social ills. A survey of more than 40 years of research shows an abundance of evidence that group approaches are associated with clients' improvement in a variety of settings and situations (Barlow et al., 2004; Burlingame, Fuhriman, & Johnson, 2004).

Barlow (2008) reports that group therapy is being utilized increasingly in many settings and adds that groups are no longer viewed as a second-choice form of treatment. Instead, group therapy is seen as "a potent force for change in the world of mental health, global politics, ethnic strife, and more" (p. 241). Barlow cites studies that have demonstrated group therapy to be as effective as individual treatment and, in some cases, more effective. Practitioners need to be able to assess whether clients are better served by being in a group rather than being in individual therapy. Practitioners should know about the availability of groups and the suitability of a group for a particular client.

Our illustrations of important ethical considerations in this chapter are drawn from a broad spectrum of groups, including therapy groups, counseling groups, personal-growth groups, and psychoeducational groups. Obviously, these groups differ with respect to their member population, purpose, focus, and procedures, as well as in the level of training required for the facilitators of these groups. Although these distinctions are important, all groups face some common ethical concerns: training group leaders, co-leadership issues, the ethical issues surrounding group membership, confidentiality in groups, values, uses of group techniques, and issues concerning consultation, referral, termination, and follow-up. These ethical issues are the subject of this chapter.

Ethical Issues in Training and Supervision of Group Leaders

For competent group leaders to emerge, training programs must make group work a priority. Such is not always the case, and some graduate training programs do not require even one group course. Other training programs offer a sequence of two or three courses in group work, but most have only one group course (Wilson, Rapin, & Haley-Banez, 2004). Most group courses include both the didactic and experiential aspects of group process.

With proper training in group work, competent practitioners will discover their limitations and recognize the kinds of groups they are competent to lead. Ethical practitioners familiarize themselves with referral resources and refrain from working with client populations that need special assistance beyond their level of competence. The American Group Psychotherapy Association (AGPA, 2002) has this guideline pertaining to competence:

> The group psychotherapist must be aware of his/her own individual competencies, and when the needs of the patient/client are beyond the competencies of the psychotherapist, consultation must be sought from other qualified professionals or other appropriate sources. (3.1.)

In addition, group workers must remain current and increase their knowledge and skills through activities such as continuing education, supervision, and participation in various personal and professional development activities (ASGW, 2008).

Specialized training is essential for practitioners to become competent group facilitators (Markus & King, 2003). When it comes to training doctoral level psychologists, comprehensive training standards have not been universally and rigorously followed. In a survey of group psychotherapy training during predoctoral psychology internships, Markus and King found that, much like graduate school programs, predoctoral clinical psychology internships do not routinely provide adequate group therapy training. The results of this survey suggest that there is a lack of depth and breadth of group therapy didactic offerings to psychology interns.

Barlow (2008) maintains that groups can be used effectively for both prevention and education. "Through ever-growing research and continuing improvements in clinical application, groups remain a powerful intervention tool across the life span, positively impacting childhood, adult, and geriatric disorders" (p. 244). Barlow emphasizes the importance of adequate training for practitioners who are interested in conducting groups so that they can effectively and ethically maximize the unique group properties in their work.

Professional Training Standards*

The ASGW (2000) "Professional Standards for the Training of Group Workers" specifies two levels of competencies and related training. First is a set of *core knowledge* and *skill competencies* that provide the foundation on which *specialized* training is built. At a minimum, one group course should be included in a training program, and it should be structured to help students acquire the basic knowledge and skills needed to facilitate a group. These group skills are best mastered through supervised practice, which should include a minimum of 10 hours (with 20 hours recommended) of observation and participation in a group experience. Specific course experiences can be developed from the knowledge and skill objectives delineated for these areas: nature and scope of practice; assessment of group members; planning group interventions with

*Adapted from "Professional Standards for the Training of Group Workers," adopted January 22, 2000, in *The Group Worker: Association for Specialists in Group Work, 29*(3), (Spring 2000), 1–10. The ASGW is a division of the American Counseling Association, 5999 Stevenson Avenue, Alexandria, VA 22304.

emphasis on environmental contexts and the implication of diversity; implementation of specific group interventions; co-leadership practices; evaluation of process and outcomes; and ethical practice, best practice, and diversity-competent practice (Wilson et al., 2004).

Once counselor trainees have mastered these core knowledge and skills domains, they can acquire training in group work specializations in one or more of these four areas: (1) task groups, (2) psychoeducational groups, (3) group counseling, and (4) group psychotherapy. The ASGW (2000) standards detail specific knowledge and skills competencies for these specialties and recommend the number of hours of supervised training necessary for each.

Our Views on the Ethical Training of Group Workers

Professional codes, legislative mandates, and institutional policies alone will not assure competent group leadership. Group counselor trainees need to confront the typical ethical dilemmas they will face in practice and learn ways to clarify their views on these issues. This can best be done by including ethics in the trainees' academic program as well as discussing ethical issues that grow out of the students' experiences in practicum, internship, and field-work. One effective way to teach ethical decision making is by presenting trainees with case vignettes of typical problems that occur in group situations and encouraging discussion of the ethical issues and pertinent guidelines. We tell both students and professionals who attend our workshops that they will not always have the answers to dilemmas they encounter in their groups. Ethical decision making is an ongoing process that takes on new forms and increased meaning as practitioners gain experience. Group leaders need to be receptive to self-examination and to questioning the professionalism of their group practice if they hope to become competent, ethical group practitioners. Brabender (2006) describes the ethical group leader as "an individual in possession of ethical and legal knowledge, technical skills, and personal qualities predisposing him or her to strive to achieve moral excellence in his or her group psychotherapy practice" (p. 411).

In addition to learning about ethical decision making regarding dilemmas encountered in group work, we highly recommend three other experiences as adjuncts to a training program for group workers: (1) personal experience in a self-exploration group; (2) personal (individual) psychotherapy; and (3) supervision.

Self-exploration groups.   Group leaders need to demonstrate the willingness to do for themselves what they expect members in their groups to do: Expand their awareness of self and the effect of that self on others. As an adjunct to formal course work and internship training, participation in a therapeutic group is extremely valuable. One of the best ways to learn how to assist group members in their struggles is to be a member of a group yourself. If a self-exploration group or personal therapy is a program requirement, it is ethically imperative that students are made aware of this requirement at an orientation meeting during the admission process or prior to the time they enroll in a program.

Personal psychotherapy. Sometimes issues surface in a group experience that may be more appropriately dealt with in personal (individual) therapy. We also encourage individual therapy as a way of enhancing trainees' abilities to understand both themselves and others, which is essential for ethical practice. Yalom (2005) believes that extensive self-exploration is necessary if trainees are to perceive countertransference feelings, recognize blind spots and biases, and use their personal attributes effectively in groups.

Supervision. Markus and King (2003) maintain that comprehensive training must include intensive supervision by a competent group therapist. Although Markus and King endorse group supervision of group leader trainees as a powerful cognitive and emotional learning experience, they report that the majority of internships that provide supervision of group trainees tend to use the one-to-one model rather than offer opportunities for group supervision.

Group supervision with group counselors provides trainees with many experiential opportunities to learn about the process and development of a group. In their investigation of group supervision with group counselors, Christensen and Kline (2000) emphasize that supervisees have many opportunities to learn through both participation and observation. Their investigation lent support to the numerous benefits of group supervision, a few of which include enhancement of knowledge and skills; ability to practice techniques in a safe and supportive environment; integration of theory and practice; richer understanding of patterns of group dynamics; opportunities to test one's assumptions; personal development through connection with others; and opportunities for self-disclosure and for giving and receiving feedback. Group supervision creates the foundation for future ethical practice.

Workshops that provide supervision for group trainees help them to develop the skills necessary for effective and ethical intervention. Also, this format helps interns learn a great deal about their response to criticism, competitiveness, need for approval, concern over being competent, and power struggles. In working with both university students learning about group approaches and professionals who want to upgrade their skills, we often use a five-day intensive workshop, which we find to be very effective.

As you consider some of the ethical issues in the training of group leaders, reflect on these questions for yourself:

- What makes you qualified to lead groups?
- Can you think of safeguards to minimize the potential risks of combining experiential and didactic methods?
- Does ethical practice demand that group leaders receive some personal therapy? Should this be group therapy or experience in a personal-growth group?
- What are your reactions to the suggestions we offered for training group workers?

Ethical Issues in the Diversity Training of Group Workers

The U.S. population is increasingly diverse, so it is essential that group counselors become diversity-competent practitioners (Bemak & Chung, 2004). An integral part of the training of group leaders is promoting sensitivity and competence in addressing diversity in all forms of group work. According to Debiak (2007), the importance of multicultural competence for group psychotherapists has emerged as an ethical imperative. To fail to address diversity issues that arise in a group is to fail the members. Attending to and addressing diversity is an ethical mandate, but this practice is also a route to more effective group work. We agree with Debiak's contention that it is the responsibility of training programs to create safe opportunities for a trainee's cultural self-explorations.

The "Principles for Diversity Competent Group Workers" (ASGW, 1999), and the "Best Practice Standards" (ASGW, 2008) address issues such as race, class, gender, sexual orientation, and ability. These principles emphasize the acquisition of awareness, knowledge, and skills that will equip group leaders to work ethically and effectively with the diversity within their groups. Trainees in group work need to be exposed to both courses and experiential practice so that diversity themes become an integral part of their way of thinking and practicing.

Social justice is a dynamic issue that inevitably surfaces when people from diverse backgrounds participate in a group, and group practitioners have an opportunity to transform the group experience rather than perpetuating racism, classism, sexism, and heterosexism (MacNair-Semands, 2007). The group leader should work toward healing experiences rather than allowing potentially harmful interactions to occur. Group leaders can challenge group members to expand their perspectives to understand nuances in the interactions of culturally diverse members.

As you recall from Chapter 4, most of the ethics codes of the various professional organizations now give increasing attention to applying cultural perspectives when working with diverse client populations. Guidelines for competence in diversity issues in group practice are discussed in a variety of sources, some of which include ASGW (1999, 2008), APA (1993), Bemak and Chung (2004), and DeLucia-Waack and Donigian (2004). Based on these sources, we have adapted the following ethical guidelines for group practice:

- Group counselors emphasize appreciation, respect, and acceptance in cultural and racial identity for all cultures.
- Group counselors strive to understand how their cultural background interrelates with people from other cultural backgrounds.
- Group counselors consider the impact of adverse social, environmental, and political factors in assessing problems and designing interventions.

- Group counselors acquire the knowledge and skills necessary for effectively working with the diverse range of members in their groups. They seek consultation, supervision, and further education to fill any gaps and remain current.

- Group counselors are aware of problems involved in stereotyping and avoid making the erroneous assumption that there are no differences between group members from the same ethnic, racial, or other group.

- Group counselors respect the roles of family and community hierarchies within a client's culture.

- Group counselors assist members in determining those instances when their difficulties stem from others' racism or bias, so they do not inappropriately personalize problems.

- Group counselors inform members about basic values that are implicit in the group process (such as self-disclosure, reflecting on one's life, and taking risks).

If group counselors do not understand how their own cultural background influences their own thinking and behavior, there is little chance they can understand how their group members are influenced by their cultural thinking and behavior. The characteristics of the culturally competent counselor discussed in Chapter 4 are equally relevant for practitioners who work with groups. The ASGW (2008) guidelines provide general guidance for acquiring awareness of and sensitivity to client differences in groups:

> Group Workers practice with broad sensitivity to client differences including but not limited to ethnic, gender, religious, sexual, psychological maturity, economic class, family history, physical characteristics or limitations, and geographic location. Group Workers continuously seek information regarding the cultural issues of the diverse population with whom they are working both by interaction with participants and from using outside resources. (B.8.)

In addition, social justice and advocacy competencies are basic for group workers who practice ethically and responsibly. Although it is not realistic to assume that leaders will have knowledge about every culture, it is important that counselors understand that each person participates in a group from his or her own unique perspective (DeLucia-Waack & Donigian, 2004). For a more detailed treatment of diversity issues in group work, see DeLucia-Waack and Donigian (2004), *The Practice of Multicultural Group Work: Visions and Perspectives From the Field.* For a description of social justice and advocacy competencies that can be applied to group work, see *ACA Advocacy Competencies: A Social Justice Framework for Counselors* (Ratts, Toporek, & Lewis, 2010).

As you read the following case, consider how you could increase your own sensitivity to individuals from cultural groups different from your own.

■ The Case of John.

John comes from a lower-middle-class neighborhood in an eastern city, has struggled to get a college degree, and has finally attained a master's degree in counseling. He is proud of his accomplishments and considers himself to be sensitive to his own background and to those who struggle with similar problems. He has moved to the West Coast and has been hired to work in a high school with a culturally diverse student population.

As a high school counselor, John starts a group for at-risk adolescents. His goals for this group are as follows: (1) to instill pride so that group members will see their present environment as an obstacle to be overcome, not suffered with; (2) to increase self-esteem and to challenge group members to fight the negativism they may encounter in their home and school environments; (3) to teach group members to minimize their differences in terms of the larger community (for example, he points out how some of their idioms and ways of speaking separate them from the majority and reinforce differences and stereotypes); and (4) to teach group members how to overcome obstacles in a nonsupportive environment.

John does not work very closely with teachers, administrators, or other school counselors in the district. He views them as being more interested in politics and red tape and as actually giving very little energy to personal counseling in the school. He has little to do with the families of the adolescents, because he sees them as being too willing to accept handouts and welfare and as not being very interested in becoming self-sufficient and independent. He tells his group members: "What you have at home with your families has obviously not worked for you. What you have in this group is the opportunity to change."

- Does John's background and experiences qualify him as a culturally competent group counselor? Why or why not?
- What are John's assumptions?
- What was John's internal dialogue?
- If John had become familiar with the environment of this particular group, would he have expressed the same goals?
- If you were John's supervisor, how would you work with him?

Commentary. We disagree with John's axiom that simply because he could obtain a graduate degree (against difficult odds) anybody could have the same success. John is a well-intentioned school counselor who disregarded the particular needs of the students in his school and his group. Instead, he imposed his personal values in terms of language and upward mobility on the group.

John made no attempt to become aware of the unique struggles or values of the high school students he serves. He stereotyped the parents of his group members in a very indirect, but powerful fashion and set up potential conflicts between group members and their families. John acted insensitively to the families of his group members. Most ethics codes require therapists to respect community and family traditions and to utilize these as potential resources in therapy when appropriate. John failed to pay attention to the potential healing power of the community, which can be a powerful therapeutic force for change.

John seems to lack specific training that would assist him in developing multicultural competence as a group worker. In working with groups characterized by diversity, it is critical that John be aware of the assumptions he makes about people from diverse ethnic and cultural groups, and from an ethical standpoint, he should adapt his practices to the needs of the members in his group. John needs to make sure that the goals and processes of his group match the cultural values and personal goals of the members of the group. To be able to make interventions that are appropriate for members' unique cultural backgrounds, John must have an understanding of the ways diversity influences group process. John will need to be aware of his own cultural bias and be willing to reflect on the assumptions underlying his methods and practices. ASGW (2008) emphasizes the importance of self-awareness for group workers: "Group Workers are aware of and monitor their strengths and weaknesses and the effects these have on group members. They explore their own cultural identities and how these affect their values and beliefs about group work" (B.l.).

Ethical Considerations in Co-Leadership

If you lead groups, you will probably work with a co-leader at some time. Co-leader relationships can either enhance or complicate the group process, which raises a multitude of potential ethical issues. The group can benefit from the insights and feedback of two leaders. Co-leaders who complement and balance each other can provide useful modeling for members. Furthermore, co-leaders can share the responsibilities and provide mutual support.

Along with the advantages of co-leadership, there are some disadvantages that can raise ethical concerns. Luke and Hackney (2007) found that one of the primary disadvantages involves relationship difficulties between the leaders. Other potential drawbacks to the co-leadership model include ineffective communication, competition between leaders, and overdependence on the co-leader. Unresolved conflicts between the leaders can result in splitting within the group. Luke and Hackney's review highlights the necessity for group leaders to attend to their own individual development, their development as a co-leading team, and the development of the group they are facilitating. It is challenging for group leaders to divide their time to these multiple areas of development, yet doing so is essential for a successful group.

Okech and Kline's (2006) study underscores the importance of co-leaders being committed to identifying and working through issues that interfere with them working effectively in the group. One path is through regular supervision as a basic part of learning how to facilitate groups. Okech and Kline recommend that supervision should include opportunities for co-leaders to explore their personal beliefs and perspectives about co-facilitation. This discussion should include their perceptions and reactions to each other as a co-leading team. Okech and Kline report that effective co-leader relationships require commitment to establishing and maintaining these relationships.

At this point, clarify your own position on co-leadership in group work:

- What would you most appreciate in a co-leader?
- Do you prefer working alone to co-leading a group, and why?
- If you found that you and your co-leader clashed on many issues and approached groups very differently, what would you do?
- What ethical implications are involved when a great deal of time during the sessions is taken up with power struggles and conflicts between the co-leaders?
- In what ways could you be most helpful to your co-leader?
- What do you know about yourself that would make it difficult for your co-leader to work with you?
- How would you handle the situation if your co-leader were acting unethically?

Ethical Issues in Forming and Managing Groups

How can group leaders make potential members aware of the services they are providing? What information do clients have a right to expect before they decide to attend a group? **Informed consent** is a process of presenting basic information about group treatment to potential group members to enable them to make better decisions about whether or not to enter and how to participate in a group (Fallon, 2006). Leaders have the responsibility of ensuring that members become aware of their rights (as well as their responsibilities) as group participants.

It is a good policy to provide a professional disclosure statement to group members that includes written information on a variety of topics pertaining to the nature of the group, including therapists' qualifications, techniques often used in the group, the rights and obligations of group members, and the risks and benefits of participating in the group. Other information potential members should have includes alternatives to group treatment; policies regarding appointments, fees, and insurance; and the nature and limitations of confidentiality in a group.

Fallon (2006) suggests that an overly lengthy informed consent process can emphasize the legalistic aspects, which could replace a collaborative working relationship with a legalistic framework. Group leaders should not overwhelm members with too much information at one time. In his study of informed consent, Pomerantz (2005) makes the point that clients should be informed at the outset that informed consent is an ongoing process rather than a one-time event. The section on informed consent in Chapter 5 applies to both individual and group counseling. Refer to that discussion for further details.

Screening and Selection of Group Members

Not everyone will benefit from a group experience, and some people may be psychologically harmed by certain group experiences. Therefore, group leaders are faced with the difficult task of determining who should be included in a group and who should not. Many group leaders do not screen participants, for various reasons. Some practitioners are theoretically opposed to the notion of using screening as a way of determining who is suitable for a group, and some maintain that they simply do not have the time to carry out effective screening, or doing so is not realistic in their work setting. Others believe that ethical practice demands careful screening and preparation of all candidates. Is it unethical to fail to screen prospective group candidates?

Unless careful selection criteria are employed, Yalom (2005) argues that group therapy clients may end up discouraged and may not be helped. He maintains that it is easier to identify the people who should be excluded from group therapy than those who should be included. Citing clinical studies, he lists the following as poor candidates for a heterogeneous outpatient intensive therapy group: brain-damaged people, paranoid individuals, hypochondriacs, those who are actively addicted to drugs or alcohol, acutely psychotic individuals, and antisocial personalities. In terms of criteria for inclusion, he contends that the client's level of motivation to work is the most important variable. From his perspective, groups are useful for people who have problems in the interpersonal domain, such as loneliness, inability to make or maintain intimate contacts, feelings of unlovability, fears of being assertive, and dependency issues. Clients who lack meaning in life, who suffer from generalized anxiety, who are searching for an identity, who fear success, and who are compulsive workers might also profit from a group experience.

The ACA (2005) identifies the counselor's ethical responsibility for screening prospective group members as follows:

> Counselors screen prospective group counseling/therapy participants. To the extent possible, counselors select members whose needs and goals are compatible with goals of the group, who will not impede the group process, and whose well-being will not be jeopardized by the group experience. (A.8.a.)

As a general ethical guideline, we think that some type of screening, which involves interviewing and evaluating potential members, should be employed to select suitable members. In addition, what is best for the group as a whole needs to be considered in selecting members for that group. More specifically, the question can be framed thusly: Is it appropriate for *this* person to become a participant in *this* type of group, with *this* leader, at *this* time? Screening should not be done for the comfort of the group leader, nor should it be done arbitrarily to unfairly discriminate against certain members.

Not all theoretical orientations favor or agree with the notion of screening, nor would they view screening as an ethical mandate. For example, practitioners with a transactional analysis orientation often do not conduct screening. Many Adlerians believe screening does not fit with the democratic spirit of their theory. Some maintain that screening is done more for the comfort of the group leader than for the good of the client. If a practitioner does not screen because of a theoretical value, we do not think this constitutes unethical practice.

■ The Case of Angela.

Angela is a counselor in a busy community agency that is understaffed, and counselors are increasingly expected to design groups as a way to meet the diverse needs of clients in the agency. Angela decides to organize a personal-growth group by sending colleagues a memorandum asking for candidates for her group. There are no provisions for individual screening of potential members, no written announcement informing the members of the goals and purposes of the group, and no preparation for incoming members. No information is given to the members about the leader's background, possible techniques to be used, expectations for participation, or how to get the most from the group experience. Angela asks the receptionist to admit the first 10 people who come to enroll, assuming that the interest of these people is a sign that they are ready for a group experience. The receptionist puts people into the group as they inquire, irrespective of the nature of their problems, and they are told when to come in for the first meeting.

- Can Angela's failure to screen members for her group be justified on ethical and clinical grounds?
- What are some alternatives to screening, if doing so is impractical?
- What potential problems do you see in the way Angela formed her group?

Commentary. We realize that in some settings it is impractical to screen members prior to forming a group. In Angela's agency, where it is not possible to conduct screening interviews, one alternative is to use the initial session to provide orientation for the participants and to present informed consent guidelines. We think Angela was remiss in not doing any kind of screening to determine whether those who were applying were ready for this kind of group experience. Simply filling the group by admitting the first 10 people who wanted to sign up is not an effective way to form a group. At the very least, she could have made provisions for candidates to meet with her briefly to ask questions about the group.

The kind of screening and preparation that are required depend on the theoretical orientation of the group therapist, the type of group being offered, the potential members who are being considered for the group, and how the group fits into the overall treatment program of the agency.

Preparing Group Participants

To what extent are group counselors ethically responsible for helping participants to benefit from their group experience? Many practitioners do very little to prepare members for a group. They are opposed to preparation on the grounds that it could inhibit a group's spontaneity and autonomy. Others take the position that members need to be provided with some structure to derive maximum gains.

Yalom (2005) advocates exploring group members' misconceptions and expectations, predicting early problems, and providing a conceptual framework that includes guidelines for effective group behavior. He views this preparatory process as more than the dissemination of information. He contends that it reinforces the therapist's respect for the client, demonstrates that therapy is a collaborative venture, and shows that the therapist is willing to share his or her knowledge with the client. This cognitive approach to preparation has the goals of providing a rational explanation of the group process, clarifying how members are expected to behave, and raising expectations about what the group can accomplish.

■ The Case of Denise.

Denise assumes that the more information about group process she provides to group members, the more the members will attempt to please her. To avoid this, Denise does not give information out before members actually meet, either in writing or orally, nor does she establish group rules and group norms. This leader is convinced that informed consent is not really possible, and she prefers to have an open discussion in the group that allows members to formulate rules that make sense to them. If members flounder in defining goals, Denise believes this is part of the group process; therefore, she does not expect members to identify specific goals to guide their participation in a group. Denise thinks members should follow their own spontaneous paths rather than learning about group norms and other expected group behavior from the group leader.

- Do you think an argument could be made for not giving information to potential members before they decide to join a group? Explain.
- What do you think of Denise's approach to formulating group rules and norms with the group members?
- If you were forming a group, how would you take care of the informed consent process?

Commentary. We respect differences in leadership styles. Some leaders prefer a structured approach, whereas others prefer giving the group members maximum freedom to decide how they will function as a group. Denise's approach is to allow the group to define its own direction; she assumes that the members can formulate their own norms governing behavior in the group. We do not think Denise is behaving unethically with respect to allowing group members to formulate the group rules and norms for their group. However, by not providing any information about the group before it begins, Denise is not attending to the informed consent process. Most codes of ethics agree on the importance of providing informed consent so that clients know what they are agreeing to before they make a commitment.

In our experience in working with groups, we have found that providing members with basic information about group process tends to eliminate some of the difficulties typically encountered in the early stages of a group. Our preparation procedures apply to most types of groups, with some modifications. At both the screening session and the initial group meeting, we explore the members' expectations, clarify goals and objectives, discuss procedural details, explore the possible risks and values of group participation, and discuss guidelines for getting the most from a group experience. See M. Corey, Corey, and Corey (2010), for more detailed discussion on this topic.

As part of member preparation, we include a discussion of the values and limitations of groups, the psychological risks involved in group participation, and ways of minimizing these risks. We also allow time for dealing with misconceptions that people have about groups and for exploring the fears or reservations the members may have. In most of our groups, members do have certain fears about what they will experience; until we acknowledge these fears and talk about them, very little productive work can occur. We also ask members to spend time before they come to the group defining what they most want to achieve and formulating personal goals that will guide their participation.

We believe appropriate orientation and preparation are basic to effective and ethical group work practices, but we realize that others disagree with us when it comes to the comprehensive kind of preparation we think is useful. Write down some things you might do to prepare people for a group. What ethical concerns do you have regarding preparation? What do you think would occur if you did little in the way of preparing group members?

Involuntary Participation

Voluntary participation is an important beginning point for a successful group experience. Members will make significant changes only to the extent that they actively seek something for themselves. Unfortunately, not all groups are composed of clients who have chosen to be there. Are there situations in which it is ethical to require or mandate people to participate in a group? How is informed consent especially critical in groups where attendance is mandatory? Can involuntary groups be successful?

Mandatory participation in a group raises a different set of ethical issues. Greater effort needs to be directed toward fully informing members of the nature and goals of the group, procedures to be used, the rights of members to decline certain activities, the limits of confidentiality, and what effect their level of participation in the group will have on critical decisions about them outside of the group. When attendance at group sessions is required, group leaders must be certain that group members understand their rights and their responsibilities, and counselors must at all times show their respect for these mandated members.

Consider these questions on the ethics of involuntary membership:

- Do you think members can benefit from a group experience even if they are required to attend? Why or why not?
- What strategy might a leader use to foster more effective group participation while still giving the members true freedom of choice?
- From an ethical perspective, is it required that members of an involuntary group give consent? To what degree should members be informed about the consequences of their level of participation in a group?

Freedom to Leave a Group

Once members make a commitment to be a part of a group, do they have the right to leave at any time they choose? Procedures for leaving a group should be explained to all members during the initial session. Ideally, the leader and the member cooperate to determine whether a group experience is proving to be productive or counterproductive. We take the position that clients have a responsibility to the leader and to other members to explain why they want to leave. There are several reasons for this policy. It can be psychologically damaging to members to leave without having been able to discuss what they considered threatening or negative in the experience. Further, it is unfortunate if members leave a group because of a misunderstanding about some feedback they have received. Such a termination can be harmful to group cohesion, for the members who remain may think that they caused a particular member's departure. We tell our members that they have an obligation to attend all sessions and to inform us if they decide to withdraw. Although members have a right to leave, we ask them to talk about it out of respect for the needs of the remaining members. However, we do not think it is ethical to use undue pressure to keep these members, and we are alert to other members' pressuring a person to stay.

Psychological Risks

The fact that groups can be powerful catalysts for personal change means that they are also risky. Our goal is not to make sure that all members are comfortable as much as to create a safe environment where they can take risks and explore their discomfort. Although we don't think groups can be free of risks, ethical practice demands that group practitioners inform prospective participants of the potential hazards involved in the group experience. Fallon (2006) suggests that explaining both the potential benefits and risks of group therapy is an essential part of the informed consent process. However, merely informing participants does not absolve leaders of all responsibility. Group leaders have an ethical responsibility to take precautionary measures to reduce unnecessary psychological risks. ACA's (2005) guideline is this: "In a group setting, counselors take reasonable precautions to protect clients from physical, emotional, or psychological trauma" (A.8.b.).

Group leaders have a significant role in preventing damaging group experiences. Smokowski, Rose, and Bacallao (2001) remind us that group leaders have a great deal of power, prestige, and status within their groups and caution that "many leaders are not able to responsibly manage, or even recognize, their power and influence" (p. 228). The outcomes of a group are very much related to what leaders bring to a group and to their actions. Smokowski and colleagues studied damaging experiences in therapeutic groups and identified a variety of factors or events that result in members having a negative group experience, some of which include lack of leader support; an aggressive and harshly confrontational leadership style; premature pressure to disclose; passive leadership style; misuse of a leader's power and influence; lack of acceptance for diverse points of view; lack of clarity about group norms; and negative norms that coerce participation or encourage excessive confrontation. Smokowski and colleagues state that group leaders are in a position to either promote or prevent damaging group experiences and conclude: "Leaders who are aggressive and overstimulating in their use of confrontation and leaders who choose to sit passively by while the group works out its difficulties tended to precipitate damaging group experiences" (p. 246).

Although all risks cannot be eliminated, certain safeguards can be taken during the course of a group to avoid disastrous outcomes. Here are some of the risks that participants should know about (M. Corey, Corey, & Corey, 2010):

- Members may experience some disruptions in their lives as a result of their work in the group.
- Group participants are often encouraged to be completely open. In this quest for self-revelation, privacy is sometimes surrendered.
- A related risk is group pressure. The participants' right not to explore certain issues or to stop at a certain point should be respected. Also, members should not be coerced into participating in an exercise.
- Scapegoating is another potential hazard in groups. Unchallenged projection and blaming can have dire effects on the target person. Moreno (2007) contends that scapegoating is destructive. Not only is damage done to the individual being scapegoated, but the group suffers in the depth and progress of their work.
- Confrontation can be used or misused in groups. Harmful attacks on others should not be permitted.
- Even though a counselor may continue to stress the necessity not to discuss with outsiders what goes on in the group, there is no guarantee that all members will respect the confidential nature of their exchanges.

One way to minimize psychological risks in groups is to use a contract, in which leaders specify what their responsibilities are and members specify their commitment to the group by declaring what they are willing to do. If members and leaders operate under a contract that clarifies expectations, there is less chance for members to be exploited or damaged by a group experience.

Of course, a contract approach is not the only way to reduce potential risks, nor is it sufficient in itself to do so. One of the most important safeguards is the leader's training in group process. Group counselors have the major ethical responsibility for preventing needless harm to members. To fulfill this role, group leaders should have a clear grasp of the boundaries of their competence. As a rule, leaders should conduct only those types of groups for which they have been sufficiently prepared. Working with an experienced co-leader is one good way to learn and also a way to reduce potential risks.

Confidentiality in Groups

The ethical, legal, and professional aspects of confidentiality (discussed in Chapter 6) have a different application in group situations. Are members of a group under the same ethical and legal obligations as the group leader not to disclose the identities of other members or the content of what was shared in the group? The legal concept of privileged communication is not always recognized in a group setting, unless there is a statutory exception. However, protecting the confidentiality of group members is an ethical mandate, and it is the responsibility of the counselor to address this at the outset of a group. The American Group Psychotherapy Association (AGPA, 2002) states: "The group therapist is knowledgeable about the limits of privileged communication as they apply to group therapy and informs group members of those limits" (2.2). The group therapist is expected to safeguard the members' right to privacy by judiciously protecting the identity of the members and protecting information of a confidential nature. Group leaders also have the ethical responsibility of informing members of the limits of confidentiality within the group setting, their responsibilities to other group members, and the absence of legal privilege concerning what is shared in a group (Wheeler & Bertram, 2008).

From the beginning of a group we discuss with members the purpose and limits of confidentiality. The APA (2002) ethical standard also recognizes the limits of confidentiality in group therapy: "When psychologists provide services to several persons in a group setting, they describe at the outset the roles and responsibilities of all parties and the limits of confidentiality" (10.03.). ACA's (2005) ethics code specifies that "counselors clearly explain the importance and parameters of confidentiality for the specific group being entered" (B.4.a.). Another ACA (2005) standard pertains to the respect for confidentiality: "Counselors do not share confidential information without client consent or without sound legal or ethical justification" (B.1.c.). Finally, multicultural considerations pertaining to confidentiality are contained in this ASGW (2008) guideline: "Group Workers maintain awareness and sensitivity regarding the cultural meaning of confidentiality and privacy. Group Workers respect differing views towards disclosure of information" (A.6.).

The ASGW (2008) "Best Practice Guidelines" state the following regarding confidentiality:

> Group Workers define confidentiality and its limits (for example, legal and ethical exceptions and expectations; waivers implicit with treatment plans, documentation, and insurance usage). Group Workers have the responsibility to inform all group participants of the need for confidentiality and potential consequences of breaching confidentiality; and that legal privilege does not apply to group discussions (unless provided by state statute). (A.7.d.)

Although most writers on ethical issues in group work make the point that confidentiality cannot be guaranteed, they also talk about the importance of teaching group members ways of avoiding breaking confidences. Because of the complex kinds of groups, the nature of ethical issues that can arise also becomes more complex. In individual psychotherapy, the therapist can ensure the client's confidentiality, yet in group therapy leaders cannot always prevent other members from disclosing personal information about members in the group. Although group leaders are themselves ethically and legally bound to maintain confidentiality, a group member who violates another member's confidences faces no legal consequences (Lasky & Riva, 2006).

▪ **The Case of Pierre.**

Pierre briefly discusses confidentiality at the first group session, saying "Anything that happens here, stays here." He tells members that it is not necessary to go into detail in talking about confidentiality "because everyone in here already knows that confidentiality is a given." Pierre does not let members know that confidentiality cannot be guaranteed in his group, nor does he inform them of the limitations of confidentiality in a group setting. Pierre does not invite members to raise questions they might have about confidentiality because he is anxious for his group to start working.

- How do evaluate the ethical appropriateness of Pierre's approach to discussing confidentiality in his group?
- What specific aspects of confidentiality would you most want to inform members of in your group?
- What potential problems, if any, do you see in the way Pierre explained confidentiality to group members?

Commentary. We think Pierre is guilty of oversimplification in stating that confidentiality is a given and that members are familiar with its importance. Members may be mistaken in their assumption that confidentiality can be guaranteed in a group setting. It would be wise for Pierre to encourage members to raise any concerns they have about confidentiality at any point during the course of the group. In discussing the importance of confidentiality in the group, Pierre could point out how confidentiality can be violated in subtle ways and how confidences are often divulged without malice. Most people do not maliciously attempt to hurt others by talking with people outside the group about specific members. However, it is tempting for members to share their experiences with other people, and in so doing they sometimes make inappropriate disclosures. Because of this tendency to want to share with outsiders, we caution participants about how easily and unintentionally the confidentiality of the group can be compromised. We tell members that they are less likely to break confidentiality if they talk only about their own personal insights.

It is our position that leaders need periodically to reaffirm to group members the importance of not discussing with outsiders what has occurred in the group. We talk with each prospective member about the necessity of maintaining confidentiality to establish the trust and cohesion required if participants are to reveal themselves in significant ways. We discuss this point during the screening interviews, again during the pregroup or initial meetings, at times during the course of a group when it seems appropriate, and again at termination. A full discussion of confidentiality is critical because it respects the rights of group members to make autonomous choices and enhances the overall group experience (Lasky & Riva, 2006).

How to encourage confidentiality. Confidentiality in group situations is not easily enforced. Because members cannot assume that anything they say or hear in the group will remain confidential, they should be able to make an informed choice about how much to reveal. Members should be informed that absolute confidentiality in groups is difficult and at times even unrealistic (Lasky & Riva, 2006). As a way to safeguard group members' confidentiality, some group leaders have developed a written contract in which each participant pledges to keep confidential other group members' identities and disclosures. This contract can include a termination policy if a member breaches the confidentiality of another group member (Knauss, 2006).

If you were to lead a group, which of the following measures might you take to ensure confidentiality? Check any of the statements that apply:

_____ 1. I would keep reinforcing the importance of confidentiality at group meetings.

_____ 2. I would require group members to sign a statement saying that they fully understand their commitment to maintain the confidential character of the group.

_____ 3. I would let members know that they would be asked to leave the group if they violated confidentiality.

_____ 4. With the permission and knowledge of the members, I would tape-record all the sessions.

_____ 5. I would leave it up to group members to decide how they want to deal with confidentiality issues in their group.

Exceptions to confidentiality in groups. Group counselors have an ethical responsibility to define clearly what confidentiality means, explain its importance, and inform members of the difficulties involved in enforcing it. Although group counselors are expected to stress the importance of confidentiality and set a norm, they also are expected to inform members about its limits. For example, if members pose a danger to themselves or to others, the group therapist has an ethical and legal obligation to take appropriate steps to protect the group member and society in general (AGPA, 2002). The other limitations of confidentiality discussed in Chapter 6 also apply to group work.

It is a good practice for group facilitators to give a written statement to each member outlining the nature, purposes, and limitations of confidentiality and acknowledging specific situations that would require the breaching of confidences. It seems that such straightforwardness with members from the outset does a great deal to create trust, for at least members know the consequences of certain revelations to the group.

Of course, it is imperative that those who lead groups become familiar with the state laws that have an impact on their practice. For instance, all states have had mandatory child abuse reporting laws since 1967. Most states also have mandatory elder abuse and dependent adult abuse reporting laws. The great majority of states currently have laws requiring counselors to report clients' threats to harm themselves or others.

If you lead a group at a correctional institution or an inpatient facility, you may have to record in a member's chart certain behaviors or verbalizations that he or she exhibits in the group. At the same time, your responsibility to your clients requires you to inform them that you are documenting their verbalizations and behaviors and that this information is accessible to other staff.

Confidentiality with minors.   Encouraging confidentiality is a special challenge for counselors who offer groups for children and adolescents in school settings. On this matter, ASCA's (2004) *Ethical Standards for School Counselors* provides an important guideline:

> The professional school counselor establishes clear expectations in the group setting and clearly states that confidentiality in group counseling cannot be guaranteed. Given the developmental and chronological ages of minors in schools, the counselor recognizes the tenuous nature of confidentiality for minors renders some topics inappropriate for group work in a school setting. (A.6.c.)

Group leaders have a responsibility in groups that involve children and adolescents to take measures to increase the chances that confidentiality will be kept. It is important to work cooperatively with parents and legal guardians as well as to enlist the trust of the young members. It is also useful to teach minors, using a vocabulary they understand, about the nature, purposes, and limitations of confidentiality. It is a good idea for leaders to encourage members to initiate discussions on confidentiality whenever this becomes an issue for them.

Do parents/legal guardians have a right to information that is disclosed by their children in a group? The answer to that question depends on whether we are looking at it from a legal, ethical, or professional viewpoint. State laws differ regarding counseling minors. It is important for group leaders to be aware of the laws related to working with minors in the state where they are practicing. Circumstances in which a minor may seek professional help without parental consent, defining an emancipated minor, or the rights of parents (or legal guardians) to have access to the records regarding the professional help received by their minor child vary according to state statutes.

Before any minor enters a group, it is a good practice to obtain written permission from the parents. Such a statement should include a brief description of the purpose of the group, the importance of confidentiality as a prerequisite to accomplishing these purposes, and your intention not to violate any confidences. Although it may be useful to give parents information about their child, this can be done without violating confidences. At the first session it is helpful to inform and discuss with minors their concerns about confidentiality and how it will be maintained. Such practices can strengthen the child's trust in the counselor.

Confidentiality and online group work.   Ethical considerations pertaining to confidentiality and the questionable effectiveness of online counseling may be a factor in its limited uses in educational and practice settings (Krieger & Stockton, 2004). Humphreys, Winzelberg, and Klaw (2000) take the position that online group psychotherapy cannot ethically be conducted over the Internet, except in very limited circumstances. Protecting clients' privacy and confidentiality is a very difficult matter. In addition, individuals cannot be reliably identified over the Internet. A person with access to a client's computer could sign into online group counseling by using the password and the name of the actual client. The implications for lack of confidentiality and privacy are obvious here. Because of the difficulty of maintaining the confidential nature of a group, we are opposed to online group counseling on both ethical and clinical grounds.

Humphreys and colleagues (2000) state that some kinds of peer groups and self-help groups do utilize Internet technology, but they add that the astonishing growth in the technology has outpaced the development of formal ethical guidelines for practitioners involved in online groups. Humphreys and colleagues write about a therapist's ethical responsibilities in self-help groups, discussion groups, and support groups that operate on the Internet, and they offer practical strategies for avoiding ethical problems. See Malone, Miller, and Walz (2007) and Malone (2007a, 2007b) for a discussion of online technologies for distance counseling.

Values in Group Counseling

Group counselors have the responsibility of being aware of their own values and the potential impact they have on the interventions they are likely to make. The group leader's central function is to help members find answers that are congruent with their own values, not to short-circuit the members' exploration by providing them with answers. We suggest that you refer to the discussion of value conflicts in Chapter 3 and consider specific areas in which you might be inclined to impose your values in the groups you lead. Reflect on any tendencies you may have to lead your clients in a certain direction, and think about ways to minimize the chances of imposing your values on them.

Certain behaviors of group leaders reveal their values: (a) demonstrating acceptance of the person of the client; (b) avoiding responding to sarcastic remarks with sarcasm; (c) being honest with members rather than harboring hidden agendas; (d) avoiding judgments and labeling of members, and instead describing the behavior of members; (e) stating observations and hunches in a tentative way rather than dogmatically; (f) letting members who are difficult know how they are affecting them in a nonblaming way; (g) detecting their own countertransference reactions; (h) avoiding misuse of their power; (i) providing both support and caring confrontations;

and (j) avoiding meeting their own needs at the expense of the members (M. Corey, Corey, & Corey, 2010).

Ethics in the Use of Group Techniques

Group techniques can be used to facilitate the movement of a group and to deepen and intensify certain feelings. We think leaders should have a clear rationale for using each technique. This is an area in which theory can be a useful guide for practice.

Techniques can also be abused or used in unethical ways. Here are some ways leaders might employ techniques unethically:

- Using techniques with which they are unfamiliar
- Using techniques to enhance their power
- Using techniques whose sole purpose is to create intensity because of the leader's need for intensity
- Using techniques to pressure members, even when they have expressed a desire not to participate in an exercise

We use these guidelines in our practice as ways to effectively use techniques in a group:

- Techniques used have a therapeutic purpose and are grounded in some theoretical framework.
- The client's self-exploration and self-understanding is fostered.
- Techniques are devised for the unique needs of various cultural and ethnic groups.
- Techniques are modified so that they are suitable for the client's cultural and ethnic background.
- Techniques are used to enhance the group process rather than to cover up the leader's incompetence.
- Techniques are introduced in a timely and sensitive manner and are abandoned if they are not working.
- The tone of a leader is consistently invitational; members are given the freedom either to participate in or to skip a given experiment.
- Leaders use techniques in which they have received training and supervision.

Although it is unrealistic to expect that leaders will always know exactly what will result from an intervention, they should know how to cope with unexpected outcomes. For example, guided fantasies into times of loneliness as a child or physical exercises designed to release anger can lead to intense emotional experiences. If leaders use such techniques, they must be ready to deal with any emotional release. It is essential that group counselors become aware of the potential for encouraging catharsis to fulfill their own needs.

Some leaders push people to express anger, and they develop techniques to focus bring about this catharsis. Although these are legitimate feelings, expressing anger in the group may satisfy the leader's agenda more than it meets the needs of the members. This question ought to be raised frequently: "Whose needs are primary, and whose needs are being met—the members' or the leader's?"

How can leaders determine whether they are competent to use a certain technique? Some leaders who have received training in the use of a technique may hesitate to use it (out of fear of making a mistake); other leaders may not have any reservations about trying out new techniques. It is useful if leaders have experienced these techniques as members of a group and have a clear rationale for using them.

Another major issue pertaining to the use of group techniques relates to providing immediate help for any group member who shows extreme distress during or at the end of a group session, especially if techniques were used to elicit intense emotions. Although some unfinished business promotes growth, there is an ethical issue in the use of a technique that incites strong emotional reactions if the client feels abandoned at the end of a session because time has run out. Leaders must take care to allow enough time to deal adequately with the reactions that were stimulated in a session. It is unwise to introduce techniques in a session when there is not enough time to work through the feelings that might result or in a setting where there is no privacy or where the physical setup would make it harmful to employ certain techniques.

Our position on the ethical use of techniques is that group leaders need to learn about potential adverse effects. One way for group leaders to learn is by taking part in groups themselves. By being a group member and first experiencing a range of techniques, a therapist can develop a healthy respect for using techniques appropriately to meet clients' needs. In our training workshops for group leaders, we encourage spontaneity and inventiveness in the use of techniques, but we also stress the importance of striking a balance between creativity and irresponsibility. The reputation of group work has suffered from the actions of irresponsible practitioners, mostly those who use techniques randomly without a clear rationale or without any sense of the potential outcome of techniques. If the group leader has a strong academic background, has had extensive supervised group experience, has participated in his or her own therapy or personal-growth experience, and has a basic respect for clients, he or she is not likely to abuse techniques.

Ethics in the Consultation Process

Group counselors need to be aware of their limitations in working with certain types of clients. The willingness to consult with other professionals demonstrates wisdom and good faith on the practitioner's part. For example, diversity-competent group workers are willing to seek consultation with traditional healers and religious or spiritual healers in the treatment of a diverse range of problems of individual members.

It is a good ethical practice for leaders to explain to members their policies about consultation. When are they likely to consult? What measures do they take to protect confidentiality? Are they willing to have between-session consultations with group members? When and how might they refer? Here are some ethical guidelines pertaining to the consultation and referral process:

- Group counselors can seek consultation and supervision when they are faced with ethical concerns or difficulties that interfere with carrying out their leadership functions.
- Leaders need to develop sensitivity to situations in which a referral is appropriate.
- Group workers learn about the resources within the community and help members make use of these resources.

As we discussed earlier, one way to protect against a malpractice suit is to demonstrate that consultation procedures were used in dealing with an ethical dilemma. If group workers consult supervisors or other professionals, and if they document such consultations, they are demonstrating good clinical practice, adhering to ethical guidelines, and minimizing their chances of malpractice.

Ethical Issues Concerning Termination

The final phase in the life of a group is critical, for this is when members have the task of consolidating their learning. At this time members need to be able to express what the group experience has meant to them and to state where they intend to go from here. Neglecting the process of termination can easily leave the members with unfinished work and will limit opportunities for them to conceptualize what they learned from a group experience. For many group members endings are difficult because they realize that time is limited in their group. The ending of a group often triggers other losses that members have experienced. Thus, the termination of a group may involve a grieving process. It is important for leaders to focus on these feelings of loss. These feelings need to be identified and explored, although they probably cannot be alleviated. Members need to face the reality of termination and learn how to say good-bye. If the group has been truly therapeutic, the members will be able to extend their learning outside the group, even though they may well experience a sense of sadness and loss.

The Termination Phase in a Closed Group

Mangione, Forti, and Iacuzzi (2007) state that endings in a therapeutic group are frequently emotionally charged and complex events, and they can be fraught with ethical dilemmas. In a *closed* group the task of leaders is to help members review their individual work and the evolving patterns from the first to the final session. Informed consent involves talking with group members from the beginning of a group experience about the ending and how to terminate productively.

The termination phase of a group provides an opportunity for members to clarify the meaning of their experience, to consolidate the gains they have made, and to make decisions about the new behaviors they want to carry away from the group and apply to their everyday lives. The following questions are relevant during the termination of a group:

- What ethical responsibilities do group leaders have for assisting participants to develop a conceptual framework that will make sense of, integrate, and consolidate what they have learned in their group?

- To what degree is it the leader's responsibility to ensure that members are not left with excessive unfinished business at the end of the group?

- How can group leaders help participants translate what they have learned as a result of the group into their daily lives? Should leaders assume that this translation will occur automatically, or must they prepare members for maximizing their learning?

The final phase of group work may be the one that leaders handle most ineptly, possibly owing to their lack of training or partly because of their own resistance to termination. Avoiding acknowledgment of a group's termination may reflect discomfort on the leader's part in dealing with endings and separations. A group facilitator who does not have a clear picture of his or her own vulnerabilities pertaining to loss or endings will likely find it difficult to facilitate members' expressions of their feelings over endings. Mangione and colleagues maintain that group workers must be aware of their personal limitations pertaining to endings or loss if they expect to act ethically and effectively in assisting members to deal with termination. When termination is not dealt with, the group misses an opportunity to explore concerns that may affect many members, and the clients' therapy is jeopardized. When learning is not conceptualized, the ability to bring the meaning of the experience to real life is severely diminished. A discussion of endings is crucial to adequate closure. The termination process tends to be most meaningful when members have the opportunity to share their thoughts and feelings associated with this transition (Shapiro & Ginzberg, 2002).

Termination of Members in an Open Group

An *open* group has different challenges from a closed group because members leave the group and new members are incorporated into the group at various times. Here are some tasks to be accomplished with a person who is leaving an open group:

- It is important to teach members in an open group to give adequate notice when they decide it is time to terminate. This policy will ensure that members have time to address any unfinished business with themselves or others in the group.

- If the member's intention to leave is not adequately discussed in the group, this can undermine potentially valuable group experiences. A successful termination can be viewed as a gift to the member who is terminating as well as to the remaining members of the group (Shapiro & Ginzberg, 2002).

- An ideal termination is one that has been mutually agreed upon by the member and the leader and for which there is sufficient time to work through the process of loss and separation (Fieldsteel, 2005).

- It is essential to assist those members who are leaving to review what they have learned in the group and, specifically, what they intend to do with this learning.

- Remaining group members often have reactions about the loss of a member, and it is important that they have an opportunity to express their thoughts and feelings.

Follow-Up and Evaluation

Throughout the life of a group, group leaders assist members in assessing their own progress and monitor their style of modeling. In this sense, evaluation is an ongoing process whereby members are taught how to determine whether the group is helping them attain their personal goals. But group counselors also must assess both the process and the outcomes of their groups. Once a group has ended, follow-up group sessions provide an opportunity to do this. In our opinion, follow-up activities are useful to the members and to the group counselor as well. Both short-term follow-up (after one month) and long-term follow-up (after three months to a year) can be invaluable measures of accountability. For more discussion on termination issues, see M. Corey, Corey, and Corey (2010).

Chapter Summary

Along with the growing popularity of group approaches to counseling and therapy comes a need for ethical and professional guidelines for those who lead groups. There are many types of groups, and there are many possible uses of groups in various settings. In this chapter we have discussed some ethical issues that are related to most groups. To become competent group leaders, counselors require adequate education and supervised experience in facilitating a group. Meeting the professional training standards for group workers is essential. As is true in any form of counseling, achieving diversity competence is basic to becoming an ethical and effective group worker.

We also looked at the advantages and disadvantages of a co-leadership model of group work. Co-leadership can enhance what members learn in a group, but it is essential that the co-leaders work together well as a team and model a respectful relationship.

Conducting a group entails attending to a host of ethical issues, including providing informed consent, screening and selecting group members, and preparing members for a meaningful group. Leaders working with involuntary groups are challenged to establish procedures for members who want to leave the group, address psychological risks of group participation, and explore members' concerns about confidentiality. In addition, we discussed some ethical issues pertaining to dealing with values in group counseling, the use of group techniques, consultation practices, and dealing ethically and effectively with termination of members in both a closed group and an open group. With respect to these and other issues, we have stressed the importance of formulating your own views on ethical practice in leading groups, after carefully considering the ethics codes of your professional organization, and as well, the best practice guidelines and training standards of ASGW.

Suggested Activities

1. Replicate the initial session of a group. Two students can volunteer to co-lead and approximately eight other students can become group members. Assume that the group is a personal-growth group that will meet for a predetermined number of weeks. The co-leaders' job is to orient and prepare the members by describing the group's purpose, giving an overview of group process concepts, and talking about ground rules for effective group participation. If time allows, members can express any fears and expectations they have about being involved in the group, and they can also raise questions they would like to explore.

2. Practice conducting screening interviews for potential group members. One person volunteers to conduct interviews, and another student can role play a potential group member. Allow about 10 minutes for the interview. Afterward, the prospective client can talk about what it was like to be interviewed, and the group leader can share his or her experience.

3. As part of your job, you are expected to lead a group consisting of involuntary members. How will this fact affect your approach? What might you do differently with this group compared with a group of voluntary members? Have several students play the reluctant members while others practice dealing with them.

4. You are leading a counseling group with high school students. A member comes to the group obviously incoherent and disruptive. How do you deal with him? Discuss in class how you would deal with this situation, or demonstrate how you might respond by having a fellow student play the part of the adolescent.

5. Again, assume that you are leading a high school counseling group. An angry father who gave written permission for his son's

participation comes to your office and demands to know what is going on in your group. He is convinced that his son's participation in the group is an invasion of family privacy. As a group leader, how would you deal with his anger? To make the situation more real and interesting, have someone role play the father.

6. Selecting a good co-leader for a group is important, for not all matches of co-leaders are productive. Form dyads and negotiate with your partner to determine whether the two of you would be effective if you were to lead a group together. You might discuss matters such as potential power struggles, competitiveness, compatibility of views and philosophy, your differing styles and how they might complement or interfere with each other, and other issues that you think would have a bearing on your ability to work as a team.

Chapter 23

Pre-Chapter Self-Inventory

Directions: For each statement, indicate the response that most closely identifies your beliefs and attitudes. Use the following code:

5 = I *strongly agree* with this statement.

4 = I *agree* with this statement.

3 = I am *undecided* about this statement.

2 = I *disagree* with this statement.

1 = I *strongly disagree* with this statement.

_____ 1. It is important to include people from the client's environment in his or her treatment.

_____ 2. Community workers need to take an active role in seeking solutions to the social and political conditions related to human suffering.

_____ 3. Mental health experts need to devote more of their energies to preventing emotional and behavioral disorders rather than just treating them.

_____ 4. With increasing attention being paid to the community mental health approach and less funding being provided, the role of the professional needs to expand to include a variety of indirect services to clients as well as direct clinical services.

_____ 5. The use of nonlicensed workers is a valuable, cost-effective, and ethical way to deal with the shortage of professional help and budget constraints.

_____ 6. I want to actively advocate for my profession within the community, educating community members about what we do and dispelling myths or misconceptions about the role of mental health professionals.

_____ 7. In working with a variety of client groups in the community, it is essential for community workers to be skilled in out-of-office strategies and roles such as change agent, outreach, consulting, and advocacy.

_____ 8. Human-service workers need to understand the community in which they operate, including its needs, assets, and issues.

_____ 9. It is possible to work within the framework of a system and still be effective.

_____ 10. When I think of my experience in working in an agency or an institution, I am convinced of the necessity to initiate significant changes in the organization.

_____ 11. I frequently have good ideas and proposals, and I see myself as being willing to do the work necessary to translate these plans into actual programs.

_____ 12. Ethical practice requires that we look for ways to involve and mobilize resources and assets in the community to identify problems and find solutions.

_____ 13. Although I might be unable to bring about major changes in an institution or system, I am confident that I can make changes within the boundaries of my own position.

_____ 14. I can see that I might fall into complacency and rarely question what I am doing or how I could do my work more effectively, which could be unethical.

_____ 15. It would be unethical to accept a position with an agency whose central aims I disagreed with.

_____ 16. Human-service workers should be able to identify indigenous leaders in the community and work with them to improve conditions in the community.

_____ 17. A central role in human services is the development of leadership among community members.

_____ 18. As a professional working in the community, one of my main goals is to empower people in the community to become increasingly self-reliant.

_____ 19. As a counselor I am part of a system, and I have an ethical responsibility to work toward changing those aspects of the system that are ineffective.

_____ 20. I place a special value on meaningful contact with colleagues so as not to become excessively narrow in my thinking.

Introduction

The aspirations and difficulties of clients intertwine with those of many other people and, ultimately, with those of the community at large. Working with people in individual, couples, family, and group therapy are some ways for professionals to promote mental and emotional health. Working in the community has an expansive focus that can have an impact on the total milieu of people's lives and foster real and lasting community change. Community work requires a range of skills, some of which include connecting people with each other, developing leadership, acting as an advocate, and inspiring confidence. Practitioners can help create ripples within segments of the community even in small ways if they are committed to becoming grassroots change agents.

To be effective community workers, we must develop a set of personal competencies, such as cultural self-awareness, that allow us to work with those who differ from us. From an ethical perspective, we must first work on better understanding ourselves as cultural beings if we hope to implement the skills of bringing about community change. By understanding our personal culture, we can build a foundation for engaging in meaningful dialogue in a culturally diverse environment (Hogan, 2007).

As you recall from Chapter 11, systems theories are based on the premise that the identified client's problem might be a symptom of how the family system functions, not just a symptom of the individual's internal dynamics. When the community mental health movement came into existence, it took the family systems perspective a step further and holds that the entire community is the best focus of treatment. By looking at the whole community, it is possible to discover strengths within the community and to develop ways to bring these strengths to work for the community. Feminist therapy likewise addresses the need to consider the social, cultural, historical, political, and economic context that contributes to a person's problems in order to understand and help that person. It is our contention that individual, family, group, community, and feminist perspectives all have a special place as each one addresses a specific and complementary need that is not addressed by the others. These theoretical frameworks need not compete with one another; the field is enriched by all approaches.

The foundation of all ethical practice is promoting the welfare of clients. More often than not, this challenges us to look at the community as a whole to identify assets and opportunities as well as to identify problems and find solutions. If community workers ignore community needs because they seem overwhelming, and overlook the abilities, strengths, and resources within the community, this poses an ethical concern.

In this chapter we focus on the community itself as the client and target for change. In *Promoting Community Change,* Mark Homan (2008) captures the spirit of **community** in this definition:

> A community is a number of people who share a distinct location, belief, inter-est, activity, or other characteristic that clearly identifies their commonality and differentiates them from those not sharing it. This common distinction is sufficiently evident that members of the community are able to recognize it, even though they may not currently have this recognition. Effectively act-ing on their recognition may lead members to more complete personal and mutual development. (p. 98)

The ethical issues we discuss here are faced by many workers in community agency settings. We use the term **community agency** broadly to include any institution—public or private, nonprofit or for-profit—designed to provide a wide range of social and psychological services to the community. Likewise, when we speak of a **community worker**, we refer to a diverse pool of human-service workers whose primary duties include serving individuals within the community in a variety of community groups. Community workers include, but are not limited to, social workers, community organizers and developers, clinical mental health counselors, psychologists, psychiatrists, nurses, coun-selors, couples and family therapists, and human-service workers with vary-ing degrees of education and training.

Even if you don't plan to work in a community agency setting, you need to know how to mobilize community resources. Examine your own commit-ment to working in the community by thinking about these questions:

- What sense do you have of the social and psychological needs in your community and of the assets and resources within the community to deal with them?
- If clients ask what resources are available to them, would you know where to refer them?
- What forces within your community exacerbate the problems individu-als and groups are experiencing?
- What are the main assets available to empower people in your community?
- What factors contribute to the strength and development of your community?
- How do you see your role in improving your community?

This chapter will also examine an issue of particular importance to the community worker: namely, how the system affects the counselor and how to thrive and survive while working in the system. In examining the counselor's relationship to the community, we address the ethical dimensions of practice. If practitioners are limited in their ability to adapt their roles to the needs of the community, they are not likely to be effective in reaching those who most need assistance. Likewise, if the community does not understand what community mental health workers can do, they are less likely to use their services.

Ethical Practice in Community Work

The ethics codes of professional practice reinforce the practitioner's responsibility to the community and to society (see the Ethics Codes box titled "Responsibilities to Community and Society"). It is left to community workers to identify strategies for becoming more responsive to the community.

Community organizers typically work with community residents, constituency groups, local institutions, and government decision makers. Hardina (2004) asserts that most community practice activities occur outside traditional agency settings and involve the use of power and influence to bring about social change. One of the primary objectives of community practice is constituency self-determination. Community organizers must first

Ethics Codes

Responsibilities to Community and Society

National Organization for Human Services (2000)

Human service professionals keep informed about current social issues as they affect the client and the community. They share that information with clients, groups and community as part of their work. (Statement 11.)

Human service professionals act as advocates in addressing unmet client and community needs. Human service professionals provide a mechanism for identifying unmet client needs, calling attention to these needs, and assisting in planning and mobilizing to advocate for those needs at the local community level. (Statement 13.)

Human service professionals advocate for the rights of all members of society, particularly those who are members of minorities and groups at which discriminatory practices have historically been directed. (Statement 16.)

American School Counselor Association (2004)

The professional school counselor:
   (a) Collaborates with agencies, organizations and individuals in the community in the best interest of students and without regard to personal reward or remuneration.
   (b) Extends his/her influence and opportunity to deliver a comprehensive school counseling program to all students by collaborating with community resources for student success. (D.2.)

determine the primary recipient of their interventions. Is the client or constituent an individual, a group of people, or society in general? Those who engage in community work often encounter ethical dilemmas different from those common to clinical practice. Practitioners need to acquire adequate tools to deal effectively with these ethical challenges.

The Community Mental Health Orientation

While the traditional approach to understanding and treating human problems focuses on resolution of internal conflicts as a pathway to individual change, the community approach focuses on ways of changing the environmental factors causing individual problems. The community mental health perspective is relevant to all communities, but it is particularly relevant to underserved communities.

The community orientation requires practitioners to design interventions that go beyond the office. Counselors trained in individual therapy who work in the community need to develop a more expansive notion of who the client is. "Clients" are primarily constituency group members, residents of target communities, and people who have been marginalized (Hardina, 2004). The community orientation is based on the premise that the community itself is the most appropriate focus of attention, rather than the individual, and the community also is the most potent resource for solutions. As Mark Homan stresses, healthy communities believe more in their abilities than in their problems (personal communication, December 7, 2008). The ethical imperative is to do what best serves the "community as the client":

> Just like an individual or a family, a community has resources and limitations. Communities have established coping mechanisms to deal with problems. To promote change in a community, the community must believe in its own ability to change and must take responsibility for its actions or inactions. (Homan, 2008, p. 22)

The need for diverse and readily accessible treatment programs has been a key factor in the development of the community mental health orientation. Environmental factors cause or contribute to the problems of many groups in society, and a process that considers both the individual and the environment is often most beneficial to clients.

The focus of community work is on preventing rather than remediating problems. Additionally, members of the community are encouraged to take control of and master their own problems so that traditional intervention will become less necessary (Trull, 2005). Lewis, Lewis, Daniels, and D'Andrea (2003) define **community counseling** as "a comprehensive helping framework of intervention strategies and services that promotes the personal development and well-being of all individuals and communities" (p. 6). They describe the activities that make up a comprehensive community counseling model as having the following four components: (1) direct client services, (2) indirect client services, (3) direct community services, and (4) indirect community services. Let's examine each of these components separately.

1. **Direct client services** focus on outreach activities to a population that might be at risk for developing mental health problems. Community counselors provide help to clients either facing crises or dealing with ongoing stressors that overwhelm them. By reaching out to schools and communities that would be receptive to help, community workers can offer a variety of personal, career, family, and counseling services to at-risk groups (Lewis et al., 2003). This population would also include referrals from the courts, churches, probation departments, and drug and alcohol treatment centers. Direct client service providers empower clients with skills, knowledge, and understanding that will help them cope with external stressors (Toporek, Lewis, & Crethar, 2009).

2. **Indirect client services** consist of client advocacy and consultation, and include active intervention for and with an individual or a group such as people without jobs, people without homes, people with disabilities, or persons living with AIDS. Community workers need to become advocates, speaking up on their clients' behalf and actively intervening in their clients' situation (Lewis et al., 2003). Advocacy requires focused efforts to change existing policy or to influence proposed policy on behalf of specific underrepresented groups (Ezell, 2001). Mark Homan has a different point of view on advocacy (personal communication, December 7, 2008). He makes a subtle, but important distinction, of working *with* groups, rather than *for* groups. For Homan, advocacy requires working with groups to build their capacity and power and use it, along with ours, to make change. As much as possible, advocacy involves creating partnerships by working with groups in a collaborative way rather than merely providing services for these groups. This difference is reflected in the ACA *Advocacy Competencies* described by Toporek and colleagues (2009), wherein the counselor works as an advocate both *with* and *on behalf* of clients.

3. **Direct community services** in the form of *preventive education* are geared to the population at large. Examples of these programs include life planning workshops, value clarification seminars, interpersonal skills training, marriage education, and teaching parents about their legal rights and responsibilities. Because the emphasis is on prevention, these programs help people develop a wider range of competencies. The focus of preventive programs is on teaching effective living and problem-solving competencies.

4. **Indirect community services** are attempts to change the social environment to meet the needs of the population as a whole and are carried out by influencing public policy. The focus is on promoting systemic change by working closely with those is the community who develop public policy. The overall goal is the reduction of health problems, both mental and physical. Lee and Rodgers (2009) define the process of

systemic change as increasing public awareness, affecting public policy, and influencing legislation.

Community counseling calls for practitioners who (a) are familiar with resources within the community that they can refer clients to, when necessary; (b) have a basic knowledge of the cultural background of their clients; (c) possess skills that can be used as needed by clients; (d) have the ability to balance various roles as professionals; (e) are able to identify and work with professionals and nonprofessionals in the community who have the ability to be change agents for their community; (f) are willing to be advocates for policy changes in the community; and (g) have the ability to connect with the community and to connect community members with each other.

Social Justice Perspective

Social justice rests on the assumption that all people have a right to equitable treatment and a fair allocation of societal resources, including decision making (Crethar et al., 2008). Social justice addresses issues of oppression, privilege, and social inequities. Social justice and advocacy increasingly are being viewed as areas of major concern for all counselors (Roysircar, 2009; Steele, 2008).

Ideally, all mental health professionals are committed to promoting change on both individual and community levels; however, practitioners do not all have

Ethics Codes

Social Justice Advocacy

National Association of Social Workers (2008)

(a) Social workers should engage in social and political action that seeks to ensure that all persons have equal access to the resources, employment, services, and opportunities that they require in order to meet their basic human needs and to develop fully. Social workers should be aware of the impact of the political arena on practice, and should advocate for changes in policy and legislation to improve social conditions in order to meet basic human needs and promote social justice.

(b) Social workers should act to expand choice and opportunity for all persons, with special regard for vulnerable, disadvantaged, oppressed, and exploited persons and groups.

(c) Social workers should promote conditions that encourage respect for cultural and social diversity within the United States and globally. Social workers should promote policies and practices that demonstrate respect for difference, support the expansion of cultural knowledge and resources, advocate for programs and institutions that demonstrate cultural competence, and promote policies that safeguard the rights of and confirm equity and social justice for all people.

(continued on next page)

(d) Social workers should act to prevent and eliminate domination of, exploitation of, and discrimination against any person, group, or class on the basis of race, ethnicity, national origin, color, sex, sexual orientation, gender identity or expression, age, marital status, political belief, religion, immigration status, or mental or physical disability. (6.04.)

Canadian Association of Social Workers (1994)

A social worker shall advocate change: (a) in the best interest of the client, and (b) for the overall benefit of society, the environment and the global community. (10)

A social worker shall identify, document and advocate for the elimination of discrimination. (10.1.)

A social worker shall advocate for the equal distribution of resources to all persons. (10.2.)

A social worker shall advocate for the equal access of all persons to resources, services and opportunities. (10.3.)

A social worker shall advocate for a clean and healthy environment and shall advocate the development of environmental strategies consistent with social work principles. (10.4.)

A social worker shall provide reasonable professional services in a state of emergency. (10.5.)

A social worker shall promote social justice. (10.6.)

Feminist Therapy Institute (2000)

A feminist therapist seeks multiple avenues for impacting change, including public education and advocacy within professional organizations, lobbying for legislative actions, and other appropriate activities. (V.A.)

A feminist therapist actively questions practices in her community that appear harmful to clients or therapists. She assists clients in intervening on their own behalf. As appropriate, the feminist therapist herself intervenes, especially when other practitioners appear to be engaging in harmful, unethical, or illegal behaviors. (V.B.)

the same areas of interest and expertise. Counselors with a community orientation are committed to making society a better place by challenging systemic inequities. Some of the ethics codes refer to the role of social justice advocacy as an ethical mandate (see the Ethics Codes box titled "Social Justice Advocacy").

The goal of counseling from a social justice perspective is to promote the empowerment of people who are marginalized and oppressed in our society (Herlihy & Watson, 2007). This perspective reflects a valuing of fairness and equitable treatment for marginalized individuals and groups of people who do not share equally in society (Constantine, Hage, Kindaichi, & Bryant, 2007). Counselors who base their practice on aspirational ethics will need to involve themselves in opposing all forms of discrimination and oppression and be committed to challenging inherent inequities in social systems.

The Goals of Social Justice and Advocacy

Counselors must be willing to work outside of traditional school and agency settings to lower societal barriers that impede optimum human functioning (Steele, 2008). Some of these societal barriers include limited access to health care, poverty, segregation, racism, sexism, and discrimination, all of which are conditions that create barriers to participating fully in society. Steele states that the goal of the social justice and advocacy approach is to work toward ending oppressive society practices.

Herlihy and Watson (2007) state that a social justice perspective involves thinking about the therapeutic enterprise and ethics beyond a traditional framework.

> In order to effect social change, many counselors will need to reconceptualize how they traditionally have perceived the counseling process. They will no longer be able to view counseling as a one-on-one, in-the-office encounter, nor will they be able to assume that the problems a client brings to counseling originate within him or her. In other words, counseling for social justice requires a paradigm shift. (p. 181)

To be able to translate this paradigm shift into one's actual counseling practice, it is necessary to acquire a set of social justice and advocacy competencies. In a review and analysis of courses dealing with multicultural competence and social justice issues in counseling and counseling psychology programs, Pieterse and colleagues (2009) found that, by and large, instructors in training programs are attempting to provide multicultural instruction that is consistent with the accepted awareness, knowledge, and skills paradigm of multicultural counseling competencies. It is also evident that attempts are being made to incorporate a social justice perspective in multicultural counseling course work.

Homan (2008) emphasizes that we need to change conditions that affect people, not just change people who are affected by conditions. Homan believes that all human-service workers face the challenge of seeking changes in the way things are in the community. If we are interested in changing societal conditions, Hogan (2007) believes we need to recognize that our own cultural framework is the starting point for how we engage the world. Understanding ourselves as cultural beings powerfully influences our perceptions, as well as the methods we use in our professional work.

Pack-Brown, Thomas, and Seymour (2008) claim that using the community counseling model can assist students in developing an ethical sense from a multicultural and social justice perspective. Students need to think about the cultural values of the community where they work and the degree to which their intervention strategies are likely to advance the mental health of clients in the community. It is essential that students recognize how their values and the values of culturally diverse communities align. Sometimes the cultural values of the community may not be congruent with the values of the community worker. What is the practitioner to do when there is a conflict between a community agency's program and the personal values of the practitioner? Reflect on the following case of a social worker who is seeking advice.

■ The Case of Lupe.

Lupe is a social worker in a community mental health agency that is sponsoring workshops aimed at preventing the spread of AIDS. The agency has attempted to involve the local churches in these workshops. One church withdrew its support because the workshops encouraged "safer" sexual practices, including the use of condoms, as a way of preventing AIDS. A church official contended that the use of condoms is contrary to church teachings. Being a member of this church, Lupe finds herself struggling with value conflicts. She believes the teachings of her church and thinks the official had a right to withdraw his support of these workshops. But she also is aware that many people in the community she serves are at high risk for contracting AIDS because of both drug use and sexual practices. In an attempt to resolve this value conflict, Lupe seeks out several of her colleagues, each of whom provides some advice.

Colleague A: I hope you tell your clients and others in the community that you have value conflicts between agency practice and your religious beliefs and, for that reason, you are voluntarily resigning from the agency.

Colleague B: Be up front with the people you come in contact with by telling them of your values and providing them with adequate referrals so they can get information about prevention of this disease. You do owe it to them not to steer them in the direction you think they should move.

Colleague C: It is best that you not disclose your values or let them know that you agree with the church's views. Instead, work toward changing their behavior and modifying their values directly. After all, in this case the end justifies the means.

If Lupe were to seek you out and ask for your advice, consider what you would say to her. In formulating your position, answer these questions:

- Which of her colleagues comes closest to your thinking, and why?
- With which colleague do you find yourself disagreeing the most, and why?
- Would it be ethical for Lupe not to disclose her values to her clients? Why or why not?
- What are the potential consequences if Lupe imposes her moral beliefs on the population she is serving? Is it her ethical and moral duty to the community to develop a program aimed at prevention of AIDS? Explain.
- How would you advise Lupe, and what does your response tell you about your values?

Commentary. This case highlights a conflict between the social worker's personal values and her agency's requirements in a community context. Lupe should identify any conflicts between her ethical duty to avoid harm and promote her clients' best interests and the church's teachings, and then abide by the ethical mandate. We would remind Lupe that just as in individual counseling, she is committed to working for the best interests of her client, in this case, the community as a whole. Lupe's failure to provide necessary information to members of the community puts the community at risk of harm. Because the teachings of the church prevent such a partnership, Lupe may need to enlist other community groups in her efforts to provide outreach regarding methods of safer sex. Even though Lupe's values are congruent with the church's position, ethically she cannot replace community values with her personal values.

Advocacy Competencies

Mental health practitioners especially need to function as advocates for clients who are marginally acculturated and who need remediation of a problem that results from discrimination and oppression. Lee and Hipolito-Delgado (2007) indicate that counselors function as **advocates** when they use their skills in helping clients challenge institutional barriers that impede their personal, social, academic, or career goals. They add: "When necessary, counselors need to be willing to act on behalf of marginalized or disenfranchised clients and to actively challenge longstanding traditions, preconceived notions, or regressive policies and procedures that may stifle human development" (p. xvi). Steele (2008) claims that *social justice* and *advocacy* both emphasize the relationship between social factors such as poverty, racism, and mental health problems. **Social justice advocacy** is defined by Steele as "professional practice, research, or scholarship intended to identify and intervene in social policies and practices that have a negative impact on the mental health of clients who are marginalized on the basis of social status" (pp. 75–76).

Counselors who have a social justice advocacy perspective demonstrate leadership abilities and understand the importance of speaking out to empower individuals, families, and their community (Ratts & Hutchins, 2009). Lee and Rodgers (2009) assert that counselors must have the courage of their convictions and articulate social injustices to those in power in the public arena. It takes courage "to intervene not only into the lives of clients but also into the larger social/political arena for the benefit of an individual client as well as to foster social justice for all" (p. 286).

Advocacy competence is "the ability, understanding, and knowledge to carry out advocacy ethically and effectively" (Toporek et al., 2009). To become competent client advocates, counselors need to develop a greater awareness of their own beliefs, attitudes, and biases as they relate to the impact that social and political factors have on marginalized and underserved populations. Practitioners serve their clientele at three levels of advocacy intervention: (a) the individual client/student level, (b) the community/school level, and (c) the public/societal level. Within each of these levels, counselors act *with* and on *behalf of* their clients and others in their clients' environments.

At the *individual client/student level,* practitioners work with their clients in individual counseling situations to help them develop the critical consciousness and skills that underlie their empowerment. Practitioners work with persons from marginalized groups to help them learn to advocate for themselves. At the individual client/student level, practitioners advocate on their clients' behalf when clients believe such advocacy is useful in helping them to overcome the challenges facing them. Particular care must be taken to protect clients' confidentiality and safety when providing this form of advocacy.

Advocacy at the *community/school level* typically includes consulting with other allies in their clients' communities to determine how mental health professionals can be supportive in advancing the ongoing empowerment of these communities. As in the client/student level, it is important that practitioners work as much as possible in concert with the populations for which they advocate. This assures that the advocacy efforts selected accurately reflect the needs, values, and culture of the community. For an in-depth treatment of the client/ student and community/school levels of advocacy, see Ratts and Hutchins (2009) and Toporek, Lewis, and Crethar (2009).

Advocacy at the *public/societal level* includes public education and legal and social policy advocacy. Educational services are targeted at increasing the public's awareness of the adverse impact of social injustices on the wellness and welfare of various populations served by counselors. Social policy and legal advocacy generally comes in the form of lobbying interventions with elected officials and other policymakers as well as those who execute the laws and policies. An in-depth discussion on community collaboration and systems advocacy in the public arena can be found in Lopez-Baez and Paylo (2009) and Lee and Rodgers (2009).

Ethical practice requires counselors to assume an advocacy role that is focused on affecting public opinion, public policy, and legislation (ACA, 2005; Lee & Rodgers, 2009). To effectively serve as client advocates, counselors must understand the impact of political, social, economic, and cultural factors on human development (Lewis, Arnold, House, & Toporek, 2002). Practitioners also need to develop an awareness of their own beliefs and attitudes regarding social issues and marginalized populations, the scope of their knowledge, and their level of skill at intervening within the different domains of advocacy. Finally, multicultural competence is essential in understanding the cultural relevance and appropriateness of advocacy interventions as counselors bring their own attitudes and beliefs to the sociopolitical history of their communities. For a comprehensive discussion of social justice and systems changes as applied to working with diverse client populations, see *ACA Advocacy Competencies: A Social Justice Framework for Counselors* (Ratts, Toporek, & Lewis, 2010).

Roles of Helpers Working in the Community

No matter what setting we choose for our work, we must be aware of the broader context of human problems in order to be effective and practice ethically. The challenge is to think beyond the needs of the individual to the needs and strengths of the community at large, in much the same way that practitioners include the family when addressing the needs of the child.

Outreach interventions. As we indicated in Chapter 4, to meet the needs of many ethnic and culturally diverse clients, traditional counselors must have a different vision and master different skills, such as outreach interventions. Providing services in nontraditional settings outside the office may be clinically and ethically indicated and may be most beneficial to clients. On this point, Knapp and Slattery (2004) indicate that home-based services often are the only way some people can get services due to transportation problems, mobility issues, or cultural barriers to office-based treatment. Home-based services can lead to ethical challenges in managing professional boundaries. When working in the homes of clients, Knapp and Slattery recommend that therapists emphasize informed consent, especially about therapeutic boundaries.

The outreach approach may include both developmental and educational efforts, such as skills training, stress management, and consultation. Outreach activities also include family preservation services, the goal of which is to develop a treatment plan with a family to maintain children's safety in their own homes. Community counselors also attempt to change the dysfunctional system that is producing problems for individuals, families, and communities. The focus is on looking at the problem in its community context rather than dealing only with the problem within the individual.

School counselors as cultural mediators. School counselors are called upon to do outreach work in the community and to design ways to build bridges between the school and the community. Portman (2009) believes the changing role of the school counselor encompasses **cultural mediation**, which involves the counselor engaging in "prevention, intervention, and/or remediation activities that facilitate communication and understanding between culturally diverse human systems that aid the educational progress of all students" (p. 23). If school counselors hope to make effective interventions, it is essential that they connect with the community as a cultural mediator. Some functions of a cultural mediator in a school system include communicating with families and community organizations regarding cultural diversity, facilitating access to community resources and social service agencies, creating a supportive and encouraging culturally diverse school and community climate, and serving as an information hub for culturally diverse families. Cultural consultation facilitates linkages between the school counselor and members of the community. Portman forecasts the future of school counselors as cultural mediators by emphasizing their role as community consultants and social advocates: "school counselors may intervene for culturally diverse students in educational systems and communities to eliminate institutional barriers and cultural insensitivities" (p. 25).

A developmental versus a service approach. Homan (2008) compares the functions of workers who operate within a developmental approach with those who rely on a service orientation. The **developmental approach** is grounded on strengths, focuses on assets and capacities, promotes capability and power, changes conditions, and is aimed at prevention. This approach builds on identifying resources within the individual, the group, or the community that can be more fully activated. In contrast, a **service approach** focuses on problems to be solved and holes to fill. It is concerned more with maintaining rather than changing conditions and is oriented toward fixing problems rather than preventing them. A service orientation relies on experts and reinforces power imbalances, whereas a developmental approach relies on partnerships and equalizes power relationships. In the alternative roles described in the following section, counselors focus their work within a developmental framework to empower their community clients.

Alternative Counselor Roles

Community-oriented counseling emphasizes the necessity of recognizing and dealing with environmental conditions that often create problems for ethnically diverse client groups. This is known as a psychosocial approach. Rather than operating in a singular role, as is the case with many traditional counselors, the emphasis of the community perspective is on alternative ways of helping clients. Atkinson (2004) suggests these alternative roles for counselors who work in the community: advocate, change agent, consultant, adviser, facilitator of indigenous support systems, and facilitator of indigenous healing methods. These alternative roles embody fundamental principles of social justice and activism that are aimed at client empowerment (Constantine et al., 2007; Crethar et al., 2008).

Constantine and colleagues (2007) provide the following example to illustrate the multiple roles open to counselors who pursue a social justice advocacy model. A Black gay male is consistently denied promotion in his firm, even though he has an exceptional sales record. He seeks counseling to deal with his depression arising from feeling powerless in his work situation. Although a conventional therapeutic approach could help this client achieve his stated goal, other avenues are open for a wider exploration of this client's issues. For example, the counselor could help the client identify his experiences with racial and sexual discrimination, serve as an adviser or consultant in helping the client identify possible legal recourses to his situation, or encourage the client to join a gay men's support group to discuss issues of discrimination and possible action strategies. The counselor can take various alternative roles or combine conventional and alternative strategies. Constantine and colleagues believe "that counselors and counseling psychologists committed to principles of social justice must develop skills in creativity and courage in order to ameliorate the consequences of social injustice" (p. 26).

Advocate.   Because marginalized clients are often oppressed to some degree by the dominant society, they can be helped by counselors who are willing to speak on their behalf or to argue for a cause. Competencies required for counselors to act in the role of advocate on the individual, community, and societal levels were discussed earlier in the chapter.

Change agent.   Counselors can confront and bring about change within the system that contributes to, if not creates, many of the problems clients face. In the role of **change agents**, counselors assist clients in recognizing oppressive forces in the community as a source of their problem; they also teach clients strategies for dealing with these environmental problems. A change agent recognizes that healthy communities produce healthy people. Homan (2008) believes that effective human-service workers are change agents: "All workers must accept the simple fact that improvement means that something has to change—and they will play a part in promoting that change" (p. 64). The main purpose of community change is to foster healthy communities. In their role of change agent, workers must sometimes educate organizations to change their culture to meet the needs of the community.

Consultant.   Operating as **consultants**, counselors encourage clients from diverse cultures to learn skills they can use to interact successfully with various forces within their community. In this role, the client and counselor cooperate in addressing unhealthy forces within the system. They work with clients from diverse racial, ethnic, and cultural backgrounds to design preventive programs aimed at eliminating the negative impacts of racism and oppression. The role of consultant can be seen as the role of a teacher. Often the "teacher" is less of a threat and more socially acceptable to members of non-Western cultures than the "counselor," even though the same professional may be performing both functions.

Adviser.   The counselor as **adviser** initiates discussions with clients about ways to deal with environmental problems that contribute to their personal problems. In many ways, this is a social work approach that considers the person-in-the-environment rather than simply addressing problems within the individual. For example, recent immigrants may need advice on immigration paperwork, coping with problems they will face in the job market, or problems that their children may encounter at school.

Facilitator of indigenous support systems.   All cultural groups have some form of social support aimed at preventing or remediating psychological and social problems. Many ethnically diverse clients, people in rural environments, and older people would not consider seeking professional help in the traditional sense. They may not feel comfortable or safe with helping professionals who are not members of their indigenous frameworks of helping (Constantine et al., 2007). However, they may be willing to put their faith in family members or close friends, or turn to other social support systems within their own communities. Community workers need to be aware of cultural factors that may be instrumental in contributing to a client's problem or resources that might help alleviate or solve the client's problem. Counselors can play an important role by encouraging clients to make full use of **indigenous support systems** (such as family and friendship networks) within their own communities.

Facilitator of indigenous healing systems. Mental health practitioners need to learn what kinds of healing resources exist within a client's culture. In many cultures individuals with problems are more likely to put their trust in traditional healers. For that reason, counselors need to be aware of **indigenous healing systems** (such as religious leaders and institutions, energy healers, and respected community leaders) and be willing to work collaboratively with them when it is to the benefit of the client. Ignoring these indigenous resources can have a negative effect on the client's welfare, and therefore, has ethical implications. One such example of a conflict between indigenous healing and mainstream medicine is explored in Fadiman's (1997) book, *The Spirit Catches You and You Fall Down*. This conflict resulted in the death of a child.

Constantine and colleagues (2004) present a comprehensive literature review and discuss the cultural relevance of alternative healing practices in promoting psychological, physical, and spiritual well-being in people of color. They suggest that counselors exercise due care in making referrals to indigenous helping resources so as not to jeopardize clients' physical and mental health. Constantine and her colleagues encourage counselors to be open to learning about indigenous healing resources, especially with clients from cultures that may mistrust Western mental health approaches. By assuming an open stance, "counselors may be able to recognize potential similarities and differences between indigenous and Western approaches to helping and may begin to bridge the gaps between traditional helping institutions and the cultures of the individuals they serve" (p. 120).

In summary, we see it as ethically incumbent on practitioners who work in the community to assume some or all of the alternative roles described above when needed to benefit their clients and provide optimal and at times alternative care.

Educating the Community

There are many reasons for the underuse of available mental health resources. Clients may be unaware of their existence; they may not be able to afford the services; they may have misconceptions about the nature and purpose of counseling; they may be reluctant to recognize their problems; they may harbor the attitude that they should be able to solve their own problems; they may feel a social stigma attached to seeking professional help; or they may perceive that these resources are not intended for them because the services are administered in a culturally insensitive way. One of the major barriers to clients making use of social and psychological services is that access to these services is confusing and sometimes humiliating.

One goal of the community approach is to educate the public and attempt to change the attitudes of the community about mental health and the attitudes toward those who deliver mental health services. Many people still cling to a very narrow definition of mental illness. Widespread misconceptions include the notion that once people suffer from any kind of emotional disturbance they can never be cured, the idea that people with emotional and behavioral disorders are merely deficient in "willpower," and the belief that the mentally ill are always dangerous and should be separated from the community lest they "contaminate" or harm others. Professionals face real challenges in combating these misconceptions, but unless this is done many people will not seek professional help. Practitioners are ethically bound to actively work at presenting mental health services in a way that is understandable to and respectful of the community at large.

Influencing Policymakers

The challenges facing community workers can be overwhelming, especially with current constraints on funding and the bureaucratic malaise. How can dedicated community workers continue to develop social programs if they are constantly faced with the possibility that their programs will be cut back or canceled? There is little room for staff members to initiate innovative social programs when the agencies themselves are concerned with mere survival.

One way community workers can initiate change is by organizing within an agency or even several agencies and developing a collective voice. Practitioners can empower a community to organize political action to influence the state and national government to fulfill their responsibilities. This action may involve providing funds, technical assistance, legal protection, or other support a smaller community requires to flourish (Homan, 2008).

■ The Case of a Nonprofit Agency Designed to Educate the Community.

The Coalition for Children, Adolescents and Parents (CCAP) is a community agency aimed at the prevention of adolescent pregnancy. This small grassroots agency in Orange County, California, applies outreach strategies to educate the community as a way to meet a critical need in the community (Hogan-Garcia & Scheinberg, 2000). For the past 20 years, CCAP has served as a model of how to involve the community in a project to enhance the community. From its inception, a high priority has been given to hiring a multiethnic staff that could serve and mirror the community. The staff is committed to understanding each other, rather than allowing their differences to separate them, and staff members meet frequently for cultural sharing as a way to better understand each other and themselves. Those who work at the agency have opportunities to critically examine their ethnocentric assumptions about the world and the community. All the members of the agency staff are committed to clarifying and understanding personal values, beliefs, and behaviors.

One of the early projects designed by CCAP involved outreach and education in the Latino community to prevent the spread of HIV. A Latina staff member conducted interviews with 30 mothers in the community regarding their understanding of HIV, human sexuality, and teen pregnancy. From this contact with these mothers, a group of leaders (*comadres*) was formed to educate the community. The women who served as leaders met for monthly meetings, which were held at a neighborhood center. Eventually, the women invited their husbands into the classes. This project was funded by an external source, and the agency was required to report to the funders about the outcomes of the project. Hogan-Garcia and Scheinberg (2000) summarize these outcomes thusly:

> By the end of the contract year, the agency had exceeded the expectations of funders with the project and the Comadres Project had spread the word about HIV prevention to friends, neighbors, and family members. The empowerment of disenfranchised women and men continued beyond the contract term. CCAP staff continued to meet with and follow this special group of friends. Three women went back to school, a group of the women formed a Spanish-speaking PTA group, and one went on to become a school board member. (p. 28)

In 2000 the agency served more than 12,000 clients, providing after-school recreational services, tutoring, academic enrichment programs, physical examinations, parenting education, conflict resolution, cultural-diversity training, school-based group counseling, a homeless shelter, drug abuse prevention, and child care training.

> *Commentary.* This agency is an example of an effective collaboration committed to ensuring that the members of the community have a full voice in determining the nature of community services. Because the individuals on the staff believe in the value of understanding cultural diversity, they are able to serve as a bridge between the mainstream and minority communities. This is also a good example of *developing* leadership rather than simply providing leadership.

■ The Case of Maribel.

Maribel is the director of a community clinic in an inner-city neighborhood. Her agency provides birth control counseling and funding for abortion to low-income women. As the time approaches for her to submit her request for financing to the state government, she is contacted by a local politician who is adamantly opposed to abortion. He informs her that if she requests funding for abortion he will do everything in his power not only to deny the money but also to reduce the overall funding for the agency. Faced with the prospect of radically reduced funds, Maribel omits her request for money for abortion services.

- In light of the threats that were made, did Maribel act in the best interest of her community? Can you see any justification for her action? What ethical concerns are raised by her decision?
- How ethically bound was Maribel to disclose the coercive attempts of the influential politician, even though it was only her word against his?
- What would you have done in her place?

Commentary. Maribel is obviously faced with a very difficult situation. She has the task of doing what is in the best interests of the community (her client). Her program is designed to address critical needs in the community, but these needs are being compromised due to a politician's threat. To serve her community effectively, Maribel may have to become an advocate for change and initiate actions aimed at changing policies that would lessen such threats in the future. In addition, Maribel can work with community members to empower their voices for change that will benefit the whole community.

Promoting Change in the Community

Homan (personal communication, December 7, 2008) poses a question that has significant implications for community work: Are you willing to honestly examine who owns the project or the change? From Homan's perspective, if we are just doing things we think are right *for* people, rather than the project really being theirs to take charge of, we may just be politely reasserting a form of social control. While some client/constituent groups do not have the immediate skills, or even the time to take care of every aspect of a change project, they can learn skills and receive support for their work. Thus, the matter of "who owns" the project is an important ethical concern.

Homan (2008) emphasizes the notion that promoting community change is a broader issue than merely solving the problems of the community. He raises a series of questions that community workers need to address in their change efforts (p. 55):

- Is there an identified community? If so, who has defined it, and how have they defined it?
- Does the project build skills of community members? Can these skills be identified?
- Does the project produce new leaders and new teachers?
- Who owns the project? How is this seen? Who holds decision-making authority? If ownership is external, what processes are in place to transfer ownership to the members of the community?

- Does the project produce new community resources that can exist apart from the project or after the intended life of the project?
- Do the benefits or resources created by the project in turn create new benefits or resources?
- Which community capacities or assets will the project build upon? How will these be expanded by the project?
- Which community conditions does the project intend to change?

The answers to these questions can provide community workers with a framework for developing the capacity within a community to recognize conditions that need to be changed and the willingness and ability to take action to bring this change about. Practitioners working in the community need to develop the capacities of community members to strengthen their own community. As Homan (2008) puts this: "Community capacity is the ability of a community to effectively act on its own behalf to provide for the well being and draw forth the contribution of its members" (p. 52).

Ways to Involve Yourself in the Community

Consider your responsibility to teach constituents to use the resources available to them in their communities. Here is a list of things you might do to link residents to the environment in which they live. Rate each of these activities, using the following code:

A = I would do this on a *regular basis*.

B = I would do this *occasionally*.

C = I would do this *rarely*.

_____ 1. I would work with agencies to assess community needs.

_____ 2. I would familiarize myself with available community resources so that I could refer people to appropriate sources of further help.

_____ 3. With my clients' permission, I would enlist people who had a direct influence on their lives.

_____ 4. I would connect my clients to both formal and informal support systems and resources that are already available in the community.

_____ 5. I would work actively with groups committed to bringing about change in the community.

_____ 6. I would bring together clients who are affected by a common condition and help them work out strategies to change the condition that affects them.

_____ 7. I would encourage efforts to make the community's helping network more responsive.

_____ 8. I would provide training to key people from various cultural groups in peer-counseling skills so that they could work with those people who might not seek professional services from an agency.

_____ 9. I would work with politicians who were actively involved in helping the community.

If you plan on going into one of the mental health professions, you are likely to spend some time working in a community agency setting, and you will be working with many different facets of the community. If you were to work in such a setting at this time, consider the following questions:

- How would you go about learning what it takes to become an effective agent for change in the community?
- What skills do you already have that can be applied to community change?
- What is the most essential skill you need to acquire?
- What fears or concerns do you have of working in the community?
- How would you translate your ideas into a practical set of strategies aimed at community change?
- How aware are you of your beliefs and attitudes toward the people you serve, and how might this affect the way you work?

Working Within a System

One of the major challenges for counselors who work in the community is to learn how to make the system work for the clients they serve and, secondarily, work for themselves so that in the process they do not lose their ability to be effective. Working in a system can put an added strain on the counselor due to the monumental amount of paperwork required to justify continued funding, high caseloads, and a multitude of policy directives. Another source of strain is the counselor's relationships with those who administer the agency or institution, who may have long forgotten the practicalities involved in providing direct services to clients. Conversely, practitioners who deal with clients directly may have little appreciation for the intricacies with which administrators must contend in managing and funding their programs. If communication is poor and problem solving is inadequate, tension and problems are inevitable. The ultimate challenge is to empower the community to address its own problems. This will be difficult if the system trying to effect change is itself impaired.

The Challenge of Maintaining Integrity in an Agency Environment

Many professionals struggle with the issue of how to work within a system while retaining their integrity and vitality. Although working in an organization is oftentimes frustrating, counselors need to examine their attitude, which might be part of the problem. Blaming others does not effect change. Focusing on the things that can be changed fosters a sense of personal power that may allow for progress.

Practitioners need to evaluate the options they have in responding to unacceptable circumstances. Homan (2008) raises some thought-provoking questions in this regard:

- If you respond to the presence of disturbing social conditions within your midst by attempting to mainly soften the pain they cause, does this imply tolerance for these problems in the system?
- If you genuinely believe that your efforts make a difference, should you accept limitations on your efforts?
- To what degree is it your ethical responsibility to work toward shaping the system that shapes your practice?

Homan suggests that simply putting up with problems within a system is rarely gratifying and that workers gain professional satisfaction by actively taking steps to promote positive changes:

> I believe that you do have options for challenging the circumstances that lead to the problems you confront. And I believe that you have options for creating conditions that permit you to do effective work. In my experience, workers who have acted thoughtfully and purposefully to confront and resolve systemic problems have produced many positive results. (p. 71)

Recognizing the need for action is the first step toward responding to unacceptable circumstances. Once a problem has been identified, you will respond in one of four ways (Homan, 2008, p. 79):

- You can change your perception by identifying the situation as acceptable.
- You can leave the situation, either by emotionally withdrawing or by physically leaving.
- You can recognize the situation as unacceptable and then decide to adjust to the situation.
- You can identify the situation as unacceptable and do what you can to change it.

Each of these actions has consequences for both you and your clients. If you recognize that you do have choices in how you respond to unacceptable situations, you may be challenged to take action to change these circumstances. From an ethical perspective, you are expected to alert your employer to circumstances that may impair your ability to reach clients.

Homan (personal communication, December 7, 2008) also points out that agencies can become skilled and creative at strengthening their financial base, consistent with their mission, rather than just learning skills about how to deal with cutbacks. However, we need to recognize that sometimes a worker's physical and mental health may be at risk in a dysfunctional system.

In such a case, the only viable option might be to withdraw from the system to prevent serious health problems or burnout.

By creating and participating in support groups, those who work in an agency might find ways to collectively address problems in the system of which they are a part. A case can be made for the value of support groups in agency settings. These groups create an internal subculture that provides some support in dealing with bureaucratic pressure. Workers alone would have difficulty changing large organizations, but when they unite, they have a greater opportunity for effecting change.

◼ The Case of Toni.

For 19 years Toni has worked with women in recovery in a community agency that is funded by a grant. To prevent burnout, she and her coworkers organized a support group among the community workers in the agency. Her group consists of about 15 people, some of whom are case managers, treatment counselors, nurses, social workers, and supervisors. They meet at the agency during work hours twice a month for up to 2 hours. During these sessions the workers have opportunities to talk about difficult clients or stressful situations they are facing on the job or in their personal lives. Personal concerns sometimes have an impact on workers' abilities to function professionally, and members are able to use the support within the group as a way to deal with personal issues.

Unfortunately, because of cuts in many of the nonprofit grants, many of the benefits they previously had have been cut. Toni says,

I have recently been hard hit by these cuts. The grant on which I have been working for the past 19 years was recently cut by 10%. To make ends meet in the organization, many employees have been laid off, which has resulted in greater workloads for those remaining. These cutbacks were especially felt in the counseling area. We have lost a treatment counselor as well as two social workers, one based at the intensive day treatment program and the other at a hospital-based clinic. All of us are feeling the increased stress resulting from these losses. We have been forced to let go of our bi-monthly stress reduction meetings that over the years have been so valuable to us. This has left me alone in the clinic and hospital area without backup. Being unable to have someone to consult with on a daily basis has greatly increased my stress level. I am quickly realizing how important our meetings were to the welfare of the organization, as well as to the clients. Exploring new ways to manage our work-related stress is a top priority for our agency now. (Toni Wallace, personal communication, December 23, 2004)

- ▪ If you worked in an agency, would you want this kind of group?
- ▪ Do you think members of this group could effect change in the agency?

- How would you cope with the cutbacks and the loss of a program you valued?
- How might you deal with the demands of an increased workload due to layoffs?

Commentary. Toni's case represents a familiar scenario that mental health workers will increasingly face in these difficult financial times. Workers in community agencies will be expected to meet the demands placed upon them with fewer staff and resources to accomplish the job. Self-care is extremely important in this situation. One way for Toni to take care of herself is by finding ways to meet with colleagues outside of the agency to discuss how others are dealing with the demands of their work situation. In addition, Toni could increase her focus on self-care outside of her work environment.

Relationships Between Community Worker and Agency

The ethical violations in a community agency are more complex and difficult to resolve than violations pertaining to individual counseling. If a worker is not motivated, the system may tolerate this lack of motivation. If the system violates the rights of the client (community), then this is a real challenge to address. There is no easy solution to the problem of a system abusing clients, but clearly the people seeking help are vulnerable and need to be protected. Correcting systemic abuse demands the willingness of those involved in the system to practice aspirational ethics and take action.

Moving toward empowerment.   We suggest you respond to the following questions to clarify your position on ways in which you could increase your chances of assuming power within the system:

- What would you do if the organization for which you worked instituted a policy to which you were opposed?
- What would you do if you believed strongly that certain changes needed to be made in your institution but your colleagues disagreed?
- How would you attempt to make contact with your colleagues if members of the staff seemed to work largely in isolation from one another?
- If the staff seemed to be divided by jealousies, hostilities, or unspoken conflicts, how would you intervene?
- Can you image circumstances in which you might bypass the agency administrators and approach the board of directors?
- Would you be willing to organize clients to promote change within your agency?
- What do you consider to be the ethics involved in staying with a job after you have done everything you can to bring about change, but to no avail?

Now let's look at some examples that illustrate issues discussed in this chapter. Try to imagine yourself in each of these situations, and ask yourself how you would deal with them.

■ The Case of Adriana.

Adriana works in a community mental health clinic, and most of her time is devoted to dealing with crisis situations. The more she works with people in crisis, the more she is convinced that the focus of her work should be on preventive programs designed to educate the public. Adriana comes to believe strongly that there would be far fewer clients in distress if people were effectively contacted and motivated to participate in growth-oriented educational programs. She develops detailed, logical, and convincing proposals for programs she would like to implement in the community, but these proposals are consistently rejected by the director of her center. Because the clinic is partially funded by the government for the express purpose of crisis intervention, the director feels uneasy about approving any program that does not relate directly to this objective.

If you were in Adriana's place, which of the following courses of action would you choose?

_____ 1. I would do what the director expected.

_____ 2. I would continue to work toward a compromise and try to find some way to make room for my special project. I would work with the director until I convinced her to permit me to launch my program in some form.

_____ 3. If I could not do what I deemed important, I would have to consider looking for another job.

_____ 4. I would involve clients in setting the direction for the proposal and providing the necessary support to secure approval.

_____ 5. I would examine the director's responses and try to incorporate them into my approach.

_____ 6. I would get several other staff members together, pool our resources, and look for ways to implement the program as a group.

_____ 7. With my director's approval, I would try to obtain a grant for a pilot program in the community.

Commentary. Adriana has tried repeatedly to convince the director of the center that preventive programs would help to avert crises and improve community health. One alternative role open to her is to advocate for policy changes in government regulations. By joining forces with others in her agency, they could work toward an expanded definition of crisis intervention to include preventive measures.

As a mental health practitioner, you may need to decide how you will work within a system and how you can be most effective. Study the agency's philosophy before you accept a position, and determine whether the agency's norms, values, and expectations coincide with what you expect from the position. If you are not able to support the philosophy and policies of that agency, you are almost certain to experience conflicts, if not failure. It will be up to you to find your own answers to questions such as these:

- To what degree is my philosophy of helping compatible with the agency where I work?
- How can I meet the requirements of an institution and at the same time do what I most believe in?
- What can I do to bring about change in a particular system?
- Would I consider mobilizing clients to promote changes in the community? in my own agency?
- At what point does the price of attempting to work within an organized structure become too high?
- What special ethical obligations am I likely to face in working in a system?

■ The Case of Ronnie.

Ronnie, an African American student, moved with his family into a mostly White community and attends high school there. Almost immediately he became the butt of racial jokes and experienced social isolation. A teacher noticed his isolation and sent him to the school counselor. It is evident to the counselor that Ronnie is being discriminated against, not only by many of the students but also by some of the faculty. The counselor has no reason to doubt the information provided by Ronnie because she is aware of racism in the school and in the community. She determines that it would be much more practical to help Ronnie learn to ignore the prejudice than to try to change the racist attitudes of the school and the community.

- How do you evaluate this counselor's decision? What are its ethical ramifications? Does she have an obligation to work to change community attitudes?
- If you were consulted by this counselor, what suggestions would you make?
- Does a school system have an ethical obligation to attempt to change attitudes of a community that discriminates against some of its citizens?
- What are the risks of not addressing the problem of racism?
- How might a counselor assist Ronnie in becoming empowered using a social justice approach?

Commentary. This counselor is struggling with the nature of the challenge and seems ill equipped to take it on. She may fear reprisals if she acts on values that are not shared by many in the community. She may want to do what is needed to promote the well-being of her client, yet she may be struggling with self-doubts and with anxiety about not being accepted by some faculty members. Although this counselor seems unwilling or perhaps is unable to confront racism within the school setting, she has an ethical duty to advocate for change in the school community. By talking with the teacher who sent Ronnie to her, she may be able to begin to gather a coalition for change in the school community. She might consider presenting workshops and classroom guidance activities on racism in the school. The counselor also may be able to gain the support of the school administration if she approaches the problem in a noncombative manner. In this case, the client is the school community, and Ronnie's troubles will not be resolved without community change.

Chapter Summary

The primary focus of this chapter has been on the importance of working in the community as a change agent. The community mental health orientation is one way to meet the increasing demand for a variety of services. Too often mental health professionals have been denied the opportunity to devise programs that address the diverse needs of the community. Over the past few years some alternatives to conventional therapy have arisen, creating new roles for counselors who work in a community agency setting. If you seek a full-time career in an agency, it is essential to consider how you can work *with* the system for the benefit of you and your clients. As Homan (1999) puts it: "If you treat people as if they are allies, they are more likely to become allies; if you treat them as enemies, they are more likely to become enemies" (p. 141). Counselors also need to be aware of social justice issues that are manifested in the community. Becoming increasingly aware of how oppression and discrimination operate in the lives of our clients is a fundamental part of ethical practice. Practitioners are expected to translate this awareness into various forms of social action.

We encourage you to think of ways to accept the responsibility of working effectively in an organization and thus increasing your effectiveness as a professional. We also recommend that you make efforts to educate community members about what community practitioners actually do. Finally, we ask you to reflect on the major causes of disillusionment that often accompany working in a system and to find creative ways to retain your vitality, both as a person and as a professional.

Suggested Activities

1. Retake the self-assessment at the end of Chapter 1, which surveys your attitudes about ethical and professional issues. Cover your initial answers when you complete the self-assessment, and compare your responses now to see whether your thinking has changed. In addition, circle the 10 questions that are most significant to you or that you are most interested in pursuing further. Bring these to class and discuss them in small groups. Write down a few of the most important things you have learned in this course and from this book. You might also write down some questions that remain unanswered for you. Exchange your ideas with other students.

2. In small groups discuss your thoughts about the relationship between the social justice perspective and ethical practice. What relationship do you see between advocacy competencies and multicultural competencies? Which of the advocacy competencies would you most want to incorporate into your practice in the community?

3. Reflect on and discuss alternative roles human-service professionals might play when working in the community. Identify which of the following roles you think you could assume as a community worker: (a) advocate, (b) change agent, (c) consultant, (d) adviser, (e) facilitator of indigenous support systems, (f) facilitator of indigenous healing systems, or (g) all of the above roles. In small groups discuss in which of these roles you would feel least comfortable functioning, and why. How could you learn to carry out professional roles in the community different from those in which you were trained?

4. An issue you may well face in your practice is how to get through the hesitation people have toward asking for professional assistance. How would you respond to clients who have questions such as these: "What will people think if they find out that I am coming for professional help?" "Shouldn't I really be able to solve my problems on my own? Isn't it a sign of weakness that I need others to help me?" "Will I really be able to resolve my problems by consulting you?" Share your responses in dyads or in small groups.

5. How familiar are you with the resources that exist in your community? Would you know where to refer clients for special needs? Investigate a community mental health center in your area and find the answers to questions such as these:

- Where would I send a family who needed help?
- Where would I send a family who has a child with a learning or developmental disability?
- Where would I refer a couple seeking help for relationship problems?
- What website resources would I recommend?
- What facilities are available to treat drug and alcohol abuse?

- Is crisis intervention available?
- Are health and medical services available at the center?
- What groups are offered?
- Is individual counseling available? for whom? at what fee? long-term? short-term?
- Are hotline services available for people in crisis?

6. Suppose you were applying for a job in a community mental health center. How would you respond to the following questions during the interview?

- Many of our clients represent a range of diverse cultural and ethnic backgrounds. To what degree do you think you will be able to work with them?
- How much do you understand about your own acculturation process? How will this help or hinder you in working with our clientele?
- What will be your biggest challenge in forming trusting relationships with clients who are culturally different from you?

7. Several students can interview a variety of professionals in the mental health field about the major problems they encounter in their institution. What barriers do they meet when they attempt to implement programs? How do they deal with obstacles? Compare the responses of experienced and inexperienced personnel without revealing the identities of the persons interviewed.

8. After recognizing that a problem exists within the organization for which you work, identify skills you would need to make the desired changes. How might you go about developing strategies for getting support from coworkers if you were interested in changing an agency?

9. Consider asking professionals how they view workers who organize and mobilize clients, particularly toward making changes in the agency in which the professional works.

10. Interview clients in an agency and get their perceptions of how community workers have involved them in changing the conditions they face.

11. Some websites offer useful information pertaining to topics addressed in this chapter. Choose several topics that interest you and check these resources to see what information is available.

- Welfare Information Network: www.welfareinfo.org
- The Web Counseling Site: http://home.nww.net/willcars/index.html
- Addiction: www.jointogether.org or www.atforum.com
- Multicultural Services: www.mc-memhr.org
- Child Welfare League of America: www.handsmt.org/cwla
- National Institute on Drug Abuse: www.nida.nih.gov

- Substance Abuse and Mental Health Services Administration: www.samhsa.gov
- Mental Retardation: www.thearc.org
- National Coalition for the Homeless: www.ari.net/hone/nch
- Homeless Population Resources: www.homeless.org
- Psychosocial Rehabilitation: www.ucpsychrehab.org
- Posttraumatic Stress Disorder: www.ncptsd.org
- Program for Assertive Community Treatment: www.nami.org/about/pactfact.html
- Crisis Counseling: www.crisiscounseling.com
- Suicide Crisis Intervention: www.mhsantuary.com
- Prevention: www.prevention.org
- Advocacy Institute: www.advocacy.com
- Law and Social Policy: www.clasp.org
- International Critical Incident Stress Foundation: www.icisf.org

Authors' Concluding Commentary

We have raised some of the ethical and professional issues that you most likely will encounter in your counseling practice and have tried to stimulate you to think most likely will about your own guidelines for professional practice. If one fundamental question can serve to tie together all the issues we have discussed, it is this: "Who has the right to counsel another person?" This question can be the basis for self-examination whenever you have concerns about clients. At times you may be troubled and believe that you have no right to counsel others. This may be because you are not doing in your own life what you are challenging your clients to do. Occasional self-doubt is far less damaging, in our view, than a failure to question. Complacency will stifle your growth as a practitioner. Your commitment to ongoing self-exploration and self-care will make you a more effective helper.

Developing a sense of professional and ethical responsibility is a task that is never really finished. There are no final or universal answers to many of the questions we have posed. For ourselves, we hope never to reach the point where we think we have figured it all out and no longer need to reexamine our assumptions and practices. The issues raised in this book demand periodic reflection and an openness to change. Give careful thought to your own values and ethics. Be willing to rethink your positions as you gain more experience. When you are interested in what you do and in the people you serve, you will be not only an ethical practitioner but also an interesting one.